Linux for Programmers and Users

Trademark Information

Linux for Programmers and Users

Glass / Ables

PEARSON
Prentice
Hall

Upper Saddle River, NJ 07458

Library of Congress Cataloging-in-Publication Data
On file

Vice President and Editorial Director, ECS: *Marcia J. Horton*
Executive Editor: *Tracy Dunkelberger*
Assistant Editor: *Carole Snyder*
Editorial Assistant: *Christianna Lee*
Executive Managing Editor: *Vince O'Brien*
Managing Editor: *Camille Trentacoste*
Production Editor: *Donna Crilly*
Director of Creative Services: *Paul Belfanti*
Art Director and Cover Manager: *Jayne Conte*
Cover Designer: *Bruce Kenselaar*
Managing Editor, AV Management and Production: *Patricia Burns*
Art Editor: *Gregory Dulles*
Manager, Cover Visual Research and Permissions: *Karen Sanatar*
Manufacturing Manager, ESM: *Alexis Heydt-Long*
Manufacturing Buyer: *Lisa McDowell*
Executive Marketing Manager: *Robin O'Brien*
Marketing Assistant: *Barrie Reinhold*
Cover Image: *Natalie Racioppa / Photodisc Red / Getty Images.com*

PEARSON
Prentice Hall

© 2006 Pearson Education, Inc.
Pearson Prentice Hall
Pearson Education, Inc.
Upper Saddle River, NJ 07458

Pearson Prentice Hall® is a trademark of Pearson Education, Inc.

The author and publisher of this book have used their best efforts in preparing this book. These efforts include the development, research, and testing of the theories and programs to determine their effectiveness. The author and publisher make no warranty of any kind, expressed or implied, with regard to these programs or the documentation contained in this book. The author and publisher shall not be liable in any event for incidental or consequential damages in connection with, or arising out of, the furnishing, performance, or use of these programs.

Printed in the United States of America.

ISBN 0-13-185748-7

Pearson Education Ltd., *London*
Pearson Education Australia Pty. Ltd., *Sydney*
Pearson Education Singapore, Pte. Ltd.
Pearson Education North Asia Ltd., *Hong Kong*
Pearson Education Canada, Inc., *Toronto*
Pearson Educación de Mexico, S.A. de C.V.
Pearson Education—Japan, *Tokyo*
Pearson Education Malaysia, Pte. Ltd.
Pearson Education, Inc., *Upper Saddle River, New Jersey*

*To all those who work to leave our world a little
better than they found it.*

Table of Contents

Preface

About the Authors

Graham Glass graduated from the University of Southampton, England, with a Bachelor's degree in Computer Science and Mathematics. He immigrated to the United States and obtained his Master's degree in Computer Science from the University of Texas at Dallas. He then worked as a UNIX/C systems analyst and became heavily involved with research in neural networks and parallel distributed processing. He later taught at the University of Texas at Dallas, covering a wide variety of courses including UNIX, C, assembly language, programming languages, C++, and Smalltalk. He co-founded ObjectSpace, which specialized in object-oriented training, consulting, and products. He then founded The Mind Electric, which produced a Java web services platform called Glue and a platform for shared SOA infrastructure called Fabric. The Mind Electric was acquired by webMethods, where Graham is now the Chief Technology Officer. In his spare time, he reads, runs, swims, cycles, dives, skis, travels, and maintains a blog.

King Ables earned his Bachelor's degree in Computer Science from the University of Texas at Austin in 1982. He has been a UNIX user, developer, systems administrator, or consultant since 1979 and a Linux user since late in the last century. He has worked in academia, at small startup companies, and in large corporations, and is currently an independent consultant specializing in IT services and network security. He has developed UNIX and Linux product software and systems tools, delivered support and training services, and written product documentation and training materials. He has authored or co-authored two books on UNIX, written many magazine articles on various UNIX topics, and is a co-inventor of an e-commerce privacy mechanism that was awarded a software patent. His professional interests include networking, security, and privacy, but he likes hiking, mountain biking, and skiing just a bit more.

About the Book

This book is an outgrowth of the popularity of Linux. Its original version, *UNIX for Programmers and Users*, written by Graham and updated in subsequent editions by King has been widely used in classroom settings and is popular with professionals new to UNIX or UNIX programming. The increasing popularity of Linux created a demand for a Linux version of such a book, especially in classrooms where Linux is emerging as the platform of choice for computer science students.

Graham wrote the original version in response to the need for course material for university students as well as professional programmers, taking great care to include many different types of users in his target audience. He created a book that was helpful to everyone from a complete beginner to an experienced programmer and allowed instructors to teach a variety of courses. The widespread use of Linux has led to the same need for Linux users and instructors.

When my editors at Prentice-Hall first approached me about creating a Linux version of the book, my flippant response was "Fine, change 'UNIX' to 'Linux' on the cover and ship it!" That response was made in jest, of course, but I also thought it was rooted in some amount of truth. I had used many versions of both UNIX and Linux in the past several years, and they seemed all the same to me (which is a strength of both Linux and UNIX). But this similarity is only skin deep.

Experienced UNIX users will feel very comfortable with Linux because it adheres to a specified standard for portable operating systems, which means that it provides a specific set of commands, applications, library functions, and system calls. Most of the commands and system calls behave similarly to, if not exactly the same as, those in most versions of UNIX. Some Linux commands have been renamed for various reasons, but in most cases the old UNIX name is usually available as an equivalent.

While, on the surface, Linux looks just like UNIX (which is the whole idea behind having a standard), the implementation is another story. With the benefit of thousands of volunteer programers unencumbered by marketing departments and product release schedules (i.e., "business issues") but armed with years of advances in operating-systems understanding, Linux is actually a significant improvement of an already good idea. When you look "under the hood," you will find that Linux is a much cleaner implementation because it doesn't suffer from the long evolution and tangled code base that plagues many versions of UNIX today.

And so this Linux-specific book is actually very different from its UNIX counterpart. Even where the substance is similar to UNIX, the details and examples may vary greatly. Substantive differences include a new chapter on installing Linux and largely revised chapters on the internal workings of Linux and system administration.

While we could not possibly cover every detail of every command or application that comes with Linux (without creating a multivolume set!), we try to cover the basics and the most often used utilities to provide a solid foundation upon which you can continue to build your understanding of Linux and the GNU utilities.

Organization of the Book

Linux is a big thing. To describe it fully requires an explanation of many topics from different angles, which is exactly what I've provided. This book is split into several sections, each designed for a particular kind of user. I recommend that the various categories of user read the chapters as follows:

Category of user	Chapters
Day-to-day casual users	Chapter 1, "What Is Linux?" Chapter 2, "Installing Your Linux System" (if necessary) Chapter 3, "GNU Utilities for Nonprogrammers"
Advanced users	The previous chapters and: • Chapter 4, "GNU Utilities for Power Users" • Chapter 5, "The Linux Shells" • your choice of shell chapter(s) • Chapter 9, "Networking and the Internet" • Chapter 10, "The Linux Desktop"
Applications programmers	The above chapters and: • Chapter 11, "C Programming Tools" • Chapter 12, "Systems Programming"
Wizards	Everything (of course!)

Layout of the Chapters

Every chapter in this book has a standard prologue, as follows:

Motivation

Why it's useful to learn the material that follows.

Prerequisites

What the reader should know in order to successfully negotiate the chapter.

Objectives

A list of the topics that are presented.

Presentation

A description of the method by which the topics are presented.

Utilities

A list of the utilities that are covered in the chapter (when appropriate).

System Calls

A list of the system calls that are covered in the chapter (when appropriate).

Shell Commands

A list of the shell commands that are covered in the chapter (when appropriate).

In addition, every chapter ends with a review section, which contains the following:

Checklist

A recap of the topics.

Quiz

A quick self-test.

Exercises

A list of exercises, rated *easy, medium,* or *hard.*

Projects

One or more related projects, rated *easy, medium,* or *hard.*

A Guide for Teachers

As I mentioned earlier, this book was originally written for an audience of undergraduate and graduate students. I suggest that a lecture series based on this book could be designed as follows.

If the students don't know the C language, then a medium-paced course could begin with:

a. Chapter 1, "What Is Linux?"

b. Chapter 3, "GNU Utilities for Nonprogrammers"

c. Chapter 5, "The Linux Shells"

d. Chapter 11, "C Programming Tools"

The lecturer could then introduce the students to the C language, and use the contents of Chapter 12, "Systems Programming" for class exercises and projects.

If the students already know the C language, then a medium-paced course could include:

a. Chapter 1, "What Is Linux?"

b. Chapter 3, "GNU Utilities for Nonprogrammers"

c. Chapter 5, "The Linux Shells"

d. Chapter 6, "The Bourne Again Shell"

e. Chapter 11, "C Programming Tools"

f. Chapter 12, "Systems Programming"

g. Chapter 13, "Linux Internals"

Projects focusing on parallel processing and interprocess communication will ensure that the students end up with a good knowledge of Linux fundamentals.

Nomenclature

There are references throughout this book to Linux utilities, shell commands (that is, commands that are part of a command shell itself), and system calls (Linux library functions). It's quite easy to confuse these three things, so I adopted a consistent way to differentiate them:

- Linux utilities are always written in boldface, like this: "the **mkdir** utility makes a directory."
- Shell commands are always written in italics, like this: "the *history* command lists your previous commands."
- System calls are always followed by parentheses, like this: "the fork () system call duplicates a process."

Formal descriptions of utilities, shell commands, and system calls are supplied in a box, using a modified-for-Linux Backus-Naur notation. The conventions of this notation are fairly simple and are described fully in the Appendix. As an example, here's a description of the Linux **man** utility:

Utility: **man** [*chapter*] *word*
    man -k *keyword*

The first usage of **man** displays the manual entry associated with *word*. A value for *chapter* is optional. If no chapter number is specified, the first entry found is displayed. The second usage of **man** displays a list of all the manual entries that contain *keyword*.

Formal descriptions of all utilities, shell commands, system calls, and library functions used in the book are cross-referenced in the appendix. Regular references are included in the index.

Sample Linux command sessions are presented in a Courier font. Keyboard input from the user is always displayed in italics, and annotations are always preceded by ellipses (. . .). Here's an example:

```
$ ls                    ... generate a directory listing.
myfile.txt    yourfile.txt
$ whoami
ables
$ _                     ... a new prompt is displayed.
```

References to Other Books

For the same reason that it's good to reuse existing code, it's also good to use other people's reference material when it doesn't interfere with the natural flow of the presentation. Information that we consider to be too specialized for this book is noted with a reference to a publication listed in the Bibliography at the end of this book. For example:

"... for more information on virtual memory, see p. 116 of [Bar, 2000]."

The information in brackets is usually the name of the primary author and the year of publication; in this case this book is entitled *Linux Internals*. Where we reference specific pages, it is, of course, possible that future editions of these books will have different page numbers. The reference will hopefully still remain reasonably close to the quoted page number.

Source Code Availability Online

Source code examples of any "significant" length used in this edition can be found on the web at:

`http://www.prenhall.com/glass`

(You can type this string into a web browser or see Chapter 9, "Networking and the Internet," for more information on FTP.)

Acknowledgments

First of all, thanks go to Graham Glass for his original work and his assistance and support for my work to keep it up-to-date and to develop this Linux version. Also thanks to all those who found the UNIX edition useful and expressed a desire for a Linux edition.

I must also thank thousands of people, most of whom I've never met, but without whom this Linux edition would have no need to fill. Linus Torvalds and his legion of contributors to Linux, as well as Richard Stallman and his Free Software Foundation members and followers, have changed the business of software development.

Those who have been of great help to me personally throughout this process include reviewers Dean Mellas of Cerritos College, Ramon Mata-Toledo and Josh Blake of James Madison University, William D. Leahy Jr. of The Georgia Institute of Technology, Bob Kramer of Youngstown State University, Shawn M. Crowley of The University of Buffalo, and Sydney Shewchuk of Heald College. Other colleagues and friends to whom I owe a debt are David Carver and Judy Ashworth, who provided excellent feedback that helped make this edition much better, and Chris and Dana Dodge and Dan and Denise Downs, who donated equipment to my home computer "lab."

As always, the folks at Prentice Hall have been nothing but helpful, encouraging, and supportive, especially Petra Recter, Kate Hargett, Camille Trentacoste, Marcia Horton, Michael Giacobbe, Tracy Dunkelberger, Donna Crilly, Sarah Parker, Christianna Lee, and John Keegan.

Special thanks to Paul Becker and Alan Apt for starting me on this road and for their continued friendship and encouragement.

And lastly, my eternal gratitude to all my friends and my sister, Kat, for keeping me sane through the last couple of years. Without them, you would not be holding this book.

King Ables

1

What Is Linux?

Motivation

Linux is a popular operating system in the engineering and information technology world and has lately been growing in popularity in the business world. Knowledge of its functions and purpose will help you to understand why so many people choose to use it, and will make your own use of Linux more effective.

Prerequisites

To fully understand this chapter, you should have a little experience with using a computer and a familiarity with basic computer terms such as *program*, *file*, and *CPU*.

Objectives

In this chapter, I describe the basic components of a computer system, define the term *operating system*, and explain why Linux is so successful. I also present Linux from several different perspectives, ranging from that of a nonprogrammer to that of an advanced systems programmer.

Presentation

To begin with, I describe the main bits and pieces that make up a typical computer system. I then show how a special program called an *operating system* is needed to control these pieces effectively, and present a short list of operating system facilities and standards. Following this is a look at where Linux came from and a description of the basic UNIX and Linux philosophies that act as a framework for the information presented in the rest of this book.

1

1.1 Computer Systems

A typical single-user computer system is built out of many parts, including a central processing unit (CPU), memory, disks, a monitor, and a keyboard. Small systems like this may be connected together to form larger computer networks, enabling tasks to be distributed among individual computers. Figure 1–1 is an illustration of such a network.

The hardware that goes to make up a computer network is only half the story; the software that runs on the computer is equally important. Let's take a closer look at the various hardware and software components of a computer system.

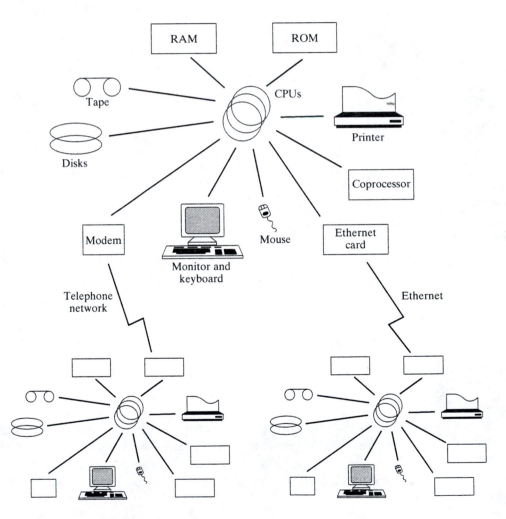

Figure 1–1   A typical computer network.

1.2 Hardware

Computer systems, whether large or small, multi-user or single-user, expensive or cheap, include most of the following pieces of hardware:

1.2.1 Central Processing Unit (CPU)

This reads machine code (instructions in a form that a computer can understand) from memory and executes it. A CPU is often likened to the "brain" of a computer.

1.2.2 Bus

This is the connection, or data path, between the CPU and the system memory and devices of a computer system. All data that moves from a disk drive into memory, or from memory to the CPU, travels across the system's bus.

1.2.3 Random Access Memory (RAM)

This holds the machine code and data that are accessed by the CPU. RAM normally forgets everything it holds when the power is turned off.

1.2.4 Read-Only Memory (ROM)

This holds both machine code and data. Its contents may not be changed and are remembered even when the power is turned off.

1.2.5 Disk(s)

These hold large amounts of data and code on a magnetic or optical medium, and remember it all even when the power is turned off. Floppy disks are generally removable, whereas hard disks are not. Hard disks can hold a lot more information than floppy disks.

1.2.6 CD-ROM Drives

These allow digitally published information on a compact disc to be read by the computer. The information may be in a data stream or may constitute a file system that the operating system can read as if it were on a hard disk drive.

1.2.7 Monitor(s)

These display information and come in two flavors: monochrome and color. Monochrome monitors are rare in newer computer systems.

1.2.8 Graphics Card(s)

These allow the CPU to display information on a monitor. Many graphics cards have on-board processors to decrease the load on the system processor.

1.2.9 Keyboard

This allows a user to enter alphanumeric information. There are several different kinds of keyboards available, depending partly on the language of the user. For example, Japanese keyboards are much larger than Western keyboards, as their alphabet is much larger. The Western keyboards are often referred to as QWERTY keyboards, as these are the first six letters on the upper left-hand side of the keyboard.

1.2.10   Mouse

This allows a user to position things easily on the screen using short movements of the hand. Most mice have "tails" that connect them to the computer, but some have radio or infrared connections that make the tail unnecessary.

1.2.11   Printer(s)

These allow a user to obtain hard copies of information. Some printers print characters only, whereas others may print graphics.

1.2.12   Tape(s)

These are generally used for making backup copies of information stored on disks. They are slower than disks but store large amounts of data in a fairly cheap way.

1.2.13   Modem

A modem allows you to communicate with other computers across a telephone line. Different modems allow different rates of communication. Most modems even correct for errors that are caused by a poor telephone connection.

1.2.14   Network Interface

A network interface card (NIC) allows your computer to communicate with other computers across a high-speed link.

1.2.15   Other Peripherals

There are many other kinds of peripherals that computer systems can support, including graphics tablets, optical scanners, array processors, sound cards, voice recognition cards, and synthesizers (to name a few).

You cannot just connect these pieces of hardware together and have a working computer system—you must also have some software that controls and coordinates it all. The ability to share peripherals, to share memory, to communicate between machines, and to run more than one program at a time is made possible by a special kind of program called an *operating system*.

1.3   Operating System

The components of a computer system can't function together without an operating system. Many different operating systems are available for PCs, minicomputers, and mainframes—the most common ones being Linux, OpenVMS, MacOS, various versions of UNIX, and Windows. Linux and UNIX are available for many different hardware platforms, whereas most other operating systems are tied to a specific hardware family. This is one of the first good things about Linux—it's available for just about any machine.

Some operating systems are very large and include the command interpreter, windowing capability, and tools built into the operating system code. Linux is different. The part of Linux that can be considered the running "system" is known as the Linux kernel and provides only the "core" capabilities and interfaces for moving data between devices and managing running processes. The commands, editors, programs, windowing systems, and most of the other parts of the system with which people interface run separately from the kernel code.

Of the operating systems listed above, only Linux, OpenVMS, and UNIX allow more than one user to use the computer system at a time, providing a multi-user environment. Some businesses still buy a powerful minicomputer with twenty or more terminals and then use UNIX as the operating system that shares the CPUs, memory, and disks among the users. Now that workstation hardware is relatively inexpensive, every user can run a UNIX or Linux system on his or her desk.

1.4   Software

One way to describe the hardware of a computer system is that it provides a framework for executing programs and storing files. The kinds of programs that run on Linux platforms vary widely in size and complexity, but tend to share certain common characteristics. Here is a list of useful facts concerning Linux programs and files:

- A *file* is a collection of data that is usually stored on disk, although some files are stored on tape. Linux treats peripherals as *special* files, so that terminals, printers, and other devices are accessible in the same way as disk-based files.
- A *program* is a collection of bytes representing code and data that are stored in a file.
- When a program is started, it is loaded from disk into RAM (actually, only parts of it are loaded, but we'll come to that later). When a program is running it is called a *process*.
- Most processes read and write data from files.
- Processes and files have an *owner* and may be protected against unauthorized access.
- Linux supports a hierarchical directory structure.
- Files and processes have a "location" within the directory hierarchy. A process may change its own location and/or the location of a file.
- Linux provides services for the creation, modification, and destruction of programs, processes, and files.

Figure 1–2 is an illustration of a tiny Linux directory hierarchy that contains four files and a process running the "sort" utility.

1.5   Sharing Resources

Another operating system function that Linux provides is the sharing of limited resources among competing processes. Limited resources in a typical computer system include CPUs, memory, disk space, and peripherals such as printers. Here is a brief outline of how these resources are shared:

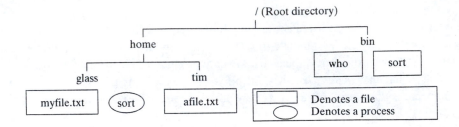

Figure 1–2 Directory hierarchy.

- Linux shares *CPUs* among processes by dividing each second of CPU time into equal-sized "slices" and then allocating them to processes based on a priority scheme. Important processes are allocated more slices than others.
- Linux shares *memory* among processes by dividing RAM up into thousands of equal-sized "pages" of memory, and then allocating them to processes based on a priority scheme. Only those portions of a process that actually need to be in RAM are ever loaded from disk. Pages of RAM that are not accessed for a while are saved back to disk so that the memory may be reallocated to other processes.
- Linux shares *disk space* among users by dividing the disks into thousands of equal-sized "blocks" and then allocating them to users as necessary. A single file is built out of one or more blocks.

Chapter 13, "Linux Internals," contains more details on how these sharing mechanisms are implemented. We've now looked at every major role that Linux plays as an operating system except one—as a medium for communication.

1.6   Communication

The components of a computer system cannot achieve very much when they work in isolation:

- A process may need to talk to a graphics card to display output.
- A process may need to talk to a keyboard to get input.
- A network mail system needs to talk to other computers to send and receive mail.
- Two processes need to talk to each other in order to collaborate on a single problem.

Linux provides several different ways for processes and peripherals to talk to each other, depending on the type and speed of the communication. For example, one way that a process can talk to another process is via an interprocess communication mechanism called a "pipe." A pipe is a one-way medium-speed data channel that allows two processes on the same machine to talk. If the processes are on different machines connected by a network, then a mechanism called a "socket" may be used instead. A socket is a two-way high-speed data channel.

It is becoming quite common nowadays for different pieces of a problem to be tackled by different processes on different machines. For example, there is a graphics system called the X Window System that works by using something termed a "client-server" model. One computer (the X "server") is used to control a graphics terminal and to draw the various lines, circles, and windows, while another computer (the X "client") generates the data that is to be displayed. Arrangements like this are examples of distributed processing, where the burden of computation is spread among many computers. In fact, a single X server may service many X clients. Figure 1–3 is an illustration of an X-based system.

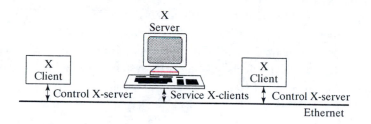
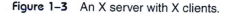

Figure 1–3   An X server with X clients.

We will discuss the X Window System further in Chapter 10, "The Linux Desktop."

1.7 Utilities

Even the most powerful operating system isn't worth much to the average user unless there is useful software available for it. Linux distributions come complete with at least two hundred small utility programs, including a couple of text editors, a C/C++ compiler, a sorting utility, a graphical user interface, several command shells, and text-processing tools. Through the open source movement and commercial resources, many other popular packages like spreadsheets, compilers, and desktop publishing tools are also available.

1.8 Programmer Support

Any good operating system must also provide an environment in which programmers can develop new and innovative software to address the changing needs of the user community. Linux caters very well to programmers. It is an example of an "open" system, which means that the internal software architecture is well documented and available in source code form, either free of charge or for a relatively small fee. The features of Linux—such as parallel processing, interprocess communication, and file handling—are all easily accessible from a programming language such as C via a set of functions known as "system calls." Many facilities that were difficult to use on older operating systems are now within the reach of every systems programmer.

1.9   Standards

In "the old days," a computer ran an operating system that was designed and developed to run only on that specific computer. Another computer built by another company ran a different operating system, so not only was it difficult to move application software to another system, it was difficult to even use the other system if you didn't already know the operating system.

When UNIX, the predecessor and inspiration for Linux, was created, the authors wrote a great deal of the code in the C programming language. This made it relatively easy to port UNIX to different hardware platforms. This is an important benefit and has contributed a great deal to the proliferation and success of UNIX.

Over time, this portability led to the definition of a standard for the interfaces and behavior of a "portable operating system." Today, POSIX 1003.1 is *the* standard for UNIX and UNIX-like operating systems and is maintained by IEEE and The Open Group. Because Linux implements this POSIX standard, it "looks and feels" like a UNIX system even though no code[1] from any UNIX implementation is used in Linux. For more information about UNIX standards, visit the following web sites:

```
http://www.ieee.org
http://www.opengroup.org
http://www.unix.org
```

1.10 Linux Lineage

Linux has emerged as the most successful operating system adhering to the POSIX standard for a portable operating system. This is largely due to the already existing popularity of UNIX, the availability of Linux for many different platforms, and the freedom of use and low cost for Linux because of its distribution as open software. In order to understand what Linux is, you have to know a little something about its roots.

1.10.1   UNIX

A computer scientist named Ken Thompson was interested in building a system for a game called "Space Wars," which required a fairly fast response time. The operating system that he was using, MULTICS[2], didn't give him the performance that he needed, so he decided to build his own operating system on a spare PDP-7 system. He called it UNICS because the "UNI" part of the name implied that it would do one thing well, as opposed to the "MULTI" part of the "MULTICS" name, which he felt tried to do many things without much success. He wrote his operating system in assembly language, and the first version was very primitive; it was only a single-user system, it had no network capability, and it had a poor memory management system

---

1.   A pending lawsuit by SCO against IBM disputes this. SCO alleges that IBM has used some original UNIX code in their distribution(s) of Linux. Should this turn out to be true, the code will most certainly be removed, so even if this is an issue, it is only a temporary one.

2.   The Multiplexed Information and Computing Service, originally developed by Bell Labs, MIT, and General Electric.

for sharing memory between processes. However, it was efficient, compact, and fast, which was exactly what he wanted.

A few years later, a colleague of Ken's, Dennis Ritchie, suggested that they rewrite his operating system using the C language, which Dennis had recently developed from a language called B. The idea that an operating system could be written in a high-level language was an unusual approach at that time. Most people felt that compiled code would not run fast enough[3] and that only direct use of machine language was sufficient for such an important component of a computer system. Fortunately, C was slick enough that the conversion was successful, and the new operating system suddenly had a huge advantage over other operating systems—its source code was understandable. Only a small percentage of the original source code remained in assembly language, which meant that porting the operating system to a different machine was possible. As long as the target machine had a C compiler, most of the operating system would work with no changes; only the assembly-language sections had to be rewritten.

Bell Laboratories started using this prototype version of what was by then called UNIX in its patent department, primarily for text processing, and a number of UNIX utilities that are found in modern UNIX systems were originally designed during this time period. Examples of these utilities are **nroff** and **troff**. But because AT&T was prohibited from selling software due to antitrust regulations in the early 1970s, Bell Laboratories licensed UNIX source code to universities free of charge, hoping that enterprising students would enhance the system and further its progress into the marketplace.

Indeed, graduate students at the University of California at Berkeley (Bill Joy, co-founder of Sun Microsystems, among them) took the task to heart and made some huge improvements over the years, including the first good memory management system and the first real networking capability. In the late 1970s, the university began to distribute its own version of UNIX, called the Berkeley Software Distribution (BSD UNIX), to the general public. The differences between these versions of UNIX can still be seen in some versions of UNIX to this day.

With the breakup of the Bell System and release from many antitrust restrictions, AT&T was free to start selling UNIX licenses in the mid 1980s. AT&T UNIX had proceeded through releases known as System III and System V. By the end of the 1980s, workstation hardware was becoming economical and UNIX was infiltrating businesses and engineering environments, because companies like Sun (who commercialized BSD UNIX) and AT&T were selling and supporting its use.

Both System V and BSD UNIX have their own strengths and weaknesses, as well as a lot of commonality. Two consortiums of leading computer manufacturers gathered behind these two versions of UNIX, each believing its own version to be the best. UNIX International, headed by AT&T and Sun, backed the latest version of System V UNIX, called System V Release 4. The Open Software Foundation (OSF), headed by IBM, Digital Equipment Corporation, and Hewlett-Packard, attempted to create the successor to BSD UNIX called OSF/1. Both

---

3. Compiler technology has also improved greatly since then, so code most compilers produce is much more efficient.

groups complied with a set of standards created by the Portable Operating System Interface (POSIX) committee of The Institute of Electrical and Electronics Engineers (IEEE). The OSF project has fallen by the wayside in recent years, leaving System V as the apparent "winner" of the "UNIX wars," although most of the best features of BSD UNIX have been rolled into most System V-based versions of UNIX. Hence, Solaris (from Sun Microsystems), HP-UX (from Hewlett-Packard), AIX (from IBM), and IRIX (from Silicon Graphics, Inc.), while all System V-based, also include most of the different features of BSD UNIX at varying levels of completeness.

While the so-called "UNIX wars" (BSD vs. System V) were playing out, however, the watershed event that would lead to the evolution of Linux was brewing.

1.10.2   Open Source Software and the Free Software Foundation

The UNIX community has a long tradition of software being available in source code form, either free or charge or for a reasonably small fee, enabling people to learn from or improve the code in order to evolve the state of the art. UNIX itself started out this way, and many individual components related to (and in many cases now a part of) UNIX share this tradition. So it's no surprise that in a world of otherwise proprietary, shrink-wrapped software, where you buy what's available and conform your requirements so that they are satisfied by the software, those who support the idea of freely available source code have banded together.

One of the first proponents of the idea of freely available software was Richard Stallman, one of the founders of the Free Software Foundation in the mid-1980s. Stallman had already written a version of the popular Emacs text editor and made it publicly available. He believed that everyone should have the right to obtain, use, view, and modify software. He started the GNU[4] Project whose goal was to reproduce popular UNIX tools, and ultimately an entire UNIX-like operating system, in new code that could be freely distributed because it did not contain any licensed code as UNIX did. Early products included a version of the popular text editor Emacs and the GNU C Compiler. Today, GNU applications are numerous and popular, but the kernel itself proved to be more challenging. Work continues on GNU Hurd, a Mach-based Unix-like kernel, that will complete FSFs goal of providing a free and standard operating system and tools.

The "free" in FSFs philosophy of free software does not mean the software is available at no cost, but rather that it comes with the freedom to use, view, and modify it. Up to this point, when someone wanted to give away their software, they simply stated that it belonged to the public domain. However, this allowed people to change it and include it in proprietary software, thus removing the freedom for others that had allowed them to use it. In order to retain their ownership and rights to GNU software but still provide for its use by the widest possible audience, the FSF developed the GNU General Public License (GPL) under which GNU software is licensed to the world. The GNU GPL provides for the copying, use, modification, and redistribution of GNU software provided that the same freedom to use, modify, and distribute is passed on

---

4.   GNU is a recursive acronym standing for "GNUs not UNIX" and pronounced "guh-NEW."

to anyone who uses your version of the software. Where a *copyright* is used to protect the rights of the owner, the goal here is to protect the rights of the recipient of a distribution of the software as well. Thus, the FSF coined the term *copyleft* to describe this somewhat inverted meaning. [Fink, 2003] is an excellent examination of the phenomenon of open source software, why it came about, where it works, and where it does not. For more information on the Free Software Foundation and the GNU Project, visit their web site:

```
http://www.fsf.org
```

1.10.3   Linus

In 1991, Linus Torvalds, a student at the University of Helsinki in Finland, posted a message to an Internet newsgroup, asking if anyone was interested in helping him develop a UNIX-like kernel. He had been playing with Minix, a small UNIX-like kernel developed by Andrew Tanenbaum for teaching operating system concepts, but Minix's role was to be small and demonstrate concepts, not to be a "real" operating system. Linus and like-minded programmers found each other and began to develop their own kernel code.

When he started his work, Linus had no intention of it becoming anything more than a hobby. Because he wanted others to be able to use it freely, Linus released Linux (standing for "Linus' Minix") 1.0 under the GNU GPL in 1994.

At first, Linus and a few friends maintained and modified the source code, but today thousands of volunteer developers around the world contribute new code and fixes. The combination of the Linux kernel and GNU utilities allows one to create a complete UNIX-like operating system, running on many different hardware platforms, and available in source form so you can make your own bug fixes and enhancements to it.

Linux shares no common code with any version of UNIX but adheres to the POSIX operating system standard, so it is indistinguishable from UNIX to the casual user. And because it has been written with the benefit of years of operating systems knowledge, in many places it is actually a significant improvement over UNIX.

With the release of Linux 2.0 in 1996, Linux became a major competitor to other popular operating systems, including commercial versions of UNIX.

1.11 Linux Packaging

Linus and his group of volunteer programmers developed a kernel, which is the core part of the operating system. But if you installed a kernel on a machine without the hundreds of tools, utilities, and applications that users require, it would not be of much use to most people. To complement the Linux kernel, the UNIX-like tools developed by the Free Software Foundation can be added to the kernel code and packaged as a *distribution* of open source software.

The distinction between the Linux kernel and the GNU utilities is an important one. While most people refer to a complete system as Linux, this is strictly not correct. Linux is technically only the kernel itself; most of the command utilities and applications come from the GNU Project.

Many companies and organizations have created their own distributions of Linux and the GNU utilities, as we will see in Chapter 2, "Installing Your Linux System." When you receive a Linux distribution from a vendor, it was packaged and perhaps modified or added to by that vendor, but contains code from Linus and his kernel team and the FSF GNU Project. Because it is all covered by the GNU GPL, you are free to use and modify all of the code in any way you wish, as long as, if you redistribute it, you do so also under the terms of the GNU GPL (thus allowing anyone else to use and modify any code you might have added).

More information on Linux, Linux distributions, download locations, and documentation, can be found on the following web site:

```
http://www.linux.org
```

1.12 The Linux and UNIX Philosophy

So what is Linux? Let's be clear, Linux is not UNIX. It shares no code with UNIX. But because both operating systems adhere to the same POSIX standard, they look and act almost alike, so for most people, the fact that they are not the same thing is only a technicality. But it is an extremely important technicality!

Linux is a complete reimplementation. Because it shares no common code with any version of UNIX, it does not connect into the UNIX "family tree." Even so, Linux has strong philosophical connections and design influences derived from virtually all versions of UNIX. When one talks about the philosophy of Linux and GNU utilities, it is truly to talk about the UNIX philosophy.

The original UNIX system was lean and mean. It had a very small number of utilities and virtually no network or security functionality. The original designers of UNIX had some pretty strong notions about how utilities should be written: a program should do one thing, do it well, and complex tasks should be performed by using these utilities together. To this end, they built a special mechanism called a "pipe" into the heart of UNIX to support their vision. A pipe allows a user to specify that the output of one process is to be used as the input to another process. Two or more processes may be connected in this fashion, resulting in a "pipeline" of data flowing from the first process through to the last (Figure 1–4).

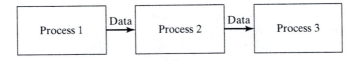

Figure 1–4   A pipeline.

The nice thing about pipelines is that many problems can be solved by such an arrangement of processes. Each process in the pipeline performs a set of operations upon the data and then passes the results on to the next process for further processing. For example, imagine that you wish to obtain a sorted list of all the users on the system. There is a utility called **who** that outputs an unsorted list of the users, and another utility called **sort** that outputs a sorted version of its input. These two utilities may be connected together with a pipe so that the output from **who** passes directly into **sort**, resulting in a sorted list of users (Figure 1–5).

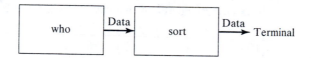

Figure 1–5   A pipeline that sorts.

This is a more powerful approach to solving problems than writing a fresh program from scratch every time or using two programs but having to store the intermediate data in a temporary file in order for the next program to have access to it.

The UNIX (and therefore Linux) philosophy for solving problems can thus be stated:

- If you can solve the problem by combining multiple existing utilities using pipes, do it; *otherwise*
- ... ask people on the network if they know how to solve it. If they do, great; *otherwise*
- ... if you could solve the problem with the aid of some other hand-written utilities, write the utilities yourself and add them into the repertoire. Design each utility to do one thing well and one thing only, so that each may be reused to solve other problems.
  If more utilities won't do the trick
- ... write a program to solve the problem (typically in C, C++, or Java).

Inside Linux is hidden another more subtle philosophy that is slowly eroding. The original system was designed by programmers who liked to have the power to access data or code anywhere in the system, regardless of who owned it. To support this capability, they built the concept of a "super-user" into UNIX, which meant that certain privileged individuals could have special access rights. For example, the system administrator of a UNIX system always has the capability of becoming a super-user so that he/she may perform cleanup tasks such as terminating rogue processes or removing unwanted users from the system. The concept of super-user has security implications that are a little frightening. Anyone with the right password could potentially wipe out an entire system, or extract top-security data with relative ease.

1.13 Linux Features

Here is a recap of the features that Linux provides:

- It allows many users to access a computer system at the same time.
- It supports the creation, modification, and destruction of programs, processes, and files.
- It provides a directory hierarchy that gives a location to processes and files.

- It shares CPUs, memory, and disk space in a fair and efficient manner between competing processes.
- It allows processes and peripherals to talk to each other, even if they're on different machines.
- It comes complete with a large number of standard utilities.
- There are plenty of high-quality, commercially available software packages available for most versions.
- It allows programmers to easily access operating features via a well-defined set of system calls, which are analogous to library functions.
- It is a standard, portable, open source operating system, and thus is available on a wide variety of platforms.

Because it provides all the features expected of a modern operating system, doing it in a way that is well documented, accessible, and adheres to a defined standard, and because its implementation is open source and freely available, Linux has made, and will continue to make, its mark on modern operating system design.

Throughout this book references to web sites are listed for various specific topics relevant to the topic at hand. In addition to all future specific references, there are a number of useful web sites containing a great deal of valuable information about Linux (Figure 1–6).

`http://www.kernel.org/`	The Linux Kernel Archives
`http://www.li.org/`	Linux International
`http://www.linux.org/`	The Linux Home Page at Linux Online
`http://www.linuxhq.com/`	Linux HeadQuarters
`http://www.linuxjournal.com/`	Linux Journal
`http://www.tldp.org/`	The Linux Documentation Project

Figure 1–6   Useful Linux web sites.

1.14 The Rest of This Book

As you can probably tell by now, Linux is a fairly substantial topic, and can only be properly digested in small portions. In order to aid this process, and to allow individual readers to focus on the subjects that they find most applicable, I decided to write this book's chapters based on the different kinds of Linux user. These users tend to fall into one of several categories:

- *Nonprogrammers*, who occasionally want to perform simple tasks like sending and receiving electronic mail, using a spreadsheet, or doing some word processing.
- *Shell Users*, who use background processing and write small scripts from within a convenient interface.

- *Advanced Nonprogrammers*, who use more complex facilities like file stream editors and file processing.
- *Advanced Shell Users*, who write programs in a high-level command language for performing useful tasks such as automatic backups, monitoring disk usage, and performing software installations.
- *Programmers*, who write programs in a general-purpose language such as C for speed and efficiency.
- *System Programmers*, who write programs that require a good knowledge of the underlying computer system, including network communications and advanced file access.
- *System Architects*, who invent better computer systems. These people provide a vision and a framework for the future.
- *System Administrators*, who make sure that the computer system runs smoothly and that the users are generally satisfied.

To begin with, read the chapters that interest you the most. Then go back and fill in the gaps when you have the time. If you're unsure of which chapters are most appropriate for your skill level, read the introductory section "About This Book" for some hints.

CHAPTER REVIEW

Checklist

In this chapter, I mentioned:

- the main hardware components of a computer system
- the purpose of an operating system
- the meaning of the terms *program*, *process*, and *file*
- the layout of a hierarchical directory structure
- that Linux shares CPUs, memory, and disk space among competing processes
- that Linux supports communication between processes and peripherals
- that Linux comes complete with a multitude of standard utilities
- that most major software packages are available on Linux systems
- that Linux is an "open" system as well as an open source system
- the Free Software Foundation
- the history of Linux and UNIX
- that Linux has a rosy future

Quiz

1. What are the two main versions of UNIX that influenced Linux, and how did each begin?
2. Write down five main functions of an operating system.
3. What is the difference between a *process* and a *program*?
4. What is the UNIX/Linux philosophy?
5. What is the difference between an "open system" and an open source system?

Exercises

1. Identify one or two other popular or historical operating systems and compare their features with those of Linux. [level: *medium*]

Projects

1. Compare two Linux distributions. What tools do they share? Name some tools that are unique to one distribution. [level: *easy*]

2

Installing Your Linux System

Motivation

In the past, when someone became a new UNIX user, the system was usually owned and provided by the user's workplace or school. Linux is popular at universities and in business, but is also a great operating system for personal use. Therefore, you may be planning to set up your very own Linux system. This chapter will help make this task less intimidating.

Prerequisites

A beginner with no Linux experience should find this chapter helpful. General familiarity with computers and having read Chapter 1, "What Is Linux?" will help.

Objectives

In this chapter, I describe the issues involved in choosing a particular Linux distribution, methods of obtaining the software, and, in general, how to go about installing it on your system. Because each installation is different, you will need to consult the installation guide or other documentation for the distribution of Linux you choose to install.

Presentation

We begin by looking at the hardware required to run Linux and the more popular distributions of Linux from which you are likely to choose. Once you decide what to install, we will discuss options and issues related to getting and installing Linux on your computer.

2.1   Introduction

You may be reading this book in order to learn to use Linux in a place that already has Linux computers available for you to use. In that case, this chapter will give you an appreciation of what it took to set them up, but you can just start using Linux without having to do your own installation.

It is just as likely that you either need or want to run Linux on a computer of your own (at home, perhaps). In this case, you will need to get Linux and install it before you can begin your "real work."

So many choices are available to you, it may seem overwhelming. Because you are free to choose any Linux distribution you wish, I cannot possibly go through a step-by-step installation process for all of them. If I were to pick a single distribution to cover, this book would be much less useful to anyone who picked a different distribution (which, by definition, would be most people). In order to be most useful to the widest possible audience, we will not limit our discussions to any single distribution, but instead, we'll examine the myriad of issues and decisions you will make on your way to installing any distribution of Linux on your system. You should consult the specific installation documentation for your chosen distribution.

2.2   Make Sure Your Hardware Will Support Linux

While Linux runs on a wide variety of hardware platforms, it is wise to take a few minutes to be sure that the computer you have (or get) will support it effectively.

2.2.1   CPU Type

Linux probably runs on more Intel-based (or Intel clone) computers than any other type of hardware (most likely because there are more of those out in the world). But in addition to the "typical" PC processors manufactured by companies like Intel, AMD, and Cyrix, some of the other CPU families that can run Linux include:

- 68000 (Motorola)
- Alpha (DEC, now part of HP)
- Itanium (HP and Intel)
- MIPS (SGI)
- PA-RISC (HP)
- PowerPC (IBM and Freescale Semiconductor, formerly part of Motorola)
- RS6000 (IBM)
- SPARC (Sun Microsystems)
- Vax (DEC, now part of HP)

The Intel Pentium I is probably the oldest Intel processor you would want to use. Some distributions compile specifically for Pentium, so earlier processors will not work, but even when an 80486 system, for example, will run Linux, it does so poorly. I have found a Pentium II (with enough memory) to be quite acceptable for most uses.

2.2.2   Bus Architecture

Most modern PCs have two types of bus architectures: the Peripheral Component Interconnect (PCI) and the Industry Standard Architecture (ISA). The PCI bus is a 32-bit bus and is faster than older bus architectures (and its extended version, PCI-X, is faster yet). The ISA bus, one of those older architectures, is a 16-bit bus, and is slower than a PCI bus, but remains in many PCs for backward compatibility with old hardware. The original ISA bus was 8 bits in the first IBM PC in the 1980s and was later expanded to 16 bits. The Extended ISA (EISA) bus, a 32-bit extension of the ISA bus, is also supported by the Linux kernel.

Linux sometimes needs extra drivers for older devices connected to the ISA bus, but it works well with most PCI-based devices.

2.2.3   Memory

Like any complex operating system, Linux requires a significant amount of memory in order to run effectively. The table in Figure 2–1 shows recommended amounts of memory for various types of Linux installations.

Minimum memory for a system without the graphical user interface	64 MB
Minimum memory for a typical graphical workstation	128 MB
Recommended memory for a typical workstation	256 MB (or more)

Figure 2–1   Linux memory guidelines.

Note that Linux will run on systems with less memory, but it will not do so well. Of course, the more memory you have, the better any system will run.

2.2.4   Disk

Nearly all operating systems take up more disk space with every release, and Linux is no different. A full installation of Linux, depending on your distribution, requires about 3 gigabytes[1] (GB) of disk space. You can, however, install a useful Linux system in much less. Figure 2–2 provides some estimates for space for common uses of Linux.

Most Intel-based PC systems contain disk drives that use the Integrated Device Electronics (IDE) interface, and Linux finds these just fine. Some higher-end PCs might have Small Computer Systems Interface (SCSI) disks and, while Linux comes with SCSI drivers, the boot kernels do not always find these devices by default. You may need to consult the specific installation guide to find out how to load SCSI drivers if Linux doesn't "see" the disks when it starts.

---

1.   1 GB = 1,024 megabytes (MB).

Minimal system without many optional software applications	500 MB to 1 GB
Typical Linux workstation including common user applications	1–2 GB
Linux workstation or server including many optional software packages	2–4 GB
Full Linux installation including everything on your installation media	4–12 GB depending on distribution selected

Figure 2–2   Linux disk space guidelines.

2.2.5   Display, Keyboard, and Mouse

The vast majority of displays, keyboards, and mouse devices that work on PCs will work for Linux. As with other hardware, very old devices might not be supported. Sometimes a very new device is not recognized because no one has (yet) contributed a new driver for it.

Many distributions of Linux initially default to using a 640×480 display for greatest compatibility with the greatest number of monitors and video cards. After Linux is installed, you have the opportunity to reconfigure the display to a higher resolution based on what your video card can support.

Linux supports most PC keyboards and both PS/2 and serial mouse devices without having to specify a driver, but you might have to select the type of device from a list.

2.3   Choose Your Linux Distribution

If there is a disadvantage to Linux, it is that there are so many distributions from which to choose! Many large companies, small companies, and even individuals create their very own distributions of Linux, often to address specific needs. This is the strength of Open Software, but it might not seem like it when all you want is to pick one to run on *your* desktop. Linux distributions are available for all manners of boot media, hardware platforms, and user environments. Several distributions of Linux (e.g., Knoppix, Linspire, MEPIS, and SuSE) can run "live" directly off a CD-ROM, without having to be installed on the hard drive. FeatherLinux can be booted from a USB pen drive. Yellow Dog Linux runs on an Apple Power Mac.

The good news is that only a few distributions are widely deployed. While many more distributions exist than could be discussed here, we can limit ourselves to a discussion of the most popular and least expensive distributions. A great deal of information on these (and many other) distributions can be found at the following web sites:

```
http://www.linux.org
http://www.distrowatch.com
```

The code for Linux and the GNU utilities is open source, so there is no charge for the code itself. However, depending on the distribution you select and the packaging, media, and support that does or does not come with it, you may pay "real money" for it. Most of the distributions we survey here can be downloaded, and all are available on CD-ROM for nominal fees, as we will see later.

2.3.1 Debian

Debian GNU/Linux is a truly noncommercial distribution of Linux in that it is managed by volunteer developers worldwide and not any corporate entity. Debian has been ported to more different hardware platforms than most other distributions.

Although Debian has a reputation for being a bit hard to install, this is being actively addressed by the development of a new install program. There are many options during Linux installation, and the current Debian installation requires that the user be knowledgeable about these options. The installation is text based (rather than using a graphical interface), which seems more difficult to novice users. The X Window System must be configured in a separate step after installation, so Debian initially comes up without a graphical display.

Once Debian is installed, however, it receives high marks for its Advanced Packaging Tool, which is used to install Linux packages rather than the more common Red Hat Package Manager (RPM).

Debian is a very reliable distribution and popular with experienced users. For more information about Debian GNU/Linux, see these web sites:

```
http://www.debian.org/
http://www.aboutdebian.com/
```

2.3.2 Fedora

Red Hat, Inc., was founded in 1994 and was an early, and arguably the most successful, commercial producer of a Linux distribution. Over time, Red Hat has focused on business customers who wanted higher levels of support for enterprise applications. With the addition of the Red Hat Certified Engineer (RHCE) certification program, corporate users felt confident that the information, update, and support resources would be available long into the future.

This success took Red Hat away from the smaller customer and individual Linux user. To avoid neglecting this large and loyal class of user, Red Hat created an entity they named Project Fedora, a community-directed project separate from the retail offerings of the company. The objective of Project Fedora is to provide a new distribution at a fast development pace, so it's always on the leading edge of new functionality, while accepting slightly less stability. The distribution produced by Project Fedora is known as Fedora Core Linux and is popular due to its ease of installation and use. While Red Hat sponsors Project Fedora, they do not support the Fedora Core distribution as they do their commercial Red Hat distributions.

Like most distribution creators, Red Hat adds quite a few enhancements to the basic GNU/Linux system. Fedora Core comes with Red Hat's Disk Druid graphical disk partitioning tool as well as the Red Hat Package Manager (RPM), which is now found in many Linux distributions.

Fedora Core includes a nice graphical installation tool and is better than many other distributions at recognizing a variety of devices during installation. It also does a nice job of helping you decide which optional packages to install.

Officially, Fedora Core is listed as experimental and not for critical environments, but for many uses, Fedora Core is quite satisfactory. In business enterprise and other more critical environments, you are more likely to encounter Red Hat's Enterprise distributions. For more information on Fedora Core and Red Hat, see:

```
http://fedora.redhat.com/
http://www.fedoranews.org/
http://www.redhat.com
```

2.3.3   Mandrake

Mandrake Linux is a commercial distribution, created by MandrakeSoft, a French company founded by Linux enthusiasts in 1998. Mandrake was originally based on an early Red Hat distribution, but many features have been added since. Mandrake is arguably the most popular distribution today.

Mandrake's popularity is largely due to its ease of installation. The graphical installation program includes an excellent disk partitioning tool that can even shrink a Windows partition to make room for Linux (more about that later). Mandrake also does excellent hardware detection. In fact, it was the only distribution I installed that did not have even a minor failure or misstep due to unrecognized hardware or partitioning problems. This is probably one reason Mandrake is very popular with beginners. The installation tool is also helpful when selecting which optional packages to install.

For more information on Mandrake Linux, see:

```
http://www.mandrakesoft.com
http://www.mandrakelinux.com
```

2.3.4   Slackware

Slackware Linux was the first distribution of Linux, originally created by Patrick J. Volkerding while at Moorhead State University (and he is still heavily involved today). Somewhat like Debian, Slackware is a noncommercial distribution and tries to stay more traditional and closer to a "pure" Linux distribution.

The installation process is text, not graphical, so it can be more intimidating for novice users. To install, you boot the kernel and then run a disk partitioning tool (**fdisk** or **cfdisk**) manually, and then run the setup program. Like Debian, the X Window System must be configured in a separate step after installation, so Slackware initially comes up without a graphical display.

What Slackware lacks in bells and whistles, it makes up for in stability. Experienced users (with whom Slackware is most popular) appreciate that it doesn't clutter things up with a lot of "unnecessary" third-party code.

One way Slackware differs from most other Linux distributions is that it uses BSD-style boot scripts when booting instead of the more common System V style. It also includes its own package tool (called **pkgtool**) instead of RPM, but **pkgtool** can read RPM-format package files.

For more information on Slackware, visit their web site:

```
http://www.slackware.com
```

2.3.5   SuSE

SuSE Linux was originally created in Germany, and has been a favorite in Europe. It is a derivative of the Slackware distribution but with the typical additional features of a commercial distribution. SuSE is now owned by Novell and is becoming a favorite in the United States.

SuSE adds its own graphical installation and configuration tool called YaST (which stands for "Yet another Setup Tool"). YaST performs the installation (sometimes in text mode, which is a bit painful), including disk partitioning, and is also the main system configuration tool on a running system. This consistency is comforting and provides a single place to do everything. SuSE also provides a unified X Window System configuration tool called SaX2. Like many distributions, SuSE uses RPM for packages.

For more information on SuSE Linux, visit their web site:

```
http://www.suse.com
```

2.3.6   TurboLinux

While American readers may not run into TurboLinux very much, Linux users in other parts of the world will. TurboLinux is the leading supplier of Linux in the Asia Pacific region and is very popular there because of its excellent multibyte language support (thus it runs well in Chinese, Korean, and Japanese). TurboLinux includes an easy-to-use installation program. TurboLinux is a wholly owned subsidiary of Livedoor, a Tokyo-based information technology company, who acquired it in mid-2004.

For more information on TurboLinux, see:

```
http://www.turbolinux.com/
```

2.4   Consider Optional Software Packages

Once you decide which distribution you want, you will also want to decide how much of it to install. You don't have to decide on each and every package, either before you begin the installation or even while you install your Linux distribution. You can install additional packages later. There are, however, a few important things you should think about up front in order for the installation to go more smoothly.

You should consider things like whether you'll have a graphical workstation or a text-only interface, whether or not you'll be connected to a network, and what kind of work you plan to do with your new Linux system. Of course, you can simply install everything that comes with your distribution if you have the disk space.

2.4.1   X Window System

The X Window System is the graphical user interface for Linux-based systems (and is discussed in more detail in Chapter 10, "The Linux Desktop"). Unless you plan to use your Linux system as a server or only for command-line functions, you probably want to install the X Window System.

Until mid-2004, XFree86 was the open source version of the X Window System used in most distributions of Linux. Due to changes in the licensing, something to which free software fans are unaccustomed, many distributions have chosen to move to an implementation provided by the X.org Foundation. You may see either package, depending on which distribution or even which version of a distribution you choose to install.

It is likely that one or the other will be available, but not both, so if you plan to use your Linux computer as a workstation, plan to install whichever X Window System software is included with the distribution. For more information on open source implementations of the X Window System, see the following web sites:

```
http://www.x.org
http://www.xfree86.org
```

2.4.2   Desktop Environments

If you plan to run your Linux system as a graphical workstation, then in addition to the X Window System, you'll want a *desktop environment*. Where the X Window System provides the basic windowing functions and interfaces to the screen, a desktop environment provides the interfaces that a person uses, like the icons, menus, and toolbars that make up a virtual desktop on the screen.

Two desktop environments have emerged as the main players in Linux environments and are now used in many UNIX environments as well: the GNU Object Model Environment (GNOME) and the K Desktop Environment (KDE). Both come with most distributions of Linux, although each distribution generally displays a preference by specifying one it will install by default (e.g., Fedora defaults to GNOME, Mandrake to KDE). Both desktop environments provide a menu bar of useful applications, a status bar showing running processes and other status information, as well as their own unique window applications (such as file managers and window managers).

If you have never used either GNOME or KDE, you will probably want to install both (if you have the disk space) and try them. Debate rages over which is "better," and they each have legions of fans. On the surface, they both let your system behave like a "typical" window-based system. The differences are more in the philosophy of the designers and what problems they were trying to address. To greatly oversimplify, many feel GNOME is simple but elegant and KDE is complex but flexible. Which you prefer is largely a matter of personal taste.

2.4.2.1   GNOME

GNOME originally grew from code written for a GNU image library. It is a user desktop as well as a development platform for graphical applications that can be written in a variety of languages. Developers with the GNOME Project have invested a great deal of effort in human interface and usability issues. In the UNIX tradition, it embraces simplicity, providing the basic necessities of a desktop environment, but does not overload the user with options. GNOME is Open Software. Figure 2–3 shows an example of a GNOME desktop.

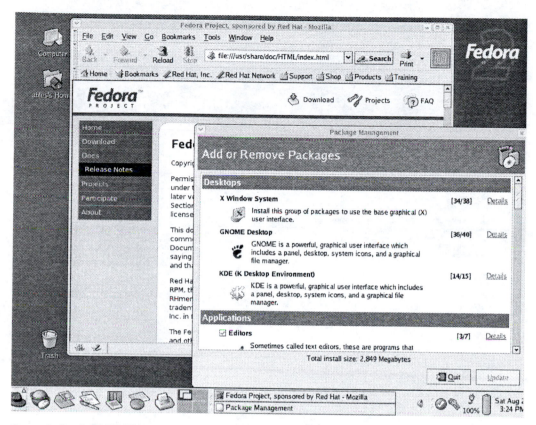

Figure 2-3 A GNOME desktop on Fedora Core Linux.

2.4.2.2 KDE

KDE is also a user desktop and development platform. It provides more applications specific to the KDE environment and tries to serve more purposes for more types of users. While this gives many users, especially novices, more options and capability, it also makes the desktop environment seem busier. Some people don't like that KDE's roots were in some licensed software, but they have worked hard to remove those restrictions, and today KDE is all Open Software. Figure 2–4 shows an example of a KDE desktop.

If you want to install only one, you should visit both project's web sites and read about their capabilities in detail:

```
http://www.kde.org
http://www.gnome.org
```

I might even go so far as to say that both web sites have a "feel" that is similar to the desktop environments, so if you find one web site more useful or comfortable than the other, that might tell you something.

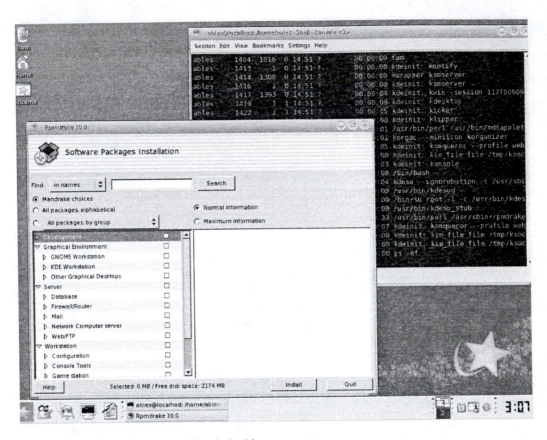

Figure 2–4   A KDE desktop on Mandrake Linux.

2.4.3   Networking

If you are installing your Linux computer in an environment where it will be connected to a local network, there are some things you will likely need to know to install Linux. Your network or systems administrator should be able to provide you with the information you need. Most installation programs have a section where they let you set this information. When installing Slackware Linux, you have to run the **network** utility to set up the network during the installation process. You can also define all the network-related information after installation is complete, but be sure you select enough so that the network services and utilities get installed if you will need them.

The first thing to find out is whether your local network runs a Dynamic Host Configuration Protocol (DHCP) server. If hosts on the network use DHCP to gather information about themselves when they boot, then you may not need to configure much of it yourself (but you'll need your systems administrator to add information for your new machine to the DHCP server). A computer using DHCP sends out a broadcast as it boots up, effectively saying "Who am I" and should receive its name, network address, and everything else it needs to operate on the network.

If your network doesn't use DHCP, then you will need to have your network administrator assign values for (or help you choose) the following items:

- a hostname for your computer
- an IP address
- a netmask
- a default gateway address
- a name server address

The specifics about these items are discussed in more detail in Chapter 9, "Networking and the Internet."

If you are on a local network, then you should also install packages containing network services and tools. If you plan to allow other computers to access the file systems on your Linux computer, you should also install NFS (Sun's Network File System) and Samba.

You should also find out if your local network runs IP (IPv4) or IPv6. Some Linux distributions default to using IPv6 (the latest version of the Internet Protocol networking protocol) and in some environments this can actually cause performance problems. If your network is still running IPv4 (most probably do), you may wish to disable IPv6 in your Linux system.

2.4.4   Office Tools

A nice suite of office productivity tools is available with most distributions of Linux (and if not, you can download the latest version of the software from the web site below). Sun Microsystems sponsors and participates in the open source project OpenOffice.org, which provides a suite of tools with similar functionality to those in Microsoft's Office Suite. Based on Sun's StarOffice (which cannot be completely released as open source due to licensing restrictions on parts of it), OpenOffice.org tools are also able to import and export data from and to the Microsoft applications, so that you can exchange information with Microsoft users.

OpenOffice.org boasts 16 million downloads and includes the following applications:

- Writer—word-processing tool for reports, documents, newsletters, and brochures
- Calc—spreadsheet
- Impress—presentation creator with drawing tools, animation, and special effects
- Draw—drawing tool for everything from simple diagrams to 3D and specialized images
- Base—database user tools that support dBASE, ODBC, and JDBC databases

If you plan to do any sort of writing or presentation creation on your Linux system, these tools are a must. For more information about OpenOffice.org or to download the latest version, see their web site:

```
http://www.openoffice.org
```

2.4.5   Programming Languages and Tools

Linux comes with GNU C and C++ compilers, Perl, and Python. Java comes with many distributions, but if your distribution doesn't have it, you can download it from the Sun Java web site:

```
http://java.sun.com/linux/
```

2.5   Design Your System

Now that you've decided what distribution and what tools to put on your system, you should think about how to lay out the file system(s). It is possible to simply install Linux from a CD-ROM, take all the default sizes and placements of components, and get a running system. But you'll be happier later if you take a few minutes to think about what you need from your Linux system and design an appropriate plan.

2.5.1   How Do You Want To Run Linux?

The ideal situation is that you have a PC that you no longer use and can put Linux on it. This way you don't risk losing any data by doing something wrong during the installation of Linux. Used computer stores sell older models at a fraction of the price of a new system. If you already have or can justify buying a spare system, I would strongly recommend going with a completely separate system. However, this is not always possible. If you must use a PC that already runs Windows, you have several different options.

Some distributions can run Linux "live" off a CD—Knoppix, Linspire, MEPIS, and SuSE, to name but a few. Be sure the distribution you choose supports running directly from the CD without having to install files on the system.

Another option is to run Linux from within Windows. A commercial product called VMware (`www.vmware.com`) can emulate PC hardware, allowing you to install Linux running under VMware.

The most likely option is that you will install Linux on your system alongside Windows. If you install Linux along with any other operating system, you create a *dual-boot* system, because you can boot one of two different operating systems. You can also put multiple distributions of Linux on a system (if you have enough disk space) and create a *multiboot* system.

WARNING: Only create a dual-boot system if you have the media to enable you to reinstall your original system should it become necessary, and be sure to back up everything on your existing system first! If you make a mistake during the Linux installation, it is possible to wipe out everything on the system, including any existing operating system and data. If you could not reinstall and restore your original system on an empty disk, you should not attempt to create a dual-boot system!

2.5.2   Disk Partitioning

If you plan to install Linux software on your hard drive, you will need to create one or more *partitions* on the disk. A partition is an area of the disk that is treated as a separate unit. The disk may contain only one partition (the whole disk) or it may be divided into smaller units.

Partitioning a disk is, without question, the most intimidating step of the installation process. If you are trying to keep existing data already on your computer (like an existing Windows partition, for example), it is also the most dangerous. When setting up one or more partitions for Linux to use, you must be careful to avoid overwriting any existing data you wish to preserve.

Every disk drive has a *partition table*, where information about each partition is stored. Most partition tables allow four entries.

2.5.2.1   Partition Types

Most disk drives support two types of partitions: primary and extended (or logical) partitions. A primary partition has an entry in the partition table and points to a fixed area on the disk. An extended partition has an entry in the partition table but points to a group of one or more logical partitions. This is useful when you need more than the four partitions that a partition table could support.

You can use either type of partition: to Linux they all work the same. Some partitioning tools don't even show you the difference between primary and extended partitions, they just start using extended partitions when it becomes necessary.

2.5.2.2   Partitioning for Linux

A Linux file system is a hierarchical grouping of names beginning at the root (/) of a directory tree. This is known as the root file system. The simplest partitioning for a Linux system is to put the entire root file system in a single partition. You also have the option of creating other partitions for parts of the Linux file system, as we'll see later.

One other partition is required on a Linux system, a *swap* partition. This partition is used by the virtual memory manager to swap data in and out of memory while the system is running. This is not a file system but rather a raw area on disk in which the kernel can "scribble." This partition is typically 1.5–2 times the size of the amount of real memory in your system. For example, if your system has 256 MB of memory, your swap partition should be at least 256 MB, but performance will improve if you make it 384 MB or more.

If you have two empty disk drives on your system, you can create swap partitions, each of half the total required size, on each disk. This spreads the swapping activity across different devices and will speed things up somewhat. In this case, any single swap partition should still be big enough to be useful to the system, so don't make them smaller than 64 MB, even if together they will add up to more swap space than you think you need.

If you have two disk drives, but you know one is substantially faster than the other one, use the faster one for the swap partition if possible.

If you dual-boot or multiboot a system with more than one distribution of Linux, you can create just one swap partition on the system and configure all the Linux distributions to use that same partition. Nothing is stored in a swap partition, it is simply an area where the memory manager can write while Linux is running, and since only one distribution of Linux will be running at any one time, they can all use the same swap partition.

2.5.2.3   Partitioning for Linux and Windows

If you must install Linux on a system where Windows is already installed, then you can only create Linux partitions out of free space that Windows is not using. Most Windows systems are installed using all of the disk space on the system, though, so this will be your first problem: how do you free up disk space and make it available to Linux?

If you are really lucky, you have (or could put) a second disk drive in your system. If you have a spare disk drive that Windows is not currently using, then you have a place to put Linux and you don't need to worry about changing anything on the Windows disk drive (however, you still must be very careful that you don't accidentally do anything to the Windows drive during the Linux installation process). Many PCs, however, have only one large disk drive, in which case, you must create your Linux partitions on the same disk drive. This will involve shrinking the existing Windows partition to make room, as we'll see a bit later.

2.5.3   Linux File Systems

A partition is merely an area on the disk drive that can hold data. For Linux to be able to read and write directories and files, a partition must contain a *file system*. A file system is a data infrastructure that keeps track of file names and their associated data blocks in a hierarchical structure that makes it easy for humans to navigate around. For the purposes of installing Linux, it is not necessary to have more than a high-level understanding of what a file system is and how it works. Most distributions of Linux come with several different file systems from which to choose.

2.5.3.1   Types of File Systems

Many different file system implementations exist, each with its own advantages and disadvantages for certain types of operations. For example, a *journaling* file system maintains transaction information about file operations to increase integrity of the file system in the event of a system failure.

All Linux distributions support these common file systems:

- ext2—the Second Extended file system, the standard Linux file system (listed in some setup programs as "native Linux")
- ext3—a journaling version of ext2, faster and more reliable

Many distributions include one or more alternate journaling file systems:

- IBM JFS—IBM's journaling file system
- ReiserFS—Hans Reiser's high-performance journaling file system
- XFS—SGI's journaling file system

You may choose any file system available in your distribution's installation program. Most people choose ext2 (linux native) or ext3 unless they have a preference or a need for one of the more specialized file systems.

2.5.3.2   Organization of File Systems

The Linux directory tree, beginning at the root (/), is made up of one or more file systems. The important issue for installation is how, if at all, you want to divide your Linux file system across your available partitions. You may put all your files in the root (/) file system, create a second partition for the swap partition, and run with only those two partitions. This works fine for most individual workstations. Depending on your intended use of the system, however, you might want to separate certain directories into their own partitions. When you separate a directory onto its own partition, it is connected into the root directory at a *mount point*, a directory in the root file system.

The Linux boot files are stored in the /boot directory. This directory is sometimes put in its own small partition to guarantee it stays located at the beginning of a disk drive. This is mostly a historical requirement for old boot hardware that could only read a limited area of the disk and is usually not an issue today.

On a system with many users (such as a server), home directories are often created in a standard place like /home. If /home is part of the root file system, then users can fill up your system's root disk. If you make /home a separate file system and then mount that file system, it looks the same to the users, but they can only fill up that partition, not the root file system. If users do fill up /home, the root file system will still have space, so the system itself will continue to run fine. Users will no longer be able to create new files, but that is a less severe problem than the system's being unable to create new files.

System directories that are used for a lot of temporary data are also good candidates for separate file systems. The /var directory is used to store data such as files to be sent to printers and e-mail messages as they are sent and received. If /var is a separate partition, then these processes won't fail if other partitions are full. The /tmp directory is another place for temporary files that could be segregated from the rest of the system this way, in case some program went crazy creating files.

Even system directories like /usr and /opt, where system files and optional software may be installed, could be put in separate partitions. Of course it is more work to set up separate partitions, but depending on your system usage, it could be worth the effort.

2.5.3.3   Size of File Systems

It is hard to say exactly how much space you'll need for various Linux file systems. A good rule of thumb for /boot (if you make it a separate partition) is at least 10 MB. It only stores files required for booting (the kernel and associated files) so it doesn't require much space.

The minimum amount of space in which you would ever want to install Linux would be about 500 MB, and so the smallest root file system (/) you would want would be about that. The more optional software you add, the bigger you'll want this file system (see Figure 2–2 earlier in this chapter).

If you split the entire file system across multiple partitions, you should still never make the root smaller than 500 MB. How big you make the other partitions (especially a directory for users' home directories) is mainly a factor of how much disk space you have available.

2.5.3.4   Sharing File Systems

If you plan to dual-boot your system with Windows or another distribution of Linux, there are a couple of miscellaneous issues you should keep in mind.

Windows partitions can be mounted and read by Linux. Some file systems can be mounted read-write, some can only be mounted read-only. I would recommend you mount any Windows file system read-only so that files are not accidentally altered.

Do not share /boot partitions between different distributions of Linux. Linux expects to be able to write what it needs in /boot, including files that may have the same names between different distributions, so one distribution could overwrite files (e.g., the kernel) of another distribution.

2.5.4   Boot Loaders

What we refer to as "booting" a computer derived from the word "bootstrap" (as in, to pull yourself up by your bootstraps). The hardware knows how to load a small program from a known location and execute it. That program, in turn, knows where the "real" operating system is located and loads it.

When the boot process starts, the computer loads the contents of the Master Boot Record (MBR) from the first sector of the first disk and executes that program. On a Windows machine, this program then loads Windows, and your PC boots up. On a Linux machine, it's more or less the same. The Linux *boot loader* program loads the kernel, and Linux boots up.

Most distributions of Linux come with a choice of boot loaders: the original, LILO (the LInux LOader), and the more recent GRUB (the GNU GRand Unified Boot loader). Both do basically the same job: they create boot code to allow you to boot one or more operating systems. Both can install themselves in the MBR, in the first sector of the root partition, or on a floppy disk.

If you install the boot code into the MBR, you will overwrite whatever boot code is already there (e.g., Windows boot code). GRUB and LILO both preserve the option to boot Windows in their boot menus, but I would recommend against altering the MBR if you plan to continue to boot Windows in addition to Linux.

If you install the boot loader to the first sector of the root drive, you still depend on the Windows boot code to find it and transfer control to it. Windows code is notorious for "not playing well with others," and for this reason, I would not recommend this option.

If you plan to dual-boot your Linux system with Windows, you can install the boot loader on the floppy drive (usually /dev/fd0). This removes the need to install a boot loader on your hard drive, and you can leave the Windows boot code in the MBR as it is. When you want to boot Linux, put the floppy with the boot loader into the floppy drive and boot, but if the floppy is not in the drive, Windows will boot. This is by far the safest way to configure a dual-boot system. Be sure to specify /dev/fd0 as the boot location when installing the boot loader in the installation process in this case.

If you are installing a single distribution on a system by itself, then you probably won't be changing the boot loader information, you'll just keep what the installation sets up to boot Linux. If you are installing a multiboot system, you may modify the boot loader information from time to time as you install other operating systems.

2.5.5   Boot Floppy

During the Linux installation process of most distributions, you have the option of creating a boot floppy (you can also create it with the **mkbootdisk**[2] command after Linux is running). This is a floppy disk that can be used to boot Linux in the case of a system crash or other failure that

---

2.   SuSE has removed **mkbootdisk** and provides this function through the YaST console.

damages the boot sector of your hard drive. You should always make the boot floppy. You may never use it, and it may seem unnecessary, but it only takes a few minutes, and if you ever need it and don't have it, you could wind up reinstalling your entire system. A boot floppy is a cheap insurance policy.

Here's my personal story for recommending making a boot floppy. One of the systems I built in preparation to write this Linux edition was a dual-boot system with Mandrake Linux and Windows XP. Everything was working fine until one day I powered up the system and got the message "Lilo timestamp mismatch" and then nothing; no boot menu, no Windows, and no Linux. I couldn't reinstall LILO since I couldn't boot Linux. Because I hadn't made a boot floppy (this was a test system, after all), I had to reinstall both Windows and Linux. Don't let this happen to a system you care about!

You can also use a boot floppy to boot Linux instead of a floppy with a boot loader installed. The floppy disk contains somewhat different information in this case, but the end result is the same. A boot floppy allows you modify kernel parameters and location in the event a "normal boot" is not working because of a failure. But the default behavior is to boot the kernel on your hard drive just like a boot loader.

2.6 Get Linux

Once you have your hardware ready and have decided which distribution you want to run, all you have to do is go get it! There are many ways you can obtain Linux installation media or images. That is both a blessing and a curse. The blessing is that for nearly any type of machine with any limitation you can imagine, there will be some viable option for getting Linux onto your computer. The curse is that there are so many options, it may be hard to decide which one is the best.

Linux itself is free of any license fee because it is distributed under the GNU Public License. This is also true for the GNU utilities that go along with the Linux kernel to make up a typical Linux distribution. Because the GPL allows it to be redistributed free of charge, this means you can borrow CDs from a friend who has them and copy them or install from them (something that is generally forbidden with copyrighted commercial software).

Even if you don't know anybody who already has a copy, most distributions are available for free download or on moderately priced CD-ROMs. While there is no license fee for the software, companies that sell Linux distributions often include media, documentation and/or support in their price, so you're getting more than just "free software" for the price.

2.6.1 CD-ROM

The simplest installation method is to get access to Linux on some type of static media, usually a set of compact discs. CDs are easy to buy, move, and store. Should you ever need to reinstall your Linux machine, you can just get out your CDs and go to work. The disadvantage of CDs is you generally have to purchase them. However, since Linux is open source software, the cost of the CDs usually reflects only the cost of manufacturing and does not include expensive software licensing.

In preparing to write this book, I purchased the most recently available version of seven different Linux distributions (for a Pentium-based platform[3]) on CD-ROM and spent less than $100 (Figure 2–5).

Debian GNU/Linux (7 CDs, includes source code)	$17
Fedora Core (4 CDs)	$ 9
Linspire Live	$ 7
Mandrake Linux (4 CDs)	$12
Slackware Linux (4 CDs)	$10
SuSE Linux Personal (2 CDs, includes a printed installation guide and a "live" version)	$29
TurboLinux	$ 8

Figure 2–5   Approximate cost of some popular Linux distributions.

The difference in price is usually explained by how many CDs make up the distribution, how much packaging is included, and whether any paper documentation (like an installation guide) is included.

Linux is available for purchase in many places; a good web search will turn up many sites from which you can buy a distribution. The web sites I have found most useful are:

```
http://www.easylinuxcds.com
http://www.linuxcentral.com
```

2.6.2   Download

If you are installing Linux in an environment with existing Linux machines (such as a medium-to-large company or a university), there may be copies of installation images available on the local network. You might be able to copy install images from another machine via any number of network utilities as long as you have a network card in your computer. Talk to your systems administrator, or someone knowledgeable about such things, as the details of exactly what steps to take vary greatly depending on where the data resides and what kind of network interface you have in your system.

If you have a connection to the internet, you can also download installation images from www.linux.org as well as most web sites of companies who manufacture their own Linux distribution. Downloading installable images involves copying standard ISO install images and writing them onto a CD or local hard disk. This is truly only an option if you have a high-speed connection to the internet, and even then it is very time consuming. At some point, the

---

3.   Linux distributions for larger or more sophisticated hardware platforms are sometimes more expensive.

time required for this activity (not to mention the cost of the blank CD-ROMs) outweighs the relatively low price of a media-only copy from a vendor. Unless others at your company or school are experienced in such activities, I would highly recommend purchasing an inexpensive distribution.

2.7 Install Linux

As I mentioned at the beginning of this chapter, since you are free to install any distribution of Linux you wish, it isn't possible to provide an exact list of steps you'll need to install your specific distribution of Linux. Although they may do it differently, every distribution's installation program performs more or less the same set of tasks to get Linux and the GNU utilities installed on your computer.

2.7.1 Get the Documentation for Your Distribution
The first thing you should do is get installation instructions for your Linux distribution. Most CD-ROMs have either text files or HTML files (suitable for viewing with a web browser). The names and locations of these files may vary, but look for files or directories containing the following text:

- doc or docu—directory containing documentation files
- README—generally a file that you should read first
- HOWTO—often contains installation steps
- release_notes—Distribution release notes sometimes contain the installation instructions
- HTML or htm—web page files are generally documentation of some kind
- FAQ—frequently asked questions
- install—notes about installation or a directory containing notes

For example, Debian documentation can be found on the CD-ROM in the install/doc directory, Slackware provides a nice install manual on the first source CD-ROM as well as a text Slackware-HOWTO file on the boot CD, and Mandrake provides an installation manual called install.htm on the CD-ROM. You may also find installation notes on the web sites of the various distribution sponsors.

2.7.2 Boot
The easiest way to get started is to boot Linux from the CD-ROM. Unless your PC is very old, this should be supported. If it is not, you may be able to change the boot settings to look at the CD-ROM drive in your system's BIOS setup program. Linux recognizes most modern CD-ROM drives. If you cannot boot the CD-ROM, you will need to boot with a boot floppy.

2.7.3 Partition Disks
As we saw previously, this is the dangerous step where you can damage any data that is already on your computer. In case you've missed it thus far, I cannot stress strongly enough how important it is that you make a backup copy of all data on the system that you care about before you attempt to repartition a disk. This is your final warning.

When running a partitioning tool, whether a graphical tool, **fdisk** or **cfdisk**, you will refer to disk partitions by their *device names*. These are names of special files in the /dev directory that identify each physical device. These special files are discussed in more detail in Chapter 13, "Linux Internals" For now, the types of names you're likely to encounter are:

- /dev/fd0—first floppy disk drive
- /dev/fd1—second floppy disk drive
- /dev/hda—first IDE hard drive
- /dev/hdb—second IDE hard drive
- /dev/sda—first SCSI hard drive
- /dev/sdb—second SCSI hard drive

Note that while nearly all systems have a /dev/fd0 (floppy drive), you may see some or none of the other names, depending on the disk drives on your system. Also note that links from /dev/fd0 to the actual floppy device are set up at install time. If you install on a laptop when a removable floppy drive is not present, these links will likely not be set up properly. If you later install your floppy drive and Linux isn't able to access it as /dev/fd0, try other device names in the IDE sequence (e.g., /dev/hdc worked for me). If your CD-ROM drive is an IDE device, it should also be accessible as one of the "hd" devices. One of the hardware browser/management tools can help you identify disk drive devices (e.g., Fedora's Hardware Browser **hwbrowser** or Mandrake's Harddrake tool).

Each of the hard drives that are divided into multiple partitions will also have device names for each partition. For example, the first partition on /dev/hda is called /dev/hda1, the second partition is called /dev/hda2, and so on.

As you create partitions and assign them to parts of your Linux file system, be sure to keep notes about which partition/device contains which file system. If you create more than a couple of partitions it can quickly get confusing, and if you haven't written it down you won't remember it later!

Also remember that some disk partitioning tools don't show you the difference between primary and extended partitions, you just go from /dev/hda2 to /dev/hda5 (this is because /dev/hda4 was created as an extended partition). Mandrake's Disk Drake tool creates extended partitions as necessary without asking you. Fedora's Disk Druid allows you to "force" a partition to be primary, but will choose for you if you don't specify it.

All distributions of Linux include **fdisk** and **cfdisk**, tools to create disk partitions. Most distribution providers have created their own disk partitioning tools and no longer use **fdisk** and **cfdisk**. Some of the more "bare bones" distributions (e.g., Debian and Slackware) still rely on **cfdisk** (although a new Debian installation tool is in the works). **fdisk** is a purely command-line oriented tool while **cfdisk** is a full-screen tool with good help information available within the program.

Whatever partitioning tool you use, the general process is to define the partitions and assign a mount point (or set it as a swap partition) and then write the partition table out to disk. Until you write the partition table to the disk, you have not changed data on the disk. Once you update the partition table, data in partitions that are no longer defined is lost (the data is still on the disk, but now there is no way to access it) because the new partition table is in effect.

Part of the partitioning process is also to reformat the partitions. This is not necessary if a partition was not changed and it had been formatted previously. However, it is usually a good idea to let the system reformat everything to be sure about what you're getting. Unless you know your disk is in good shape, I would also recommend letting it do the bad-block check during the format (it takes longer, but it could save you headaches later if the disk has any bad-blocks).

2.7.4   Resize a Windows Partition

If you plan to dual-boot your Linux system with Windows, you may need to shrink the size of the Windows partition in order to have enough free space in which to install Linux. The first thing you want to do is boot Windows and run SCANDISK or CHKDSK to make sure the Windows file system has no errors. Then you should run DEFRAG to defragment the disk and move all of your data to the front part of the disk. The details of this vary a bit between different versions of Windows. Consult the DEFRAG report to determine which are the last disk blocks used by Windows. This will be the limit to how much you can shrink your Windows partition, and you should leave at least an extra 20–25% free space so you'll have some room for new files when you run Windows.

Once you have determined the correct new size for your Windows partition, you must shrink the Windows partition so that you can create the Linux partition(s) in the freed space. An old program called FIPS could resize (and shrink) a FAT or FAT32 file system, commonly used in Windows 95/98 and Windows ME. If your Windows system uses the FAT file system format, you might find a copy of FIPS in your Linux distribution (e.g., Mandrake and TurboLinux provide it in the "dostools" directory, Debian puts it in the "tools" directory).

Windows XP provides no tools to shrink its NTFS file system (it has some disk management tools but they can only expand a file system). One alternative is to purchase one of a number of commercial partitioning tools. One such tool with a fine reputation for ease of use and reliability is Symantec's PartitionMagic.

Some Linux distributions (e.g., Mandrake, SuSE) have very good disk partitioning utilities that can also shrink NTFS partitions. However you choose to shrink an existing Windows partition, BE VERY CAREFUL and only proceed through steps you completely understand. If you are not sure, ask someone who has done it before. There is no "undo" if you overwrite a disk partition that contained data you wanted!

2.7.5   System Setup

After the disk partitions have been created, the installation will begin. This is all part of the same process in most distributions. In a more simple process like Debian, after you run **cfdisk**, the next utility to run is **setup**.

In the system setup part of installation, you will set things like:

- language
- keyboard, mouse, and monitor
- time and time zone

- security settings
- printer
- network
- optional software components/packages
- root password
- set up a new account for one or more users

Linux uses Coordinated Universal Time (UTC), which is (for our purposes) equivalent to Greenwich Mean Time (GMT), to represent the time to the machine. When time is displayed by an application, it uses calls that look up time-zone information and display the time appropriately. In this way, users on a machine working from different time zones can still have their local time displayed properly, but the internal representation of time is still in UTC/GMT.

This can be a problem if you dual-boot with Windows, because Windows stores the local time internally. When you set the time on Linux, however, it asks if the time is local or UTC, so you can select local.

Some distributions allow you to specify a security setting that will install or configure security functions, like firewalls, automatically.

2.7.6   The Boot Loader

During the installation process, you will have the option to install (or not install) a boot loader. LILO is the standard boot loader for Linux, but some distributions include GRUB and install it by default (e.g., Fedora and SuSE).

The LILO boot loader consists of a **lilo** command utility that writes the boot code into the boot device listed in /etc/lilo.conf. This file also contains all the information about the various operating systems and boot parameters. After editing the configuration file, run **lilo** to install a new boot loader.

GRUB provides more capability, but with that comes more options and a more sophisticated interface. GRUB includes a command shell called **grub** that can modify boot information and write the new boat loader out to disk.

A Windows PC contains boot code in the MBR that will boot Windows. During Linux installation, you can overwrite this code with LILO or GRUB code to boot Linux. Boot loaders *usually* preserve the Windows boot information and create a boot loader that will list Windows as one of the boot options. But it is safer to only write boot loader code into the MBR if you do not plan to boot Windows anymore (i.e., if you're installing Linux in place of Windows), because once you overwrite the MBR, the original Windows boot code will be gone. You can rewrite the MBR from the Windows Recovery Console in Windows XP (or with FDISK in earlier versions), but if you have trouble booting Windows again, this won't help you. Even though boot loaders can install themselves in such a way that they can still let you boot Windows, I would recommend that you write your boot loader to a floppy disk instead and leave your Windows boot code alone. If you do choose to rewrite your MBR, be sure Windows shows up in the list of boot options before you allow the installation procedure to write it to the disk.

CHAPTER REVIEW

Checklist

In this chapter, I mentioned:

- the hardware requirements to run Linux
- the variety of Linux distributions available
- Linux packages
- disk partitioning and Linux file system organization
- boot loaders and boot floppies
- ways to get your own distribution of Linux

Quiz

1. What are the minimum disk space and memory required for a system to run Linux reasonably well?
2. How many primary partitions can be created on a disk drive?
3. What is the minimum number of disk partitions required to run Linux?
4. What is a dual-boot system?
5. What is the major difference between the ext2 and ext3 file systems?
6. Describe the function of a boot loader.

Exercises

1. Find three Linux distributions not mentioned in this chapter and state why someone might choose each of them over the more popular distributions. [level: *medium*]

Projects

1. Obtain a distribution of Linux and install it (you saw that one coming, right?). [level: *easy*]

3

GNU Utilities for Nonprogrammers

Motivation

This section contains the absolute basics that you really need to know in order to be able to do anything useful with Linux.

Prerequisites

In order to understand this chapter, you must have already read Chapter 1, "What Is Linux?" It also helps if you have access to a Linux system so that you can try out the various Linux/GNU features that I discuss.

Objectives

In this chapter, I'll show you how to log on and off a Linux system, how to change your password, how to get online help when you're stuck, how to stop a program, and how to use the file system. I'll also introduce you to the mail system so that you can enter the world of computer networking.

Presentation

The information in this section is presented in the form of a couple of sample Linux terminal sessions. If you don't have access to a Linux system, march through the sessions anyway and try them out later.

Utilities

This section introduces the following utilities, listed in alphabetical order:

cancel	head	mv
cat	lp	newgrp
chgrp	lpr	passwd
chmod	lprm	pwd
chown	lpq	rm
clear	lpstat	rmdir
cp	ls	stty
date	mail	tail
emacs	man	tset
file	mkdir	vim
groups	more	wc

Shell command

This section introduces the following shell command:

    cd

3.1   Obtaining an Account

In order to login on a Linux system, you'll need to get an account. If you will be using someone else's Linux computer, they can create an account for you. If you have installed your own Linux system, you should have already created your own account during the installation process. If not, you must login as "root" (the administrator account) for now and create your own account. See page 584 of Chapter 14, "System Administration" for information on creating and maintaining user accounts. It is extremely important to create your own account rather than simply using the root account. The root account has full system privileges and if you use that account all the time, it is much too easy to accidentally delete or damage critical system files.

3.2   Logging In

In order to use a Linux system, you must first "log in" with a suitable "username." A username is a unique name that distinguishes you from the other users of the system. For example, my own username is "ables." Your username and initial password are assigned to you by the system administrator, or set during installation. It's sometimes necessary to press the *Enter* key (also known as the *Return* key) a couple of times to make the system give you a login prompt. Many Linux machines display a login box rather than a text prompt. You are first prompted for your username and then for your password. When you enter your password, the letters that you type are not displayed for security reasons. Linux is case sensitive, so make sure that the case of the letters is matched exactly. Depending on how your system is set up, you should then see either a $ or a % prompt, or the X Window System graphical interface may be started. Here's an example login:

```
Fedora Core release 2 (Tettnang)
Kernel 2.6.5-1.358 on an i686

bluenote login: ables
Password:       ...what I typed here is secret and doesn't show.
Last login: Sun Feb 15 18:33:26 from dialin
$ _
```

It's quite common for the system to immediately ask you which kind of terminal you're using. This is so that it can set special characters like the backspace and cursor movement keys to their correct values. You are usually allowed to press the *Enter* key for the default terminal setting, and I suggest that you do this when you log in for the first time. I'll show you later how to change the terminal type if necessary. Other possible events that might occur when you log in are:

- A help system recognizes that you're a first-time user and asks you whether you'd like a guided tour of Linux.
- The "news of the day" messages are displayed to your screen, informing you of scheduled maintenance times and other useful information.

On a system with a fully installed X Window System, after typing in your password, the Desktop Environment takes a minute to start up. You are then presented with a graphical desktop (similar to the examples in Chapter 2, "Installing Your Linux System").

3.3 Shells

The $ or % prompt that you see when you first log in or start a terminal window is displayed by a special kind of program called a *shell*. A shell is a program that acts as a middleman between you and the Linux operating system. It lets you run programs, build pipelines of processes, save output to files, and run more than one program at the same time. A shell executes all of the commands that you enter. The three most popular shells in Linux environments are:

- the Bourne Again shell (bash)
- the Korn shell (ksh)
- the C shell (csh)

All of these shells share a similar set of core functionality, together with some specialized properties. The Korn shell and Bash are both supersets of the original UNIX Bourne shell. Bash, the newest of all these shells, is quickly becoming the most popular, as it includes many of the most popular features of the others as well as compatibility with the original Bourne shell. This book contains information on how to use all three shells, each discussed in a separate chapter.

Chapter 5, "The Linux Shells," describes the core functionality found in all Linux command shells, and subsequent chapters describe the specialized features of each shell.

Each shell has its own programming language. One reasonable question to ask is: Why would you write a program in a shell language rather than a language like C or Java? The answer is that the shell languages are tailored to manipulating files and processes in the Linux system, which makes them more convenient in many situations. In this chapter the only shell facilities that I use are the abilities to run utilities and to save the output of a process to a file. Let's go ahead and run a few simple GNU utilities.

3.4 Running a GNU Utility

As we saw in Chapter 1, "What Is Linux?," most of the utility commands that are part of a Linux distribution come from the Free Software Foundation's GNU Project. Therefore, they are strictly not Linux utilities but GNU utilities. People tend to use these descriptions interchangeably, however, since they come packaged in a Linux distribution.

To run a utility, simply enter its name and press the *Enter* key. From now on, when I mention that you should enter a particular bit of text, I also implicitly mean that you should press the *Enter* key after the text. This tells the shell that you've entered the command and that you wish it to be executed.

Not all systems have exactly the same utilities installed, so if a particular example doesn't work, don't be flustered. One utility that every system has is called **date**, which displays the current date and time:

```
$ date       ... run the date utility.
Mon Sep  6 11:25:51 CDT 2004
$ _
```

Whenever I introduce a new utility, I'll write a small synopsis of its typical operation in the format shown in Figure 3–1. It's self-explanatory, as you can see. I use a modified-for-Linux BNF (Backus-Naur Form) notation for the syntax description, which is fully documented in the Appendix.

Please note that I do not list every different kind of option or present a particularly detailed description—this is best left to the manual pages available on your Linux system.

Utility: **date** [*yymmddhhmm* [*.ss*]]

Without any arguments, **date** displays the current date and time. If arguments are provided, **date** sets the date to the supplied setting, where *yy* is the last two digits of the year, the first *mm* is the number of the month, *dd* is the number of the day, *hh* is the number of hours (use the 24-hour clock), and the last *mm* is the number of minutes. The optional *ss* is the number of seconds. Only a super-user may set the date.

Figure 3–1   Description of the **date** command.

Another useful utility is **clear**, which clears your screen (Figure 3–2).

Utility: **clear**

This utility clears your screen.

Figure 3–2   The **clear** command.

3.5   Input, Output, and Error Channels

In the example of the **date** command above, the output was written to the terminal window. Linux can write to files, but there are three default I/O channels that are always assumed active for every command or program.

- Standard input, known as "stdin," where a program expects to find input.
- Standard output, known as "stdout," where a program writes its output by default.
- Standard error, known as "stderr," where a program writes error messages.

By default, all three I/O channels are the terminal running the command or program. This enables commands to interact with the terminal easily and still use input from other places and write output to other places when necessary. The default I/O channels can be easily changed on the command line by using "redirection." We'll see examples of I/O redirection later in this chapter. For details on how the Linux I/O channels work see Chapter 12, "Systems Programming."

3.6   Obtaining Online Help: man

There are bound to be many times when you're at your terminal and you can't quite remember how to use a particular utility. Alternatively, you may know what a utility does, but don't remember what it's called. You may also want to look up an argument not described in this text. Linux systems have a utility called **man** (short for "manual") which puts this information at your fingertips. **man** works as shown in Figure 3–3.

Utility: **man** [*section*] *word*
       man -k *keyword*

The manual pages are online copies of the Linux documentation, which is divided into eight or nine sections, depending on your Linux distribution. They contain information about utilities, system calls, file formats, and shells. When **man** displays help about a given utility, it indicates in which section the entry appears.

The first usage of **man** displays the manual entry associated with *word*. If no section number is specified, the first entry that it finds is displayed.

The second usage of **man** displays a list of all the manual entries that contain *keyword*.

Figure 3–3   The **man** command.

The typical division of topics in manual page sections is as follows:

1. User Commands
2. System Calls
3. Library Functions
4. Special Files
5. File Formats
6. Games
7. Miscellaneous
8. System Administration and Privileged Commands
9. Kernel Interfaces (not included in all distributions)

Sometimes, there is more than one manual entry for a particular word. For example, there is a utility called **chmod** and a system call called chmod (), and there are manual pages for both (in sections 1 and 2). By default, **man** displays the manual pages for the first entry that it finds, so it will display the manual page for the **chmod** utility.

Here's an example of **man** in action:

```
$ man -k permission    ...search for keyword 'permission'.
chmod               (1) - change file access permissions
console.perms [console] (5) - permissions control file for users at
the system console
access              (2) - check user's permissions for a file
chmod               (2) - change permissions of a file
fchmod [chmod]      (2) - change permissions of a file
ioperm              (2) - set port input/output permissions
...
q        ...man uses the more command, use 'q' to quit.
$ man chmod    ...select the first manual entry.
CHMOD(1)              User Commands              CHMOD(1)


NAME
       chmod - change file access permissions

SYNOPSIS
       chmod [OPTIONm]... MODEm[,MODEm]... FILEm...
       chmod [OPTIONm]... OCTAL-MODEm FILEm...
       chmod [OPTIONm]... --reference=RFILEm FILEm...


DESCRIPTION
       This manual page documents the GNU version of chmod.
...
q
$ man 2 chmod    ...select the manual entry from section 2.
```

```
CHMOD(2)              Linux Programmer's Manual              CHMOD(2)

NAME
      chmod, fchmod - change permissions of file

SYNOPSIS
      #include <sys/types.h>
      #include <sys/stat.h>

      int chmod(const char *path, mode_t mode);
      int fchmod(int fildes, mode_t mode);

DESCRIPTION
      The mode of the file given by path or referenced by
      fildes is changed.
...
q
$ _
```

3.7 Special Characters

Some characters are interpreted specially when typed in a Linux terminal window. These characters are sometimes called *metacharacters*, and may be listed by using the **stty** utility with the **-a** (all) option. The **stty** utility is discussed fully at the end of this chapter. Here's an example:

```
$ stty -a        ...obtain a list of terminal metacharacters
speed 38400 baud; rows 35; columns 80; line = 233;
intr = ^C; quit = ^\; erase = ^?; kill = ^U; eof = ^D; eol = <undef>;
eol2 = <undef>; start = ^Q; stop = ^S; susp = ^Z; rprnt = ^R;
werase = ^W; lnext = ^V; flush = ^O; min = 1; time = 0;
-parenb -parodd cs8 -hupcl -cstopb cread -clocal -crtscts
-ignbrk brkint ignpar -parmrk -inpck -istrip -inlcr -igncr icrnl ixon
-ixoff -iuclc -ixany imaxbel
opost -olcuc -ocrnl onlcr -onocr -onlret -ofill -ofdel nl0 cr0 tab0
bs0 vt0 ff0
isig icanon iexten echo echoe echok -echonl -noflsh -xcase -tostop
-echoprt echoctl echoke
$ _
```

The ^ in front of each letter means that the *Control* key must be pressed at the same time as the letter. The default meaning of each option is shown in Figure 3–4.

Option	Meaning
erase	Backspace one character.
kill	Erase all of the current line.
werase	Erase the last word.
rprnt	Reprint the line.
flush	Ignore any pending input and reprint the line.
lnext	Don't treat the next character specially.
susp	Suspend the process for a future awakening.
intr	Terminate (interrupt) the foreground job with no core dump.
quit	Terminate the foreground job and generate a core dump.
stop	Stop/restart terminal output.
eof	End-of-input.

Figure 3–4   stty options.

Some of these characters won't mean much to you until you read some more chapters of this book, but there are a few worth mentioning immediately: *Control-C*, *Control-S*, *Control-Q*, and *Control-D*.

3.7.1   Terminating a Process: *Control-C*

Often when you run a program you wish to stop it before it's finished. The standard way to do this in Linux is to press the keyboard sequence *Control-C*. Although there are a few programs that are immune to this form of process termination, most processes are immediately killed, and your shell prompt is returned. Here's an example:

```
$ man chmod
CHMOD(1)                   User Commands                    CHMOD(1)

NAME
       chmod - change file access permissions

SYNOPSIS
^C        ...terminate the job and go back to the shell.
$ _
```

3.7.2   End-of-Input: *Control-D*

Many utilities may take their input from either a file or the keyboard. If you instruct a utility to do the latter, you must tell the utility when the input from the keyboard is finished. To do this, type a *Control-D* on a line of its own after the last line of input. *Control-D* means "end-of-input." For example, the **mail** utility allows you to send mail from the keyboard to a named user:

```
$ mail tim          ...send mail to my friend tim.
Hi Tim,             ...input is entered from the keyboard.
  I hope you get this piece of mail. How about building a country
one of these days?

- with best wishes from Graham
^D               ...tell the terminal that there's no more input.
$ _
```

The **mail** utility is fully described later in this chapter.

3.8   Setting Your Password: passwd

After you first log in to a Linux system, it's a good idea to change your initial password if you didn't create your own account (someone set it, so you know at least one other person knows it). A password should generally be at least six letters long, and *should not* be a word from a dictionary or a proper noun. This is because it's quite easy for someone to set up a computer program that runs through all the words in a standard dictionary and tries them as your password.

To set your password, use the **passwd** utility (Figure 3–5).

Utility: **passwd**

passwd allows you to change your password. You are prompted for your old password and then twice for the new one (since what you type isn't shown on the screen, you would not know if you made a typo). The new password may be stored in an encrypted form in the password file "/etc/passwd" or in a "shadow" file (for more security) depending on which was selected during the installation of your Linux system.

Figure 3–5   Description of the **passwd** command.

Here's an example, with the passwords shown. Note that you wouldn't normally be able to see the passwords, as Linux turns off the keyboard echo when you enter them.

```
$ passwd
Changing password for user ables.
Changing password for ables
(current) UNIX password: penguin      ... poor choice.
New UNIX password: GWK145W            ... better choice.
Retype new UNIX password: GWK145W
passwd: all authentication tokens updated successfully.
$ _
```

Yes, in many current versions of Linux, the **passwd** utility really does print the first message twice and refer to the password as a "UNIX" password.

If you forget your password, the only thing to do is to contact your system administrator and ask for a new password. If you can become the administrator, you can set a new password without knowing the old password.

3.9 Logging Out

If you are simply logged in on the Linux console (i.e., not running a graphical desktop environment), then to leave the system just type the keyboard sequence *Control-D* at your shell prompt.[1] This tells your login shell that there is no more input for it to process, causing it to disconnect you from the system. Most systems then display a "login:" prompt and wait for another user to log in. Here's an example:

```
$ ^D      ...I'm done!
Fedora Core release 2 (Tettnang)
Kernel 2.6.5-1.358 on an i686

bluenote login:    ...wait for another user to log in.
```

If you are running a graphical desktop environment, each one has a menu selection that allows you to log out. Graphical desktops are discussed in more detail in Chapter 10, "The Linux Desktop."

Congratulations! You've now seen how you can log into a Linux system, execute a few simple utilities, change your password, and then log out. In the next few sections I'll describe some more utilities that allow you to explore the directory hierarchy and manipulate files.

3.10 Poetry in Motion: Exploring the File System

I decided that the best way to illustrate some common Linux utilities was to describe a session that used them in a natural fashion. One of my hobbies is to compose music, and I often use the Linux system to write lyrics for my songs. The next few sections are a running commentary on the Linux utilities that I used to create a final version of one of my song's lyrics, called "Heart To Heart." Figure 3–6 shows the approximate series of events that took place, together with the utility that I used at each stage.

---

1.   The C-shell can be set to ignore ^D for logout, since you might type it by accident. In this case, you must type the "logout" command instead.

Action	Utility
I displayed my current working directory.	pwd
I wrote the first draft and stored it in a file called "heart."	cat
I listed the directory contents to see the size of the file.	ls
I displayed the "heart" file using several utilities.	cat, more, page, head, tail
I renamed the first draft "heart.ver1."	mv
I made a directory called "lyrics" to store the first draft.	mkdir
I moved "heart.ver1" into the "lyrics" directory.	mv
I made a copy of "heart.ver1" called "heart.ver2."	cp
I edited the "heart.ver2" file.	vi
I moved back to my home directory.	cd
I made a directory called "lyrics.final."	mkdir
I renamed the "lyrics" directory to "lyrics.draft."	mv
I copied the "heart.ver5" file from "lyrics.draft" to "lyrics.final," renaming it "heart.final."	cp
I removed all the files from the "lyrics.draft" directory.	rm
I removed the "lyrics.draft" directory.	rmdir
I moved into the "lyrics.final" directory.	cd
I printed the "heart.final" file.	lpr
I counted the words in "heart.final."	wc
I listed the file attributes of "heart.final."	ls
I looked at the file type of "heart.final."	file
I obtained a list of my groups.	groups
I changed the group of "heart.final."	chgrp
I changed the permissions of "heart.final."	chmod

Figure 3–6 Script of upcoming examples.

3.11 Printing Your Shell's Current Working Directory: pwd

Every Linux process has a location in the directory hierarchy, termed its *current working directory*. When you log into a Linux system, your shell starts off in a particular directory called your "home directory." In general, every user has a different home directory, which often begins with the prefix "/home." For example, my own home directory is called "/home/glass." The system administrator assigns these home directory values. To display your shell's current working directory, use the **pwd** utility (Figure 3–7).

Utility: **pwd**

Prints the current working directory.

Figure 3–7　Description of the **pwd** command.

To illustrate this utility, here's what happened when I logged into Linux to start work on my song's lyrics:

```
Fedora Core release 2 (Tettnang)
Kernel 2.6.5-1.358 on an i686

bluenote login: glass
Password:        ...secret.
$ pwd
/home/glass
$ _
```

Figure 3–8 is a diagram that indicates the location of my login Korn shell in the directory hierarchy.

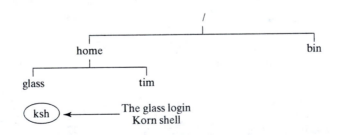

Figure 3–8　The login shell starts at the user's home directory.

3.12 Absolute and Relative Pathnames

Before I continue with the sample Linux session, it's important to introduce you to the idea of *pathnames*.

Two files in the same directory may not have the same name, although it's perfectly OK for several files in *different* directories to have the same name. For example, Figure 3–9 shows a small hierarchy that contains a "ksh" process and three files called "myFile."

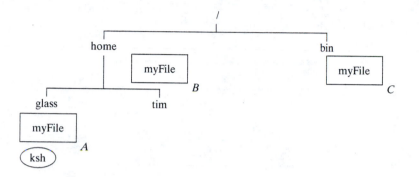

Figure 3–9   Different files may have the same name.

Although these files have the same name, they may be unambiguously specified by their *pathname* relative to "/," the root of the directory hierarchy. A pathname is a sequence of directory names that lead you through the hierarchy from a starting directory to a target file. A pathname relative to the root directory is often termed an *absolute* or *full* pathname. Figure 3–10 shows the absolute pathnames of the "A," "B," and "C" instances of "myFile."

File	Absolute PathName
A	/home/glass/myFile
B	/home/myFile
C	/bin/myFile

Figure 3–10   Absolute pathnames.

A process may also unambiguously specify a file by using a pathname *relative* to its current working directory. The Linux file system supports special fields that may be used when supplying a relative pathname (Figure 3–11).

For example, Figure 3–12 shows the pathnames of the three instances of "myFile" relative to the "ksh" process located in the "/home/glass" directory.

Field	Meaning
.	current directory
..	parent directory

Figure 3–11   Current and parent directories.

File	Relative Pathname
A	myFile
B	../myFile
C	../../bin/myFile

Figure 3–12   Relative pathnames.

Note that the pathname "myFile" is equivalent to "./myFile," but the second form is usually not used unless you need to specify a command in your current directory when "." is not in your search path (more on this later).

3.13 Creating a File

I already had an idea of what the first draft of my song's lyrics would look like, so I decided to store them in a file called "heart." Ordinarily, I would use a Linux editor such as **vim** or **emacs** to create the file, but this is a beginner's chapter, so I used a simpler utility called **cat** to achieve the same result. Figure 3–13 describes how **cat** works.

Utility: **cat** -n { *fileName* }*

The **cat** utility takes its input from standard input or from a list of files and displays them to standard output. The **-n** option adds line numbers to the output. **cat** is short for "concatenate," which means "to connect in a series of links."

Figure 3–13   Description of the **cat** command.

By default, the *standard input* of a process is the keyboard and the *standard output* is the screen. We can send the standard output of a process to a file instead of the screen by making use of a shell facility called *output redirection*. If you follow a command by a > character and the name of a file, the output from the command is saved to the file. If the file doesn't already exist, it is created; otherwise, its previous contents are overwritten. Right now, use this feature without worrying how it works; Chapter 5, "The Linux Shells," explains it all in detail. To create the first draft of my lyrics, I entered the following text at the shell prompt:

```
$ cat > heart     ...store keyboard input a the file 'heart'.
I hear her breathing,
I'm surrounded by the sound.
Floating in this secret place,
I never shall be found.
^D  ...tell cat that the end-of-input has been reached.
$ _
```

3.14 Listing the Contents of a Directory: ls

Once the "heart" file was created, I wanted to confirm its existence in my home directory and see how many bytes of storage it used. To do this, I used the **ls** utility, which lists information about a file or a directory. Figure 3–14 describes how **ls** works.

Utility: **ls** -adglsFGR { *fileName* }* { *directoryName* }*

With no arguments at all, **ls** lists all of the files in the current working directory in alphabetical order, excluding files whose name starts with a period. The **-a** option causes such files to be included in the listing. Files that begin with a period are sometimes known as "hidden" files. To obtain a listing of directories other than the current directory, place their names after the options. To obtain listings of specific files, place their names after the options. The **-d** option causes the details of the directories themselves to be listed, rather than their contents. The **-g** option lists a file's group. The **-l** option generates a long listing, including permission flags, the file's owner, and the last modification time. The **-s** option causes the number of disk blocks that the file occupies to be included in the listing (a block is typically between 512 and 4K bytes). The **-F** option causes a character to be placed after the file's name to indicate the type of the file: * means an executable file, / means a directory file, @ means a symbolic link, and = means a socket. The **-G** option causes group information to be omitted from the listing. The **-R** option recursively lists the contents of a directory and its subdirectories.

Figure 3–14   Description of the **ls** command.

Some of the **ls** options described in Figure 3–14 won't mean a lot right now, but will become increasingly relevant as this book progresses.

Here's an example of **ls**:

```
$ ls                ...list all files in current directory.
heart
$ ls -lG heart      ...long listing of 'heart'.
-rw-r--r--  1   glass    106   Jan 30 19:46    heart
$ _
```

I'll describe the exact meaning of each field in the long directory listing later in this chapter, but for now I'll give you a brief overview (Figure 3–15).

Field #	Field value	Meaning
1	-rw-r--r--	The type and permission mode of the file, which indicates who can read, write, and execute the file.
2	1	The hard link count (discussed much later in this book).
3	glass	The username of the owner of the file.
4	106	The size of the file (in bytes).
5	Jan 30 19:46	The time that the file was last modified.
6	heart	The name of the file.

Figure 3–15   Description of output from the **ls** command.

You may obtain even more information by using additional options:

```
$ ls -alFs          ...extra-long listing of current dir.
total 3             ...total number of blocks of storage.
1 drwxr-xr-x  3   glass    cs    512   Jan 30 22:52 ./
1 drwxr-xr-x 12   root     cs   1024   Jan 30 19:45 ../
1 -rw-r--r--  1   glass    cs    106   Jan 30 19:46 heart
$ _
```

The **-s** option generates an extra first field, which tells you how many disk blocks the file occupies. On my Linux system, each disk block is 1024 bytes long, which implies that my 106-byte file actually takes up 1024 bytes of physical storage. This is a result of the physical implementation of the file system, which is described in Chapter 13, "Linux Internals." The **-a** option causes **ls** to include a listing of all *hidden* files, which are files whose name begins with a period. "." and ".." are hidden files that correspond to the current directory and its parent directory, respectively. The **-F** option appends a / to all files that are directories.

3.15 Listing the Contents of a File: cat/more/head/tail

To check the contents of the "heart" file that I had created in my home directory "/home/glass," I listed its contents to the screen using the **cat** utility. Notice that I supplied **cat** with the name of the file that I wanted to display:

```
$ cat heart     ...list the contents of the 'heart' file.
I hear her breathing,
I'm surrounded by the sound.
Floating in this secret place,
I never shall be found.
$ _
```

cat can actually take any number of files as arguments, in which case they are listed together, one following the other. **cat** is good for listing small files, but doesn't pause between screens of output. The **more** utility is better suited for viewing larger files, because it provides advanced facilities such as the ability to scroll backward through a file. Figure 3–16 gives some notes on each utility.

Utility: **more** -f [+*lineNumber*] { *fileName* }*

The **more** utility allows you to scroll through a list of files, one page at a time. By default, each file is displayed starting at line 1, although the + option may be used to specify the starting line number. The **-f** option tells **more** not to fold long lines. After each page is displayed, **more** displays the message "-- More --" to indicate that it's waiting for a command. To list the next page, press the space bar. To list the next line, press the *Enter* key. To quit from **more**, press the *q* key. To obtain help on the multitude of other commands, press the *h* key.

Figure 3–16   Description of the **more** command.

While we're on the topic of listing files, there are a couple of handy utilities called **head** and **tail** that allow you to peek at the start and end of a file, respectively. Figures 3–17 and 3–18 describe how they work.

Utility: **head** -n { *fileName* }*

The **head** utility displays the first *n* lines of a file. If *n* is not specified, it defaults to 10. If more than one file is specified, a small header identifying each file is displayed before its contents.

Figure 3–17   Description of the **head** command.

Utility: **tail** -n { *fileName* }*

The **tail** utility displays the last *n* lines of a file. If *n* is not specified, it defaults to 10. If more than one file is specified, a small header identifying each file is displayed before its contents.

Figure 3–18   Description of the **tail** command.

In the following example, I displayed the first two lines and last two lines of my "heart" file:

```
$ head -2 heart        ...list the first two lines
I hear her breathing,
I'm surrounded by the sound.
$ tail -2 heart        ...list the last two lines
Floating in this secret place,
I never shall be found.
$ _
```

3.16 Renaming a File: mv

Now that I'd created the first draft of my lyrics, I wanted to create a few more experimental versions. To indicate that the file "heart" was really the first generation of many versions to come, I decided to rename it "heart.ver1" by using the **mv** utility, which works as described in Figure 3–19.

Utility: **mv** -i *oldFileName newFileName*
  mv -i {*fileName*}* *directoryName*
  mv -i *oldDirectoryName newDirectoryName*

The first form of **mv** renames *oldFileName* as *newFileName*. If the label *newFileName* already exists, it is replaced. The second form allows you to move a collection of files to a directory, and the third form allows you to move an entire directory. None of these options actually moves the physical contents of a file if the destination location is within the same file system as the original; instead, they just move labels around the hierarchy. **mv** is therefore a very fast utility. The **-i** option prompts you for confirmation if *newFileName* already exists.

Figure 3–19   Description of the **mv** command.

Here's how I renamed the file using the first form of the **mv** utility:

```
$ mv heart heart.ver1        ...rename to "heart.ver1".
$ ls
heart.ver1
$ _
```

The second and third forms of the **mv** utility are illustrated later in this chapter.

3.17 Creating a Directory: mkdir

Rather than clog up my home directory with the many versions of "heart," I decided to create a subdirectory called "lyrics" in which to keep them all. To do this, I used the **mkdir** utility, as described in Figure 3–20.

Utility: **mkdir** [-p] *newDirectoryName*

The **mkdir** utility creates a directory. The **-p** option creates any parent directories in the *newDirectoryName* pathname that do not already exist. If *newDirectoryName* already exists, an error message is displayed and the existing file is not altered in any way.

Figure 3–20   Description of the **mkdir** command.

Here's how I did it:

```
$ mkdir lyrics          ...create a directory called "lyrics".
$ ls -1FG               ...confirm.
-rw-r--r--  1  glass    106  Jan 30  23:28    heart.ver1
drwxr-xr-x  2  glass    512  Jan 30  19:49    lyrics/
$ _
```

The letter "d" at the start of the permission flags of "lyrics" indicates that it's a directory file.

In general, you should keep related files in their own separate directory. If you name your directories sensibly, it'll make it easy to track down files weeks, or even years, after you create them.

Once the "lyrics" directory was created, the next step was to move the "heart.ver1" into its new location. To do this, I used **mv**, and confirmed the operation using **ls**:

```
$ mv heart.ver1 lyrics  ...move into "lyrics"
$ ls                    ...list the current directory.
lyrics/                 ..."heart.ver1" has gone.
$ ls lyrics             ...list the "lyrics" directory.
heart.ver1              ..."heart.ver1" has moved.
$ _
```

3.18 Moving to a Directory: cd

Although I could remain in my home directory and access the various versions of my lyric files by preceding them with the prefix "lyrics/", this would be rather inconvenient. For example, to edit the file "heart.ver1" with the Linux **vim** editor, I'd have to do the following:

```
$ vim lyrics/heart.ver1         ...invoke the vim editor.
```

In general, it's a good idea to move your shell into a directory if you intend to do a lot of work there. To do this, use the *cd* command. *cd* isn't actually a Linux or GNU utility, but instead is an example of a shell built-in command. Your shell recognizes it as a special keyword and executes it directly. Notice that I write shell commands using italics, in adherence to the nomenclature that I described at the start of this book. Figure 3–21 shows how *cd* works:

Shell Command: cd [directoryName]

The *cd* (change directory) shell command changes a shell's current working directory to be *directoryName*. If the *directoryName* argument is omitted, the shell is moved to its owner's home directory.

Figure 3–21 Description of the *cd* shell command.

The following example shows how I moved into the "lyrics" directory and confirmed my new location using **pwd**:

```
$ pwd                ...display where I am.
/home/glass
$ cd lyrics          ...move into the "lyrics" directory.
$ pwd                ...display where I am now.
/home/glass/lyrics
$ _
```

Figure 3–22 illustrates the shell movement caused by the previous *cd* command:

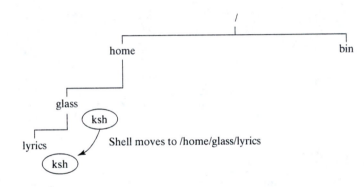

Figure 3–22   *cd* moves a shell.

Since "." and ".." refer to your shell's current working directory and parent directory, respectively, you may move up one directory level by typing "cd ..". Here's an example:

```
$ pwd                ...display current position.
/home/glass/lyrics
$ cd ..              ...move up one level.
$ pwd                ...display new current position.
/home/glass
$ _
```

3.19 Copying a File: cp

After moving into the "lyrics" directory, I decided to work on a second version of my lyrics. I wanted to keep the first version for posterity, so I copied "heart.ver1" into a new file called "heart.ver2" and then edited the new file. To copy the file I used the **cp** utility, which works as described in Figure 3–23.

> *Utility:* **cp** -i *oldFileName newFileName*
>   **cp** -ir { *fileName* }* *directoryName*
>
> The first form of **cp** copies *oldFileName* to *newFileName*. If the label *newFileName* already exists, it is replaced. The **-i** option prompts you for confirmation if *newFileName* already exists. The second form of **cp** copies a list of files into *directoryName*. The **-r** option causes any source files that are directories to be recursively copied, thus copying the entire directory structure.

Figure 3-23 Description of the **cp** command.

cp actually does two things:

- It makes a physical copy of the original file's contents.
- It creates a new label in the directory hierarchy that points to the copied file.

The new copy of the original file can therefore be edited, removed, and otherwise manipulated without having any effect on the original file. Here's how I copied the "heart.ver1" file:

```
$ cp heart.ver1 heart.ver2              ...copy to "heart.ver2".
$ ls -lG heart.ver1 heart.ver2          ...confirm.
-rw-r--r--  1      glass   106   Jan 30   23:28 heart.ver1
-rw-r--r--  1      glass   106   Jan 31   00:12 heart.ver2
$ _
```

3.20 Editing a File: vim

At this point, I edited the "heart.ver2" file using an editor called **vim**. The way that the **vim** editor works is described later in this chapter, together with information about another editor called **emacs**. For the time being, assume that I edited "heart.ver2" to look like this:

```
$ vim heart.ver2                        ...edit the file.
... editing session takes place here.
$ cat heart.ver2                        ...list the file.
I hear her breathing,
I'm surrounded by the sound.
Floating in this secret place,
I never shall be found.

She pushed me into the daylight,
I had to leave my home.
But I am a survivor,
And I'll make it on my own.
$ _
```

After creating five versions of my song's lyrics, my work was done. I moved back to my home directory and created a subdirectory called "lyrics.final" in which to store the final version of my lyrics. I also renamed the original "lyrics" directory to "lyrics.draft," which I felt was a better name.

```
$ cd                       ...move back to my home directory.
$ mkdir lyrics.final       ...make the final lyrics directory.
$ mv lyrics lyrics.draft   ...rename the old lyrics dir.
$ _
```

The final version of my lyrics was stored in a file called "heart.ver5" in the "lyrics.draft" directory, which I then copied into a file called "heart.final" in the "lyrics.final" directory:

```
$ cp lyrics.draft/heart.ver5 lyrics.final/heart.final
$ _
```

3.21 Deleting a Directory: rmdir

Although posterity is a good reason for keeping old things around, it can interfere with your disk usage in a multi-user system. I therefore decided to remove the "lyrics.draft" directory to avoid exceeding my modest disk quota. Before I removed it, I archived its contents using the **cpio** utility, which is described in Chapter 4, "GNU Utilities for Power Users" To remove the directory, I used the **rmdir** utility (Figure 3–24).

Utility: **rmdir** { *directoryName* }+

The **rmdir** utility removes all of the directories in the list of directory names. A directory must be empty before it can be removed. To recursively remove a directory and all of its contents, use the **rm** utility with the **-r** option (described shortly).

Figure 3–24 Description of the **rmdir** command.

I tried to remove the "lyrics.draft" directory while it still contained the draft versions, and received the following error message:

```
$ rmdir lyrics.draft
rmdir: lyrics.draft: Directory not empty
$ _
```

To remove the files from the "lyrics.draft" directory, I made use of the **rm** utility, described next.

3.22 Deleting a File: rm

The **rm** utility allows you to remove a file's label from the hierarchy. When no more labels reference a file, Linux removes the file itself. In most cases, every file only has one label, so the act of removing the label causes the file's physical contents to be deallocated. However, in Chapter 4, "GNU Utilities for Power Users," I'll show you some occasions where a single file has more than one label. In these cases, a label may be removed without affecting the file that it refers to. Figure 3–25 describes **rm**.

Utility: **rm** -fir {*fileName*} *

The **rm** utility removes a file's label from the directory hierarchy. If the filename doesn't exist, an error message is displayed. The **-i** option prompts the user for confirmation before deleting a filename; press **y** to confirm, and **n** otherwise. If *fileName* is a directory, the **-r** option causes all of its contents, including subdirectories, to be recursively deleted. The **-f** option inhibits all error messages and prompts.

Figure 3–25 Description of the **rm** command.

To remove every file in the "lyrics.draft" directory, I moved into the "lyrics.draft" directory and used **rm**:

```
$ cd lyrics.draft        ...move to "lyrics.draft" dir.
$ rm heart.ver1 heart.ver2 heart.ver3 heart.ver4 heart.ver5
$ ls                     ...nothing remains.
$ _
```

Now that all the files were erased, I moved back to my home directory and erased the draft directory:

```
$ cd                     ...move to my home directory.
$ rmdir lyrics.draft     ...this time it works.
$ _
```

As you'll see in Chapter 5, "The Linux Shells," there's a much easier way to erase a collection of files when you're using a shell. I could have written the following instead:

```
$ cd lyrics.draft        ...move into "lyrics.draft" directory.
$ rm *                   ...erase all files in current dir.
```

Even better, I could have used the more advanced **-r** option of **rm** to delete the "lyrics.draft" directory and all of its contents with just one command:

```
$ cd                     ...move to my home directory.
$ rm -r lyrics.draft     ...recursively delete directory.
$ _
```

3.23 Printing a File: lp/lpstat/cancel

Now that the hard work is done, I want to obtain a printout of my lyrics to sing from. I can use the GNU utility, patterned after the System V UNIX utility, called **lp** (Figure 3–26).

Utility: **lp** [-d *destination*] [-n *copies*] { *fileName* }*

lp prints the named files to the printer specified by the **-d** option. If no files are specified, standard input is printed instead. By default, one copy of each file is printed, although this may be overridden using the **-n** option.

Figure 3–26   Description of the **lp** command.

lp causes a numbered print job to be started for the specified files. You may find the status of a particular job and/or printer by using the **lpstat** utility (Figure 3–27).

Utility: **lpstat** *[destination]*

lpstat displays the status of all print jobs sent to any printer with the **lp** command. If a printer destination is specified, **lpstat** reports queue information for that printer only. **lpstat** displays information about the user, the name and size of the job, and a print request ID.

Figure 3–27   Description of the **lpstat** command.

If for some reason you wish to cancel a print job, you may do so by using the **cancel** utility (Figure 3–28). You will need the request ID displayed by **lpstat**.

Utility: **cancel** { *request-ID* }+

cancel removes all of the specified jobs from the printer queue. If you're a super-user, then you may cancel any queued job.

Figure 3–28   Description of the **cancel** command.

You may obtain a list of the printers on your system from your system administrator.

In the following example, I started by ordering a printout of "heart.final" from the "lwcs" printer. I then decided to order two more copies, and obtained a printer status. Finally, I changed my mind and canceled the last print job.

```
$ lp -d lwcs heart.final      ...order a printout.
request id is lwcs-37 (1 file)
$ lpstat lwcs              ...look at the printer status.
printer queue for lwcs
lwcs-36          ables      priority 0  Mar 18 17:02 on lwcs
     inventory.txt                     457 bytes
lwcs-37          glass      priority 0  Mar 18 17:04 on lwcs
     heart.final                       213 bytes
$ lp -n 2 -d lwcs heart.final          ...order two more copies.
request id is lwcs-38 (1 file)
$ lpstat lwcs      ...look at the printer status again.
printer queue for lwcs
lwcs-37          glass      priority 0  Mar 18 17:04 on lwcs
     heart.final                       213 bytes
lwcs-38          glass      priority 0  Mar 18 17:05 on lwcs
     heart.final    2 copies           213 bytes
$ cancel lwcs-38           ...remove the last job.
request "lwcs-38" cancelled
$ _
```

In the next example, I used the keyboard to compose a quick message for the printer:

```
$ lp -d lwcs              ...print from standard input.
Hi there,
This is a test of the print facility.
- Graham
^D       ...end of input.
request id is lwcs-42 (standard input)
$ _
```

3.24 Printing a File: lpr/lpq/lprm

BSD UNIX provided its own print commands, and both sets of commands are supported by Linux. These commands cover the same basic functions of print, check the queue, cancel the job, but have different names and arguments.

To print my file using such a system, use the **lpr** utility, which works as shown in Figure 3–29.

Utility: **lpr** -m [-P*printer*] [-#*copies*] { *fileName* }*

lpr prints the named files to the printer specified by the **-P** option. If no printer is specified, the printer in the environment variable $PRINTER is used (for more information about environment variables, refer to Chapter 5, "The Linux Shells"). If no files are specified, standard input is printed instead. By default, one copy of each file is printed, although this may be overridden using the **-#** option. The **-m** option causes mail to be sent to you when printing is complete.

Figure 3–29   Description of the **lpr** command.

lpr causes a numbered print job to be started for the specified files. You may find the status of a particular job and/or printer by using the **lpq** utility (Figure 3–30).

Utility: **lpq** -l [-P*printer*] { *job#* }* {*userId* }*

lpq displays the status of jobs on the printer specified by the **-P** option. If no printer is specified, the printer in the environment variable $PRINTER is used. **lpq** displays information pertaining to the specified jobs and/or the jobs of the specified users. If no jobs or users are specified, the status of all jobs on the specified printer is displayed. The **-l** option generates extra information.

Figure 3–30   Description of the **lpq** command.

If for some reason you wish to cancel a print job, you may do so by using the **lprm** utility:

Utility: **lprm** [-P*printer*] [-] { *job#* }* { *username* }*

lprm cancels all of the specified jobs on the printer specified by the **-P** option. If no printer is specified, the printer in the environment variable $PRINTER is used. The - option cancels all of the print jobs started by you. If you are the super-user, then you may cancel all of the jobs owned by a particular user by specifying their username.

Figure 3–31   Description of the **lprm** command.

You may obtain a list of the printers on your system from your system administrator.

As in our previous example, I started by ordering a printout of "heart.final" from the "lwcs" printer. I then decided to order two more copies, and obtained a printer status. Finally, I changed my mind and canceled the last print job.

```
$ lpr -Plwcs heart.final        ...order a printout.
$ lpq -Plwcs glass       ...look at the printer status.
lwcs is ready and printing
Rank    Owner  Job  Files         Total Size
active  glass  731  heart.final  213 bytes
$ lpr -#2 -Plwcs heart.final        ...order two more copies.
$ lpq -Plwcs glass       ...look at the printer status again.
lwcs is ready and printing
Rank    Owner  Job  Files         Total Size
active  glass  731  heart.final  213 bytes
active  glass  732  heart.final  426 bytes
$ lprm -Plwcs 732        ...remove the last job.
centaur: dfA732vanguard dequeued
centaur: cfA732vanguard.utdallas.edu dequeued
$ _
```

In the next example, I used the keyboard to compose a quick message for the printer, and requested mail notification of job completion:

```
$ lpr -m -Plwcs        ...print from standard input.
Hi there,
This is a test of the print facility.
- Graham
^D         ...end of input.
$                       ...wait a little.
$ mail                  ...read my mail.
Mail version 8.1 6/6/93.  Type ? for help.
>N 1 daemon@utdallas.edu Sat Jan 31 18:04  15/502  printer job
& 1                     ...read the first mail message.
From: daemon@utdallas.edu
To: glass@utdallas.edu
Subject: printer job
Date: Tue, 31 Jan 2005 18:04:32 -0600

Your printer job (stdin)
Completed successfully
& q                     ...quit out of mail.
$ _
```

3.25 Counting Words in a File: wc

I was quite interested to find out how many characters, words, and lines were in the "heart.final" file (even though printing it gave me a byte count). To do this, I used the **wc** utility, described in Figure 3–32.

Utility: **wc** -lwc { *fileName* }*

The **wc** utility counts the lines, words, and/or characters in a list of files. If no files are specified, standard input is used instead. The **-l** option requests a line count, the **-w** option requests a word count, and the **-c** option requests a character count. If no options are specified, then all three counts are displayed. A word is defined by a sequence of characters surrounded by tabs, spaces, or newlines.

Figure 3–32   Description of the **wc** command.

Here's an example of **wc**:

```
$ wc heart.final        ...obtain a word count.
  9    43     213 heart.final
$ _
```

3.26 File Attributes

Now that I've introduced you to some of the common file-oriented utilities, it's time to look at the various file attributes. I used **ls** to obtain a long listing of "heart.final," and got the following output:

```
$ ls -lsF heart.final
1 -rw-r--r--   1   glass  cs   213   Jan 31 00:12   heart.final
$ _
```

Each field is the value of a file attribute, described by the Figure 3–33.

Field #	Field value	Meaning
1	1	The number of blocks of physical storage occupied by the file.
2	-rw-r--r--	The type and permission mode of the file—which indicates who can read, write, and execute the file.
3	1	The hard link count (discussed in Chapter 4, "GNU Utilities for Power Users").
4	glass	The username of the owner of the file.
5	cs	The group name of the file.
6	213	The size of the file, in bytes.
7	Jan 31 00:12	The date and time that the file was last modified.
8	heart.final	The name of the file.

Figure 3–33   File attributes.

The next few sections describe the meaning of the individual fields, in increasing order of difficulty.

3.26.1 File Storage

The number of blocks of physical storage is shown in field 1 and is useful if you want to know how much actual disk space a file is using. It's possible to create sparse files that seem to be very large in terms of field 6 but actually take up very little physical storage. Sparse files are discussed in detail in Chapter 12, "Systems Programming."

3.26.2 Filenames

The name of the file is shown in field 8. A Linux filename may be up to 255 characters in length. You may use any printable[2] characters you want in a filename except the slash (/), although I recommend that you avoid the use of any character that is special to a shell (like <, >, *, ?, or the tab) as these can confuse both the user and the shell. Unlike some operating systems, there's no

---

2.   Some nonprintable characters are valid in filenames, but can result in unexpected behavior when displayed or used, so their use is discouraged.

requirement that a file end in an extension such as ".c" and ".h," although many GNU utilities, such as the C compiler, will only accept files that end with a particular suffix. Thus, the filenames "heart" and "heart.final" are both perfectly legal. The only filenames that you definitely *can't* choose are "." and "..", as these are predefined filenames that correspond to your current working directory and its parent directory, respectively.

3.26.3   File Modification Time

Field 7 shows the time that the file was last modified, and is used by several utilities. For example, the **make** utility, described in Chapter 11, "C Programming Tools," uses the last modification time of files to control its dependency checker. The **find** utility, described in Chapter 4, "GNU Utilities for Power Users," may be used to find files based on their last modification time.

3.26.4   File Owner

Field 4 tells you the owner of the file. Every Linux process has an owner, which is typically the same as the username of the person who started it. For example, my login shell is owned by "glass," which is my username. Whenever a process creates a file, the file's owner is set to the process's owner. This means that every file that I create from my shell is owned by "glass," the owner of the shell itself. Chapter 12, "Systems Programming," contains more information on processes and ownership.

Note that while the text string known as the username is typically how we refer to a user, internally Linux represents this as an integer known as the *user ID*. The username is easier for humans to understand than a numeric ID. Therefore I will refer to the textual name as *username* while using *user ID* to refer to the numeric value itself.

3.26.5   File Group

Field 5 shows the file's group. Every Linux user is also a member of a group. This membership is initially assigned by the system administrator, and is used as part of the Linux security mechanism. For example, my group name is "cs." Every Linux process also belongs to a specific group, usually the same as that of the user that started the process. My login shell belongs to the group name "cs." Because a file created by a process is assigned to the same group as that of the creating process, this means that every file that I create from my shell has the group name "cs." Chapter 12, "Systems Programming," contains more information on processes and groups. The use of groups in relation to the Linux security mechanism is described in the next few sections.

As with the user ID, the group is usually referenced by the text string name, but is represented internally as an integer value called the *group ID*. Therefore I will refer to the textual name as *group name* while using *group ID* when referring to the numeric value itself.

3.26.6   File Types

Field 2 describes the file's type and permission settings. In the previous **ls** example:

```
1 -rw-r--r--  1 glass  cs  213  Jan 31 00:12 heart.final
```

the first character of field 2 indicates the type of the file, which is encoded as shown in Figure 3–34.

Character	File type
-	regular file
d	directory file
b	buffered (block-oriented) special file (such as a disk drive)
c	unbuffered (character-oriented) special file (such as a terminal)
l	symbolic link
p	pipe
s	socket

Figure 3–34   File types.

In the example, the type of "heart.final" is indicated as a regular file. You'll encounter symbolic links in Chapter 4, "GNU Utilities for Power Users," pipes and sockets in Chapter 12, "Systems Programming," and buffered/unbuffered special files in Chapter 13, "Linux Internals."

A file's type can often be determined by using the file utility (Figure 3–35).

Utility: **file** { *fileName* }+

The **file** utility attempts[a] to describe the contents of the *fileName* arguments, including the language that any text is written in. When using **file** on a symbolic link file, **file** reports on the file that the link is pointing to, rather than the link itself.

---

a.   While **file** is quite useful, it is not 100% accurate and can be fooled by some file formats.

Figure 3–35   Description of the **file** command.

For example, when I ran **file** on "heart.final," I saw this:

```
$ file heart.final        ...determine the file type.
heart.final: ascii text
$ _
```

3.26.7   File Permissions

The next nine characters of field 2 indicate the file's permission settings. In the current example, the permission settings are "rw-r--r--":

```
1 -rw-r--r--  1  glass  cs  213  Jan 31 00:12 heart.final
```

These nine characters should be thought of as being arranged in three groups of three characters, as in Figure 3–36.

User (owner)	Group	Others
rw-	r--	r--
Read permission	**Write permission**	**Execute permission**
r	w	x

Figure 3–36   File permissions.

If a dash occurs instead of a letter, then the permission is denied. The meaning of the read, write, and execute permissions depends on the type of the file (Figure 3–37).

	Regular file	**Directory file**	**Special file**
read	The process may access the contents.	The process may read the directory (i.e., list the names of the files that it contains).	The process may read from the file using the read () system call.
write	The process may change the contents.	The process may add or remove files to/from the directory.	The process may write to the file using the write () system call.
execute	The process may execute the file (which only makes sense if it's a program).	The process may access files in the directory or any of its subdirectories.	No meaning.

Figure 3–37   Permission meanings for file types.

When a process executes, it has four values related to file permissions:

1. a *real* user ID
2. an *effective* user ID
3. a *real* group ID
4. an *effective* group ID

When you log in, your login shell process has its real and effective user IDs set to your own user ID, and its real and effective group IDs set to your group ID. When a process runs, the file permissions apply as follows:

- If the process's effective user ID is the same as the owner of the file, the **User** permissions apply.
- If the process's effective user ID is different from the owner of the file, but its effective group ID matches the file's group ID, then the **Group** permissions apply.
- If neither the process's effective user ID nor its effective group ID matches, the **Others** permissions apply.

The permission system is therefore a three-tier arrangement that allows you to protect your files from general users but at the same time allows access by certain groups. Later in this chapter I'll illustrate the use of permission settings to good effect and describe the utilities that are used to alter them.

Note that only a process's effective user and group IDs affect its permissions, its real user and group IDs are only used for accounting purposes. Note also that a process's access rights depend ordinarily on who *executes* the process, and not on who *owns* the executable. There are some occasions where this is undesirable (e.g., in a game that maintains a file of the best scores of previous players). Obviously, the game program itself must have permission to alter this file when it is executing, but the player that executes the game program should not. This seems impossible, based on the permission rules that I just described. To get around this problem, Linux provides two special file permissions called "*set user ID*" and "*set group ID*." When an executable with "set user ID" permission is exec'ed, the process's effective user ID becomes that of the executable. Similarly, when an executable with "set group ID" permission is exec'ed, the process's effective group ID is copied from the executable. In both cases, the real user/group ID is unaffected. In the case of our game, the executable and the score file are both owned by a different user, and the program executable has "set user ID" permission. The score file only has write permission for its owner, thus protecting general users from modifying it. When a player executes the game program, the process executes with the effective user ID of the game, and thus is able to modify the score file.

"Set user ID" and "set group ID" permissions are indicated by an "s" instead of an "x" in the user and group clusters, respectively. They may be set using the **chmod** utility, described shortly, and by the chmod () system call, described in Chapter 12, "Systems Programming."

Here are a few other notes relating to file permissions:

• When a process creates a file, the default permissions given to that file are modified by a special value called the *umask*. The umask value is usually set a sensible default, so we will wait to discuss it further in Chapter 5, "The Linux Shells."
• The super-user automatically has all access rights, regardless of whether they're granted or not.
• It's perfectly possible, although unusual, for the owner of a file to have fewer permissions than the group or anyone else.

3.26.8   Hard Link Count

Field 3 of the output from the **ls** command shows the file's hard link count, which indicates how many labels in the hierarchy are pointing to the same physical file. Hard links are rather advanced, and are discussed in conjunction with the **ln** utility in Chapter 4, "GNU Utilities for Power Users"

3.27 Groups

Now that you've read about file permissions, it's time to see how they can come in handy. Recall that the "heart.final" file's user and group names were "glass" and "cs," respectively, inherited from my login shell:

```
$ ls -l heart.final
-rw-r--r--  1  glass  cs   213  Jan 31 00:12 heart.final
$ _
```

The original permission flags allow anyone to read it but only the owner to write it. What I really wanted to do was to set up a new group called "music" and allow anyone in the "music" group to read my work. I, the owner, would retain read and write permissions, and anyone else would be denied all access rights.

The only way to create a new group is to ask the system administrator to add it. The actual way that a new group is added is described in Chapter 14, "System Administration." After a new group is added, any user who wants to be a part of that group must also ask the system administrator. At this time, I mailed a request to the system administrator for a new "music" group and asked for myself and my friend Tim to be added to the group. When I received a confirmation of the request, it was time to update my file attributes.

3.28 Listing Your Groups: groups

Before changing my file's group setting, I wanted to confirm that I was now an official member of the "music" group. The **groups** utility allows you to list all of the groups that you're a member of (Figure 3–38).

Utility: **groups** [*userId*]

When invoked with no arguments, the **groups** utility displays a list of all the groups that you are a member of. If the name of a user is specified, a list of that user's groups are displayed.

Figure 3–38 Description of the **groups** command.

Here's what I saw when I executed **groups**:

```
$ groups        ...list my groups.
cs    music
$ _
```

3.29 Changing a File's Group: chgrp

The first step toward protecting my lyrics was to change the group name of "heart.final" from "cs" to "music." I did this by using the **chgrp** utility, described in Figure 3–39.

Utility: **chgrp** -R *groupname* { *fileName* }*

The **chgrp** utility allows a user to change the group of files that he/she owns. A super-user can change the group of any file. All of the files that follow the *groupname* argument are affected. The **-R** option recursively changes the group of the files in a directory.

Figure 3–39 Description of the **chgrp** command.

I used **chgrp** like this:

```
$ ls -l heart.final
-rw-r--r-- 1 glass   cs    213 Jan 31 00:12 heart.final
$ chgrp music heart.final        ...change the group.
$ ls -l heart.final              ...confirm it changed.
-rw-r--r-- 1 glass  music 213 Jan 31 00:12 heart.final
$ _
```

You may also use **chgrp** to change the group of a directory.

3.30 Changing a File's Permissions: chmod

Now that the file's group was changed, it was necessary to update its permissions, or mode, to deny all access rights to general users. To do this, I used the **chmod** utility (Figure 3–40).

Utility: **chmod** -R *change* { , *change* }*{ *fileName* }+

The **chmod** utility changes the modes of the specified files according to the *change* parameters, which may take the following forms:

  clusterSelection+newPermissions (add permissions)

  clusterSelection-newPermissions (subtract permissions)

and

  clusterSelection=newPermissions (assign permissions absolutely)

where *clusterSelection* is any combination of:

- u (user/owner)
- g (group)
- o (others)
- a (all)

and *newPermissions* is any combination of

- r (read)
- w (write)
- x (execute)
- s (set user ID/set group ID)

The **-R** option recursively changes the modes of the files in directories. Please see the following text for examples. Changing a directory's permission settings doesn't change the settings of the files that it contains.

Figure 3–40 Description of the **chmod** command.

To remove read permission from others, I used **chmod** as follows:

```
$ ls -l heart.final              ...before.
-rw-r--r-- 1 glass      music 213 Jan 31 00:12    heart.final
$ chmod o-r heart.final          ...remove read for others.
```

```
$ ls -l heart.final             ...after.
-rw-r----- 1 glass        music 213 Jan 31 00:12     heart.final
$ _
```

Figure 3–41 gives some other examples of **chmod**.

Requirement	Change parameters
Add group write permission.	g+w
Remove user read and write permission.	u-rw
Add execute permission for user, group, and others.	a+x
Give the group just read permission.	g=r
Add write permission for user, and remove read from group.	u+w, g-r

Figure 3–41   File permission specifications for the **chmod** command.

I recommend that you protect your login directory from unauthorized access by not granting write permission for anyone but yourself, and by restricting read and execute permission to yourself and members of your group. Here's an example of how to do this:

```
$ cd                          ...change to home directory.
$ ls -lGd .                   ...list attributes of home dir.
drwxr-xr-x 45 glass             4096 Apr 29 14:35   .
$ chmod o-rx                  ...update permissions.
$ ls -lGd                     ...confirm.
drwxr-x--- 45 glass             4096 Apr 29 14:35   .
$ _
```

Note that I used the **-d** option of **ls** to ensure that the attributes of my home directory were displayed, rather than the attributes of its files.

The **chmod** utility allows you to specify the new permission setting of a file as an octal number. Each octal digit represents a permission triplet. For example, if you wanted a file to have the following permission settings:

```
rwxr-x--
```

then the octal permission setting would be 750, calculated in Figure 3–42.

	User	Group	Others
setting	rwx	r-x	---
binary	111	101	000
octal	7	5	0

Figure 3–42   Permission of 750 for the **chmod** command.

The octal permission setting would be supplied to **chmod** as follows:

```
$ chmod 750 .          ...update permissions.
$ ls -ldG              ...confirm.
drwxr-x--- 45 glass      4096 Apr 29 14:35  .
$ _
```

3.31 Changing a File's Owner: chown

If for some reason you ever want to relinquish ownership of a file, you may do so by using the **chown** utility (Figure 3–43).

Utility: **chown** -R *newUserId* { *fileName* }+

The **chown** utility allows a super-user to change the ownership of files. All of the files that follow the *newUserId* argument are affected. The **-R** option recursively changes the owner of the files in directories.

Figure 3–43   Description of the **chmod** command.

Linux allows only a super-user to change the ownership of a file. Several occasions when the system administrator needs to use **chown** are described in Chapter 14, "System Administration."

If I had been a super-user, I could have executed the following sequence of commands to change the ownership of "heart.final" to "tim" and then back to "glass" again:

```
# ls -l heart.final             ...before.
-rw-r----- 1  glass  music 213  Jan 31 00:12 heart.final
# chown tim heart.final         ...change the owner to "tim".
# ls -l heart.final             ...after.
-rw-r----- 1  tim    music 213  Jan 31 00:12 heart.final
# chown glass heart.final       ...change the owner back.
# _
```

3.32 Changing Groups: newgrp

If you're a member of several groups and then you create a file, to what group does the file belong? Well, although you may be a member of several groups, only one of them is your *effective* group at any given time. When a process creates a file, the group ID of the file is set to the process's *effective* group ID. This means that when you create a file from the shell, the group ID of the file is set to the effective group ID of your shell. In this example session, I was a member of the "cs" and "music" groups, and my login shell's effective group name was "cs."

The system administrator is the one who chooses which one of your groups is used as your login shell's effective group ID. The only way to permanently alter your login shell's effective group ID is to ask the system administrator to change it. However, you may create a shell with a different effective group ID by using the **newgrp** utility (Figure 3–44).

Utility: **newgrp** { - | *groupname* }

The **newgrp** utility, when invoked with a group name as an argument, creates a new shell
with an effective group ID corresponding to the group name. The old shell sleeps until you
exit the newly created shell. You must be a member of the group that you specify. If you use a
dash (-) instead of a group name as the argument, a shell is created with the same settings as
the shell that was created when you logged into the system.

Figure 3–44   Description of the **newgrp** command.

In the following example, I created a file called "test1" from my login shell, which had an
effective group of "cs." I then created a temporary shell with an effective group of "music" and
then created a file called "test2." I then terminated the shell and went back to the original shell,
where I obtained a long listing of both files:

```
$ date > test1          ...create from a "cs" group shell.
$ newgrp music          ...create a "music" group shell.
$ date > test2          ...create from a "music" group shell.
^D       ...terminate the new shell.
$ ls -l test1 test2     ...look at each file's attributes.
-rw-r--r--   1    glass  cs     29 Jan 31 22:57   test1
-rw-r--r--   1    glass  music  29 Jan 31 22:57   test2
$ _
```

3.33 Poetry in Motion: Epilogue

This concludes the "Poetry in Motion" series of examples. During this series, you were introduced to many useful Linux concepts and GNU utilities. I thoroughly recommend that you try
them out before progressing further through this book, as this will help you retain and understand the Linux basics. The remainder of this chapter covers the two most popular Linux editors
and explains how you can alter your terminal settings so that they work correctly. It also contains
some information on using the Linux e-mail system.

3.34 Determining Your Terminal's Type: tset

Several GNU utilities, including the two standard editors **vim** and **emacs**, need to know what
kind of terminal you're using so that they can control the screen correctly. In most cases, you're
working in a terminal window or on the console itself, and the system already knows those
types, so you shouldn't need to help it out. But if you are connected to a Linux system via the
network or a dial up line from another type of system, it might not realize that the special characters used to drive your terminal will be different.

The type of your terminal is stored by your shell in something called an *environment variable*. Environment variables are described in more detail in Chapter 5, "The Linux Shells." You may think of them as being rather like global variables that hold strings.

Before **vim** or **emacs** can work correctly, your shell's TERM environment variable must be set to your terminal type. There are several ways that this variable can be set:

- Your shell startup file, described in the next section, can set TERM directly by containing a line of the form: "setenv TERM vt100" (C shell) or "TERM=vt100 ; export TERM" (Korn and Bash shells). This is only practical if you know the type of your terminal in advance and you always log into the same terminal.
- You can manually set TERM from a shell.

If it is necessary to manually set your terminal type, the best way is to use **tset** from your login shell. Figure 3–45 describes how **tset** works.

Utility: **tset** -s [-e*c*] [-i*c*] {-m *portId*:[?]*terminalType*}*

tset is a utility that tries to determine your terminal's type and then resets it for standard operation.

If the **-s** option is not used, **tset** assumes that your terminal type is already stored in the TERM environment variable, and resets it using terminal capability information stored in "/etc/termcap" or the *terminfo* database.

If you use the **-s** option, **tset** examines the "/etc/ttys" file and tries to map your terminal's port to a terminal type listed there. It then generates shell commands to standard output that, when executed, cause the TERM and TERMCAP environment variables to be set properly. **tset** uses the contents of the SHELL environment variable to determine which kind of shell commands to generate. Filename expansion must be temporarily inhibited during the execution of the command sequence that **tset** generates, since there could be special characters that might be misinterpreted by the shell. Examples of this follow shortly.

The **-e** option sets the terminal's erase character to *c* instead of the default *Control-H* setting. Control characters may be indicated either by typing the character directly or by preceding the character by a ^ (i.e., use ^h to indicate *Control-H*).

The **-i** option sets the terminal's interrupt character to *c* instead of the default *Control-C* setting. Control characters may be indicated as described in the previous paragraph.

The "/etc/ttys" mappings may be overridden or supplemented by using the **-m** option. The sequence "-m *pp:tt*" tells **tset** that if the terminal's port type is *pp*, then it should assume that the terminal is of type *tt*. If a question mark (?) is placed after the colon (:), **tset** displays *tt* and asks the user to either press *Enter* to confirm that the terminal type is indeed *tt*, or to enter the actual terminal type that **tset** should use.

Figure 3–45 Description of the **tset** command.

In the following example, I found out my actual port name by using the **tty** utility (described in Chapter 4, "GNU Utilities for Power Users") and then examined the output from the **tset** command:

```
$ tty                ...display my terminal's port id.
/dev/pts/1
$ tset -s            ...call tset.
TERM=xterm;          ...shell command generated by tset.
$ _
```

The previous example is only provided to illustrate how **tset** does its stuff. To actually make **tset** change the TERM and TERMCAP variables, which after all is the reason for using it in the first place, you must 'eval' its output. The *eval* shell command is described fully on page 197 in Chapter 5, "The Linux Shells." Here's a more realistic example of **tset**:

```
$ set noglob         ...temporarily inhibit filename expansion.
$ eval `tset -s`     ...evaluate output from tset.
$ unset noglob        ...re-enable filename expansion.
$ echo $TERM          ...look at the new value of TERM.
network               ...the terminal type that tset found.
$ _
```

Unfortunately, the terminal type *network* is not very useful, as it assumes that my terminal has almost no capabilities at all. The **tset** command may be presented with a rule that tells it, "If the terminal type is discovered to be network, assume that the terminal is a vt100." Here is the variation of **tset** that does this:

```
$ set noglob             ...disable filename expansion.
$ eval `tset -s -m 'network:vt100'`    ...provide rule
$ unset noglob          ...re-enable filename expansion.
$ echo $TERM            ...display new TERM setting.
vt100                   ...this is the terminal type that tset used.
$ _
```

If you aren't sure what type of terminal you might be on when you log in from the network, you can have **tset** prompt you for confirmation (or let you set something else):

```
$ set noglob             ...disable filename expansion.
$ eval `tset -s -m 'network:?vt100'`    ...provide rule but ask.
Terminal type? [vt100] xterm        ...specify xterm, hit <Enter>.
$ unset noglob          ...re-enable filename expansion.
$ echo $TERM            ...display new TERM setting.
xterm                   ...this is the terminal type that tset used.
$ _
```

In summary, it's wise to contain a command in your shell's startup file that calls **tset** to set your terminal type. Shell startup files are described in Chapter 5, "The Linux Shells." The simplest form of **tset** is the following:

C shell

```
setenv TERM vt100
tset
```

Bash/Korn shell

```
TERM=vt100; export TERM
tset
```

The more sophisticated form of **tset** searches the "/etc/ttys" file for your terminal type, and should look somewhat like this:

C shell

```
set noglob
eval `tset -s -m 'network:?vt100'`
unset noglob
```

Bash/Korn shell

```
eval `tset -s -m 'network:?vt100'`
```

3.35 Changing a Terminal's Characteristics: stty

All terminals have the ability to process certain characters in a special manner; these characters are called *metacharacters*. Examples of metacharacters include the backspace character and the *Control-C* sequence, which is used to terminate programs. The default metacharacter settings may be overridden using the **stty** utility, described in Figure 3–46.

Utility: **stty** -a { *option* }* { *metacharacterString* <*value*>} *

The **stty** utility allows you to examine and set a terminal's characteristics. **stty** supports the modification of over one hundred different settings, so I've only listed the most common ones here. Consult **man** for more details. To list a terminal's current settings, use the **-a** option. To alter a particular setting, supply one or more of the following options:

OPTION	MEANING
-echo	Don't echo typed characters.
echo	Echo typed characters.
-raw	Enable the special meaning of metacharacters.
raw	Disable the special meaning of metacharacters.
-tostop	Allow background jobs to send output to the terminal.
tostop	Stop background jobs that try to send output to the terminal.
sane	Set the terminal characteristics to sensible default values.

You may also set the mappings of metacharacters by following the name of its corresponding string with its new value. A control character may be indicated by preceding the character with a ^ or by typing a \ followed by the actual control character itself. Here are the common metacharacter strings together with their meanings:

OPTION	MEANING
erase	Backspace one character.
kill	Erase all of the current line.
lnext	Don't treat the next character specially.
susp	Suspend the process for a future awakening.
intr	Terminate (interrupt) the foreground job with no core dump.
quit	Terminate the foreground job with a core dump.
stop	Stop/restart terminal output.
eof	End-of-input.

Figure 3–46 Description of the **stty** command.

Here's an example of **stty** in action:

```
$ stty -a      ...display current terminal settings.
speed 38400 baud; rows 35; columns 80; line = 233;
intr = ^C; quit = ^\; erase = ^?; kill = ^U; eof = ^D; eol = <undef>;
eol2 = <undef>; start = ^Q; stop = ^S; susp = ^Z; rprnt = ^R;
werase = ^W; lnext = ^V; flush = ^O; min = 1; time = 0;
```

```
-parenb -parodd cs8 -hupcl -cstopb cread -clocal -crtscts
-ignbrk brkint ignpar -parmrk -inpck -istrip -inlcr -igncr icrnl ixon
-ixoff -iuclc -ixany imaxbel
opost -olcuc -ocrnl onlcr -onocr -onlret -ofill -ofdel nl0 cr0 tab0
bs0 vt0 ff0
isig icanon iexten echo echoe echok -echonl -noflsh -xcase -tostop
-echoprt echoctl echoke
$ stty erase ^b        ...set erase key to Control-B.
$ stty erase ^h        ...set erase key to Control-H
$ _
```

Invoke **stty** from your shell's startup file if your favorite metacharacter mappings differ from the norm. **stty** is useful when building shells that need to turn keyboard echoing on and off; an example of such a script is included in Chapter 8, "The C Shell." Here's an example that uses **stty** to turn off keyboard echoing:

```
$ stty -echo      ...turn echoing off.
$ stty echo       ...turn echoing back on again.
$ _
```

Note that the last line of input (*stty echo*) would not ordinarily be seen due to the inhibition of echoing caused by the preceding line!

Now that you've seen how to set your terminal type and alter its settings, you can use full-screen editors like **vim** and **emacs**.

3.36 Editing a File: vim

The two most common Linux text editors are **vi** and **emacs**. This section and the next contain enough information about each editor to allow you to perform essential editing tasks. They also contain references to other books for obtaining more advanced information.

3.36.1   Starting vim

Bill Joy of Sun Microsystems, Inc., originally developed **vi** (standing for **vi**sual editor) for BSD UNIX while at the University of California at Berkeley. **vi** proved so popular in the UNIX world that it was later adopted as a standard utility for System V and most other versions of UNIX. Today **vi** is found on virtually every UNIX system. The version of **vi** contributed to the GNU Project started out as a different full-screen editor, but it is compatible with **vi**. Because it was "vi with some improvements," it was renamed **vim**. Conveniently, most shell startup scripts created for Linux users define an alias for "vi" that points to **vim**, so old UNIX hacks can still type **vi** and feel like they're using **vi**. Those wanting to learn everything about **vim** can also run the **vimtutor** training program.

To start **vim** with a blank slate, enter the command **vim** without any parameters. To edit an existing file, supply the name of the file as a command-line parameter (i.e., "*vim filename*"). When **vim** is started with a new or empty file, lines past the end of the file containing no data are indicated by tilde characters (~). **vim** then enters *command mode* and awaits instructions. To conserve space, I'll draw screens that are only six lines long. For example, Figure 3–47 shows what I saw when I executed **vim** with no parameters.

```
~
~
~
~
~
~
                                              0,0-1        All
```

Figure 3–47 Example of the screen when starting **vim**.

In the lower right-hand corner, you see the line number and character indentation of the current location of the cursor and how far into the file you are positioned (this is usually a percentage value; "All" means you're looking at the entire file, and other values you might see here are "Top" and "Bot" for top and bottom of the file).

Command mode is one of the two modes that **vim** may be in; the other mode is called *text entry mode*. Since it's easier to describe command mode when there's some text on the screen, I'll start by describing text entry mode.

3.36.2 Text Entry Mode

To enter text entry mode from command mode, press one of the keys listed in Figure 3–48. Each key enters you into text entry mode in a slightly different way.

Key	Action
i	Text is inserted in front of the cursor.
I	Text is inserted at the beginning of the current line.
a	Text is appended after the cursor.
A	Text is appended to the end of the current line.
o	Text insertion point is opened after the current line.
O	Text insertion point is opened before the current line.
R	Text is replaced (overwritten).

Figure 3–48 Text input commands in **vim**.

Any text that you enter at this point will be displayed on the screen. To move to the next line, press the *Enter* key. You may use the backspace key to delete the last character that you entered. You may still move around the screen using the cursor keys even when you're in text entry mode.

To go from text entry mode to command mode, press the *Esc* or *Escape* key.

To enter a short four-line poem, I pressed the **a** key to add characters in text entry mode, entered the text of the poem, and then pressed the *Esc* key to return to command mode. Figure 3–49 shows what I ended up with.

```
I always remember standing in the rains,
On a cold and damp september,
Brown Autumn leaves were falling softly to the ground,
Like the dreams of a life as they slide away.
~
~                                                    4,45          All
```

Figure 3–49   Editing a file with **vim**.

The next section describes the editing features of **vim** that allowed me to change this poem to something a little more appealing.

3.36.3   Command Mode

To edit text, you must enter command mode. To travel from text entry mode to command mode, press the *Esc* key. If you accidentally press the *Esc* key when in command mode, nothing bad happens (depending on your terminal settings, you may hear a beep or bell that tells you are already in command mode).

vim's editing features are selected by pressing special character sequences. For example, to erase a single word, position the cursor at the beginning of a particular word and press the **d** key followed by the **w** key (**d**elete **w**ord).

Some editing features require parameters, and are accessed by pressing the colon (:) key, followed by the command sequence, followed by the *Enter* key. When the colon key is pressed, the remainder of the command sequence is displayed at the bottom of the screen. In the following example, the *Enter* key is indicated as *<Enter>*. The < and > characters act as delimiters and should not be entered. For example, to delete lines 1 through 3, you'd enter the following command sequence:

```
:1,3d<Enter>
```

Some editing features, such as the block delete command that I just described, act upon a range of lines. **vim** accepts a couple of formats for a line range:

- To select a single line, state its line number.
- To select a block of lines, state the first and last line numbers inclusively, separated by a comma.

vim allows you to use $ to denote the line number of the last line in the file, and . to denote the line number of the line currently containing the cursor. **vim** also allows you to use arithmetic expressions when stating line numbers. For example, the sequence

```
:.,.+2d<Enter>
```

would delete the current line and the two lines that follow it. Figure 3–50 shows some other examples of line ranges.

Range	Selects
1,$	All of the lines in the file.
1,.	All of the lines from the start of the file to the current line, inclusive.
.,$	All of the lines from the current line to the end of the file, inclusive.
.-2	The single line that's two lines before the current line.

figure 3–50 Specifying a line range in vim.

In what follows, the term *<range>* indicates a range of lines in the format described above.

3.36.4   Memory Buffer and Temporary Files

While you are editing your file, **vim** stores a copy of your file in memory and makes the changes to that copy of your file. The disk file is not modified until you explicitly tell **vim** to write the file or you exit **vim** with one of the commands that also writes the file (discussed below). For this reason, I recommend that you not spend hours and hours editing a file without either writing or exiting **vim** and getting back in on a regular basis. If your system were to crash (for whatever reason) while you were editing, all changes you made since the last time you either wrote the file or started **vim** would be lost.

Even if the system does crash while you are editing, all may not be lost. **vim** also uses a temporary file to manage the in-memory copy of your file while you edit (if your file is very large, it won't all be kept in memory at the same time). **vim** may be able to recover the file using the **-r** argument. While this is a nice feature, it is much safer to not depend on this and just write the file periodically. Even though today's systems are much more reliable, it is still wise to save your work often.

3.36.5   Common Editing Features

The most common **vim** editing features can be grouped into the following categories:

- moving the cursor
- deleting text
- replacing text
- pasting text

- searching text
- search/replace text
- saving/loading files
- miscellaneous (including how to quit **vi**)

These categories are described and illustrated in the subsections that follow, using the sample poem that I entered at the start of this section.

3.36.6   Cursor Movement

Figure 3–51 is a table of the common cursor movement commands.

Movement	Key sequence
Up one line	<cursor up> or **k**
Down one line	<cursor down> or **j**
Right one character	<cursor right> or **l** (will not wrap around)
Left one character	<cursor left> or **h** (will not wrap around)
To start of line	^
To end of line	$
Back one word	**b**
Forward one word	**w**
Forward to end of current word	**e**
To top of screen	**H**
To middle of screen	**M**
To bottom of screen	**L**
Down a half screen	*Control-D*
Forward one screen	*Control-F*
Up a half screen	*Control-U*
Back one screen	*Control-B*
To line *nn*	:*nn*<Enter> (*nn***G** also works)
To end of file	**G**

Figure 3–51   Cursor movement commands in **vim**.

For example, to insert the word "Just" before the word "Like" on the fourth line, I moved the cursor to the fourth line, pressed the **i** key to enter text entry mode, entered the text, and pressed the *Esc* key to return to command mode. To move the cursor to the fourth line, I used the key sequence :**4**<Enter> (or I could have used **4G**).

3.36.7 Deleting Text

Figure 3–52 is a table of the common text deletion commands.

Item to delete	Key sequence
Character	Position the cursor over the character and then press **x**.
Word	Position the cursor at start of word and then press **dw**.
Line	Position the cursor anywhere the line and then press **dd** (typing a number ahead of **dd** will cause **vim** to delete the specified number of lines beginning with the current line).
Current position to end of current line	Press **D**.
Block of lines	:*<range>*d*<Enter>*

Figure 3–52   Commands that delete text in **vim**.

For example, to delete the word "always," I typed **:1<Enter>** to move to the start of line one, pressed **w** to move forward one word, and then typed the letters **dw**. To delete the trailing "s" on the end of "rains" on the first line, I moved my cursor over the letter "s" and then pressed the **x** key. My poem now looked as shown in Figure 3–53.

```
I remember standing in the rain,
On a cold and damp september,
Brown Autumn leaves were falling softly to the ground,
Just Like the dreams of a life as they slide away.
~
~                                              4,1        All
```

Figure 3–53   Our file after deleting some text.

3.36.8 Replacing Text

Figure 3–54 is a table of the common text replacement commands.

Item to replace	Key sequence
Character	Position the cursor over the character, press **r**, and then type the replacement character.
Word	Position the cursor at start of word, press **cw**, and then type the replacement text followed by *Esc*.
Line	Position the cursor anywhere in line, press **cc**, and then type the replacement text followed by *Esc*.

Figure 3–54   Commands that replace text in **vim**.

For example, to replace the word "standing" by "walking," I moved to the start of the word and then typed the letters **cw**. I then typed the word "walking" and pressed the *Esc* key. To replace the lowercase "s" of september by an uppercase "S," I positioned the cursor over the "s," pressed the **r** key, and then pressed the "S" key.

I then performed a few more tidy-up operations, replacing "damp" by "dark," "slide" by "slip," and the "L" of "like" by "l". Figure 3–55 shows the final version of the poem.

```
I remember walking in the rain,
On a cold and dark September,
Brown Autumn leaves were falling softly to the ground,
Just like the dreams of a life as they slip away.
~
~                                    4,1         All
```

Figure 3–55   Our file after replacing text.

3.36.9   Pasting Text

vim maintains a paste buffer that may be used for copying and pasting text between areas of a file. Figure 3–56 is a table of the most common pasting operations.

Action	Key sequence
Copy (**yank**) lines into paste buffer.	:*\<range>***y**<*Enter*>
Copy (**yank**) current line into paste buffer.	**Y**
Insert (put) paste buffer after current line.	**p** or **:pu**<*Enter*> (contents of paste buffer are unchanged)
Insert paste buffer after line *nn*.	**:***nn***pu**<*Enter*> (contents of paste buffer are unchanged)

Figure 3–56   Commands that paste text in **vim**.

For example, to copy the first two lines into the paste buffer and then paste them after the third line, I entered the following two commands:

```
:1,2y
:3pu
```

The poem then looked as shown in Figure 3–57.

```
I remember walking in the rain,
On a cold and dark September,
Brown Autumn leaves were falling softly to the ground,
I remember walking in the rain,
On a cold and dark September,
Just like the dreams of a life as they slip away.
```

Figure 3–57   Our file after pasting text.

To restore the poem, I typed **:4,5d**<*Enter*>.

3.36.10 Searching

vim allows you to search forward and backward through a file, relative to the current line, for a particular substring. Figure 3–58 is a table of the most common search operations.

Action	Key sequence
Search forward from current position for string *sss*.	*/sss/*<*Enter*>
Search backward from current position for string *sss*.	*?sss?*<*Enter*>
Repeat last search.	**n**
Repeat last search in the opposite direction.	**N**

Figure 3–58   Search commands in **vim**.

The trailing "/" and "?" in the first two searches are optional (**vim** figures out what you mean when you type *Enter*, but it's a good habit to be in, since you can add other commands after that rather than simply hitting *Enter*.

For example, I searched for the substring "ark" from line 1 of the poem by entering the following commands:

```
:1<Enter>
/ark/<Enter>
```

vim positioned the cursor at the start of the substring "ark" located in the word "dark" on the second line (Figure 3–59).

```
I remember walking in the rain,
On a cold and dark September,
Brown Autumn leaves were falling softly to the ground,
Just like the dreams of a life as they slip away.
~
~
                                           4,1         All
```

Figure 3–59   Searching in **vim**.

3.36.11 Search/Replace

You may perform global "search and replace" operations by using the following commands in Figure 3–60.

Action	Key sequence
Replace the first occurrence of *sss* on each line with *ttt*.	:*\<range\>*s/ *sss*/ *ttt*/*\<Enter\>*
Replace every occurrence of *sss* on each line with *ttt* (global replace).	:*\<range\>*s/ *sss*/ *ttt*/g*\<Enter\>*

Figure 3–60   Searching and replacing in **vim**.

For example, to replace every occurrence of the substring "re" by "XXX," I entered the command displayed in Figure 3–61.

```
I XXXmember walking in the rain,
On a cold and dark September,
Brown Autumn leaves weXXX falling softly to the ground,
Just like the dXXXams of a life as they slip away.
~
:1,$s/re/XXX/g
```

Figure 3–61   Example of searching and replacing in **vim**.

3.36.12 Saving/Loading Files

Figure 3–62 is a table of the most common save/load file commands.

Action	Key sequence
Save file as \<name\>.	:**w** *\<name\> \<Enter\>*
Save file with current name.	:**w***\<Enter\>*
Save file with current name and exit.	:**wq***\<Enter\>* (**ZZ** also works)
Save only certain lines to another file.	:*\<range\>* **w** *\<name\> \<Enter\>*
Read in contents of another file at current position.	:**r** *\<name\> \<Enter\>*
Discard current file and edit file \<name\> instead.	:**e** *\<name\> \<Enter\>*
Edit next file on initial command line.	:**n***\<Enter\>*

Figure 3–62   Commands that write to and read from files in **vim**.

For example, I saved the poem in a file called "rain.doc" by entering the command displayed in Figure 3–63.

```
I remember walking in the rain,
On a cold and dark September,
Brown Autumn leaves were falling softly to the ground,
Just like the dreams of a life as they slip away.
~


:w rain.doc
```

Figure 3–63   Example of writing a buffer to a file in **vim**.

     vim tells you how many bytes a file occupies when you save it.

     If you place more than one file on the command line when you first invoke **vim**, it starts by loading the first file. You may edit the next file by using the key sequence **:n.**

3.36.13 Miscellaneous

Figure 3–64 is a list of the most common miscellaneous commands, including the commands for quitting **vi.**

Action	Key sequence
Redraw screen.	*Control-L*
Undo the last operation.	**u**
Undo multiple changes made on current line.	**U**
Join next line with current line.	**J**
Repeat the last operation.	**.**
Execute *command* in a subshell and then return to **vim**.	**:!**<*command*> <*Enter*>
Execute *command* in a subshell and read its output into the edit buffer at the current position.	**:r !**<*command*> <*Enter*>
Quit **vim** if work is saved.	**:q**<*Enter*>
Quit **vim** and discard unsaved work.	**:q!**<*Enter*>

Figure 3–64   Miscellaneous **vim** commands.

     Control-L is particularly useful for refreshing the screen if a message pops up and messes up your screen, or if some static interferes with your modem connection during a **vim** session.

     To finally quit **vim** after saving the final version of the poem, I typed the command illustrated in Figure 3–65.

```
I remember walking in the rain,
On a cold and dark September,
Brown Autumn leaves were falling softly to the ground,
Just like the dreams of a life as they slip away.
~
:q
```

Figure 3–65   Quitting **vim**.

3.36.14 Customizing vim

vim can be customized by setting options that determine its behavior in certain situations. The ":set" command is used to set and unset **vim**'s options. By typing ":set all" you will see a list of all the options supported by your version of **vim** and their current settings. Settings are either toggled (on or off) or set to a numeric or string value. Figure 3–66 shows the most commonly used options.

Option	Description	Default setting
autoindent	When set, subsequent lines you type are indented to the same point as the previous line.	off
ignorecase	When set, during searches and substitutes, the upper- and lowercase characters both satisfy the match criteria.	off
number	When set, **vim** displays line numbers on the left-hand side of the screen.	off
showmode	Causes **vim** to indicate when you are in a text input mode (open, insert, append, or replace) rather than the normal command mode.	on
showmatch	Causes **vim** to briefly move the cursor back to the opening parenthesis or brace when you type the matching closing one.	off

Figure 3–66   Commands to customize **vim**.

To turn autoindent on, type ":set autoindent<Enter>". To turn autoindent off again, type ":set noautoindent<Enter>".

3.36.15 Keeping Your Customizations

You don't want to have to type every ":set" command you want every time you enter **vim**. You would quickly decide most settings weren't worth that much effort. But you can create a special file in your home directory that **vim** recognizes and put your preferred settings there. Then every time you run **vim**, your settings will be the way you want them (and you can always modify the file as you find others you like).

To make **vim** set autoindent and ignorecase every time we run it, create a file called ".exrc" (note that the filename begins with a period; this is a special convention that we will see again later when we look at command shells). In that file, put the following lines:

```
set autoindent
set ignorecase
set nonumber
```

We don't really need to set "nonumber" since its initial value is off, but this shows how you would turn an option off if the default was that it was set. Now every time you start **vim**, autoindent and ignorecase will be on.

3.37 Editing a File: emacs

Emacs (Editor MACroS) is a popular editor that is found on many UNIX systems and was one of the first contributions of the GNU Project to the world of open source software. Emacs had its start in the Lisp-based Artificial Intelligence community. In 1975, Richard Stallman and Guy Steele wrote the original version. Stallman later rewrote it from scratch, and this version is the one available on Linux and for other platforms from the Free Software Foundation (FSF).

3.37.1   Starting emacs

To start **emacs** with a blank file, enter the command **emacs** with no parameters. To edit an existing file, specify its name as a command-line parameter. You can run **emacs** in a terminal window, or it can also start up in it own window when you're using a graphical desktop on Linux. GNU Emacs also includes a tutorial as part of the program.

Assuming that you supply no parameters, your screen will initially look something like Figure 3–67.

```
GNU Emacs 21.3.2 (i386-mandrake-linux-gnu, X toolkit)
 of 2004-02-12 on ke.mandrakesoft.com, modified by Mandrake
Copyright (C) 2001 Free Software Foundation, Inc.


--- Emacs:  *scratch*      (Fundamental) --L1- All ----------
```

Figure 3–67   Example of starting **emacs**.

I'll draw screens that are only about six lines long to conserve space. The second-from-bottom line is called the *mode line*, and contains information in the following left-to-right order:

- If the first three dashes contain a **, this means that the current file has been modified.
- The name that follows "Emacs:" is the name of the current file. If no file is currently loaded, the name *scratch* is used instead.

- The current editing mode is then shown between parentheses. In this case, it's *Fundamental*, which is the standard editing mode.
- L with a number indicates the line number of the line where the cursor is positioned.
- The next entry indicates your relative position in the file as a percentage. If the file is very small and fits completely on the screen, then *All* is displayed. If you're at the top or the bottom of a file, then *Top* or *Bot* is displayed, respectively.

3.37.2   emacs Commands

Unlike **vim**, **emacs** doesn't distinguish between text entry mode and command mode. To enter text, simply start typing. The initial **emacs** welcome banner automatically disappears when you type the first letter. Long lines are not automatically broken, so you must press the *Enter* key when you wish to start a new line. Lines longer than the screen width are indicated by a \ (backward slash) character at the end of the screen, and the remainder of the line is "wrapped" onto the next line (Figure 3–68).

```
This is a long line that illustrates the way unbroken lines a \
re displayed.
This is a much shorter line.
-** Emacs:  *scratch*       (Fundamental) --L2-- All ---------
```

Figure 3–68   How **emacs** wraps long lines.

emacs' editing features are accessed via either a control sequence or a metasequence. I'll indicate control sequences by prepending the name of the key with the prefix "Control-". For example, the sequence

```
Control-H t
```

means "Press and hold the *Control* key and then press the **H** key (for control sequences, it doesn't matter whether you use uppercase or lowercase, so I suggest that you use lowercase, as it's easier). Then release both keys and press the **t** key on its own." Similarly, metasequences use the *Esc* key. For example, the sequence:

```
Esc x
```

means "Press the *Esc* key (but don't hold it) and then press the **x** key." The next few sections contain many examples of **emacs** command sequences. If you ever accidentally press *Esc* followed by *Esc*, **emacs** warns you that you're trying to do something advanced and suggests that you press the **n** key to continue. Unless you're a seasoned **emacs** user, it's good advice.

3.37.3   Getting Out of Trouble

Whenever you're learning a new editor, it's quite easy to get lost and confused. Here are a couple of useful command sequences to return you to a sane state:

- The command sequence *Control-G* terminates any **emacs** command, even if it's only partially entered, and returns **emacs** to the state where it's waiting for a new command.

- The command sequence *Control-X* **1** closes all **emacs** windows except your main file window. This is useful, as several **emacs** options create a new window to display information, and it's important to know how to close them once you've read their contents.

3.37.4   Getting Help

There are several ways to obtain help information about **emacs**. One of the best ways to get started with **emacs** is to read the self-describing help tutorial. I suggest that you do this before anything else. To read the tutorial, use the command sequence *Control-H* **t**. The tutorial will appear and give you directions on how to proceed.

3.37.5   Leaving emacs

To leave **emacs** and save your file, use *Control-X Control-C*. If you haven't saved your file since it was last modified, you'll be asked whether you want to save it.

3.37.6   emacs Modes

emacs supports several different modes for entering text, including Fundamental, Lisp Interaction, and C. Each mode supports special features that are customized for the particular kind of text that you're editing. **emacs** starts in Fundamental mode by default, which is the mode that I'll be using during my description of **emacs**. For more information about modes, consult the **emacs** tutorial.

3.37.7   Entering Text

To enter text, simply start typing. For example, Figure 3–69 shows a short four-line poem.

```
There is no need for fear in the night,
You know that your Mommy is there,
To watch over her babies and hold them tight,
When you are in her arms you can feel her sigh all night.
-** Emacs:  *scratch*      (Fundamental) --L4-- All -------
```

Figure 3–69   Entering text in **emacs**.

The next section describes the editing features of **emacs** that allowed me to change this poem to something a little better.

3.37.8   Common Editing Features

The most common **emacs** editing features can be grouped into the following categories:

- moving the cursor
- deleting, pasting, and undoing text
- searching text
- search/replace text
- saving/loading files
- miscellaneous

These categories are described and illustrated in the subsections that follow, using the sample poem that I entered at the start of this section.

3.37.9 Moving the Cursor

Figure 3–70 is a table of the common cursor movement commands.

Movement	Key sequence
Up one line	<cursor up> or *Control-P* (previous)
Down one line	<cursor down> or *Control-N* (next)
Right one character	<cursor right> or *Control-F* (forward, wraps around)
Left one character	<cursor left> or *Control-B* (backward, wraps around)
To start of line	*Control-A* (a is first letter)
To end of line	*Control-E* (end)
Back one word	*Esc* **b** (back)
Forward one word	*Esc* **f** (forward)
Down one screen	*Control-V*
Up one screen	*Esc* **v**
Start of file	*Esc* <
End of file	*Esc* >

Figure 3–70 Moving the cursor in **emacs**.

For example, to insert the words "worry or" before the word "fear" on the first line, I moved the cursor to the first line of the file by typing *Esc* < and then moved forward several words by using the *Esc* **f** sequence. I then typed in the words, which were automatically inserted at the current cursor position.

3.37.10 Deleting, Pasting, and Undoing

Figure 3–71 is a table of the common deletion commands.

Item to delete	Key sequence
Character before cursor	<delete> key
Character after cursor	*Control-D*
Word before cursor	*Esc* <delete>
Word after cursor	*Esc* **d**
To end of current line	*Control-K*
Sentence	*Esc* **k**

Figure 3–71 Delete, paste, and undo in **emacs**.

Whenever an item is deleted, **emacs** remembers it in an individual "kill buffer." A list of kill buffers is maintained so that deleted items may be retrieved long after they have been removed from the display. To retrieve the last killed item, use *Control-Y*. After you have typed *Control-Y*, you may type *Esc* **y** to replace the retrieved item with the previously deleted item. Every time you type *Esc* **y**, the retrieved item moves one step back through the kill buffer list.

You may append the next deleted item onto the end of the last kill buffer rather than create a new one by typing *Esc Control-W* immediately prior to the delete command. This is useful if you wish to cut different bits and pieces out of a file and then paste them all together back into one place.

You may undo editing actions one at a time by typing *Control-X* **u** for each action that you wish to undo. Figure 3–72 is a summary of the kill buffer and undo commands.

Action	Key sequence
Insert last kill buffer.	*Control-Y*
Retrieve previous kill.	*Esc* **y**
Append next kill.	*Esc Control-W*
Undo.	*Control-X* **u**

Figure 3–72   The kill buffer in **emacs**.

3.37.11 Searching

emacs allows you to perform something called an *incremental search*. To search forward from your current cursor position for a particular sequence of letters, type *Control-S*. The prompt "I-search:" is displayed on the bottom line of the screen, indicating that **emacs** wants you to enter the string that you wish to search for. As you enter the character sequence, **emacs** searches to find the first string from your initial cursor position that matches what you've entered so far; in other words, partial substrings are found as you enter the full string. To terminate the search and leave your cursor at its current position, press *Esc*. If you delete characters in the full string before pressing the *Esc* key, **emacs** moves back to the first match of the remaining substring. To repeat a search, don't press *Esc*, but instead press *Control-S* to search forward or *Control-R* to search backward. Figure 3–73 is a summary of the searching commands.

3.37.12 Search/Replace

To perform a global search/replace, type *Esc* **x** followed by the string "repl s" followed by *Enter*. **emacs** then prompts you for the string to replace. Enter the string and press *Enter*. **emacs** then prompts you for the replacement string. Enter the string and press *Enter*. **emacs** then performs the global text substitution.

Action	Key sequence
Search forward for *str*.	*Control-S str*
Search backward for *str*.	*Control-R str*
Repeat last search forward.	*Control-S*
Repeat last search backward.	*Control-R*
Leave search mode.	*Esc*

Figure 3–73   Searching in **emacs**.

3.37.13 Saving/Loading files

To save your current work to a file, type *Control-X Control-S*. If your work hasn't been associated with a filename yet, you are prompted for a filename. Your work is then saved into its associated file.

To edit another file, type *Control-X Control-F*. You are prompted for the new filename. If the file already exists, its contents are loaded into **emacs**; otherwise, the file is created.

To save your file and then quit out of **emacs**, type *Control-X Control-C*.

Figure 3–74 is a summary of the save/load commands.

Action	Key sequence
Save current work.	*Control-X Control-S*
Edit another file.	*Control-X Control-F*
Save work and then quit.	*Control-X Control-C*

Figure 3–74   Saving and loading files in **emacs**.

3.37.14 Miscellaneous

To redraw the screen, type *Control-L*. To place **emacs** into auto-wrap mode, which automatically inserts line breaks when words flow past the end of a line, type *Esc* **x** auto-fill-mode and press *Enter*. To leave this mode, repeat the command again.

3.38 Electronic Mail: mail

It is useful to know how to use the Linux electronic mail facility from the very beginning, as it's a convenient way to ask your systems administrator or other seasoned users questions about Linux. The command-line interface is **mail**.

mail has a large number of features, so in accordance with the initial aim of this book, I shall only describe what I consider to be the most useful; consult **man** for more information. Figure 3–75 gives a description of **mail**.

Utility: **mail** [-f *fileName*] { *userId*]*

mail allows you to send and read mail. If a list of usernames is supplied, mail reads standard input, mails it to the specified users, and then terminates. Usernames can be a combination of the following forms:

- a local user name (i.e., login name)
- an Internet address of the form name@hostname.domain
- a filename
- a mail group

If no usernames are specified, **mail** assumes that you wish to read mail from a mail folder. The folder "/var/spool/mail/<username>" is read by default, where <username> is your own username, although this may be overridden by using the **-f** option. **mail** prompts you with an & and then awaits commands. A list of the most useful command-mode options is contained in the next few pages.

When **mail** is invoked, it begins by reading the contents of the mail startup file, which may contain statements that customize the **mail** utility. By default, mail reads the file ".mailrc" in your home directory, although the name of this file may be overridden by setting the environment variable MAILRC. Environment variables are discussed in Chapter 5, "The Linux Shells."

There are a large number of customizable options. The most important option is the ability to define mail groups (also sometimes called aliases), which are variables that denote a group of users. To specify a mail group, place a line of the form:

```
group name {userId}+
```

into the **mail** startup file. You may then use *name* as an alias for the specified list of users, either on the command line or in command mode.

Figure 3–75   Description of the **mail** command.

Figure 3–76 is a list of the most useful **mail** commands that are available from command mode.

Command	Meaning
?	Display help.
copy [*mesgList*] [*fileName*]	Copy messages into *fileName* without marking them as "saved."
delete [*mesgList*]	Delete specified messages from system mailbox.
file [*fileName*]	Read mail from mailbox *fileName*. If no filename is given, display the name of the current mailbox together with the number of bytes and messages that it contains.
headers [*message*]	Display page of message headers that include *message*.
mail { *userId* }+	Send mail to specified users.
print [*mesgList*]	Display specified messages using **more**.
quit	Exit **mail**.
reply [*mesgList*]	Mail response back to senders of message list.
save [*mesgList*] [*fileName*]	Save specified messages to *fileName*. If no filename is given, save them in a file called "mbox" in your home directory by default.

Figure 3–76   **mail** commands.

In these commands *mesgList* describes a collection of one or more mail messages using the syntax shown in Figure 3–77.

Syntax	Meaning
.	Current message.
nn	Message number *nn*.
^	First undeleted message.
$	Last message.
*	All messages.
nn-mm	Messages numbered *nn* through *mm* inclusive.
user	All messages from user.

Figure 3–77   Message designators in **mail**.

As you'll see in the examples that follow, these **mail** commands may be invoked by their first letter only; i.e., you can use "p" instead of "print."

3.38.1   Sending Mail

The easiest way to send mail is to enter the mail directly from the keyboard and terminate the message by pressing *Control-D* on a line of its own:

```
$ mail tim              ...send some mail to the local user tim.
Subject: Mail Test      ...enter the subject of the mail
Hi Tim,
 How is Amanda doing?
- with best regards from Graham
^D        ...end of input; standard input is sent as mail.
$ _
```

I wanted to create a mail group called "music" that would allow me to send mail to all of the people in my band. To do this, I created a file called ".mailrc" in my home directory to look like this:

```
group music jeff richard kelly bev
```

This allowed me to send mail as follows:

```
$ mail music            ...send mail to each member of the group.
Subject: Music
Hi guys
 How about a jam sometime?

- with best regards from Graham.
^D                      ...end of input.
$ _
```

For mail messages that are more than just a few lines long, it's a good idea to compose the message using a text editor, save it in a named file, and then redirect the input of **mail** from the file:

```
$ mail music < jam.txt      ...send jam.txt as mail.
$ _
```

To send mail to users on the Internet, use the standard Internet addressing scheme "user@hostname":

```
$ mail glass@utdallas.edu < mesg.txt      ...send it.
$ _
```

3.38.2   Reading Mail

When mail is sent to you, it is stored in a file called "/var/spool/mail/<username>", where <user-name> is equal to your login name. Files that hold mail are termed "mail folders." For example, my own incoming mail is held in the mail folder "/var/spool/mail/glass." To read a mail folder, type **mail** followed by an optional folder specifier. You are notified if no mail is currently present:

```
$ mail    ...try reading my mail from the default folder.
No mail for glass
$ _
```

If mail is present, **mail** displays a list of the incoming mail headers and then prompts you with an ampersand. Press *Enter* to read each message in order, and press **q**(uit) to exit mail. The mail that you read is appended by default to the mail folder "mbox" in your home directory, which you may read at a later time by typing the following in your home directory:

```
$ mail -f mbox      ...read mail saved in the mbox folder.
```

In the examples that follow, I've deleted some of **mail**'s verbose information so that the output fits in a reasonable amount of space. In the following example, I read two pieces of mail from my friend Tim and then exited **mail**:

```
$ ls -lG /var/spool/mail/glass          ...see if mail is present.
-rw-------  1 glass     758 Mar 12 14:32 /var/spool/mail/glass
$ mail                        ...read mail from default folder.
Mail version 8.1 6/6/93.  Type ? for help.
"/var/spool/mail/glass": 2 messages 2 unread
>U  1 tim@utdallas.edu Sat Mar 12 14:32 11/382  Mail test
 U  2 tim@utdallas.edu Sat Mar 12 14:32 11/376  Another
& <Enter>        ...press enter to read message #1.
From tim@utdallas.edu Sat Mar 12 14:32:33 2005
To: glass@utdallas.edu
Subject: Mail test
hi there
& <Enter>        ...press enter to read message #2.
From tim@utdallas.edu Sat Mar 12 14:32:33 2005
To: glass@utdallas.edu
Subject: Another
hi there again
& <Enter>        ...press enter to read next message.
At EOF       ...there are none!
& q      ...quit mail.
Saved 2 messages in /home/glass/mbox
$ _
```

To respond to a message after reading it, use the **r**(eply) option. To save a message to a file, use the **s**(ave) option. If you don't specify a message **list**, mail selects the current message by default. Here's an example:

```
& 15          ...read message #15.
From ssmith@utdallas.edu Tue Mar 15 23:27:11 2005
To: glass@utdallas.edu
Subject: Re: come to a party
The SIGGRAPH party begins Thursday NIGHT at 10:00 PM!!
Hope you don't have to teach Thursday night.
& R           ...reply to ssmith.
To: ssmith@utdallas.edu
Subject: Re: come to a party
Thanks for the invitation.
- see you there
^D            ...end of input.
& s ssmith.party        ...save the message from ssmith.
"ssmith.party" [New file] 27/1097
& q           ...quit from mail.
$ _
```

Caution: "R" replies to the sender and "r" replies to everyone. This is not very intuitive and causes many people some problems when they reply to everyone in the header of the message when they only intended to respond to the sender.

It's possible that you'll receive quite a bit of "junk mail"; to delete messages that aren't worth reading, use the *d*(elete) option:

```
& d1-15         ...delete messages 1 thru 15 inclusive.
& d*            ...delete all remaining messages.
```

3.38.3 Contacting the System Administrator

The system administrator's mailing address is usually "root" or possibly "sysadmin." Typically, the alias "postmaster" should direct mail to the person in charge of e-mail-related issues.

CHAPTER REVIEW

Checklist

In this chapter, I described:

- how to obtain a Linux account
- how to log in and out of a Linux system
- the importance of changing your password
- the function of a shell

- how to run a utility
- how to obtain online help
- the special terminal metacharacters
- the most common file-oriented utilities
- two Linux editors
- how to set up your terminal correctly
- how to send electronic mail

Quiz

1. What is one way that hackers try to break Linux security?
2. What's the best kind of password?
3. What Linux command do you use to change the name or location of a file?
4. Is Linux case-sensitive?
5. Name the three most common Linux command shells.
6. Why are shells better suited than C programs for some tasks?
7. How do you terminate a process?
8. How do you indicate the end-of-input when entering text from the keyboard?
9. How do you terminate a shell?
10. What term is given to the current location of a process?
11. What attributes does every file have?
12. What is the purpose of groups?
13. How do permission flags relate to directories?
14. Who may change the ownership of a file?

Exercises

1. Describe how the **mv** command moves a file even though it doesn't touch the data blocks belonging to the file. [level: *easy*]
2. Explain why a process may have only *one* current group. [level: *medium*]
3. Even seemingly trivial inventions such as a flashing cursor and a scrolling window have been granted patents. Many software designers construct programs only to find that they have unintentionally re-invented someone else's patented invention. Do you think that patents are fair, and if not, can you think of a better mechanism to protect intellectual property? [level: *medium*]
4. Design a file security mechanism that alleviates the need for the "set user ID" feature. [level: *hard*]

Project

1. Use both **vim** and **emacs** to edit a file. Perform basic operations like adding text, deleting text, changing text on a line, and writing the file and exiting. Notice how in **vim** you're only in text input mode when you want to be, but in **emacs** you're in text input mode by

default. Which feels more comfortable to you? If you have previous experience with a different screen-oriented editor, how do **vim** and **emacs** compare? [level: *easy*]

2. Set up two new groups (you may need assistance from a system administrator if you do not have access to the root password, or see "Substituting a User: su" on page 139). Experiment with the group-related utilities and explore the permissions system. [level: *medium*]

GNU Utilities for Power Users

Motivation

In addition to the common file-oriented GNU utilities found on a Linux system, there are plenty of other utilities that process text, schedule commands, archive files, and sort files. This chapter contains descriptions and examples of the most useful utilities that will increase your productivity.

Prerequisites

In order to understand this chapter, you should have already read Chapter 1, "What Is Linux?," and Chapter 3, "GNU Utilities for Nonprogrammers"

Objectives

In this chapter, I'll show you how to use about thirty useful utilities.

Presentation

The information in this section is presented in the form of several sample Linux sessions.

Utilities

This chapter introduces the following utilities, listed in alphabetical order:

at	cpio	diff
cmp	crontab	egrep

fgrep	od	tr
find	perl	tty
gawk	sed	ul
grep	sort	umount
gunzip	su	uniq
gzip	tar	whoami
ln	time	zcat
mount		

4.1   Introduction

In this chapter, I introduce about thirty useful utilities. Rather than describe them in alphabetical order, I've grouped them into fairly logical sets, as shown in Figure 4–1.

Section	Utilities
Filtering files	egrep, fgrep, grep, uniq
Sorting files	sort
Comparing files	cmp, diff
Archiving files	tar, cpio
Searching for files	find
Scheduling commands	at, crontab
Programmable text processing	gawk, perl
Hard and soft links	ln
Switching users	su
Transforming files	gzip, gunzip, sed, tr, ul, zcat
Looking at raw file contents	od
Mounting file systems	mount, umount
Identifying shells	whoami
Timing execution of a command	time

Figure 4–1   Advanced Linux/GNU utilities.

The remainder of this chapter goes through each group in turn, describing the utilities using worked examples.

4.2   Filtering Files: grep, egrep, fgrep, and uniq

Often it's handy to be able to filter the contents of a file, selecting only those lines that match some kind of criteria. The utilities that do this include the following:

- **egrep**, **fgrep**, and **grep**, which filter out all lines that do not contain a specified pattern
- **uniq**, which filters out duplicate adjacent lines

The next few subsections describe these utilities.

4.2.1   Filtering Patterns: egrep/fgrep/grep

egrep, **fgrep**, and **grep** allow you to scan a file and filter out all of the lines that don't contain a specified pattern. They are very similar in nature, the main difference being the kind of text patterns that each can filter. I'll begin by describing the common features of all three, and then finish up by illustrating the differences. Figure 4–2 gives a brief synopsis of the three utilities.

Utility: **grep** -hilnvw *pattern* { *fileName* } *
       fgrep -hilnvwx *string* { *fileName* } *
       egrep -hilnvw *pattern* { *fileName* } *

grep (Global or Get Regular Expression and Print) is a utility that allows you to search for a pattern in a list of files. If no files are specified, it searches standard input instead. *pattern* may be a regular expression. All lines that match the pattern are displayed to standard output. If more than one file is specified, each matching line is preceded by the name of the file unless the **-h** option is specified. The **-n** option precedes each matching line by its line number. The **-i** option causes the case of the patterns to be ignored. The **-l** option displays a list of the files that contain the specified pattern. The **-v** option causes grep to display all of the lines that don't match the pattern. The **-w** option restricts matching to occur on whole words only. **fgrep** (Fixed grep) is a fast version of **grep** that can only search for fixed strings. **egrep** (Extended grep) supports matching with regular expressions. **fgrep** supports an additional option; the **-x** option outputs only lines that are exactly equal to *string*.

  For more information about regular expressions, consult the Appendix.

Figure 4–2   Description of the **grep** command.

  To obtain a list of all the lines in a file that contain a string, follow **grep** by the string and the name of the file to scan. Here's an example:

```
$ cat grepfile                  ...list the file to be filtered.
Well you know it's your bedtime,
So turn off the light,
Say all your prayers and then,
Oh you sleepy young heads dream of wonderful things,
Beautiful mermaids will swim through the sea,
```

```
And you will be swimming there too.
$ grep the grepfile            ...search for the word "the".
So turn off the light,
Say all your prayers and then,
Beautiful mermaids will swim through the sea,
And you will be swimming there too.
$ _
```

Notice that words that contain the string "the" also satisfied the matching condition. Here's an example of the **-w** and **-n** options:

```
$ grep -wn the grepfile        ...be more particular this time!
2:So turn off the light,
5:Beautiful mermaids will swim through the sea,
$ _
```

To display only those lines in a file that don't match, use the **-v** option:

```
$ grep -wnv the grepfile       ...reverse the filter.
1:Well you know it's your bedtime,
3:Say all your prayers and then,
4:Oh you sleepy young heads dream of wonderful things,
6:And you will be swimming there too.
$ _
```

If you specify more than one file to search, each selected line is preceded by the name of the file in which it appears. In the following example, I searched my C source files for the string "x". Please consult Chapter 5, "The Linux Shells," for a description of the shell wildcard mechanism.

```
$ grep -w x *.c        ...search all files ending in ".c".
a.c:test (int x)
fact2.c:long factorial (x)
fact2.c:int x;
fact2.c:  if ((x == 1) || (x == 0))
fact2.c:    result = x * factorial (x-1);
$ grep -wl x *.c        ...list names of matching files.
a.c
fact2.c
$ _
```

fgrep, **grep**, and **egrep** all support the options that I've described so far. The difference between them is that each allows a different kind of text pattern to be matched (Figure 4–3).

Utility	Kind of pattern that may be searched for
fgrep	Fixed string only.
grep	Regular expression.
egrep	Extended regular expression.

Figure 4–3   The differences in the **grep** command family.

For information about regular expressions and extended regular expressions, consult the Appendix.

To illustrate the use of **grep** and **egrep** regular expressions, here is a piece of text followed by the lines of text that would match various regular expressions. When using **egrep** or **grep**, place regular expressions inside single quotes to prevent interference from the shell. In the examples in Figures 4–4 and 4–5 the portion of each line of this example text that satisfies the regular expression is italicized.

```
Well you know it's your bedtime,
So turn off the light,
Say all your prayers and then,
Oh you sleepy young heads dream of wonderful things,
Beautiful mermaids will swim through the sea,
And you will be swimming there too.
```

4.2.1.1   Matching Patterns

grep pattern	Lines that match
.nd	Say all your prayers *and* then,
	Oh you sleepy young heads dream of w*ond*erful things,
	And you will be swimming there too.
^.nd	*And* you will be swimming there too.
sw.*ng	And you will be *swimming* there too.
[A-D]	*B*eautiful mermaids will swim through the sea,
	*A*nd you will be swimming there too.
\.	And you will be swimming there too. *(the "." matches)*
a.	*Sa*y all your prayers and then,
	Oh you sleepy young he*ad*s dream of wonderful things,
	Be*au*tiful mermaids will swim through the sea,

Figure 4–4   Pattern matching in **grep**. (Part 1 of 2)

grep pattern	Lines that match
a.$	Beautiful mermaids will swim through the s*ea*,
[a-m]nd	Say all your prayers *and* then,
[^a-m]nd	Oh you sleepy young heads dream of w*onde*rful things, *And* you will be swimming there too.

Figure 4–4   Pattern matching in **grep**. (Part 2 of 2)

egrep Pattern	Lines that match
s.*w	Oh you *sleepy young heads dream of* wonderful things, Beautiful mermaids *will swi*m through the sea, And you will be s*wi*mming there too.
s.+w	Oh you *sleepy young heads dream of* wonderful things, Beautiful mermaid*s will swi*m through the sea,
off|will	So turn *off* the light, Beautiful mermaids *will* swim through the sea, And you *will* be swimming there too.
im*ing	And you will be swimming there too.
im?ing	<no matches>

Figure 4–5   Pattern matching in **egrep**.

4.2.2   Removing Duplicate Lines: uniq

The **uniq** utility displays a file with all of its identical adjacent lines replaced by a single occurrence of the repeated line (Figure 4–6).

Utility: **uniq** -c -number [*inputfile* [*outputfile*]]

uniq is a utility that displays its input file with all adjacent repeated lines collapsed to a single occurrence of the repeated line. If an input file is not specified, standard input is read. The **-c** option causes each line to be preceded by the number of occurrences that were found. If *number* is specified, then *number* fields of each line are ignored.

Figure 4–6   Description of the **uniq** command.

Here's an example:

```
$ cat animals          ...look at the test file.
cat   snake
monkey  snake
```

```
dolphin  elephant
dolphin  elephant
goat  elephant
pig  pig
pig  pig
monkey  pig
$ uniq animals              ...filter out duplicate adjacent lines.
cat  snake
monkey  snake
dolphin  elephant
goat  elephant
pig  pig
monkey  pig
$ uniq -c animals           ...display a count with the lines.
   1 cat  snake
   1 monkey  snake
   2 dolphin  elephant
   1 goat  elephant
   2 pig  pig
   1 monkey  pig
$ uniq -1 animals           ...ignore first field of each line.
cat  snake
dolphin  elephant
pig  pig
$ _
```

4.3 Sorting Files: sort

The **sort** utility sorts a file in ascending or descending order based on one or more *sort fields*, and works as described in Figure 4–7.

Utility: **sort** -tc -r { *sortField* -bfMn }* { *fileName* }*

sort is a utility that sorts lines in one or more files based on a sorting criterion. By default, lines are sorted into ascending order. The **-r** option specifies descending order instead. Input lines are split into fields separated by spaces and/or tabs. To specify a different character for the field separator, use the **-t** option. By default, all of a line's fields are considered when the sort is being performed. This may be overridden by specifying one or more sort fields, whose format is described later in this section. Individual sort fields may be customized by following them by one or more options. The **-f** option causes **sort** to ignore the case of the field. The **-M** option sorts the field in month order. The **-n** option sorts the field in numeric order. The **-b** option ignores leading spaces.

Figure 4–7 Description of the **sort** command.

Individual fields are ordered lexicographically, which means that corresponding characters are compared based on their ASCII value (see **man ascii** for a list of all characters and their
corresponding values). Two consequences of this are that an uppercase letter is "less" than its
lowercase equivalent, and a space is "less" than a letter. In the following example, I sorted a
text file in ascending order and descending order using the default ordering rule:

```
$ cat sortfile            ...list the file to be sorted.
jan  Start chapter 3   10th
Jan  Start chapter 1   30th
 Jan  Start chapter 5  23rd
 Jan  End chapter 3  23rd
Mar  Start chapter 7  27
 may  End chapter 7  17th
Apr  End Chapter 5  1
 Feb  End chapter 1  14
$ sort sortfile           ...sort it.
 Feb  End chapter 1  14
 Jan  End chapter 3  23rd
 Jan  Start chapter 5  23rd
 may  End chapter 7  17th
Apr  End Chapter 5  1
Jan  Start chapter 1  30th
Mar  Start chapter 7  27
jan  Start chapter 3  10th
$ sort -r sortfile        ...sort it in reverse order.
jan  Start chapter 3  10th
Mar  Start chapter 7  27
Jan  Start chapter 1  30th
Apr  End Chapter 5  1
 may  End chapter 7  17th
 Jan  Start chapter 5  23rd
 Jan  End chapter 3  23rd
 Feb  End chapter 1  14
$ _
```

To sort on a particular field, you must specify the starting field number using a + prefix, followed by the noninclusive stop field number using a - prefix. Field numbers start at index 0. If
you leave off the stop field number, all fields following the start field are included. In the next
example, I sorted the same text file on the first field only, which is number zero:

```
$ sort +0 -1 sortfile        ...sort on first field only.
 Feb  End chapter 1  14
 Jan  End chapter 3  23rd
 Jan  Start chapter 5  23rd
 may  End chapter 7  17th
```

```
Apr   End Chapter 5   1
Jan   Start chapter 1   30th
Mar   Start chapter 7   27
jan   Start chapter 3   10th
$ _
```

Note that the leading spaces were counted as being part of the first field, which resulted in a strange sorting sequence. Additionally, I would have preferred the months to be sorted in correct order, with "Jan" before "Feb", etc. The **-b** option ignores leading blanks and the **-M** option sorts a field based on a month order. Here's an example that worked better:

```
$ sort +0 -1 -bM sortfile              ...sort on first month.
 Jan   End chapter 3   23rd
 Jan   Start chapter 5   23rd
Jan   Start chapter 1   30th
jan   Start chapter 3   10th
 Feb   End chapter 1   14
Mar   Start chapter 7   27
Apr   End Chapter 5   1
 may   End chapter 7   17th
$ _
```

The example text file was correctly sorted by month, but the dates were still out of order. You may specify multiple sort fields on the command line to deal with this problem. The **sort** utility first sorts all of the lines based on the first sort specifier, and then uses the second sort specifier to order lines that compared equally by the first specifier. Therefore, to sort the example text file by month and date, it had to be sorted based on the first field and then the fifth. In addition, the fifth field had to be sorted numerically by using the **-n** option.

```
$ sort +0 -1 -bM +4 -n sortfile
jan   Start chapter 3   10th
 Jan   End chapter 3   23rd
 Jan   Start chapter 5   23rd
Jan   Start chapter 1   30th
 Feb   End chapter 1   14
Mar   Start chapter 7   27
Apr   End Chapter 5   1
 may   End chapter 7   17th
$ _
```

Characters other than spaces often delimit fields. For example, the "/etc/passwd" file contains user information stored in fields separated by colons. You may use the **-t** option to specify an alternative field separator. In the following example, I sorted a file based on fields separated by : characters.

```
$ cat sortfile2            ...look at the test file.
jan:Start chapter 3:10th
Jan:Start chapter 1:30th
Jan:Start chapter 5:23rd
Jan:End chapter 3:23rd
Mar:Start chapter 7:27
may:End chapter 7:17th
Apr:End Chapter 5:1
Feb:End chapter 1:14
$ sort -t: +0 -1 -bM +2 -n sortfile2   ...colon delimiters.
jan:Start chapter 3:10th
Jan:End chapter 3:23rd
Jan:Start chapter 5:23rd
Jan:Start chapter 1:30th
Feb:End chapter 1:14
Mar:Start chapter 7:27
Apr:End Chapter 5:1
may:End chapter 7:17th
$ _
```

sort contains several other options that are too detailed to describe here; I suggest that you use the **man** utility to find out more about them.

4.4   Comparing Files: cmp and diff

There are two utilities that allow you to compare the contents of two files:

- **cmp,** which finds the first byte that differs between two files
- **diff,** which displays all the differences and similarities between two files

The next few subsections describe these utilities.

4.4.1   Testing for Sameness: cmp

The **cmp** utility determines whether two files are the same (Figure 4–8).

Utility: **cmp** -ls *fileName1 fileName2* [*offset1*] [*offset2*]

cmp is a utility that tests whether two files are identical. If *fileName1* and *fileName2* are exactly equal, then **cmp** returns the exit code 0 and displays nothing; otherwise, it returns the exit code 1 and displays the offset and line number of the first mismatched byte. If one file is a prefix of the other, then the EOF message is displayed for the file that is shorter. The **-l** option displays the offset and values of all mismatched bytes. The **-s** option causes all output to be inhibited. The optional values *offset1* and *offset2* specify the starting offset in *fileName1* and *fileName2*, respectively, that the comparison should begin.

Figure 4–8   Description of the **cmp** command.

In the following example, I compared the files "lady1," "lady2," and "lady3":

```
$ cat lady1              ...look at the first test file.
Lady of the night,
I hold you close to me,
And all those loving words you say are right.
$ cat lady2              ...look at the second test file.
Lady of the night,
I hold you close to me,
And everything you say to me is right.
$ cat lady3              ...look at the third test file.
Lady of the night,
I hold you close to me,
And everything you say to me is right.
It makes me feel,
I'm so in love with you.
Even in the dark I see your light.
$ cmp lady1 lady2        ...files differ.
lady1 lady2 differ: char 48, line 3
$ cmp lady2 lady3        ...file2 is a prefix of file3.
cmp: EOF on lady2
$ cmp lady3 lady3        ...files are exactly the same.
$ _
```

The **-l** option displays the byte offset and values of every byte that doesn't match:

```
$ cmp -l lady1 lady2     ...display bytes that don't match.
   48 141 145
   49 154 166
   ...
   81 145  56
   82  40  12
cmp: EOF on lady2        ...lady2 is smaller than lady1.
$ _
```

4.4.2   File Differences: diff

The **diff** utility compares two files and displays a list of editing changes that would convert the first file into the second file (Figure 4–9).

Utility: **diff** -i -dflag *fileName1 fileName2*

diff is a utility that compares two files and outputs a description of their differences. See the rest of this section for information on the format of this output. The **-i** flag makes **diff** ignore the case of the lines.

Figure 4–9 Description of the **diff** command.

There are three kinds of editing changes: adding lines (a), changing lines (c), and deleting lines (d). Figure 4–10 shows the format that diff uses to describe each kind of edit, where *firstStart* and *firstStop* denote line numbers in the first file, and *secondStart* and *secondStop* denote line numbers in the second file.

Additions
firstStart **a** *secondStart, secondStop*
> lines from the second file to add to the first file

Deletions
firstStart, firstStop **d** *lineCount*
< lines from the first file to delete

Changes
firstStart, firstStop **c** *secondStart, secondStop*
< lines in the first file to be replaced
--
> lines in the second file to be used for the replacement

Figure 4–10   The meaning of output produced by **diff**.

In the following example, I compared several text files to observe their differences:

```
$ cat lady1      ...look at the first test file.
Lady of the night,
I hold you close to me,
And all those loving words you say are right.
$ cat lady2      ...look at the second test file.
Lady of the night,
I hold you close to me,
And everything you say to me is right.
$ cat lady3      ...look at the third test file.
Lady of the night,
I hold you close to me,
And everything you say to me is right.
It makes me feel,
I'm so in love with you.
Even in the dark I see your light.
$ cat lady4      ...look at the fourth test file.
Lady of the night,
I'm so in love with you.
Even in the dark I see your light.
$ diff lady1 lady2   ...compare lady1 and lady2.
3c3
```

```
< And all those loving words you say are right.
--
> And everything you say to me is right.
$ diff lady2 lady3      ...compare lady2 and lady3.
3a4,6
> It makes me feel,
> I'm so in love with you.
> Even in the dark I see your light.
$ diff lady3 lady4      ...compare lady3 and lady4.
2,4d1
< I hold you close to me,
< And everything you say to me is right.
< It makes me feel,
$ _
```

4.5 Finding Files: find

The **find** utility can do much more than simply locate a named file; it can perform actions on a set of files that satisfy specific conditions. For example, you can use **find** to erase all of the files belonging to a user *tim* that haven't been modified for 3 days. Figure 4–11 gives a formal description.

Utility: **find** *pathList expression*

The **find** utility recursively descends through *pathList* and applies *expression* to every file. The syntax of *expression* is described below, together with some examples of **find**.

Figure 4–11 Description of the **find** command.

Figure 4–12 is a table that describes the syntax of *expression*.

Expression	Value/action
-name *pattern*	True if the file's name matches *pattern*, which may include the shell metacharacters *, [,], and ?.
-perm *oct*	True if the octal description of the file's permission flags is exactly equal to *oct*.
-type *ch*	True if the type of the file is *ch* (b = block, c = char, etc.).
-user *userId*	True if the owner of the file is *userId*.
-group *groupId*	True if the group of the file is *groupId*.
-atime *count*	True if the file has been accessed within *count* days.

Figure 4–12 **find** expressions. (Part 1 of 2)

Expression	Value/action
-mtime *count*	True if the contents of the file have been modified within *count* days.
-ctime *count*	True if the contents of the file have been modified within *count* days or if any of its attributes have been altered.
-exec *command*	True if the exit code from executing *command* is 0. *command* must be terminated by an escaped semicolon (\;). If you specify { } as a command-line argument, it is replaced by the name of the current file.
-print	Prints out the name of the current file and returns true.
-ls	Displays the current file's attributes (equivalent of ls -dils) and returns true.
-cpio *device*	Writes the current file in cpio format to *device* and returns true.
!*expression*	Returns the logical negation of *expression*.
expr1 [-a] *expr2*	Short-circuiting and; if *expr1* is false, it returns false and *expr2* is not executed. If *expr1* is true, it returns the value of *expr2*.
expr1 -o *expr2*	Short-circuiting or; if *expr1* is true, it returns true. If *expr1* is false, it returns the value of *expr2*.

Figure 4-12   find expressions. (Part 2 of 2)

Here are some examples of **find** in action:

```
$ find . -name '*.c' -print    ...print c source files in the
        ...current directory or any of
        ...its subdirectories.
./proj/fall.89/play.c
./proj/fall.89/referee.c
./proj/fall.89/player.c
./rock/guess.c
./rock/play.c
./rock/player.c
./rock/referee.c
$ find . -mtime 14 -ls          ...ls modified files
        ...during the last 14 days.
286580 16 -rw-r--r--  1 glass  cs 14151 May  1 16:58 ./stty.txt
286377  4 -rw-r--r--  1 glass  cs    48 May  1 14:02 ./file.doc
284428  4 -rw-r--r--  1 glass  cs    10 May  1 14:02 ./rain.doc
287331 16 -rw-r--r--  1 glass  cs 14855 May  1 16:58 ./tset.txt
288646 48 -rw-r--r--  1 glass  cs 47794 May  2 10:56 ./mail.txt
$ find . -name '*.bak' -ls -exec rm {} \;
                ...ls and then remove all files
                ...that end with ".bak".
```

```
285451  4 -rw-r--r--  1 glass  cs      9 May 16 12:01 ./a.bak
282849  4 -rw-r--r--  1 glass  cs      9 May 16 12:01 ./b.bak
284438 16 -rw-r--r--  1 glass  cs 15630 Jan 26 00:14 ./s6/g.bak
284427 20 -rw-r--r--  1 glass  cs 18481 Jan 26 12:59 ./s6/g2.bak
$ find . \( -name  '*.c' -o -name '*.txt' \) -print
                    ...print the names of all files that
                    ...end in ".c" or ".txt".
./proj/fall.89/play.c
./proj/fall.89/referee.c
./proj/fall.89/player.c
./rock/guess.c
./rock/play.c
./rock/player.c
./rock/referee.c
./stty.txt
./tset.txt
./mail.txt
$ _
```

4.6   Archiving Files: cpio, tar, and dump/restore

There are several occasions when you'll want to save some files to a secondary storage medium such as a disk or tape:

- for daily, weekly, or monthly backups
- for transport between non-networked Linux or UNIX machines
- for posterity

Three GNU archiving programs are available in Linux environments, each having its own strengths and weaknesses:

- **cpio**, which allows you to save directory structures onto a single backup volume. It's handy for saving small quantities of data, but the single-volume restriction makes it useless for large backups.
- **tar**, which allows you to save directory structures onto a single backup volume. It's specially designed to save files onto tape, so it always archives files onto the end of the storage medium. As before, the single-volume restriction makes it unusable for large backups.
- **dump** and **restore**, which allow you to save a file system to multiple backup volumes. **dump** is especially useful for doing total and incremental backups.

You can write archive information to a tape device or create regular files that can later be copied to an external drive (like a Zip drive), a spare internal disk drive, or a CD writer. You can store archive files anywhere you can store a regular file.

4.6.1   Copying Files: cpio

The **cpio** utility allows you to create and access special cpio-format files. These special format files are useful for backing up small subdirectories. Figure 4–13 describes how **cpio** works.

Utility: **cpio** -ov
      cpio -idtu *patterns*
      cpio -pl *directory*

cpio allows you to create and access special cpio-format files.

      The **-o** option takes a list of filenames from standard input and creates a cpio-format file that contains a backup of the files. The **-v** option causes the name of each file to be displayed as it's copied.

      The **-i** option reads a cpio-format file from standard input and re-creates all of the files from the input channel whose name matches a specified pattern. By default, older files are not copied over younger files. The **-u** option causes unconditional copying. The **-d** option causes directories to be created if they are needed during the copy process. The **-t** option causes a table of contents to be displayed instead of performing the copy.

      The **-p** option takes a list of filenames from standard input and copies their contents to a named directory. This option is useful for copying one subdirectory to another place, although most uses of this option can be performed more easily using the **cp** utility with the **-r** (recursive) option. The **-l** option creates links instead of performing physical copies whenever possible.

Figure 4–13   Description of the **cpio** command.

      To demonstrate the **-o** and **-i** options, I created a backup version of all the C source files in my current directory, deleted the source files, and then restored them.

```
$ ls -lG *.c                    ...list the files to be saved.
-rw-r--r--  1 glass    172 Jan  5 19:44 main1.c
-rw-r--r--  1 glass    198 Jan  5 19:44 main2.c
-rw-r--r--  1 glass    224 Jan  5 19:44 palindrome.c
-rw-r--r--  1 glass    266 Jan  5 23:46 reverse.c
$ ls *.c | cpio -ov > backup    ...save in "backup".
main1.c
main2.c
palindrome.c
reverse.c
3 blocks
$ ls -lG backup         ...examine "backup".
-rw-r--r--    1 glass   1536 Jan  9 18:34 backup
$ rm *.c                ...remove the original files.
$ cpio -it < backup     ...restore the files.
main1.c
main2.c
palindrome.c
reverse.c
3 blocks
```

```
$ ls -lG *.c                    ..confirm their restoration.
-rw-r--r--  1 glass     172 Jan  5 19:44 main1.c
-rw-r--r--  1 glass     198 Jan  5 19:44 main2.c
-rw-r--r--  1 glass     224 Jan  5 19:44 palindrome.c
-rw-r--r--  1 glass     266 Jan  5 23:46 reverse.c
$ _
```

To back up all of the files that match the pattern "*.c", including subdirectories, use the output from the **find** utility as the input to **cpio**. The **-depth** option of **find** recursively searches for matching patterns. In the following example, note that I escaped the * character in the argument to the **-name** option so that it was not expanded by the shell:

```
$ find . -name \*.c -depth -print | cpio -ov > backup2
main1.c
main2.c
palindrome.c
reverse.c
tmp/b.c
tmp/a.c
3 blocks
$ rm -r *.c              ...remove the original files.
$ rm tmp/*.c            ...remove the lower-level files.
$ cpio -it < backup2    ...restore the files.
main1.c
main2.c
palindrome.c
reverse.c
tmp/b.c
tmp/a.c
3 blocks
$ _
```

To demonstrate the **-p** option, I obtained a list of all the files in my current directory that were modified in the last two days (using the **find** utility) and then copied them into the parent directory. Without the **-l** option, the files were physically copied, resulting in a total increase in disk usage of 153 blocks. With the **-l** option, however, the files were linked, resulting in no disk usage at all.

```
$ find . -mtime -2 -print | cpio -p ..          ...copy
153 blocks
$ ls -lG ../reverse.c           ...look at the copied file.
-rw-r--r--  1 glass       266 Jan  9 18:42 ../reverse.c
$ find . -mtime -2 -print | cpio -pl ..         ...link
0 blocks
$ ls -lG ../reverse.c           ...look at the linked file.
-rw-r--r--  2 glass       266 Jan  7 15:26 ../reverse.c
$ _
```

4.6.2   Tape Archiving: tar

The **tar** utility was designed specifically for maintaining an archive of files on a magnetic tape. When you add a file to an archive file using **tar**, the file is *always* placed on the end, since you cannot modify the middle of a file that is stored on tape. Figure 4–14 shows how **tar** works.

Utility: **tar** -cfrtuvxz [*tarFileName*] *fileList*

tar allows you to create and access special tar-format archive files. The **-c** option creates a tar-format file. Use the **-f** option followed by a filename to specify the destination for the tar-format file. The **-v** option causes verbose output. The **-x** option allows you to extract named files, and the **-t** option generates a table of contents. The **-r** option unconditionally appends the listed files to the archive file. The **-u** option appends only files that are more recent than those already archived. The **-z** option filters the archive through **gzip** to compress or uncompress it. If the file list contains directory names, the contents of the directories are appended/ extracted recursively.

Figure 4–14   Description of the **tar** command.

In the following example, I saved all of the files in the current directory to the archive file "tarfile":

```
$ ls                    ...look at the current directory.
main1       main2       palindrome.c      reverse.h
main1.c     main2.c     palindrome.h      tarfile
main1.make  main2.make  reverse.c         tmp/
$ ls tmp                ...look in the "tmp" directory.
a.c         b.c
$ tar -cvf tarfile .    ...archive the current directory.
./main1.c
/main2.c
...
/main2
/tmp/b.c
/tmp/a.c
$ ls -lG tarfile        ...look at the archive file "tarfile".
-rw-r--r--  1 glass     65536 Jan 10 12:44 tarfile
$ _
```

To obtain a table of contents of a **tar** archive, use the **-t** option:

```
$ tar -tvf tarfile      ...look at the table of contents.
drwxr-xr-x 496/62         0 2005-01-10 12:10:22 ./
```

```
-rw-r--r-- 496/62      172 2005-01-10 12:10:24 ./main1.c
-rw-r--r-- 496/62      198 2005-01-09 12:10:24 ./main2.c
...
-rw-r--r-- 496/62    24576 2005-01-07 12:24:54 ./main2
drwxr-xr-x 496/62        0 2005-01-10 12:10:28 ./tmp/
-rw-r--r-- 496/62        9 2005-01-10 12:10:29 ./tmp/b.c
-rw-r--r-- 496/62        9 2005-01-10 12:10:29 ./tmp/a.c
$
```

To unconditionally append a file to the end of a tar archive, use the **-r** option followed by a list of files and/or directories to append. Notice in the following example that the tar archive ended up holding two copies of "reverse.c":

```
$ tar -rvf tarfile reverse.c          ...unconditionally append.
reverse.c
$ tar -tvf tarfile                    ...look at the table of contents.
drwxr-xr-x 496/62        0 2005-01-10 12:10:24 ./
-rw-r--r-- 496/62      172 2005-01-10 12:32:33 ./main1.c
...
-rw-r--r-- 496/62      266 2005-01-09 12:32:34 ./reverse.c
...
-rw-r--r-- 496/62      266 2005-01-10 12:32:56 reverse.c
$ _
```

To append a file only if it isn't in the archive or if it has been modified since it was last archived, use the **-u** option instead of **-r**. In the following example, note that "reverse.c" was not archived because it hadn't been modified:

```
$ tar -rvf tarfile reverse.c          ...unconditionally append.
reverse.c
$ tar -uvf tarfile reverse.c          ...conditionally append.
$ _
```

To extract a file from an archive file, use the **-x** option followed by a list of files and/or directories. If a directory name is specified, it is recursively extracted:

```
$ rm tmp/*                ...remove all files from "tmp".
$ tar -vxf tarfile ./tmp  ...extract archived "tmp" files.
./tmp/b.c
./tmp/a.c
$ ls tmp                  ...confirm restoration.
a.c          b.c
$ _
```

Unfortunately, **tar** doesn't support pattern matching of the name list, so to extract files that match a particular pattern, be crafty and use **grep** as part of the command sequence—like this:

```
$ tar -xvf tarfile 'tar -tf tarfile | grep '.*\.c''
./main1.c
./main2.c
./palindrome.c
./reverse.c
./tmp/b.c
./tmp/a.c
$ _
```

If you change into another directory and then extract files that were stored using relative path-names, the names are interpreted as being relative to the current directory. In the following example, I restored "reverse.c" from the previously created tar file to a new directory "tmp2". Note that each copy of "reverse.c" overwrote the previous one, so that the latest version was the one that was left intact:

```
$ mkdir tmp2                          ...create a new directory.
$ cd tmp2                             ...move there.
$ tar -vxf ../tarfile reverse.c       ...restore single file.
reverse.c
reverse.c
$ ls -lG                              ...confirm restoration.
total 1
-rw-r--r--   1 glass          266 Jan 10 12:48 reverse.c
$ _
```

4.6.3   Incremental Backups: Dump and Restore

The **dump** and **restore** commands were originally part of BSD UNIX but became common in other versions of UNIX and are included in most Linux distributions for backing up ext2 and ext3 format file systems. Here's a system administrator's typical backup strategy:

- Perform a monthly total file system backup.
- Perform a daily incremental backup, storing only those files that were changed since the last incremental backup. Daily dumps may be made at different *backup levels*, so only files backed up since the last lower-level incremental backup will be backed up again.

This kind of backup strategy is supported nicely by the **dump** and **restore** utilities. Figure 4–15 describes how **dump** works.

Utility: **dump** [*level*] [-f *dumpFile*] [-w] *fileSystem*
    dump [*level*] [-f *dumpFile*] [-w] { *fileName* }+

The **dump** utility has two forms. The first form of the **dump** utility copies files from the specified file system to *dumpFile*, which is "/dev/rmt0" by default (this will vary depending on your available tape or disk device). If the dump level is specified as *n*, then all of the files that have been modified since the last dump at a lower level than *n* are copied. For example, a level 0 dump will always dump all files, whereas a level 2 dump will dump all of the files modified since the last level 0 or level 1 dump. If no dump level is specified, it is set to 9. The **-w** option causes **dump** to display a list of all the file systems that need to be dumped instead of performing a backup.

The second form of **dump** allows you to specify the names of files to be dumped.

Both forms prompt the user to insert and/or remove dump media when necessary. For example, a large system dump to a tape drive often requires an operator to remove a full tape and replace it with an empty one.

When a dump is performed, information about the dump is recorded in the "/etc/dump-dates" file for use by future invocations of **dump**.

Figure 4–15 Description of the **dump** command.

Here's an example of **dump** which performs a level 0 dump of the file system on /dev/hda0 to the tape drive /dev/rmt0:

```
$ dump 0 -f /dev/rmt0 /dev/hda0
```

The **restore** utility allows you to restore files from a **dump** backup, and works as shown in Figure 4–16.

Utility: **restore** -irtx [-f *dumpFile*] { *fileName* }*

The **restore** utility allows you to restore a set of files from a previous dump file found on *dumpFile*. The **-r** option causes every file on *dumpFile* to be restored into the current directory, so use this option with care. The **-t** option causes a table of contents of *dumpFile* to be displayed instead of restoring any files. The **-x** option causes **restore** to extract only the specified filenames from *dumpFile*. If a filename is the name of a directory, its contents are recursively restored.

The **-i** option causes **restore** to read the table of contents of *dumpFile* and then enter an interactive mode that allows you to choose the files that you wish to restore. For more information on this interactive mode, consult **man restore**.

Figure 4–16 Description of the **restore** command.

In the following example, I used **restore** to extract a couple of previously saved files from the dump device "/dev/rmt0":

```
$ restore -x -f /dev/rmt0 wine.c hacking.c
```

4.7 Scheduling Commands: crontab and at

There are two utilities that allow you to schedule commands to be executed at a later point in time:

- **crontab**, which allows you to create a scheduling table that describes a series of jobs to be executed on a periodic basis
- **at**, which allows you to schedule jobs to be executed on a one-time basis

The subsections that follow describe each utility.

4.7.1   Periodic Execution: Crontab

The **crontab** utility allows you to schedule a series of jobs to be executed on a periodic basis and works as described in Figure 4–17.

Utility: **crontab** *crontabName*
     crontab [-u *userName*] -ler

crontab is the user interface to the Linux cron system. When used without any options, the crontab file called *crontabName* is registered and its commands are executed according to the specified timing rules. The **-l** option lists the contents of a registered crontab file. The **-e** option edits and then registers a registered crontab file. The **-r** option removes a registered crontab file. The **-l, -e,** and **-r** options may be used by a super-user to access another user's crontab file by using the **-u** option. The anatomy of a crontab file is described shortly.

Figure 4–17   Description of the **crontab** command.

To use **crontab**, you must prepare an input file that contains lines of the format:

```
minute   hour   day   month   weekday   command
```

where the values of each field are as shown in Figure 4–18.

Files of this nature are called "crontab" files. Whenever the current time matches a line's description, the associated command is executed by /bin/sh (which is Bash on a Linux system). If any of the first five fields contain an * instead of a number, the field always matches. The standard output of the command is automatically sent to the user via **mail**. Any characters following a % are copied into a temporary file and used as the command's standard input. Here is a sample crontab file that I created in my home directory and called "crontab.cron":

```
$ cat crontab.cron              ...list the crontab file.
0  8  *  *  1-5    echo Welcome to work
*  *  *  *  *      echo One Minute Passed > /dev/pts/1
30 14 1  1,4,7,10  *    mail users % Quarterly Meeting At 3pm
$ _
```

Field	Valid value
minute	0–59
hour	0–23
day	1–31
month	1–12
weekday	1–7 (1 = Mon, 2 = Tue, 3 = Wed, 4 = Thu, 5 = Fri, 6 = Sat, 7 = Sun, but 0 can be used for Sunday as well) or the name of the day
command	any Linux command

Figure 4–18 crontab field meanings and values.

The first line causes the message "Welcome to work" to be mailed to me at 8 a.m. every weekday morning. The next line echoes "One Minute Passed" every minute to the device "/dev/pts/1", which happens to be my terminal. The last line sends mail to all users on the first day of January, April, July, and October, at 2:30 p.m. to remind them of an impending meeting.

There is a single process called "cron" (or sometimes "crond") that is responsible for executing the commands in registered crontab files in a timely fashion. It is started when the Linux system is booted and does not stop until the Linux system is shut down. Copies of all registered crontab files are stored in the directory "/var/spool/cron" in a file named the same as the username.

To register a crontab file, use the **crontab** utility with the name of the crontab file as the single argument:

```
$ crontab crontab.cron          ...register the crontab file.
$ _
```

If you already have a registered crontab file, the new one is registered in place of the old one. To list the contents of your registered crontab, use the **-l** option. To list someone else's, add their name as an argument. Only a super-user can use this option. In the example that follows, note that one of my previously registered crontab file entries triggered coincidentally after I used the **crontab** utility.

```
$ crontab -l    ...list contents of current crontab file.
0  8  *  *  1-5    echo Welcome to work
*  *  *  *  *      echo One Minute Passed > /dev/pts/1
30 14 1  1,4,7,10  *  mail users % Quarterly Meeting At 3pm
$ One Minute Passed  ...output from one crontab command.
```

To edit your crontab file and then resave it, use the **-e** option. To remove a registered crontab file, use the **-r** option:

```
$ crontab -r           ...remove my crontab file.
$ _
```

A super-user may create files called "/etc/cron.allow" or "/etc/cron.deny" to either enable only specific users or prevent individual users from using the crontab facility. Each file consists of a list of user names on separate lines. If neither of the files exist, all users may use **crontab**.

4.7.2   One-Time Execution: at

The **at** utility allows you to schedule one-time commands or scripts (Figure 4–19).

Utility: **at** -csm *time* [*date* [, *year*]] [+*increment*] [-f *script*]
    atrm { *jobId* }+
    atq

at allows you to schedule one-time commands and/or scripts. It supports a flexible format for time specification. If the **-f** option is specified, commands will be taken from the file *script*, otherwise commands are read from stdin. Commands are run by /bin/sh, which on Linux is Bash. If no script name is specified, **at** takes a list of commands from standard input. The output from the script is sent to the user via e-mail when the job is complete. The **-m** option instructs **at** to send you mail even if there is no output. **atrm** removes the specified jobs from the **at** queue. The **atq** command and lists the pending jobs. A job is removed from the **at** queue after it has executed.

    time is in the format HH or HHMM followed by an optional A.M./P.M. specifier, and *date* is spelled out using the first three letters of the day and/or month. The keyword "now" may be used in place of the time sequence. The keywords "today" and "tomorrow" may be used in place of *date*. If no *date* is supplied, then **at** uses the following rules:

- If *time* is after the current time, then *date* is assumed to be "today".
- If *time* is before the current time, then *date* is assumed to be "tomorrow".

The stated time may be augmented by an *increment*, which is a number followed by "minutes," "hours," "days," "weeks," "months," or "years".

Figure 4–19 Description of the **at** command.

In the following example, I scheduled an **at** job to send a message to my terminal device.

```
$ cat at.sh          ...look at the script to be scheduled.
echo at done > /dev/pts/1          ...echo output to terminal.
$ date               ...look at current time.
Sat Jan 22 17:30:42 CST 2005
$ at now + 2 minutes -f at.sh     ...schedule script to
... execute in 2 minutes
job 2519 at 2005-01-22 17:32
$ atq                             ...look at the at schedule.
2519     2005-01-22 17:32 a ables
$ _
at done                           ...output from scheduled script.
$ at 17:35 -f at.sh        ...schedule the script again.
job 2520 at 2005-01-22 17:35
$ atrm 2520                       ...deschedule.
$ atq                             ...look at the at schedule.
$ _
```

Here are some more examples of legal **at** time formats:

```
0934am Sep 18
9:34 Sep 18, 2005
11:00pm tomorrow
now + 1 day
9pm Jan 13
10pm Wed
```

If you omit the command name, **at** displays a prompt and then waits for a list of commands to be entered from standard input. To terminate the command list, press a *Control-D*. Here's an example:

```
$ at 8pm       ...enter commands to be scheduled from keyboard.
at> echo at done > /dev/pts/1
at> ^D              ...end-of-input.
job 2530 at 2005-01-22 20:00
$ _
```

You may program a script to reschedule itself by calling **at** within the script:

```
$ cat at2.sh          ...a script that reschedules itself.
date > /dev/pts/1
# Reschedule script
at now + 2 minutes -f at2.sh
$ _
```

A super-user may create files called "/etc/at.allow" or "/etc/at.deny" to enable and inhibit individual users from using the **at** facility. Each file should consist of a list of user names on separate lines. If neither file exists, all users may use **at**.

4.8 Programmable Text Processing: gawk

The **gawk** utility scans one or more files and performs an action on all of the lines that match a particular condition. The actions and conditions are described by a **gawk** program, and range from the very simple to the complex.

gawk is a GNU reimplementation of the UNIX **awk** command. **awk** got its name from the combined first letters of its authors' surnames: Aho, Weinberger, and Kernighan. It borrows its control structures and expression syntax from the C language. If you already know C, then learning **awk/gawk** is quite straightforward.

awk/gawk is a comprehensive utility—so comprehensive, in fact, that there's a book on it! Because of this, I've attempted to describe only the main features and options of **gawk**; however, the material in this section will allow you to write a good number of useful applications. Figure 4–20 provides a synopsis of **gawk**.

Utility: **gawk** -Fc [-f *fileName*] *program* { *variable=value* }* { *fileName* }*

gawk is a programmable text-processing utility that scans the lines of its input and performs actions on every line that matches a particular criterion. A **gawk** program may be included on the command line, in which case it should be surrounded by single quotes; alternatively, it may be stored in a file and specified using the **-f** option. The initial values of variables may be specified on the command line. The default field separators are tabs and spaces. To override this, use the **-F** option followed by the new field separator. If no filenames are specified, **gawk** reads from standard input.

Figure 4–20 Description of the **gawk** command.

The next few subsections describe the various **gawk** features and include many examples.

4.8.1 gawk Programs

A **gawk** program may be supplied on the command line, but it's much more common to place it in a text file and specify the file using the **-f** option. If you decide to place a **gawk** program on the command line, surround it by single quotes.

When **gawk** reads a line, it breaks it into fields that are separated by tabs and/or spaces. The field separator may be overridden by using the **-F** option, as you'll see later in this section. A **gawk** program is a list of one or more commands of the form:

```
[ condition ] [ \{ action \} ]
```

where *condition* is one of the following:

- the special token BEGIN or END
- an expression involving logical operators, relational operators, and/or regular expressions

and *action* is a list of one or more of the following kinds of C-like statements, terminated by semicolons:

- **if** (conditional) statement [**else** statement]
- **while** (conditional) statement
- **for** (expression; conditional; expression) statement
- **break**
- **continue**
- variable=expression
- **print** [list of expressions] [> expression]
- **printf** format [, list of expressions] [> expression]
- **next** (skips the remaining patterns on the current line of input)
- **exit** (skips the rest of the current line)
- { list of statements }

action is performed on every line that matches *condition*. If *condition* is missing, *action* is performed on every line. If *action* is missing, then all matching lines are simply sent to standard output. The statements in a **gawk** program may be indented and formatted using spaces, tabs, and newlines.

4.8.2   Accessing Individual Fields

The first field of the current line may be accessed by $1, the second by $2, etc. $0 stands for the entire line. The built-in variable **NF** is equal to the number of fields in the current line. In the following example, I ran a simple **gawk** program on the text file "float" to insert the number of fields into each line:

```
$ cat float                      ...look at the original file.
Wish I was floating in blue across the sky,
My imagination is strong,
And I often visit the days
When everything seemed so clear.
Now I wonder what I'm doing here at all...
$ gawk '{ print NF, $0 }' float    ...execute the command.
9 Wish I was floating in blue across the sky,
4 My imagination is strong,
6 And I often visit the days
5 When everything seemed so clear.
9 Now I wonder what I'm doing here at all...
$ _
```

4.8.3   BEGIN and END

The special condition BEGIN is triggered before the first line is read, and the special condition END is triggered after the last line has been read. When expressions are listed in a print statement, no space is placed between them, and a newline is printed by default. The built-in variable

FILENAME is equal to the name of the input file. In the following example, I ran a program that displayed the first, third, and last fields of every line:

```
$ cat gawk2                    ...look at the gawk script.
BEGIN { print "Start of file:", FILENAME }
{ print $1 $3 $NF }     ...print 1st, 3rd, and last field.
END { print "End of file" }
$ gawk -f gawk2 float           ...execute the script.
Start of file: float
Wishwassky,
Myisstrong,
Andoftendays
Whenseemedclear.
Nowwonderall...
End of file
$ _
```

4.8.4   Operators

When commas are placed between the expressions in a **print** statement, a space is printed. All of the usual C operators are available in **gawk**. The built-in variable **NR** contains the line number of the current line. In the next example, I ran a program that displayed the first, third, and last fields of lines 2..3 of "float":

```
$ cat gawk3                    ...look at the gawk script.
NR > 1 && NR < 4 { print NR, $1, $3, $NF }
$ gawk -f gawk3 float       ...execute the script.
2 My is strong,
3 And often days
$ _
```

4.8.5   Variables

gawk supports user-defined variables. There is no need to declare a variable. A variable's initial value is a null string or zero, depending on how you use it. In the next example, the program counted the number of lines and words in a file as it echoed the lines to standard output:

```
$ cat gawk4                    ...look at the gawk script.
BEGIN { print "Scanning file" }
{
 printf "line %d: %s\n", NR, $0;
 lineCount++;
 wordCount += NF;
}
END { printf "lines = %d, words = %d\n", lineCount, wordCount }
$ gawk -f gawk4 float       ...execute the script.
```

```
Scanning file
line 1: Wish I was floating in blue across the sky,
line 2: My imagination is strong,
line 3: And I often visit the days
line 4: When everything seemed so clear.
line 5: Now I wonder what I'm doing here at all...
lines = 5, words = 33
$ _
```

4.8.6   Control Structures

gawk supports most of the standard C control structures. In the following example, I printed the fields in each line backward:

```
$ cat gawk5              ...look at the gawk script.
{
  for (i = NF; i >= 1; i--)
    printf "%s ", $i;

 printf "\n";
}
$ gawk -f gawk5 float      ...execute the script.
sky, the across blue in floating was I Wish
strong, is imagination My
days the visit often I And
clear. so seemed everything When
all... at here doing I'm what wonder I Now
$ _
```

4.8.7   Extended Regular Expressions

The condition for line matching can be an extended regular expression, which is defined in the Appendix of this book. Regular expressions must be placed between / characters. In the next example, I displayed all of the lines that contained a "t" followed by an "e," with any number of characters in between. For the sake of clarity, I've italicized the character sequences of the output lines that satisfied the condition.

```
$ cat gawk6              ...look at the script.
/t.*e/ { print $0 }
$ gawk -f gawk6 float      ...execute the script.
Wish I was floating in blue across the sky,
And I often visit the days
When everything seemed so clear.
Now I wonder what I'm doing here at all...
$ _
```

4.8.8   Condition Ranges

A condition may be two expressions separated by a comma. In this case, **gawk** performs *action* on every line from the first line that matches the first condition to the next line that satisfies the second condition:

```
$ cat gawk7              ...look at the gawk script.
/strong/ , /clear/ { print $0 }
$ gawk -f gawk7 float    ...execute the script.
My imagination is strong,
And I often visit the days
When everything seemed so clear.
$ _
```

4.8.9   Field Separators

If the field separators are not spaces, use the **-F** option to specify the separator character. In the next example, I processed a file whose fields were separated by colons:

```
$ cat gawk3               ...look at the awk script.
NR > 1 && NR < 4 { print $1, $3, $NF }
$ cat float2              ...look at the input file.
Wish:I:was:floating:in:blue:across:the:sky,
My:imagination:is:strong,
And:I:often:visit:the:days
When:everything:seemed:so:clear.
Now:I:wonder:what:I'm:doing:here:at:all...
$ gawk -F: -f gawk3 float2        ...execute the script.
My is strong,
And often days
$ _
```

4.8.10   Built-in Functions

gawk supports several built-in functions, including exp (), log (), sqrt (), int (), and substr (). The first four functions work just like their standard C counterparts. The substr (*str*, *x*, *y*) function returns the substring of *str* from the *x*th character and extending *y* characters. Here's an example of these functions:

```
$ cat test          ...look at the input file.
1.1 a
2.2 at
3.3 eat
4.4 beat
$ cat gawk8         ...look at the gawk script.
```

```
{
 printf "$1 = %g ", $1;
 printf "exp = %.2g ", exp ($1);
 printf "log = %.2g ", log ($1);
 printf "sqrt = %.2g ", sqrt ($1);
 printf "int = %d ", int ($1);
 printf "substr (%s, 2, 2) = %s\n", $2, substr($2, 2, 2);
}
$ gawk -f gawk8 test        ...execute the script.
$1 = 1.1 exp = 3 log = 0.095 sqrt = 1 int = 1 substr (a, 2, 2) =
$1 = 2.2 exp = 9 log = 0.79 sqrt = 1.5 int = 2 substr (at, 2, 2) = t
$1 = 3.3 exp = 27 log = 1.2 sqrt = 1.8 int = 3 substr (eat, 2, 2) = at
$1 = 4.4 exp = 81 log = 1.5 sqrt = 2.1 int = 4 substr (beat, 2, 2) = ea
$ _
```

4.9 Hard and Soft Links: ln

The **ln** utility allows you to create both hard links and symbolic (soft) links between files, as described in Figure 4–21.

Utility: **ln** -sF *original* [*newLink*]
     ln -sF { *original* }+ *directory*

ln is a utility that allows you to create hard links or symbolic (soft) links to existing files.

To create a hard link between two regular files, specify the existing file label as the *original* filename and the new file label as *newLink*. Both labels will then refer to the same physical file, and this arrangement will be reflected in the hard-link count shown by the **ls** utility. The file can then be accessed via either label, and is removed from the file system only when all of its associated labels are deleted. If *newLink* is omitted, the last component of *original* is assumed. If the last argument is the name of a directory, then hard links are made from that directory to all of the specified original filenames. Hard links may not span file systems.

The **-s** option causes **ln** to create symbolic links. A symbolic link is a new file that contains a pointer (by name) to another file. A symbolic link may span file systems since there is no explicit connection to the destination file other than the name. Note that if the file pointed to by a symbolic link is removed, the symbolic-link file still exists but will result in an error if accessed.

The **-F** option allows a super-user to create a hard link to a directory.

For further information about how hard links are represented in the file system, see the discussion of Linux file systems in Chapter 13, "Linux Internals."

Figure 4–21 Description of the **ln** command.

In the following example, I added a new label "hold" to the file referenced by the existing label "hold.3". Note that the hard-link count field incremented from one to two when the hard link was added, and then back to one again when the hard link was deleted:

```
$ ls -lG      ...look at the current directory contents.
total 3
-rw-r--r--  1 glass       124 Jan 12 17:32 hold.1
-rw-r--r--  1 glass        89 Jan 12 17:34 hold.2
-rw-r--r--  1 glass        91 Jan 12 17:34 hold.3
$ ln hold.3 hold          ...create a new hard link.
$ ls -lG                  ...look at the new directory contents.
total 4
-rw-r--r--  2 glass        91 Jan 12 17:34 hold
-rw-r--r--  1 glass       124 Jan 12 17:32 hold.1
-rw-r--r--  1 glass        89 Jan 12 17:34 hold.2
-rw-r--r--  2 glass        91 Jan 12 17:34 hold.3
$ rm hold                 ...remove one of the links.
$ ls -lG                  ...look at the updated directory contents.
total 3
-rw-r--r--  1 glass       124 Jan 12 17:32 hold.1
-rw-r--r--  1 glass        89 Jan 12 17:34 hold.2
-rw-r--r--  1 glass        91 Jan 12 17:34 hold.3
$ _
```

A series of hard links may be added to an existing directory if the directory's name is specified as the last argument to **ln**. In the following example, I created links in the "tmp" directory to all of the files matched by the pattern "hold.*":

```
$ mkdir tmp               ...create a new directory.
$ ln hold.* tmp           ...create a series of links in "tmp".
$ ls -lG tmp              ...look at the contents of "tmp".
total 3
-rw-r--r--  2 glass       124 Jan 12 17:32 hold.1
-rw-r--r--  2 glass        89 Jan 12 17:34 hold.2
-rw-r--r--  2 glass        91 Jan 12 17:34 hold.3
$ _
```

A hard link may not be created from a file on one file system to a file on a different file system. To get around this problem, create a *symbolic* (or soft) link instead. A symbolic link may span file systems. To create a symbolic link, use the **-s** option to **ln**. In the following example, I tried to create a hard link from my home directory to the file "/usr/include/stdio.h". Unfortunately, that file was on a different file system, and so **ln** failed. However, **ln** with the **-s** option succeeded. When **ls** is used with the **-F** option, symbolic links are followed by the @ character.

By default, **ls** displays the contents of the symbolic link; to obtain information about the file that the link refers to, use the **-L** option.

```
$ ln /usr/include/stdio.h stdio.h        ...hard link.
ln: stdio.h: Cross-device link
$ ln -s /usr/include/stdio.h stdio.h     ...symbolic link.
$ ls -lG stdio.h          ...examine the file.
lrwxrwxrwx  1 glass  20 Jan 12 17:58 stdio.h -> /usr/include/stdio.h
$ ls -F                      ...@ indicates a sym. link.
stdio.h@
$ ls -lGL stdio.h                ...look at the link itself.
-rw-r--r--  1 root      27839 May 11  07:40 stdio.h
$ cat stdio.h                    ...look at the file.
/* Define ISO C stdio on top of C++ iostreams.
   Copyright (C) 1991,1994-2002,2003 Free Software Foundation
   This file is part of the GNU C Library.

...
$ _
```

4.10 Identifying Shells: whoami

Let's say that you come across a vacated system and there's a shell prompt on the screen. Obviously someone was working on the Linux system and forgot to log off. You wonder curiously who that person was. To solve the mystery, you can use the **whoami** utility, which displays the owner of a shell (Figure 4–22).

Utility: **whoami**

Displays the owner of a shell.

Figure 4-22 Description of the **whoami** command.

For example, when I executed **whoami** at my system, I saw this:

```
$ whoami
glass
$ _
```

4.11 Substituting a User: su

A lot of people think that **su** stands for "super-user," but it doesn't. Instead, it stands for "substitute user," and allows you to create a subshell owned by another user (Figure 4–23).

Utility: **su** [-] [*userName*] [*args*]

su creates a temporary shell with *userName*'s real and effective user/group IDs. If *userName* is not specified, "root" is assumed and the new shell's prompt is set to a # as a reminder. While you're in the subshell, you are effectively logged on as that user; when you terminate the shell with a *Control-D*, you are returned to your original shell. Of course, you must know the other user's password to use this utility. The SHELL and HOME environment variables are set from *userName*'s entry in the password file. If *userName* is not "root," the USER environment variable is also set. The new shell does not go through its login sequence unless the - option is supplied. All other arguments are passed as command-line arguments to the new shell.

Figure 4–23   Description of the **su** command.

Here's an example of **su**:

```
$ whoami              ...find out my current username.
glass
$ su                  ...substitute user.
Password: <enter super-user password here>
$ whoami        ...confirm my current username has changed.
root
$ ... perform super-user tasks here
$ ^D                  ...terminate the child shell.
$ whoami        ...confirm current username is restored.
glass
$ _
```

The **su** command is probably most often used to become the super-user. If you will act as the system administrator or have a need to become the super-user on a regular basis, you should also see the description of the **sudo** command on page 577.

4.12 Transforming Files

There are several utilities that perform a transformation on the contents of a file, including the following:

- **gzip**, **gunzip**, and **zcat**, which convert a file into a space-efficient intermediate format and then back again. These utilities are useful for saving disk space.
- **sed**, a general-purpose programmable stream editor that edits a file according to a pre-prepared set of instructions.
- **tr**, which maps characters from one set to another. This utility is useful for performing simple mappings such as converting a file from uppercase to lowercase.
- **ul**, which converts embedded underline sequences in a file to a form suitable for a particular terminal type.

The next few subsections contain a description of each utility.

4.12.1   Compressing Files: gzip and gunzip

The GNU file compression utility is called **gzip**. The utility to uncompress the file, as you might guess, is **gunzip**. Figure 4–24 resolves these utilities.

Utility: **gzip** -cv { *fileName* }+
    gunzip -cv { *fileName* }+
    zcat { *fileName* }+

gzip replaces a file by its compressed version, appending a ".gz" suffix. The **-c** option sends the result to standard output rather than overwriting the original file. The **-v** option displays the amount of compression that takes place.

The **gunzip** command uncompresses a file created by **gzip**.

zcat is equivalent to **gunzip -c**.

Figure 4–24   Description of the **gzip**, **gunzip**, and **zcat** commands.

This is how to use **gzip** and **gunzip**:

```
$ ls -lG palindrome.c reverse.c
 -rw-r--r--    1 ables         224 Jul  1 14:14 palindrome.c
 -rw-r--r--    1 ables         266 Jul  1 14:14 reverse.c
$ gzip -v palindrome.c  reverse.c
palindrome.c:          34.3% -- replaced with palindrome.c.gz
reverse.c:             39.4% -- replaced with reverse.c.gz
$ ls -lG palindrome.c.gz reverse.c.gz
 -rw-r--r--    1 ables         178 Jul  1 14:14 palindrome.c.gz
 -rw-r--r--    1 ables         189 Jul  1 14:14 reverse.c.gz
$ gunzip -v *.gz
palindrome.c.gz:       34.3% -- replaced with palindrome.c
reverse.c.gz:          39.4% -- replaced with reverse.c
$ ls -lG palindrome.c reverse.c
 -rw-r--r--    1 ables         224 Jul  1 14:14 palindrome.c
 -rw-r--r--    1 ables         266 Jul  1 14:14 reverse.c
$ _
```

4.12.2   Stream Editing: sed

The stream **ed**itor utility **sed** scans one or more files and performs an editing action on all of the lines that match a particular condition. The actions and conditions may be stored in a **sed** script. **sed** is useful for performing simple repetitive editing tasks.

sed is a fairly comprehensive utility. Because of this, I've only attempted to describe the main features and options of **sed**; however, the material in this section will allow you to write a good number of useful **sed** scripts.

Figure 4–25 gives a synopsis of **sed**.

Utility: **sed** [-e *script*] [-f *scriptfile*] { *fileName* }*

sed is a utility that edits an input stream according to a script that contains editing commands. Each editing command is separated by a newline, and describes an action and a line or range of lines to perform the action upon. A **sed** script may be stored in a file and executed by using the **-f** option. If a script is placed directly on the command line, it should be surrounded by single quotes. If no files are specified, **sed** reads from standard input. The format of **sed** scripts is described in the following sections.

Figure 4–25   Description of the **sed** command.

4.12.2.1 **sed** commands

A **sed** script is a list of one or more of the commands shown in Figure 4–26, separated by newlines.

Command syntax	Meaning
address **a** text	Append *text* after the line specified by *address*.
addressRange c\ text	Replace the text specified by *addressRange* with text.
addressRange **d**	Delete the text specified by *addressRange*.
address **i** text	Insert *text* after the line specified by *address*.
address **r** *name*	Append the contents of the file *name* after the line specified by *address*.
addressRange s/*expr*/*str*/	Substitute the first occurrence of the regular expression *expr* by the string *str*.
addressRange s/*expr*/*str*/**g**	Substitute every occurrence of the regular expression *expr* by the string *str*.

Figure 4–26   Editing commands in **sed**.

The following rules apply:

• *address* must be either a line number or a regular expression. A regular expression selects all of the lines that match the expression. You may use $ to select the last line.

- *addressRange* can be a single address or a couple of addresses separated by commas. If two addresses are specified, then all of the lines between the first line that matches the first address and the first line that matches the second address are selected.
- If no address is specified, then the command is applied to all of the lines.

4.12.2.2 Substituting Text

In the following example, I supplied the **sed** script on the command line. The script inserted a couple of spaces at the start of every line.

```
$ cat arms                    ...look at the original file.
People just like me,
Are all around the world,
Waiting for the loved ones that they need.
And with my heart,
I make a simple wish,
Plain enough for anyone to see.
$ sed 's/^/  /' arms > arms.indent    ...indent the file.
$ cat arms.indent             ...look at the result.
  People just like me,
  Are all around the world,
  Waiting for the loved ones that they need.
  And with my heart,
  I make a simple wish,
  Plain enough for anyone to see.
$ _
```

To remove all of the leading spaces from a file, use the substitute operator in the reverse fashion:

```
$ sed 's/^ *//' arms.indent    ...remove leading spaces.
People just like me,
Are all around the world,
Waiting for the loved ones that they need.
And with my heart,
I make a simple wish,
Plain enough for anyone to see.
$ _
```

4.12.2.3 Deleting Text

The next example illustrates a script that deleted all of the lines that contained the character 'a':

```
$ sed '/a/d' arms        ...remove all lines containing an 'a'.
People just like me,
$ _
```

To delete only those lines that contain the *word* 'a', I surrounded the regular expression by
escaped angled brackets (\< and \>):

```
$ sed '/\<a\>/d' arms
People just like me,
Are all around the world,
Waiting for the loved ones that they need.
And with my heart,
Plain enough for anyone to see.
$ _
```

4.12.2.4 Inserting Text

In the next example, I inserted a copyright notice at the top of the file by using the insert command. Notice that I stored the **sed** script in a file and executed it by using the **-f** option.

```
$ cat sed5                     ...look at the sed script.
1i\
Copyright 1992, 1998, & 2002 by Graham Glass\
All rights reserved\
$ sed -f sed5 arms             ...insert a copyright notice.
Copyright 1992, 1998, & 2002 by Graham Glass
All rights reserved
People just like me,
Are all around the world,
Waiting for the loved ones that they need.
And with my heart,
I make a simple wish,
Plain enough for anyone to see.
$ _
```

4.12.2.5 Replacing Text

To replace lines, use the change function. In the following example, I replaced the group of lines
1..3 with a censored message:

```
$ cat sed6                     ...list the sed script.
1,3c\
Lines 1-3 are censored.
$ sed -f sed6 arms             ...execute the script.
Lines 1-3 are censored.
And with my heart,
I make a simple wish,
Plain enough for anyone to see.
$ _
```

To replace individual lines with a message rather than an entire group, supply a separate command for each line:

```
$ cat sed7                    ...list the sed script.
1c\
Line 1 is censored.
2c\
Line 2 is censored.
3c\
Line 3 is censored.
$ sed -f sed7 arms            ...execute the script.
Line 1 is censored.
Line 2 is censored.
Line 3 is censored.
And with my heart,
I make a simple wish,
Plain enough for anyone to see.
$ _
```

4.12.2.6 Inserting Files

In the following example, I inserted a message after the last line of the file:

```
$ cat insert          ...list the file to be inserted.
The End
$ sed '$r insert' arms          ...execute the script.
People just like me,
Are all around the world,
Waiting for the loved ones that they need.
And with my heart,
I make a simple wish,
Plain enough for anyone to see.
The End
$ _
```

4.12.2.7 Multiple **sed** Commands

This last example illustrates the use of multiple **sed** commands. I inserted a "<<" sequence at the start of each line, and appended a ">>" sequence to the end of each line:

```
$ sed -e 's/^/<< /' -e 's/$/ >>/' arms
<< People just like me, >>
<< Are all around the world, >>
<< Waiting for the loved ones that they need. >>
<< And with my heart, >>
<< I make a simple wish, >>
<< Plain enough for anyone to see. >>
$ _
```

4.12.3   Translating Characters: tr

The **tr** utility maps the characters in a file from one character set to another (Figure 4–27).

Utility: **tr** -cds *string1 string2*

tr maps all of the characters in its standard input from the character set *string1* to the character set *string2*. If the length of *string2* is less than the length of *string1*, it's padded by repeating its last character; in other words, the command *"tr abc de"* is equivalent to *"tr abc dee"*.

A character set may be specified using the [] notation of shell filename substitution:

- To specify the character set a, d, and f, simply write them as a single string: *adf*.
- To specify the character set a through z, separate the start and end characters by a dash: *a-z*.

By default, **tr** replaces every character of standard input in *string1* by its corresponding character in *string2*.

The **-c** option causes *string1* to be complemented before the mapping is performed. *Complementing* a string means that it is replaced by a string that contains every ASCII character except those in the original string. The net effect is that every character of standard input that *does not* occur in *string1* is replaced.

The **-d** option causes every character in *string1* to be deleted from standard input.

The **-s** option causes every repeated output character to be condensed into a single instance.

Figure 4–27   Description of the **tr** command.

Here are some examples of **tr** in action:

```
$ cat go.cart              ...list the sample input file.
go cart
racing
$ tr a-z A-Z < go.cart     ...translate lower to uppercase.
GO CART
RACING
$ tr a-c D-E < go.cart     ...replace abc by DEE.
go EDrt
rDEing
$ tr -c a X < go.cart      ...replace every non-a with X.
XXXXaXXXXXaXXXXX$          ...even last newline is replaced.
$ tr -c a-z '\012' < go.cart   ...replace non-alphas with
go                             ...ASCII 12 (newline).
```

```
cart
racing
$ tr -cs a-z '\012' < go.cart      ...repeat, but condense
go                                 ...repeated newlines.
cart
racing
$ tr -d a-c < go.cart              ...delete all a-c characters.
go rt
ring
$ _
```

4.12.4 Converting Underline Sequences: ul

The **ul** utility transforms a file that contains underlining characters so that it appears correctly on a particular terminal type. This is useful with commands like **man** that generate underlined text. Figure 4–28 describes how **ul** works.

Utility: **ul** -t*terminal* { *filename* }*

ul is a utility that transforms underline characters in its input so that they will display correctly on the specified terminal. If no terminal is specified, the one defined by the TERM environment variable is assumed. The "/etc/termcap" file (or terminfo database) is used by **ul** to determine the correct underline sequence.

Figure 4–28   Description of the **ul** command.

For example, let's say that you want to use the **man** utility to produce a document that you wish to print on a simple ASCII-only printer. The **man** utility generates underline characters for your current terminal, so to filter the output so that it's suitable for a dumb printer, pipe the output of **man** through **ul** with the "dumb" terminal setting. Here's an example:

```
$ man who | ul -tdumb > man.txt
$ head man.txt            ...look at the first 10 lines.
WHO(1)                   User Commands                   WHO(1)

NAME
    who - show who is logged on

SYNOPSIS
    who [OPTION]... [ FILE | ARG1 ARG2 ]

DESCRIPTION
$ _
```

4.13 Looking at Raw File Contents: od

The octal dump utility, **od**, allows you to see the contents of a nontext file in a variety of formats. Figure 4–29 describes how it works.

Utility: **od** -abcdfhilox *fileName* [*offset*[.][b]]

od displays the contents of *fileName* in a form specified by one of several options:

OPTION	MEANING
-a	Interpret bytes as characters, and print as ASCII names (i.e., 0 = null).
-b	Interpret bytes as unsigned octal.
-c	Interpret bytes as characters, and print in C notation (i.e., 0 = \0).
-d	Interpret two-byte pairs as unsigned decimal.
-f	Interpret four-byte pairs as floating point.
-h	Interpret two-byte pairs as unsigned hex.
-i	Interpret two-byte pairs as signed decimal.
-l	Interpret four-byte pairs as signed decimal.
-o	Interpret two-byte pairs as unsigned octal.
-s[n]	Look for strings of minimum length n (default 3), terminated by null characters.
-x	Interpret two-byte pairs as hex.

By default, the contents are displayed as a series of octal numbers. *offset* specifies where the listing should begin. If the offset ends in **b**, then it is interpreted as a number of blocks; otherwise, it is interpreted as an octal number. To specify a hex number, precede it by **x.** To specify a decimal number, end it with a period.

Figure 4–29   Description of the **od** command.

In the following example, I displayed the contents of the "/bin/od" executable as octal numbers, and then as characters:

```
$ od /usr/bin/od        ...dump the "/bin/od" file in octal.
0000000 042577 043114 000401 000001 000000 000000 000000 000000
0000020 000002 000003 000001 000000 107020 004004 000064 000000
0000040 101244 000000 000000 000000 000064 000040 000010 000050
0000060 000031 000030 000006 000000 000064 000000 100064 004004
0000100 100064 004004 000400 000000 000400 000000 000005 000000
0000120 000004 000000 000003 000000 000464 000000 100464 004004
0000140 100464 004004 000023 000000 000023 000000 000004 000000
...
$ od -c /usr/bin/od     ...dump "/bin/od" as characters.
0000000 177   E   L   F 001 001 001  \0  \0  \0  \0  \0  \0  \0  \0  \0
0000020 002  \0 003  \0 001  \0  \0  \0 020 216 004  \b   4  \0  \0  \0
0000040 304 202  \0  \0  \0  \0  \0  \0   4  \0      \0  \b  \0   (  \0
0000060 031  \0 030  \0 006  \0  \0  \0   4  \0  \0  \0   4 200 004  \b
0000100   4 200 004  \b  \0 001  \0  \0  \0 001  \0  \0 005  \0  \0  \0
0000120 004  \0  \0  \0 003  \0  \0  \0   4 001  \0  \0   4 201 004  \b
0000140   4 201 004  \b 023  \0  \0  \0 023  \0  \0  \0 004  \0  \0  \0
...
$ _
```

You may search for strings of a minimum length by using the **-s** option. Any series of characters followed by an ASCII null is considered to be a string.

```
$ od -s7 /usr/bin/od    ...search for strings 7 chars or more.
0000464 /lib/ld-linux.so.2
0003121 libc.so.6
0003142 putc_unlocked
0003160 getopt_long
0003174 __fpending
0003225 setvbuf
0003235 mbrtowc
0003263 strtoumax
0003312 iswprint
...
$ _
```

4.14 Mounting File Systems: mount and umount

A super-user may extend the file system by using the **mount** utility (Figure 4–30).

Utility: **mount** *-ooptions* -t *type* [*deviceName directory*]
    umount *deviceName*

mount is a utility that allows you to "splice" a device's file system into the root hierarchy. When used without any arguments, **mount** displays a list of the currently mounted devices. To specify special options, follow **-o** by a list of valid codes. These codes include **rw**, which mounts a file system for read/write, and **ro**, which mounts a file system for read-only. Use *type* to specify the file system type (e.g., ext2, ext3, etc.). The **umount** utility unmounts a previously mounted file system.

Figure 4–30   Description of the **mount** and **umount** commands.

In the following example, I spliced the file system contained on the "/dev/dsk2" device onto the "/usr" directory. Notice that before I performed the mount, the "/usr" directory was empty; after the mount, the files stored on the "/dev/dsk2" device appeared inside this directory.

```
$ mount                 ...list the currently mounted devices.
/dev/dsk1 on /  type ext2 (rw)
$ ls /usr               .../usr is currently empty.
$ mount /dev/dsk2 /usr  ...mount the /dev/dsk2 device.
$ mount                 ...list the currently mounted devices.
/dev/dsk1 on / type ext2 (rw)
/dev/dsk2 on /usr type ext2 (rw)
$ ls /usr    ...list the contents of the mounted device.
bin/    etc/    include/ lost+found/ src/     ucb/
demo/   games/  lib/     pub/        sys/     ucblib/
dict/   hosts/  local/   spool/      tmp/
$ _
```

To unmount a device, use the **umount** utility. In the following example, I unmounted the "/dev/dsk2" device and then listed the "/usr" directory. The files were no longer accessible.

```
$ umount /dev/dsk2     ...unmount the device.
$ mount                ...list the currently mounted devices.
/dev/dsk1 on / type ext2 (rw)
$ ls /usr              ...note that /usr is empty again.
$ _
```

4.15 Identifying Terminals: tty

The **tty** utility identifies the name of your terminal (Figure 4–31).

> *Utility*: **tty**
>
> **tty** displays the pathname of your terminal. It returns zero if its standard input is a terminal; otherwise, it returns 1.

Figure 4–31 Description of the **tty** command.

In the following example, my login terminal was the special file "/dev/pts/1":

```
$ tty          ...display the pathname of my terminal.
/dev/pts/1
$ _
```

4.16 Timing Execution: time

It is sometimes useful to know how long it takes to run a specific command or program (or more to the point, to know how long it takes relative to how long something else takes) (Figure 4–32).

> *Utility*: **time** [-p] *command-line*
>
> The **time** command can be used to report the execution time of any Linux command specified by *command-line*. Time is reported in both elapsed time and CPU time (CPU time is expressed as two values, user time and system time). When the **-p** option is used, **time** reports in the traditional UNIX format.

Figure 4–32 Description of the **time** command.

For example:

```
$ time -p sort allnames.txt >sortednames.txt

real    0m 4.18s
user    0m 1.85s
sys     0m 0.14s
$ _
```

This command tells us it took over 4 seconds of "wall clock" time to sort our file. But the total CPU time used was 1.99 seconds (user time plus system time).

The **time** command is particularly useful when testing programs or scripts on small amounts of data where you can't "feel" the difference in the time required because they run so fast, but you know that when you run on your large amount of "real data," you'll want your program to be as efficient as possible.

4.17 Rolling Your Own Programs: Perl

When your task requires combining several of the utilities we've examined, you might write a shell script, as we will see in the next few chapters. Shell scripts are slower than C programs, since they are interpreted instead of compiled, but they are also much easier to write and debug. C programs allow you to take advantage of many more Linux features, but generally require more time both to write and to modify.

In 1986, Larry Wall found that shell scripts weren't enough and C programs were overkill for many purposes. He set out to write a scripting language that would be the best of both worlds. The result was Perl. The **P**ractical **E**xtraction **R**eport **L**anguage addressed many of Larry's problems generating reports and other text-oriented functions, although it also provides easy access to many other Linux facilities that shell scripts do not.

The Perl language syntax will look familiar to shell and C programmers, since much of the syntax was taken from elements of both. I can only hope to give you a high-level view of Perl here. Like **awk/gawk**, entire books have been written on Perl that describe it in detail (e.g., [Medinets, 1996], [Wall, 1996]). That level of detail is beyond the scope of this book. But by whetting your appetite with an introduction, I'm sure you'll want to find out more about Perl.

4.17.1   Getting Perl

Perl comes with all Linux distributions. Perl is also available for all versions of UNIX and even runs on MacOS and Windows. You do have to watch out for inconsistencies in system calls and file system locations of data files, but your code will require very few changes to run properly on different platforms.

The best source for all things Perl is:

`http://www.perl.com`

This site contains distributions of Perl for various platforms in the "downloads" section as well as documentation and links to many other useful resources.

But the biggest advantage of Perl is that it is free. Perl itself is licensed by a variation of the GNU Public License, known as the Artistic License. This does not impact any code you write in Perl. You are free to use and distribute your own code in any way you see fit. And you generally don't need to worry about redistributing Perl for someone to be able to run your code, since it is so freely available.

4.17.2   Running Perl

Figure 4–33 demonstrates the most commonly used arguments to Perl.

Utility: **perl** [-c] *fileName*
        perl -v

perl interprets and executes the Perl script code in *fileName*. If the **-c** argument is present, the script is checked for syntax but not executed. When the **-v** argument is used, Perl prints version information about itself.

Figure 4–33   Description of the **perl** command.

In most cases, you simply run a Perl script in a file with the following command:

```
$ perl file.pl
```

4.17.3   Printing Text

Without the ability to print output, most programs wouldn't accomplish much. So in the UNIX tradition, I'll start our Perl script examples with one that prints a single line:

```
print "hello world.\n";
```

Just from this simple example, you can infer that each line in Perl must end with a semicolon (;). Also note the "\n" is used (as in the C programming language) to print a newline character at the end of the line.

4.17.4   Variables, Strings, and Integers

To write useful programs, of course, requires the ability to assign and modify values like strings and integers. Perl provides variables much like the shells. These variables can be assigned any type of value, Perl keeps track of variable type for you. The major difference between Perl variables and shell variables is that the dollar sign is not simply used to expand the value of the variable but is *always* used to denote the variable. Even when assigning a value to a variable:

```
$i = 3;
```

you put the $ on the variable. This is probably the most difficult adjustment for seasoned shell programmers to make.

In addition to all of the "typical" mathematical operators (add, subtract, etc.), integers also support a *range operator* ".." which is used to specify a range of integers. This is useful when building a loop around a range of values, as we will see later.

Strings, as in most languages, are specified by text in quotation marks. Strings also support a concatenation operator "." which puts strings together.

```
print 1, 2, 3..15, "\n";     # range operator
print "A", "B", "C", "\n";   # strings
$i = "A" . "B" ;             # concatenation operator
print "$i", "\n" ;
```

The previous example lines of Perl generate the following output:

```
123456789101112131415
ABC
AB
```

You can see that each value, and only each value, is printed, giving you control over all spacing.

4.17.5   Arrays

Most programming languages provide *arrays*, which are lists of data values. Arrays in Perl are quite simple to use, as they are dynamically allocated (you don't have to define how large they will be, and if you use more than what is currently allocated, Perl will allocate more space and enlarge the array). The syntax is probably new, however. Rather than using a dollar sign, as you do with Perl variables, you denote an array by an at sign (@):

```
@arr = (1,2,3,4,5);
```

This line defines the array "arr" and puts 5 values in it. You could also define the same array with the line:

```
@arr = (1..5);
```

using the range operator with integers.

You can access a single element with a subscript in brackets, like:

```
print @arr[0],"\n";
```

As with most array implementations, the first element is numbered zero. Using the definition from before, this line would print "1" since it's the first value.

If you print an array without subscripts, all defined values are printed. If you use the array name without a subscript in a place where a scalar value is expected, the number of elements in the array is used.

```
@a1 = (1);             # array of 1 element
@a2 = (1,2,3,4,5);     # array of 5 elements
@a3 = (1..10);         # array of 10 elements

print @a1, " ", @a2, " ", @a3, "\n";

print @a1[0], " ", @a2[1], " ", @a3[2], "\n";

# using as scalar will yield number of items
print @a2 + @a3, "\n";
```

will result in the following output:

```
1 12345 12345678910
1 2 3
15
```

A special type of array provided in Perl is the *associative array*. Whereas you specify an index or position of a normal array with an integer between zero and the maximum size of the array, an associative array can have indices in any order and of any value.

Consider, for example, an array of month names. You can define an array called $month with 12 values of "January," "February," and so on (since arrays begin with index 0, you either remember to subtract one from your index or you define an array of 13 values and ignore $month[0], starting with $month[1]="January").

But what if you are reading month names from the input and want to look up the numeric value? You could use a **for** loop to search through the array until you found the value that matched the name you read, but that requires extra code. Wouldn't it be nice if you could just index into the array with the name? With an associative array you can:

```
@month{'January'} = 1;
@month{'February'} = 2;
     .
     .
     .
```

and so on. Then you can read in the month name and access its numeric value this way:

```
$monthnum = $month{$monthname};
```

without having to loop through the array and search for the name. Rather than setting up the array one element at a time, as we did above, you can define it at the beginning of your Perl program like this:

```
%month = ("January", 1, "February", 2, "March", 3,
          "April", 4, "May", 5, "June", 6,
          "July", 7, "August", 8, "September", 9,
          "October", 10, "November", 11, "December", 12);
```

The set of values that can be used in an associative array, or the keys to the array, are returned as a regular array by a call to the Perl function **keys()**:

```
@monthnames = keys(%month);
```

If you attempt to use a value as a key that is not a valid key, a null or zero (depending on how you use the value) will be returned.

4.17.6 Mathematical and Logical Operators

Once you have your variables assigned, the next thing you usually want to do with them is change their values. Most operations on values are familiar from C programming. The typical operators add, subtract, multiply, and divide are +, −, *, and /, respectively, for both integers and real numbers. Integers also support the C constructs to increment and decrement before and after the value is used and logical ANDs and ORs. Notice in this example that I have to backslash the

$ used in print statement text, since I don't want the value of the variable in those places, but I actually want the name with the $ prepended to it:

```
$n = 2;
print ("\$n=", $n, "\n");

$n = 2 ; print ("increment after \$n=", $n++, "\n");
$n = 2 ; print ("increment before \$n=", ++$n, "\n");
$n = 2 ; print ("decrement after \$n=", $n--, "\n");
$n = 2 ; print ("decrement before \$n=", --$n, "\n");

$n = 2;                          # reset
print ("\$n+2=", $n + 2, "\n");
print ("\$n-2=", $n - 2, "\n");
print ("\$n*2=", $n * 2, "\n");
print ("\$n/2=", $n / 2, "\n");

$r = 3.14;                       # real number
print ("\$r=", $r, "\n");

print ("\$r*2=", $r * 2, "\n"); # double
print ("\$r/2=", $r / 2, "\n"); # cut in half

print ("1 && 1 -> ", 1 && 1, "\n");
print ("1 && 0 -> ", 1 && 0, "\n");
print ("1 || 1 -> ", 1 || 1, "\n");
print ("1 || 0 -> ", 1 || 0, "\n");
```

This script generates the following output:

```
$n=2
increment after $n=2
increment before $n=3
decrement after $n=2
decrement before $n=1
$n+2=4
$n-2=0
$n*2=4
$n/2=1
$r=3.14
$r*2=6.28
$r/2=1.57
1 && 1 -> 1
1 && 0 -> 0
1 || 1 -> 1
1 || 0 -> 1
```

4.17.7 String Operators

Operations on string types are more complex and usually require using string functions (discussed later). The only simple operation that makes sense for a string (since you can't add or subtract a string) is concatenation. Strings are concatenated with the "." operator.

```
$firstname = "Bob";
$lastname = "Smith";
$fullname = $firstname . " " . $lastname;
print "$fullname\n";
```

results in the output:

```
Bob Smith
```

However, several simple matching operations are available:

```
if ($value =~ /abc/) { print "contains 'abc'\n"};
$value =~ s/abc/def/;    # change 'abc' to 'def'
$value =~ tr/a-z/A-Z/;   # translate to upper case
```

The experienced Linux or UNIX user will recognize the substitute syntax from **vi** and **sed** as well as the translation syntax based on the **tr** command.

4.17.8 Comparison Operators

You'll also want operators to compare values to one another. Comparison operators are the usual suspects (Figure 4–34).

Operation	Numeric values	String values
Equal to	==	eq
Not equal to	!=	ne
Greater than	>	gt
Greater than or equal to	>=	ge
Less than	<	lt
Less than or equal to	<=	le

Figure 4–34 Perl comparison operators.

In the case of greater-than or less-than comparisons with strings, this compares their sorting order. In most cases you're usually most concerned with comparing strings for equivalence (and lack thereof).

4.17.9   If, While, For and foreach Loop Constructs

An essential part of any programming language is the ability to execute different statements depending on the value of a variable and create loops for repetitive tasks or indexing through array values. If statements and while loops in Perl are similar to those in the C language.

In an "if" statement, a comparison operator is used to compare two values, and different sets of statements are executed depending on the result of the comparison (true or false):

```
$i = 0;
if ( $i == 0 ) {
    print "it's true\n";
} else {
    print "it's false\n";
}
```

results in "it's true" being printed. As with C, other comparison operators can be != (not equal), < (less than), > (greater than), among others.

You could also loop in a while statement to print the text until the comparison was no longer true:

```
while ( $i == 0 ) {
    print "it's true\n";
    ...
    <do some things that may modify the value of $i>
    ...
}
```

Perl also handles both "for" loops from C and "foreach" loops from the C shell:

```
for ($i = 0 ; $i < 10 ; $i++ ) {
    print $i, " ";
}
print "\n";
```

counts from 0 to 9 and prints the value (without a newline until the end) and generates:

```
0 1 2 3 4 5 6 7 8 9
```

A foreach loop looks like this:

```
foreach $n (1..15) {
    print $n, " ";
}
print "\n";
```

and generates about what you would expect:

```
1 2 3 4 5 6 7 8 9 10 11 12 13 14 15
```

4.17.10 File I/O

One big improvement in Perl over shell scripts is the ability to do input and output to specific files rather than just the standard input, output, or error channels. You still can access standard input and output:

```
while (@line=<stdin>) {
   foreach $i (@line) {
      print "->", $i;              # also reads in EOL
   }
}
```

This script will read each line from the standard input and print it. However, perhaps you have a specific data file you wish to read from:

```
$FILE="info.dat";
open (FILE);                       # name of var, not eval
@array = <FILE>;
close (FILE);
foreach $line (@array) {
   print "$line";
}
```

This Perl script opens "info.dat" and reads all its lines into the array called "array" (clever name, wouldn't you say?). It then does the same as the previous script and prints out each line.

4.17.11 Functions

To be able to effectively separate various tasks a program performs, especially if the same task is needed in several places, a language needs to provide a *subroutine* or *function* capability. The Korn shell provides a weak type of function implemented through the command interface, and it is the only major shell that provides functions at all. Of course, the C language does, but script writers had a harder time of it before Perl came along.

Perl functions are simple to use, although the syntax can get complicated. A simple example of a Perl function will give you the idea:

```
sub pounds2dollars {
   $EXCHANGE_RATE = 1.54;          # modify when necessary
   $pounds = $_[0];
   return ($EXCHANGE_RATE * $pounds);
}
```

This function changes a value specified in pounds sterling (British money) into US dollars (given an exchange rate of $1.54 to the pound, which can be modified as necessary). The special variable $_[0] references the first argument to the function. To call the function, our Perl script would look like this:

```
$book = 3.0;                          # price in British pounds
$value = pounds2dollars($book);
print "Value in dollars = $value\n";
```

When we run this script (which includes the Perl function at the end), we get:

```
Value in dollars = 4.62
```

In the next section, we'll see an example of a function that returns more than one value.

4.17.12 Library Functions

One capability that is conspicuously absent from shell scripting is that of making Linux system calls. Perl provides an interface to many Linux system calls. The interface is via Perl library functions, not directly through the system call library, therefore its use is dependent on the implementation and version of Perl, and you should consult the documentation for your version for specific information. When an interface is available, it is usually very much like its C library counterpart.

Without even realizing it, we looked at a few Perl functions in previous sections when we saw the use of open(), close(), and print(). Another simple example of a useful system-level function is:

```
exit(1);
```

to exit a Perl program and pass the specified return code to the shell. Perl also provides a special exit function to print a message to stdout and exit with the current error code:

```
open(FILE) or die("Cannot open file.");
```

Thus if the call to open() fails, the die() function will be executed, causing the error message to be written to stdout and the Perl program to exit with the error code returned by the failure from open().

Some string functions to assist in manipulating string values are length(), index(), and split():

```
$len = length($fullname);
```

sets the $len variable to the length of the text stored in the string variable $fullname. To locate one string inside another:

```
$i = index($fullname, "Smith");
```

The value of $i will be zero if the string begins with the text you specify as the search string (the second argument). To divide up a line of text based on a delimiting character (for example, if you want to separate the tokens from the Linux password file into its various parts):

```
($username, $password, $uid, $gid, $name, $home, $shell)
                              = split(/:/, $line)
```

In this case, the split() function returns an array of values found in the string specified by $line and separated by a colon. We have specified separate variables in which to store each item in this array so we can use the values more easily than indexing into an array.

Another common function provides your Perl program with the time and date:

```perl
($s, $m, $h, $dy, $mo, $yr, $wd, $yd, $dst) = gmtime();
$mo++;                      # month begins counting at zero
$yr+=1900;                  # Perl returns years since 1900
print "The date is $mo/$dy/$yr.\n";
print "The time is $h:$m:$s.\n";
```

The code above produces the following result:

```
The date is 3/25/2005.
The time is 13:40:27.
```

Note that gmtime() returns 9 values. The Perl syntax is to specify these values in parentheses (as you would if you were assigning multiple values to an array).

4.17.13 Command-Line Arguments

Another useful capability is to be able to pass command-line arguments to a Perl script. Shell scripts provide a very simple interface to command-line arguments, while C programs provide a slightly more complex (but more flexible) interface. The Perl interface is somewhere in between:

```perl
$n = $#ARGV+1;  # number of arguments (beginning at zero)
print $n, " args: \n";
for ( $i = 0 ; $i < $n ; $i++ ) {
    print "    @ARGV[$i]\n";
}
```

This Perl script prints the number of arguments that were supplied on the **perl** command (after the name of the Perl script itself) and then prints out each argument on a separate line.

We can modify our pounds-to-dollars script from before to allow a value in British pounds to be specified on the command line:

```perl
if ( $#ARGV < 0 ) {  # if no argument given
    print "Specify value in to convert to dollars\n";
    exit
}
$poundvalue = @ARGV[0];      # get value from command line

$dollarvalue = pounds2dollars($poundvalue);
```

```
print "Value in dollars = $dollarvalue\n";

sub pounds2dollars {
   $EXCHANGE_RATE = 1.54;   # modify when necessary

   $pounds = $_[0];
   return ($EXCHANGE_RATE * $pounds);
}
```

4.17.14 A Real-World Example

All of these short examples should have given you the flavor for how Perl works, but so far we haven't done anything that's really very useful. So let's take what we've seen and write a Perl script to print out a table of information about a loan. We define a command with the syntax shown in Figure 4–35.

Utility: **loan** -a amount -p payment -r rate

loan prints a table given a loan amount, interest rate, and payment to be made each month. The table shows how many months will be required to pay off the loan as well as how much interest and principal will be paid each month. All arguments are required.

Figure 4–35 Description of the **loan** command written in Perl.

The Perl script loan.pl is available online (see the Preface for more information) and looks like this:

```
# show loan interest

$i=0;
while ( $i < $#ARGV) {                    # process args
   if ( @ARGV[$i] eq "-r" ) {
      $RATE=@ARGV[++$i];                  # interest rate
   } else {
      if ( @ARGV[$i] eq "-a" ) {
         $AMOUNT=@ARGV[++$i];             # loan amount
      } else {
         if ( @ARGV[$i] eq "-p" ) {
            $PAYMENT=@ARGV[++$i];  # payment amount
         } else {
            print "Unknown argument (@ARGV[$i])\n";
            exit
         }
      }
   }
   $i++;
```

```perl
}

if ($AMOUNT == 0 || $RATE == 0 || $PAYMENT == 0) {
    print "Specify -r rate -a amount -p payment\n";
    exit
}

print "Original balance: \$$AMOUNT\n";
print "Interest rate:    ${RATE}%\n";
print "Monthly payment:  \$$PAYMENT\n";
print "\n";
print "Month\tPayment\tInterest\tPrincipal\tBalance\n\n";

$month=1;
$rate=$RATE/12/100;        # get actual monthly percentage rate
$balance=$AMOUNT;
$payment=$PAYMENT;

while ($balance > 0) {
# round up interest amount
    $interest=roundUpAmount($rate * $balance);
    $principal=roundUpAmount($payment - $interest);
    if ( $balance < $principal ) {      # last payment
        $principal=$balance;            # don't pay too much!
        $payment=$principal + $interest;
    }
    $balance = roundUpAmount($balance - $principal);
    print
"$month\t\$$payment\t\$$interest\t\t\$$principal\t\t\$$balance\n";
    $month++;
}

sub roundUpAmount {
#
# in: floating point monetary value
# out: value rounded (and truncated) to the nearest cent
#
    $value=$_[0];

    $newvalue = ( int ( ( $value * 100 ) +.5 ) ) / 100;

    return ($newvalue);
}
```

If I want to pay $30 a month on my $300 credit card balance and the interest rate is 12.5% APR, my payment schedule looks like this:

```
$ perl loan.pl -r 12.5 -a 300 -p 30
Original balance: $300
Interest rate:      12.5%
Monthly payment:   $30
```

Month	Payment	Interest	Principal	Balance
1	$30	$3.13	$26.87	$273.13
2	$30	$2.85	$27.15	$245.98
3	$30	$2.56	$27.44	$218.54
4	$30	$2.28	$27.72	$190.82
5	$30	$1.99	$28.01	$162.81
6	$30	$1.7	$28.3	$134.51
7	$30	$1.4	$28.6	$105.91
8	$30	$1.1	$28.9	$77.01
9	$30	$0.8	$29.2	$47.81
10	$30	$0.5	$29.5	$18.31
11	$18.5	$0.19	$18.31	$0

```
$ _
```

So I find it will take 11 months to pay off the balance at $30 per month, but the last payment will only be $18.31. If I want to pay it off faster than that, I know I need to raise my monthly payment!

CHAPTER REVIEW

Checklist

In this chapter, I described utilities that:

- filter files
- sort files
- compare files
- archive files
- find files
- schedule commands
- support programmable text processing
- create hard and soft links
- substitute users
- check for mail
- transform files

- look at raw file contents
- mount file systems
- prepare documents
- allow you to write Perl scripts

Quiz

1. Under what circumstances would you archive files using **tar**?
2. How would you convert the contents of a file to uppercase?
3. What is the difference between **cmp** and **diff**?
4. Describe what it means to "mount" a file system.
5. Which process serves the **crontab** system?
6. What additional functionality does an *extended* regular expression have?
7. What are the main differences between **sed** and **gawk**?
8. When do you need the **su** command?
9. What argument causes **gzip** to write the compressed file to stdout rather than a file?
10. Under what circumstances would you use a symbolic link instead of a hard link?
11. What are the drawbacks of using a symbolic link?
12. What are some ways that Perl makes script programming easier than conventional shell scripts?

Exercises

1. Ask your system administrator (or someone knowledgeable) to demonstrate the use of **tar** to produce a backup tape of your files. [level: *easy*]
2. Explain how you would use **crontab** to schedule a script that finds and removes your old temporary files in /tmp at the start of each day. [level: *medium*]

Projects

1. Write a command pipeline to find files in a directory hierarchy (e.g. your home directory) that have not been accessed for 30 days and compress them. [level: *easy*]
2. Modify the **loan** Perl script so that you can pass a list of payments to it rather than using the same payment value for every month. [level: *medium*]

5

The Linux Shells

Motivation

A shell is a program that sits between you and the raw Linux operating system. There are three shells that are commonly used by Linux users—the Bourne Again shell (bash), the Korn shell (ksh), and the C shell (tcsh). All of these shells share a common core set of operations that make life in the Linux system a little easier. For example, all shells allow the output of a process to be stored in a file or "piped" to another process. They also allow the use of wildcards in filenames, so it's easy to say things like "list all of the files whose name ends with the suffix '.c'." This chapter describes all of the common core shell facilities, and subsequent chapters describe the special features of each individual shell.

Prerequisites

In order to understand this chapter, you should have already read Chapter 1, "What Is Linux?" and Chapter 3, "GNU Utilities for Nonprogrammers" Some of the utilities that I mention are described fully in Chapter 4, "GNU Utilities for Power Users"

Objectives

In this chapter, I'll explain and demonstrate the common shell features, including I/O redirection, piping, command substitution, and simple job control.

Presentation

The information in this section is presented in the form of several sample command sessions. If you don't have access to a Linux system, march through the sessions anyway and hopefully you'll be able to try them out later.

Utilities

This section introduces the following utilities, listed in alphabetical order:

chsh	kill	ps
echo	nohup	sleep

Shell Commands

This section introduces the following shell commands, listed in alphabetical order:

echo	exit	tee
eval	kill	umask
exec	shift	wait

5.1   Introduction

A shell is a program that is an interface between a user and the raw operating system. It makes basic facilities such as multitasking and piping easy to use, as well as adding useful file-specific features such as wildcards and I/O redirection. There are three shells in common use today, listed here in approximate order of popularity:

- the Bourne Again shell (bash)
- the Korn shell (ksh)
- the C shell (csh)

All of these shells come with Linux, but they may not all be installed on your system depending on your selection of optional packages. The names vary a bit between UNIX and Linux systems. The major difference is that /bin/sh is the Bourne shell on a UNIX system but on a Linux system it is a symbolic link to /bin/bash. The shells and their common naming are shown in Figure 5–1.

Shell	Linux	UNIX
Bash	sh or bash	bash
Korn shell	ksh, pdksh, or zsh	ksh
C shell	csh or tcsh	csh

Figure 5–1   Comparison of Linux and UNIX shell names.

The shell that you use is a matter of personal taste based on its power, compatibility, and availability. The Korn shell was designed to be upward compatible with the original UNIX Bourne shell, and incorporates the best features of the Bourne and C shells plus some more of its own. Bash also takes a "best of all worlds" approach, including features from all the other major shells. Bash is the default shell on Linux systems, but we will examine all three shells in the subsequent chapters.

5.2 Selecting a Shell

When you first get an account on a Linux machine, the account will use Bourne Again Shell (/bin/bash) as its login shell. But using **bash** is not a requirement, you can choose any shell to be your login shell.

To change your default login shell, use the **chsh** utility (Figure 5–2).

Utility: **chsh**

---

chsh allows you to change your default login shell. It prompts you for the full pathname of the new shell, which is then used as your shell for subsequent logins.

Figure 5–2   Description of the **chsh** command.

In order to use **chsh**, you must know the full pathnames of the shells (Figure 5–3).

Shell	Full pathname
Bash	/bin/bash (or /bin/sh)
Korn	/bin/ksh
C	/bin/tcsh (or /bin/csh)

Figure 5–3   Common shell locations.

In the following example, I changed my default login shell from Bash to a C shell:

```
$ chsh                  ...change the login shell.
Changing shell for glass
Password:               ...must verify you are who you say.
New shell [/bin/bash]: /bin/tcsh     ...enter full pathname.
$ ^D                    ...terminate login shell.

login: glass            ...log back in again.
Password:               ...secret.
% _                     ...this time I'm in a C shell.
```

Another way to find out the full pathname of your login shell is to type the following:

```
$ echo $SHELL     ...display the name of my login shell.
/bin/tcsh         ...full pathname of the C shell.
$ _
```

This example illustrated the *echo* shell command and a shell variable called *SHELL*. Both of these new facilities—echoing and variables—are discussed later in this chapter.

5.3   Shell Operations

When a shell is invoked, either automatically during a login, or manually from a keyboard or script, it follows a preset sequence:

1. It reads a special startup file, typically located in the user's home directory, that contains some initialization information. Each shell's startup sequence is different, so I'll leave the specific details to later chapters.
2. It displays a prompt and waits for a user command.
3. If the user enters a *Control-D* character on a line of its own, this is interpreted by the shell as meaning "end-of-input," and causes the shell to terminate; otherwise, the shell executes the user's command and returns to step 2.

Commands range from simple utility invocations like this:

```
$ ls
```

to complex-looking pipeline sequences like this:

```
$ ps -ef | sort | ul -tdumb | lp
```

If you ever need to enter a command that is longer than a line on your terminal, you may terminate a portion of a command by a backslash (\) character, and the shell allows you to continue the command on the next line:

```
$ echo this is a very long shell command and needs to \
be extended with the line continuation character. Note \
that a single command may be extended for several lines.
this is a very long shell command and needs to be extended with
the line continuation character. Note that a single command may
be extended for several lines.
$ _
```

5.4   Executable Files Versus Built-in Commands

Most Linux commands invoke utility programs that are stored in the directory hierarchy. Utilities are stored in files that have execute permission. For example, when you type:

```
$ ls
```

the shell locates the executable program called "ls," which is typically found in the "/bin" directory, and executes it. The way that the shell finds a utility is described later in this chapter. In addition to its ability to locate and execute utilities, the shell contains several built-in commands, which it recognizes and executes internally. I'll describe two of the most useful ones now: *echo* and *cd*.

5.4.1   Displaying Information: echo

The built-in echo command displays its arguments to standard output (Figure 5–4).

Shell Command: **echo** {*arg*}*

---

echo is a built-in shell command that displays all of its arguments to standard output. By default, it appends a newline to the output.

Figure 5–4   Description of the *echo* shell command.

All of the shells we will see contain this built-in function, but you may also invoke the utility called **echo** (found in /bin) instead. This is sometimes useful, as some arguments and subtle behavior may vary between the different built-ins and it can be confusing if you write scripts in more than one of these shells. We'll look at writing shell scripts shortly.

5.4.2   Changing Directories: cd

The built-in *cd* command changes the current working directory of the shell to a new location, and was described fully in Chapter 3, "GNU Utilities for Nonprogrammers."

5.5   Metacharacters

Some characters are processed specially by the shell, and are known as *metacharacters*. All shells share a core set of common metacharacters, whose meanings are given in Figure 5–5.

Symbol	Meaning
>	Output redirection; writes standard output to a file.
>>	Output redirection; appends standard output to a file.
<	Input redirection; reads standard input from a file.
*	File substitution wildcard; matches zero or more characters.
?	File substitution wildcard; matches any single character.
[...]	File substitution wildcard; matches any character between brackets.

Figure 5–5   Shell metacharacters. (Part 1 of 2)

Symbol	Meaning
`command`	Command substitution; replaced by the output from *command*.
|	Pipe symbol; sends the output of one process to the input of another.
;	Used to sequence commands.
||	Conditional execution; executes a command if the previous one failed.
&&	Conditional execution; executes a command if the previous one succeeded.
(...)	Groups commands.
&	Runs a command in the background.
#	All characters that follow up to a newline are ignored by the shell and programs (i.e., a comment).
$	Expands the value of a variable.
\	Prevents special interpretation of the next character.
<<*tok*	Input redirection; reads standard input from script up to *tok*.

Figure 5–5   Shell metacharacters. (Part 2 of 2)

When you enter a command, the shell scans it for metacharacters and processes them specially. When all metacharacters have been processed, the command is finally executed. To turn off the special meaning of a metacharacter, precede it by a \ character. Here's an example:

```
$ echo hi > file      ...store output of echo in "file".
$ cat file            ...look at the contents of "file".
hi
$ echo hi \> file     ...inhibit > metacharacter.
hi > file             ...> is treated like other characters.
$ _                   ...and output comes to terminal instead
```

This chapter describes the meaning of each metacharacter in the order listed in Figure 5–5.

5.6   Redirection

The shell redirection facility allows you to:

- store the output of a process to a file (*output redirection*)
- use the contents of a file as input to a process (*input redirection*)

Let's have a look at each facility, in turn.

5.6.1   Output Redirection

Output redirection is handy because it allows you to save a process's output into a file so it can be listed, printed, edited, or used as input to a future process. To redirect output, use either the > or >> metacharacters. The sequence

```
$ command > fileName
```

sends the standard output of *command* to the file with name *fileName*. The shell creates the file with name *fileName* if it doesn't already exist; otherwise, it overwrites its previous contents. If the file already exists and doesn't have write permission, an error occurs. In the following example, I created a file called "alice.txt" by redirecting the output of the **cat** utility. Without parameters, **cat** simply copies its standard input—which in the case is this keyboard—to its standard output.

```
$ cat > alice.txt                    ...create a text file.
In my dreams that fill the night,
I see your eyes,
^D                                   ...end-of-input.
$ cat alice.txt                      ...look at its contents.
In my dreams that fill the night,
I see your eyes,
$ _
```

The sequence

```
$ command >> fileName
```

appends the standard output of *command* to the file with name *fileName*. The shell creates the file with name *fileName* if it doesn't already exist. In the following example, I appended some text to the existing "alice.txt" file:

```
$ cat >> alice.txt            ...append to the file.
And I fall into them,
Like Alice fell into Wonderland.
^D                            ...end-of-input.
$ cat alice.txt               ...look at the new contents.
In my dreams that fill the night,
I see your eyes,
And I fall into them,
Like Alice fell into Wonderland.
$ _
```

By default, both forms of output redirection leave the standard error channel connected to the terminal. However, both shells have variations of output redirection that allow them to redirect the standard error channel. The C, Korn, and Bash shells also provide protection against accidental overwriting of a file due to output redirection. These facilities are described in later chapters.

5.6.2   Input Redirection

Input redirection is useful because it allows you to prepare a process's input and store it in a file for later use. To redirect input, use either the < or << metacharacters. The sequence:

```
$ command < fileName
```

executes *command* using the contents of the file *fileName* as its standard input. If the file doesn't exist or doesn't have read permission, an error occurs. In the following example, I sent myself the contents of "alice.txt" via the **mail** utility:

```
$ mail glass < alice.txt            ...send myself mail.
$ mail                              ...look at my mail.
Mail version 8.1 6/6/93.  Type ? for help.
>N  1 glass@utdallas.edu Mon Feb  2 13:29   17/550
& 1                                ...read message #1.
From: Graham Glass <glass@utdallas.edu>
To: glass@utdallas.edu
In my dreams that fill the night,
I see your eyes,
And I fall into them,
Like Alice fell into Wonderland
& q                                ...quit mail.
$ _
```

When the shell encounters a sequence of the form:

```
$ command << word
```

it copies its standard input up to but not including the line starting with *word* into a buffer and then executes *command* using the contents of the buffer as its standard input. This facility is used almost exclusively to allow shell programs (*scripts*) to supply the standard input to other commands as inline text, and is revisited in more detail later on in this chapter.

5.7   Filename Substitution (Wildcards)

All shells support a wildcard facility that allows you to select files from the file system that satisfy a particular name pattern. Any word on the command line that contains at least one of the wildcard metacharacters is treated as a pattern, and is replaced by an alphabetically sorted list of all the matching filenames. This act of pattern replacement is called *globbing*. The wildcards and their meanings listed in Figure 5–6.

Wildcard	Meaning
*	Matches any string, including the empty string.
?	Matches any single character.
[..]	Matches any one of the characters between the brackets. A range of characters may be specified by separating a pair of characters by a dash.

Figure 5–6   Shell wildcards.

You may prevent the shell from processing the wildcards in a string by surrounding the string by single quotes (apostrophes) or double quotes. See the "quoting" section later in this chapter for more details. A / character in a filename must be matched explicitly. Here are some examples of wildcards in action:

```
$ ls -FR              ...recursively list my current directory.
a.c   b.c   cc.c  dir1/  dir2/

dir1:
d.c  e.e

dir2:
f.d  g.c
$ ls *.c                       ...any text followed by ".c".
a.c   b.c   cc.c
$ ls ?.c                       ...one character followed by ".c".
a.c   b.c
$ ls [ac]*             ...any string beginning with "a" or "c".
a.c   cc.c
$ ls [A-Za-z]*         ...any string beginning with a letter.
a.c   b.c   cc.c
$ ls dir*/*.c          ...all ".c" files in "dir*" directories.
dir1/d.c  dir2/g.c
$ ls */*.c             ...all ".c" files in any subdirectory.
dir1/d.c  dir2/g.c
$ ls *2/?.? ?.?
a.c   b.c   dir2/f.d  dir2/g.c
$ _
```

The result of a pattern that has no matches is shell-specific. Some shells have a mechanism for turning off wildcard replacement.

5.7.1   Pipes
The shell allows you to use the standard output of one process as the standard input of another process by connecting the processes together using the pipe (|) metacharacter. The sequence

```
$ command1 | command2
```

causes the standard output of *command1* to "flow through" to the standard input of *command2*. Any number of commands may be connected by pipes. A sequence of commands chained together in this way is called a *pipeline*.

Pipelines support one of the basic Linux philosophies, which is that large problems can often be solved by a chain of smaller processes, each performed by a relatively small, reusable utility.

The standard error channel is not piped through a standard pipeline, although some shells support this capability.

In the following example, I piped the output of the **ls** utility to the input of the **wc** utility to count the number of files in the current directory. See Chapter 3, "GNU Utilities for Nonprogrammers" for a description of **wc**.

```
$ ls              ...list the current directory.
a.c    b.c    cc.c    dir1    dir2
$ ls | wc -w      ...count the entries.
      5
$ _
```

Figure 5–7 illustrates the pipeline.

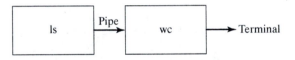

Figure 5–7   A simple pipeline.

In the next example, I piped the contents of the "/etc/passwd" file into the **gawk** utility to extract the first field of each line. The output of **gawk** was then piped to the sort utility, which sorted the lines alphabetically. The result was a sorted list of every user on the system. The **gawk** utility is described fully in Chapter 4, "GNU Utilities for Power Users."

```
$ head -4 /etc/passwd       ...look at the password file.
root:eJ2S10rVe8mCg:0:1:Operator:/:/bin/csh
nobody:*:65534:65534::/:
daemon:*:1:1::/:
sys:*:2:2::/:/bin/csh
$ cat /etc/passwd | gawk -F: '{ print $1 }' | sort
ables
adm
bin
daemon
glass
mail
news
```

```
nobody
root
sync
tim
uucp
$ _
```

Figure 5–8 illustrates the pipeline:

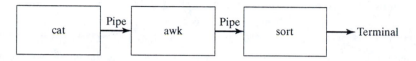

Figure 5–8   A pipeline that sorts.

There's a very handy utility called **tee** that allows you to copy the output of a pipe to a file and still allow it to flow down the pipeline. As you might have guessed, the name of this utility comes from the "T" connections that plumbers use. Figure 5–9 describes how **tee** works.

Utility: **tee** -ia {fileName}+

The **tee** utility copies its standard input to the specified files and to its standard output. The **-a** option causes the input to be appended to the files rather than overwriting them. The **-i** option causes interrupts to be ignored.

Figure 5–9   Description of the **tee** command.

In the following example, I copied the output of **who** to a file called "who.capture," and also let it pass through to **sort**:

```
$ who | tee who.capture | sort
ables     pts/6    May  3 17:54 (gw.waterloo.com)
glass     pts/0    May  3 18:49 (blackfoot.utdall)
posey     pts/2    Apr 23 17:44 (:0.0)
posey     pts/4    Apr 23 17:44 (:0.0)
$ cat who.capture              ...look at the captured data.
glass     pts/0    May  3 18:49 (blackfoot.utdalla)
posey     pts/2    Apr 23 17:44 (:0.0)
posey     pts/4    Apr 23 17:44 (:0.0)
ables     pts/6    May  3 17:54 (gw.waterloo.com)
$
```

Notice that the output captured is directly from the **who** utility before the list is sorted.

5.8   Command Substitution

A command surrounded by grave accents (`) is executed and its standard output is inserted in
the command in its place. Any newlines in the output are replaced by spaces. For example:

```
$ echo the date today is `date`
the date today is Wed Feb 2 00:41:55 CST 2005
$ _
```

It's possible to do some crafty things by combining pipes and command substitution. For example, the **who** utility (described in Chapter 9, "Networking and the Internet") produces a list of all
the users on the system, and the **wc** utility (described in Chapter 3, "GNU Utilities for Nonprogrammers") counts the number of words/lines in its input. By piping the output of **who** to the **wc**
utility, it's possible to count the number of users on the system:

```
$ who            ...look at the output of who.
posey    ttyp0   Jan 22 15:31   (blackfoot:0.0)
glass    ttyp3   Feb  3 00:41   (bridge05.utdalla)
huynh    ttyp5   Jan 10 10:39   (atlas.utdallas.e)
$ echo there are `who | wc -l` users on the system
there are 3 users on the system
$ _
```

The result of command substitution may be used as part of another command. For example, the
vim utility allows you to specify a list of files to be edited on the command line, which are then
visited by the editor one after the other. The **grep** utility, described in Chapter 4, "GNU Utilities
for Power Users" has a **-l** option that returns a list of all the files on the command line that contain a specified pattern. By combining these two features using command substitution, it's possible to specify using a single command that **vim** be invoked upon all files ending in ".c" that
contain the pattern "debug":

```
$ vim `grep -l debug *.c`
```

5.9   Sequences

If you enter a series of simple commands or pipelines separated by semicolons, the shell will
execute them in sequence, from left to right. This facility is useful for type-ahead (and think-
ahead) addicts who like to specify an entire sequence of actions at once. Here's an example:

```
$ date; pwd; ls        ...execute three commands in sequence.
Wed Feb  2 00:11:10 CST 2005
/home/glass/wild
a.c   b.c   cc.c  dir1  dir2
$ _
```

Each command in a sequence may be individually I/O redirected:

```
$ date > date.txt; ls; pwd > pwd.txt
a.c         b.c         cc.c        date.txt   dir1       dir2
$ cat date.txt                ...look at output of date.
Wed Feb  2 00:12:16 CST 2005
$ cat pwd.txt                 ...look at output of pwd.
/home/glass
$ _
```

5.9.1   Conditional Sequences

Every Linux process terminates with an exit value. By convention, an exit value of 0 means that the process completed successfully, and a nonzero exit value indicates failure. All built-in shell commands return 1 if they fail. You may construct sequences that make use of this exit value:

- If you specify a series of commands separated by && tokens, the next command is executed only if the previous command returns an exit code of 0.
- If you specify a series of commands separated by || tokens, the next command is executed only if the previous command returns a nonzero exit code.

The && and || metacharacters therefore mirror the operation of their counterpart C operators.

For example, if the C compiler **gcc** compiles a program without fatal errors, it creates an executable program called "a.out" and returns an exit code of 0; otherwise, it returns a nonzero exit code. The following conditional sequence compiles a program called "myprog.c" and only executes the "a.out" file if the compilation succeeds:

```
$ gcc myprog.c && a.out
```

The following example compiles a program called "myprog.c" and displays an error message if the compilation fails:

```
$ gcc myprog.c || echo compilation failed.
```

Exit codes are discussed in more detail toward the end of this chapter.

5.10 Grouping Commands

Commands may be grouped by placing them between parentheses, which causes them to be executed by a child shell (*subshell*). The group of commands shares the same standard input, standard output, and standard error channels, and may be redirected and piped as if it were a simple command. Here are some examples:

```
$ date; ls; pwd > out.txt          ...execute a sequence
Wed Feb  2 00:33:12 CST 2005       ...output from date.
```

```
a.c        b.c                      ...output from ls.
$ cat out.txt                       ...only pwd was redirected.
/home/glass
$ (date; ls; pwd) > out.txt         ...group and then redirect.
$ cat out.txt                       ...all output was redirected.
Wed Feb  2 00:33:28 CST 2005
a.c
b.c
/home/glass
$ _
```

5.11 Background Processing

If you follow a simple command, pipeline, sequence of pipelines, or group of commands by the & metacharacter, a subshell is created to execute the commands as a background process. The background process runs concurrently with the parent shell, and does not take control of the keyboard. Background processing is therefore very useful for performing several tasks simultaneously, as long as the background tasks do not require keyboard input. In windowed environments, it's more common to run each command within its own window than to run many commands in one window using the background facility. When a background process is created, the shell displays some information that may be used to control the process at a later stage. The exact format of this information is shell-specific.

In the following example, I executed a **find** command in the foreground to locate the file called "a.c". This command took quite a while to execute, so I decided to run the next **find** command in the background. The shell displayed the background process's unique process ID number and then immediately gave me another prompt, allowing me to continue my work. Note that the output of the background process continued to be displayed at my terminal, which was inconvenient. In the next few sections, I'll show you how you can use the process ID number to control the background process, and how to prevent background processes from messing up your terminal.

```
$ find . -name a.c -print     ...search for "a.c".
./wild/a.c
./reverse/tmp/a.c
$ find . -name b.c -print &    ...search in the background.
27174                          ...process ID number
$ date                         ...run "date" in the foreground.
./wild/b.c                     ...output from background "find".
Wed Feb  2 18:10:42 CST 2005   ...output from date.
$ ./reverse/tmp/b.c            ...more from background "find"
        ...came after we got the shell prompt so we don't
        ...get another one.
```

You may specify several background commands on a single line by separating each command by
an ampersand:

```
$ date & pwd &          ...create two background processes.
27310                           ...process ID of "date".
27311                           ...process ID of "pwd".
/home/glass                     ...output from "date".
$ Wed Feb  2 18:37:22 CST 2005  ...output from "pwd".
$ _
```

5.12 Redirecting Background Processes

To prevent the output from a background process from arriving at your terminal, redirect its output to a file. In the following example, I redirected the standard output of the **find** command to a
file called "find.txt". As the command was executing, I watched it grow using the **ls** command:

```
$ find . -name a.c -print > find.txt &
27188                   ...process ID of "find".
$ ls -lG find.txt       ...look at "find.txt".
-rw-r--r-- 1 glass        0 Feb  3 18:11 find.txt
$ ls -lG find.txt       ...watch it grow.
-rw-r--r-- 1 glass       29 Feb  3 18:11 find.txt
$ cat find.txt          ...list "find.txt".
./wild/a.c
./reverse/tmp/a.c
$ _
```

Another alternative is to mail it to yourself:

```
$ find . -name a.c -print | mail glass &
27193
$ gcc program.c         ...do other useful work.
$ mail                  ...read my mail.
Mail version 8.1 6/6/93.  Type ? for help.
>N  1 glass@utdallas.edu Mon Feb  3 18:12   10/346
& 1
From: Graham Glass <glass@utdallas.edu>
To: glass@utdallas.edu

./wild/a.c              ...the output from "find".
./reverse/tmp/a.c
& q
$ _
```

Some utilities also produce output on the standard error channel, which must be redirected *in addition* to standard output. The next chapter describes in detail how this is done, but I'll supply an example in Bash and the Korn shell now, just in case you're interested:

```
$ man ps > ps.txt &          ...save documentation in background.
27203
$ Reformatting page.  Wait   ...shell prompt comes here.
done                         ...standard error messages.
man ps > ps.txt 2>&1 &       ...redirect error channel too.
27212
$ _          ...all output is redirected.
```

5.13 Shell Programs (Scripts)

Any series of shell commands may be stored inside a regular text file for later execution. A file that contains shell commands is called a *script*. Before you can run a script, you must give it execute permission by using the **chmod** utility. Then, to run it, you only need to type its name. Scripts are useful for storing commonly used sequences of commands, and range in complexity from simple one-liners to full blown programs. The control structures supported by the languages built into the shells are sufficiently powerful to enable scripts to perform a wide variety of tasks. System administrators find scripts particularly useful for automating repetitive administrative tasks such as warning users when their disk usage goes beyond a certain limit.

When a script is run, the system determines which shell the script was written for, and then executes the shell using the script as its standard input. The system decides which shell the script is written for by examining the first line of the script. Here are the rules that it uses:

- If the first line is just a #, then the script is interpreted by the shell from which you executed this script as a command.
- If the first line is of the form #! *pathName*, then the executable program *pathName* is used to interpret the script.
- If neither rule 1 nor rule 2 applies, then the script is interpreted by Bash.

If a # appears on any other line apart from the first line, all characters up to the end of that line are treated as a comment. Scripts should be liberally commented in the interests of maintainability.

When you write your own scripts, I recommend that you use the #! form to specify which shell the script is designed for, as it's completely unambiguous and doesn't require the reader to be aware of the default rules (especially since the default is different for UNIX and Linux).

Here is an example that illustrates the construction and execution of two scripts, one for the C shell, and the other for the Korn shell:

```
$ cat > script.csh          ...create the C shell script.
#!/bin/csh
# This is a sample C shell script.
```

```
echo -n the date today is     # in csh, -n omits newline
date                          # output today's date.
^D                      ...end-of-input.
$ cat > script.ksh      ...create the Korn shell script.
#!/bin/ksh
# This is a sample Korn shell script.
echo "the date today is \c"   # in ksh, \c omits the nl
date                          # output today's date.
^D                      ...end-of-input.
$ chmod +x script.csh script.ksh    ...make them executable.
$ ls -lFG script.csh script.ksh     ...look at attributes.
-rwxr-xr-x  1 glass       138 Feb  1 19:46 script.csh*
-rwxr-xr-x  1 glass       142 Feb  1 19:47 script.ksh*
$ ./script.csh          ...execute the C shell script.
the date today is Tue Feb  1 19:50:00 CST 2005
$ ./script.ksh          ...execute the Korn shell script.
the date today is Tue Feb  1 19:50:05 CST 2005
$ _
```

The ".csh" and ".ksh" extensions of my scripts are used only for clarity; scripts can be called anything at all, and don't even need an extension.

Note the usage of "\c" and "-n" in the above examples of the **echo** command. Different versions of "/bin/echo" use one or the other to omit the newline. It may also depend on the shell being used. If the shell has a built-in *echo* function, then the specifics of "/bin/echo" won't matter. You'll want to experiment with your particular shell and echo combination; it isn't quite as simple as I implied in the above comments.

5.14 Subshells or Child Shells

When you log into a Linux system, you execute an initial login shell. This initial shell executes any simple commands that you enter. However, there are several circumstances when your current shell (the parent process) creates a new shell (a child process) to perform some tasks:

- When a grouped command is executed, such as (ls; pwd; date), the parent shell creates a child shell to execute the grouped commands. If the command is not executed in the background, the parent shell sleeps until the child shell terminates.
- When a script is executed, the parent shell creates a child shell to execute the commands in the script. If the script is not executed in the background, the parent shell sleeps until the child shell terminates.
- When a background job is executed, the parent shell creates a child shell to execute the background commands. The parent shell continues to run concurrently with the child shell.

A child shell is often called a *subshell*. Just like any other Linux process, a subshell has its own current working directory, and so *cd* commands executed in a subshell do not affect the working directory of the parent shell:

```
$ pwd               ...display my login shell's current dir.
/home/glass
$ (cd /; pwd)       ...the subshell moves and executes pwd.
/                   ...output comes from the subshell.
$ pwd               ...my login shell never moved.
/home/glass
$ _
```

Every shell contains two data areas: an environment space and a local variable space. A child shell inherits a copy of its parent's environment space and a clean local variable space (Figure 5–10).

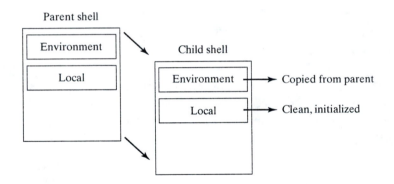

Figure 5–10 Child shell data spaces.

5.15 Variables

The shell supports two kinds of variables—*local* and *environment* variables. Both kinds of variables hold data in a string format. The main difference between them is that when a shell invokes a subshell, the child shell gets a copy of its parent shell's environment variables, but not its local variables. Environment variables are therefore used for transmitting useful information between parent shells and their children.

Every shell has a set of predefined environment variables, usually initialized by the startup files described in later chapters. Similarly, every shell has a set of predefined local variables that have special meanings to the shell. Other environment and local variables may be created as needed, and are particularly useful when writing scripts. Figure 5–11 is a list of the predefined environment variables that are common to all shells.

Name	Meaning
$HOME	The full pathname of your home directory.
$PATH	A list of directories to search for commands.
$MAIL	The full pathname of your mailbox.
$USER	Your username.
$SHELL	The full pathname of your login shell.
$TERM	The type of your terminal.

Figure 5-11 Predefined shell variables.

The syntax for assigning variables differs between shells, but the way that you access them is the same; if you prepend a $ to the name of a variable, this token sequence is replaced by the shell with the value of the named variable.

To create a variable, simply assign it a value; a variable does not have to be declared. The details of how variables are assigned are left to the specific shell chapters, but for now it's enough to know that the syntax for assigning a variable in the Bash and the Korn shell is as follows:

```
variableName=value          ...place no spaces around the =.
```

In the following example, I displayed the values of some common shell environment variables:

```
$ echo HOME = $HOME, PATH = $PATH        ...list two variables.
HOME = /home/glass, PATH = /bin:/usr/bin:/usr/sbin
$ echo MAIL = $MAIL                      ...list another.
MAIL = /var/mail/glass
$ echo USER = $USER, SHELL = $SHELL, TERM=$TERM
USER = glass, SHELL = /bin/sh, TERM=vt100
$ _
```

The next example illustrates the difference between local and environment variables. I assigned values to two local variables and then made one of them an environment variable by using the shell *export* command. I then created a child shell and displayed the values of the variables that I had assigned in the parent shell. Note that the value of the environment variable was copied into the child shell, but the value of the local variable was not. Finally, I typed a *Control-D* to terminate the child shell and restart the parent shell, and then displayed the original variables:

```
$ firstname=Graham            ..set a local variable.
$ lastname=Glass              ...set another local variable.
$ echo $firstname $lastname   ...display their values.
```

```
Graham Glass
$ export lastname        ...make "lastname" an environment var.
$ sh                     ...start a child shell; the parent sleeps.
$ echo $firstname $lastname       ...display values again.
Glass                    ...note that firstname wasn't copied.
$ ^D                     ...terminate child; the parent awakens.
$ echo $firstname $lastname       ...they remain unchanged.
Graham Glass
$ _
```

There are several common built-in variables that have a special meaning (Figure 5–12).

Name	Meaning
$$	The process ID of the shell.
$0	The name of the shell script (if applicable).
$1..$9	$n refers to the nth command-line argument (if applicable).
$*	A list of all the command-line arguments.

Figure 5–12 Special built-in shell variables.

The first special variable is especially useful for creating temporary filenames, and the rest are handy for accessing command-line arguments in shell scripts. Here's an example that illustrates all of the common special variables:

```
$ cat script.sh                          ...list the script.
echo the name of this script is $0
echo the first argument is $1
echo a list of all the arguments is $*
echo this script places the date into a temporary file
echo called $1.$$
date > $1.$$      # redirect the output of date.
ls $1.$$          # list the file.
rm $1.$$          # remove the file.
$ ./script.sh paul ringo george john        ...execute it.
the name of this script is script.sh
the first argument is paul
a list of all the arguments is paul ringo george john
this script places the date into a temporary file
called paul.24321
paul.24321
$ _
```

5.16 Quoting

There are often times when you want to inhibit the shell's wildcard-replacement, variable-substitution, and/or command-substitution mechanisms. The shell's quoting system allows you to do just that. Here's the way it works:

- Single quotes (') inhibit wildcard replacement, variable substitution, and command substitution.
- Double quotes (") inhibit wildcard replacement only.
- When quotes are nested, only the outer quotes have any effect.

The following example illustrates the difference between the two different kinds of quotes:

```
$ echo 3 * 4 = 12          ...remember, * is a wildcard.
3 a.c b.c c.c 4 = 12
$ echo "3 * 4 = 12"        ...double quotes inhibit wildcards.
3 * 4 = 12
$ echo '3 * 4 = 12'        ...single quotes inhibit wildcards.
3 * 4 = 12
$ name=Graham
```

By using single quotes (apostrophes) around the text, we inhibit all wildcarding, variable, and command substitutions:

```
$ echo 'my name is $name - date is `date` '
my name is $name and the date is `date`
```

By using double quotes around the text, we inhibit wildcarding, but allow variable and command substitutions:

```
$ echo "my name is $name - date is `date`"
my name is Graham - date is Wed Feb  2 23:14:56 CST 2005
$ _
```

5.17 Here Documents

Earlier in the chapter, I briefly mentioned the << metacharacter. I delayed its full description until now, as really it's only used in conjunction with scripts and variables. When the shell encounters a sequence of the form:

```
$ command << word
```

it copies its own standard input up to but not including the line starting with *word* into a shell buffer, and then executes *command* using the contents of the buffer as its standard input. Obviously, you should choose a sensible value for *word* that is unusual enough not to occur naturally in the text that follows. If no line containing just *word* is encountered, Bash and the Korn shell stop copying input when they reach the end of the script, whereas the C shell issues an error message. All references to shell variables in the copied text are replaced by their values. The most common use of the << metacharacter is to allow scripts to supply the standard input of other commands as inline text, rather than having to use auxiliary files. Scripts that use << are sometimes called *here documents*. Here's an example of a here document:

```
$ cat here.sh            ...look at an example of a "here" doc.
mail $1 << ENDOFTEXT
Dear $1,
 Please see me regarding some exciting news!
- $USER
ENDOFTEXT
echo mail sent to $1
$ ./here.sh glass        ...send mail to myself using the script.
mail sent to glass
$ mail                   ...look at my mail.
Mail version 8.1 6/6/93.  Type ? for help.
>N  1 glass@utdallas.edu Mon Feb  2 13:34    12/384
& 1                      ...read message #1.
From: Graham Glass <glass@utdallas.edu>
To: glass@utdallas.edu

Dear glass,
 Please see me regarding some exciting news!

- glass

& q                      ...quit out of mail.
$ _
```

5.18 Job Control

Convenient multitasking is one of the best features of Linux, so it's important to be able to obtain a listing of your current processes and control their behavior. There are two utilities and one built-in command that allow you to do this:

- **ps**, which generates a list of processes and their attributes, including their name, process ID number, controlling terminal, and owner
- **kill**, which allows you to terminate a process based on its ID number
- **wait**, which allows a shell to wait for one of its child processes to terminate

The next few sections describe these facilities in more detail.

5.18.1   Process Status: ps
The **ps** utility allows you to monitor the status of processes (Figure 5–13).

Utility: **ps** -efl

---

ps generates a listing of process status information. By default, the output is limited to processes created by your current shell. The **-e** option instructs **ps** to include all running processes. The **-f** option causes **ps** to generate a full listing. The **-l** option generates a long listing. The meaning of each **ps** column is described in the text that follows.

Figure 5–13 Description of the **ps** command.

In the following example, I made use of the **sleep** utility to delay a simple echo statement, and placed the command in the background. I then executed the ps utility to obtain a list of my shell's associated processes. Each "sh" process was a Bash shell process; one of them was my login shell, and the other was the subshell created to execute the command group.

```
$ (sleep 10; echo done) &        ...delayed echo in background.
27387                            ...the process ID number.
$ ps                             ...obtain a process status list.
  PID TTY          TIME CMD
27355 pts/3     00:00:01 sh              ...the login shell.
27387 pts/3     00:00:00 sh              ...the subshell.
27388 pts/3     00:00:00 sleep 10        ...the sleep.
27389 pts/3     00:00:00 ps              ...the ps command itself!
$ done     ...the output from the background process.
```

For the record, Figure 5–14 describes the **sleep** utility.

Utility: **sleep** *seconds*

The **sleep** utility sleeps for the specified number of seconds and then terminates.

Figure 5–14 Description of the **sleep** command.

The meanings of the common column headings of **ps** output are given in Figure 5–15.

Column	Meaning
S	The process state.
UID	The effective user ID of the process.
PID	The process ID.
PPID	The parent process ID.

Figure 5–15 **ps** output column meanings. (Part 1 of 2)

Column	Meaning
C	The percentage of CPU time that the process used in the last minute.
PRI	The process priority.
SZ	The size of the process's data and stack in kilobytes.
STIME	The time the process was created, or the date if created before today.
TTY	The controlling terminal.
TIME	The amount of CPU time used so far (MM:SS).
CMD	The name of the command.

Figure 5–15 **ps** output column meanings. (Part 2 of 2)

The S field encodes the process's state as described in Figure 5–16.

Letter	Meaning
O	Running on a processor.
R	Runable.
S	Sleeping.
T	Suspended.
Z	Zombie process.

Figure 5–16 Process state codes reported by **ps**.

The meanings of most of these terms are described later in the book; only the R and S fields will make sense right now. Here's an example of some user-oriented output from **ps**:

```
$ (sleep 10; echo done) &
27462
$ ps -f              ...request user-oriented output.
UID        PID  PPID  C STIME TTY          TIME CMD
glass     24379 23708  0 16:41 pts0     00:00:00 ksh
glass     24382 24379  0 16:41 pts0     00:00:00 sleep 10
glass     24803 24382  0 17:28 pts0     00:00:00 ps -f
$ done               ...output from previous command
```

If you're interested in tracking the movements of other users on your system, try the **-e** and **-f**
option of **ps:**

```
$ ps -ef           ...list all users' processes.
UID         PID  PPID  C STIME TTY        TIME CMD
root          1     0  0 Aug25 ?      00:00:02 init [5]
root          2     1  0 Aug25 ?      00:00:00 [ksoftirqd/0]
root          3     1  0 Aug25 ?      00:00:00 [events/0]
root          4     1  0 Aug25 ?      00:00:01 [kblockd/0]
root          5     1  0 Aug25 ?      00:00:00 [kapmd]
root          7     1  0 Aug25 ?      00:00:00 [pdflush]
root          8     1  0 Aug25 ?      00:00:05 [kswapd0]
root        742     1  0 Aug25 ?      00:00:00 syslogd -m 0
root        750     1  0 Aug25 ?      00:00:00 klogd -2
daemon      965     1  0 Aug25 ?      00:00:00 /usr/sbin/atd
root       1003   948  0 Aug25 ?      00:00:00 -:0
root       1078     1  0 Aug25 ?      00:00:00 crond
glass      1362  1282  0 Aug25 ?      00:03:01 magicdev
glass      1376     1  0 Aug25 ?      00:00:00 /usr/lib/gconfd
glass      1463  1282  0 Aug25 ?      00:00:00 kwrapper
glass     23708 23693  0 15:51 pts0   00:00:00 bash
root      24379 23708  0 16:41 pts0   00:00:00 su
root      24382 24379  0 16:41 pts0   00:00:00 bash
root      24805 24382  0 17:28 pts0   00:00:00 ps -ef
$ _
```

The Korn shell automatically terminates background processes when you log out, whereas the C
and Bash shells allow them to continue. If you're using the Korn shell and you want to make a
background process immune from this effect, use the **nohup** utility to protect it (Figure 5–17).

Utility: **nohup** *command*

The **nohup** utility executes *command* and makes it immune to the hangup (HUP) and terminate (TERM) signals. The standard output and error channels of *command* are automatically
redirected to a file called "nohup.out," and the process's priority value is increased by five,
thereby reducing its priority. This utility is ideal for ensuring that background processes are
not terminated when your login shell is exited.

Figure 5–17 Description of the **nohup** command.

If you execute a command using **nohup**, log out, and then log back in again, you won't see the
command on the output of a regular **ps**. This is because a process loses its control terminal when
you log out, and continues to execute without it. To include a list of all the processes without
control terminals in a **ps** output, use the **-x** option.

Here's an example of this effect:

```
$ nohup sleep 10000 &              ...nohup a background process.
27406
nohup: appending output to 'nohup.out'  ...message from "nohup".
$ ps                               ...look at processes.
 PID TT STAT   TIME COMMAND
27399 pts/3    00:00:00 bash
27406 pts/3    00:00:00 sleep 10000
27407 pts/3    00:00:00 ps
$ ^D                               ...log out.

login: glass       ...log back in.
Password:          ...secret.
$ ps               ...the background process is not seen.
 PID TT STAT   TIME COMMAND
27409 pts/4    00:00:00 bash
27411 pts/4    00:00:00 ps
$ ps -x            ...the background process may be seen.
 PID   TT  STAT  TIME  COMMAND
...                ...along with lots of other output
27406 ?        S     00:00 sleep 10000
27409 pts/4    Ss    00:00 bash
27412 pts/4    R+    00:00 ps -x
$ _
```

For more information about control terminals, consult Chapter 12, "Systems Programming"

5.18.2   Signaling Processes: kill

If you wish to terminate a process before it completes, use the **kill** command. Most shells contain a built-in command called **kill** in addition to the standard utility. Both versions of **kill** support the functionality described in Figure 5–18.

Utility/Shell Command: **kill** [-*signalId*] {*pid* }+
    kill -l

kill sends the signal with code *signalId* to the list of numbered processes. *signalId* may be the number or name of a signal. By default, **kill** sends a TERM signal (number 15), which causes the receiving processes to terminate. To obtain a list of the legal signal names, use the **-l** option. To send a signal to a process, you must either own it or be a super-user. For more information about signals, refer to Chapter 12, "Systems Programming."

    Processes may protect themselves from all signals except the KILL signal (number 9). Therefore, to ensure a kill, send signal number 9 (note that sending a KILL will not allow a process to clean up and terminate normally, as many programs do when they receive a TERM signal).

Figure 5–18 Description of the **kill** command.

In the following example, I created a background process and then killed it. To confirm the termination, I obtained a **ps** listing:

```
$ (sleep 10; echo done) &&      ...create background process.
27390                           ...process ID number.
$ kill 27390                    ...kill the process.
$ ps                            ...it's gone!
 PID TT STAT  TIME COMMAND
27355 pts/3   00:00:00 bash
27394 pts/3   00:00:00 ps
$ _
```

The following example illustrates the use of the **-l** option and a named signal. The signal names are listed in numeric order, starting with signal #1.

```
$ kill -1                        ...list the signal names.
 1) SIGHUP       2) SIGINT       3) SIGQUIT      4) SIGILL
 5) SIGTRAP      6) SIGABRT      7) SIGBUS       8) SIGFPE
 9) SIGKILL     10) SIGUSR1     11) SIGSEGV     12) SIGUSR2
13) SIGPIPE     14) SIGALRM     15) SIGTERM     17) SIGCHLD
18) SIGCONT     19) SIGSTOP     20) SIGTSTP     21) SIGTTIN
22) SIGTTOU     23) SIGURG      24) SIGXCPU     25) SIGXFSZ
26) SIGVTALRM   27) SIGPROF     28) SIGWINCH    29) SIGIO
30) SIGPWR      31) SIGSYS      35) SIGRTMIN    36) SIGRTMIN+1
37) SIGRTMIN+2  38) SIGRTMIN+3  39) SIGRTMIN+4  40) SIGRTMIN+5
41) SIGRTMIN+6  42) SIGRTMIN+7  43) SIGRTMIN+8  44) SIGRTMIN+9
45) SIGRTMIN+10 46) SIGRTMIN+11 47) SIGRTMIN+12 48) SIGRTMIN+13
49) SIGRTMIN+14 50) SIGRTMAX-14 51) SIGRTMAX-13 52) SIGRTMAX-12
53) SIGRTMAX-11 54) SIGRTMAX-10 55) SIGRTMAX-9  56) SIGRTMAX-8
57) SIGRTMAX-7  58) SIGRTMAX-6  59) SIGRTMAX-5  60) SIGRTMAX-4
61) SIGRTMAX-3  62) SIGRTMAX-2  63) SIGRTMAX-1  64) SIGRTMAX
$ (sleep 10; echo done) &
27490           ...process ID number.
$ kill -KILL 27490       ...kill the process with signal #9.
$ _
```

5.18.3   Waiting For Child Processes: wait

A shell may wait for one or more of its child processes to terminate by executing the built-in **wait** command (Figure 5–19).

Shell Command: **wait** [*pid*]

wait causes the shell to suspend until the child process with the specified process ID number terminates. If no arguments are supplied, the shell waits for all of its child processes.

Figure 5–19 Description of the *wait* shell command.

In the following example, the shell waited until both background child processes had terminated before continuing:

```
$ (sleep 30; echo done 1) &          ...create a child process.
[1] 24193
$ (sleep 30; echo done 2) &          ...create a child process.
[2] 24195
$ echo done 3; wait; echo done 4     ...wait for children.
done 3
done 1              ...output from first child.
done 2              ...output from second child.
done 4
$ _
```

This facility is generally useful only in advanced shell scripts.

5.19 Finding a Command: $PATH

When a shell processes a command, it first checks to see whether it's a built-in; if it is, the shell executes it directly. *echo* is an example of a built-in shell command:

```
$ echo some commands are executed directly by the shell
some commands are executed directly by the shell
$ _
```

If it isn't a built-in command, the shell looks to see if the command begins with a / character. If it does, it assumes that the first token is the absolute pathname of a command, and tries to execute the file with the stated name. If the file doesn't exist or isn't an executable, an error occurs:

```
$ /bin/ls                ...full pathname of the ls utility.
script.csh  script.ksh
$ /bin/nsx               ...a nonexistent filename.
bash: /bin/nsx: not found
$ /etc/passwd            ...the name of the password file.
bash: /etc/passwd: Permission denied     ...it's not executable.
$ _
```

If it isn't a built-in command or a full pathname, the shell searches the directories whose names are stored in the PATH environment variable. Each directory in the PATH variable (from left to right) is searched for an executable matching the command name. If a match is found, the file is executed. If a match isn't found in any of the directories, or the file that matches is not executable, an error occurs. The contents of the PATH variable may be changed using the methods described in later chapters, thereby allowing you to tailor the search path to your needs. The original search path is usually initialized by the shell's startup file, and typically includes all of the standard Linux directories that contain executable utilities. Here are some examples:

```
$ echo $PATH
/bin:/usr/bin:/usr/local/bin      ...directories searched.
$ ls                              ...located in "/bin".
script.csh   script.ksh
$ nsx                             ...not located anywhere.
bash: nsx: not found
$ _
```

An important note about the $PATH variable: Traditionally, UNIX shells included your current directory (".") in the search path, usually at the end. This is convenient for running shell scripts and compiled programs that you are working on. When you include "." in your $PATH, you can type "a.out" to run a compiled C program rather than having to specify "./a.out" (which explicitly tells the shell that a.out is in the current directory). This may seem trivial, but over the years, having "." in your search path has come to be viewed as a security risk. Someone could plant a program called (for example) ls in a directory that did something nefarious. Then they could try to trick you to going to that directory, and when you typed "ls" then their program might run instead.

Default shell startup files on Linux systems do not include the current directory in the path. Therefore, it is necessary to reference any file you are executing (e.g., a compiled C binary or a shell script) relative to the current directory (i.e., "./test.ksh"). Some of the examples in this book may not always do this, in which case it is presumed that the current directory (".") is included in the search path, even though this is not recommended for most users.

5.20 Superseding Standard Utilities

Users often create a "bin" subdirectory in their home directory and place this subdirectory *before* the traditional "bin" directories in their PATH setting. This allows them to supersede default GNU utilities with their own "homebrewed" versions, since they will be located by the search process ahead of their standard counterparts. If you choose to do this, you should take great care, as scripts run from a shell expect to use standard utilities and might be confused by the nonstandard utilities that actually get executed. In the following example, I inserted my own "bin" directory into the search path sequence, and then overrode the standard "ls" utility with my own version:

```
$ mkdir bin          ...make my own personal "bin" directory.
$ cd bin             ...move into the new directory.
$ cat > ls           ...create a script called "ls".
echo my ls
^D      ...end-of-input.
$ chmod +x ls        ...make it executable.
```

```
$ echo $PATH           ...look at the current PATH setting.
/bin:/usr/bin:/usr/sbin
$ echo $HOME           ...get pathname of my home directory.
/home/glass
$ PATH=/home/glass/bin:$PATH        ...update.
$ ls                              ...call "ls".
my ls              ...my own version overrides "/bin/ls".
$ _
```

Note that only this shell and its child shells would be affected by the change to PATH; all other shells would be unaffected.

5.21 Termination and Exit Codes

Every Linux process terminates with an exit value. By convention, an exit value of 0 means that the process completed successfully, and a nonzero exit value indicates failure. All built-in commands return 1 if they fail. In Bash and the Korn, the special shell variable $? always contains the value of the previous command's exit code. In the C shell, the $status variable holds the exit code. In the following example, the **date** utility succeeded, whereas the **gcc** and **gawk** utilities failed:

```
$ date                          ...date succeeds.
Wed Feb  2 22:13:38 CST 2005
$ echo $?                       ...display its exit value.
0                               ...indicates success.
$ gcc prog.c            ...compile a nonexistent program.
gcc: prog.c: No such file or directory.
gcc: no input files
$ echo $?                       ...display its exit value.
1                               ...indicates failure.
$ gawk                  ...use gawk incorrectly.
Usage: gawk [POSIX or GNU style options] -f progfile [--] file
Usage: gawk [POSIX or GNU style options] [--] 'program' file ...
...
$ echo $?                       ...display its exit value.
1                               ...indicates failure.
$ _
```

Any script that you write should always explicitly return an exit code. To terminate a script, use the built-in *exit* command (Figure 5–20).

Shell Command: **exit** *number*

exit terminates the shell and returns the exit value *number* to its parent process. If *number* is omitted, the exit value of the previous command is used.

Figure 5–20   Description of the *exit* shell command.

If a shell doesn't include an explicit *exit* statement, the exit value of the last command is returned by default. The script in the following example returned an exit value of 3:

```
$ cat script.sh              ...look at the script.
echo this script returns an exit code of 3
exit 3
$ ./script.sh                ...execute the script.
this script returns an exit code of 3
$ echo $?                    ...look at the exit value.
3
$ _
```

The next chapter contains some examples of scripts that make use of a command's exit value.

5.22 Common Core Built-Ins

There are a large number of built-in commands that are supported by command shells, of which only a few are common to all. This section describes the most useful common core built-in commands.

5.22.1 eval

Figure 5–21 describes the *eval* shell command.

Shell Command: **eval** *command*

The *eval* shell command executes the output of *command* as a regular shell command. It is useful when processing the output of utilities that generate shell commands (e.g., **tset**).

Figure 5–21   Description of the *eval* shell command.

In the following example, I executed the result of the *echo* command, which caused the variable *x* to be set:

```
$ echo x=5           ...first execute an echo directly.
x=5
$ eval `echo x=5`    ...execute the result of the echo.
$ echo $x            ...confirm that x was set to 5.
5
$ _
```

For a more complex example, see the description of **tset** in Chapter 3, "GNU Utilities for Non-programmers"

5.22.2 exec

Figure 5–22 describes the *exec* shell command.

Shell Command: **exec** *command*

The *exec* shell command causes the shell's image to be replaced with *command* in the process' memory space. If *command* is successfully executed, the shell that performed the *exec* ceases to exist. If this shell was a login shell, then the login session is terminated when *command* terminates.

Figure 5–22   Description of the *exec* shell command.

In the following example, I exec'ed the **date** command from my login shell, which caused the **date** utility to run and then my login process to terminate:

```
$ exec date           ...replace shell process by date process.
Tue Feb  1 18:55:01 CDT 2005            ...output from date.

login: _              ...login shell is terminated.
```

5.22.3   shift
Figure 5–23 describes the *shift* shell command.

Shell Command: **shift**

The *shift* shell command causes all of the positional parameters $2..$n to be renamed $1..$(n-1), and $1 to be lost. It's particularly handy in shell scripts when cycling through a series of command-line parameters. If there are no positional arguments left to shift, an error message is displayed.

Figure 5–23   Description of the *shift* shell command.

In the following example, I wrote a C shell script to display its arguments before and after a shift.

```
$ cat shift.csh           ...list the script.
#!/bin/csh
echo first argument is $1, all args are $*
shift
echo first argument is $1, all args are $*
$ ./shift.csh a b c d        ...run with four arguments.
first argument is a, all args are a b c d
first argument is b, all args are b c d
$ ./shift.csh a              ...run with one argument.
```

```
first argument is a, all args are a
first argument is , all args ar
$ ./shift.csh                ...run with no arguments.
first argument is , all args are
shift: No more words         ...error message.
$ _
```

5.22.4 umask

When a C program creates a file, it supplies the file's original permission settings as an octal parameter to the system call open (). For example, to create a file with read and write permission for the owner, group, and others, it would execute a system call like this:

```
fd = open ("myFile", O_CREAT | O_RDWR, 0666);
```

For information on the encoding of permissions as octal numbers, see Chapter 3, "GNU Utilities for Nonprogrammers." For information on the open () system call, see Chapter 12, "Systems Programming." When the shell performs redirection using (using the ">" character), it uses a system call sequence similar to the one shown above to construct a file with octal permission 666. However, if you try creating a file using redirection with the ">" character, you'll probably end up with a file that has a permission setting of 644 octal:

```
$ date > date.txt
$ ls -lG date.txt
-rw-r--r--  1 glass      29 May  3 18:56 date.txt
$ _
```

The reason for this is that every Linux process contains a special quantity called a *umask* value, which is used to restrict the permission settings that it requests when a file is created. The default umask value of a shell is 0022 octal. The set bits of a umask value mask out the set bits of a requested permission setting. In the example shown above, the requested permission 0666 was masked with 0022 to produce the final permission 0644, as shown in Figure 5–24.

	r	w	x	r	w	x	r	w	x
original	1	1	0	1	1	0	1	1	0
mask	0	0	0	0	1	0	0	1	0
final	1	1	0	1	0	0	1	0	0

Figure 5–24 Bit-by-bit example of the effect of the umask setting.

If a file already exists before it is redirected to, the original file's permission values are retained and the umask value is ignored.

Figure 5–25 describes how the *umask* command may be used to manipulate the umask value.

Shell Command: **umask** [*octalValue*]

The *umask* shell command sets the shell's umask value to the specified octal number, or displays the current umask value if the argument is omitted. A shell's umask value is retained until changed. Child processes inherit their umask value from their parent.

Figure 5–25   Description of the *umask* shell command.

In the following example, I changed the umask value to 0 and then created a new file to illustrate its effect:

```
$ umask              ...display current umask value.
0022                 ...mask write permission of group/others.
$ umask 0            ...set umask value to 0.
$ date > date2.txt    ...create a new file.
$ ls -lG date2.txt
-rw-rw-rw-  1 glass    29 May  3 18:56 date2.txt
$ _
```

CHAPTER REVIEW

Checklist

In this chapter, I described:

1. the common functionality of the popular Linux shells
2. the common shell metacharacters
3. output and input redirection
4. filename substitution
5. pipes
6. command substitution
7. command sequences
8. grouped commands
9. the construction of scripts
10. the difference between local and environment variables
11. the two different types of quoting
12. basic job control
13. the mechanism that the shell uses to find commands
14. several core built-in commands

Quiz

1. Can you change your default login shell?
2. What shell command is used to change your current directory?
3. What is the difference between a built-in command and a utility?
4. How can you make a script executable?
5. Describe a common use for command substitution.
6. Describe the meaning of the terms *parent shell*, *child shell*, and *subshell*.
7. How do you think the **kill** command got its name?
8. Describe a way to override a standard utility.
9. What is a good *umask* value, and why?

Exercises

1. Write a script that creates three background processes, waits for them all to complete, and then displays a simple message. [level: *easy*]
2. Experiment with the *exec* command by writing a series of three shell scripts called "a.sh," "b.sh," and "c.sh" that each display their name, execute **ps**, and then *exec* the next script in the sequence. Observe what happens when you start the first script by executing exec a.sh. [level: *medium*]
3. Why is the file that is created in the following session unaffected by the umask value? [level: *medium*]

```
$ ls -lG date.txt
-rw-rw-rw-  1 glass       29 Aug 20 21:04 date.txt
$ umask 0077
$ date > date.txt
$ ls -lG date.txt
-rw-rw-rw-  1 glass       29 Aug 20 21:04 date.txt
$ _
```

Project

1. Compare and contrast the Linux shell features against the graphical shells available on Windows. Which do you think is better? [level: *medium*]

6

The Bourne Again Shell

Motivation

Bash, a.k.a. the Bourne Again shell, originally written by Brian Fox of the Free Software Foundation, is the default shell for Linux users. Bash is an attempt to create a "best of all shells" that not only provides backward compatibility with the original UNIX Bourne shell, but also the most useful features of both the C shell and Korn shell. Another advantage is that Bash, as an open software product, is freely available and can be found in all Linux distributions, and it can be downloaded and installed on just about any version of UNIX if it isn't already present.

Prerequisites

You should have already read Chapter 5, "The Linux Shells," and have experimented with some of the core shell facilities.

Objectives

In this chapter, I'll explain and demonstrate the facilities of Bash.

Presentation

The information in this section is presented in the form of several sample Linux sessions.

Shell Commands

This section describes the following shell commands, listed in alphabetical order:

alias	for..do..done	readonly
bg	function	return
builtin	history	select..do..done
case..in..esac	if..then..elif..then..else..fi	set
cd	jobs	source
declare	kill	trap
dirs	local	unalias
env	popd	unset
export	pushd	until..do..done
fg	read	while..do..done

6.1   Introduction

Bash is the shell of choice on Linux systems. It implements all the core facilities described in Chapter 5, "The Linux Shells," and is compatible with the original UNIX Bourne shell (so Bourne shell scripts run under Bash). Bash conforms to the POSIX standard for command shells (IEEE 1003.2). Bash also implements the best features from the original UNIX C shell.

On Linux systems, Bash is installed as /bin/bash, but /bin/sh is a pointer to /bin/bash, since any script expecting Bourne shell functionality will run properly under Bash.

The following features of Bash that are new or a bit different from what has been discussed in previous chapters include:

- • variable manipulation
- • command-line processing, aliases, and history
- • arithmetic, conditional expressions, control structures
- • directory stack
- • job control
- • shell functions

6.2   Startup

Bash, like other shells, is a program. When a new Bash shell starts, it executes commands in the file ".bashrc" in the home directory of the user running Bash. The one exception is when Bash is started as a login shell, in which case it runs the commands in the file ".bash_profile" in the user's home directory instead. So if you want your ".bashrc" file to be executed in your login shell as well, you have to add this to your ".bash_profile" file:

```
if [ -f ~/.bashrc ]; then
  . ~/.bashrc
fi
```

We'll see how and why that works later in the chapter. This is often found by default in ".bash_profile" files on a system.

In addition to these two files, the system administrator can put initialization commands appropriate for all users in the file "/etc/profile" which Bash will also read and execute. Note that Bash will read the "/etc/profile" file first, before running any initialization files belonging to the user.

6.3 Variables

Bash allows creation and use of shell variables for the following purposes:

- Value assignment and access
- Defining and using lists of values
- Testing a value or for existence of a variable
- Reading or writing a variable's value

6.3.1 Creating/Assigning a Simple Variable

To assign a value to a simple variable, the syntax is similar to that of other shells (Figure 6–1).

```
{name=value}+
```

Figure 6–1 Example of assigning a simple variable.

If a variable doesn't exist, it is implicitly created; otherwise, its previous value is overwritten. A newly created variable is always local, although we may turn it into an environment variable using a method that I'll describe shortly. To assign a value that contains spaces, surround the value by quotes. Here are some examples:

```
$ teamname="Denver Broncos"
$ gameswon=12
$ gameslost=3
```

The *set* built-in command can be used to set and display shell settings and to display the value of shell variables (Figure 6–2).

Shell command: **set**

The *set* built-in displays all variables set in the shell.

Figure 6–2 Example of the *set* built-in to display shell variables and values.

The *set* built-in has many arguments and uses, which we'll discuss in several places in this chapter. Its simplest use is simply to display shell variables and their values:

```
$ set
gameslost=3
gameswon=12
teamname="Denver Broncos"
$ _
```

Other output that *set* would produce has been omitted for clarity. The *set* built-in also has several other options, some of which we'll use later. Figure 6–3 is a list of the most useful options.

Option	Meaning
-o allexport | -a	Export all created or modified variables and functions.
-o emacs	Set command edit style to behave like **emacs**.
-o ignoreeof	Interactive shell will not exit on EOF (e.g., if you typed *Control-D* by accident).
-o noclobber | -C	Prevent output redirection from overwriting existing files.
-o noglob | -f	Disable filename substitution (a.k.a. globbing).
-o posix	Cause Bash behavior to always adhere to the POSIX 1003.2 Shell standard.
-o verbose | -v	Print shell input lines as they are read (useful for debugging scripts).
-o vi	Set command edit style to behave like **vi.**

Figure 6–3   Some useful *set* built-in options.

6.3.2   Accessing Simple Variables

Figure 6–4 lists the methods Bash supports for accessing the value of simple variables.

Syntax	Action
$*name*	Replaced by the value of *name*.
${*name*}	Replaced by the value of *name*. This form is useful if the expression is immediately followed by an alphanumeric that would otherwise be interpreted as part of the variable name.
${*name-word*}	Replaced by the value of *name* if set, and *word* otherwise.

Figure 6–4   Accessing the value of a simple variable. (Part 1 of 2)

Syntax	Action
${name+word}	Replaced by *word* if *name* is set, and nothing otherwise.
${name=word}	Assigns *word* to the variable *name* if *name* is not already set, and then is replaced by the value of *name*.
${name?word}	Replaced by name if *name* is set. If *name* is not set, *word* is displayed to the standard error channel and the shell is exited. If *word* is omitted, then a standard error message is displayed instead.
${#name}	Replaced by the length of the value of *name*.
${#name[*] }	Replaced by the number of elements in the array *name*.
${name:+word } ${name:=word } ${name:?word } ${name:+word }	Work like their counterparts that do not contain a :, except that *name* must be set *and* non-null instead of just set.
${name#pattern} ${name##pattern}	Removes a leading *pattern* from *name*. The expression is replaced by the value of *name* if name doesn't begin with *pattern*, and with the remaining suffix if it does. The first form removes the smallest matching pattern, and the second form removes the largest matching pattern.
${name%pattern} ${name%%pattern}	Removes a trailing *pattern* from *name*. The expression is replaced by the value of *name* if *name* doesn't end with *pattern*, and with the remaining prefix if it does. The first form removes the smallest matching pattern, and the second form removes the largest matching pattern.

Figure 6–4 Accessing the value of a simple variable. (Part 2 of 2)

The following examples illustrate each access method. In the first example, I used braces to append a string to the value of a variable:

```
$ verb=sing           ...assign a variable.
$ echo I like $verbing     ...there's no variable "verbing".
I like
$ echo I like ${verb}ing   ...now it works.
I like singing
$ _
```

Here's an example that uses command substitution to set the variable startDate to the current date if it's not already set:

```
$ startDate=${startDate-`date`}  ...if not set, run date.
$ echo $startDate              ...look at its value.
```

```
Wed May 4 06:56:51 CST 2005
$ _
```

In the next example, I set the variable x to a default value and printed its value, all at the same time:

```
$ echo x = ${x=10}      ...assign a default value.
x = 10
$ echo $x               ...confirm the variable was set.
10
$ _
```

In the following example, I displayed messages based on whether certain variables were set or not:

```
$ flag=1                           ...assign a variable.
$ echo ${flag+'flag is set'}       ...conditional message #1.
flag is set
$ echo ${flag2+'flag2 is set'}     ...conditional message #2.
                                   ...result is null

$ _
```

In the next example, I tried to access an undefined variable called *grandTotal* and received an error message instead:

```
$ total=10                             ...assign a variable.
$ value=${total?'total not set'}       ...accessed OK.
$ echo $value                          ...look at its value.
10
$ value=${grandTotal?'grand total not set'}  ...not set.
grandTotal: grand total not set
$ _
```

In this example, I ran a script that used the same access method as the previous example. Note that the script terminated when the access error occurred:

```
$ cat script.sh                 ...look at the script.
value=${grandTotal?'grand total is not set'}
echo done        # this line is never executed.
$ script.sh                      ...run the script.
script.sh: grandTotal: grand total is not set
$ _
```

In this final example, I'll modify some variable values:

```
$ echo $PWD     ...display the current working directory.
/home/glass/dir1
$ echo $HOME
```

```
/home/glass
$ echo ${PWD#$HOME/}            ...remove leading $HOME/
dir1
$ fileName=menu.sh              ...set a variable.
$ echo ${fileName%.sh}.bak      .. .remove trailing ".sh"
menu.bak                        ...and add ".bak".
$ _
```

6.3.3   Creating/Assigning a List Variable

List variables, or arrays, are created with the *declare* built-in command (Figure 6–5), although simply using a variable in the form of an array will also work.

Shell command: **declare** [-ax] [*listname*]

If the named variable does not already exist, it is created. If an array name is not specified when **-a** is used, *declare* will display all currently defined arrays and their values. If the **-x** option is used, the variable is exported to subshells. *declare* writes its output in a format that can be used again as input commands. This is useful when you want to create a script that sets variables as they are set in your current environment.

Figure 6–5   Example of the *declare* shell command.

Here is an example of how you might create a list of teams:

```
$ declare -a teamnames
$ teamnames[0]="Dallas Cowboys"
$ teamnames[1]="Washington Redskins"
$ teamnames[2]="New York Giants"
```

In reality, if you omit the *declare* command, the other lines will still work as expected.

6.3.4   Accessing List Variables

Once you build a list of values, you will want to use them for something. When accessing array values, you can always put braces around the variable name to explicitly distinguish it from other text that might be around it (to prevent the shell from trying to use other text as part of the variable name (Figure 6–6).

${*name*[*index*]}	Access the *index*th element of the array $*name*.
${*name*[*]} or ${*name*[@]}	Access all elements of the array $*name*.
${#*name*[*]} or ${#*name*[@]}	Access the number of elements in the array $*name*.

Figure 6–6   Accessing the value(s) of a list variable.

The braces are required when using arrays to distinguish between other shell operators. Suppose, for example, we have our list of 32 NFL teams stored as $teamname[0] .. $teamname[31]. One might use this information this way:

```
$ echo "There are ${#teamnames[*]} teams in the NFL"
There are 32 teams in the NFL
$ echo "They are: ${teamnames[*]}"
...
```

6.3.5   Building Lists

You can build an array or list variable in one of two ways. If you know how many elements you will need, you can use the *declare* built-in command to define the space and assign the values into specific locations in the list. If you don't know, or don't care, how many elements will be in the list, you can simply list them and they will be added in the order you specify.

For example, to define our list of NFL teams, of which we know (at least today) there are 32, you might define it as follows:

```
$ declare -a teamnames
$ teamnames[0]="Dallas Cowboys"
$ teamnames[1]="Washington Redskins"
$ teamnames[2]="New York Giants"
  ...
$ teamnames[31]="Houston Texans"
```

This can also be done in a single (though long) command:

```
$ declare -a teamnames
$ teamnames=([0]="Dallas Cowboys" \
            [1]="Washington Redskins" \
  ...
            [31]="Houston Texans")
```

The backslash is used to tell the shell that the command is continued on the next line.

Even though we know the number of teams ahead of time, we don't need to know this to define the array. We could have also done it this way:

```
$ teamnames = ("Dallas Cowboys" "Washington Redskins" \
            "New York Giants" "New York Jets"    \
  ...
            "Houston Texans")
```

Note that if you have sparsely populated the array—that is, you have not assigned values in consecutive locations but skipped around—when you ask for the number of values in the array, the value will be the actual number of populated elements, not the largest index defined. For example:

```
$ mylist[0]=27
$ mylist[5]=30
$ echo ${#mylist[*]}        ...number of elements in mylist[]
2
$ declare -a               ...display defined element values
declare -a mylist='([0]="27" [5]="30")'
$ _
```

6.3.6   Destroying lists

List variables can be deallocated or destroyed using the *unset* built-in to Bash (Figure 6–7).

Shell command: **unset** *name*
        unset *name*[*index*]

Deallocates the specified variable or element in the list variable.

Figure 6–7   Description of the *unset* shell command.

If you have finished using an array, you can deallocate the space used by the array by destroying it completely. It is more likely you will want to remove a specific element in the array.

```
$ unset teamnames[17]
```

Now our array contains 31 names instead of 32.

6.3.7   Reading a Variable from Standard Input

The *read* command allows you to read variables from standard input (Figure 6–8).

Shell Command: **read** { *variable* }+

read reads one line from standard input and then assigns successive words from the line to the specified variables. Any words that are left over are assigned to the last-named variable.

Figure 6–8   Description of the *read* shell command.

If you specify just one variable, the entire line is stored in the variable. Here's an example script that prompts a user for his or her full name:

```
$ cat script.sh                    ...list the script.
echo "Please enter your name: \c"
read name                          # read just one variable.
echo your name is $name            # display the variable.
$ bash script.sh                   ...run the script.
Please enter your name: Graham Walker Glass
your name is Graham Walker Glass    ...whole line was read.
$ _
```

Here's an example that illustrates what happens when you specify more than one variable:

```
$ cat script.sh                    ...list the script.
echo "Please enter your name: \c"
read firstName lastName        # read two variables.
echo your first name is $firstName
echo your last name is $lastName
$ bash script.sh                   ...run the script.
Please enter your name: Graham Walker Glass
your first name is Graham          ...first word.
your last name is Walker Glass     ...the rest.
$ bash script.sh                   ...run it again.
Please enter your name: Graham
your first name is Graham          ...first word.
your last name is                  ...only one.
$ _
```

6.3.8   Exporting Variables

In all shells, variables are local to the specific shell and, unless otherwise specified, are not passed to subshells. The *export* command allows you to mark local variables for export to the environment (Figure 6–9).

Shell Command: **export** { *variable* }+

export marks the specified variables for export to the environment. If no variables are specified, a list of all the variables marked for export during the shell session is displayed.

Figure 6-9   Description of the *export* shell command.

Although it's not necessary, I tend to use uppercase letters to name environment variables. The **env** utility allows you to modify and list environment variables (Figure 6–10).

Utility: **env** { *variable=value* }* [*command*]

env assigns values to specified environment variables, and then executes an optional command using the new environment. If variables or command are not specified, a list of the current environment is displayed.

Figure 6-10   Description of the **env** command.

In the following example, I created a local variable called DATABASE, which I then marked for export. When I created a subshell, a copy of the environment variable was inherited:

```
$ export                   ...list my current exports.
export TERM                ...set in my ".profile" startup file.
```

```
$ DATABASE=/dbase/db        ...create a local variable.
$ export DATABASE          ...mark it for export.
$ export                   ...note that it's been added.
export DATABASE
export TERM
$ env                      ...list the environment.
DATABASE=/dbase/db
HOME=/home/glass
LOGNAME=glass
PATH=:/bin:/usr/bin
SHELL=/bin/bash
TERM=xterm
USER=glass
$ bash                     ...create a subshell.
$ echo $DATABASE           ...a copy was inherited.
/dbase/db
$ ^D                       ...terminate subshell.
$ _
```

Bash provides a shell option that allows you to specify that, by default, all shell variables be exported to any subshells created. Shell options are defined with the *set* built-in (Figure 6–11).

Shell command: **set** -o allexport

Tell the shell to export all variables to subshells.

Figure 6–11   Example of the *set* built-in to export all variables.

6.3.9   Read-Only Variables

The *readonly* command allows you to protect variables against modification (Figure 6–12).

Shell Command: **readonly** { *variable* }*

readonly makes the specified variables read-only, protecting them against future modification. If no variables are specified, a list of the current read-only variables is displayed. Copies of exported variables do not inherit their read-only status.

Figure 6–12   Description of the *readonly* shell command.

In the following example, I protected a local variable from modification. I then exported the variable and showed that its copy did not inherit the read-only status:

```
$ password=Shazam          ...assign a local variable.
$ echo $password           ...display its value.
Shazam
```

```
$ readonly password        ...protect it.
$ readonly                 ...list all read-only variables.
readonly password
$ password=Phoombah        ...try to modify it.
password: is read only
$ export password          ...export the variable.
$ password=Phoombah        ...try to modify it.
password: is read only
$ bash                     ...create a subshell.
$ readonly        ...the exported password is not read-only.
$ echo $password           ...its value was copied correctly.
Shazam
$ password=Alacazar        ...but its value may be changed.
$ echo $password           ...echo its value.
Alacazar
$ ^D                       ...terminate the subshell.
$ echo $password           ...echo original value.
Shazam
$ _
```

6.3.10 Predefined Variables

Like most shells, Bash defines some variables when it starts (Figure 6–13).

Name	Value
$-	The current shell options assigned from the command line or by the built-in set command—discussed later.
$$	The process ID of this shell.
$!	The process ID of the last background command.
$#	The number of positional parameters.
$?	The exit value of the last command.
$@	An individually quoted list of all the positional parameters.
$_	The last parameter of the previous command.
$BASH	The full pathname of the Bash executable.
$BASH_ENV	Location of Bash's startup file (default is ~/.bashrc).
$BASH_VERSINFO	A read-only array of version information.
$BASH_VERSION	Version string.

Figure 6–13 Bash predefined variables. (Part 1 of 3)

Name	Value
$DIRSTACK	Array defining the directory stack (discussed later).
$ENV	If this variable is not set, the shell searches the user's home directory for the ".profile" startup file when a new login shell is created. If this variable is set, then every new shell invocation runs the script specified by ENV.
$EUID	Read-only value of effective user ID of user running Bash.
$HISTFILE	Location of file containing shell history (default ~/.bash_history).
$HISTFILESIZE	Maximum number of lines allowed in history file (default is 500).
$HISTSIZE	Maximum number of commands in history (default is 500).
$HOSTNAME	Hostname of machine where Bash is running.
$HOSTTYPE	Type of host where Bash is running.
$IFS	When the shell tokenizes a command line prior to its execution, it uses the characters in this variable as delimiters. IFS usually contains a space, a tab, and a newline character.
$LINES	Used by *select* to determine how to display the selections.
$MAILCHECK	How often (seconds) to check for new mail.
$OLDPWD	The previous working directory of the shell.
$OSTYPE	Operating system of machine where Bash is running.
$PPID	The process ID number of the shell's parent.
$PPID	Read-only process ID of the parent process of Bash.
$PS1	This contains the value of the command-line prompt, and is $ by default. To change the command-line prompt, simply set PS1 to a new value.
$PS2	This contains the value of the secondary command-line prompt that is displayed when more input is required by the shell, and is > by default. To change the prompt, set PS2 to a new value.
$PS3	The prompt used by the *select* command, #? by default.
$PWD	The current working directory of the shell.
$RANDOM	A random integer.
$REPLY	Set by a *select* command.

Figure 6–13 Bash predefined variables. (Part 2 of 3)

Name	Value
$SHLVL	Level of shell (incremented once each time a Bash process is started, it shows how deeply the shell is nested).
$UID	Read-only value of user ID of user running Bash.

Figure 6-13   Bash predefined variables. (Part 3 of 3)

Here's a small shell script that illustrates the first three variables. In this example, the C compiler (**gcc**) was invoked on a file that didn't exist, and therefore returned a failure exit code.

```
$ cat script.sh                        ...list the script.
echo there are $# command line arguments: $@
gcc $1                      # compile the first argument.
echo the last exit value was $?    # display exit code.
$ script.sh nofile tmpfile          ...execute the script.
there are 2 command line arguments: nofile tmpfile
gcc: nofile: No such file or directory
gcc: no input files
the last exit value was 1           ...gcc errored.
$ _
```

The next example illustrates how $! may be used to kill the last background process:

```
$ sleep 1000 &        ...bg process, bash does not report PID.
$ kill $!             ...kill it!
29455 Terminated
$ echo $!             ...the process ID is still remembered.
29455
$ _
```

Here's a small example that illustrates the predefined variables used to set the command-line prompt. I set my prompt to something different by assigning a new value to PS1, and I set PS2 to a new value and illustrated an occasion where the secondary prompt is displayed.

```
$ PS1="bash? "               ...set a new primary prompt.
bash? string="a long\        ...assign a string over 2 lines
>  string"                   ...">" is the secondary prompt.
bash? echo $string           ...look at the value of "string".
a long string
bash? PS2="??? "             ...change the secondary prompt.
bash? string="a long\        ...assign a long string.
??? string"                  ..."???" is new secondary prompt.
bash? echo $string           ...look at the value of "string".
a long string
bash? _
```

6.4 Command Shortcuts

Bash provides a few ways to shorten commands and arguments you type at the keyboard.

6.4.1 Aliases

Bash allows you to define your own commands with the *alias* built-in command (Figure 6–14).

Shell Command: **alias** [-p] [*word*[=*string*]]

If you alias a new command word equal to string, then when you type the command word the string will be used in its place (and any succeeding arguments will be appended to string) and the command will be evaluated. In the usage "alias *word*" any alias defined for word will be printed. Its simplest usage "alias" will print all defined aliases. If the **-p** argument is used, the aliases are printed in a format suitable for input to the shell (so if you've manually set up aliases you like, you can write them to a file to include in your .bashrc file).

Figure 6–14   Description of the *alias* shell command.

Here is an example of defining and using Bash command aliases:

```
$ alias dir="ls -aF"
$ dir
./     main2.c     p.reverse.c      reverse.h
../    main2.o     palindrome.c     reverse.old
$ dir *.c
main2.c    p.reverse.c    palindrome.c
$
```

To cause an alias to no longer have a special definition, use the *unalias* built-in (Figure 6–15).

Shell Command: **unalias** [-a] {*word*}+

Remove the specified alias(es). If "-a" is used, remove all aliases.

Figure 6–15   Description of the *unalias* shell command.

You might wish to undefine an alias when you want the normal behavior of a command that you normally alias to a different behavior (e.g., in our above example, if you no longer want *dir* to use the **ls** command because there is another **dir** command on the system).

6.4.2 Command History

Bash maintains a historical record of the commands you type. With the commands maintained in this history, you can selectively re-execute commands or cause them to be modified and executed with changes.

6.4.2.1   Storage of Commands

Commands you have typed to the shell are stored in a history file defined by the $HISTFILE shell variable. By default, the value specifies the file ".bash_history" in the user's home directory. This file can hold a maximum of $HISTFILESIZE entries, the default value being 500.

6.4.2.2   Reading Command History

To see your shell history, use the built-in *history* command (Figure 6–16).

Shell Command: **history** [-c] [*n*]

Print out the shell's current command history. If a numeric value *n* is specified, show only the last *n* entries in the history list. If "-c" is used, clear the history list.

Figure 6–16   Description of the *history* shell command.

6.4.2.3   Command Re-execution

Bash honors the "!" metacharacter to re-execute commands from the history list in the forms listed in Figure 6–17.

Form	Action
!!	Replaced with the text of the last command.
!*number*	Replaced with command number *number* in the history list.
!-*number*	Replaced with the text of the command *number* commands back from the end of the list (!-1 is equivalent to !!).
!*prefix*	Replaced with the text of the last command that started with *prefix*.
!?*substring*?	Replaced with the text of the last command that contained *substring*.

Figure 6–17   Command re-execution metacharacters in Bash.

6.4.2.4   History substitution

Sometimes you want to do more than simply re-execute a command that you have previously used. You may want to modify the command slightly (change a filename or a single argument to a long command).

Figure 6–18 describes the simplest form of history substitution.

---

*^string1^string2^*

Substitute *string2* for *string1* in the previous command and executes it.

Figure 6–18   Description of simple history substitution in Bash.

This is useful when you make a minor mistake in a command and don't want to have to retype the entire command, such as in:

```
$ lp financial_report_july_2003.txt
lp: File not found.
$ ^2003^2004^
lp financial_report_july_2004.txt
request id is lwcs-37 (1 file)
$ _
```

Or, perhaps you wish to substitute something in an earlier command (because you have issued other commands to find out what was wrong, so now the command you want to repeat isn't the most recent command in this history list); Figure 6–19 shows how it's done.

!command:s/string1/string2/

string2 is substituted for *string1* in the most recent command that begins with the text specified by *command*.

Figure 6–19   Example of more complex history substitution in Bash.

For example:

```
$ lp financial_report_july_2003.txt
lp: file not found.
$ ls
financial_report_july_2004.txt          financial_report_may_2004.txt
financial_report_june_2004.txt
$ !lp:s/2003/2004/
request id is lwcs-37 (1 file)
$ _
```

6.4.2.5   Command Editing

Bash provides a fairly sophisticated command-editing capability. Both **emacs** and **vi** styles of editing are supported; **emacs** is the default. Since, in **emacs**, you are always in text input mode, you can type **emacs** movement characters at any time while typing a command.

So, for example, if you've left out a word, you can back up with *Control-B* and insert it. To access your history list of previous commands, you can use *Control-P* to move "up" as if your history list were a file. On most keyboards, the directional arrow keys can also be used for cursor movement in all four directions.

Most other **emacs** movement commands are supported; see the section "Editing a File: Emacs" in Chapter 3, "GNU Utilities for Nonprogrammers," for more information.

Bash also allows **vi** users the same luxury, but this must be set using the *set* built-in, as shown in Figure 6–20.

Shell command: **set** –o vi

Tell the shell to use **vi**-style command editing. If you ever want to return to the default **emacs**-style, substitute "emacs" for "vi" in the above command.

Figure 6–20   Example of the *set* built-in to set the command-line edit style.

Because **vi** has two modes, "command mode" and "text input mode," while typing a normal command, Bash treats you as if you are in text input mode. Therefore, to access the **vi** command-editing features, you have to hit the *ESCAPE* key, just as you would in **vi** to get back into command mode. Once you do that, you can move around just as you would in **vi** ("h" to back up in the command, or "k" to back up to previous commands in the history list).

See the section "Editing a File: vi" in Chapter 3, "GNU Utilities for Nonprogrammers," for more information.

6.4.3   Auto-Completion

Bash can complete a filename, command name, username or shell variable name that you've begun typing if you've typed enough to uniquely identify it. To have Bash attempt to complete the current argument of your command, type the *TAB* character. If matching filenames are available but the text you've typed does not identify one completely, text that the possible names have in common will be filled in to the point where they no longer have characters in common. This gives you the option of having the shell fill in long filenames where only a few characters at the end are different (like a sequence number or a date). Then you can type only the part that is unique to the file you wish to access. Typing a second *TAB* character will show all possible matches.

6.5   Tilde Substitution

Any token of the form *~name* is subject to *tilde substitution*. The shell checks the password file to see if *name* is a valid user name, and if it is, replaces the *~name* sequence with the full pathname of the user's home directory. If it isn't, the *~name* sequence is left unchanged. Tilde substitution occurs *after* aliases are processed. Figure 6–21 is a table of the tilde substitutions, including the special cases ~+ and ~-:

Tilde sequence	Replaced by
~	$HOME
~user	home directory of *user*
~/pathname	$HOME/*pathname*
~+	$PWD (current working directory)
~-	$OLDPWD (previous working directory)

Figure 6–21 Tilde substitutions in Bash.

The predefined local variables PWD and OLDPWD are described later in this chapter. Here are some examples of tilde substitution:

```
$ pwd
/home/glass            ...current working directory.
$ echo ~
/home/glass            ...my home directory.
$ cd /                 ...change to root directory.
$ echo ~+
/                      ...current working directory.
$ echo ~-
/home/glass            ...previous working directory.
$ echo ~dcox
/home/dcox             ...another user's home directory.
$ _
```

6.6 Redirection

Bash supplies an additional redirection capability over the standard shell redirection, the ability to strip leading tabs off of "here" documents. Figure 6–22 shows the augmented syntax.

command << [-] *word*

Figure 6–22 Redirection with a "here" document in Bash.

If *word* is preceded by a -, then leading tabs are removed from the lines of input that follow. Here's an example:

```
$ cat <<- ENDOFTEXT
>            this input contains
>       some leading tabs
>ENDOFTEXT
this input contains
some leading tabs
$ _
```

This allows "here" text in a script to be indented to match the nearby shell commands without affecting how the text is used.

6.7 Command Substitution

In addition to the older method of command substitution—surrounding the command with grave accents—Bash allows you to perform command substitution using the syntax in Figure 6–23.

```
$( command )
```

Figure 6–23   Command substitution in Bash.

Note that the $ that immediately precedes the open parentheses is part of the syntax, and is *not* a prompt. Here's an example:

```
$ echo there are $(who | wc -1) users on the system
there are 6 users on the system
$ _
```

To substitute the contents of a file into a shell command, you may use $(<*file*) as a faster form of $(cat *file*).

6.8 Arithmetic

To perform an arithmetic operation in Bash, you simply put the operation inside a double set of parentheses (Figure 6–24).

```
(( operation ))
```

Figure 6–24   Syntax of an arithmetic operation.

Common numeric operations include those listed in Figure 6–25.

+ -	Addition, subtraction.
++ --	Increment, decrement.
* / %	Multiplication, division, remainder.
**	Exponentiation.

Figure 6–25   Arithmetic operators.

Integer arithmetic is faster than floating-point arithmetic. If you know your variable will always be an integer (like a counter or array index), you can use the *declare* built-in to declare it to be an integer (Figure 6–26).

Shell command: **declare** -i *name*

This form of *declare* defines the variable *name* as an integer value

---

Figure 6–26   Using the *declare* built-in to define a variable as an integer.

After we look at some simple conditional expressions, we'll combine them into a simple math script.

6.9   Conditional Expressions

You can also compare values (usually stored in shell variables) with each other and branch to different commands depending on the outcome of the comparison. We'll see in the next section on control structures how you control what you do after the comparison.

6.9.1   Arithmetic Tests

Like arithmetic operations, arithmetic tests are enclosed in double parentheses. The types of comparisons you can do include those in Figure 6–27.

<= >= < >	Less than or equal to, greater than or equal to, less than, greater than comparisons.
== !=	Equal, not equal.
!	Logical NOT.
&&	Logical AND.
||	Logical OR.

Figure 6–27   Arithmetic conditional operators.

This all makes it simple to do a bit of math in a Bash script. We'll count up to 20 and test to see what numbers divide into 20 evenly (don't worry too much about the *while* construct just yet, we'll see it a bit later):

```
$ cat divisors.sh
#!/bin/bash
#
declare -i testval=20
declare -i count=2      # start at 2, 1 always works

while (( $count <= $testval )); do
  (( result = $testval % $count ))
  if (( $result == 0 )); then    # evenly divisible
    echo " $testval is evenly divisible by $count"
  fi
  (( count++ ))
done
$ bash divisors.sh
 20 is evenly divisible by 2
 20 is evenly divisible by 4
 20 is evenly divisible by 5
 20 is evenly divisible by 10
 20 is evenly divisible by 20
$ _
```

6.9.2   String Comparisons

String conditional operators are listed in Figure 6–28.

-n *string*	True if length of string is non-zero.
-z *string*	True if length of string is zero.
string1 == *string2*	True if strings are equal.
string1 != *string2*	True if strings are not equal.

Figure 6–28   String conditional operators.

6.9.3   File-Oriented Expressions

File-oriented conditional operator are listed in Figure 6–29.

-a *file*	True if the file exists.
-b *file*	True if the file exists and is a block-oriented special file.
-c *file*	True if the file exists and is a character-oriented special file.

Figure 6–29   File-oriented conditional operators. (Part 1 of 2)

-d *file*	True if the file exists and is a directory.
-e *file*	True if the file exists.
-f *file*	True if the file exists and is a regular file.
-g *file*	True if the file exists and its "set group ID" bit is set.
-p *file*	True if the file exists and is a named pipe.
-r *file*	True if the file exists and is readable.
-s *file*	True if the file exists and has a size greater than zero.
-t *fd*	True if the file descriptor is open and refers to the terminal.
-u *file*	True if the file exists and its "set user ID" bit is set.
-w *file*	True if the file is writable.
-x *file*	True if the file exists and is executable.
-O *file*	True if the file exists and is owned by the effective user ID of the user.
-G *file*	True if the file exists and is owned by the effective group ID of the user.
-L *file*	True if the file exists and is a symbolic link.
-N *file*	True if the file exists and has been modified since it was last read.
-S *file*	True if the file exists and is a socket.
file1 –nt *file2*	True if *file1* is newer than *file2*.
file1 –ot *file2*	True if *file1* is older than *file2*.
file1 –ef *file2*	True if *file1* and *file2* have the same device and inode numbers.

Figure 6–29   File-oriented conditional operators. (Part 2 of 2)

A simple example of a file operation might be:

```
$ cat owner.sh
#!/bin/bash
#

if [ -O /etc/passwd ]; then
    echo "you are the owner of /etc/passwd."
else
    echo "you are NOT the owner of /etc/passwd."
fi
$ bash owner.sh
```

```
you are NOT the owner of /etc/passwd.
$_
```

6.10 Control Structures

To take advantage of the comparisons described above, you can use various commands that control what command is executed next. While these structures can be used in the interactive Bash shell, they are most often used when writing Bash shell scripts.

6.10.1 case .. in .. esac

The *case* statement lets you specify multiple actions to be taken when the value of a variable matches one or more values (Figure 6–30).

Shell command: **case**
case *word* **in**
  pattern { | *pattern* }*) *commands* ;;

  ...

esac

Execute the commands specified by *commands* when the value of *word* matches the pattern specified by *pattern*. The ")" indicates the end of the list of patterns to match. The ";;" is required to indicate the end of the commands to be executed.

Figure 6–30 Description of the *case* shell command.

For example, a section of Bash shell script to print out the home location of the NFL teams listed in our earlier example might look like this:

```
case ${teamname[$index]} in
   "Dallas Cowboys") echo "Dallas, TX" ;;
   "Denver Broncos") echo "Denver, CO" ;;
   "New York Giants"|"New York Jets") echo "New York, NY";;
   . . .
   *) echo "Unknown location" ;;
esac
```

Note the special use of the pattern "*" as the last pattern. If you go through all the patterns and have never matched anything, this is useful to catch this situation. It is permissible to not match any patterns, in which case, none of the commands will be executed.

Here's an example script called "menu.sh" that makes use of a *case* control structure (this script is also available online; see the Preface for information):

```
#!/bin/bash
echo menu test program
```

```
stop=0                         # reset loop termination flag.
while test $stop -eq 0         # loop until done.
do
 cat << ENDOFMENU              # display menu.
 1   : print the date.
 2, 3: print the current working directory.
 4   : exit
ENDOFMENU
 echo
 echo -n 'your choice? '       # prompt.
 read reply                    # read response.
 echo
 case $reply in                # process response.
   "1")
     date                      # display date.
     ;;
   "2"|"3")
     pwd                       # display working directory.
     ;;
   "4")
     stop=1                    # set loop termination flag.
     ;;
   *)                          # default.
     echo illegal choice       # error.
     ;;
 esac
 echo
done
```

Here's the output from the "menu.sh" script:

```
$ bash menu.sh
menu test program
 1   : print the date.
 2, 3: print the current working directory.
 4   : exit

your choice? 1

Thu May  5 07:09:13 CST 2005

 1   : print the date.
 2, 3: print the current working directory.
 4   : exit

your choice? 2
```

```
/home/glass

  1   : print the date.
  2, 3: print the current working directory.
  4   : exit

your choice? 5

illegal choice

  1   : print the date.
  2, 3: print the current working directory.
  4   : exit

your choice? 4

$ _
```

6.10.2   if .. then .. elif .. then .. else .. fi

The *if* statement lets you compare two or more values and branch to a block of commands depending on how the values relate (Figure 6–31).

Shell command: **if**
if *test1*; **then**
  commands1;
[**elif** *test2*; **then**
  commands2;]
[**else** *commands3*;]
fi

test1 is a conditional expression (discussed above), which, if true, causes the commands specified by *commands1* to be executed. If *test1* tests false, then if an "elif" structure is present, the next test, *test2*, is evaluated ("else if"). If *test2* evaluates to true, then the commands in *commands2* are executed. The "else" construct is used when you always want to run commands after a test evaluated as false.

Figure 6–31   Description of the *if* shell command.

As an example, let's assume we have a special case for a couple of our NFL teams when printing information about them. We might determine which file of information to print like this:

```
# $index has been set to some arbitrary team in the list
#
if [ "${teamname[$index]}" == "Minnesota Vikings" ]; then
```

```
    cat "vikings.txt"       # print "special" info
elif [ "${teamname[$index]}" == "Chicago Bears" ]; then
    cat "bears.txt"         # ditto
else
    cat "nfl.txt"   # for everyone else, print the standard
fi
```

6.10.3   for .. do .. done

The *for* construct is best used when you have a known set of items you wish to iterate over (e.g., a list of hostnames, filenames, or something of that sort) (Figure 6–32). You might use a comparison to jump out of such a loop, or you might simply wish to process each item in the list sequentially.

Shell command: **for**

for *name* **in** *word* { *word* }*

do

  commands

done

Perform *commands* for each *word* in list with $*name* containing the value of the current *word*.

Figure 6–32   Description of the *for* shell command.

One example of this use might be if you needed to sort the contents of all text files in a directory:

```
$ ls
abc.txt      def.txt      ghi.txt
$ for file in *.txt
do
  sort $file > $file.sorted
done
$ ls
abc.txt             def.txt             ghi.txt
abc.txt.sorted      def.txt.sorted      ghi.txt.sorted
$ _
```

6.10.4   while/until .. do .. done

The *while* and *until* constructs work in a similar fashion, performing a loop while or until a test condition is met ("while" in the case that the condition is initially true and you want to loop until it becomes false, "until" in the case that the condition is initially false and you want to loop until it becomes true), as described in Figure 6–33.

Shell commands: **while/until**

while *test*
do
  commands
done

until *test*
do
  commands
done

In a *while* statement, perform *commands* as long as the expression *test* evaluates to true. In an *until* statement, perform *commands* as long as the expression *test* evaluates to false (i.e., until *test* is true).

Figure 6–33 Description of the *while* and *until* shell commands.

These constructs are useful when you don't know exactly when the status of the test condition will be changed. Here's an example of a script that uses an *until* control structure:

```
$ cat until.sh        ...list the script.
x=1
until [ $x -gt 3 ]
do
 echo x = $x
 (( x = $x + 1 ))
done
$ bash until.sh        ...execute the script.
x = 1
x = 2
x = 3
$ _
```

Here's an example of a script that uses a *while* control structure to generate a small multiplication table:

```
$ cat multi.sh          ...list the script.
if [ $# -lt 1 ]; then
    echo "Usage: multi number"
    exit
fi
x=1                           # set outer loop value
while [ $x -le $1 ]           # outer loop
do
```

```
    y=1                           # set inner loop value
    while [ $y -le $1 ]
    do                            # generate one table entry
       (( entry = $x * $y ))
       echo -e -n "$entry\t"
       (( y = $y + 1 ))           # update inner loop count
    done
    echo                          # blank line
    (( x = $x + 1 ))              # update outer loop count
done
$ bash multi.sh 7        ...execute the script.
1       2       3       4       5       6       7
2       4       6       8       10      12      14
3       6       9       12      15      18      21
4       8       12      16      20      24      28
5       10      15      20      25      30      35
6       12      18      24      30      36      42
7       14      21      28      35      42      49
```

6.10.5   trap

The *trap* command allows you to specify a command that should be executed when the shell receives a signal of a particular value. Figure 6–34 gives the syntax.

Shell command: **trap** [[*command*] { *signal* } +]

The *trap* command instructs the shell to execute *command* whenever any of the numbered signals *signal* are received. If several signals are received, they are trapped in numeric order. If a signal value of 0 is specified, then *command* is executed when the shell terminates. If *command* is omitted, then the traps of the numbered signals are reset to their original values. If *command* is an empty string, then the numbered signals are ignored. If *trap* is executed with no arguments, a list of all the signals and their *trap* settings is displayed. For more information on signals and their default actions, see Chapter 12, "Systems Programming."

Figure 6–34 Description of the *trap* shell command.

Here's an example of a script that uses the *trap* control structure. When a *Control-C* was typed, the shell executed the *echo* command followed by the exit command:

```
$ cat trap.sh                         ...list the script.
trap 'echo Control-C; exit 1' 2    # trap Ctl-C (signal #2)
while test 1
do
 echo infinite loop
 sleep 2                              # sleep for two seconds.
```

```
done
$ bash trap.sh              ...execute the script.
infinite loop
infinite loop
^C                          ...I typed a Control-C here.
Control-C                   ...displayed by the echo command.
$ _
```

6.11 Functions

Bash allows you to define functions that may be invoked as shell commands. Parameters passed to functions are accessible via the standard positional parameter mechanism. Functions must be defined before they are used. There are two ways to define a function, as shown in Figure 6–35.

---

function *name*

{

  list of commands

}

     or the keyword **function** may be omitted:

name ()

{

  list of commands.

}

Figure 6–35   A Bash *function* declaration.

To invoke a function, supply its name followed by the appropriate parameters. For obvious reasons, the shell does not check the number or type of the parameters.

Here's an example of a script that defines and uses a function that takes no parameters:

```
$ cat func1.sh             ...list the script.
message ()     # no-parameter function.
{
 echo hi
 echo there
}
i=1
while (( i <= 3 ))
do
 message    # call the function.
 let i=i+1 # increment loop count.
done
$ sh func1.sh              ...execute the script.
hi
there
```

```
hi
there
hi
there
$ _
```

6.11.1   Using Parameters

As I mentioned previously, parameters are accessible via the standard positional mechanism. Here's an example of a script that passes parameters to a function:

```
$ cat func2.sh               ...list the script.
f ()
{
 echo parameter 1 = $1       # display first parameter.
 echo parameter list = $*    # display entire list.
}
# main program.
f 1                          # call with 1 parameter.
f cat dog goat               # call with 3 parameters.
$ sh func2.sh                    ...execute the script.
parameter 1 = 1
parameter list = 1
parameter 1 = cat
parameter list = cat dog goat
$ _
```

6.11.2   Returning from a Function

The *return* command returns the flow of control back to the caller, and has the following syntax shown in Figure 6–36.

```
return [ value ]
```

Figure 6–36   Bash function *return* statement.

When *return* is used without an argument, the function call returns immediately with the exit code of the last command that was executed in the function; otherwise, it returns with its exit code set to *value*. If a *return* command is executed from the main script, it's equivalent to an *exit* command. The exit code is accessible from the caller via the $? variable. Here's an example function that multiplies its arguments and returns the result:

```
$ cat func3.sh              ...list the script.
f ()       # two-parameter function.
{
 (( returnValue = $1 * $2 ))
```

```
  return $returnValue
}
# main program.
f 3 4                        # call function.
result=$?                    # save exit code.
echo return value from function was $result
$ sh func3.sh                ...execute the script.
return value from function was 12
$ _
```

6.11.3   Access to Functions

Functions can be exported to subshells in Bash. This is accomplished with the *export* built-in, described in Figure 6–37.

Shell command: **export** -f *functionname*

The *export* built-in command used with the **-f** option exports a function to a subshell the same way exported shell variable values are exported to subshells.

Figure 6–37   Description of the *export* shell command used to export a function.

Bash also provides a built-in command called *local* (Figure 6–38) to restrict a variable to be local only to the current function (i.e., its value cannot be passed to a subshell).

Shell command: **local** *name*[=*value*]

The *local* built-in command defines a variable to be local only to the current function. A variable name can be listed or a value can be assigned in the same statement.

Figure 6–38   Description of the *local* shell command.

Another useful built-in command used when writing functions is the *builtin* built-in command (Figure 6–39).

Shell command: **builtin** [*command* [*args*]]

The *builtin* shell built-in runs the named shell built-in *command*, and passes it *args* if present. This is useful when you are writing a shell function that has the same name as an existing built-in but within the function you still want to run the built-in rather than recursively call the function.

Figure 6–39   Description of the *builtin* shell command.

6.11.4   Recursion

With careful thought, it's perfectly possible to write recursive functions. Here are two example scripts that implement a recursive version of factorial (). The first uses the exit code to return the result and the second uses standard output to echo the result. Note these scripts are available online; see the Preface for more information.

6.11.4.1 Recursive Factorial, Using Exit Code

```
factorial ()        # one-parameter function
{
 if (( $1 <= 1 ))
 then
   return 1                    # return result in exit code.
 else
   typeset tmp                 # declare two local variables.
   typeset result
   (( tmp = $1 - 1 ))
   factorial $tmp              # call recursively.
   (( result = $? * $1 ))
   return $result             # return result in exit code.
 fi
}
# main program.
factorial 5                    # call function
echo factorial 5 = $?          # display exit code.
```

6.11.4.2 Recursive Factorial, Using Standard Output

```
factorial ()        # one-parameter function
{
 if (( $1 <= 1 ))
 then
   echo 1                      # echo result to standard output.
 else
   typeset tmp                 # declare two local variables.
   typeset result
   (( tmp = $1 - 1 ))
   (( result = `factorial $tmp` * $1 ))
   echo $result          # echo result to standard output.
 fi
}
#
echo factorial 5 = `factorial 5`      # display result.
```

6.11.5 Sharing Functions

To share the source code of a function between several scripts, place it in a separate file and then read it using the "." or *source* built-in commands at the start of the scripts that use the function (Figure 6–40).

Shell Command: **source** *fileName*
   . *fileName*

source (or ".") causes a shell to execute every command in the script called *fileName* without invoking a subshell. It is perfectly legal for *fileName* to contain further *source* commands. If an error occurs during the execution of *fileName*, control is returned to the original shell.

Figure 6–40   Description of the *source* and "." shell commands.

In the following example, assume that the source code of one of the previous factorial scripts was saved in a file called "fact.sh":

```
$ cat script.sh                       ...list the script.
. fact.sh                  # read function source code.
echo factorial 5 = `factorial 5`   # call the function.
$ sh script.sh                        ...execute the script.
factorial 5 = 120
$ _
```

6.12 Menus: select

The *select* command allows you to create simple menus, and has the syntax shown in Figure 6–41.

---

select *name* [**in** {*word* }+]
do
   list
done

Figure 6–41   Description of the *select* shell command.

The *select* command displays a numbered list of the words specified by the *in* clause to the standard error channel, displays the prompt stored in the special variable PS3, and then waits for a line of user input. When the user enters a line, it's stored in the predefined variable REPLY, and then one of three things occurs:

• If the user entered one of the listed numbers, *name* is set to that number, the commands in list are executed, and then the user is prompted for another choice.

- If the user entered a blank line, the selection is displayed again.
- If the user entered an illegal choice, *name* is set to null, the commands in the list are executed, and then the user is prompted for another choice.

The next example is a recoding of the menu-selection example from earlier in the chapter. It replaces the while loop and termination logic with a simpler *select* command.

```
$ cat newmenu.sh          ...list the script.
echo menu test program
select reply in "date" "pwd" "pwd" "exit"
do
 case $reply in
   "date")
     date
     ;;
   "pwd")
     pwd
     ;;
   "exit")
     break
     ;;
   *)
     echo illegal choice
     ;;
 esac
done
$ sh newmenu.sh           ...execute the script.
menu test program
1) date
2) pwd
3) pwd
4) exit
#? 1
Fri May  6 21:49:33 CST 2005
#? 5
illegal choice
#? 4
$ _
```

6.13 Directory Access and the Directory Stack

Bash provides a built-in version of *cd* that works as shown in Figure 6–42.

Shell Command: **cd** { *name* }
      cd *oldName newName*

The first form of the *cd* command is processed as follows:

- If *name* is omitted, the shell moves to the home directory specified by $HOME.
- If *name* is equal to -, the shell moves to the previous working directory that is kept in $OLDPWD.
- If *name* begins with a /, the shell moves to the directory whose full name is *name*.
- If *name* begins with anything else, the shell searches through the directory sequence specified by $CDPATH for a match, and moves the shell to the matching directory. The default value of $CDPATH is null, which causes *cd* to search only the current directory.

If the second form of *cd* is used, the shell replaces the first occurrence of the token *oldName* by the token *newName* in the current directory's full pathname, and then attempts to change to the new pathname. The shell always stores the full pathname of the current directory in the variable PWD. The current value of $PWD may be displayed by using the built-in command *pwd*.

Figure 6–42   Description of the *cd* shell command.

Here's an example of *cd* in action:

```
$ CDPATH=.:/usr   ...set my CDPATH.
$ cd dir1         ...move to "dir1", located under ".".
$ pwd
/home/glass/dir1
$ cd include      ...move to "include", located in "/usr".
$ pwd             ...display the current working dir.
/usr/include
$ cd -            ...move to my previous directory.
$ pwd             ...display the current working dir.
/home/glass/dir1
$ _
```

Bash provides a directory stack mechanism allowing you to easily move back and forth between different directories. The entire stack is stored in the string array $DIRSTACK, allowing easy access to any item in the stack from a Bash shell script.

To push the current directory onto the directory stack and *cd* to a new directory, use the *pushd* built-in command (Figure 6–43).

Shell command: **pushd** [-n] [*dir*]

pushd saves the current directory as the most recent addition to (i.e., on top of) the directory stack. A subsequent *popd* will retrieve this directory. Then *pushd* changes directories to the directory specified. If no new directory is specified, the current directory and the top directory on the stack are swapped (i.e., you pop the current top of the stack and *cd* there and push the directory you were in onto the stack). If the **-n** argument is present, do not *cd* to the new directory, simply push the current directory onto the stack.

Figure 6–43   Description of the *pushd* shell command.

When it's time to return to a previous directory, use the *popd* built-in to retrieve previous locations and *cd* there (Figure 6–44).

Shell command: **popd** [-n]

popd retrieves the last directory that was pushed onto the stack and changes directory to that location. The entry is removed from the stack. If the **-n** argument is present, do not *cd* to the new directory, simply remove it from the top of the stack.

Figure 6–44   Description of the *popd* shell command.

In addition to contents of the stack being available in the $DIRSTACK shell variable, the *dirs* built-in command will print (or empty) the contents of the directory stack (Figure 6–45).

Shell command: **dirs** [-cp]

If no arguments are given, *dirs* simply prints out the contents of the directory stack. The **-p** option causes the directories to be printed one per line. The **-c** option causes the directory stack to be cleared.

Figure 6–45   Description of the *dirs* shell command.

6.14 Job Control

Job control allows you to suspend and resume the execution of a process begun from the Bash command line. Typing a *Control-Z* while a process is running will suspend it. You can then use the *bg* or *fg* shell commands to resume it in the background or foreground, respectively, as described in Figures 6–48 and 6–49.

To see all jobs associated with the current shell, use the *jobs* built-in (Figure 6–46).

Shell command: **jobs** [-lrs]

jobs displays a list of all the shell's jobs. When *jobs* is used with the **-l** option, process IDs are included in the listing. If the **-r** option is used, list only currently running jobs. If the **-s** option is used, list only currently stopped jobs.

Figure 6–46   Description of the *jobs* shell command

6.14.1   Specifying a Job

Each of the job control commands (bg, fg, and kill) requires that a job be specified upon which to act. Figure 6–47 shows the forms available to specify a Bash job.

Form	Specifies
%*integer*	The job number *integer*.
%*prefix*	The job whose name starts with *prefix*.
%+	The job that was last referenced.
%%	Same as %+.
%-	The job that was referenced second to last.
%*name*	Refers to a process whose name begins with *name*.
%?*name*	Refers to a process where *name* appears anywhere in the command line.

Figure 6–47   Job specifications in Bash.

The specifier must uniquely identify a job. If more than one job matches the specifier, Bash reports an error.

6.14.2   bg

Figure 6–48 describes the *bg* shell command.

Shell Command: **bg** [%*job*]

bg resumes the specified job as a background process. If no job is specified, the last-referenced job is resumed.

Figure 6–48   Description of the *bg* shell command.

In the following example, I started a foreground job and then decided it would be better to run it in the background. I suspended the job using *Control-Z* and then resumed it in the background.

```
$ man bash | ul -tdumb > bash.txt  ...start in foreground.
^Z                                 ...suspend it.
[1] + Stopped            man bash | ul -tdumb > bash.txt
$ bg %1                  ...resume it in background.
[1]   man bash | ul -tdumb > bash.txt&
$ jobs                         ...list current jobs.
[1] + Running            man bash | ul -tdumb > bash.txt
$ _
```

6.14.3   fg

Figure 6–49 describes the *fg* shell command.

Shell Command: **fg** [*%job*]

fg resumes the specified job as the foreground process. If no job is specified, the last-referenced job is resumed.

Figure 6–49   Description of the *fg* shell command.

In the following example, I brought a background job into the foreground using *fg*:

```
$ sleep 1000 &                     ...start a background job.
[1]   27143
$ man bash | ul -tdumb > bash.txt &   ...start another.
[2]   27144
$ jobs                         ...list the current jobs.
[2] + Running            man bash | ul -tdumb > bash.txt &
[1] - Running            sleep 1000 &
$ fg %ma                       ...bring job to foreground.
man bash | ul -tdumb > bash.txt    ...command is redisplayed.
$ _
```

6.14.4   kill

Use the *kill* built-in to send a signal to a job (Figure 6–50).

> *Shell command*: **kill** [-s *signame*] [-n *signum*] *jobspec* or *pid*
>
> *kill* sends the specified signal to the specified process. Either *jobspec* (e.g., "%1") or a process ID is required. If the **-s** option is used, *signame* is a valid signal name (e.g., SIGINT). If the **-n** option is used, *signum* is the signal number. If neither **-s** nor **-n** is used, a SIGTERM signal is sent to the process.

Figure 6–50   Description of the *kill* shell command.

6.15 Command-Line Options

Bash supports many command-line options. Some of the most useful are shown in Figure 6–51.

-c *string*	Run *string* as a shell command.
-s	Read commands from standard input.
--login	Run Bash as a login shell. This is useful if you can't set Bash to be your login shell with **chsh**.
--noprofile	Ignore Bash profile files (systemwide and user versions).
--norc	Ignore Bash rc files (~/.bashrc).
--posix	Run in Posix mode (same as *set –o posix*).
--verbose	-v	Print shell input lines as they are read (same as *set –o verbose*).

Figure 6–51   Some Bash command-line options.

CHAPTER REVIEW

Checklist

In this chapter, I described:

- Bash startup files
- using shell variables
- using aliases, the history mechanism, and command-line editing
- arithmetic, conditionals, and control structures
- functions
- using the directory stack
- job control

Quiz

1. Describe a common use of the built-in variable $$.
2. What is the easiest way to re-execute your ".profile" file?

3. Why are braces ({ }) required around list variables?
4. Why is the alias mechanism useful?
5. What characters surround an arithmetic expression in a Bash script?
6. How are functions made available to subshells?
7. How do you change your command-editing mode from **emacs** to **vim**?
8. Name one method used to define a shell variable in a subshell (i.e., pass the value to the subshell).
9. What shell variable contains the directory stack?

Exercises

1. Rewrite the loan Perl program from Chapter 4, "GNU Utilities for Power Users" (beginning on page 162) in Bash. [level: *medium*]
2. Write a utility called **junk** that satisfies the following specification:

Utility: **junk** [-l] [-p] { *fileName* }*

junk is a replacement for the **rm** utility. Rather than removing files, it moves them into the subdirectory ".junk" in your home directory. If ".junk" doesn't exist, it is automatically created. The **-l** option lists the current contents of the ".junk" directory, and the **-p** option purges ".junk".

Here's an example of junk at work:

```
$ ls -lG reader.c        ...list existing file.
-rw-r--r--  1 glass    2580 May  4 19:17 reader.c
$ junk reader.c          ...junk it!
$ ls -lG reader.c        ...confirm that it was moved.
reader.c not found
$ junk badguy.c          ...junk another file.
$ junk -l                ...list contents of "junk" directory.
-rw-r--r--  1 glass      57 May  4 19:17 badguy.c
-rw-r--r--  1 glass    2580 May  4 19:17 reader.c
$ junk -p                ...purge junk.
$ junk -l                ...list junk.
$ _
```

Remember to comment your script liberally. [level: *medium*]

Projects

1. Create a process management utility that allows you to kill processes based on their CPU usage. This kind of utility would be especially useful to system administrators (see Chapter 14, "System Administration"). [level: *easy*]

2. Write a Bash script called **mv** (which replaces the GNU utility **mv**) that tries to rename the specified file (using the GNU utility **mv**), but if the destination file exists, instead creates an index number to append to the destination file, a sort of version number. So if I type:

```
$ mv a.txt b.txt
```

but b.txt already exists, **mv** will move the file to b.txt.1. Note that if b.txt.1 already exists, you must rename the file to b.txt.2, and so on, until you can successfully rename the file to a name that does not already exist. [level: *medium*]

3. Write a crafty script called **ghoul** that is difficult to kill; when it receives a SIGINT (from a *Control-C*), it should create a copy of itself before dying. Thus, every time an unwary user tries to kill a ghoul, another ghoul is created to take its place! Of course, **ghoul** can still be killed by a SIGKILL (-9) signal. [level: *hard*]

7

The Korn Shell

Motivation

The Korn shell, originally designed by David Korn, is a powerful superset of the original UNIX Bourne shell, and offers improvements in job control, command-line editing, and programming features. It is very popular in UNIX environments and is available on most Linux systems.

Prerequisites

You should already have read Chapter 5, "The Linux Shells."

Objectives

In this chapter, I explain and demonstrate the Korn-specific facilities.

Presentation

The information in this section is presented in the form of several sample Linux command sessions.

Shell Commands

This section introduces the following shell commands, listed in alphabetical order:

alias	env	fg
bg	export	function
cd	fc	jobs

kill	readonly	trap
let	return	typeset
print	select	unalias
read	set	

7.1   Introduction

The Korn shell is available for Linux as the Public Domain Korn Shell (pdksh), a public domain reimplementation that is intended to be a clone of the UNIX ksh. Although sometimes not installed in the default set of Linux packages, pdksh is included in most Linux distributions. Another Linux shell, the Z shell (zsh, written by Paul Falstad), also implements most features of the Korn shell, but does not claim complete compatibility with the original Korn shell.

The Korn shell supports all of the shell facilities described in Chapter 5, "The Linux Shells," as well as the control structures and conditional expressions described in Chapter 6, "The Bourne Again Shell." The following features unique to the Korn shell are discussed in this chapter:

- command customization using aliases
- access to previous commands via a history mechanism (through **vi**-like and **emacs**-like command-line editing features)
- functions
- advanced job control
- several new built-in commands

7.2   Startup

The Korn shell is a regular C program whose executable file is stored as "/bin/ksh." If your chosen shell is "/bin/ksh," an interactive Korn shell is invoked automatically when you log into a Linux system. You may also invoke a Korn shell manually from a script or from a terminal by using the command **ksh. ksh** has several command-line options that are described at the end of this chapter.

When a Korn shell is invoked, the startup sequence is different for interactive shells and noninteractive shells (Figure 7–1).

Step	Shell type	Action
1	interactive only	Execute commands in "/etc/profile" if it exists.
2	interactive only	Execute commands in $HOME/.profile if it exists.
3	both	Execute commands in the file named by $ENV if it exists.

Figure 7–1 Korn shell startup sequence.

The value $ENV is usually set to $HOME/.kshrc in the $HOME/.profile script. After reading the startup files, an interactive Korn shell then displays its prompt and awaits user commands. The standard Korn shell prompt is $, although it may be changed by setting the local variable PS1. Here's an example of a Korn shell ".profile" script, which is executed exactly once at the start of every login session:

```
TERM=xterm; export TERM          # my terminal type.
ENV=~/.kshrc; export ENV         # environment filename.
HISTSIZE=100; export HISTSIZE    # remember 100 commands.
MAILCHECK=60; export MAILCHECK   # seconds between checks.
set -o ignoreeof      # don't let Control-D log me out.
set -o trackall       # speed up file searches.
stty erase '^H'       # set backspace character.
tset                  # set terminal.
```

Some of these commands won't mean much to you right now, but their meaning will become clear as the chapter progresses.

Here's an example of a Korn shell ".kshrc" script, which typically contains useful Korn-shell specific information required by all shells, including those that are created purely to execute scripts:

```
PATH='.:~/bin:/bin:/usr/bin:/usr/local/bin'
PS1='! $ ';export PS1   # put command number in prompt.
alias h="fc -l"         # set up useful aliases.
alias ll="ls -l"
alias rm="rm -i"
alias cd="cdx"
alias up="cdx .."
alias dir="/bin/ls"
alias ls="ls -aF"
alias env="printenv|sort"

# function to display path and directory when moving
function cdx
{
 if 'cd' "$@"
 then
   echo $PWD
   ls -aF
 fi
}
```

Every Korn shell executes this script when it begins, including all subshells.

7.3   Variables

The command ksh can perform the following variable-related operations:

- simple assignment and access
- testing of a variable for existence
- reading a variable from standard input
- making a variable read-only
- exporting of a local variable to the environment

The Korn shell also defines several local and environment variables in addition to those mentioned in Chapter 5, "The Linux Shells."

7.3.1   Creating/Assigning A Variable

The Korn shell syntax for assigning a value to a variable is:

```
{name=value}+
```

If a variable doesn't exist, it is implicitly created; otherwise, its previous value is overwritten. A newly created variable is always local, although it may be turned into an environment variable using a method that I'll describe shortly. To assign a value that contains spaces, surround the value by quotes. Here's an example:

```
$ firstName=Graham lastName=Glass age=29    ...assign vars.
$ echo $firstName $lastName is $age
Graham Glass is 29                           ...simple access.
$ name=Graham Glass                          ...syntax error.
Glass: not found
$ name="Graham Glass"            ...use quotes to build strings.
$ echo $name                                 ...now it works.
Graham Glass
$ _
```

7.3.2   Accessing A Variable

ksh supports the access methods listed in Figure 7–2.

Syntax	Action
$*name*	Replaced by the value of *name*.
${*name*}	Replaced by the value of *name*. This form is useful if the expression is immediately followed by an alphanumeric that would otherwise be interpreted as part of the variable name.

Figure 7–2   Korn shell variable access. (Part 1 of 2)

Syntax	Action
${name-word}	Replaced by the value of *name* if set, and *word* otherwise.
${name+word}	Replaced by *word* if *name* is set, and nothing otherwise.
${name=word}	Assigns *word* to the variable *name* if *name* is not already set, and then is replaced by the value of *name*.
${name?word}	Replaced by name if *name* is set. If *name* is not set, *word* is displayed to the standard error channel and the shell is exited. If *word* is omitted, then a standard error message is displayed instead.

Figure 7-2   Korn shell variable access. (Part 2 of 2)

If a variable is accessed before it is assigned a value, it returns a null string.

I personally find these variable access techniques to be "hack" methods of dealing with certain conditions, and hardly ever use them. However, it's good to be able to understand code that uses them. The following examples illustrate each access method. In the first example, I used braces to append a string to the value of a variable:

```
$ verb=sing              ...assign a variable.
$ echo I like $verbing   ...there's no variable "verbing".
I like
$ echo I like ${verb}ing ...now it works.
I like singing
$ _
```

Here's an example that uses command substitution to set the variable *startDate* to the current date if it's not already set:

```
$ startDate=${startDate-`date`}  ...if not set, run date.
$ echo $startDate                ...look at its value.
Wed May 4 06:56:51 CST 2005
$ _
```

In the next example, I set the variable *x* to a default value and printed its value, all at the same time:

```
$ echo x = ${x=10}       ...assign a default value.
x = 10
$ echo $x                ...confirm the variable was set.
10
$ _
```

In the following example, I displayed messages based on whether certain variables were set or not:

```
$ flag=1                              ...assign a variable.
$ echo ${flag+'flag is set'}          ...conditional message #1.
flag is set
$ echo ${flag2+'flag2 is set'}        ...conditional message #2.
                                      ...result is null
$ _
```

In the next example, I tried to access an undefined variable called *grandTotal* and received an error message instead:

```
$ total=10                            ...assign a variable.
$ value=${total?'total not set'}      ...accessed OK.
$ echo $value                         ...look at its value.
10
$ value=${grandTotal?'grand total not set'}  ...not set.
grandTotal: grand total not set
$ _
```

In the final example, I ran a script that used the same access method as the previous example. Note that the script terminated when the access error occurred:

```
$ cat script.sh                ...look at the script.
value=${grandTotal?'grand total is not set'}
echo done          # this line is never executed.
$ script.sh                    ...run the script.
script.sh: grandTotal: grand total is not set
$ _
```

7.3.3   Reading a Variable from Standard Input

The *read* command allows you to read variables from standard input (Figure 7–3).

Shell Command: **read** { *variable* }+

read reads one line from standard input and then assigns successive words from the line to the specified variables. Any words that are left over are assigned to the last-named variable.

Figure 7–3   Description of the *read* shell command.

If you specify just one variable, the entire line is stored in the variable. Here's an example script that prompts a user for his or her full name:

```
$ cat script.sh                    ...list the script.
echo "Please enter your name: \c"
read name                    # read just one variable.
echo your name is $name      # display the variable.
$ ksh script.sh                    ...run the script.
Please enter your name: Graham Walker Glass
your name is Graham Walker Glass     ...whole line was read.
$ _
```

Here's an example that illustrates what happens when you specify more than one variable:

```
$ cat script.sh                    ...list the script.
echo "Please enter your name: \c"
read firstName lastName      # read two variables.
echo your first name is $firstName
echo your last name is $lastName
$ ksh script.sh                    ...run the script.
Please enter your name: Graham Walker Glass
your first name is Graham          ...first word.
your last name is Walker Glass     ...the rest.
$ ksh script.sh                    ...run it again.
Please enter your name: Graham
your first name is Graham          ...first word.
your last name is                  ...only one.
$ _
```

7.3.4   Exporting Variables

The *export* command allows you to mark local variables for export to the environment and works as described in Figure 7–4.

Shell Command: **export** { *variable* }+

export marks the specified variables for export to the environment. If no variables are specified, a list of all the variables marked for export during the shell session is displayed.

Figure 7–4   Description of the *export* shell command.

Although it's not necessary, I tend to use uppercase letters to name environment variables. The **env** utility (Figure 7–5) allows you to modify and list environment variables.

Utility: **env** { *variable=value* }* [*command*]

env assigns values to specified environment variables, and then executes an optional command using the new environment. If variables or command are not specified, a list of the current environment is displayed.

Figure 7–5 Description of the **env** command.

In the following example, I created a local variable called DATABASE, which I then marked for export. When I created a subshell, a copy of the environment variable was inherited:

```
$ export                    ...list my current exports.
export TERM                 ...set in my ".profile" startup file.
$ DATABASE=/dbase/db        ...create a local variable.
$ export DATABASE           ...mark it for export.
$ export                    ...note that it's been added.
export DATABASE
export TERM
$ env                       ...list the environment.
DATABASE=/dbase/db
HOME=/home/glass
LOGNAME=glass
PATH=:/bin:/usr/bin
SHELL=/bin/ksh
TERM=xterm
USER=glass
$ ksh                       ...create a subshell.
$ echo $DATABASE            ...a copy was inherited.
/dbase/db
$ ^D                        ...terminate subshell.
$ _
```

7.3.5   Read-Only Variables

The *readonly* command allows you to protect variables against modification, and works as described in Figure 7–6.

Shell Command: **readonly** { *variable* }*

readonly makes the specified variables read-only, protecting them against future modification. If no variables are specified, a list of the current read-only variables is displayed. Copies of exported variables do not inherit their read-only status.

Figure 7–6 Description of the *readonly* shell command.

In the following example, I protected a local variable from modification. I then exported the variable and showed that its copy did not inherit the read-only status:

```
$ password=Shazam          ...assign a local variable.
$ echo $password           ...display its value.
Shazam
$ readonly password        ...protect it.
$ readonly                 ...list all read-only variables.
readonly password
$ password=Phoombah        ...try to modify it.
password: is read only
$ export password          ...export the variable.
$ password=Phoombah        ...try to modify it.
password: is read only
$ ksh                      ...create a subshell.
$ readonly        ...the exported password is not read-only.
$ echo $password           ...its value was copied correctly.
Shazam
$ password=Alacazar        ...but its value may be changed.
$ echo $password           ...echo its value.
Alacazar
$ ^D                       ...terminate the subshell.
$ echo $password           ...echo original value.
Shazam
$ _
```

7.3.6   Predefined Local Variables
In addition to the core predefined local variables, the Korn shell defines those in Figure 7–7.

Name	Value
$@	An individually quoted list of all the positional parameters.
$#	The number of positional parameters.
$?	The exit value of the last command.
$!	The process ID of the last background command.
$-	The current shell options assigned from the command line or by the built-in set command—discussed later.
$$	The process ID of this shell.

Figure 7–7   Korn shell predefined local variables.

Here's a small shell script that illustrates the first three variables. In this example, the C compiler (**gcc**) was invoked on a file that didn't exist, and therefore returned a failure exit code.

```
$ cat script.sh                        ...list the script.
echo there are $# command line arguments: $@
gcc $1                     # compile the first argument.
echo the last exit value was $?    # display exit code.
$ script.sh nofile tmpfile           ...execute the script.
there are 2 command line arguments: nofile tmpfile
gcc: nofile: No such file or directory
gcc: no input files
the last exit value was 1             ...gcc errored.
$ _
```

The next example illustrates how $! may be used to kill the last background process:

```
$ sleep 1000 &     ...bg process, ksh does not report PID.
$ kill $!          ...kill it!
29455 Terminated
$ echo $!          ...the process ID is still remembered.
29455
$ _
```

7.3.7   Predefined Environment Variables

In addition to the core predefined environment variables (listed in Chapter 3, "GNU Utilities for Nonprogrammers"), the Korn shell defines those in Figure 7–8.

Name	Value
$IFS	When the shell tokenizes a command line prior to its execution, it uses the characters in this variable as delimiters. IFS usually contains a space, a tab, and a newline character.
$PS1	This contains the value of the command-line prompt, and is $ by default. To change the command-line prompt, simply set PS1 to a new value.
$PS2	This contains the value of the secondary command line-prompt that is displayed when more input is required by the shell, and is > by default. To change the prompt, set PS2 to a new value.
$ENV	If this variable is not set, the shell searches the user's home directory for the ".profile" startup file when a new login shell is created. If this variable is set, then every new shell invocation runs the script specified by ENV.

Figure 7–8   Korn shell predefined environment variables.

Here's a small example that illustrates the predefined environment variables used to set the command-line prompt. I set my prompt to something different by assigning a new value to PS1, and I set PS2 to a new value and illustrated an occasion where the secondary prompt is displayed.

```
$ PS1="ksh? "            ...set a new primary prompt.
ksh? string="a long\     ...assign a string over 2 lines
>  string"               ...">" is the secondary prompt.
ksh? echo $string        ...look at the value of "string".
a long string
ksh? PS2="??? "          ...change the secondary prompt.
ksh? string="a long\     ...assign a long string.
??? string"              ..."???" is new secondary prompt.
ksh? echo $string        ...look at the value of "string".
a long string

ksh? _
```

7.4 Aliases

The Korn shell allows you to create and customize your own commands by using the *alias* command (Figure 7–9).

Shell Command: **alias** [-tx] [*word* [= *string*]]

alias supports a simple form of command-line customization. If you alias *word* to be equal to *string* and then later enter a command beginning with *word*, the first occurrence of *word* is replaced by *string* and then the command is reprocessed. If you don't supply *word* or *string*, a list of all the current shell aliases is displayed. If you only supply *word*, then the string currently associated with the alias *word* is displayed. If you supply *word* and *string*, the shell adds the specified alias to its collection of aliases. If an alias already exists for *word*, it is replaced. If the replacement string begins with word, it is not reprocessed for aliases to prevent infinite loops. If the replacement string ends with a space, then the first word that follows is processed for aliases.

Figure 7–9 Description of the *alias* shell command.

Here's an example of *alias* in action:

```
$ alias dir='ls -aF'     ...register an alias.
$ dir                    ...same as typing "ls -aF".
./          main2.c      p.reverse.c        reverse.h
../          main2.o      palindrome.c       reverse.old
$ dir *.c                ...same as typing "ls -aF *.c".
main2.c      p.reverse.c      palindrome.c
```

```
$ alias dir              ...definition of "dir".
dir=ls -aF
$ _
```

In the following example, I defined a command in terms of itself:

```
$ alias ls='ls -aF'      ...no problem.
$ ls *.c                 ...same as typing "ls -aF *.c".
main2.c    p.reverse.c        palindrome.c
$ alias dir='ls'         ...define "dir" in terms of "ls".
$ dir                    ...same as typing "ls -aF".
./          main2.c     p.reverse.c      reverse.h
../         main2.o     palindrome.c     reverse.old
$ _
```

7.4.1   Aliasing Built-In Commands
All built-in commands may be aliased except for the following: *case, do, done, elif, else, esac, fi, for, function, if, select, then, time, until, while, {, }.*

7.4.2   Removing an Alias
To remove an alias, use the *unalias* command (Figure 7–10).

Shell Command: **unalias** { *word* } +

unalias removes all the specified aliases.

Figure 7–10   Description of the *unalias* shell command.

Here's an example of *unalias*:

```
$ alias dir              ...look at an existing alias.
dir=ls
$ unalias dir            ...remove the alias.
$ alias dir              ...try looking at the alias again.
dir alias not found
$ _
```

7.4.3   Predefined Aliases
For convenience, the shell predefines the aliases shown in Figure 7–11.

Alias	Value
false	let 0
functions	typeset -f
history	fc -l
integer	typeset -i
r	fc -e -
true	:
type	whence -v
hash	alias -t

Figure 7–11 Korn shell predefined aliases.

The uses of these aliases will become more apparent as the chapter progresses. For example, the "r" alias is particularly useful, as it allows you to recall previous commands without having to use the tedious sequence "fc -e -".

7.4.4   Some Useful Aliases

Figure 7–12 is a grab-bag of useful aliases that I've gathered from various sources.

Alias	Value
rm	rm -i This causes **rm** to prompt for confirmation.
mv	mv -i This causes **mv** to prompt for confirmation.
ls	ls -aF This causes **ls** to display more information.
env	printenv | sort This displays a sorted list of the environment variables.
ll	ls -l This allows you to obtain a long directory listing more conveniently.

Figure 7–12 Some useful aliases.

For some other interesting aliases, please see "Aliases" in Chapter 8, "The C Shell."

7.4.5   Tracked Aliases

One common use of aliases is as a shorthand for full pathnames, to avoid the lookup penalty of the standard search mechanism as it scans the directories specified by $PATH. You may arrange for the full pathname replacement to occur automatically by making use of the *tracked alias* facility. All aliases listed with the **-t** option are flagged as tracked aliases, and the standard search mechanism is used to set their initial value. From then on, a tracked alias is replaced by its value, thereby avoiding the search time. If no aliases follow the **-t** option, a list of all the currently tracked aliases is displayed.

```
$ alias -t more        ...define a tracked alias for more.
$ alias -t             ...look at all tracked aliases.
more=/bin/more         ...its full pathname is stored.
$ _
```

The "-o trackall" option of *set* (described later in this chapter) tells the shell to track all commands automatically.

```
$ set -o trackall      ...all commands are now tracked.
$ date                 ...execute date.
Fri May  6 00:54:44 CST 2005
$ alias -t             ...look at all tracked aliases.
date=/bin/date         ...date is now tracked.
more=/bin/more
$ _
```

Since the value of a tracked alias is dependent on the value of $PATH, the values of all tracked aliases are re-evaluated every time the PATH variable is changed. If PATH is unset, the values of all tracked aliases are set to null, but remain tracked.

7.4.6   Sharing Aliases

To make an alias available to a child shell, you must mark it as an *export alias* by using the **-x** option of *alias*. All aliases listed with the **-x** option are flagged as export aliases. If no aliases follow the **-x** option, a list of all currently exported aliases is displayed. Note that if the value of an alias is changed in a child shell, it does not affect the value of the original alias in the parent shell.

```
$ alias -x mroe='more'  ...add an export alias.
$ alias -x              ...list exported aliases.
autoload=typeset -fu    ...a standard alias.
...                     ...other aliases are listed here.
ls=ls -F
mroe=more               ...the alias I just added.
...                     ...other aliases are listed here.
type=whence -v
vi=/usr/bin/vi
$ cat test.ksh          ...a script using the new alias.
```

```
mroe main2.c
$ ksh test.ksh          ...run the script. mroe works!
/* MAIN2.C */

#include "stdio.h"
#include "palindrome.h"

main ()

{
 printf ("palindrome (\"cat\") = %d\n",
palindrome ("cat"));
 printf ("palindrome (\"noon\") = %d\n",
palindrome ("noon"));
}
$ _
```

7.5   History

The Korn shell keeps a record of commands entered from the keyboard so that they may be edited and re-executed at a later stage. This facility is known as a *history* mechanism. The built-in command *fc* (**fix c**ommand) gives you access to history. There are two forms of *fc*. The first, simpler form allows you to re-execute a specified set of previous commands, and the second, more complex form allows you edit them before re-execution.

7.5.1   Numbered Commands

When you're using history, it's very handy to arrange for your prompt to contain the "number" of the command that you're about to enter. To do this, set the primary prompt variable (PS1) to contain a ! character:

```
$ PS1='! $ '          ...set PS1 to contain a !.
103 $ _                ...prompt for command #103.
```

7.5.2   Storage of Commands

The Korn shell records the last $HISTSIZE commands in the file $HISTFILE. If the environment variable HISTSIZE is not set, a default value of 128 is used. If HISTFILE is not set, or the named file is not writable, then the file $HOME/.sh_history is used by default. All the Korn shells that specify the same history file will share it. Therefore, as long as you don't change the value of $HISTFILE during a login session, the commands entered during that session are available as history at the next session. The file is not strictly a text file, but each command string is in the file (along with other housekeeping data). In the following example, I examined the history file where commands are stored using the **strings** command:

```
$ echo $HISTSIZE          ...set in ".profile".
100
$ echo $HISTFILE          ...not set previously.
```

```
$ strings $HOME/.sh_history | tail -3   ...display last 3 lines.
echo $HISTSIZE
echo $HISTFILE
tail -3 $HOME/.sh_history
$ _
```

7.5.3   Command Re-execution

The *fc* command allows you to re-execute previous commands. The first, simpler form of *fc* works as described in Figure 7–13.

Shell Command: **fc** -e - [*old=new*] *prefix*

This form of the *fc* command re-executes the last command beginning with *prefix* after optionally replacing the first occurrence of the string *old* by the string *new*. *prefix* may be a number, in which case the numbered event is re-executed.

Figure 7–13   Description of the *fc* shell command used for re-executing a command.

Here's an example of *fc* in action:

```
360 $ fc -e - ech    ...last command starting with "ech".
echo $HISTFILE
361 $ fc -e - FILE=SIZE ech  ...replace "FILE" by "SIZE".
echo $HISTSIZE
100
362 $ fc -e - 360            ...execute command # 360.
echo $HISTFILE
363 $ _
```

The token "r" is a predefined alias for "fc -e -", which allows for a more convenient way to re-execute commands:

```
364 $ alias r         ...look at "r"'s alias.
r=fc -e -
365 $ r 364           ...execute command # 364.
alias r
r=fc -e -
366 $ _
```

7.5.4   Editing Commands

The Korn shell allows you to pre-edit commands before they are re-executed by using a more advanced form of the *fc* command, described in Figure 7–14.

Shell Command: **fc** [-e editor] [-nlr] [start] [end]

This form of *fc* invokes the editor called *editor* upon the specified range of commands. When the editor is exited, the edited range of commands is then executed. If *editor* is not specified, then the editor whose pathname is stored in the environment variable FCEDIT is used. The value $FCEDIT is "/bin/ed" by default, and I *don't* recommend that you use this default. I personally prefer "/bin/vim" (the full pathname of the **vim** editor on a Linux system), as I'm most familiar with the UNIX **vi** editor. If no other options are specified, the editor is invoked upon the last command.

When you enter the editor, you may edit the command(s) as you wish and then save the text. When you exit the editor, the Korn shell automatically echoes and executes the saved version of the command(s).

To specify a particular command either by its index or by its prefix, supply the number or the prefix as the value of *start* but don't supply a value for *end*. To specify a range of commands, set the value of *start* to select the first command in the series, and set the value of *end* to select the last command in the series. If a negative number is supplied, it's interpreted as an offset to the current command.

The **-l** option causes the selected commands to be displayed but not executed. In this case, if no command series is specified, the last sixteen commands are listed. The **-r** option reverses the order of the selected commands, and the **-n** option inhibits the generation of command numbers when they are listed.

Figure 7–14   Description of the *fc* shell command used for command editing.

The following example illustrates the method of editing and re-execution:

```
371 $ whence vim          ...find the location of "vim".
/bin/vim
372 $ FCEDIT=/bin/vim      ...set FCEDIT to full path.
373 $ fc 371               ...edit command # 371.
...enter vim, edit the command to say "whence ls", save, quit vi
whence ls                 ...display edited commands.
/bin/ls                   ...output from edited command.
374 $ fc 371 373           ...edit commands # 371..373.
...enter vim and edit a list of the last three commands.
...assume that I deleted the first line, changed the remaining
...lines to read "echo -n hi" and "echo there", and then quit.
echo -n "hi "             ...display edited commands.
echo there
hi there                  ...output from edited commands.
375 $ _
```

Here's an example of the **-l** option:

```
376 $ fc -l 371 373      ...list commands with numbers.
371 $ whence vim
372 $ FCEDIT=/bin/vim
373 $ fc 371
377 $ fc -6              ...edit command # 371.
...edit command to say "whence ls" and then quit.
whence ls               ...display edited command.
/bin/ls                 ...output by command.
378 $ _
```

7.6 Editing Commands

The Korn shell contains simplified built-in versions of the **vi**, **gmacs**, and **emacs** editors that may be used to edit the current command or previous commands. To select one of these built-in editors, set either the VISUAL or the EDITOR variable to a string that ends in the name of one of these editors. In the following example, I selected the **vi** editor:

```
380 $ VISUAL=vi          ...select the built-in "vi" editor.
381 $ _
```

Each built-in editor is now described separately.

7.6.1 The Built-In vi Editor

This description assumes that you are familiar with the **vi/vim** editors. If you're not, please consult the description of the **vim** editor in Chapter 3, "GNU Utilities for Nonprogrammers."

To edit the current line, press the *Esc* key to enter the built-in **vi** editor's control mode and make the required changes. To enter append or insert mode from control mode, press the **a** key or the **i** key, respectively. To go back to control mode from either of these modes, press the *Esc* key. To re-execute the command, press the *Enter* key. Be warned that if you type a *Control-D* inside the editor, it terminates the shell, not just the editor.

When in control mode, key sequences fall into one of several categories:

- standard **vi** key sequences (described in Chapter 3, "GNU Utilities for Nonprogrammers").
- additional movement.
- additional searching.
- filename completion.
- alias replacement.

The last four categories of key sequences are described in the following subsections.

7.6.1.1 Additional Movement

The cursor up (**k** or -) and cursor down (**j** or +) keys select the previous and next commands in the history list, respectively. This allows you to easily access history from within the built-in editor. To load a command with a particular number, enter command mode and then enter the number of the command followed by the **G** key. Here's an example:

```
125 $ echo line 1
line 1
126 $ echo line 2
line 2
127 $ ...at this point, I pressed the Esc key followed by
      ...k twice (up, up). This loaded command #125 onto
      ...the command line, which I then executed by
      ...pressing the Enter key.
line 1
128 $ ...at this point, I pressed Esc followed by 125G.
      ...This loaded command #125 onto the command line,
      ...which I then executed by pressing the Enter key.
line 1
129 $ _
```

7.6.1.2 Additional Searching

The standard search mechanisms /*string* and ?*string* search backward and forward through history, respectively. Here's an example:

```
127 $ echo line 1
line 1
138 $ echo line 2
line 2
139 $ ...at this point, I pressed the Esc key followed
      ...by /ech, which loaded the last command
      ...containing "ech" onto the command line.
      ...Then I pressed n to continue the search to
      ...the next command that matched. Finally, I
      ...pressed the Enter key to execute the command.
line 1
$ _
```

7.6.1.3 Filename Completion

If you type an asterisk (*) in control mode, it is appended to the word that the cursor is over and then processed as if it were a wildcard by the filename substitution mechanism. If no match occurs, a beep is sounded—otherwise, the word is replaced by an alphabetical list of all the matching filenames and the editor enters input mode automatically. Here's an example:

```
114 $ ls m*
m               m3          main.c          mbox
m1              madness.c   main.o          mon.out
m2              main        makefile        myFile
115 $ ls ma  ...at this point I pressed the Esc key
             ...the * key, and then the Enter key.
```

```
115 $ ls madness.c main main.c main.o makefile
madness.c      main.c           makefile
main           main.o
116 $ _
```

If you type an equal sign (=) in control mode, the editor displays a numbered list of all the files that have the current word as a prefix and then redraws the command line:

```
116 $ ls ma       ...at this point I pressed the Esc key
                  ...and then the = key.

1) madness.c
2) main
3) main.c
4) main.o
5) makefile
116 $ ls ma_      ...back to the original command line.
```

If you type a \ in control mode, the editor attempts to complete the current filename in an unambiguous way. If a completed pathname matches a directory, a / is appended; otherwise, a space is appended. Here's an example:

```
116 $ ls ma    ...at this point I pressed the Esc key
               ...and then the \ key.
               ...No completion was performed, since "ma"
               ...is a prefix of more than one file.
116 $ ls mak   ...at this point I pressed the Esc key
               ...and then the \ key. The editor
               ...completed the name to be "makefile".
116 $ ls makefile _
```

7.6.1.4 Alias Replacement

If you find yourself typing the same pattern again and again from the editor, you can make good use of the alias replacement mechanism. If you give _letter an alias of word, the sequence @letter is replaced by word when you're in command mode. In the following example, the letter **i** at the start of the alias causes the built-in editor to go into insert mode, and the literal Esc at the end of the string causes it to leave **vi** mode:

```
123 $ alias _c='icommon text^['      ...^[ was Control-V
                                     ...followed by Esc
124 $ echo       ...at this point I pressed Esc followed by @c.
124 $ echo common text_
```

7.6.2   The Built-in emacs/gmacs Editor

This description assumes that you are familiar with the **emacs** editor. If you're not, please consult the description of the **emacs** editor in Chapter 3, "GNU Utilities for Nonprogrammers."

Most of the **emacs** key sequences are supported. You may move the cursor and manipulate text using the standard **emacs** key sequences. To re-execute the command, press the *Enter* key.

The main difference between the built-in editor and standard **emacs** is that the cursor-up, cursor-down, search-forward, and search-backward key sequences operate on the history list. For example, the cursor-up key sequence, *Control-P*, displays the previous command on the command line. Similarly, the search-backward key sequence, *Control-R string,* displays the last command that contains *string.*

7.7 Arithmetic

The *let* command allows you to perform arithmetic (Figure 7–15).

Shell Command: **let** *expression*

The *let* command performs double-precision integer arithmetic, and supports all of the basic math operators using the standard precedence rules. Here they are grouped in descending order of precedence:

OPERATOR	MEANING
-	unary minus
!	logical negation
* / %	multiplication, division, remainder
+ -	addition, subtraction
<= >= < >	relational operators
== !=	equality, inequality
=	assignment

All of the operators associate from left to right except for the assignment operator. Expressions may be placed between parentheses to modify the order of evaluation. The shell doesn't check for overflow, so beware! Operands may be integer constants or variables. When a variable is encountered, it is replaced by its value, which in turn may contain other variables. You may explicitly override the default base (10) of a constant by using the format *base#number* where *base* is a number between 2 and 36. You must not put spaces or tabs between the operands or operators. You must not place a $ in front of variables that are part of an expression.

Figure 7–15 Description of the *let* shell command.

Here are some examples:

```
$ let x = 2 + 2        ...expression contains spaces.
ksh: =: syntax error   ...no spaces or tabs allowed!
$ let x=2+2            ...OK.
$ echo $x
4
```

```
$ let y=x*4              ...don't place $ before variables.
$ echo $y
16
$ let x=2#100+2#100      ...add two numbers in base 2.
$ echo $x
8                        ...number is displayed in base 10.
$ _
```

7.7.1   Preventing Metacharacter Interpretation

Unfortunately, the shell interprets several of the standard operators, such as <, >, and *, as meta-characters, so they must be quoted or preceded by a backslash (\ ) to inhibit their special meaning. To avoid this inconvenience, there is an equivalent form of *let* that automatically treats all of the tokens as if they were surrounded by double quotes, and allows you to use spaces around tokens. The token sequence:

```
(( list ))
```

is equivalent to:

```
let " list "
```

Note that double quotes do not prevent the expansion of variables. I personally *always* use the ((..)) syntax instead of *let*. Here's an example:

```
$ (( x = 4 ))            ...spaces are OK.
$ (( y = x * 4 ))
$ echo $y
16
$ _
```

7.7.2   Testing Values

Arithmetic values may be used by decision-making control structures, such as an *if* statement:

```
$ (( x = 4 ))           ...assign x to 4.
$ if (( x > 0 ))        ...OK to use in a control structure.
> then
>   echo x is positive
> fi
x is positive           ...output from control structure.
$ _
```

For simple arithmetic tests, I recommend using ((..)) instead of **test** expressions.

7.8 Tilde Substitution

Any token of the form *~name* is subject to *tilde substitution*. The shell checks the password file
to see if *name* is a valid user name, and if it is, replaces the *~name* sequence with the full pathname of the user's home directory. If it isn't, the *~name* sequence is left unchanged. Tilde substitution occurs *after* aliases are processed. Figure 7–16 is a table of the tilde substitutions,
including the special cases ~+ and ~-.

Tilde sequence	Replaced by
~	$HOME
~user	home directory of *user*
~/pathname	$HOME/*pathname*
~+	$PWD (current working directory)
~-	$OLDPWD (previous working directory)

Figure 7–16   Tilde substitutions in the Korn shell.

The predefined local variables PWD and OLDPWD are described later in this chapter.
Here are some examples of tilde substitution:

```
$ pwd
/home/glass          ...current working directory.
$ echo ~
/home/glass          ...my home directory.
$ cd /
$ echo ~+
/                    ...current working directory.
$ echo ~-
/home/glass          ...previous working directory.
$ echo ~dcox
/home/dcox           ...another user's home directory.
$ _
```

7.9 Menus: select

The *select* command allows you to create simple menus, and has the syntax shown in Figure 7–17.

```
select name [ in {word }+ ]
do
  list
done
```

Figure 7–17   Description of the *select* shell command.

The *select* command displays a numbered list of the words specified by the *in* clause to the standard error channel, displays the prompt stored in the special variable PS3, and then waits for a line of user input. When the user enters a line, it's stored in the predefined variable REPLY, and then one of three things occurs:

- If the user entered one of the listed numbers, *name* is set to that number, the commands in list are executed, and then the user is prompted for another choice.
- If the user entered a blank line, the selection is displayed again.
- If the user entered an illegal choice, *name* is set to null, the commands in list are executed, and then the user is prompted for another choice.

The next example is a recoding of the menu selection example from Chapter 6, "The Bourne Again Shell." It replaces the while loop and termination logic with a simpler *select* command.

```
$ cat menu.ksh              ...list the script.
echo menu test program
select reply in "date" "pwd" "pwd" "exit"
do
  case $reply in
    "date")
      date
      ;;
    "pwd")
      pwd
      ;;
    "exit")
      break
      ;;
    *)
      echo illegal choice
      ;;
  esac
done
$ ksh menu.ksh                    ...execute the script.
menu test program
1) date
2) pwd
3) pwd
4) exit
#? 1
Fri May  6 21:49:33 CST 2005
#? 5
illegal choice
#? 4
$ _
```

7.10 Functions

The Korn shell allows you to define functions that may be invoked as shell commands. Parameters passed to functions are accessible via the standard positional parameter mechanism. Functions must be defined before they are used. There are two ways to define a function, as shown in Figure 7–18.

---

function *name*
{
  list of commands
}
     or the keyword **function** may be omitted:
name ()
{
  list of commands.
}

Figure 7–18 The Korn shell *function* declaration.

I personally favor the second form because it looks more like the C language. To invoke a function, supply its name followed by the appropriate parameters. For obvious reasons, the shell does not check the number or type of the parameters.

Here's an example of a script that defines and uses a function that takes no parameters:

```
$ cat func1.ksh          ...list the script.
message ()     # no-parameter function.
{
 echo hi
 echo there
}
i=1
while (( i <= 3 ))
do
 message    # call the function.
 let i=i+1 # increment loop count.
done
$ ksh func1.ksh              ...execute the script.
hi
there
hi
there
hi
there
$ _
```

7.10.1   Using Parameters

As I mentioned previously, parameters are accessible via the standard positional mechanism.
Here's an example of a script that passes parameters to a function:

```
$ cat func2.ksh                 ...list the script.
f ()
{
  echo parameter 1 = $1      # display first parameter.
  echo parameter list = $*   # display entire list.
}
# main program.
f 1                            # call with 1 parameter.
f cat dog goat                 # call with 3 parameters.
$ ksh func2.ksh                  ...execute the script.
parameter 1 = 1
parameter list = 1
parameter 1 = cat
parameter list = cat dog goat
$ _
```

7.10.2   Returning from a Function

The *return* command returns the flow of control back to the caller (Figure 7–19).

```
return [ value ]
```

Figure 7–19   Korn shell function *return* statement.

When *return* is used without an argument, the function call returns immediately with the
exit code of the last command that was executed in the function; otherwise, it returns with its exit
code set to *value*. If a *return* command is executed from the main script, it's equivalent to an *exit*
command. The exit code is accessible from the caller via the $? variable. Here's an example function that multiplies its arguments and returns the result:

```
$ cat func3.ksh            ...list the script.
f ()     # two-parameter function.
{
  (( returnValue = $1 * $2 ))
  return $returnValue
}
# main program.
f 3 4                        # call function.
result=$?                    # save exit code.
echo return value from function was $result
$ ksh func3.ksh                  ...execute the script.
return value from function was 12
$ _
```

7.10.3   Context

A function executes in the same context as the process that calls it. This means that it shares the same variables, current working directory, and traps. The only exception to this is the "trap on exit"; a function's "trap on exit" executes when the function returns.

7.10.4   Local Variables

The *typeset* command (described in more detail later in this chapter) has some special function-oriented facilities. Specifically, a variable created using the *typeset* function is limited in scope to the function in which it's created and all of the functions that the defining function calls. If a variable of the same name already exists, its value is overwritten and replaced when the function returns. This property is similar (but not identical) to the scoping rules in most traditional high-level languages. Here's an example of a function that declares a local variable using *typeset*:

```
$ cat func4.ksh            ...list the script.
f ()  # two-parameter function.
{
  typeset x              # declare local variable.
  (( x = $1 * $2 ))      # set local variable.
  echo local x = $x
  return $x
}
# main program.
x=1                       # set global variable.
echo global x = $x        # display value before function call.
f 3 4                     # call function.
result=$?                 # save exit code.
echo return value from function was $result
echo global x = $x        # value of global after function.
$ ksh func4.ksh           ...execute the script.
global x = 1
local x = 12
return value from function was 12
global x = 1
$ _
```

7.10.5   Recursion

With careful thought, it's perfectly possible to write recursive functions. Here are two example scripts that implement a recursive version of factorial (). The first uses the exit code to return the result and the second uses standard output to echo the result. Note these scripts are available online; see the Preface for more information.

7.10.5.1 Recursive Factorial, Using Exit Code

```
factorial ()        # one-parameter function.
{
 if (( $1 <= 1 ))
```

```
then
   return 1                    # return result in exit code.
else
   typeset tmp                 # declare two local variables.
   typeset result
   (( tmp = $1 - 1 ))
   factorial $tmp              # call recursively.
   (( result = $? * $1 ))
   return $result             # return result in exit code.
 fi
}
# main program.
factorial 5                    # call function.
echo factorial 5 = $?          # display exit code.
```

7.10.5.2 Recursive Factorial, Using Standard Output

```
factorial ()        # one-parameter function.
{
 if (( $1 <= 1 ))
 then
    echo 1                     # echo result to standard output.
 else
    typeset tmp                # declare two local variables.
    typeset result
    (( tmp = $1 - 1 ))
    (( result = 'factorial $tmp' * $1 ))
    echo $result        # echo result to standard output.
 fi
}
#
echo factorial 5 = 'factorial 5'    # display result.
```

7.10.6 Sharing Functions

To share the source code of a function between several scripts, place it in a separate file and then read it using the "." built-in command at the start of the scripts that use the function. In the following example, assume that the source code of one of the previous factorial scripts was saved in a file called "fact.ksh":

```
$ cat script.ksh                    ...list the script.
. fact.ksh                 # read function source code.
echo factorial 5 = 'factorial 5'   # call the function.
$ ksh script.ksh                    ...execute the script.
factorial 5 = 120
$ _
```

7.11 Job Control

The Korn shell supports the job control commands shown in Figure 7–20.

Command	Function
jobs	Lists your jobs.
bg	Places a specified job into the background.
fg	Places a specified job into the foreground.
kill	Sends an arbitrary signal to a process or job.

Figure 7–20 Korn shell job control commands.

The next few sections provide a description of each job control facility and examples of their use.

7.11.1 Jobs

Figure 7–21 describes the *jobs* shell command.

Shell Command: **jobs** [-l]

jobs displays a list of all the shell's jobs. When used with the **-l** option, process IDs are added to the listing. The syntax of each line of output is:

job#   [+\-]   *PID   Status   Command*

where a + means that the job was the last job to be placed into the background, and a - means that it was the second-to-last job to be placed into the background. *Status* may be one of the following:

- Running
- Stopped (suspended)
- Terminated (killed by a signal)
- Done (zero exit code)
- Exit (nonzero exit code)

The only real significance of the + and - is that they may be used when specifying the job in a later command (see "Specifying a Job," below).

Figure 7–21 Description of the *jobs* shell command.

Here's an example of *jobs* in action:

```
$ jobs                              ...no jobs right now.
$ sleep 1000 &                      ...start a background job.
[1]    27128
$ man ls | ul -tdumb > ls.txt &    ...another bg job.
[2]    27129
$ jobs -l                           ...list current jobs.
[2] + 27129  Running     man ls | ul -tdumb > ls.txt &
[1] - 27128  Running     sleep 1000 &
$ _
```

7.11.2   Specifying a Job

The *bg, fg,* and *kill* commands that I'm about to describe allow you to specify a job using one of several forms, as listed in Figure 7–22.

Form	Specifies
%integer	The job number *integer*.
%prefix	The job whose name starts with *prefix*.
%+	The job that was last referenced.
%%	Same as %+.
%-	The job that was referenced second to last.

Figure 7–22   Job specifications in the Korn shell.

The descriptions that follow contain examples of job specification.

7.11.3   bg

Figure 7–23 describes the *bg* shell command.

Shell Command: **bg** [%job]

bg resumes the specified job as a background process. If no job is specified, the last-referenced job is resumed.

Figure 7–23   Description of the *bg* shell command.

In the following example, I started a foreground job and then decided it would be better to run it in the background. I suspended the job using *Control-Z* and then resumed it in the background.

```
$ man ksh | ul -tdumb > ksh.txt    ...start in foreground.
^Z                                 ...suspend it.
[1] + Stopped                 man ksh | ul -tdumb > ksh.txt
$ bg %1                       ...resume it in background.
[1]    man ksh | ul -tdumb > ksh.txt&
$ jobs                             ...list current jobs.
[1] +  Running                man ksh | ul -tdumb > ksh.txt
$ _
```

7.11.4   fg

Figure 7–24 describes the *fg* shell command.

Shell Command: **fg** [*%job*]

fg resumes the specified job as the foreground process. If no job is specified, the last-referenced job is resumed.

Figure 7–24   Description of the *fg* shell command.

In the following example, I brought a background job into the foreground using *fg*:

```
$ sleep 1000 &                           ...start a background job.
[1]    27143
$ man ksh | ul -tdumb > ksh.txt &     ...start another.
[2]    27144
$ jobs                                ...list the current jobs.
[2] +  Running            man ksh | ul -tdumb > ksh.txt &
[1] -  Running            sleep 1000 &
$ fg %ma                              ...bring job to foreground.
man ksh | ul -tdumb > ksh.txt         ...command is redisplayed.
$ _
```

7.11.5   kill

Figure 7–25 describes the *kill* shell command.

Shell Command: **kill** [-l] [*-signal*] { *process* | *%job* }+

kill sends the specified signal to the specified job or processes. A process is specified by its PID number. A signal may be specified either by its number or symbolically, by removing the "SIG" prefix from its symbolic constant in "/usr/include/sys/signal.h." To obtain a list of the signal names, use the **-l** option. If no signal is specified, the TERM signal is sent. If the TERM or HUP signals are sent to a suspended process, it is sent the CONT signal, which causes it to resume.

Figure 7–25   Description of the *kill* shell command.

The following example demonstrates the use of *kill*:

```
$ man ksh | ul -tdumb > ksh.txt &    ...start a bg job.
[1]   27160
$ kill -9 %1            ...kill it via a job specifier.
[1] + Killed            man ksh | ul -tdumb > ksh.txt &
$ man ksh | ul -tdumb > ksh.txt &  ...start another.
[1]   27164
$ kill -KILL 27164         ...kill it via a process ID.
[1] + Killed            man ksh | ul -tdumb > ksh.txt &
$ _
```

7.12 Enhancements

In addition to the new facilities that have already been described, the Korn shell also offers some enhancements to older shells in the following areas:

- redirection
- pipes
- command substitution
- variable access
- extra built-in commands

7.12.1   Redirection

The Korn shell supplies a minor extra redirection facility—the ability to strip leading tabs off "here" documents. Figure 7–26 gives the augmented syntax.

```
command << [-] word
```

Figure 7–26   Redirection with a "here" document in the Korn shell.

If *word* is preceded by a -, then leading tabs are removed from the lines of input that follow. Here's an example:

```
$ cat <<- ENDOFTEXT
>           this input contains
>      some leading tabs
>ENDOFTEXT
this input contains
some leading tabs
$ _
```

This allows "here" text in a script to be indented to match the nearby shell commands without affecting how the text is used.

7.12.2   Pipes

The |& operator supports a simple form of concurrent processing. When a command is followed
by |&, it runs as a background process whose standard input and output channels are connected
to the original parent shell via a two-way pipe. When the original shell generates output using a
print -p command (discussed later in this chapter), it is sent to the child shell's standard input
channel. When the original shell reads input using a *read -p* command (also discussed later in
this chapter), it is taken from the child shell's standard output channel. Here's an example:

```
$ date |&                  ...start child process.
[1]    8311
$ read -p theDate          ...read from standard output of child.
[1] +  Done      date |&   ...child process terminates.
$ echo $theDate            ...display the result.
Tue May 10 21:36:57 CDT 2005
$ _
```

7.12.3   Command Substitution

In addition to the older method of command substitution—surrounding the command with grave
accents—the Korn shell also allows you to perform command substitution using the syntax shown
in Figure 7–27.

```
$( command )
```

Figure 7–27   Command substitution in the Korn shell.

Note that the $ that immediately precedes the open parentheses is part of the syntax, and is
not a prompt. Here's an example:

```
$ echo there are $(who | wc -1) users on the system
there are 6 users on the system
$ _
```

To substitute the contents of a file into a shell command, you may use **$(<file)** as a faster form of
$(cat file).

7.12.4   Variables

The Korn shell supports the following additional variable facilities:

- more flexible access methods
- more predefined local variables
- more predefined environment variables
- simple arrays
- a *typeset* command for formatting the output of variables

The next few subsections describe each feature.

7.12.4.1 Flexible Access Methods

In addition to the typical variable access methods, the Korn shell supports some more complex access methods (Figure 7–28).

Syntax	Action
${#*name*}	Replaced by the length of the value of *name*.
${#*name*[*] }	Replaced by the number of elements in the array *name*.
${*name*:+*word* } ${*name*:=*word* } ${*name*:?*word* } ${*name*:+*word* }	Work like their counterparts that do not contain a :, except that *name* must be set *and* non-null instead of just set.
${*name*#*pattern*} ${*name*##*pattern*}	Removes a leading *pattern* from *name*. The expression is replaced by the value of *name* if name doesn't begin with *pattern*, and with the remaining suffix if it does. The first form removes the smallest matching pattern, and the second form removes the largest matching pattern.
${*name*%*pattern*} ${*name*%%*pattern*}	Removes a trailing *pattern* from *name*. The expression is replaced by the value of *name* if *name* doesn't end with *pattern*, and with the remaining prefix if it does. The first form removes the smallest matching pattern, and the second form removes the largest matching pattern.

Figure 7–28   Korn shell variable access methods.

Here are some examples of these features:

```
$ fish='smoked salmon'        ...set a variable.
$ echo ${#fish}     ...display the length of the value.
13
$ cd dir1                     ...move to directory.
$ echo $PWD    ...display the current working directory.
/home/glass/dir1
$ echo $HOME
/home/glass
$ echo ${PWD#$HOME/}          ...remove leading $HOME/
dir1
$ fileName=menu.ksh           ...set a variable.
$ echo ${fileName%.ksh}.bak   ...remove trailing ".ksh"
menu.bak                      ...and add ".bak".
$ _
```

7.12.4.2 Predefined Local Variables

In addition to the common predefined local variables, the Korn shell supports those listed in Figure 7–29.

Name	Value
$_	The last parameter of the previous command.
$PPID	The process ID number of the shell's parent.
$PWD	The current working directory of the shell.
$OLDPWD	The previous working directory of the shell.
$RANDOM	A random integer.
$REPLY	Set by a *select* command.
$SECONDS	The number of seconds since the shell was invoked.
$CDPATH	Used by the *cd* command.
$COLUMNS	Sets the width of the edit window for the built-in editors.
$EDITOR	Selects the built-in editor type.
$ENV	Selects the name of the Korn shell startup file.
$FCEDIT	Defines the editor that is invoked by the fc command.
$HISTFILE	The name of the history file.
$HISTSIZE	The number of history lines to remember.
$LINES	Used by *select* to determine how to display the selections.
$MAILCHECK	Tells the shell how many seconds to wait between mail checks. The default value is 600.
$MAILPATH	This should be set to a list of filenames, separated by colons. The shell checks these files for modification every $MAILCHECK seconds.
$PS3	The prompt used by the *select* command, #? by default.
$TMOUT	If set to a number greater than zero and more than $TMOUT seconds elapse between commands, the shell terminates.
$VISUAL	Selects the built-in editor type.

Figure 7–29 Korn shell predefined local variables.

Here are some examples of these predefined variables:

```
$ echo hi there    ...display a message to demonstrate $_.
hi there
$ echo $_          ...display last arg of last command.
```

```
there
$ echo $PWD            ...display the current working dir.
/home/glass
$ echo $PPID           ...display the shell's parent pid.
27709
$ cd /                 ...move to the root directory.
$ echo $OLDPWD         ...display last working directory.
/home/glass
$ echo $PWD            ...display current working directory.
/
$ echo $RANDOM $RANDOM    ...display two random numbers.
32561 8323
$ echo $SECONDS        ...display seconds since shell began.

918
$ echo $TMOUT          ...display the timeout value.
0                      ...no timeout selected.
$ _
```

7.12.4.3 One-Dimensional Arrays

The Korn shell supports simple one-dimensional arrays. To create an array, simply assign a value to a variable name using a subscript between 0 and 511 in brackets. Array elements are created as needed. The syntax is given in Figure 7–30.

To set the value of an array element:

name[*subscript*]=*value*

To access the value of an array element:

${*name*[*subscript*]}

Figure 7–30 Korn shell array definition and use.

If you omit *subscript*, the value of 0 is used by default. Here's an example that uses a script to display the squares of the numbers between 0 and 9:

```
$ cat squares.ksh                      ...list the script.
i=0
while (( i < 10 ))
do
  (( squares[$i] = i * i ))  ...assign individual element.
  (( i = i + 1 ))            ...increment loop counter.
done
echo 5 squared is ${squares[5]}  ...display one element.
```

```
echo list of all squares is ${squares[*]} ...display all.
$ ksh squares.ksh                           ...execute the script.
5 squared is 25
list of all squares is 0 1 4 9 16 25 36 49 64 81
$ _
```

7.12.4.4 Typeset
Figure 7–31 describes the *typeset* shell command.

Shell Command: **typeset** { - HLRZfilrtux [*value*] [*name* [=*word*]]}*

typeset allows the creation and manipulation of variables. It allows variables to be formatted, converted to an internal integer representation for speedier arithmetic, made read-only, made exportable, and switched between lowercase and uppercase.

   Every variable has an associated set of flags that determine its properties. For example, if a variable has its "uppercase" flag set, it will always map its contents to uppercase, *even when they are changed.* The options to *typeset* operate by setting and resetting the various flags associated with named variables. When an option is preceded by -, it causes the appropriate flag to be turned *on.* To turn a flag *off* and reverse the sense of the option, precede the option by a + instead of a -.

Figure 7–31   Description of the *typeset* shell command.

   There now follows a list of the options to *typeset* with illustrations of their usage. I've split the descriptions up into related sections to make things a little easier.

   Formatting   In all of the formatting options, the field width of *name* is set to *value* if present; otherwise, it is set to the width of *word* (Figure 7–32).

Option	Meaning
L	Turn the L flag on and turn the R flag off. Left justify *word* and remove leading spaces. If the width of *word* is less than *name's* field width, then pad it with trailing spaces. If the width of *word* is greater than *name's* field width, then truncate its end to fit. If the Z flag is set, leading zeroes are also removed.
R	Turn the R flag on and turn the L flag off. Right justify word and remove trailing spaces. If the width of *word* is less than *name's* field width, then pad it with leading spaces. If the width of *word* is greater than *name's* field width, then truncate its end to fit.
Z	Right justify word and pad with zeroes if the first nonspace character is a digit and the L flag is off.

Figure 7–32   Formatting with the *typeset* shell command.

Case With the case options (Figure 7–33), the value can be converted to upper or lower case.

Option	Meaning
l	Turn the l flag on and turn the u flag off. Convert word to lowercase.
u	Turn the u flag on and turn the l flag off. Convert word to uppercase.

Figure 7–33 Changing the case of characters with the *typeset* shell command.

Here's an example that left justifies all the elements in an array and then displays them in uppercase:

```
$ cat justify.ksh          ...list the script.
wordList[0]='jeff'         # set three elements.
wordList[1]='john'
wordList[2]='ellen'
typeset -uL7 wordList       # typeset all elements in array.
echo ${wordList[*]}         # beware! shell removes nonquoted spaces
echo "${wordList[*]}"       # works OK.
$ ksh justify.ksh           ...execute the script.
JEFF JOHN ELLEN
JEFF    JOHN    ELLEN
$ _
```

Miscellaneous

Figure 7–34 shows miscellaneous *typeset* shell command options.

Option	Meaning
f	The only flags that are allowed in conjunction with this option are **t**, which sets the trace option for the named functions, and **x**, which displays all functions with the x attribute set.
t	Tags name with the token *word*.

Figure 7–34 Miscellaneous *typeset* shell command options.

In the following example, I selected the function factorial () to be traced using the **-ft** option, and then ran the script:

```
$ cat func5.ksh           ...list the script.
factorial ()              # one-parameter function
{
 if (( $1 <= 1 ))
```

```
then
  return 1
else
  typeset tmp
  typeset result
  (( tmp = $1 - 1 ))
  factorial $tmp
  (( result = $? * $1 ))
  return $result
  fi
}
#
typeset -ft factorial    ...select a function trace.
factorial 3
echo factorial 3 = $?
$ ksh func5.ksh          ...execute the script.
+ let   3 <= 1           ...debugging information.
+ typeset tmp
+ typeset result
+ let   tmp = 3 - 1
+ factorial 2
+ let   2 <= 1
+ typeset tmp
+ typeset result
+ let   tmp = 2 - 1
+ factorial 1
+ let   1 <= 1
+ return 1
+ let   result = 1 * 2
+ return 2
+ let   result = 2 * 3
+ return 6
factorial 3 = 6
$ _
```

7.12.4.5 Typeset With No Named Variables

If no variables are named, then the names of all the parameters that have the specified flags set
are listed. If no flags are specified, then all the parameters and their flag settings are listed.
Here's an example:

```
$ typeset        ...display a list of all typeset variables.
export NODEID
export PATH
...
leftjust 7 t
export integer MAILCHECK
$ typeset -i   ...display list of integer typeset vars.
```

```
LINENO=1
MAILCHECK=60
...
$ _
```

7.12.5   Built-Ins
The Korn shell includes the following built-in commands:

- cd
- set
- *print* (an enhancement of the *echo* command)
- read
- test
- trap

The next few subsections contain a description of each built-in.

7.12.5.1 Cd
The Korn shell's version of *cd* supports several new features (Figure 7–35).

Shell Command: **cd** { *name* }
       cd *oldName newName*

The first form of the *cd* command is processed as follows:

- If *name* is omitted, the shell moves to the home directory specified by $HOME.
- If *name* is equal to -, the shell moves to the previous working directory that is kept in $OLDPWD.
- If *name* begins with a /, the shell moves to the directory whose full name is *name*.
- If *name* begins with anything else, the shell searches through the directory sequence specified by $CDPATH for a match, and moves the shell to the matching directory. The default value of $CDPATH is null, which causes *cd* to search only the current directory.

If the second form of *cd* is used, the shell replaces the first occurrence of the token *oldName* by the token *newName* in the current directory's full pathname, and then attempts to change to the new pathname. The shell always stores the full pathname of the current directory in the variable PWD. The current value of $PWD may be displayed by using the built-in command *pwd*.

Figure 7–35 Description of the *cd* shell command.

Here's an example of *cd* in action:

```
$ CDPATH=.:/usr   ...set my CDPATH.
$ cd dir1         ...move to "dir1", located under ".".
```

```
$ pwd
/home/glass/dir1
$ cd include        ...move to "include", located in "/usr".
$ pwd               ...display the current working dir.
/usr/include
$ cd -              ...move to my previous directory.
$ pwd               ...display the current working dir.
/home/glass/dir1
$ _
```

7.12.5.2 Set

The *set* command (Figure 7–36) allows you to set and unset flags that control shellwide characteristics.

Shell Command: **set** [+-aefhkmnostuvx] [+-o *option*] { *arg* } *

The Korn shell version of *set* supports all of the Bourne *set* features plus a few more. The various features of *set* do not fall naturally into categories, so I'll just list each one together with a brief description. An option preceded by a + instead of a - reverses the sense of the description.

Figure 7–36   Description of the *set* shell command.

Figure 7–37 is a list of the options to *set*.

Option	Meaning
a	All variables that are created are automatically flagged for export.
f	Disable filename substitution.
h	All non-built-in commands are automatically flagged as tracked aliases.
m	Place all background jobs in their own unique process group and display notification of completion. This flag is automatically set for interactive shells.
n	Accept but do not execute commands. This flag has no effect on interactive shells.
o	This option is described separately below.
p	Set $PATH to its default value, cause the startup sequence to ignore the $HOME/.profile file and read "/etc/suid_profile" instead of the $ENV file. This flag is set automatically whenever a shell is executed by a process in "set user ID" or "set group ID" mode. For more information on "set user ID" processes, consult Chapter 12, "Systems Programming."

Figure 7–37   *set* shell command options (Part 1 of 2)

Option	Meaning
s	Sort the positional parameters.
--	Do not change any flags. If no arguments follow, all of the positional parameters are unset.

Figure 7–37 *set* shell command options (Part 2 of 2)

7.12.5.3 The **-o** Option

The **-o** option of *set* takes an argument. The argument frequently has the same effect as one of the other flags to *set*. If no argument is supplied, the current settings are displayed. Figure 7–38 is a list of the valid arguments and their meanings.

Option	Meaning
allexport	Equivalent to the a flag.
errexit	Equivalent to the e flag.
bgnice	Background processes are executed at a lower priority.
emacs	Invokes the built-in **emacs** editor.
gmacs	Invokes the built-in **gmacs** editor.
ignoreeof	Don't exit on *Control-D*. **exit** must be used instead.
keyword	Equivalent to the k flag.
markdirs	Append trailing / to directories generated by filename substitution.
monitor	Equivalent to the m flag.
noclobber	Prevents redirection from truncating existing files.
noexec	Equivalent to the n flag.
noglob	Equivalent to the f flag.
nolog	Do not save function definitions in history file.
nounset	Equivalent to the u flag.
privileged	Same as **-p**.
verbose	Equivalent to the v flag.
trackall	Equivalent to the h flag.

Figure 7–38 **set -o** arguments.

Option	Meaning
vi	Invokes the built-in **vi** editor.
viraw	Characters are processed as they are typed in **vi** mode.
xtrace	Equivalent to the x flag.

Figure 7–38 **set -o** arguments.

I can set the **ignoreeof** option in my ".profile" script to protect myself against accidental *Control-D* logouts like this:

```
set -o ignoreeof
```

7.12.5.4 print

The *print* command is a more sophisticated version of *echo*, and allows you to send output to a arbitrary file descriptor. Figure 7–39 describes how it works.

Shell Command: **print** -npsuR [*n*] { *arg* }*

By default, *print* displays its arguments to standard output, followed by a newline. The **-n** option inhibits the newline, and the **-u** option allows you to specify a single-digit file descriptor *n* for the output channel. The **-s** option causes the output to be appended to the history file instead of an output channel. The **-p** option causes the output to be sent to the shell's two-way pipe channel. The **-R** option causes all further words to be interpreted as arguments.

Figure 7–39 Description of the *print* shell command.

Here's an example:

```
121 $ print -u2 hi there       ...send output to stderr.
hi there
122 $ print -s echo hi there  ...append to history.
124 $ r 123                    ...recall command #123.
echo hi there
hi there
125 $ print -R -s hi there     ...treat "-s" as an arg.
-s hi there
126 $ _
```

7.12.5.5 read

Figure 7–40 describes how the Korn shell's *read* command works.

> *Shell Command*: **read** -prsu [*n*] [*name?prompt*] { *name* }*
>
> The Korn shell *read* command reads one line from standard input and then assigns successive words from the line to the specified variables. Any words that are left over are assigned to the last-named variable. The **-p** option causes the input line to be read from the shell's two-way pipe. The **-u** option causes the file descriptor *n* to be used for input. If the first argument contains a ?, the remainder of the argument is used as a prompt.

Figure 7–40 Description of the *read* shell command.

Here's an example:

```
$ read 'name?enter your name '
enter your name Graham
$ echo $name
Graham
$ _
```

7.12.5.6 test
The Korn shell version of *test* accepts several new operators, listed in Figure 7–41.

Operator	Meaning
-L *fileName*	Return true if *fileName* is a symbolic link.
file1 -nt *file2*	Return true if *file1* is newer than *file2*.
file1 -ot *file2*	Return true if *file1* is older than *file2*.
file1 -ef *file2*	Return true if *file1* is the same file as *file2*.

Figure 7–41 Test operators unique to the Korn shell *test* shell command.

The Korn shell also supports a more convenient syntax for *test* (Figure 7–42).

```
[[ testExpression ]]
```

which is equivalent to:

```
test textExpression
```

Figure 7–42 Two forms of *test* in the Korn shell.

I prefer the more modern form of *test* that uses the double brackets, as it allows me to write more readable programs. Here's an example of this newer form of *test* in action:

```
$ cat test.ksh          ...list the script.
i=1
```

```
while [[ i -le 4 ]]
do
 echo $i
 (( i = i + 1 ))
done
$ ksh test.ksh           ...execute the script.
1
2
3
4
$ _
```

7.12.5.7 trap

The Korn shell's *trap* command works as shown in Figure 7–43.

Shell Command: **trap** [*command*] [*signal*]

The Korn shell *trap* command instructs the shell to execute *command* whenever any of the numbered signals *signal* are received. If several signals are received, they are trapped in numeric order. If a signal value of 0 is specified, then *command* is executed when the shell terminates. If *command* is omitted, then the traps of the numbered signals are reset to their original values. If *command* is an empty string, then the numbered signals are ignored. If arg is -, then all of the specified signal actions are reset to their initial values. If an EXIT or 0 signal value is given to a *trap* inside a function, then *command* is executed when the function is exited. If *trap* is executed with no arguments, a list of all the signals and their *trap* settings is displayed. For more information on signals and their default actions, see Chapter 12, "Systems Programming."

Figure 7–43 Description of the *trap* shell command.

In the following example, I set the EXIT trap inside a function to demonstrate local function traps:

```
$ cat trap.ksh                    ...list the script.
f ()
{
 echo 'enter f ()'
 trap 'echo leaving f...' EXIT    # set a local trap
 echo 'exit f ()'
}
# main program.
trap 'echo exit shell' EXIT       # set a global trap.
f                                 # invoke the function f ().
$ ksh trap.ksh                    ...execute the script.
```

```
enter f ()
exit f ()
leaving f...                    ...local EXIT is trapped.
exit shell                      ...global EXIT is trapped.
$ _
```

7.13 Sample Project: junk

To illustrate some of the Korn shell capabilities, I present a Korn shell version of the "junk" script project that was suggested at the end of Chapter 6, "The Bourne Again Shell." Figure 7–44 defines the **junk** utility about to be described.

Utility: **junk** -lp { *fileName*]*

junk is a replacement for the **rm** utility. Rather than removing files, it moves them into the subdirectory ".junk" in your home directory. If ".junk" doesn't exist, it is automatically created. The **-l** option lists the current contents of the ".junk" directory, and the **-p** option purges ".junk".

Figure 7–44   Description of the **junk** shell script.

The Korn shell script that is listed below (and available online—see the Preface for more information) uses a function to process error messages, and uses an array to store filenames. The rest of the functionality should be pretty easy to follow from the embedded comments.

7.13.0.1 junk

```
#!/bin/ksh
# junk script
# Korn shell version
# author: Graham Glass
# 9/25/91
#
# Initialize variables
#
fileCount=0        # the number of files specified.
listFlag=0         # 1 if list option (-)used.
purgeFlag=0        # 1 if purge (-p) option used.
fileFlag=0         # 1 if at least one file is specified.
junk=~/.junk       # the name of the junk directory.
#
error ()
{
#
```

```
# Display error message and quit
#
cat << ENDOFTEXT
Dear $USER, the usage of junk is as follows:
  junk -p means "purge all files"
  junk -l means "list junked files"
  junk <list of files> to junk them
ENDOFTEXT
exit 1
}
#
# Parse command line
#
for arg in $*
do
  case $arg in
    "-p")
      purgeFlag=1
      ;;

    "-l")
      listFlag=1
      ;;

    -*)
      echo $arg is an illegal option
      ;;

    *)
      fileFlag=1
      fileList[$fileCount]=$arg       # append to list
      let fileCount=fileCount+1
      ;;
  esac
done
#
# Check for too many options
#
let total=$listFlag+$purgeFlag+$fileFlag
if (( total != 1 ))
then
 error
fi
#
# If junk directory doesn't exist, create it
#
if [[ ! (-d $junk) ]]
then
```

```
  'mkdir' $junk            # quoted just in case it's aliased.
fi
#
# Process options
#
if (( listFlag == 1 ))
then
  'ls' -lF $junk           # list junk directory.
  exit 0
fi
#
if (( purgeFlag == 1 ))
then
  'rm' $junk/*             # remove files in junk directory.
  exit 0
fi
#
if (( fileFlag == 1 ))
then
  'mv' ${fileList[*]} $junk   # move files to junk dir.
  exit 0
fi
#
exit 0
```

Here's some sample output from **junk**:

```
$ ls *.ksh                        ...list some files to junk.
fact.ksh*    func5.ksh*     test.ksh*    trap.ksh*
func4.ksh*   squares.ksh*   test2.ksh*
$ junk func5.ksh func4.ksh     ...junk a couple of files.
$ junk -l                      ...list my junk.
total 2
-rwxr-xr-x 1 glass apollocl  205 Feb  6 22:44 func4.ksh*
-rwxr-xr-x 1 glass apollocl  274 Feb  7 21:02 func5.ksh*
$ junk -p                      ...purge my junk.
$ junk -z                      ...try a silly option.
-z is an illegal option
Dear glass, the usage of junk is as follows:
  junk -p means "purge all files"
  junk -l means "list junked files"
  junk <list of files> to junk them
$ _
```

7.14 Command-Line Options

If the first command-line argument is a -, the Korn shell is started as a login shell. In addition to this, the Korn shell supports the flags of the built-in set command (including **-x** and **-v**) and those listed in Figure 7–45.

Option	Meaning
-c *string*	Create a shell to execute the command *string*.
-s	Create a shell that reads commands from standard input and sends shell messages to the standard error channel.
-i	Create an interactive shell; like the **-s** option except that the SIGTERM, SIGINT, and SIGQUIT signals are all ignored. For information about signals, consult Chapter 12, "Systems Programming."
fileName	Execute the shell commands in *fileName* if the **-s** option is not used. *fileName* is $0 within the *fileName* script.

Figure 7–45   Korn shell command-line options.

CHAPTER REVIEW

Checklist
In this chapter, I described:

- the creation of a Korn shell startup file
- aliases and the history mechanism
- the built-in **vi** and **emacs** line editors
- arithmetic
- functions
- advanced job control

Quiz

1. Why is the alias mechanism useful?
2. How can you re-edit and re-execute previous commands?
3. Does the Korn shell support recursive functions?
4. How can you find a list of signals supported by the *kill* built-in command?
5. Which shell variable contains the name of the shell startup file?
6. Describe the two forms of arithmetic expressions supported by the Korn shell.
7. How do you make a shell variable accessible to a subshell?
8. What command is used to catch signals in a shell script?

Exercises

1. Rewrite the **junk** script of this chapter to be menu driven. Use the *select* command. [level: *easy*]
2. Write a function called **dateToDays** that takes three parameters—a month string such as Sep, a day number such as 18, and a year number such as 1962—and returns the number of days from Jan 1 1900 to the date. [level: *medium*]
3. Create a script called **pulse** that takes two parameters—the name of a script and an integer. **pulse** should execute the specified script for the specified number of seconds, suspend it for the same number of seconds, and continue this cycle until the specified script is finished. [level: *hard*]

Projects

1. Write a skeleton script that allows system administration tasks to be performed automatically from a menu-driven interface. Useful tasks to automate include:

   • automatic deletion of core files
   • automatic warnings to users that use a lot of CPU time or disk space
   • automatic archiving

   Don't worry about making them do anything just yet; we'll fill this in at the end of Chapter 14, "System Administration." For now, concentrate on making the menu and task selection work properly and just use the echo or print commands to print out what would happen for each selection. [level: *easy*]

2. Write an alias manager script that allows you to choose DOS emulation, VMS emulation, or none. [level: *medium*]

8

The C Shell

Motivation

The C shell was designed to more closely adhere to the C language syntax and control structures. It was the first shell to support advanced job control, and became a favorite of early UNIX developers. Many C shell users have changed to Bash because it provides most traditional C shell features as well as its own useful features.

Prerequisites

You should already have read Chapter 5, "The Linux Shells," and experimented with some of the core shell facilities.

Objectives

In this chapter, I explain and demonstrate the C-shell-specific facilities.

Presentation

The information in this section is presented in the form of several sample Linux command sessions and a small project.

Shell Commands

This section introduces the following shell commands, listed in alphabetical order:

alias	nice	setenv
chdir	nohup	source
dirs	notify	stop
foreach..end	onintr	suspend
glob	popd	switch..case..endsw
goto	pushd	unalias
history	rehash	unhash
if..then..else..endif	repeat	while..end
logout	set	

8.1   Introduction

The C shell is available on Linux as /bin/tcsh, and is completely compatible with the UNIX C shell with some enhancements of its own. A link from /bin/csh to /bin/tcsh is provided, so UNIX users can reference it as **csh**.

The C shell supports all of the core shell facilities described in Chapter 5, "The Linux Shells," plus the following new features:

- several ways to set and access variables
- a built-in programming language that supports conditional branching, looping, and interrupt handling
- command customization using aliases
- access to previous commands via a history mechanism
- advanced job control
- filename completion and command editing

8.2   Startup

The C shell is a regular C program whose executable file is stored as "/bin/tcsh". If your chosen shell is "/bin/tcsh", an interactive C shell is invoked automatically when you log into a Linux system. You may also invoke a C shell manually from a script or from a terminal by using the command **tcsh. tcsh** has several command-line options that are described at the end of this chapter.

When a C shell is started as a login shell, a global login initialization file, "/etc/login" may also be executed. This is useful for setting up environment variables (such as PATH) to contain information about the local environment.

When a C shell is invoked, the startup sequence is different for login shells and nonlogin shells (Figure 8–1).

Step	Shell type	Action
1	both	Execute commands in $HOME/.tcshrc or $HOME/.cshrc if it exists.
2	login only	Execute commands in global login initialization file if it exists.
3	login only	Execute commands in $HOME/.login if it exists.

Figure 8–1 C shell startup sequence.

Note that the ".tcshrc" (or if not found, ".cshrc") file is run before either type of login initialization file. This may seem counterintuitive and has been the cause of much unexpected behavior when users are crafting their initialization files. The way to keep this straight is to remember that the C shell always runs its own initialization file immediately upon starting, then determines if the shell is a login shell which would require running the other initialization files.

Once an interactive shell starts and finishes running all the appropriate initialization files, it displays its prompt and awaits user commands. The standard C shell prompt is %, although it may be changed by setting the local variable $prompt, described shortly.

The ".login" file typically contains commands that set environment variables such as TERM, which contains the type of your terminal, and PATH, which tells the shell where to search for executable files. Put things in your ".login" file that need to be set only once (environment variables whose values are inherited by other shells) or make sense only for an interactive session only (like specifying terminal settings). Here's an example of a ".login" file:

```
echo -n "Enter your terminal type (default is vt100): "
set termtype = $<
set term = vt100
if ("$termtype" != "") set term = "$termtype"
unset termtype
set path=(. /bin /usr/bin /usr/local/bin )
stty erase "^?" kill "^U" intr "^C" eof "^D" crt crterase
set cdpath = (~)
set history = 40
set notify
set prompt = "! % "
set savehist = 32
```

The ".tcshrc" file generally contains commands that set common aliases (discussed later) or anything else that only applies to the current shell. The "rc" suffix stands for "**r**un **c**ommands." Here's an example of a ".tcshrc" file:

```
alias h history
alias ll ls -l
alias ls ls -F
alias rm rm -i
alias m more
```

8.3 Variables

The C shell supports local and environment variables. A local variable may hold either one value, in which case it's called a *simple* variable, or more than one value, in which case it's termed a *list*. This section describes the C shell facilities that support variables.

8.3.1 Creating/Assigning Simple Variables

To assign a value to a simple variable, use the built-in *set* command (Figure 8–2).

---

set {*name* [=*word*]}*

If no arguments are supplied, a list of all the local variables is displayed. If *word* is not supplied, *name* is set to a null string. If the variable *name* doesn't exist, it is implicitly created.

Figure 8–2 Description of the *set* shell command.

Here are some examples:

```
% set flag           ...set "flag" to a null string.
% echo $flag         ...nothing is printed, as it's null.

% set color = red    ...set "color" to the string "red".
% echo $color
red
% set name = Graham Glass        ...beware! Must use quotes.
% echo $name         ...only the first string was assigned.
Graham
% set name = "Graham Glass"      ...now it works as expected.
% echo $name
Graham Glass
% set                ...display a list of all local variables.
argv  ()
cdpath      /home/glass
color       red
cwd         /home/glass
flag
...
name        Graham Glass
term        vt100
user        glass
% _
```

8.3.2 Accessing a Simple Variable

In addition to the simple variable access syntax (*$name*), the C shell supports the complex access methods listed in Figure 8–3.

Syntax	Action
${*name*}	Replaced by the value of *name*. This form is useful if the expression is immediately followed by an alphanumeric that would otherwise be interpreted as part of the variable's name.
${*?name*}	Replaced by 1 if *name* is set and 0 otherwise.

Figure 8–3   Accessing C shell variables.

Here are some examples that illustrate these access methods. In the first example, I used braces to append a string to the value of a variable:

```
% set verb = sing
% echo I like $verbing
verbing: Undefined variable.
% echo I like ${verb}ing
I like singing
% _
```

In the following example, I used a variable as a simple flag in a conditional expression:

```
% cat flag.csh          ...list the script.
#
set flag                ...set "flag" to a null string.
if (${?flag}) then      ...branch if "flag" is set.
 echo flag is set
endif
% tcsh flag.csh         ...execute the script.
flag is set
% _
```

8.3.3   Creating/Assigning List Variables

To assign a list of values to a variable, use the built-in *set* command with the syntax shown in Figure 8–4.

---

set {*name* = ({ *word*}*) }*

If the named variable doesn't exist, it is implicitly created. The named variable is assigned to a copy of the specified list of words.

Figure 8–4   Description of the *set* shell command setting a list variable.

Here's an example:

```
% set colors = ( red yellow green )     ...set to a list.
% echo $colors                          ...display entire list.
red yellow green
% _
```

8.3.4   Accessing a List Variable

The C shell supports a couple of ways to access a list variable. Both of these methods have two forms, the second of which is surrounded by braces. The second form is useful if the expression is immediately followed by an alphanumeric that would otherwise be interpreted as part of the variable's name. Figure 8–5 describes the access methods:

Syntax	Action
$name[selector] ${name[selector]}	Both forms are replaced by the element of *name* whose index is specified by the value of *selector. selector* may be either a single number, a range of numbers in the format *start-end*, or a *. If *start* is omitted, 1 is assumed. If *end* is omitted, the index of the last element is assumed. If a * is supplied, then all of the elements are selected. The first element of a list has index 1.
$#name ${#name}	Both forms are replaced by the number of elements in *name*.

Figure 8–5   Accessing C shell list variables.

Here are some examples:

```
% set colors = ( red yellow green )     ...set to a list.
% echo $colors[1]                       ...display first element.
red
% echo $colors[2-3]           ...display 2nd and 3rd.
yellow green
% echo $colors[4]             ...illegal access.
colors: Subscript out of range.
% echo $#colors               ...display size of list.
3
% _
```

8.3.5   Building Lists

To add an element onto the end of a list, set the original list equal to itself plus the new element, surrounded by parentheses; if you try to assign the new element directly, you'll get an error message. The following example illustrates some list manipulations:

```
% set colors = ( red yellow green )     ...set to a list.
% set colors[4] = pink                  ...try to set the 4th.
```

```
set: Subscript out of range.
% set colors = ( $colors blue )        ...add to the list.
% echo $colors        ...it works!
red yellow green blue
% set colors[4] = pink                 ...OK, since 4th exists.
% echo $colors
red yellow green pink
% set colors = $colors black           ...don't forget to use ().
% echo $colors                         ...only the first was set.
red
$ set girls = ( sally georgia )        ...build one list.
$ set boys = ( harry blair )           ...build another.
$ set both = ( $girls $boys )          ...add the lists.
$ echo $both                           ...display the result.
sally georgia harry blair
% _
```

8.3.6   Predefined Local Variables

In addition to the common predefined local variables, the C shell defines those shown in Figure 8–6.

Name	Value
$?0	1 if the shell is executing commands from a named file, and 0 otherwise.
$<	The next line of standard input, fully quoted.
$argv	A list that contains all of the positional parameters: $argv[1] is equal to $1.
$cdpath	The list of alternate directories that *chdir* uses for searching purposes.
$cwd	The current working directory.
$echo	Set if the **-x** command-line option is active.
$histchars	May be used to override the default history metacharacters. The first character is used in place of ! for history substitutions, and the second is used in place of ^ for quick command re-execution.
$history	The size of the history list.
$home	The shell's home directory.
$ignoreeof	Prevents the shell from terminating when it gets a *Control-D*.
$mail	A list of the files to check for mail. By default, the shell checks for mail every 600 seconds (10 minutes). If the first word of $mail is a number, the shell uses this value instead.

Figure 8–6   C shell predefined local variables. (Part 1 of 2)

Name	Value
$noclobber	Prevents existing files from being overridden by >, and nonexistent files from being appended to by >>.
$noglob	Prevents wildcard expansion.
$nonomatch	Prevents an error from occurring if no files match a wildcard filename.
$notify	By default, the shell notifies you of job status changes just before a new prompt is displayed. If $notify is set, the status change is displayed immediately when it occurs.
$path	Used by the shell for locating executable files.
$prompt	The shell prompt.
$savehist	The number of commands to save in the history file.
$shell	The full pathname of the login shell.
$status	The exit code of the last command.
$time	If this is set, any process that takes more than this number of seconds will cause a message to be displayed that indicates process statistics.
$verbose	Set if the -v command-line option is used.

Figure 8–6   C shell predefined local variables. (Part 2 of 2)

Here's a small shell script that uses the $< variable to obtain a user response:

```
% cat var5.csh          ...list the script.
#
echo -n "please enter your name: "
set name = $<           # take a line of input.
echo hi $name, your current directory is $cwd
% tcsh var5.csh         ...execute the script.
please enter your name: Graham
hi Graham, your current directory is /home/glass
% _.
```

8.3.7   Creating/Assigning Environment Variables

To assign a value to an environment variable, use the built-in command *setenv* (Figure 8–7).

---

setenv *name word*

If the named variable doesn't exist, it is implicitly created; otherwise, it is overwritten. Note that environment variables always hold exactly one value; there is no such thing as an environment list.

Figure 8–7   Description of the *setenv* shell command.

Here's an example of *setenv*:

```
% setenv TERM vt52          ...set my terminal type.
% echo $TERM                ...confirm.
vt52
% _
```

8.3.8   Predefined Environment Variables

In addition to the common predefined environment variables (Figure 8–8), the C shell supports the ones listed below.

Name	Value
$LOGNAME	The shell owner's username.

Figure 8–8   C shell predefined environment variables.

8.4   Expressions

The C shell supports string, arithmetic, and file-oriented expressions. Let's take a look at each kind of expression.

8.4.1   String Expressions

The C shell supports the string operators listed in Figure 8–9.

Operator	Meaning
==	Return true if the string operands are exactly equal.
!=	Return true if the string operands are unequal.
=~	Like = =, except that the right operand may contain wildcards.
!~	Like !=, except that the right operand may contain wildcards.

Figure 8–9   C shell string operators.

If either operand is a list, then the first element of the list is used for the comparison. The script in the following example used the string-matching technique to infer a user's response:

```
% cat expr1.csh                 ...list the script.
#
echo -n "do you like the C shell? " #prompt.
set reply = $<                  # get a line of input.
if ($reply == "yes") then       #check for exact match.
  echo you entered yes
else if ($reply =~ y*) then     #check for inexact match.
```

```
 echo I assume you mean yes
endif
% tcsh expr1.csh                          ...execute the script.
do you like the C shell? yeah
I assume you mean yes
% _
```

8.4.2   Arithmetic Expressions

The C shell supports the arithmetic operators listed in Figure 8–10, in descending order of precedence.

Operator(s)	Meaning
-	Unary minus
!	Logical negation
* / %	Multiplication, division, remainder
+ -	Addition, subtraction
<< >>	Bitwise left shift, bitwise right shift
<= >= <>	Relational operators
== !=	Equality, inequality
& ^ |	Bitwise and, bitwise xor, bitwise or
|| &&	Logical or, logical and

Figure 8–10   C shell arithmetic operators.

These operators work just like their standard C counterparts, except that they can only operate on integers. Expressions may be surrounded by parentheses to control the order of evaluation. When an arithmetic expression is evaluated, a null string is equivalent to zero. Any expression that uses the &, &&, ||, |, <, >, <<, or >> operators must be surrounded by parentheses to prevent the shell from interpreting these characters specially. Here's a sample script that uses a couple of operators:

```
% cat expr3.csh                          ...list the script.
#
set a = 3
set b = 5
if ($a > 2 && $b > 4) then
 echo expression evaluation seems to work
endif
% tcsh expr3.csh                          ...execute the script.
expression evaluation seems to work
% _
```

To assign the result of an expression to a variable, you may not use the *set* command. Instead, use the built-in @ command, which has the forms shown in Figure 8–11.

Use	Meaning
@	List all of the shell variables.
@*variable op expression*	Set *variable* to *expression*.
@*variable*[*index*] *op expression*	Set *index*th element of *variable* to *expression*.
where op is =, +=, -=, or /=.	

Figure 8–11   Forms of the C shell command "@".

Here are some examples:

```
% set a = 2 * 2       ...you can't use set for assignment.
set: Syntax error.
% @ a = 2 * 2         ...use @ instead.
% echo $a
4
% @ a = $a + $a       ...add two variables.
% echo $a
8
% set flag = 1
% @ b = ($a && $flag)        ...need ()s because of &&.
% echo $b
1
% @ b = ($a ^ $flag)
% echo $b
0
% _
```

You may also increment or decrement a variable by using ++ or --. For example:

```
% set value = 1
% @ value ++
% echo $value
2
% _
```

8.4.3   File-Oriented Expressions

To make file-oriented decisions a little easier to program, the C shell supports several file-specific expressions. Each expression is of the form given in Figure 8–12.

-option *filename*

where 1 (true) is returned if the selected option is true, and 0 (false) otherwise. If *fileName* does not exist or is inaccessible, all options return 0.

Figure 8–12   Description of C shell file-oriented expression.

Figure 8–13 describes each option.

Option	Meaning
r	Shell has read permission for *fileName*.
w	Shell has write permission for *fileName*.
x	Shell has execute permission for *fileName*.
e	*fileName* exists.
o	*fileName* is owned by the same user as the shell process.
z	*fileName* exists and is zero bytes in size.
f	*fileName* is a regular file (not a directory or special file).
d	*fileName* is a directory file (not a regular or special file).

Figure 8–13   Options used in file-oriented expressions.

Here's an example script that uses the **-w** option to determine whether a file is writable or not:

```
% cat expr4.csh                    ...list the script.
#
echo -n "enter the name of the file you wish to erase: "
set filename = $<              # get a line of input.
if (! (-w "$filename")) then  # check I have access.
 echo you do not have permission to erase that file.
else
 rm $filename
 echo file erased
endif
% tcsh expr4.csh                   ...execute the script.
```

```
enter the name of the file you wish to erase: /
you do not have permission to erase that file.
% _
```

8.5   Filename Completion

Like the Korn shell, the C shell provides a way to avoid typing a long filename on a command line. Whenever you type part of a filename, you can strike the *Tab* key and, if the part of the file-name you have typed so far uniquely identifies a file, the rest of the name will be added automatically. If the text does not uniquely identify a file, any text that can be completed (i.e., that is unique to all possibilities) will be filled in. You can also type a *Control-D* to see a list of the file-names that currently match the part of the name you have typed. For example:

```
% ls -al .log^D        ...show my options
.login     .logout
% ls -al .login        ...shell retyped, I added "in"
```

8.6   Command Editing

Most modern command shells feature some easy method of recalling and editing previously issued commands. The original C shell did not provide this, but **tcsh** does. The easiest way to recall a previous command is to strike the up arrow button on your keyboard. This brings the most recently typed command onto your command line. You can back up and change something, hit *Return* to issue the command again, or hit the up arrow key again to go further back in the list. The down arrow key will move you forward in the command list.

It is sometimes preferable to use commands you're already accustomed to using to edit. So tcsh provides both a **vim** and **emacs**-style interface to command editing. By default, Emacs key sequences are used (i.e., *Control-P* for up, *Control-D* for down, see "Editing a File: emacs" on page 93 for more information). You can use the **tcsh** built-in command *bindkeys* to change this to **vim** key sequences (use the command *bindkeys -v*). When using **vim**-style key sequences, you must first type an *Escape* character to tell the shell you wish to edit your command history (think of your shell as command "insert mode"; you type an *Escape* to get out of insert mode just as you would in **vim**). After typing the *Escape*, you can move up and down in the command history with "k" and "j," respectively, just as you would in **vim** (for more information see "Editing a File: vim" on page 82).

8.7   Aliases

The C shell allows you to create and customize your own commands by using the built-in command *alias* (Figure 8–14).

Shell Command: **alias** [*word* [*string*]]

alias supports a simple form of command-line customization. If you alias *word* to be equal to *string* and then later enter a command beginning with *word*, the first occurrence of *word* is replaced by *string* and then the command is reprocessed.

If you don't supply *word* or *string*, a list of all the current shell aliases is displayed. If you only supply *word*, then the string currently associated with the alias *word* is displayed. If you supply *word* and *string*, the shell adds the specified alias to its collection of aliases. If an alias already exists for *word*, it is replaced.

If the replacement string begins with *word*, it is not reprocessed for aliases to prevent infinite loops. If the replacement string contains *word* elsewhere, an error message is displayed when the alias is executed.

Figure 8-14   Description of the *alias* shell command.

Here's an example of *alias* in action:

```
$ alias dir 'ls -aF'      ...register an alias.
$ dir                     ...same as typing "ls -aF".
./          main2.c       p.reverse.c        reverse.h
../          main2.o       palindrome.c       reverse.old
$ dir *.c                 ...same as typing "ls -aF *.c".
main2.c     p.reverse.c        palindrome.c
$ alias dir   ...look at the value associated with "dir".
ls -aF
$ _
```

In the following example, I aliased a word in terms of itself:

```
% alias ls 'ls -aF'     ...define "ls" in terms of itself.
% ls *.c                ...same as typing "ls -aF *.c".
main2.c     p.reverse.c        palindrome.c
% alias dir 'ls'        ...define "dir" in terms of "ls".
% dir                   ...same as typing "ls -aF".
./          main2.c       p.reverse.c        reverse.h
../          main2.o       palindrome.c       reverse.old
% alias who 'date; who'      ...infinite loop problem.
% who
Alias loop.
% alias who 'date; /usr/bin/who'  ...full path avoids error
% who                        ...works fine now.
Fri May 13 23:33:37 CST 2005
glass               ttyp0        Feb 13 23:30   (xyplex2)
% _
```

8.7.1 Removing an Alias

To remove an alias, use the built-in command *unalias* (Figure 8–15).

Shell Command: **unalias** *pattern*

unalias removes all of the aliases that match *pattern*. If *pattern* is *, then all aliases are removed.

Figure 8–15 Description of the *unalias* shell command.

8.7.2 Useful Aliases

Figure 8–16 is a list of the useful aliases that I keep in my ".tcshrc" file, together with a brief description.

Alias	Value
cd	cd \!*; set prompt = "$cwd \! > "; ls This changes your prompt to contain both the current working directory and the last command number (see history for more details).
ls	ls -F This causes **ls** to include extra file information.
rm	rm -i This causes **rm** to ask for confirmation.
rm	mv \!* ~/tomb This causes **rm** to move a file into a special "tomb" directory instead of removing it.
h	history This allows you to obtain history information by typing just one letter.
vim	(mesg n; /usr/bin/vim \!*; mesg y) This stops people from sending you messages while you're in the **vim** editor.
mroe	more This corrects a common spelling error.
ls-l	ls -l This corrects a common spelling error.
ll	ls -l This allows you to obtain a long directory listing more conveniently.

Figure 8–16 Useful C shell aliases.

8.7.3 Sharing Aliases

To make an alias available to a subshell, place its definition in the shell's ".tcshrc" file.

8.7.4 Parameterized Aliases

An alias may refer to arguments in the original pre-aliased command by using the history mechanism described in the next section. The pre-aliased command is treated as if it were the previous command. The useful alias for *cd* that I mentioned in the previous section makes good use of this facility; the \!* part of the alias is replaced by all of the arguments in the pre-aliased command. The ! is preceded by a \ to inhibit its special meaning during the assignment of the alias:

```
alias cd 'cd \!*; set prompt = "$cwd \! > "; ls'
```

8.8 History

The C shell keeps a record of the commands that you enter from the keyboard so that they may be edited and re-executed at a later stage. This facility is sometimes known as a *history* mechanism. The ! metacharacter gives you access to history.

8.8.1 Numbered Commands

When you're using history, it's very handy to arrange for your prompt to contain the "number" of the command that you're about to enter. To do this, insert the \! character sequence into your prompt:

```
% set prompt = '\! % '        ...include event num in prompt.
1 % echo Genesis        ...this command is event #1.
Genesis
2 % _        ...the next command will be event #2.
```

8.8.2 Storage of Commands

A C shell records the last $history commands during a particular session. If $history is not set, a default value of 1 is used. If you want these commands to be accessible from the next session, set the $savehist variable. If you do this, the last $savehist commands are maintained in the file specified by the HISTFILE variable (defaults to $HOME/.history). A history file is shared by all of the interactive C shells created by the same user unless HISTFILE is purposely set to a unique value in each different shell. In the following example, I instructed my shell to remember the last 40 commands in my history list and to store the last 32 commands between sessions:

```
2 % set history = 40        ...remember the last 40 commands.
40
3 % set savehist = 32        ...save 32 across sessions.
32
4 % _
```

8.8.3 Reading History

To obtain a listing of a shell's history, use the built-in command *history* (Figure 8–17).

Shell Command: **history** [-rh] [*number*]

history allows you to access a shell's history list. If no parameters are supplied, this command lists the last $history commands. The **-r** option causes the history list to be listed in reverse order, and the **-h** option inhibits the display of event numbers. "history" is usually aliased to "h" for speed.

Figure 8–17 Description of the *history* shell command.

Here's an example:

```
4 % alias h history        ...make a useful alias.
5 % h          ...list current history.
    1  13:25   set prompt = '\! % '
    2  13:26   set history = 40
    3  13:26   set savehist = 32
    4  13:26   alias h history
    5  13:27   h
6 % h -r 3      ...list last 3 commands in reverse order.
    6  13:27   h -r 3
    5  13:27   h
    4  13:26   alias h history
7 % _
```

8.8.4 Command Re-execution

To re-execute a previous command, use the ! metacharacter in one of the forms shown in Figure 8–18.

Form	Action
!!	Replaced with the text of the last command.
!*number*	Replaced with the text of the command with the specified event number.
!*prefix*	Replaced with the text of the last command that started with *prefix*.
!?*substring*?	Replaced with the text of the last command that contained *substring*.

Figure 8–18 Command re-execution in the C shell.

These sequences may be used anywhere in a command line, although they're usually used in isolation. The recalled command is echoed to the terminal before it is executed. The value of *prefix* or *substring* may not contain a space. The special meaning of ! is not inhibited

by any kind of quote, but may be inhibited by preceding it with a space, tab, =, (, or \. Here are
some examples:

```
41 % echo event 41          ...a simple echo.
event 41
42 % echo event 42          ...another simple echo.
event 42
43 % !!                ...re-execute last command.
echo event 42          ...echo command before re-execution.
event 42
44 % !41               ...re-execute command #41.
echo event 41          ...echo command before re-execution.
event 41
45 % !ec               ...re-execute command starting with "ec".
echo event 41          ...echo command before re-execution.
event 41
46 % _
```

8.8.5   Accessing Pieces of History

You may access a portion of a previous command by using history *modifiers*. These are a collection of options that may immediately follow an event specifier. Each modifier returns a single
token or range of tokens from the specified event. Figure 8–19 is a list of the modifiers.

Modifier	Token(s) returned
:0	first
:number	(number+1)th
:start-end	(*start*+1) th through to (*end*+1)th
:^	first
:$	last
:*	second through to last

Figure 8–19   C shell history modifiers.

The colon before the ^, $, and * options is optional. To use one of these modifiers on the
last command, you may precede the modifier by "!!" or just "!". Here are some examples:

```
48 % echo I like horseback riding   ...original line.
I like horseback riding
49 % !!:0 !!:1 !!:2 !!:4             ...access specified arguments.
```

```
echo I like riding
I like riding
50 % echo !48:1-$              ...access range of arguments.
echo I like horseback riding
I like horseback riding
51 % _
```

8.8.6   Accessing Portions of Filenames

If a history modifier refers to a filename, it may be further modified in order to access a particular portion of the name. The existing modifiers may be followed immediately by the following filename modifiers (Figure 8–20).

Modifier	Part of file	Portion of the specified fileName that is returned
:h	head	The filename minus the trailing pathname.
:r	root	The filename minus the trailing .* suffix.
:e	extension	The trailing .* suffix.
:t	tail	The filename minus the leading directory path.

Figure 8–20 C shell filename modifiers.

In the following example I accessed various portions of the original filename by using this filename access facility:

```
53 % ls /usr/include/stdio.h         ...the original.
/usr/include/stdio.h
54 % echo !53:1:h           ...access head.
echo /usr/include
/usr/include
55 % echo !53:1:r           ...access root.
echo /usr/include/stdio
/usr/include/stdio
56 % echo !53:1:e           ...access extension.
echo h
h
57 % echo !53:1:t           ...access tail.
echo stdio.h
stdio.h
% _
```

8.8.7   History Substitution

The substitution modifier is replaced by the specified portion of a previous event after a textual substitution is performed. Figure 8–21 gives the syntax.

> *!event*:s/*pat1*/*pat2*/
>
> This sequence is replaced by the specified event after replacing the first occurrence of *pat1*
> by *pat2*.

Figure 8–21   Description of C shell history substitution.

Here's an example:

```
58 % ls /usr/include/stdio.h              ...the original.
/usr/include/stdio.h
58 % echo !58:1:s/stdio/signal/           ...perform substitution.
echo /usr/include/signal.h
/usr/include/signal.h
59 % _
```

It's quite common to want to re-execute the previous command with a slight modification. For example, say you misspelled the name of a file. Instead of typing "fil.txt", you meant to type "file.txt". There's a convenient shorthand way to correct such a mistake. If you type the command:

```
^pat1^pat2
```

then the previous command is re-executed after the first occurrence of *pat1* is replaced by *pat2*. This shortcut procedure applies only to the previous command. Here's an example:

```
% ls -lG fil.txt            ...whoops!
ls: File or directory "fil.txt" is not found.
% ^fil^file                 ...quick correction.
ls -lG file.txt             ...OK.
-rw-r-xr-x   1 ables         410 Jun  6 23:58 file.txt
```

8.9   Control Structures

The C shell supports a wide range of control structures that make it suitable as a high-level programming tool. Shell programs are usually stored in scripts and are commonly used to automate maintenance and installation tasks.

Several of the control structures require several lines to be entered. If such a control structure is entered from the keyboard, the shell prompts you with a ? for each additional line until the control structure is ended, at which point it executes.

There now follows a description of each control structure, in alphabetical order. I made the C shell examples correspond closely to the Bash examples so that you can compare and contrast the two shells.

8.9.1   foreach .. end

The *foreach* command allows a list of commands to be repeatedly executed, each time using a different value for a named variable. Figure 8–22 gives the syntax.

> **foreach** *name* (*wordList*)
>   *commandList*
> **end**
>
> The *foreach* command iterates the value of *name* through each item in *wordList*, executing the list of commands *commandList* after each assignment. A *break* command causes the loop to immediately end, and a *continue* command causes the loop to jump immediately to the next iteration.

Figure 8–22   Description of the *foreach* shell command.

Here's an example of a script that uses a foreach control structure:

```
% cat foreach.csh            ...list the script.
#
foreach color (red yellow green blue)        # four colors
 echo one color is $color
end
% tcsh foreach.csh                  ...execute the script.
one color is red
one color is yellow
one color is green
one color is blue
% _\
```

8.9.2   goto

The *goto* command allows you to jump unconditionally to a named label. To declare a label, simply start a line with the name of the label followed immediately by a colon. Figure 8–23 gives the syntax of a *goto* command.

> **goto** *name*
>   where later there exists a label of the form:
> name:
>
> When a *goto* statement is encountered, control is transferred to the line after the label location. The label may precede or follow the *goto* statement, even if the command is entered from the keyboard.

Figure 8–23   Description of the *goto* shell command.

Use *goto* sparingly to avoid nasty spaghettilike code (even if you like spaghetti). Here's an example of a simple *goto*:

```
% cat goto.csh               ...list the script.
#
```

```
echo gotta jump
goto endOfScript            # jump
echo I will never echo this
endOfScript:                # label
echo the end
% tcsh goto.csh             ...execute the script.
gotta jump
the end
% _
```

8.9.3   if .. then .. else .. endif

There are two forms of *if* command. Figure 8–24 gives the syntax of the first form, which supports a simple one-way branch.

---

if (*expr*) *command*

This form of the *if* command evaluates *expr*, and if it is true (nonzero), executes *command*.

Figure 8–24   Description of the *if* shell command in its simple form.

Here is an example of this form of *if*:

```
% if (5 > 3) echo five is greater than 3
five is greater than three
% _
```

The second form of the *if* command (Figure 8–25) supports alternative branching.

---

if (*expr1*) **then**
  list1
else if (*expr2*) **then**
  list2
else
  list3
endif

The *else* and *else if* portions of this command are optional, but the terminating *endif* is not. *expr1* is executed. If *expr1* is true, the commands in *list1* are executed and the *if* command is done. If *expr1* is false and there are one or more *else if* components, then a true expression following an *else if* causes the commands following the associated *then* to be executed and the *if* command to finish. If no true expressions are found and there is an *else* component, the commands following the *else* are executed.

Figure 8–25   Description of the *if* shell command with *else* clauses.

Here's an example of the second form of *if*:

```
% cat if.csh                    ...list the script.
#
echo -n 'enter a number: '      # prompt user.
set number = $<                 # read a line of input.
if ($number < 0) then
 echo negative
else if ($number == 0) then
 echo zero
else
 echo positive
endif
% tcsh if.csh                   ...execute the script.
enter a number: -1
negative
% _
```

8.9.4   onintr

The *onintr* command (Figure 8–26) allows you to specify a label that should be jumped to when the shell receives a SIGINT signal. This signal is typically generated by a *Control-C* from the keyboard, and is described in more detail in Chapter 12, "Systems Programming."

---

onintr [- | *label*]

The *onintr* command instructs the shell to jump to *label* when SIGINT is received. If the -option is used, SIGINTs are ignored. If no options are supplied, it restores the shell's original SIGINT handler.

Figure 8–26   Description of the *onintr* shell command.

Here's an example:

```
% cat onintr.csh                ...list the script.
#
onintr controlC                 # set Control-C trap.
while (1)
 echo infinite loop
 sleep 2
end
controlC:
echo control C detected
% tcsh onintr.csh               ...execute the script.
infinite loop
infinite loop
^C                              ...press Control-C.
control C detected
% _
```

8.9.5   repeat

The *repeat* command allows you to execute a single command a specified number of times. Figure 8–27 gives the syntax.

---

repeat *expr command*

The *repeat* command evaluates *expr*, and then executes *command* the resultant number of times.

Figure 8–27   Description of the *repeat* shell command.

Here is an example of the use of *repeat*:

```
% repeat 2 echo hi there            ...display two lines.
hi there
hi there
% _
```

8.9.6   switch .. case .. endsw

The *switch* command supports multiway branching based on the value of a single expression. Figure 8–28 shows the general form of a *switch* construct.

---

switch (*expr*)
  case *pattern1*:
   list
  breaksw
  case *pattern2*:
  case *pattern3*:
   list2
  breaksw
default:
  defaultList
endsw

expr is an expression that evaluates to a string. *pattern1, pattern2,* and *pattern3* may include wildcards. *list1, list2,* and *defaultList* are lists of one or more shell commands. The shell evaluates *expr* and then compares it to each pattern in turn, from top to bottom. When the first matching pattern is found, its associated list of commands is executed and then the shell skips to the matching *endsw*. If no match is found and a default condition is supplied, then *defaultList* is executed. If no match is found and no default condition exists, then execution continues from after the matching *endsw*.

Figure 8–28   Description of the *switch* shell command.

Here's an example of a script called "menu.csh" that makes use of a *switch* control structure:

```
#
echo menu test program
set stop = 0               # reset loop termination flag
while ($stop == 0)         # loop until done
 cat << ENDOFMENU          # display menu
 1   : print the date.
 2, 3: print the current working directory
 4   : exit
ENDOFMENU
 echo
 echo -n 'your choice? '   # prompt
 set reply = $<            # read response
 echo ""
 switch ($reply)           # process response
   case "1":
     date                  # display date
     breaksw
   case "2":
   case "3":
     pwd                   # display working directory
     breaksw
   case "4":
     set stop = 1          # set loop termination flag
     breaksw
   default:                # default
     echo illegal choice   # error
     breaksw
 endsw
 echo
end
```

Here's the output from the "menu.csh" script:

```
% tcsh menu.csh
menu test program
 1   : print the date.
 2, 3: print the current working directory
 4   : exit

your choice? 1

Sat May 14 00:50:26 CST 2005
```

```
1   : print the date.
2, 3: print the current working directory
4   : exit

your choice? 2

/home/glass

1   : print the date.
2, 3: print the current working directory
4   : exit

your choice? 5

illegal choice

1   : print the date.
2, 3: print the current working directory
4   : exit

your choice? 4

% _
```

8.9.7   while .. end

The built-in *while* command allows a list of commands to be repeatedly executed as long as a specified expression evaluates to true (nonzero). Figure 8–29 gives the syntax.

---

while (*expr*)
  commandlist
end

The *while* command evaluates the expression *expr*, and if it is true, proceeds to execute every command in *commandlist* and then repeats the process. If *expr* is false, the while loop terminates and the script continues to execute from the command following the end. A *break* command causes the loop to end immediately, and a *continue* command causes the loop to jump immediately to the next iteration.

Figure 8–29   Description of the *while* shell command.

Here's an example of a script that uses a *while* control structure to generate a small multiplication table:

```
% cat multi.csh              ...list the script.
#
set x = 1                    # set outer loop value
while ($x <= $1)             # outer loop
  set y = 1                  # set inner loop value
  while ($y <= $1)           # inner loop
    @ v = $x * $y            # calculate entry
    echo -n $v " "           # display entry (tab in quotes)
    @ y ++                   # update inner loop counter
  end
  echo ""                    # newline
  @ x ++                     # update outer loop counter
end
% tcsh multi.csh 7              ...execute the script.
1       2       3       4       5       6       7
2       4       6       8       10      12      14
3       6       9       12      15      18      21
4       8       12      16      20      24      28
5       10      15      20      25      30      35
6       12      18      24      30      36      42
7       14      21      28      35      42      49
% _
```

8.10 Sample Project: junk

To illustrate some of the C shell capabilities, I present a C shell version of the "junk" script project that was suggested at the end of Chapter 6, "The Bourne Again Shell." Figure 8–30 defines the **junk** utility about to be described.

Utility: **junk** -lp { *fileName* }*

junk is a replacement for the **rm** utility. Rather than removing files, it moves them into the subdirectory ".junk" in your home directory. If ".junk" doesn't exist, it is automatically created. The **-l** option lists the current contents of the ".junk" directory, and the **-p** option purges ".junk".

Figure 8–30   Description of the **junk** shell script.

The C shell script that is listed below (and available online—see the Preface for more information) uses a list variable to store filenames. The rest of the functionality should be pretty easy to follow from the embedded comments.

```
#!/bin/tcsh
# junk script
# author: Graham Glass
# 9/25/91
#
# Initialize variables
#
set fileList = ()       # a list of all specified files.
set listFlag = 0        # set to 1 if -l option is specified.
set purgeFlag = 0       # 1 if -p option is specified.
set fileFlag = 0        # 1 if at least one file is specified.
set junk = ~/.junk      # the junk directory.
#
# Parse command line
#
foreach arg ($*)
  switch ($arg)
    case "-p":
      set purgeFlag = 1
      breaksw

    case "-l":
      set listFlag = 1
      breaksw

    case -*:
      echo $arg is an illegal option
      goto error
      breaksw

    default:
      set fileFlag = 1
      set fileList = ($fileList $arg) # append to list
      breaksw
  endsw
end
#
# Check for too many options
#
@ total = $listFlag + $purgeFlag + $fileFlag
if ($total != 1) goto error
#
# If junk directory doesn't exist, create it
```

```
#
if (!(-e $junk)) then
 'mkdir' $junk
endif
#
# Process options
#
if ($listFlag) then
 'ls' -lgF $junk             # list junk directory.
 exit 0
endif
#
if ($purgeFlag) then
 'rm' $junk/*        # remove contents of junk directory.
 exit 0
endif
#
if ($fileFlag) then
 'mv' $fileList $junk        # move files to junk directory.
 exit 0
endif
#
exit 0
#
# Display error message and quit
#
error:
cat << ENDOFTEXT
Dear $USER, the usage of junk is as follows:
 junk -p means "purge all files"
 junk -l means "list junked files"
 junk <list of files> to junk them
ENDOFTEXT
exit 1
```

8.11 Enhancements

In addition to the new facilities that have already been described, the C shell also enhances the common core shell facilities in the following areas:

- a shortcut for command re-execution
- the {} metacharacters
- filename substitution
- redirection
- piping
- job control

8.11.1   Metacharacters: {}

You may use braces around filenames to save typing common prefixes and suffixes. The notation:

a{b,c}d

is textually replaced with:

abd acd

In the following example, I copied the C header files "/usr/include/stdio.h" and "/usr/include/signal.h" (which have a common prefix and suffix) into my home directory:

```
% cp /usr/include/{stdio,signal}.h .        ...copy two files.
% _
```

8.11.2   Filename Substitution

In addition to the common filename substitution facilities, the C shell supports two new features—the ability to disable filename substitution and the ability to specify what action should be taken if a pattern has no matches.

8.11.2.1 Disabling Filename Substitution

To disable filename substitution, set the $noglob variable. If this is done, wildcards lose their special meaning. The $noglob variable is not set by default. Here's an example:

```
% echo a* p*          ...one wildcard pair matches: p*
prog1.c      prog2.c  prog3.c      prog4.c
% set noglob          ...inhibit wildcard processing.
% echo a* p*
a* p*
% _
```

8.11.2.2 No-Match Situations

If several patterns are present in a command and at least one of them has a match, then no error occurs. However, if none of the patterns has a match, the shell issues an error message by default. If the $nonomatch variable is set and no matches occur, then the original patterns are used as is. The $nonomatch variable is not set by default. Here's an example:

```
% echo a* p*          ...one wildcard pair matches: p*.
prog1.c      prog2.c  prog3.c      prog4.c
% echo a* b*          ...no wildcards match.
echo: No match.       ...error occurs by default.
% set nonomatch       ...set special nonomatch variable.
% echo a* b*          ...wildcards lose their special meaning.
a* b*                 ...no error occurs.
% _
```

8.11.3   Redirection

In addition to the common redirection facilities, the C shell supports a couple of enhancements—the ability to redirect the standard error channel and the ability to protect files against accidental overwrites.

8.11.3.1 Redirecting the Standard Error Channel

To redirect the standard error channel in addition to the standard output channel, simply append an & character to the > or >> redirection operator:

```
% ls -l a.txt b.txt >list.out      ...ls sends errors to stderr
ls: File or directory "b.txt" is not found.
% ls -l a.txt b.txt >& list.out    ...also redirect stderr
% _
```

Although there's no easy way to redirect just the error channel, it can be done using the following "trick":

```
(process1 > file1) >& file2
```

This trick works by redirecting the standard output from *process1* to *file1* (which can be "/dev/null" if you don't want to save the output), allowing only the standard errors to leave the command group. The command group's output and error channels are then redirected to *file2*.

8.11.3.2 Protecting Files Against Accidental Overwrites

You may protect existing files from accidental overwrites, and nonexistent files from accidental appends, by setting the $*noclobber* variable. If a shell command tries to perform either action, it fails and issues an error message. Note that regular system calls such as write () are unaffected. $*noclobber* is not set by default. Here's an example:

```
% ls -lG errors             ...look at existing file.
-rw-r-xr-x   1 glass     225 Feb 14 10:59 errors
% set noclobber             ...protect files.
% ls a.txt >& errors        ...cannot overwrite.
errors: File exists.
% _
```

To temporarily override the effect of $*noclobber*, append a ! character to the redirection operator:

```
% ls a.txt >&! errors       ...existing file is overwritten.
% _
```

8.11.4   Piping

In addition to the common piping facilities, the C shell also allows you to pipe the standard output and standard error channel from *process1* to *process2* using the syntax in Figure 8–31.

process1 |& process2

Figure 8–31   Example of a piping of both stdout and stderr.

In the following example I piped the standard output and error channels from the **ls** utility to **more**:

```
% ls -lG a.txt b.txt |& more      ...pipe stdout and stderr.
ls: File or directory "b.txt" is not found.
-rw-r-xr-x   1 ables        988 Dec  7 06:27 a.txt
% _
```

Although there's no direct way to pipe *just* the error channel, it can be done using a "trick" similar to the one used previously to pipe only the error channel to a file:

```
(process1 > file) |& process2
```

This trick works by redirecting the standard output from *process1* to *file* (which can be "/dev/ null" if you don't want to save the output), allowing only the standard errors to leave the command group. The command group's output and error channels are then piped to *process2*, but because the standard output is now empty, the result is only the standard error output.

8.11.5   Job Control
The job control facilities of the C shell are the same as the Korn shell's, with the following additional built-in commands:

- stop
- suspend
- nice
- nohup
- notify

These commands are described below.

8.11.5.1 stop
To suspend a specified job, use the *stop* command (Figure 8–32).

Shell Command: **stop** { *%job* }*

stop suspends the jobs that are specified using the same standard job specifier format described in Chapter 7, "The Korn Shell." If no arguments are supplied, the last-referenced job is suspended.

Figure 8–32   Description of the *stop* shell command.

8.11.5.2 suspend

Figure 8–33 describes the *suspend* shell command.

Shell Command: **suspend**

suspend suspends the shell that invokes it. Doing this makes sense only when the shell is a subshell of the login shell, and it is most commonly done to suspend a shell invoked by the **su** or **script** utilities.

Figure 8–33   Description of the *suspend* shell command.

8.11.5.3 nice

To set the priority level of the shell or a command, use the *nice* command (Figure 8–34).

Shell Command: **nice** [+/- *number*] [*command*]

nice runs *command* with priority level *number*. In general, the higher the priority, the slower the process will run. Only a super-user can specify a negative priority level. If the priority level is omitted, 4 is assumed. If no arguments are specified, the shell's priority level is set.

Figure 8–34   Description of the *nice* shell command.

For more information about process priorities, consult Chapter 12, "Systems Programming."

8.11.5.4 nohup

To protect a command from hangup conditions, use the built-in *nohup* command (Figure 8–35).

Shell Command: **nohup** [*command*]

nohup executes *command* and protects it from hangup conditions. If no arguments are supplied, then all further commands executed from the shell are nohup'ed. Note that all background commands are automatically nohup'ed in the C shell.

Figure 8–35   Description of the *nohup* shell command.

8.11.5.5 notify

The shell normally notifies you of a change in a job's state just before it displays a new prompt. If you want immediate (asynchronous) notification of job state changes, use the built-in *notify* command (Figure 8–36).

> *Shell Command*: **notify** { *%job* }*
>
> *notify* instructs the shell to inform you immediately when the specified jobs change state. Jobs must be specified following the standard job specifier format described in Chapter 7, "The Korn Shell." If no job is specified, the last-referenced job is used. To enable immediate notification of all jobs, set the $notify variable.

Figure 8–36   Description of the *notify* shell command.

8.11.6   Terminating a Login Shell

The *logout* command terminates a login shell. Unlike *exit*, it cannot be used to terminate an interactive subshell. You may therefore terminate a login C shell in one of three ways:

- Type a *Control-D* on a line by itself (as long as $ignoreeof is not set).
- Use the built-in *exit* command.
- Use the built-in *logout* command.

Here's an example:

```
% set ignoreeof        ...set to prevent ^D exit.
% ^D                   ...won't work now.
Use "logout" to logout.
% logout               ...a better way to log out.

login: _
```

When a login C shell is terminated, it searches for "finish-up" files. The commands in each file, if found, are executed in sequence. The user's finish-up file is $HOME/.logout and it is executed if found. Then, if the global finish-up file "/etc/csh.logout" exists, it is executed.

A finish-up file typically contains commands for cleaning up temporary directories, other such clean-up operations, and perhaps a goodbye message.

If a non-login C shell is terminated using *exit* or *Control-D*, no finish-up files are executed.

8.12 Built-Ins

The C shell provides the following extra built-ins:

- chdir
- glob
- source

The next few subsections describe each built-in.

8.12.1   chdir

Figure 8–37 describes the *chdir* shell command.

Shell Command: **chdir** [*path*]

chdir works the same as *cd*; it changes your current working directory to the specified directory.

Figure 8–37   Description of the *chdir* shell command.

8.12.2   glob

Figure 8–38 describes the *glob* shell command.

Shell Command: **glob** { *arg* }

glob works the same as *echo*, printing a list of *args* after they have been processed by the shell metacharacter mechanisms. The difference is that the list of args is delimited by nulls (ASCII 0) in the final output instead of spaces. This makes the output ideally suited for use by C programs that like strings to be terminated by null characters.

Figure 8–38   Description of the *glob* shell command.

8.12.3   source

When a script is executed, it is interpreted by a subshell. Any aliases and/or local variable assignments performed by the script therefore have no effect on the original shell. If you want a script to be interpreted by the current shell, and thus affect it, use the built-in *source* command, as described in Figure 8–39.

Shell Command: **source** [-h] *fileName*

source causes a shell to execute every command in the script called *fileName* without invoking a subshell. The commands in the script are only placed in the history list if the **-h** option is used. It is perfectly legal for *fileName* to contain further *source* commands. If an error occurs during the execution of *fileName*, control is returned to the original shell.

Figure 8–39   Description of the *source* shell command.

In the following example, I used *source* to re-execute an edited ".login" file. The only other way to re-execute it would have been to log out and then log back in again.

```
% vim .login                    ...edit my .login file.
...
% source .login                 ...re-execute it.
Enter your terminal type (default is vt100): vt52
% _
```

8.13 The Directory Stack

The C shell allows you to create and manipulate a directory stack, which makes life a little easier when you're flipping back and forth between a small working set of directories. To push a directory onto the directory stack, use the *pushd* command (Figure 8–40).

Shell Command: **pushd** [+*number* | *name*]

pushd pushes the specified directory onto the directory stack, and works like this:

- When *name* is supplied, the current working directory is pushed onto the stack and the shell moves to the named directory.
- When no arguments are supplied, the top two elements of the directory stack are swapped.
- When *number* is supplied, the *number*th element of the directory stack is rotated to the top of the stack and becomes the current working directory. The elements of the stack are numbered in ascending order, with the top as number 0.

Figure 8–40   Description of the *pushd* shell command.

To pop a directory from the directory stack, use the *popd* command (Figure 8–41).

Shell Command: **popd** [+*number*]

popd pops a directory from the directory stack, and works like this:

- When no argument is supplied, the shell moves to the directory that's on the top of the directory stack and then pops it.
- When a *number* is supplied, the shell moves to the *number*th directory on the stack and discards it.

Figure 8–41   Description of the *popd* shell command.

The *dirs* command (Figure 8–42) lets you see the contents of the directory stack.

Shell Command: **dirs**

dirs lists the current directory stack.

Figure 8–42   Description of the *dirs* shell command.

Here are some examples of directory stack manipulation:

```
% pwd                ...I'm in my home directory.
/home/glass
% pushd /            ...go to root directory, push home dir.
/ ~                  ...displays directory stack automatically.
```

```
% pushd /usr/include        ...push another directory.
/usr/include / ~
% pushd       ...swap two stack elements, go back to root.
/ /usr/include ~
% pushd       ...swap them again, go back to "/usr/include".
/usr/include / ~
% popd        ...pop a directory, go back to root.
/ ~
% popd        ...pop a directory, go back to home.
~
% _
```

8.13.1   The Hash Table

As described in Chapter 5, "The Linux Shells," the PATH variable is used when searching for an executable file. To speed up this process, the C shell stores an internal data structure, called a *hash table*, that allows the directory hierarchy to be searched more quickly. The hash table is constructed automatically whenever the ".tcshrc" file is read. In order for the hash table to work correctly, however, it must be reconstructed whenever $PATH is changed, or whenever a new executable file is added to any directory in the $PATH sequence. The C shell takes care of the first case automatically, but *you* must take care of the second.

If you add or rename an executable in any of the directories in the $PATH sequence except your current directory, you should use the *rehash* command to instruct the C shell to reconstruct the hash table. If you wish, you may use the *unhash* command to disable the hash table facility, thereby slowing down the search process. Figure 8–43 describes how these shell commands work.

Shell Command: **rehash**
   unhash

The *rehash* shell built-in command is used to rebuild your shell's command search hash list.
The *unhash* shell built-in command is used to disable search path hashing.

Figure 8–43   Description of the *rehash* and *unhash* shell commands.

In the following example, I added a new executable into the directory "~/bin", which was in my search path. The shell couldn't find it until I performed a *rehash*.

```
% pwd                      ...I'm in my home directory.
/home/glass
% echo $PATH               ...list my PATH variable.
.:/home/glass/bin:/usr/bin:/usr/local/bin:/bin:
% cat > bin/script.csh     ...create a new script.
```

```
#
echo found the script
^D                              ...end-of-input.
% chmod +x bin/script.csh       ...make executable.
% script.csh                    ...try to run it.
script.csh: Command not found.
% rehash                        ...make the shell rehash.
% script.csh                    ...try to run it again.
found the script                ...success!
% _
```

8.14 Command-Line Options

If the first command-line argument is a -, the C shell is started as a login shell. In addition to this, the C shell supports the command-line options listed in Figure 8–44.

Option	Meaning
-c *string*	Create a shell to execute the command *string*.
-e	Shell terminates if any command returns a nonzero exit code.
-f	Start shell but don't search for or read commands from ".tcshrc" or ".cshrc."
-i	Create an interactive shell; like the -s option except that the SIGTERM, SIGINT, and SIGQUIT messages are all ignored.
-n	Parse commands but do not execute them; for debugging only.
-s	Create a shell that reads commands from standard input and sends shell messages to the standard error channel.
-t	Read and execute a single line from standard input.
-v	Causes $verbose to be set, which was described earlier.
-V	Like -v, except that $verbose is set before ".tcshrc" is executed.
-x	Causes the $echo variable to be set, which was described earlier.
-X	Like -x, except that $echo is set before ".tcshrc" is read.
fileName	Execute the shell commands in *fileName* if none of the -c, -i, -s, or -t options are used. *fileName* is $0 within the *fileName* script.

Figure 8–44   C shell command-line options.

CHAPTER REVIEW

Checklist

In this chapter, I described:

- the creation of a C shell startup file
- simple variables and lists
- expressions, including integer arithmetic
- aliases and the history mechanism
- several control structures
- job control
- several new built-in commands

Quiz

1. Why do you think integer expressions must be preceded by an @ sign?
2. What's a good way to correct a simple typing mistake on the previous command?
3. What's the function of the { } metacharacters?
4. What character can you type to complete a filename on the command line?
5. Describe the differences between the *set* and *setenv* built-in commands.
6. How do you protect files from accidental overwrites?
7. What command is used to lower the priority of a process?
8. How do you protect scripts from *Control-C* interrupts?

Exercises

1. Modify the **junk** utility from this chapter so that it is menu driven. [level: *easy*]
2. Write a utility called **hunt** that acts as a front end to **find**; it takes the name of a file as its single parameter and displays the full pathname of every filename that matches, searching downward from the current directory. [level: *medium*]

Projects

1. Write a Bash script called **mv** (which replaces the GNU utility **mv**) that tries to rename the specified file (using the GNU utility **mv**), but if the destination file exists, instead creates an index number to append to the destination file, a sort of version number. So if I type:

```
$ mv a.txt b.txt
```

but b.txt already exists, **mv** will move the file to b.txt.1. Note that if b.txt.1 already exists, you must rename the file to b.txt.2, and so on, until you can successfully rename the file to a name that does not already exist. [level: *medium*]

2. Study the current trends in object-oriented programming and then design an object-oriented shell. [level: *hard*]

9

Networking and the Internet

Motivation

The major predecessor to Linux, UNIX, was one of the first operating systems to provide access to widely distributed local networks as well as the large Internet network that spans the globe. Today, millions of users and programs share information on these networks for a myriad of reasons, from distributing large computational tasks to exchanging a good recipe for lasagna. Linux has inherited this expectation that the network is a fundamental part of any computer system. To make the best use of these network resources, you should understand the utilities that manage the exchange of information. This chapter describes the most useful network utilities and provides an overview of the worldwide network known as the Internet.

Prerequisites

In order to understand this chapter, you should have already read Chapter 1, "What Is Linux?," and Chapter 3, "GNU Utilities for Nonprogrammers." It also helps if you have access to a Linux system so that you can try out the various utilities that I discuss.

Objectives

In this chapter, I'll show you how to find out what's on the network, how to talk to other users, how to copy files across a network, and how to execute processes on other computers on the network.

Presentation

This chapter begins with an overview of network concepts and terminology, and then describes the GNU network utilities. We finish up with an examination of the history and uses of the Internet.

Commands

This section introduces the following utilities, listed in alphabetical order:

finger	rsh	users
ftp	scp	w
host	sftp	walla
hostname	slogin	who
mesg	ssh	write
rcp	talk	
rlogin	telnet	

9.1   Introduction

A network is an interconnected system of cooperating computers. Through a network, you can share resources with other users via an ever-increasing number of network applications, such as web browsers and electronic mail messaging systems.

There has been a huge explosion of network use since 1990. For example, the client-server paradigm described in Chapter 1, "What Is Linux?," has been adopted by many of the major computer corporations, and relies heavily on the operating system's network capabilities to distribute the workload between the server and its clients.

In order to prepare yourself for the advent of widespread networking, it's important to know the following items:

• common network terminology
• how networks are built
• how to talk to other people on the network
• how to use other computeras on the network

This chapter covers all of these issues and more. All of the utilities covered in this chapter can be found in most distributions, but might not have been selected at install time. Check your distribution media or your distribution's application installation tool to find missing applications. For more detailed information about Linux networking, I highly recommend [Stevens, 1998], [Anderson, 1995], and the networking section of [Nemeth, 2002].

9.2   Building a Network

One of the best ways to understand how modern networks work is to look at how they evolved. Imagine that two people in an office want to hook their computers together so that they can share data. The easiest way to do this is to connect a cable between their serial ports. This is the simplest form of *local area network* (LAN), and requires virtually no special software or hardware. When one computer wants to send information to the other, it simply sends it out of its serial port (Figure 9–1).

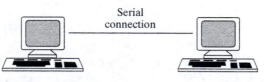

Figure 9–1   The simplest LAN.

9.2.1   Ethernets

To make things a little more interesting, let's assume that another person wants to tie into the other two guys' existing network. With three computers in the network, we need an addressing scheme so that the computers can be differentiated. We would also like to keep the number of connections down to a minimum. The most common implementation of this kind of LAN is called an *Ethernet*®. Ethernet is a hardware standard defining cabling, signaling, and behaviors that allow data to pass across a length of wire. The format of this data is defined by *network protocols* that we'll look at a bit later. The Ethernet standard was originally developed by Xerox Corporation and works like this:

- Each computer contains an Ethernet card, which is a special piece of hardware that has a unique Ethernet address.
- Every computer's Ethernet card is connected to the same single piece of wire.
- When a computer wishes to send a message to another computer with a particular Ethernet address, it broadcasts the message onto the Ethernet together with Ethernet header and trailer information that contain the Ethernet destination address. Only the Ethernet card whose address matches the destination address accepts the message.
- An attempt by two computers to broadcast to the Ethernet at the same time is known as a *collision*. When a collision occurs, they both wait a random period of time and then try again.

Figure 9–2 is a diagram of an Ethernet.

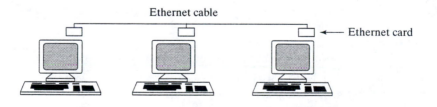

Figure 9–2   An Ethernet.

Ethernet networks can transmit data in the order of tens or hundreds megabytes per second.

9.2.2   Bridges

Let's assume that the Ethernet in the office works so well that the people in the office next door build themselves an Ethernet too. How does one computer on one Ethernet talk to another computer on another Ethernet? One solution might be to connect a special bit of hardware called a *bridge* between the networks (Figure 9–3). A bridge passes an Ethernet message between the different *segments* (wires) of the network as if both segments were a single Ethernet network cable. A bridge is used when you need to extend a network past the allowed length of a single section of wire (limited by signal degradation over a distance).

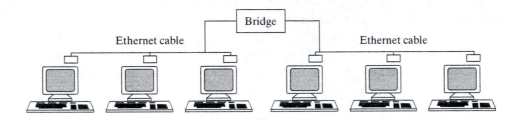

Figure 9–3   A bridge.

9.2.3   Routers

The use of bridges facilitates the construction of small serially linked sections of Ethernet, but it's a pretty inefficient way to link together large numbers of networks. For example, assume that a corporation has four LANs that it wishes to interconnect in an efficient way. Stringing them all together with bridges would cause data to pass across the "middle" sections to get to the ends when hosts on those middle sections have no interest in the data. To pass data directly from the originating network to the destination network, a *router* can be used. A router is a device that hooks together two or more networks and automatically routes incoming messages to the correct network (Figure 9–4).

9.2.4   Gateways

The final stage in network evolution occurs when many corporations wish to connect their local area networks together into a single, large wide area network (WAN). To do this, several high-capacity routers called *gateways* are placed throughout the country, and each corporation ties its LAN into the nearest gateway (Figure 9–5).

9.3   Internetworking

In order for a collection of LANs and WANs to be able route information amongst themselves, they must agree upon a networkwide addressing and routing scheme. This large-scale interconnection of different networks is known as *internetworking*. Any group of two or more networks

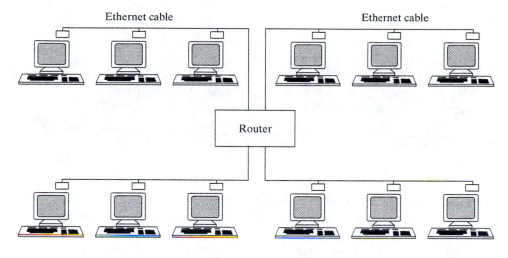

Figure 9–4 A router.

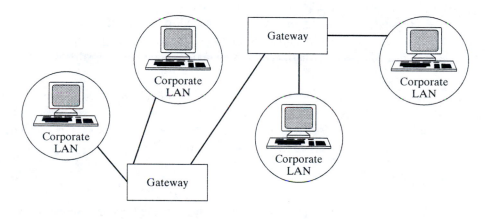

Figure 9–5 Gateways.

connected together across administrative boundaries may properly be called "an internet." However, the largest and best-known such network has become known as "the Internet."

Universities, large corporations, government offices, and military sites all have computers that are part of the Internet, which are generally linked together by high-speed data
links. The largest of these computer systems are joined together to form what is known as the
backbone of the Internet. Other smaller establishments link their LANs to the backbone via
gateways.

9.3.1   Packet Switching

Today's digital computer networks are *packet-switched* networks. When one node on the network sends a message to another node, the message is split up into small packets, each of which can be routed independently (switched) through the network.

These packets contain special information that allows them to be recombined at the destination. They also contain information for routing purposes, including the address of the source and destination nodes. The combined set of protocols is called the Transmission Control Protocol and Internet Protocol (TCP/IP) protocol suite. Linux interprocess communication (IPC) uses TCP/IP to allow Linux processes on different machines to talk to each other.

9.3.2   IP Addresses

Hosts on the Internet, as well as many private internets, also use TCP/IP to send data. While it is most popularly implemented on Ethernet networks, TCP/IP can also be used on other types of media. This makes it useful for connecting different types of networks, because not all computers are connected by Ethernet. For example, some LANs may use the IBM Token Ring system. The IP addressing system therefore uses a hardware-independent labeling scheme; the bridges, routers, and gateways transmit messages based purely on their destination IP address. The IP address is mapped to a physical hardware address only when the message reaches the destination host's LAN. Thus the computer sending the message does not need to understand hardware-specific information of the computer where the message is to be sent.

The IP addressing mechanism works the same whether or not you actually connect your computers to the Internet. When it sets up a LAN that is to be part of the Internet, an organization must get a unique address range assigned to its computers, a process we will see later.

9.3.2.1   IP (IPv4) Addresses

The most common version of the Internet Protocol (IP) in use today is still version 4. In it, an IP address is a 32-bit value that is written as 4 dot-separated numbers, each number representing 8 of the 32 bits of the address. Because each part represents an 8-bit value, the maximum value it may have is 255. Here's how his form of the IP address looks:

```
192.127.63.141
```

However, due to the explosive growth of the Internet, the seemingly endless supply of 32-bit addresses is quickly being used up. The day will come when this version of IP will no longer allow enough Internet addresses to satisfy the demand. Even when it does, local networks may continue to use IPv4 internally, as will the examples in this chapter after the next section.

9.3.2.2   IPv6 Addresses

In the early 1990s, it became clear that a new generation of IP that allowed for many more addresses would be necessary. Work began to define IPng (IP next generation), and a formal proposal for version 6 of the Internet Protocol was released in 1995.

IPv6 specifies 128-bit addresses. Although the two protocols use addresses of different lengths, both protocols can be used on the same network. This is necessary because the Internet is far too large to coordinate a "cut-over" to a new protocol at any moment in time. A smooth transition to a new addressing scheme requires the ability to evolve to it gradually rather than to require that we all wake up one day using the new protocol.

IP packets (of both versions) specify a version in the first 4 bits of the packet. Therefore, a computer that "speaks" IPv6 can still recognize and handle an IPv4 packet (if it is configured for both protocols). This allows the two protocols to coexist on the same network. The older machines can be upgraded to IPv6 as implementations become available or as the system administrators have the opportunity to upgrade, without requiring it all to happen simultaneously.

IPv6 addresses are expressed in hexadecimal format (rather than the decimal values used in IPv4), requiring two hex digits for each 8 bits, and are delimited every 16 bits by a colon (rather than a period). An IPv6 address looks like this:

```
C07F:3F8D:F11B:5810:014D:2208:BFFD:1B3D
```

In practice, many IP addresses have 8-bit or even 16-bit portions that are zero, and IPv6 also allows for dropping leading zero values as well as eliminating contiguous 16-bit values of zero. So you can actually wind up with much shorter addresses!

In addition to the addressing changes, IPv6 also provides improvements in routing and automatic configuration. While IPv6 is not currently in wide use, vendors are implementing and testing the new protocol. Over the next few years, IPv6 will be deployed across the Internet. If all goes well, people will not even notice. For more information on IPv6, visit the web site at:

```
http://www.ipv6.org
```

9.3.3   Naming

These numeric addresses are not very convenient for humans to use to access remote computers. Humans are much more used to naming things (people, pets, and cars). So we have taken to naming our computers as well.

When a *hostname* is assigned to a particular computer, a correlation can be established between its name and its numeric IP address. This way, a user can type the computer's name to reference it, and the software can translate this name to an IP address automatically.

The mapping of IP addresses to local host names is kept by the LAN's system administrator in a file called "/etc/hosts". To show you what this looks like, here's a small section of the file from UT Dallas:

```
129.110.41.1     manmax03
129.110.42.1     csservr2
129.110.43.2     ncube01
129.110.43.128   vanguard
129.110.43.129   jupiter
129.110.66.8     neocortex
129.110.102.10   corvette
```

9.3.4   Routing

The Internet Protocol performs two kinds of routing: static and dynamic. Static routing information is kept in the file "/etc/route" and is of the form: "You may get to the destination DEST via the gateway GATE with X hops." When a router has to forward a message, it can use the information in this file to determine the best route. Dynamic routing information is shared between hosts via the "/etc/routed" or "/etc/gated" daemons.[1] These programs constantly update their local routing tables based on information gleaned from network traffic, and periodically share their information with other neighboring daemons.

9.3.5   Security

It has long been known that the only way to keep any computer secure is to put it in a locked room and not connect it to a network. For most applications, however, this is not practical. The network is not only one of the most useful additions to computing, but also one of the most dangerous. The network provides a path for data to enter and leave the system, but makes no judgment about the use of the data. Therefore, it is up to the users or managers of the system to make sure "not just anyone" can gain access to the system or the data being transferred to or from the system.

9.3.5.1   User Authentication

Authentication of a user is the process of establishing that the user is who he or she claims to be. The most common user authentication mechanism is logging in with a username and password. When you access a remote machine across a network, you generally must re-authenticate in order to gain access. Another method may be to have a set of systems allow access from any of the other systems in the group by assuming you had to authenticate yourself to (log in on) the first system.

Several of the Linux networking utilities that I discuss later in this chapter allow a user with accounts on several machines to execute a command on one of these machines from another. For example, I have an account on both the "csservr2" and "vanguard" machines at UT Dallas. To execute the **date** command on the vanguard machine from the csservr2 machine I can use the **rsh** utility (discussed later in this chapter) as follows:

```
$ rsh vanguard date      ...execute date on vanguard.
```

The interesting thing about **rsh** and a few other utilities is that they are able to obtain a shell on the remote host *without requiring a password*. They can do this because of a Linux facility called *machine equivalence*. If you create a file called ".rhosts" in your home directory that contains a list of host names, then any user with the same username as your own may log into your account from these hosts without supplying a password. Both my "csservr2" and "vanguard" home directories contain a file ".rhosts" that includes the following lines:

```
csservr2.utdallas.edu
vanguard.utdallas.edu
```

---

1.   A daemon is a fancy term for a constantly running background process that is normally started when the system is booted.

We must use the "official" hostname in the ".rhosts" file which includes the Internet domain name (discussed later in this chapter).

This allows me to execute remote commands from either computer without any hassle. Linux also allows a system administrator to list globally equivalent machines in the file "/etc/hosts.equiv". Global equivalence means that *any* user on the listed machines can log into the local host without a password. For example, if the "vanguard" "/etc/hosts.equiv" file contained the lines:

```
csservr2.utdallas.edu
vanguard.utdallas.edu
```

then any user on "csservr2" could log into the "vanguard" or execute a remote command on it without a password. Global equivalence should be used with great care (if ever).

9.3.5.2   Data Encryption

Even when a user can provide authentication information to a remote system, another problem is posed by a third-party eavesdropping on the network connection and gaining access to the user-name and password the user provides to login on the remote system. Most login information, and certainly command and input data, is sent in packets across the network. This is often referred to as sending the data "in the clear" or as "clear text."

Depending on the type and extent of the network in question, this may or may not be an issue. But consider the wireless network in your local coffee shop, where your e-mail client connects to your ISP's e-mail server and passes your username and password in clear text to check your mail. Anyone on that network could conceivably copy that data and log in as you.

For this reason, many of the common network data-transfer commands now also come in a secure version that encrypts all data being sent to or received from a remote host. This is accomplished through the use of the Open Secure Shell (OpenSSH). OpenSSH is based on the Open Secure Socket Layer (OpenSSL), originally developed by Netscape Communications, to provide secure web connections so that sensitive information like credit card numbers could be sent across the Internet without fear of copying. Now the code that started the electronic commerce revolution can be used to access your own data on a remote host to keep it from prying eyes. For more information on OpenSSH and OpenSSL, visit their web sites:

```
http://www.openssh.org
http://www.openssl.org
```

9.3.6   Ports and Common Services

When one network host talks to another, it does so via a set of numbered ports. Every host supports some standard ports for common uses and allows application programs to create other ports for transient communication. The file "/etc/services" contains a list of the standard ports. Here's a snippet from the UT Dallas file:

```
echo        7/tcp
discard     9/tcp               sink null
```

```
systat      11/tcp          users
daytime     13/tcp
ftp-data    20/tcp
ftp         21/tcp
telnet      23/tcp
smtp        25/tcp          mail
time        37/tcp          timeserver
rlp         39/udp          resource
whois       43/tcp
finger      79/tcp
sunrpc      111/tcp
exec        512/tcp
login       513/tcp
```

The description of the **telnet** utility later in this chapter provides some examples where I connected to some of these standard ports.

9.3.7   Network Programming
The Linux interprocess communication allows you to communicate with other programs at a known IP address and port. This facility is described in Chapter 12, "Systems Programming."

9.4   Identifying Network Users
Linux networking is all about moving around the network and talking to other people. Therefore, a basic thing to learn is how to find out who's on a particular host. There are several utilities that do this, each with its own strengths:

- **users**, which lists all of the users on your local host
- **who**, which is like **users** except that it gives you more information
- **w**, which is like **who** except that it gives you *even more* information
- **hostname**, which displays your local host's name
- **finger**, which gives information about specific users

The next few subsections describe each of these utilities in turn.

9.4.1   Listing Users: users
The **users** utility (Figure 9–6) simply lists the current users of your local system.

Utility: **users**

users displays a simple, terse list of the users on your local host.

Figure 9–6   Description of the **users** command.

Here's an example of **users** in action:

```
$ users              ...display users on the local host.
glass posey
$ _
```

9.4.2   More User Listings: who and w

The **who** utility (Figure 9–7) supplies a little more information than the **users** utility.

Utility: **who** [*whoFile*] [am i] By default, **who** displays a list of every user on your local host.

Figure 9–7   Description of the **users** command.

Here's an example of **who**:

```
$ who          ... list all users currently on local host.
posey     pts/0   May 15 16:31 (blackfoot.utdall)
glass     pts/2   May 17 17:00 (bridge05.utdalla)
$ _
```

The **w** utility (Figure 9–8) is just as easy to use.

Utility: **w** { *userId* }* **w** displays a list that describes what each specified user is doing. In other words, it's almost the same as **who**.

Figure 9–8   Description of the **w** command.

Here's an example:

```
$ w            ...obtain more detailed information than who.
 22:25:35  up 11 days  3 users,  load average: 0.08, 0.03, 0.01
USER     TTY       LOGIN@  IDLE   JCPU   PCPU  WHAT
posey    pts/0     22:19   2days    1           csh
glass    pts/2     17:48    1      13      1    w
$ w glass   ...examine just myself.
 22:25:48  up 11 days  3 users,  load average: 0.08, 0.03, 0.01
USER     TTY       LOGIN@  IDLE   JCPU   PCPU  WHAT
glass    pts/2     17:48    1      13      1    w
$ _
```

9.4.3   Your Own Host Name: hostname

To find out the name of your local host, use **hostname** (Figure 9–9).

Utility: **hostname** [*hostName*]

When used with no parameters, **hostname** displays the name of your local host. A super-user may change this name by supplying the new host name as an argument. For more information about this file, see Chapter 14, "System Administration."

Figure 9–9   Description of the **hostname** command.

Here's an example:

```
$ hostname           ...display my host's name.
bluenote
$ _
```

9.4.4   Personal Data: finger

Once you've obtained a list of the people on your system, it's handy to be able to learn a little bit more about them. The **finger** utility allows you to do this (Figure 9–10).

Utility: **finger** {*userId* }*

finger displays information about a list of users that is gleaned from several sources:

- The user's home directory, startup shell, and full name are read from the password file "/etc/passwd".
- If the user supplies a file called ".plan" in his/her home directory, its contents are displayed as the user's "plan".
- If the user supplies a file called ".project" in his/her home directory, its contents are displayed as the user's "project".

If no usernames are listed, **finger** displays information about every user that is currently logged on. You may finger a user on a remote host by using the "@" protocol, in which case the remote host's finger daemon is used to reply to the local finger's request.

Figure 9–10   Description of the **finger** command.

I recommend that you create your own ".plan" and ".project" files in your home directory so that people can "finger" *you* back. Have fun!

In the following example, I fingered everyone on the system and then fingered myself:

```
$ finger              ...finger everyone on the system.
Login    Name         Tty    Idle   Login Time  Where
posey    John Posey   pts/0   2d    Fri 16:31   console
```

```
glass    Graham Glass pts/2         Sun 17:00   blackfoot.utdall
$ finger glass          ...finger myself.
Login name: glass              Name: Graham Glass
Directory: /home/glass         Shell: /bin/ksh
On since Mon May 17 17:47 (CDT) on pts/2 from bridge05.utdalla
No unread mail
Project: To earn an enjoyable, honest living.
Plan: To work hard and have fun and not notice the difference.
$ _
```

In the next example, I listed the three sources of **finger**'s information about me:

```
$ cat .plan              ...list the ".plan" file.
To work hard and have fun and not notice any difference.
$ cat .project           ...list the ".project" file.
To earn an enjoyable, honest living.
$ grep glass /etc/passwd  ...look at the password file.
glass:x:496:62:Graham Glass:/home/glass:/bin/ksh
$ _
```

9.5 Communicating with Network Users

There are several utilities that allow you to communicate with a user:

- **write**, which allows you to send individual lines to a user, one at a time
- **talk**, which allows you to have an interactive split-screen two-way conversation
- **wall**, which allows you to send a message to everyone on the local host
- **mail**, which allows you to send mail messages

The **mail** utility was described in Chapter 3, "GNU Utilities for Nonprogrammers," and supports the full standard Internet addressing scheme. The rest of these utilities are described in this section, together with a simple utility called **mesg** that allows you to shield yourself from other people's messages.

9.5.1   Shielding Yourself from Communication: mesg

The **write, talk,** and **wall** utilities communicate with other users by writing directly to their terminals. You may disable the ability of other users to write to your terminal by using the **mesg** utility (Figure 9–11).

Utility: **mesg** [n | y]

mesg allows you to prevent other users from writing to your terminal. It works by modifying the write permission of your tty device. The **n** and **y** arguments disable and enable writes, respectively. If no arguments are supplied, your current status is displayed.

Figure 9–11 Description of the **mesg** command.

In the following example, **mesg** prevented me from receiving a **write** message:

```
$ mesg n            ...protect terminal.
$ write glass       ...try to write to myself.
write: You have write permission turned off
$ _
```

9.5.2   Sending a Line at a Time: write
The **write** command (Figure 9–12) is a simple utility that allows you to send one line at a time to a named user.

Utility: **write** *userId* [*tty*]

write copies its standard input, one line at a time, to the terminal associated with *userId*. If the user is logged onto more than one terminal, you may specify the particular tty as an optional argument.

The first line of input that you send to a user via **write** is preceded by the message:

```
Message from yourHost!yourId on yourTty
```

so that the receiver may initiate a **write** command to talk back to you. To exit **write**, type a *Control-D* on a line of its own. You may disable writes to your terminal by using **mesg**.

Figure 9–12   Description of the **write** command.

In the following example, I received a **write** message from my friend Tim and then initiated my own **write** command to respond. We used the -o- (over) and -oo- (over and out) conventions for synchronization:

```
$
Message from tim@csservr2 on ttyp2 at 18:04
hi Graham -o-                        ...from tim.
$ write tim                 ...initiate a reply.
hi Tim -o-                       ...from me.
don't forget the movie later -oo-   ...from tim.
OK -oo-                          ...from me.
^D                          ...end of my input.
$ _
```

Although you can have a two-way conversation using **write**, it's awfully clumsy. A better way is to use the **talk** utility, which is described next.

9.5.3   Interactive Conversations: talk

The **talk** utility (Figure 9–13) allows you to have a two-way conversation across a network.

Utility: **talk** *userId* [*tty*]

The **talk** command allows you to talk to another user on the network via a split-screen inter-face. If the user is logged onto more than one terminal, you may choose a particular terminal by supplying a specific tty name.

To talk to someone, type the following at your terminal:

```
$ talk theirUserId@theirHost
```

This causes the following message to appear on their screen:

```
Message from TalkDaemon@theirHost...
talk: connection requested by yourUserId@yourHost
talk: respond with: talk yourUserId@yourHost
```

If they agree to your invitation, they'll type the following at their shell prompt:

```
$ talk yourUserId@yourHost
```

At this point, your screen divides into two portions, one containing your keyboard input, and the other containing the other guy's. Everything that you type is echoed at the other guy's ter-minal, and vice versa. To redraw the screen if it ever gets messed up, type *Control-L*. To quit from talk, press *Control-C*.

To prevent other people from talking to you, use the **mesg** utility.

Figure 9–13   Description of the **talk** command.

This is a fun utility that is worth exploring with a friend.

9.5.4   Messages to Everyone: wall

If you ever have something important to say to the world (or at least to everyone on your local host), **wall** is the way to say it. **wall** stands for write-all, and allows you to broadcast a message as described in Figure 9–14.

Utility: **wall** [*fileName*]

wall copies its standard input (or the contents of *fileName* if supplied) to the terminals of every user on the local host, preceding it with the message "Broadcast Message ...'. If a user has disabled terminal communication by using **mesg**, the message will not be received unless the user of **wall** is a super-user.

Figure 9–14   Description of the **wall** command.

In the following example, I sent a one-liner to everyone on the local host (including myself):

```
$ wall                          ...write to everyone.
this is a test of the broadcast system
^D                              ...end of input.

Broadcast Message from glass@csservr2 (ttyp2) at 18:04 ...

this is a test of the broadcast system
$ _
```

The **wall** command is most often used by system administrators to send users important, timely information (like "System going down in 5 minutes!").

9.6   Distributing Data

A very basic kind of remote operation is the transmission of files, and once again Linux has several utilities for doing this:

- **rcp** (remote copy) and **scp** (secure copy) allow you to copy files between your local Linux host and another remote Linux or UNIX host.
- **ftp** (file transfer protocol or program) and **sftp** (secure **ftp**) allow you to copy files between your local Linux host and any other host (possibly non-Linux) that supports FTP (the File Transfer Protocol). **ftp** is thus more powerful than **rcp**.
- **uucp** (unix-to-unix copy) is similar to **rcp**, and allows you to copy files between any two Linux or UNIX hosts.

subc sections that follow describe **rcp**, **scp**, **ftp**, and **sftp**.

9.6.1 Copying Files Between Two Linux or UNIX Hosts: rcp and scp

rcp and **scp** allow you to copy files between Linux or UNIX hosts (Figure 9–15).

Utility: **rcp** -p *originalFile newFile*
    rcp -pr { *fileName* }+ *directory*
    scp -p *originalFile newFile*
    scp -pr { *fileName* }+ *directory*

rcp and **scp** both allow you to copy files between Linux or UNIX hosts. Both your local host and the remote host must be registered as equivalent machines (as described in the section on Security beginning on page 342). To specify a remote file on *host*, use the syntax:

```
host:pathName
```

If *pathName* is relative, it's interpreted as being relative to your home directory on host. The **-p** option tries to preserve the last modification time, last access time, and permission flags during the copy. The **-r** option causes any file that is a directory to be recursively copied.

When **scp** is used, the TCP/IP connection to the remote host is encrypted so that a network sniffer cannot observe the data contained in the packets.

Figure 9–15 Description of the **rcp** and **scp** commands.

In the following example, I copied the file "original.txt" from the remote "vanguard" host to a file called "new.txt" on my local "csservr2" host. I then copied the file "original2.txt" from my local host to the file "new2.txt" on the remote host.

```
$ rcp vanguard:original.txt new.txt        ...remote to local.
$ rcp original2.txt vanguard:new2.txt       ...local to remote.
$ _
```

9.6.2 Copying Files Between Non-Linux/UNIX Hosts: ftp and sftp

The File Transfer Protocol is a generic protocol for the transmission of files, and is supported by many machines. You can therefore use it to transfer files from your local Linux host to any other kind of remote host as long as you know the Internet address of the remote host's ftp server. Users of non-Linux or non-UNIX computers often use **ftp** for transferring files between Linux or UNIX and their own system. Figure 9–16 gives a brief description of **ftp** and **sftp**.

Utility: **ftp** -n [*hostName*]
      sftp [user@] *hostName* [:file]

ftp and **sftp** allow you to manipulate files and directories on both your local host and a remote host.

If you supply a remote host name, **ftp** searches the ".netrc" file to see if the remote host has a passwordless anonymous **ftp** account. If it does, it uses it to log you into the remote host. Otherwise, it assumes that you have an account on the remote host and prompts you for its username and password. If the login is successful, **ftp** enters its command mode and displays the prompt "ftp>". If you don't supply a remote host name, **ftp** enters its command mode immediately and you must use the open command to connect to a remote host.

The **-n** option prevents **ftp** from attempting the initial automatic login sequence.

ftp's command mode supports many commands for file manipulation. The most common of these commands are described in Figure 9–17. You may abort file transfers without quitting **ftp** by pressing *Control-C*.

sftp opens a secure connection to the remote host and transfers files via encrypted TCP/IP packets. Once a secure connection is established, if *file* is not specified, **sftp** enters an interactive mode similar to **ftp** where files can be transferred.

Figure 9–16   Description of the **ftp** and **sftp** commands.

Figure 9–17 lists the most useful **ftp** commands that are available from its command mode.

Command	Meaning
!command	Executes *command* on local host.
append *localFile remoteFile*	Appends the local file *localFile* to the remote file *remoteFile*.
ascii	Transfers a file as ASCII text (maintains proper text format between machines whose text format may differ). ASCII transfer is the default behavior.
bell	Causes a beep to be sounded after every file transfer.
binary	Transfers a file exactly as it is with no format changes.
bye	Shuts down the current remote host connection and then quits **ftp**.

Figure 9–17   Commands within the **ftp** program. (Part 1 of 2)

Command	Meaning
cd *remoteDirectory*	Changes your current remote working directory to be *remoteDirectory*.
close	Shuts down the current remote host connection.
delete *remoteFile*	Deletes *remoteFile* from the remote host.
get *remoteFile* [*localFile*]	Copies the remote file *remoteFile* to the local file *localFile*. If *localFile* is omitted, it is given the same name as the remote file.
help [*command*]	Displays help about *command*. If *command* is omitted, a list of all **ftp** commands is displayed.
lcd *localDirectory*	Changes your current local working directory to be *localDirectory*.
ls *remoteDirectory*	Lists the contents of your current remote working directory.
mkdir *remoteDirectory*	Creates *remoteDirectory* on the remote host.
open *hostName* [*port*]	Attempts a connection to the host with name *hostName*. If you specify an optional port number, **ftp** assumes that this port is an **ftp** server.
put *localFile* [*remoteFile*]	Copies the local file *localFile* to the remote file *remoteFile*. If *remoteFile* is omitted, it is given the same name as the local file.
pwd	Displays your current remote working directory.
quit	Same as **bye**.
rename *remoteFrom remoteTo*	Renames a remote file from *remoteFrom* to *remoteTo*.
rmdir *remoteDirectory*	Deletes the remote directory *remoteDirectory*.

Figure 9-17   Commands within the **ftp** program. (Part 2 of 2)

In the following example, I copied "writer.c" from the remote host "vanguard" to my local host, and then copied "who.c" from my local host to the remote host:

```
$ ftp vanguard      ...open ftp connection to "vanguard".
Connected to vanguard.utdallas.edu.
vanguard FTP server (SunOS 5.4) ready.
Name (vanguard:glass): glass      ...login
Password required for glass.
Password:                         ...secret!
```

```
User glass logged in.
ftp> ls                  ...obtain directory of remote host.
PORT command successful.
ASCII data connection for /bin/ls (129.110.42.1,4919) (0 bytes).
...                      ...lots of files were listed here.
uniq
upgrade
who.c
writer.c
ASCII Transfer complete.
1469 bytes received in 0.53 seconds (2.7 Kbytes/s)
ftp> get writer.c           ...copy from remote host.
PORT command successful.
ASCII data connection for writer.c (129.110.42.1,4920) (1276 bytes).
ASCII Transfer complete.
local: writer.c remote: writer.c
1300 bytes received in 0.012 seconds (1e+02 Kbytes/s)
ftp> !ls                 ...obtain directory of local host.
reader.c    who.c       writer.c
ftp> put who.c           ...copy file to remote host.
PORT command successful.
ASCII data connection for who.c (129.110.42.1,4922).
ASCII Transfer complete.
ftp> quit                ...disconnect.
Goodbye.
$ _
```

9.7 Distributed Processing

The power of distributed systems becomes clearer when you start moving around the network and logging into different hosts. Some hosts supply limited passwordless accounts with usernames like "guest" so those explorers can roam the network without causing any harm, although this practice is fading away as more people abuse the privilege. These days you almost always have to have an account on a remote computer in order to login. Three utilities for distributed access are:

- **rlogin** and **slogin**, which allow you to log in to a remote Linux or UNIX host
- **rsh** and **ssh**, which allow you to execute a command on a remote Linux or UNIX host
- **telnet**, which allows you to execute commands on any remote host that has a telnet server

Of these, **telnet** is the most flexible, as other systems in addition to Linux support telnet servers. These three utilities are described in the following sections.

9.7.1 Remote Logins: rlogin and slogin

To log into a remote host, use **rlogin** (Figure 9–18).

Utility: **rlogin** -ec [-l *userId*] *hostName*
     slogin -ec [-l *userId*] *hostName*
     slogin *userID@hostName*

rlogin and **slogin** attempt to log you into the remote host *hostName*. If you don't supply a username by using the **-l** option, your local username is used during the login process.

    slogin creates a secure connection to the remote host by encrypting all packets used in the network connection.

    If the remote host isn't set as an equivalent of your local host in your "$HOME/.rhosts" file, you are asked for your password on the remote host. **slogin** will honor that file as well as information found in $HOME/.shosts on the remote host.

    Once connected, your local shell goes to sleep and the remote shell starts to execute. When you're finished with the remote login shell, terminate it in the normal fashion (usually with a *Control-D*) and your local shell will then awaken.

    There are a few special "escape commands" that you may type that have a special meaning; each is preceded by the escape character, which is a tilde (~) by default. You may change this escape character by following the **-e** option with the preferred escape character. Here is a list of the escape commands:

SEQUENCE	MEANING
~.	Disconnect immediately from remote host.
~susp	Suspend remote login session. Restart remote login using **fg**.
~dsusp	Suspend input half of remote login session, but still echo output from login session to your local terminal. Restart remote login using **fg**.

Figure 9–18 Description of the **rlogin** and **slogin** commands.

In the following example, I logged into the remote host "vanguard" from my local host "csservr2", executed the **date** utility, and then disconnected:

```
$ rlogin vanguard                    ...remote login.
Last login: Tue May 19 17:23:51 from csservr2.utdallas

vanguard% date                       ...execute a command on vanguard.
Thu May 19 18:50:47 CDT 2005
```

```
vanguard% ^D              ...terminate the remote login shell.
Connection closed.
$ _                       ...back home again at csservr2!
```

9.7.2   Executing Remote Commands: rsh and ssh

If you want to execute just a single command on a remote host, **rsh** and **ssh** are much handier than **rlogin** and **slogin** (although they are actually the same program, respectively). Figure 9–19 shows how they work.

Utility: **rsh** [-l *userId*] *hostName* [*command*]
     ssh [-l *userId*] *hostName* [*command*]
     ssh *userID@hostName* [*command*]

rsh and **ssh** attempt to create a remote shell on the host *hostName* to execute *command*. Both utilities copy standard input to *command* and copy the standard output and errors from *command* to their own standard output and error channels. Interrupt, quit, and terminate signals are forwarded to *command,* so you may *Control-C* a remote command. They terminate immediately after *command* terminates.

    If you do not supply a username by using the **-l** option, your local username is used during the connection. If no command is specified, **jsh** and **ssh** start a remote shell.

    Quoted metacharacters are processed by the remote host; all others are processed by the local shell.

    A connection created by **ssh** is encrypted.

Figure 9–19   Description of the **rsh** and **ssh** commands.

In the following example, I executed the **hostname** utility on my local "csservr2" host and the remote "vanguard" host:

```
$ hostname               ...execute on my local host.
csservr2
$ rsh vanguard hostname  ...execute on the remote host.
vanguard
$ _
```

9.7.3   Remote Connections: telnet

telnet allows you to communicate with any remote host on the Internet that has a **telnet** server. Figure 9–20 describes how it works:

Utility: **telnet** [*host* [*port*]]

telnet establishes a two-way connection with a remote port. If you supply a hostname but not a port specifier, you are automatically connected to a **telnet** server on the specified host, which typically allows you to login to the remote machine. If you don't even supply a host-name, **telnet** goes directly into command mode (in the same fashion as **ftp**).

What happens after the connection is complete depends on the functionality of the port you're connected to. For example, port 13 of any Internet machine will send you the time of day and then disconnect, whereas port 7 will echo ("ping") back to you anything that you enter from the keyboard.

To enter command mode after you've established a connection, press the sequence *Control-]*, which is the **telnet** escape sequence. This causes the command-mode prompt to be displayed, which accepts commands including the following:

COMMAND	MEANING
close	Close current connection.
open *host* [*port*]	Connect to *host* with optional *port* specifier.
quit	Exit **telnet**.
z	Suspend **telnet**.
?	Print summary of **telnet** commands.

Therefore, to terminate a **telnet** connection, press *Control-]* followed by the command **quit**.

Figure 9–20   Description of the **telnet** command.

In the following example, I used **telnet** to emulate the **rlogin** functionality by omitting an explicit port number with the **open** command:

```
$ telnet                        ...start telnet.
telnet> ?                       ...get help.
Commands may be abbreviated.  Commands are:
```

```
close           close current connection
logout          forcibly logout remote user and close the connection
display         display operating parameters
mode            try to enter line-by-line or character-at-a-time mode
open            connect to a site
quit            exit telnet
send            transmit special characters ('send ?' for more)
set             set operating parameters ('set ?' for more)
status          print status information
toggle          toggle operating parameters ('toggle ?' for more)
z               suspend telnet
?               print help information
telnet> open vanguard          ...get a login shell from vanguard.
Trying 129.110.43.128 ...
Connected to vanguard.utdallas.edu.
Escape character is '^]'.

SunOS 5.4 (vanguard)

login: glass                   ...enter my username.
Password:                      ...secret!
Last login: Wed May 18 17:22:45 from csservr2.utdalla

Thu May 19 17:23:21 CDT 2005
Erase is Backspace
vanguard% date                 ...execute a command.
Thu May 19 17:23:24 CDT 2005
vanguard% ^D           ...disconnect from remote host.
Connection closed by foreign host.
$ _                    ...telnet terminates.
```

You may specify the host name directly on the command line if you like:

```
$ telnet vanguard        ...specify host name on command line.
Trying 129.110.43.128 ...
Connected to vanguard.utdallas.edu.
Escape character is '^]'.

SunOS 5.4 (vanguard)

login: glass                   ...enter username, etc...
```

You may use **telnet** to try out some of the standard port services that I described earlier in this chapter. For example, port 13 prints the day and time on the remote host and then immediately disconnects:

```
$ telnet vanguard 13        ...what's the remote time & day?
Trying 129.110.43.128 ...
Connected to vanguard.utdallas.edu.
Escape character is '^]'.
Thu May 19 17:26:32 2005
Connection closed by foreign host        ...telnet terminates.
$ _
```

Similarly, port 79 allows you to enter the name of a remote user and obtain finger information:

```
$ telnet vanguard 79  ...manually perform a remote finger.
Trying 129.110.43.128 ...
Connected to vanguard.utdallas.edu.
Escape character is '^]'.
glass                              ...enter the username.
Login name: glass          Name: Graham Glass
Directory: /home/glass     Shell: /bin/csh
No unread mail
No Plan.
Connection closed by foreign host.  ...telnet terminates.
$ _
```

When system administrators are testing a network, they often use port 7 to check host connections. Port 7 echoes everything that you type back to your terminal, and is sometimes known as a "ping-port":

```
$ telnet vanguard 7              ...try a ping.
Trying 129.110.43.128 ...
Connected to vanguard.utdallas.edu.
Escape character is '^]'.
hi                              ...my line.
hi                              ...the echo.
there
there
^]                              ...escape to command mode.
telnet> quit                    ...terminate connection.
Connection closed.
$ _
```

telnet accepts numeric Internet addresses as well as symbolic names:

```
$ telnet 129.110.43.128 7        ... vanguard's numeric addr.
Trying 129.110.43.128 ...
Connected to 129.110.43.128.
Escape character is '^]'.
```

```
hi          ...my line.
hi          ...the echo.
^]          ...escape to command mode.
telnet> quit          ...disconnect.
Connection closed.
$ _
```

9.8   Evolution of the Internet

As local networks began to grow larger and to be connected together, an evolution began. First, some companies connected their own LANs together via private connections. Others transferred data across a network implemented on the public telephone network. Ultimately, the network research being funded by the U.S. Government brought it all together.

It may sound hard to believe, but what we know today as "the internet" was almost inevitable. Although it began in a computer lab, and at the time, most thought only high-powered computer scientists would ever use it, the way we stored and used information almost dictated that we find a better way to move information from one place to another.

Now when I watch television and see web page addresses at the end of commercials for mainstream products, I know the Internet has truly reached common usage. Not only do high-tech companies maintain web pages, even cereal companies have web sites. One may argue about the usefulness of some of these sites, but the fact that they exist tells us a great deal about how society has embraced the new technology.

It makes you wonder how we got here and where we might go with it all.

9.8.1   In The Beginning—the 1960s

In the 1960s, man was about to reach the moon, society was going through upheavals on several fronts, and technology was changing more rapidly than ever before. The Advanced Research Projects Agency (ARPA) of the Department of Defense (DoD) was attempting to develop a computer network to connect government computers (and some government contractors' computers) together. As with so many advances in our society, some of the motivation (and funding) came from a government that hoped to leverage an advance for military and/or defensive capability. High-speed data communication might help win a war at some point. Our Interstate Highway system (network) has its roots in much the same type of motivation.

In the 1960s, mainframe computers still dominated computing, and would for some time. Removable disk packs, small cartridge tapes, and compact disc technology were still in the future. Moving data from one of these mainframe computers to another usually required writing the data on a bulky tape device or some large disk device, physically carrying that medium to the other mainframe computer, and loading the data onto that computer. Although this was done, it was extremely inconvenient.

9.8.1.1   A Network Connection

Though computer networking was still in its infancy, local networks did exist, and were the inspiration for what would ultimately become the Internet. During 1968 and 1969, ARPA experimented with connections between a few government computers. The basic architecture was a 50-Kbps dedicated telephone circuit connected to a machine at each site called an Interface Message Processor (IMP). Conceptually, this is not unlike your personal Internet connection today, if you consider that your modem does the job of the IMP (of course, the IMP was a much more complex device). At each site, the IMP then connected to the computer or computers that needed to access the network.

9.8.1.2   The ARPANET

The ARPANET was born in September of 1969 when the first four IMPs were installed at the University of Southern California, Stanford Research Institute, the University of California at Santa Barbara, and the University of Utah. All of these sites had significant numbers of ARPA contractors. The success of the initial experiments between these four sites generated a great deal of interest on the part of ARPA as well as the academic community. Computing would never be the same.

9.8.2   Standardizing the Internet—the 1970s

The problem with the first connections to the ARPANET was that each IMP was, to some degree, custom designed for each site, depending on the operating systems and network configurations of their computer. Much time and effort had been expended to get this network up to four sites. Hundreds of sites would require hundreds of times this much custom work if it were done in the same fashion.

It became clear that if all the computers connected to the network in the same way and used the same software protocols, they could all connect to each other more efficiently and with much less effort at each site. But at this time, different computer vendors supplied their own operating systems with their hardware, and there was very little in the way of standards to help them interact or cooperate. What was required was a set of standards that could be implemented in software on different systems to allow sharing data in a form that different computers could understand.

Although the genesis of standard networking protocols began in the 1970s, it would be 1983 before all members of the ARPANET used them exclusively.

9.8.2.1   The Internet Protocol family

In the early 1970s, researchers began to design the Internet Protocol. The word "internet" was used since it was more generic (at the time) than ARPANET, which referred to a specific network. The word "internet" referred to the generic internetworking of computers to allow them to communicate.

The Internet Protocol is the fundamental software mechanism that moves data from one place to another across a network. Data to be sent is divided into *packets*, which is the basic data unit used on a digital computer network. IP does not guarantee that any single packet will arrive at the other end or in what order the packets will arrive, but it does guarantee that if the packet arrives, it will arrive unchanged from the original. This may not seem very useful at first, but stay with me for a moment.

9.8.2.2   TCP/IP

Once you can transmit a packet to another computer and know that, if it arrives at all, it will be correct, other protocols can be added "on top of" the basic IP to provide other functionality.

The Transmission Control Protocol (TCP) is the most often used protocol along with IP (used together they are referred to as TCP/IP). As the name might imply, TCP controls the actual transmission of the stream of data packets. TCP adds sequencing and acknowledgement information to each packet, and each end of a TCP "conversation" cooperates to make sure the original data stream is reconstructed in the same order as the original. When a single packet fails to arrive at the other end due to some failure in the network, the receiving TCP software figures this out because the packet's sequence number is missing. It can contact the sender and have it send the packet again. Alternatively, the sender, having likely not received an acknowledgment for the packet in question, will eventually retransmit the packet on its own, assuming it was not received. If it was received and only the acknowledgement was lost, the receiving TCP software, upon receiving a second copy, will drop it, since it has already received the first one. The receiver will still send the acknowledgement the sending TCP software was waiting for.

TCP is a connection-oriented protocol. An application program opens a TCP connection to another program on the other computer, and they send data back and forth to each other. When they have completed their work, they close down the connection. If one end (or a network break) closes the connection unexpectedly, this is considered an error by the other end.

9.8.2.3 UDP/IP

Another useful protocol that cooperates with IP is the User Datagram Protocol (sometimes semi-affectionately called the Unreliable Datagram Protocol). UDP provides a low-overhead method to deliver short messages over IP, but does not guarantee their arrival. On some occasions, an application needs to send status information to another application (such as a management agent sending status information to a network or systems management application), but the information is not of critical importance. If it does not arrive, it will be sent again later, unless it is unnecessary for each and every instance of the data to be received by the application. Of course, this assumes that any failure would be due to some transient condition and that "next time" the transmission will work. If it fails all the time, it would imply a network problem existed.

In a case like this, the overhead required to open and maintain a TCP connection is more work than is really necessary. You just want to send a short status message. You don't really care if the other end gets it (since if they don't, they probably will get the next one) and you certainly don't want to wait around for it to be acknowledged. So an unreliable protocol fills the bill nicely.

9.8.2.4 Internet Addressing

When an organization is setting up a LAN to be part of the Internet, it requests a unique Internet IP address from the Network Information Center (NIC). The number that is allocated depends on the size of the organization:

- A huge organization, such as a country or very large corporation, is allocated a Class A address—a number that is the first 8 bits of a 32-bit IP address. The organization is then free to use the remaining 24 bits for labeling its local hosts. The NIC rarely allocates these Class A addresses, as each one uses up a lot of the total 32-bit number space.

- A medium-sized organization, such as a mid-size corporation, is allocated a Class B address—a number that is the first 16 bits of a 32-bit IP address. The organization can then use the remaining 16 bits to label its local hosts.
- A small organization is allocated a Class C address, which is the first 24 bits of a 32-bit IP address.

For example, the University of Texas at Dallas is classified as a medium-sized organization, and its LAN was allocated the 16-bit number 33134. IP addresses are written as a series of four 8-bit numbers, with the most significant byte (8 bits) written first. All computers on the UT Dallas LAN therefore have an IP address of the form 129.110.XXX.YYY,[2] where XXX and YYY are numbers between 0 and 255.

9.8.2.5   Internet Applications

Once a family of protocols existed that allowed easy transmission of data to a remote network host, the next step was to provide application programs that took advantage of these protocols. The first applications to be used with TCP/IP were two programs that were already in wide use.

The **telnet** program was (and still is) used to connect to another computer on the network in order to login and use that computer from your local computer or terminal. This is quite useful for access to high-priced computing resources. Your organization might not have its own super-computer, but you might have access to one at another site. Telnet lets you remotely login without having to travel to the other site.

The **ftp** program was used to transfer files back and forth. While **ftp** is still available today, most people use web browsers or network file systems to move data files from one computer to another.

9.8.3   Re-Architecting and Renaming the Internet—the 1980s

As more universities and government agencies began using the ARPANET, word of its usefulness spread. Soon corporations were getting connected. At first, because of the funding involved, a corporation had to have some kind of government contract in order to qualify. Over time, this requirement was enforced less and less.

With this growth came headaches. The smaller a network is, and the fewer the nodes that are connected, the easier it is to administer. As the network grows, the complexity of managing the whole thing grows as well.

It became clear that the growth rate that the ARPANET was experiencing would soon out-grow the Defense Department's ability to manage the network.

New hosts were being added at a rate that required modifications to the network host table on a daily basis. This required each ARPANET site to download new host tables every day, if they wished to have up-to-date tables.

In addition, the number of available hostnames was dwindling, since each hostname had to be unique across the entire network.

2. $129 * 256 + 110 = 33134$

9.8.3.1 Domain Name Service

Enter DNS, the Domain Name Service. DNS and BIND, the Berkeley Internet Name Daemon, proposed the hierarchy of domain naming of network hosts and the method for providing address information to anyone on the network as they requested it.

In the new system, top-level domain names were established, under which each network site could establish a subdomain. The DoD would manage the top-level domains and delegate management of each subdomain to the entity or organization that registered the domain. The DNS/BIND software provided the method for any network site to do a lookup of network address information for a particular host.

Let's look at a real-world example of how a hostname is resolved to an address. One of the most popular top-level domains is **com**, so we'll use that in our example. The DoD maintained the server for the **com** domain. All subdomains registered in the **com** domain were known to this server. When another network host needed an address for a hostname under the **com** domain, it queried the **com** name server.

If you attempted to make a connection to **snoopy.hp.com**, your machine would not know the IP address, because there was no information in your local host table for **snoopy.hp.com**. Your machine would contact the domain name server for the **com** domain to ask it for the address. That server knows only the address for the **hp.com** name server; it does not need to know everything under that domain. But since **hp.com** is registered with it, the **com** name server can query the **hp.com** name server for the address.[3] Once a name server that has authority for the **hp.com** domain is contacted, it returns an address for **snoopy.hp.com** to the requestor (or a message that the host does not exist).

Up to this point, every host name on the ARPANET was just a name, like **utexas** for the ARPANET host at the University of Texas. Under the new system, this machine would be renamed to be a member of the **utexas.edu** domain. However, this change could not be made everywhere overnight. So for a time, a default domain **.arpa** was established. By default, all hosts began to be known under this domain (i.e., **utexas** changed its name to **utexas.arpa**). Once a site had taken that single step it could more easily become a member of its "real" domain later, since the software implemented domain names.

Once the ARPANET community adopted this system, all kinds of problems were solved. Suddenly, a hostname had to be unique only within a subdomain. HP's having a machine called **snoopy** didn't mean someone at the University of Texas couldn't also use that name, since **snoopy.hp.com** and **snoopy.utexas.edu** were different names. Duplication of names had not been such a big problem when only mainframe computers were connected to the network, but we were quickly approaching the explosion of workstations, and it would have been a huge problem

---

3.   Two options are available in the protocols. The first is that the requesting machine may be redirected to a "more knowledgeable" host and may then make follow-up requests until it obtains the information it needs. The second is that the original machine may make a single request, and each subsequent machine that doesn't have the address can make the follow-up request of the more knowledgeable host on behalf of the original host. This is a configuration option in the domain resolution software and has no effect on how many requests are made or the efficiency of the requests.

then. The other big advantage was that a single networkwide host table no longer had to be maintained and updated on a daily basis. Each site kept its own local host tables up-to-date, but would simply query the name server when an address for a host at another site was needed. By querying other name servers, you were guaranteed to receive the most up-to-date information.

The top-level domains most often encountered are listed in Figure 9–21.

Name	Category
biz	business
com	commercial
edu	educational
gov	governmental
info	unrestricted (i.e., anything)
mil	military
net	network service provider
org	nonprofit organization
XX	two-letter country code

Figure 9–21   Common top-level domain names.

For example, the University of Texas at Dallas LAN has been allocated the name "utdallas.edu". Once an organization has obtained its unique IP address and domain name, it may use the rest of the IP number to assign addresses to the other hosts on the LAN.

You can see what addresses your local DNS server returns for specific hostnames with the **host** command, available on most Linux systems (Figure 9–22).

Utility: **host** [*hostname* | *IPaddress*]

The **host** command contacts the local Name Service and requests the IP address for a given hostname. It can also do a reverse lookup, where by specifying an IP address you receive the hostname for that address.

Figure 9–22   Description of the **host** command.

host is most useful for obtaining addresses of machines in your own network. Machines at other sites around the Internet are often behind firewalls, so the address you get back may not be usable directly. However, **host** is good for finding out if domain names or web servers (machines that would need to be outside the firewall for the public to access) within domains are valid. You might see the following type of output from **host**:

```
$ host www.hp.com
www.hp.com is a nickname for www.hpgtm.speedera.net
www.hpgtm.speedera.net has address 192.151.52.187
www.hpgtm.speedera.net has address 192.6.234.8
$ host www.linux.org
www.linux.org has address 198.182.196.56
$ _
```

host displays the current IP address(es) for the hostname we requested. When a hostname doesn't exist or the DNS server can't (or won't) provide the address, we'd see something like this:

```
$ host xyzzy
Host not found.
$ _
```

9.8.3.2 DoD Lets Go

Like a parent whose child has grown up and needs its independence, the Department of Defense reached a point where its child, the ARPANET, needed to move out of the house and be on its own. The DoD originally started the network as a research project, a proof of concept. The network became valuable, so the DoD continued to run it and manage it. But as membership grew, the management of this network took more and more resources and provided the DoD fewer and fewer payoffs as non-DoD-related entities got connected. It was time for the Department of Defense to get out of the network management business.

In the late 1980s, the National Science Foundation (NSF) began to build NSFNET. NSFNET took a unique approach, in that it was constructed as a "backbone" network to which other regional networks would connect. NSFNET was originally intended to link supercomputer centers.

Using the same types of equipment and protocols as those making up the ARPANET, NSF-NET provided an alternative medium with much freer and easier access than the government-run ARPANET. To most except the programmers and managers involved, the ARPANET appears to have mutated into the Internet of today. In reality, connections to NSFNET (and their regional networks) were created and ARPANET connections were severed, but because of the sharing of naming conventions and appearances, the change was much less obvious to the casual user.

The end result was a network that worked (from the user's point of view) the same as the ARPANET had, but that, as it grew, was made up of many more corporations and nongovernment agencies. More importantly, this new network was not funded by government money; it was surviving on private funding from those using it.

9.8.4   The Web—the 1990s

The 1990s saw the Internet come into popular use. Although it had grown consistently since its inception, it still belonged predominantly to computer users and programmers. Two things happened to spring the Internet on an unsuspecting public: the continued growth of personal computers in the home and one amazingly good idea.

9.8.4.1 The "killer app"

Again, timing played a role in the history of the Internet. The network itself was growing and being used by millions of people but was still not considered mainstream. The more sophisticated home users were getting connected to the Internet via a connection to their employer's network or a subscription with a company that provided access to the Internet. These companies came to be known as *ISPs*, Internet Service Providers. In the early 1990s, only a handful of these existed, as only a few people recognized there was a business in providing Internet access to anyone who wanted it.

Then came Mosaic. Mosaic was the first "browser" and was conceived by software designers at the National Center for Supercomputing Applications (NCSA) at the University of Illinois at Urbana-Champaign. With Mosaic, a computer user could access information from other sites on the Internet without having to use the complicated and nonintuitive tools that were popular at the time (e.g., **telnet**, **ftp**).

Mosaic was (and browsers in general are) an application that displays a page of information both textually and graphically, as described by a page description language called Hyper-Text Markup Language (HTML). The most revolutionary aspect of HTML was that of a *hyperlink*, a way to link information in one place in a document to other information in another part of the document (or more generically, in another document).

By designing a page with HTML, you could display information and include links to other parts of the page or to other pages at other sites that contained related information. This created a document which could be "navigated" to allow users to obtain the specific information in which they were interested rather than having to read or search the document in a sequential fashion, as was typical at the time.

Almost overnight, servers sprang up across the Internet to provide information that could be viewed by Mosaic. Now, rather than maintaining an anonymous FTP site, a person or organization could maintain publicly accessible information in a much more presentable format. In accessing anonymous FTP sites, the users usually had to know what they were trying to find, or at best, get the README file which would help them find what they wanted. With a server that provided HTML, the users could simply point-and-click and be taken to the page containing the information they sought.

Of course, not all this magic happened automatically. Each site that maintained any information for external users had to set up a server and format the information. But this was not significantly more work than providing the information via anonymous FTP. Early on, as people switched from providing information via FTP-based tools to using web-based tools, the two alternatives were comparable in terms of the amount of effort required to make data available. As sites have become more sophisticated, the work required has increased, but the payoff in presentation has also increased.

Some of the people involved in the early releases of Mosaic later formed Netscape Communications, Inc., where they applied the lessons they had learned from early browser development and produced Netscape, the next generation in browsers. Since then, led by Netscape and Microsoft Internet Explorer, browsers have evolved to be very sophisticated applications, introducing significant advances to both browsing and publishing every year.

9.8.4.2   The Web Versus the Internet

The word "web" means many different things to different people in different contexts and causes much confusion. Before Mosaic and other browsers, there was just the Internet. As we have already seen, this is simply a worldwide network of computers. This in itself can be diagramed as a web of network connections. But this is not what the word "web" means here.

When Mosaic, using HTML, provided the capability to jump around from one place to another on the Internet, yet another conceptual "web" emerged. Not only is my computer connected to several others, forming a web, but now my HTML document is also connected to several others (by hyperlinks), creating a virtual spider web of information. This is the "web" that gave rise to the terms "web pages" and "web browsing," and is commonly referred to as "The World Wide Web."

When someone talks about "the web" today, they may mean the Internet itself or they may mean the web of information available on the Internet. Although not originally intended this way, the nomenclature "the web" and "the Internet" are often used interchangeably today. However, in proper usage, "the web" refers to the information that is available from the infrastructure of "the Internet."

9.8.4.3   Accessibility

A few ISPs had sprung up even as "the web" was coming into existence. Once the concept of "the web" gained visibility, it seemed that suddenly everyone wanted to get on the Internet. While electronic mail was always usable and remains one of the most talked-about services provided by access to the Internet, web browsing had the visibility and the public relations appeal to win over the general public.

All of a sudden, average people saw useful (or at least fun) things they could get from being connected to the Internet. It was no longer the sole domain of computer geeks. For better or worse, the Internet would change rapidly. More people, more information, and more demand caused great growth in usage and availability. Of course, with more people come more inexperienced people and more congestion. Popularity is always a double-edged sword.

Another factor boosting the general public's access to the Internet has been the geometric increase in modem speeds. While large companies have direct connections to the Internet, most individuals have dial-up connections over home phone lines requiring modems. When the top modem speed was 2400 bps (bytes per second), which wasn't all that long ago, downloading a web page would have been intolerably slow. As modem speeds have increased and high-speed digital lines have become economical for home use, it has become much more reasonable to have more than just a terminal connection via a dial-up connection.

Most of these private connections can be had for between $10 and $60 per month, depending on speed and usage, which has also played a part in attracting the general public. A bill for Internet service that is comparable with a cable bill or phone bill is tolerable. The general public likely would not accept a bill that was an order of magnitude higher than other utility bills.

9.8.4.4 Changes in the Internet

As the public has played a larger and larger part in the evolution of the Internet, some of the original spirit has changed.

The Internet was originally developed "just to prove it could be done." The original spirit of the Internet, especially in its ARPANET days, was that information and software should be free to others with similar interests and objectives. Much of the original code that ran the Internet (the TCP/ IP protocol suite and tools such as **ftp** and **telnet**, etc.) were given away by the original authors and modified by others who contributed their changes back to the original authors for "the greater good."

This was probably what allowed the Internet to grow and thrive in its youth. Today, however, business is conducted over the Internet, and much of the data is accessible for a fee. This is not to say everybody is out to do nothing but make money or that making money is bad. But it represents a significant change in the culture of the Internet.

The Internet needed its "free spirit" origins, but now that mainstream society is using the Internet, it is only natural that it would become more economically oriented. Advertising on web sites is common, and some web sites require each user to pay a subscription fee in order to be able to "login" to gain access to information. Commerce over the Internet (such as online ordering of goods and services, including online information) is expected to continue to grow long into the future.

9.8.4.5 Security

Entire books have been written about Internet security (e.g., [Cheswick, 1994]). In the future, as more commercial activity takes place across the Internet, the needs and concerns about the security of operations across the Internet will only increase.

In general, a single transfer of data is responsible for its own security. In other words, if you are making a purchase, the vendor will probably use secure protocols to acquire purchase information from you (like credit card information).

Four major risks confront an Internet web server or surfer: information copying, information modification, impersonation, and denial of service. Encryption services can prevent copying or modifying information. User education can help minimize impersonation.

The most feared (and ironically, the least often occurring) risk is the copying of information that travels across the network. The Internet is a public network, and therefore information that is sent "in the clear" (not encrypted) can, in theory, be copied by someone between the sender and the recipient. In reality, since information is divided into packets that may or may not travel the same route to their destination, it is often impractical to try to eavesdrop in order to obtain useful information.

Modification of information that is in transit poses the same problem as eavesdropping with the additional problem of making the modification. While not impossible, it is a very difficult task and usually not worth the effort.

Impersonation of a user, either through a login interface or an e-mail message, is probably the most common type of security breach. Users often do not safeguard their passwords. Once another person knows their username and password, he or she can login and have all the same rights and privileges as the legitimate user. Unfortunately, it is easy to send an e-mail message with forged headers to make it appear the message came from another user. Close examination can usually authenticate the header, but this can still lead to confusion, especially if an inexperienced user receives the message. One might also impersonate another network host by claiming to use the same network address. This is known as *spoofing*. Spoofing is not a trivial exercise, but an experienced network programmer or administrator can pull it off.

A denial-of-service attack occurs when an outside attacker sends a huge amount of information to a server to overload its capability to do its job. The server gets so bogged down that it either becomes unusable or it completely crashes.

9.8.4.6 Copyright

One of the biggest challenges in the development of information exchange on the Internet is that of copyright. In traditional print media, time is required to reproduce information, and proof of that reproduction will exist. In other words, if I reprint someone else's text without their permission, the copy I create will prove the action. On the Internet, information can be reproduced literally at the speed of light. In the amount of time it takes to copy a file, a copyright can be violated, leaving very little evidence of the action.

9.8.4.7 Censorship

In any environment where information can be distributed, there will be those who want to limit who can gain access to what information. If the information is mine and I want to limit your access to it, this is called my right to privacy. If the information is someone else's and I want to limit your access to it, this is called censorship.

This is not to say that censorship is bad. As with so much in our society, the idea alone is not the problem but rather the interpretation of the idea. Censorship on the Internet is, to put it mildly, a complex issue. Governments and organizations may try to limit certain kinds of access to certain kinds of materials (often with the best of intentions). The problem is that, since the Internet is a worldwide resource, local laws have very little jurisdiction over the whole of the Internet. How can a law in Nashville be applied to a web server in Sydney? Even if they decide the web server *is* doing something illegal, who will prosecute?

9.8.4.8 Misinformation

As much of a problem as copyrighted or offensive material may be, much more trouble is caused by information that is simply incorrect. Since there is no information authority that approves and validates information put on the net, anyone can publish anything. This is a great thing for free speech. But humans tend to believe information they see in print. I've heard innumerable stories about people acting on information they found on the web that turned out to be misleading or wrong. How much credence would you give to a rumor you were told by someone you didn't know? That's how much you should give to information you pick up off the web when you aren't sure of the source.

9.8.4.9 "Acceptable Use"

Many ISPs have an Acceptable Use policy you must adhere to in order to use their service. Over time, this may well solve many of the problems the Internet has had in its formative years. Most of these policies basically ask users to behave themselves and refrain from doing anything illegal or abusive to other users. This includes sending harassing e-mail, copying files that don't belong to you, and so on.

There is a perceived anonymity[4] of users of the Internet. If you send me an e-mail message that I disagree with, it may be difficult for me to walk over to you and yell at you personally. I might have to settle for YELLING AT YOU IN E-MAIL.[5] Because of this, people tend to behave in ways they would not in person. As the Internet and its users grow up, this problem should lessen.

9.9 Using Today's Internet

In the past, using the Internet meant keeping track of a collection of commands and ftp sites. You had to keep track of the resources as well as the method of accessing them.

Today, almost everything you access on the Internet is web-based—that is, accessible via a *web browser*. A web browser is a program, much like any other window-based program, with menu buttons, a control area, and a display area. You type in or select a web address, the browser sends the request to the specified computer on the network (either the local network or the Internet), and displays in the window the information that is returned. I won't go into detail about how to use Netscape, or any other browser, since trying it yourself is the best way to learn about web browsing. In general, all browsers have a place to type in a web address, a way to view your browser's *history* (web addresses you've previously visited), and buttons to help you move backward or forward in this list. Most allow you to save and/or print information and store web addresses in a list of "bookmarks" so you can return to the site in the future without having to remember and retype the address.

9.9.1 URLs

A *web page* is what is displayed in a browser window when you type in a particular web address. This addresses is called a *URL*, Uniform Resource Locator. For example, the URL for the Prentice Hall web site is:

```
http://www.prenhall.com
```

The components of a URL are the protocol to use to obtain the web page, the Internet

---

4.   I say "perceived" here because it is actually possible to find most people if you're willing to do enough work. Even people who have filtered threatening e-mail through "anonymous e-mail" services have been found by law enforcement. ISPs will cooperate with the authorities when arrest warrants are involved!

5.   Text in all caps is typically interpreted as equivalent to speaking the words in a loud voice. This does not apply to those few users who still use computers or terminals that can only generate uppercase characters.

address or hostname of the computer where the web page resides, an optional port number, and an optional filename. In the case of the URL above, the port number and filename were omitted, so the browser assumed port 80 and requested the default HTML file at the root of the web server document tree.

The most common protocol is **http** (HyperText Transfer Protocol), which is the protocol for accessing HTML information. An encrypted channel, Secure HTTP, specified with **https**, is used for pages or transactions involving confidential information (e.g., credit card numbers). Most web browsers also support the **ftp** protocol, which gives you a GUI-based way of accessing anonymous ftp sites through your browser. If no protocol is specified, most browsers will assume "`http://`" goes on the front of the URL, so you can usually leave that off when manually typing in a URL.

When you load a particular web page into your browser, you are typically presented with a nicely formatted display containing information and other highlighted text or icons (hyperlinks) that you can click on to be taken to other related web pages, possibly part of the current web site, or possibly managed by a completely different organization. The hyperlink is the fundamental concept at the heart of the World Wide Web. It results in a web of information, each page containing a link to many other pages. Since many web pages containing related information have links to each other, the result is a "web" of links all over the Internet.

9.9.2 Web Searches

So now that you have a browser window and can access web sites, how do you find the information you want? I could list thousands of web sites that contain interesting information, but by the time this book is published, many of them might not be available anymore. Rather than just giving you a fish, I'd rather show you how to fish so you can find anything you might need on your own.

There are more than a few web *search engines* on the Internet. These are sites that build and continuously update their database of web pages and keyword indices relating to them. Normally these are free services; the pages that show search results usually have advertising on them that sponsors pay for to support the cost of running the site.

Some common search engines, in alphabetical order, include:

- www.altavista.com
- www.excite.com
- www.google.com
- www.looksmart.com
- www.lycos.com
- www.webcrawler.com
- www.yahoo.com

I have my own preferences and so will you. Your favorite may depend on the speed of the response, the layout of the information, the quality of the findings, the ease with which you can build a query, or some of the other services the site may provide.

Today, there are so many sites on the Internet, the biggest problem with using a search engine is building a specific enough query so that you don't get thousands of links, most of which aren't what you really want.

If you are trying to find a "regular company," you can often get lucky by guessing. A URL like:

```
http://www.companyname.com
```

probably works more often than not.

9.9.3   Finding Users and Domains

The NIC provides web page access to the database of registered Internet users and Internet domains. The user database is not every Internet user, it is only users who have registered with the NIC. This usually includes system and network administrators who manage domain information for a site.

The NIC's web site is:

```
http://www.internic.net
```

and their web page can point you to the resources where you can perform all sorts of searches for domain and Internet information.

CHAPTER REVIEW

Checklist

In this chapter, I described:

- the main Linux network concepts and terminology
- utilities for listing users and communicating with them
- utilities for manipulating remote files
- utilities for obtaining remote login shells and executing remote commands
- the history of the Internet
- protocols used on the Internet
- applications that access the Internet
- the Domain Name Service used on the Internet
- the World Wide Web, web browsing, and web searching

Quiz

1. What's the difference between a bridge, a router, and a gateway?
2. What's a good way for a system administrator of a multi-user system to tell people about important events?
3. Why is **ftp** more powerful than **rcp**?
4. Why is **rcp** easier to use than **ftp**?

5. Describe some uses of common ports.
6. What does *machine equivalence* mean and how can you make use of it?
7. Why does the NIC allocate very few Class A addresses?
8. What is the difference between the *http* and *https* protocols?
9. If you were looking for Sun Microsystems' web page, what address would you try first?
10. What are the two most significant differences between the TCP and UDP protocols?

Exercises

1. Try out **rcp** and **rsh** as follows:

   • copy a single file from your local host to a remote host by using **rcp**
   • obtain a shell on the remote host using **rsh** and edit the file that you just copied
   • exit the remote shell using *exit*
   • copy the file from the remote host back to the local host using **rcp**

   [level: *easy*]
2. Use **telnet** to obtain the time of day at several remote host sites. Are the times accurate relative to each other? [level: *medium*]
3. Connect to the `www.internic.net` web site and explore it to find out what kinds of services the NIC provides. Look up information about your domain name (or your ISP's domain name). [level: *medium*]

Projects

1. Write a shell script that operates in the background on two machines and ensures that the contents of a named directory on one machine is always a mirror image of another named directory on the other machine. [level: *hard*]
2. Pretend you want to buy the latest CD of your favorite group but you don't know of an Internet site that sells them (there are many). Do a web search with several keywords (like music, CD, purchase, and the name of the group). See if you find a way to buy the CD. Explore some of the unwanted sites that come up to find out why they satisfied your search, so that you know how to make a better search next time. [level: *medium*]

10

The Linux Desktop

Motivation

The Linux graphical desktop environment is based on MIT's *X Window System*. A familiarity with the X Window System will help you effectively use any of the available Linux desktop environments.

Prerequisites

Since the X Window System takes advantage of many Linux networking facilities, you should have read or be familiar with the issues discussed in Chapter 9, "Networking and the Internet," prior to reading this chapter.

Objectives

In this chapter, I will provide you with a general overview of the major Linux desktop environments, commonly used window managers, and the X Window System upon which they all depend. Entire books cover these subjects, and we can't hope to compete with that depth, but this chapter should give you a basic understanding, so that you can get started using the Linux desktop environment, and a good foundation of knowledge upon which to build.

Presentation

First I will give you a brief history of window systems in general, followed by an examination of the X Window System, what it looks like, how it works, and the GNU utilities involved in using it. Then we'll look at the two major graphical desktop environments available in Linux distributions.

Utilities

This chapter includes a discussion of the following utilities, listed in alphabetical order:

xclock   xrdb
xhost   xterm

10.1 Introduction

In the early days of UNIX, a character terminal was the only interface to the system. You logged in and did all your work in a single, character-based terminal session. If you were lucky, it was a terminal with "smart" cursor capabilities, where you could perform full-screen manipulations by moving the cursor around on the screen (which allowed screen-oriented text editing or debugging). Usually you simply had a line-oriented terminal where you typed in a line of text (a command) and got back one or more lines of text in response. And you were happy to have it instead of the punch cards you used before that!

10.1.1 Graphical User Interfaces

As computer systems became more sophisticated, bitmapped displays (which could turn each bit on the screen on or off tather than simply displaying a character in a certain space) allowed user interfaces to become more sophisticated. The *Graphical User Interface* (GUI, often pronounced "gooey") was born.

The first computer with a semi-well-known GUI was the Xerox STAR. Purely a text-processing system, this computer was the first to use the icon representing a document that looked like a page with one corner folded over. The Xerox STAR had icons for folders, documents, and printers on a *desktop* (the screen) rather than a command-line driven interface, as had been the norm to that time.

The ability to click on a picture of a document to edit it and to drag it onto the top of a printer icon to print it, rather than having to remember what commands performed these functions, was revolutionary. Some of the engineers from Xerox moved on to Apple Computer and worked on the Apple Lisa, which led to development of the Macintosh.

UNIX vendors went through a couple of iterations of providing graphical interfaces to their systems, but under conventional windowing systems, an application could only display information on the screen of the computer on which it was running. The next step in the evolution was still to come.

10.1.2 MIT

In 1984, the Massachusetts Institute of Technology released the X Window System. Recognizing the usefulness of windowing systems, but unimpressed by what UNIX vendors had provided, students at MIT, in a move comparable to the BSD movement at Berkeley, set out to write a windowing system of their own. Digital Equipment helped initially fund Project Athena, where X had its origins.

The revolutionary idea behind the X Window System, which has yet to be rivaled in any modern computer system, is the distinction between the functions of client and server in the process of drawing an image on a computer screen. Unlike most windowing systems, X is defined by a network protocol, replacing the traditional procedure call interface. Rather than simply having an application draw its image directly to the screen, as previous window systems had done, the X Window System split the two functions apart. The X server takes care of drawing on and managing the contents of the computer's bitmapped display and communicating with all clients who wish to draw on the screen. An X client doesn't draw directly to a screen but communicates with an X server running on the computer where the screen it wishes to draw on is located. By allowing communication between two processes on the same machine or via a network connection between two processes on different machines, suddenly you gain the capability to draw graphics on a different screen. This opens the door to all sorts of new possibilities (as well as security problems).

The X Window System is often referred to simply as "X" or "X11," referring to its most recent major version. At the time of this writing, X11 is in its sixth release, hence the complete reference is X11R6. For the latest information about the X Window System, see the Open Group's X.Org Foundation web site at:

```
http://www.x.org
```

10.2 X Servers

An *X server* starts up and "takes over" the bitmapped display on a computer system. This may happen automatically when a user logs in or it may happen when the user executes a specific command, depending on the configuration of the system.

Usually at the time the X server starts, one or two *X clients* are also started. X clients are programs that will communicate with one or more X servers in order to communicate with a user. Some other program must be started that will allow the user access to the system (a screen being driven by an X server but not running any application would provide no way of running any other programs). On Linux systems, desktop tools and a window manager are started along with the X server, as we will see later.

On systems that don't start an X server for you at login time, you can log in and run the **startx** command, either by typing "startx" manually or by adding the command to your .login or .profile script so the server will be started automatically when you log in. Most Linux installation processes configure the system to start the X Window System automatically when a user logs in. In this case, a *display manager* puts up a login banner on the screen to prompt someone to log in.

10.2.1 Screen Geometry

The layout of the screen managed by the X server is called *geometry*. A bitmapped display has a certain size measured in pixels. Pixels are the dots on a display that can be set to on or off (white or black) or to some color value. A small screen might be 600×480 (a typical low-resolution PC monitor). A larger screen might be 1280×960 pixels or even larger for very high-resolution graphics screens.

Screen geometry is specified by referencing either a specific position on the screen (i.e., 500×200) or positions relative to a corner of the screen. Position $+0+0$ is the upper left corner of the screen, $-0-0$ is the lower right corner ($-0+0$ is the upper right, $+0-0$ lower left). Therefore, $+50+50$ would be 50 pixels away from the upper left corner of the screen in both the X and Y directions. We will see examples of this when we discuss X clients.

Figure 10–1 shows the positioning of various geometry specifications.

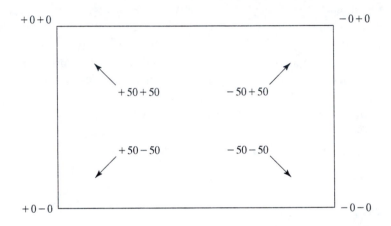

Figure 10–1   X Window System screen geometry specifications.

10.2.2   Security and Authorization

As you may have guessed by now, the ability to scribble on any computer screen in your network could lead to security problems—not so much because the act of writing on someone else's screen is anything more than annoying, if the recipient does not want it, but because I/O to an X server is just that, input and output. Write access to an X server also gives you the ability to query that system for a current copy of the display or even keyboard input.

Because of this, the X Window System has a certain amount of security built into the X server. It isn't highly rated security, but it is enough to keep the casual snoop from gaining unauthorized access.

By default, the X server running on any computer system only allows X clients on that same system to talk to it. The X server does not accept connections from "foreign" X clients without knowing who they are. This causes the default configuration of an X server to be very much like a traditional window system, where only applications running on that computer can write to that computer's display. In order to take advantage of the network capabilities of the X Window System, you must allow outside access.

The **xhost** command (an X client) is used to allow X clients on other systems to display to your system (Figure 10–2).

Utility: **xhost** [+|-][*hostname*]

The **xhost** command allows or denies access to the X server on a system. With no arguments, **xhost** prints its current settings and which hosts (if any) have access. By specifying only +, you can give access to all hosts, or by specifying only -, deny access to all hosts. When a hostname is specified after a + or -, access is granted or denied, respectively, to that host.

Figure 10–2   Description of the **xhost** command.

For example:

```
$ xhost +bluenote
```

will allow X clients running on the computer called "bluenote" to write to the display on the system where the **xhost** utility was run. Later, when whatever you needed to run is finished, you can disallow access with the command:

```
$ xhost -bluenote
```

In a secure environment where you aren't afraid of other systems writing to your display, you can allow any X client on the network to write to your display with the command:

```
$ xhost +
```

You can also take away access to all remote X clients with:

```
$ xhost -
```

10.3 Desktop Environments

A *desktop environment* (DE) is a fancy way of referring to all the programs that manage and render the conceptual desktop that is graphically represented on your screen by icons and windows. Although every DE has its own unique look and behavior, all provide the same basic set of components:

- menus providing access to objects, tasks, or applications
- icons representing devices or other objects in the system
- status bars or areas where real-time status data is displayed
- a cursor controlled by a mouse providing navigation among and interaction with desktop objects

Three major Linux desktops are in common use today: CDE, KDE, and GNOME. Other desktop environments are available, but as with the "minor" distributions of Linux, it is impossible to discuss all the various DEs in the world. Information on many other DEs, including screenshots, can be found at:

```
http://www.xwinman.org
```

10.3.1   CDE

The Common Desktop Environment (CDE) was one of the first true DEs for UNIX systems. CDE is a cooperative venture by Hewlett-Packard, IBM, SunSoft, and Novell that is common to many UNIX platforms. A commercial product (not open source), it is available for Linux and is preferred by users who frequently work on both UNIX and Linux systems.

CDE is based in large part on Hewlett-Packard's Visual User Environment (VUE) and Sun Microsystem's OpenWindows. Both are based on the OSF's Motif windowing standards, common in UNIX environments. CDE's outward appearance is very much like that of VUE, although there are also OpenWindows influences apparent throughout. CDE was the first UNIX desktop to be adopted by multiple UNIX vendors.

CDE provides a working area (desktop), icons, and a control panel made up of expandable menus and status icons. CDE also provides its own terminal application (comparable to **xterm**) and a file manager application.

Since CDE is a commercial product, it is not included in Linux distributions. For more information on CDE, including screenshots, visit the web site:

```
http://www.opengroup.org/cde/
```

10.3.2   GNOME

The GNU Network Object Model Environment (GNOME) is the GNU Project's contribution to desktop environment. Like other GNU software, it is freely available, is included in most Linux distributions, and runs on most UNIX hardware platforms as well. GNOME's goal is to provide an easy-to-use desktop for beginning users without tying the hands of experienced users.

The GNOME Desktop Environment (GDE) is made up of a working area (the desktop), icons, and a control panel made up of expandable menus and status icons (which will feel familiar to Windows users). GNOME also provides its own terminal application (comparable to **xterm**), a file manager application, and a control center for modifying system and desktop configuration information.

The subsequent screenshots in this chapter are from a system running GNOME. Another sample screenshot can be found on page 25. For more information on GNOME, including other screenshots, visit the web site:

```
http://www.gnome.org
```

10.3.3   KDE

The K Desktop Environment (KDE) has been developed by a loose group of programmers around the world. KDE is included in most Linux distributions and is available for just about every version of UNIX.

KDE attempts to provide an interface similar to those of MacOS and Windows desktops to encourage UNIX/Linux adoption in home and office environments (where MacOS and Windows have traditionally dominated). Many feel it is a "busier" desktop than some others, but also that it is more flexible and configurable.

KDE provides a working area (desktop), icons, and a control panel made up of expandable menus and status icons. KDE also provides its own terminal application (comparable to **xterm**), a file manager/browser application, and a control center for modifying system and desktop configuration information.

See page 26 for a sample screenshot of a KDE desktop. For more information on KDE, including screenshots, visit the web site:

```
http://www.kde.org
```

10.4 Window Managers

All this ability to write to a display isn't really very useful if you just sit there and watch windows pop up and go away but you can't do anything with them. This is where window managers come in. A window manager is a program (an X client) that communicates with the X server and with the keyboard and mouse on the system. It provides the interface for the user to give instructions to the X server about what to do with the windows.

Although window managers are usually run on the same computer as the display they manage, this is not a requirement. If you have a special X window manager that only runs on one specific type of computer, it is possible to set it up to manage your workstation from a remote computer. Of course, there are inherent problems in doing this. What if the remote machine running the window manager or the entire network went down? Your X server would no longer be managed, because it could not communicate with the window manager, and your keyboard and mouse likely would not respond (at least properly) to your input. But the fact that it could be done this way is a testament to the flexibility of the X Window System architecture.

An important feature provided by a window manager is the "look and feel" of the desktop. The look and feel of the interior of a window depends on the application creating the window. While all window managers provide similar basic functionality, the appearance of each can vary widely.

10.4.1   Focus

The most important job of a window manager is to maintain window *focus*. Focus is the term used to describe which window is currently selected or active. If you type on the keyboard, the window with focus is where the data will be sent. Focus is what allows you to move from one

window to another and do multiple things in different windows. Generally, a window with focus
has a different border than the other windows, although this is configurable.

Window focus can be configured so that it is set when a window border or title bar is selected
or simply when the mouse pointer is moved onto the window, depending on your preference.

10.4.2   Program Startup

Most window managers also provide a *pulldown menu* capability that can be customized to allow
you to start different often-used applications. For example, if your pointer is on the root window
(the desktop itself, not an application window) and you click and hold down the right-most mouse
button, most window managers will bring up a menu item list of things that you can select to perform a function. This list usually includes functions like starting a new terminal window or exiting
the window manager. The specific functions vary from one window manager to another and can
be heavily customized. Different mouse buttons can be customized to bring up different lists of
functions. GNOME and KDE also provide a menu from the bottom left status bar, much like the
Windows "Start" menu. Figure 10–3 is an example of a root window menu on a GNOME desktop.

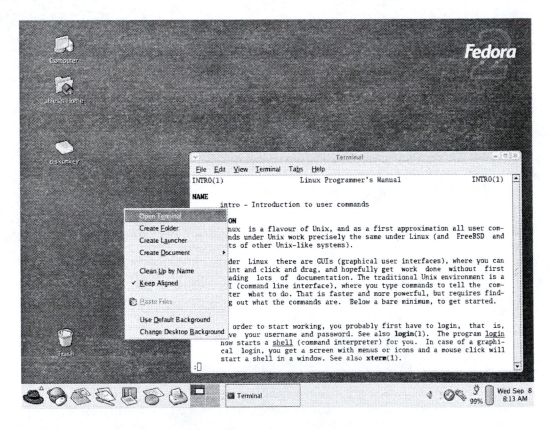

Figure 10–3   A window and a root pulldown menu.

10.4.3   Opened and Closed Windows

The window manager also takes care of displaying active windows and positioning icons that represent windows that are not open. If you start a new terminal window and are finished with it, but don't want to terminate it, as you may need it later, you can close the terminal window. The window manager will create an icon or label on the desktop or in a status bar that represents the terminal window program but is placed where it won't take up space on your desktop. You will still be able to see it and you can click on it later (or perhaps double-click, depending on the window manager you use) to have it restored (reopened). The program itself is still running while its window is *iconified,* but the window is conveniently out of your way. The X server itself knows nothing of this function, as you will see if you ever kill your window manager (all of your iconified processes pop open all over your screen!). Figure 10–4 is an example of a desktop with two open windows.

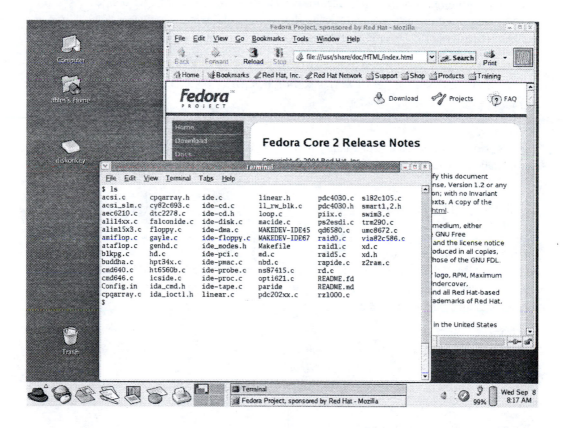

Figure 10–4   A desktop with open windows and task bar buttons.

10.4.4   Choices

Many different window managers are available for X servers. Most desktop environments include their own window manager, so you may not see the distinction between desktop environment and window manager in your day-to-day use. Historically, when you ran an X server, the window manager was the only component that provided the look and feel, and it was common to choose different window managers on a whim. Most people using a DE also use the corresponding window manager, but in most cases this is not a requirement.

The window manager provides additional components of a window that the application (the X client) does not have to worry about. The window manager draws a border around a window that can be selected with the mouse to change focus, move (drag) the window, or change its size. The window border contains a title and buttons allowing it to be moved, resized, minimized (closed to an icon), made to fill the entire screen, or terminated. These functions are processed by the X client, but the on-screen "hooks" that you use to control them are provided by the window manager.

Many window managers implement a *virtual desktop*, where a larger area of desktop is available than what the on-screen real estate supports and the window manager helps you manage which section of the larger virtual desktop is displayed on the screen.

10.4.4.1   dtwm

The Desktop Window Manager (dtwm) is part of the CDE, and is similar to vuewm, discussed below, but supports a virtual desktop.

10.4.4.2   fvwm

fvwm is popular in the Linux community because of its free availability and because it is very customizable. fvwm is included in some Linux distributions. For more information on fvwm, visit the web site:

    http://www.fvwm.org

10.4.4.3   gnome-wm

The GNOME Window Manager (gnome-wm) is the window manager used with the GNU Network Object Model Environment (GNOME). While not required, it is almost always used in conjunction with GNOME to take advantage of features known to both. gnome-wm is included in just about all Linux distributions.

10.4.4.4   icewm

The ICE Window Manager (icewm) is another grass-roots, popular window manager. It is small, fast, and easily customizable to resemble Windows so that PC users can feel comfortable using a Linux system. icewm is included in some Linux distributions. For more information on icewm, visit the web site:

    http://www.icewm.org

10.4.4.5 kwm

The K Window Manager (kwm) is used with the K Desktop Environment (KDE). While not required, it is recommended over other window managers for use with KDE because of its tight integration with KDE functionality. kwm is included in just about all Linux distributions.

10.4.4.6 mwm

The Motif Window Manager (mwm) is one of the first major window managers.

10.4.4.7 olwm

Sun Microsystems' OpenLook Window Manager (olwm) and OpenLook Virtual Window Manager (olvwm) run on Sun systems and can be used with CDE.

10.4.4.8 twm

Tom's Window Manager (twm) and Tom's Virtual twm (tvtwm) were written by Tom LaStrange to correct some of the things he didn't like about mwm. tvm is included in many Linux distributions. tvm is also sometimes called the Tab Window Manager.

10.4.4.9 vuewm

The VUE Window Manager (vuewm) is from Hewlett-Packard and runs under HP's Visual User Environment (VUE) desktop.

10.5 Widgets

A *widget* is the term used to describe each individual component of an X window. Buttons, borders, and scrolling text boxes are all widgets. Each X toolkit can define its own set of widgets. Each desktop or window manager can provide its own widget set, but nearly all widget sets have a common set of core functions that are expected by computer users.

10.5.1 Menus

Menus provide GUI access to functions provided by the application. These functions are often those not directly related to the contents of any particular window (things like opening files, setting options, and exiting). Menu buttons are found along the top of a window. Figure 10–5 shows an example of a menu pulldown.

10.5.2 Pushbuttons

Pushbuttons can be laid out in any fashion required by an application. The typical pushbutton example is the OK/Cancel *dialog box* (an additional window that pops up with new information or one that queries the user for more information). Figure 10–6 shows an example of a dialog box.

10.5.3 Check Boxes/Radio Buttons

Check boxes and *radio buttons* are both input-gathering widgets. A check box is a yes/no type of button. If checked, this item is true, yes, or present, depending on the context of the statement. Check boxes are usually square. Radio buttons are a collection of mutually exclusive selections; when one is selected, any others that were selected are deselected (like the buttons on a car radio). Radio buttons are usually round. Figure 10–7 shows an example of check boxes and radio buttons.

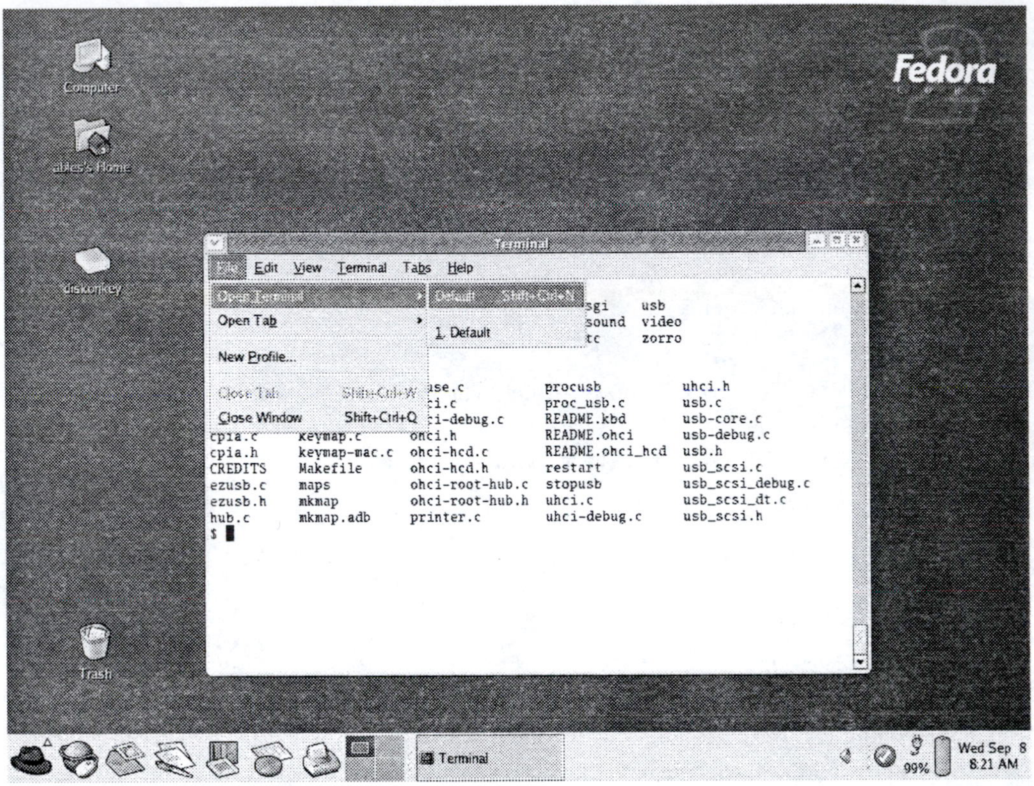

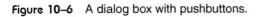

Figure 10-5   A menu pulldown.

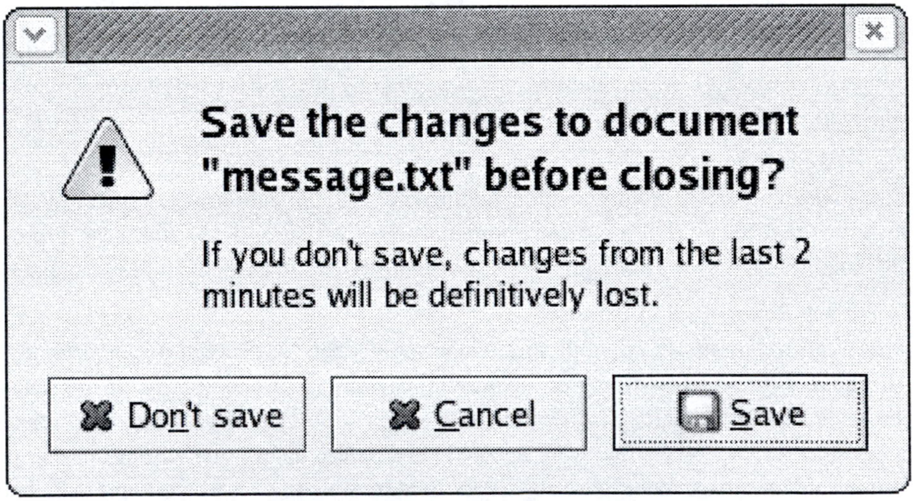

Figure 10-6   A dialog box with pushbuttons.

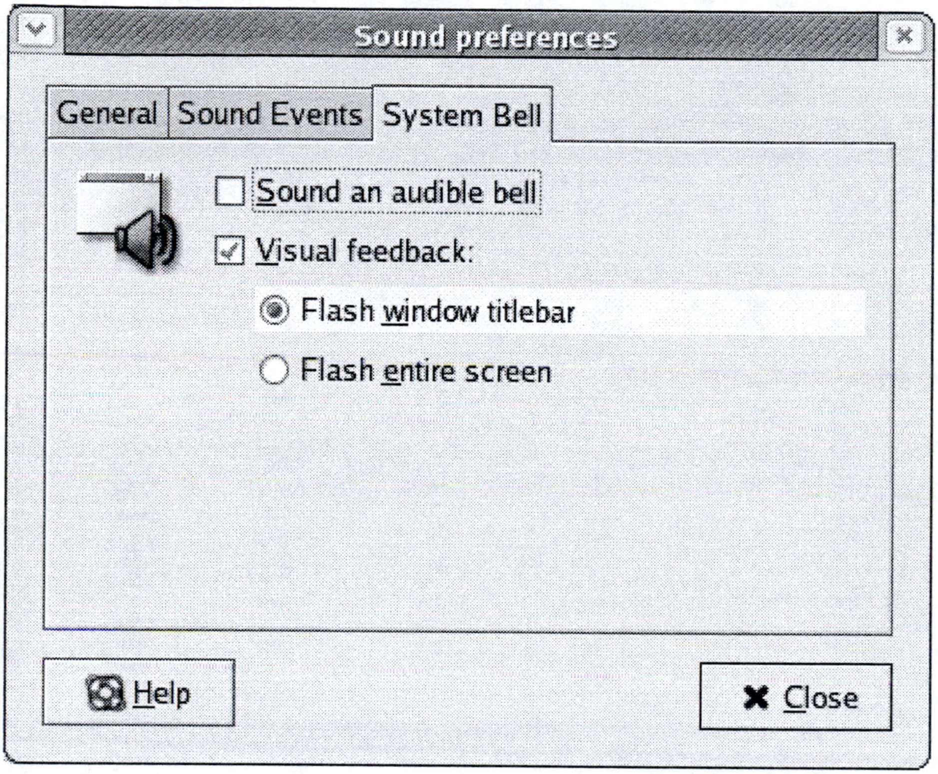

Figure 10–7   Check boxes and radio buttons.

10.5.4   Scroll Bars

Scroll bars allow you to scroll back and forth in a window or a part of a window. This is often useful when a lot of text is involved but a short display area is available so not all the text fits. Scroll bars may be either horizontal or vertical. Vertical scroll bars are generally on the right side of a window (as in Figure 10–8). Horizontal scroll bars are usually along the bottom of a window.

10.6 Desktop Operation

The exact use and behavior of functions performed on windows and icons on the desktop vary, depending on the specific window manager being used, but nearly all window managers adhere to a certain set of behaviors.

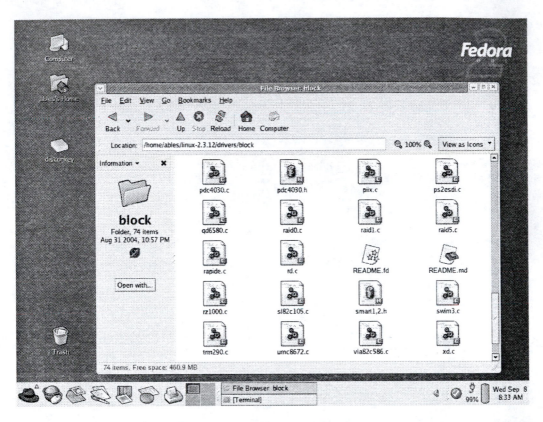

Figure 10–8   A file browser window with a scroll bar.

10.6.1   Bringing up the Root Menu

The root menu contains the basic functions needed to control your X session. The default list includes starting a terminal window, moving focus to another window, and exiting the window manager. The root menu is customizable and is often heavily customized to add often-used X applications to make them easy to start. It is possible to have a different menu brought up for each mouse button. Clicking and holding the rightmost mouse button while the cursor is over an empty spot on the desktop generally brings up a default menu.

10.6.2   Opening and Closing a Window

The act of opening and closing a window is generally tied to starting and stopping the application that creates the window. Thus, how a window is opened depends greatly on how the application is started. Closing the window, however, is common to all X applications. In addition to any application-specific exit or end process, an X window also has a box or tab in the upper right-hand corner of the window with an X in it. Clicking this box will terminate the program and close the window.

10.6.3   Minimizing a Window

When you want to work in another window but you don't yet wish to terminate a program, you can *minimize* the window to get it off your desktop. When a window is minimized, the window manager puts an icon on the desktop or in the task bar (depending on the window manager) representing the running process. You can minimize a window by clicking on the close tab in the window border (usually a box in the upper right title bar with an underscore).

10.6.4   Maximizing a Window

To reopen a window that has been minimized, double click the icon representing the closed window on the desktop or single click the tab in the status bar representing the window.

10.6.5   Moving a Window

Move a window by selecting the window border and holding down the left or middle mouse button and then dragging the window to the new location. A window border pulldown menu also usually has a "Move" selection.

10.6.6   Resizing a Window

Resize a window by selecting the resize border area of any corner or border of the window with the left mouse button and dragging the edge to the new size. When you drag a corner, both the X and Y sizes are modified. When you select a top, bottom, or side border and drag it, the window size is modified in only one direction.

10.6.7   Raising or Lowering a Window

A window can be raised to the top (over other windows) simply by selecting its border. This also sets focus on this window. Most window managers now allow you to click anywhere in the window to raise it to the top, but be careful you don't click on an action button in the window by mistake.

10.6.8   Bringing up a Window Menu

The window manager can supply a menu for each window. These menus generally provide one or more functions listed above but can also be customized. To bring up the window menu, you can either click on the menu button in the upper left corner of the window or hold down the right mouse button anywhere in the window border or title bar.

10.7 Client Applications

Every program that writes to the screen of an X server is known as an X client. Many useful X clients are included with the X Window System. Many other useful clients have been developed specifically for GNOME and KDE, but they require their expected DE in order to function properly and vary between Linux distributions. To give you a flavor of X clients, we'll stick with generic clients that are common to all desktop environments.

Here are a few of the simplest X clients that beginners tend to use first to learn the X Window System. You should consult the man page for each program to find out about optional arguments that can be used to customize the client program.

10.7.1   xclock

Figure 10–9 describes the **xclock** command, and Figure 10–10 shows an **xclock** client.

Utility: **xclock** [-digital]

The **xclock** command provides a simple clock on your desktop. The default is an analog
clock. If the **-digital** argument is specified, a digital clock is displayed instead.

Figure 10–9   Description of the **xclock** command.

The **xclock** command can be started by hand or in your initialization file.

Figure 10–10   An **xclock** client.

10.7.2   xterm

The **xterm** is probably the most commonly used X client among Linux users. It provides a terminal interface window to the system (Figure 10–11). Early windowing system users used their X terminals mostly to provide multiple terminal interfaces into the system to consolidate monitors on their desktop. As X clients become more sophisticated, **xterm** is used less and less, but it is still quite useful if you use the Linux shell interface. We saw an example of an **xterm** earlier in this chapter. The **xterm** has a myriad of arguments allowing the window's size, color, and font to be defined at the command line. See the man page for **xterm** for details.

Utility: **xterm**

The **xterm** command starts a terminal window on the desktop.

Figure 10–11   Description of the **xterm** command.

10.8 Standard X Client Arguments

Most X clients accept standard arguments that allow their size and position to be customized when started.

10.8.1   geometry

X client geometry is specified by the *-geometry* argument. You can specify not only the size of the client but the offset position where it will appear on the screen. The general format is "*XxY*" for the size followed by "*+X+Y*" for the offset position. For example, to start an **xclock** positioned 10 pixels in each direction from the upper right-hand corner of the screen and 100 pixels in both width and height, you would use the command:

```
$ xclock -geometry 100x100-10+10
```

Note that the value of the *-geometry* argument is a single shell token (there are no spaces imbedded in it).

10.8.2   Foreground and Background

Foreground and background colors can be set with the *-foreground* and *-background* arguments. The following **xterm** command will create a terminal window with cyan (a light shade of blue) letters on a black background:

```
$ xterm -foreground cyan -background black
```

I find this combination of colors very easy to work with, but everyone has his own favorite.

10.8.3   title

The *-title* argument sets the title in the title bar of a window. This is often useful to label one of many terminal windows used for a remote login session to another machine to help keep them straight, such as:

```
$ xterm -title "Remote access to mail server"
```

10.8.4   iconic

The *-iconic* argument is used to start an X client but to have the window minimized so that only the icon representing it shows up on the desktop. This is useful for an application that you will be using but don't necessarily want to use the moment it starts up (like a mail reader or web browser).

10.9 Advanced Topics

Some of the topics we want to examine here fall into one or more of the previous sections, but you needed a good foundation before we discussed these more complex capabilities of the X Window System.

10.9.1   Copy-and-Paste

The *copy-and-paste* function is one of the more useful features of the X Window System. The ability to select text in one window and copy it to another window without having to retype it is a great timesaver. I am discussing it outside the range of the window manager because, even though it "feels" like the window manager provides the capability, it is actually provided by the X server itself. You can prove this by using it even when no window manager is running.

To copy text into the copy-and-paste text buffer, you simply click and hold down the left mouse button with the pointer set at one end of the text you wish to select and drag it to the other end (you can do this either forward or backward). When you release the mouse button, the highlighted text has been copied to the buffer (unlike a PC, where you have to tell it to copy the highlighted text to the buffer). You can also click in one location and then click again while holding the *Shift* key down, and the text in between the two locations will be highlighted and copied. You then go to the window where you want to paste the text and click the middle mouse button (or both mouse buttons at once on a system that only has two buttons) and the text is inserted. Some applications will insert the text at the current cursor position, others will insert it at the point where you click the middle mouse button. This is application specific.

In the example in Figure 10–12, I found a command on a web page that I wanted to type in another window. I selected the beginning of the command and dragged the cursor to the end before letting up on the mouse button to highlight it. Then, to paste it into the other window, I simply clicked the middle button into the terminal window where I wanted to execute the command, and the text was entered into my terminal window. All that is left to do is hit the *Return* key.

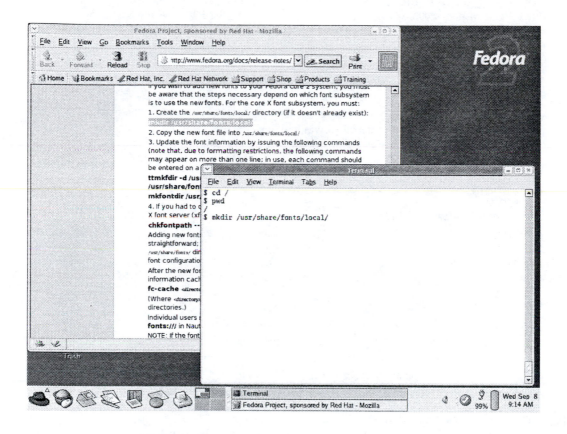

Figure 10–12   A copy-and-paste example.

10.9.2   Networking Capabilities

I mentioned earlier that the X Window System is a networked windowing system and that it is possible to display information from an X client running on one computer on an X server running on another. This capability is fundamental in the X design and is quite simple to use from any X client by specifying the **-display** argument. This is used to tell the X client which X server to contact to display its widgets. By default, the display is the local machine where the client is running. To start an **xterm** on the host "savoy," use an **xterm** command like this:

```
$ xterm -display savoy:0.0
```

The specification of ":0.0" is a method of uniquely identifying a display and X server running on the computer. While it is possible to run multiple X servers as well as to have multiple monitors connected to a single computer, in general usage each computer will have only one monitor and be running only one X server, so this value will almost always be ":0.0" to denote

this (though some X servers use only ":0"). The default display name for the local system would
be ":0.0" without a hostname.

If I type the command:

```
$ xterm -display bluenote:0.0
```

and if the user on bluenote has used the **xhost** command to allow access to the machine where I
typed this command, then the X terminal window that is created will be displayed on bluenote.

You can also set the DISPLAY environment variable to a hostname specification, and all
your X applications will use it for their display. For example, the equivalent behavior to the previous command will be seen with:

```
$ export DISPLAY="bluenote:0.0"
$ xterm
```

This is useful when you are working on a remote server (via **telnet** or **rlogin**) and need to display all your X applications on your local desktop.

10.9.3   Application Resources

Application *resources* are a Pandora's Box of detail as well as one of the most revolutionary
aspects of the X Window System. X resources allow users to customize the look and feel of their
desktop and the applications they run to a degree that no other window system provides. Here
we will take a quick look at the basics of using X resources. I would strongly urge you to read
the chapter "Setting Resources" in [Quercia, 1993] for exhaustive details.

10.9.3.1 How Resources Work

Every application, including the window manager itself, can take advantage of X resources. An
X resource is a text string, like a variable name, and a value, which is set as part of the X server.
The value of a resource is tied to a specific widget. When the X server draws a specific widget, it
looks up the value(s) associated with the widget in its list of resources and sets the described
attribute appropriately.

For example, consider the hypothetical application called **xask**. This application is simply
a dialog box containing a text message (a question) and two buttons: Yes and No. It might be
defined with (at least) the following resources:

```
xask.Button.yes.text
xask.Button.no.text
```

The application may have default values in case these resources are not set. With no resources
set, when you run **xask**, you might see a window like the one in Figure 10–13.

But what if you would rather have something more interesting than Yes and No for
choices? Maybe you need to change the language used by the application, but you do not wish to
have a separate version for each language.

Figure 10–13   The mythical **xask** application.

The answer is to customize the values with X resources. In our example, we'll set the following resources for **xask**:

```
xask.Button.yes.text: Sure
xask.Button.no.text:  No way
```

Of course, this is a trivial example, but you see the power of X resources to modify behavior of a program without changing the code. By setting the above values to those resources in the X server, the next time you run **xask**, you see the window in Figure 10–14.

Figure 10–14   The **xask** application with customized X resources.

If I set these X resources on my X server and run **xask**, and you do not set any resources on your X server and run the exact same copy of **xask**, we each will see a different window!

X resources are used to set things like sizes, colors, fonts, and values of text strings. While these are typical, there is really no limit to what you could allow to be customized in an application.

Every X application uses some number of X resources, and they should be defined in the documentation for the application. The larger (more complex) the application, the more resources it will use.

10.9.3.2 Defining Resources

Once you know what resources you want to set, how do you do it? X resources are resources of the X server, therefore they are set on the machine where the X server runs. There are many ways to load resources into an X server.

The most manual method of accessing the X resource database in the X server is with the **xrdb** command (Figure 10–15).

Utility: **xrdb** [-*query*|-*load*|-*merge*|-*remove*] [*filename*]

The **xrdb** command provides access to the X resource database for the X server. Used with the **-query** argument, **xrdb** prints the resources defined in the X server. The **-load** argument causes new resource information to be loaded into the resource database, replacing the previous information. If a filename is specified, the resource information is loaded from that file, otherwise the Standard Input channel is read to find the resource information. The **-merge** argument loads new resource information, similar to the **-load** argument, except that existing information is not removed (information about duplicate resources is overwritten). Finally, the **-remove** argument clears out the X server's resource database.

Figure 10–15 Description of the **xrdb** command.

You can add or remove individual or groups of resources anytime you wish.

Manually adding and removing X resources gets tedious very quickly. What we really want is a way to specify a resource that will apply every time we run a given application. We do this by setting up a default resource file called .Xdefaults. This file is an initialization file recognized by the X server program when run by the user. Upon startup, the X server loads all resources listed in this file. For example, if we always want our **xask** program to use the more casual text in the response buttons as in our earlier example, we can enter those resources into our .Xdefaults file, and the next time we start the X server these resources will be set. Note that we could also run **xrdb** on our .Xdefaults file itself to load or reload these resources at any time.

CHAPTER REVIEW

Checklist

In this chapter, I described:

- what a Graphical User Interface does
- MIT's X Window System
- X servers, X clients, X widgets
- desktop environments and window managers
- X application resources

Quiz

1. What is the biggest difference between the X Window System and most other graphical windowing systems?
2. Which command is used to change access permissions on an X server?
3. Which widget would you use in a window where you want to give the users a choice between several options but they can only choose one?
4. What is the X application argument used to cause the application's window to show up on a different computer's screen?
5. What attribute about an X server allows you to change the appearance of an X application without having to modify the program?

Exercises

1. Explain why a window manager is an X client. [level: *easy*]
2. Suppose that your window manager has exited and you cannot get focus in a window to type a command to bring up a new one (and that you have no root menu button that starts a new one). Explain how you might still be able to use *copy-and-paste* with your existing windows to execute a command. [level: *hard*]

Projects

1. Use the **xrdb** command to print the resource database of a running X server. Study the output to learn what types of applications use what types of resources. [level: *medium*]

11

C Programming Tools

Motivation

The most commonly used programming languages on Linux systems are C and C++. This isn't surprising, since Linux is written predominately in C and includes a C compiler. Most GNU utilities and many commercial products are written in C or C++. It's therefore likely that you will find knowledge about writing, compiling, and running C programs very useful. Of course, Linux supports many other popular programming languages, but this chapter applies primarily to the C language and its supporting tools, since these are so fundamental to Linux environments.

Prerequisites

This chapter assumes that you are at least familiar with the C language.

Objectives

In this chapter, I describe the tools that support the various different stages of program development: compiling, debugging, maintaining libraries, and profiling.

Presentation

The C programming environment is introduced in a natural fashion, with plenty of examples and small programs.

Utilities

This section introduces the following utilities, listed in alphabetical order:

ar	gprof	touch
gcc	make	
gdb	strip	

11.1 The C Language

The C language can be found in two main forms: K&R C and ANSI C. K&R, named for the authors of the first popular C programming text, Brian Kernighan and Dennis Ritchie, defines the C language as it was in the early days of UNIX. Some now refer to this as "Classic C." The American National Standards Institute defined a C standard of their own, adding some useful features and defining exact syntax for existing but not well-defined features. Most compilers support both standards.

Before we get into any source code, I'd like to make an important point: *the source code in this book does not conform to the ANSI C standard.* While ANSI C contains several nice syntactic and type-checking facilities that encourage maintainable and readable programs, I did not use these features because many major corporations and universities still use K&R C. In order to make my source code as portable and useful as possible, I tailored the code to the most reasonable lowest common denominator.

11.2 C Compilers

Traditionally, a C compiler was a standard component in UNIX, especially versions that came with source code (how else would you modify the code and create a new kernel?). Linux distributions include GNU C (**gcc**) and GNU C++ (**g++**) and will be on any system where the developer package(s) have been installed. If you're an old UNIX hack, /usr/bin/cc is a link to /usr/bin/gcc, so you can still type "cc" to invoke **gcc**. The GNU C compiler works like this:

Utility: **gcc** -cv [-o *fileName*] [-pg] { *fileName* }*

The **gcc** utility compiles C program code in one or more files and produces object modules or an executable file. Files specified should have a ".c" extension. Use the **-c** option to produce object modules suitable for linking later. Use the **-o** option to specify a filename other than the default "a.out" for the executable. Use the **-pg** option to produce profiling data for the GNU profiler **gprof**. Use the **-v** option to produce verbose commentary during the compilation and/or linking process.

Figure 11-1 Description of the **gcc** utility.

11.3 Single-Module Programs

Let's examine a C program[1] that performs a simple task: reversing a string. To begin with, I'll show you how to write, compile, link, and execute a program that solves the problem using a single source file. Then I'll explain why it's better to split the program up into several independent modules, and show you how to do this. Here's a source code listing of the first version of the reverse program:

```
1   /* REVERSE.C */
2
3   #include <stdio.h>
4
5   /* Function Prototype */
6   int reverse ();
7
8   /*********************************************************************/
9
10   main ()
11
12   {
13     char str [100]; /* Buffer to hold reversed string */
14
15     reverse ("cat", str); /* Reverse the string "cat" */
16     printf ("reverse ("cat") = %s\n", str); /* Display */
17     reverse ("noon", str); /* Reverse the string "noon" */
18     printf ("reverse ("noon") = %s\n", str); /* Display */
19   }
20
21   /*********************************************************************/
22
23   reverse (before, after)
24
25   char *before; /* A pointer to the source string */
26   char *after; /* A pointer to the reversed string */
27
28   {
29     int i;
30     int j;
31     int len;
32
33     len = strlen (before);
34
35     for (j = len - 1; i = 0; j >= 0; j--; i++) /* Reverse loop */
36       after[i] = before[j];
37
```

1.   Most of the examples used in this chapter are available online; see the Preface for more information.

```
38    after[len] = 0; /* terminate reversed string */
39  }
```

11.3.1   Compiling a C Program

To create and run the "reverse" program, I first created a subdirectory called "reverse" inside my home directory and then created the file "reverse.c" using the **emacs** editor. I then compiled the C program using the **gcc** utility.

To prepare an executable version of a single, self-contained program, follow **gcc** by the name of the source code file, which must end in a ".c" suffix. **gcc** doesn't produce any output when the compilation is successful and it has no diagnostic comments. By default, **gcc** creates an executable file called "a.out" in the current directory. To run the program, type "a.out" (or "./ a.out" if "." is not in your search path). Any errors that are encountered are sent to the standard error channel, which is connected by default to your terminal's screen.

Here's what happened:

```
$ mkdir reverse    ...create subdirectory for source code.
$ cd reverse
$ ... I created the above file in r.c using emacs.
$ gcc r.c          ...compile source.
r.c: In function 'main':
r.c:16: error: parse error before "cat"
r.c:18: error: parse error before "noon"
r.c: In function 'reverse':
r.c:35: error: parse error before ')' token
$ _
```

As you can see, **gcc** found a number of compile-time errors:

- The errors on lines 16 and 18 were due to inappropriate use of double quotes within double quotes.
- The error on line 35 was due to an illegal use of a semicolon (;).

Since these errors were easy to correct, I copied the error-laden "r.c" file to a file called "r.old1.c" and then removed the compile-time errors using **emacs**. I left the original file in the directory so that I could see the evolution of my programming attempts.

11.3.2   A Listing of the Corrected Reverse Program

Here is the corrected version of the reverse program. The lines containing the errors that I corrected are in italics:

```
1  /* REVERSE.C */
2
3  #include <stdio.h>
4
5  /* Function Prototype */
```

```
6   int reverse ();
7
8   /*******************************************************************/
9
10  main ()
11
12  {
13      char str [100]; /* Buffer to hold reversed string */
14
15      reverse ("cat", str); /* Reverse the string "cat" */
16      printf ("reverse (\"cat\") = %s\n", str); /* Display */
17      reverse ("noon", str); /* Reverse the string "noon" */
18      printf ("reverse (\"noon\") = %s\n", str); /* Display */
19  }
20
21  /*******************************************************************/
22
23  reverse (before, after)
24
25  char *before; /* A pointer to the source string */
26  char *after; /* A pointer to the reversed string */
27
28  {
29      int i;
30      int j;
31      int len;
32
33      len = strlen (before);
34
35      for (j = len - 1, i = 0; j >= 0; j--, i++) /* Reverse loop */
36          after[i] = before[j];
37
38      after[len] = 0; /* terminate reversed string */
39  }
```

11.3.3   Running a C Program

After compiling the second version, which I'll call "rfix.c", I ran it by typing the name of the executable file, "a.out". As you can see, the answers were correct:

```
$ gcc rfix.c                    ...compile source.
$ ls -lG rfix.c a.out           ...list file information.
-rwxr-xr-x  1 ables        24576 Jan  5 16:16 a.out*
-rw-r--r--  1 ables          439 Jan  5 16:15 rfix.c
$ ./a.out                       ...run the program.
reverse ("cat") = tac
reverse ("noon") = noon
$ _
```

11.3.4   Overriding the Default Executable Name

The name of the default executable, "a.out", is rather cryptic, and an "a.out" file produced by a subsequent compilation of a different program would overwrite the one that I just produced. To avoid both problems, it's best to use the **-o** option with **gcc**, which allows you to specify the name of the executable file that you wish to create:

```
$ gcc rfix.c -o rfix            ...call the executable "rfix".
$ ls -lGF rfix
-rwxr-xr-x  1 ables       24576 Jan  5 16:19 rfix*
$ ./rfix                        ...run the executable "rfix".
reverse ("cat") = tac
reverse ("noon") = noon
$ _
```

11.4 Multimodule Programs

The trouble with the way that I built the reverse program is that the reverse function cannot easily be used in other programs. For example, let's say that I wanted to write a function that returns 1 if a string is a palindrome, and 0 if it is not. A palindrome is a string that reads the same forward and backward; for example, "noon" is a palindrome, and "nono" is not. I could use the reverse function to implement my palindrome function. One way to do this is to cut-and-paste reverse () into the palindrome program file, but this is a poor technique for at least three reasons:

- Performing a cut-and-paste operation is tedious.
- If we came up with a better piece of code for performing a reverse operation, we'd have to replace every copy of the old version with the new version, which is a maintenance nightmare.
- Each copy of reverse () uses up disk space.

As I'm sure you realize, there's a better way to share functions.

11.4.1   Reusable Functions

A better strategy for sharing reverse () is to remove reverse () from the reverse program, compile it separately, and then link the resultant object module into whichever programs wish to use it. This technique avoids all three of the problems listed in the previous section and allows the function to be used in many different programs. Functions with this property are called *reusable*.

11.4.2   Preparing a Reusable Function

To prepare a reusable function, create a source code module that contains the source code of the function, together with a header file that contains the function's prototype. Then compile it into an object module by using the **-c** option of **gcc.** An object module contains machine code together with symbol-table information that allows it to be combined with other object modules when an executable file is being created. Here is a listing of our new files—first, "reverse.h":

```
1   /* REVERSE.H */
2
3   int reverse (); /* Declare but do not define this function */
```

Here is a listing of the new "reverse.c":

```
1   /* REVERSE.C */
2
3   #include <stdio.h>
4   #include "reverse.h"
5
6   /****************************************************************/
7
8   reverse (before, after)
9
10  char *before; /* A pointer to the original string */
11  char *after; /* A pointer to the reversed string */
12
13  {
14     int i;
15     int j;
16     int len;
17
18     len = strlen (before);
19
20     for (j = len - 1, i = 0; j >= 0; j--, i++) /* Reverse loop */
21        after[i] = before[j];
22
23     after[len] = 0; /* terminate reversed string */
24  }
```

Here's a listing of a main program that uses reverse ():

```
1   /* MAIN1.C */
2
3   #include <stdio.h>
4   #include "reverse.h" /* Contains the prototype of reverse () */
5
6   /****************************************************************/
7
8   main ()
9
10  {
11     char str [100];
12
13     reverse ("cat", str); /* Invoke external function */
14     printf ("reverse (\"cat\") = %s\n", str);
```

```
15    reverse ("noon", str); /* Invoke external function */
16    printf ("reverse (\"noon\") = %s\n", str);
17  }
```

11.4.3 Separately Compiling and Linking Modules

To compile each source code file separately, use the **-c** option of **gcc**. This creates a separate object module for each source code file, each with a ".o" suffix:

```
$ gcc -c reverse.c    ...compile reverse.c to reverse.o.
$ gcc -c main1.c      ...compile main1.c to main1.o.
$ ls -lG reverse.o main1.o
-rw-r--r--  1 ables       311 Jan  5 18:08 main1.o
-rw-r--r--  1 ables       181 Jan  5 18:08 reverse.o
$ _
```

Alternatively, you can place all of the source code files on one line:

```
$ gcc -c reverse.c main1.c    ...compile each .c file to .o file.
$ _
```

To link them all together into an executable called "main1", list the names of all the object modules after the **gcc** command:

```
$ gcc reverse.o main1.o -o main1    ...link object modules.
$ ls -lG main1                      ...examine the executable.
-rwxr-xr-x  1 ables     24576 Jan  5 18:25 main1*
$ ./main1                           ...run the executable.
reverse ("cat") = tac
reverse ("noon") = noon
$ _
```

In UNIX environments, one often used the stand-alone linking loader (**ld**) to link separate modules. **gcc** can do this job, and it includes many default library references that would be painful to have to manually determine and add to your command line. You can see the work **gcc** does by adding the **-v** option to the command line to generate verbose output.

11.4.4 Reusing the Reverse Function

Now that you've seen how the original reverse program may be built out of a couple of modules, let's use the reverse module again to build the palindrome program. Here's the header and source code listing of the palindrome function—first, "palindrome.h":

```
1  /* PALINDROME.H */
2
3  int palindrome (); /* Declare but do not define */
```

Here is our file "palindrome.c":

```
1   /* PALINDROME.C */
2
3   #include "palindrome.h"
4   #include "reverse.h"
5   #include <string.h>
6
7   /*************************************************************/
8
9   int palindrome (str)
10
11   char *str;
12
13  {
14     char reversedStr [100];
15     reverse (str, reversedStr); /* Reverse original */
16     return (strcmp (str, reversedStr) == 0); /* Compare the two */
17  }
```

Here's the source code of the program "main2.c" that tests the palindrome function ():

```
1   /* MAIN2.C */
2
3   #include <stdio.h>
4   #include "palindrome.h"
5
6   /*************************************************************/
7
8   main ()
9
10  {
11     printf ("palindrome (\"cat\") = %d\n", palindrome ("cat"));
12     printf ("palindrome (\"noon\") = %d\n", palindrome ("noon"));
13  }
```

The way to combine the "reverse", "palindrome", and "main2" modules is as before: compile the object modules and then link them. We don't have to recompile "reverse.c", as it hasn't changed since the "reverse.o" object file was created.

```
$ gcc -c palindrome.c      ...compile palindrome.c to palindrome.o.
$ gcc -c main2.c           ...compile main2.c to main2.o.
$ gcc reverse.o palindrome.o main2.o -o main2     ...link them.
$ ls -lG reverse.o palindrome.o main2.o main2
-rwxr-xr-x  1 ables        24576 Jan  5 19:09 main2*
-rw-r--r--  1 ables          306 Jan  5 19:00 main2.o
```

```
-rw-r--r--  1 ables        189 Jan  5 18:59 palindrome.o
-rw-r--r--  1 ables        181 Jan  5 18:08 reverse.o
$ ./main2                  ...run the program.
palindrome ("cat") = 0
palindrome ("noon") = 1
$ _
```

11.5 Archiving Modules: ar

A medium-sized C project typically uses several hundred object modules. Specifying this many object modules on a command can be tedious and error prone, so I recommend that you learn how to use the GNU archive utility, **ar**, to organize and group your object modules. An archive utility is sometimes known as a *librarian*. It allows you to perform the following tasks:

• creating a special archive format file, ending in a ".a" suffix
• adding, removing, replacing, and appending any kind of file to an archive
• obtaining an archive's table of contents

Figure 11–2 is a synopsis of **ar**.

Utility: **ar** *key archiveName* { *fileName* }*

ar allows you to create and manipulate archives. *archiveName* is the name of the archive file that you wish to access, and it should end with a ".a" suffix. *key* may be one of the following:

    d - deletes a file from an archive

    q - appends a file onto the end of an archive, even if it's already present

    r - adds a file to an archive if it isn't already there, or replaces the current version if it is

    s - builds an index (table of contents) of the library for faster access

    t - displays an archive's table of contents to standard output

    x - copies a list of files from an archive into the current directory

    v - generates verbose output

Figure 11–2 Description of the **ar** command.

When a set of object modules is stored in an archive file, it may be accessed from the **gcc** compiler by simply supplying the name of the archive file as an argument. Any object modules that are needed from the archive file are automatically linked as necessary. This greatly reduces the number of parameters to these utilities when linking large numbers of object modules.

11.5.1 Creating or Adding a File

An archive is automatically created when the first file is added. To add a file to (or replace a file in) a named archive, use the **ar** utility with the **r** option (Figure 11–3).

---

ar r *archiveName* { *fileName* }+

Figure 11–3   Adding or replacing a file in an archive.

This option adds all of the specified files to the archive file *archiveName*, replacing files if they already exist. If the archive file doesn't exist, it is automatically created. The name of the archive should have a ".a" suffix.

11.5.2   Appending a File

To append a file to a named archive, use the **ar** utility with the **q** option (Figure 11–4).

---

ar q *archiveName* { *fileName* }+

Figure 11–4   Appending a file to an archive.

This option appends all of the specified files to the archive file *archiveName*, regardless of whether they already exist. If the archive file doesn't exist, it is automatically created. This option is handy if you know that the file isn't already present, as it allows **ar** to avoid searching through the archive.

11.5.3   Obtaining a Table of Contents

To obtain a table of contents of an archive, use the **ar** utility with the **t** option (Figure 11–5).

---

ar t *archiveName*

Figure 11–5   Listing the table of contents of an archive.

11.5.4   Deleting a File

To delete a list of files from an archive, use the **ar** utility with the **d** option (Figure 11–6).

---

ar d *archiveName* {*fileName* }+

Figure 11–6   Deleting files from an archive.

11.5.5   Extracting a File

To copy a list of files from an archive to the current directory, use the **ar** utility with the **x** option (Figure 11–7). If you don't specify a list of files, then all of the files in the archive are copied.

---

ar x *archiveName* { *fileName* }+

Figure 11–7   Extracting a file from an archive.

11.5.6   Maintaining an Archive from the Command Line

Here is an example that illustrates how an archive may be built and manipulated from the command line, using the object modules built earlier in this chapter.

First, I built an archive file called "string.a" to hold all of my string-related object modules. Next, I added each module in turn using the **r** option. Finally, I demonstrated the various different **ar** options:

```
$ gcc -c reverse.c palindrome.c main2.c  ...create object files.
$ ls *.o                                 ...confirm.
main2.o     palindrome.o       reverse.o
$ ar r string.a reverse.o palindrome.o   ...add to an archive.
ar: creating string.a
$ ar t string.a        ...obtain a table of contents.
reverse.o
palindrome.o
$ gcc main2.o string.a -o main2      ...link the object modules.
$ main2                              ...execute the program.
palindrome ("cat") = 0
palindrome ("noon") = 1
$ ar d string.a reverse.o            ...delete a module.
$ ar t string.a                      ...confirm deletion.
palindrome.o
$ ar r string.a reverse.o            ...put it back again.
$ ar t string.a                      ...confirm addition.
palindrome.o
reverse.o
$ rm palindrome.o reverse.o          ...delete originals.
$ ls *.o                             ...confirm.
main2.o
$ ar x string.a reverse.o            ...copy them back again.
$ ls *.o                             ...confirm.
main2.o     reverse.o
$ _
```

11.5.7   Indexing Archives

The **ar** utility does not maintain any particular order in an archive file. This is usually fine, because **gcc** and its linker are able to extract object modules and resolve external references regardless of order. However, you could have a problem if functions in the archive call each other, depending on the order in which they are found by the linker. If object module A contains a function that calls a function in object module B, then B must appear before A in the archive. Even if you maintained your ordering properly, you could get into a circular organization where one of the modules couldn't find another one and you would wind up with an error about unresolved references to functions that you know you have in your library.

You can help the linker to resolve out-of-order object modules by adding a table of contents to each archive. This also speeds up the linking process, since it doesn't have to search through the archive for each function. On UNIX systems this is often done with the **ranlib** utility. On Linux, you need only add the **s** option to your **ar** command line, like this:

```
$ ar rs string.a reverse.o palindrome.o
```

11.5.8   Shared Libraries

Static libraries work just fine for many applications. However, as processor speed increases and the prices of disk and memory come down, code has been allowed to become more complex. Programs linked with large archive libraries will result in very large executable files (a small program that creates a single X window can be a megabyte when linked with the required X libraries).

To reduce the size of your generated object code, you can link your program with a *shared library* instead. A shared (or dynamic) library is associated with a compiled program, but its functions are loaded in dynamically as they are needed rather than all at once at load time. The resulting object code is smaller, because it does not include the object code from the library as it does when linked with a static library.

The one disadvantage of using a shared library is that your object code will have been written for a specific version of the library. If bug fixes are made but no interface changes are made, then your program will benefit from the newer library that works better. However, if calling interface changes are made, problems may (probably will) result when your program links with the newer version of the library at run time. It is therefore important to be aware of changes in supporting libraries when writing an application.

The **gcc** command honors arguments (that are passed to the linker) to allow you to specify it to build a shared library rather than a static library. These arguments are **-shared** and **-static**.

11.6 Managing Dependencies: make

You've now seen how several independent object modules may be linked into a single executable. You've also seen that the same object module may be linked into several different executables. Although multimodule programs are efficient in terms of reusability and disk space, they must also be carefully maintained. For example, let's assume that we change the source code of "reverse.c" to use pointers instead of array subscripts. This would result in a faster reverse function. In order to update the two main program executables "main1" and "main2" manually, we'd have to perform the following steps, in this order:

1. Recompile "reverse.c".
2. Link "reverse.o" and "main1.o" to produce a new version of "main1".
3. Link "reverse.o" and "main2.o" to produce a new version of "main2".

Similarly, imagine a situation where a #**define** statement in a header file is changed. All of the source code files that directly or indirectly include the file must be recompiled, and then all of the executable modules that refer to the changed object modules must be relinked.

Although this might not seem like a big deal, imagine a system with a thousand object modules and fifty executable programs. Remembering all of the relationships between the headers, source code files, object modules, and executable files would be a nightmare. Summarily recompiling everything whenever something changed would be time consuming and a waste of resources. One way to avoid these problems is to use the GNU **make** utility, which allows you to create a *makefile* that contains a list of all file interdependencies for each executable. Once such a file is created, to re-create the executable is easy; you just use the **make** command as follows:

$ *make programname*

Figure 11–8 is a synopsis of **make**.

Utility: **make** [-f *makefile*]

make is a utility that updates a file based on a series of dependency rules stored in a special format "make file". The **-f** option allows you to specify your own make filename; if none is specified, **make** will look for the files "GNUmakefile," "makefile," and "Makefile," in that order.

Figure 11–8   Description of the **make** command.

11.6.1   Make Files

To use the **make** utility to maintain an executable file, you must first create a make file. This file contains a list of all the interdependencies that exist between the files that are used to create the executable. A make file may have any name, but it is easiest to set up one make file per directory and name them "Makefile." In the following examples, I will name our make files in the form "module.make" (and use the **-f** option) so that it is clear what we expect the **make** command to do.

In its simplest form, a make file contains make rules of the form shown in Figure 11–9.

---

targetList:dependencyList

   commandList

Figure 11–9   **make** dependency specification.

Here, *targetList* is a list of target files and *dependencyList* is a list of files that the files in *targetList* depend on. *commandList* is a list of zero or more commands, separated by newlines, that reconstructs the target files from the dependency files. Each line in *commandList* must start with a tab character. Rules must be separated by at least one blank line.

For example, let's think about the file interdependencies related to the executable file "main1". This file is built out of two object modules: "main1.o" and "reverse.o". If either file is changed, then "main1" may be reconstructed by linking the files using **gcc**. Therefore, one rule in "main1.make" would be:

```
main1:      main1.o reverse.o
            gcc main1.o reverse.o -o main1
```

This line of reasoning must now be carried forward to the two object files. The file "main1.o" is built from two files, "main1.c" and "reverse.h" (remember that any file that is either directly or indirectly **#include**'d in a source file is effectively part of that file). If either file is changed, then "main1.o" may be reconstructed by compiling "main1.c". Here, therefore, are the remaining rules in "main1.make":

```
main1.o:    main1.c reverse.h
            gcc -c main1.c

reverse.o:  reverse.c reverse.h
            gcc -c reverse.c
```

11.6.2   The Order of Make Rules

The order of make rules is important. The **make** utility creates a "tree" of interdependencies by initially examining the first rule. Each target file in the first rule is a root node of a dependency tree, and each file in its dependency list is added as a leaf of each root node. In our example, the initial tree would look as shown in the Figure 11–10.

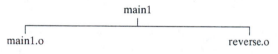

Figure 11–10   Initial **make** dependency tree.

The **make** utility then visits each rule associated with each file in the dependency list and performs the same actions. In our example, the final tree would therefore look as shown in the Figure 11–11.

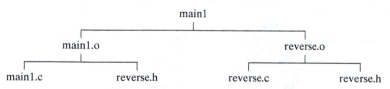

Figure 11–11   Final **make** dependency tree.

Finally, the **make** utility works up the tree from the bottom leaf nodes to the root node, looking to see if the last modification time of each child node is more recent than the last modification time of its immediate parent node. For every case where this is so, the associated parent's rule is executed. If a file is not present, its rule is executed regardless of the last modification times of its children. To illustrate this, I've numbered Figure 11–12 to illustrate the order in which the nodes would be examined.

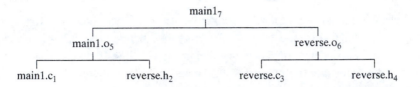

Figure 11–12   make ordering.

11.6.3   Running Make

Once a make file has been created, you're ready to run **make** to re-create the executable file whose dependency information is specified by the makefile.

To show you how this works, I deleted all of the object modules and the executable to force every command list to execute. When I then performed the make, here's what I saw:

```
$ make -f main1.make     ...make executable up-to-date.
gcc -c main1.c
gcc -c reverse.c
gcc main1.o reverse.o -o main1
$ _
```

Notice that every make rule was executed, in the exact order shown in Figure 11–12.

Since I created a second executable when I made the palindrome program, I also fashioned a second make file, called "main2.make". Here it is:

```
main2:          main2.o reverse.o palindrome.o
                gcc main2.o reverse.o palindrome.o -o main2
main2.o:        main2.c palindrome.h
                gcc -c main2.c
reverse.o:      reverse.c reverse.h
                gcc -c reverse.c
palindrome.o:   palindrome.c palindrome.h reverse.h
                gcc -c palindrome.c
```

When I performed a make using this file, I saw the following output:

```
$ make -f main2.make     ...make executable up-to-date.
gcc -c main2.c
gcc -c palindrome.c
gcc main2.o reverse.o palindrome.o -o main2
$ _
```

Notice that "reverse.c" was not recompiled. This is because the previous make had already created an up-to-date object module, and **make** only recompiles files when necessary.

11.6.4 Make Rules

The make files that I've shown you so far are larger than they need to be. This is because some of the make rules that I supplied are already known by the **make** utility in a more general way. For example, note that several of the rules are of the form:

```
xxx.o:      reverse.c reverse.h
            gcc -c xxx.c
```

where xxx varies between rules. The **make** utility contains a predefined rule similar to the following:

```
.c.o:
            gcc -c -O $<
```

This cryptic-looking rule tells the **make** utility how to create an object module from a C source code file. The existence of this general rule allows me to leave off the C recompilation rule. Here, therefore, is a sleeker version of "main2.make":

```
main2:          main2.o reverse.o palindrome.o
                gcc main2.o reverse.o palindrome.o -o main2
main2.o:        main2.c palindrome.h
reverse.o:      reverse.c reverse.h
palindrome.o:   palindrome.c palindrome.h reverse.h
```

The **make** utility also includes other inference rules. For example, **make** knows that the name of an object module and its corresponding source code file are usually related. It uses this information to infer standard dependencies. For example, it deduces that "main2.o" is dependent on "main2.c", and thus you may leave this information off the dependency list. Here is an even sleeker version of "main2.make":

```
main2:          main2.o reverse.o palindrome.o
                gcc main2.o reverse.o palindrome.o -o main2
main2.o:        palindrome.h
reverse.o:      reverse.h
palindrome.o:   palindrome.h reverse.h
```

11.6.5 Forcing Compilation

To confirm that the new version of the make file worked, I requested a make and obtained the following output:

```
$ make -f main2.make
'main2' is up to date.
$ _
```

Obviously, since I'd already performed a successful make, another one wasn't going to trigger any rules! To force a make for testing purposes, I used a handy utility called **touch**, which makes the last modification time of all the named files equal to the current system time. Figure 11–13 is a brief synopsis.

Utility: **touch** -c { *fileName* }+

touch updates the last modification and access times of the named files to the current time. By default, if a specified file doesn't exist, it is created with zero size. To prevent this, use the **-c** option.

Figure 11–13   Description of the **touch** command.

I "touched" the file "reverse.h", which subsequently caused the recompilation of several source files:

```
$ touch reverse.h        ...fool make.
$ make -f main2.make
gcc -c -O reverse.c
gcc -c -O palindrome.c
gcc main2.o reverse.o palindrome.o -o main2
$ _
```

11.6.6   Macros

The **make** utility supports primitive macros. If you specify a line of the form shown in Figure 11–14 at the top of a make file, every occurrence of $(*token*) in the make file is replaced by *replacementText*.

---

token = replacementText

Figure 11–14   A macro in **make**.

In addition to containing rules, the standard rules file contains default definitions of macros such as CFLAGS that are used by some of the built-in rules. For example, the rule that tells the make utility how to update an object file from a C source file looks like this:

```
.c.o:
        gcc -c $(CFLAGS) $<
```

The standard rules file contains a line of the form:

```
CFLAGS =    -O
```

If you wanted to recompile a suite of programs using the **-O2** option of **gcc** (for a different level of optimization), you would override the default value of CFLAGS at the top of the make file like this:

```
CFLAGS =            -O2
main2:              main2.o reverse.o palindrome.o
                    gcc main2.o reverse.o palindrome.o -o main2
main2.o:            palindrome.h
reverse.o:          reverse.h
palindrome.o:       palindrome.h reverse.h
```

To recompile the suite of programs, I used the **touch** utility to force recompilation of all the source files:

```
$ touch *.c         ...force make to recompile everything.
$ make -f main2.make
gcc -O2 -c main2.c
gcc -O2 -c palindrome.c
gcc -O2 -c reverse.c
gcc main2.o reverse.o palindrome.o -o main2
$ _
```

Notice that the **-O2** argument was not included in my **gcc** command to link everything, because I have that command defined in my make file.

11.6.7 Maintaining an Archive Using Make

Although an archive can be built and maintained from the command line, it's much better to use **make**. To refer to an object file inside an archive, place the name of the object file inside parentheses, preceded by the name of the archive. The make utility has built-in rules that take care of the archive operations automatically. Here is the updated "main2.make" file that uses archives instead of plain object files:

```
main2:              main2.o string.a(reverse.o) string.a(palindrome.o)
                    gcc main2.o string.a -o main2
main2.o:            palindrome.h
string.a(reverse.o):     reverse.h
string.a(palindrome.o): palindrome.h reverse.h
```

Here is the output from a make performed using this file:

```
$ rm *.o                        ...remove all object modules.
$ make -f main2.make            ...perform a make.
```

```
gcc -c main2.c
gcc -c reverse.c
ar rv string.a reverse.o          ...object module is saved.
a - reverse.o
ar: creating string.a
rm -f reverse.o                   ...original is removed.
gcc -c palindrome.c
ar rv string.a palindrome.o
a - palindrome.o
rm -f palindrome.o
gcc main2.o string.a -o main2     ...access archived modules.
$ _
```

Notice that the built-in make rules automatically removed the original object file once it had been copied into the archive.

11.6.8   Other Make Capabilities

As you can see, **make** is a rather complicated utility. I suggest that you consult the Linux man page and [Oram, 1991] for more details.

11.7 The GNU Profiler: gprof

It's often handy to be able to see where a program is spending its time. For example, if a greater-than-expected amount of time is being spent in a particular function, it might be worth optimizing the function by hand for better performance. The **gprof** utility allows you to obtain a program's profile (Figure 11–15).

Utility: **gprof** -b [*executableFile* [*profileFile*]]

gprof is the GNU profiler. It generates a table of time and repetitions of each function in the executable *executableFile* based on the performance trace stored in the file *profileFile*. If *profileFile* is omitted, "gmon.out" is assumed. If *executableFile* is omitted, "a.out" is assumed. The executable file must have been compiled using the **-pg** option of **gcc**, which instructs the compiler to generate special code that writes a "gmon.out" file when the program runs. The **gprof** utility then looks at this output file after the program has terminated and displays the information contained therein. The output of **gprof** is verbose (but helpful); to instruct **gprof** to be brief, use the **-b** option.

Figure 11–15   Description of the **gprof** command.

Here's an example of **gprof** in action:

```
$ main2                          ...execute the program.
palindrome ("cat") = 0           ...program output.
```

```
palindrome ("noon") = 1
$ ls -lG gmon.out              ...list the monitor output.
-rw-r-xr-x   1 ables      468 Jan  8 17:19 gmon.out
$ gprof -b main2 gmon.out      ...profile the program.
Flat profile:

Each sample counts as 0.01 seconds.
 no time accumulated

  %   cumulative   self              self    total
 time   seconds   seconds    calls  Ts/call  Ts/call  name
 0.00     0.00     0.00       2      0.00     0.00  palindrome
 0.00     0.00     0.00       2      0.00     0.00  reverse


           Call graph


granularity: each sample hit covers 2 byte(s) no time propagated

index % time    self  children    called     name
                0.00    0.00       2/2             main [9]
[1]      0.0    0.00    0.00       2           palindrome [1]
                0.00    0.00       2/2             reverse [2]
-----------------------------------------------------
                0.00    0.00       2/2             palindrome [1]
[2]      0.0    0.00    0.00       2           reverse [2]
-----------------------------------------------------

Index by function name

   [1] palindrome              [2] reverse

$ _
```

After a profile has been viewed, you may decide to do some hand tuning and then obtain another profile.

11.8 Debugging a Program: gdb

The GNU debugger **gdb** allows you to symbolically debug a program. Although it's not as slick as most commercial professional debuggers on the market, it is a handy utility that comes bundled in Linux distributions. **gdb** includes the following facilities:

- running and listing the program
- setting breakpoints
- examining variable values
- tracing execution

Figure 11–16 is a synopsis of **gdb**.

Utility: **gdb** *executableFilename*

gdb is a standard GNU/Linux debugger. The named executable file is loaded into the debugger and a user prompt is displayed. To obtain information on the various **gdb** commands, enter **help** at the prompt.

Figure 11–16   Description of the **gdb** command.

To demonstrate **gdb**, let's debug the following recursive version of palindrome ():

```
1   /* PALINDROME.C */
2
3   #include "palindrome.h"
4   #include <string.h>
5
6
7   enum { FALSE, TRUE };
8
9
10  int palindrome (str)
11
12  char *str;
13
14  {
15      return (palinAux (str, 1, strlen (str)));
16  }
17
18  /****************************************************************/
19
20  int palinAux (str, start, stop)
21
22  char *str;
23  int start;
24  int stop;
25
26  {
27      if (start >= stop)
28          return (TRUE);
29      else if (str[start] != str[stop])
30          return (FALSE);
31      else
32          return (palinAux (str, start + 1, stop - 1));
33  }
```

The basic algorithm is that it starts from each end of a string and compares the letters and quits if and when the two letters differ (false) or when the indices "cross" or become equal (true).

11.8.1 Preparing a Program for Debugging

To debug a program, it must have been compiled using the **-g** option to **gcc**, which places debugging information into the object module. Using a new palindrome module in palbug.c along with our previous reverse module and a main program to control it all, we compile this way:

```
$ make
gcc -g -c -o main2.o main2.c
gcc -g -c -o reverse.o reverse.c
gcc -g -c -o palbug.o palbug.c
gcc main2.o reverse.o palbug.o -o main2
$ _
```

Now we have a "main2" file containing an executable built from these module files.

11.8.2 Entering the Debugger

Once a program has been compiled correctly, invoke **gdb** with the name of the executable as the first argument. **gdb** presents you with a prompt. I recommend that you enter **help** at the prompt to see a list of all the **gdb** commands:

```
$ gdb main2                    ...enter the debugger.
GNU gdb 6.0-2mdk (Mandrake Linux)
Copyright 2003 Free Software Foundation, Inc.
GDB is free software, covered by the GNU General Public License,
and you are welcome to change it and/or distribute copies of it
under certain conditions.
Type "show copying" to see the conditions.
There is absolutely no warranty for GDB. Type "show warranty"
for details.
This GDB was configured as "i586-mandrake-linux-gnu"...Using
host libthread_db library "/lib/tls/libthread_db.so.1".

(gdb) help                     ...get some help.
List of classes of commands:

aliases -- Aliases of other commands
breakpoints -- Making program stop at certain points
data -- Examining data
files -- Specifying and examining files
internals -- Maintenance commands
obscure -- Obscure features
running -- Running the program
stack -- Examining the stack
status -- Status inquiries
support -- Support facilities
```

```
tracepoints -- Tracing of program execution without stopping the
program
user-defined -- User-defined commands

Type "help" followed by a class name for a list of commands in that
class.
Type "help" followed by command name for full documentation.
Command name abbreviations are allowed if unambiguous.
(gdb) _
```

Note that **gdb** prints its copyright and licensing information each time it is started, but in future examples I will omit this in the interest of brevity.

11.8.3   Running a Program

To run your program, enter the **run** command, which runs the program to completion:

```
(gdb) run
Starting program: /home/ables/main2
palindrome ("cat") = 0
palindrome ("noon") = 0

Program exited with code 030.
(gdb) _
```

But there's a problem. The string "noon" is a palindrome, even though my function reports that it isn't.

11.8.4   Listing a Program

In order to know where you're looking in your code, you can use the **list** command to list sections of the program, ten lines at a time by default, and including line numbers you'll use to reference specific statements:

```
(gdb) list
2
3        #include <stdio.h>
4        #include "palindrome.h"
5
6        /
*************************************************************/
7
8        main ()
9
10       {
11          printf ("palindrome (\"cat\") = %d\n", palindrome ("cat"));
(gdb) _
```

Our first use of the **list** command listed the ten lines following our current position (which was line 1). If ten lines aren't enough, you can specify a line range, such as:

```
(gdb) list 1,99
1          /* MAIN2.C */
2
3          #include <stdio.h>
4          #include "palindrome.h"
5
6          /
**************************************************************/
7
8          main ()
9
10         {
11            printf ("palindrome (\"cat\") = %d\n", palindrome ("cat"));
12            printf ("palindrome (\"noon\") = %d\n", palindrome ("noon"));
13         }
(gdb) _
```

We don't have 99 lines in this file, but it lists what it can. Notice, however, that **gdb** is listing the contents of main2.c. To list lines from another source file, specify the line range with a file name in the form "filename:firstline,lastline", or to list the ten lines around a specific location, use "filename:linenumber"—like this:

```
(gdb) list palbug.c:10
5
6
7          enum { FALSE, TRUE };
8
9
10         int palindrome (str)
11
12         char *str;
13
14         {
(gdb) list
15            return (palinAux (str, 1, strlen (str)));
16         }
17
18         /
**************************************************************/
19
20         int palinAux (str, start, stop)
21
22         char *str;
```

```
23      int start;
24      int stop;
(gdb) list
25
26      {
27        if (start >= stop)
28          return (TRUE);
29        else if (str[start] != str[stop])
30          return (FALSE);
31        else
32          return (palinAux (str, start + 1, stop - 1));
33      }
(gdb) _
```

Our subsequent **list** commands began a new ten-line listing from the end of the previous listing.

11.8.5 Setting a Breakpoint

To make **gdb** stop when it encounters a particular function, use the **break** command. This allows you to run a program at full speed until the function that you wish to examine more closely is executed:

```
(gdb) help breakpoints
Making program stop at certain points.

List of commands:

awatch -- Set a watchpoint for an expression
break -- Set breakpoint at specified line or function
catch -- Set catchpoints to catch events
clear -- Clear breakpoint at specified line or function
commands -- Set commands to be executed when a breakpoint is hit
condition -- Specify breakpoint number N to break only if COND is true
delete -- Delete some breakpoints or auto-display expressions
disable -- Disable some breakpoints
enable -- Enable some breakpoints
hbreak -- Set a hardware assisted breakpoint
ignore -- Set ignore-count of breakpoint number N to COUNT
rbreak -- Set a breakpoint for all functions matching REGEXP
rwatch -- Set a read watchpoint for an expression
tbreak -- Set a temporary breakpoint
tcatch -- Set temporary catchpoints to catch events
thbreak -- Set a temporary hardware assisted breakpoint
watch -- Set a watchpoint for an expression

(gdb) break palindrome
Breakpoint 1 at 0x804843e: file palbug.c, line 15.
(gdb) run
Starting program: /home/ables/main2
```

```
Breakpoint 1, palindrome (str=0x80485b8 "cat") at palbug.c:15
15          return (palinAux (str, 1, strlen (str)));
(gdb) list
10        int palindrome (str)
11
12        char *str;
13
14        {
15            return (palinAux (str, 1, strlen (str)));
16        }
17
18      /
**************************************************************/
19
(gdb) _
```

If you want to set a breakpoint at a specific line number, you can use a line number instead of a function name, like this:

```
(gdb) list
20        int palinAux (str, start, stop)
21
22        char *str;
23        int start;
24        int stop;
25
26        {
27          if (start >= stop)
28              return (TRUE);
29          else if (str[start] != str[stop])
(gdb) break 27
Breakpoint 2 at 0x8048465: file palbug.c, line 27.
(gdb) run
The program being debugged has been started already.
Start it from the beginning? (y or n) n
Program not restarted.
(gdb) continue
Continuing.

Breakpoint 2, palinAux (str=0x80485b8 "cat", start=1, stop=3) at
palbug.c:27
27          if (start >= stop)
(gdb) _
```

Notice that after I set the new breakpoint, I typed "run", but this instructs **gdb** to start the program from the beginning. Since I was in the middle of execution already, it asked me if I knew what I was doing (which, of course, I did not!). To resume execution of a program from the same place, use the **continue** command. If you type "y" in answer to the question, the program will be restarted from the beginning with all the same breakpoints that have already been set.

As with the **list** command, you can specify a line number or function name within a file with the syntax "break file:linenumber" and "break file:functionname," respectively.

```
(gdb) quit
The program is running. Exit anyway? (y or n) y
$ gdb main2                              ...begin again.
(gdb) break palbug.c:27
Breakpoint 1 at 0x8048465: file palbug.c, line 27.
(gdb) run
Starting program: /home/ables/main2

Breakpoint 1, palinAux (str=0x80485b8 "cat", start=1, stop=3) at
palbug.c:27
27        if (start >= stop)
(gdb) _
```

11.8.6   Stepping Through the Code

To step through a program one line at a time, use the **step** command. This command causes **gdb** to redisplay its prompt immediately after the next line of program has been executed, and is useful for high-resolution interrogation of a function. In the following example, I entered **step** after my program stopped at line 27.

```
(gdb) step
29        else if (str[start] != str[stop])
(gdb) step
30            return (FALSE);
(gdb) _
```

You can also step multiple lines at a time:

```
(gdb) step 5
palindrome ("cat") = 0

Breakpoint 1, palinAux (str=0x80485d5 "noon", start=1, stop=4) at
palbug.c:27
27        if (start >= stop)
(gdb) step 5
palindrome ("noon") = 0
main () at main2.c:13
13     }
(gdb) _
```

11.8.7 Examining Variable Values

The power of **gdb** is the ability to examine and change the state of the program at any point during its execution. You can stop execution and examine the value of any variable to see if they match your expectation. To print the value of a particular variable at any time, use the **print** command.

```
(gdb) help data
Examining data.

List of commands:

append -- Append target code/data to a local file
call -- Call a function in the program
delete display -- Cancel some expressions to be displayed when program
stops
delete mem -- Delete memory region
disable display -- Disable some expressions to be displayed when
program stops
disable mem -- Disable memory region
disassemble -- Disassemble a specified section of memory
display -- Print value of expression EXP each time the program stops
dump -- Dump target code/data to a local file
enable display -- Enable some expressions to be displayed when program
stops
enable mem -- Enable memory region
inspect -- Same as "print" command
mem -- Define attributes for memory region
output -- Like "print" but don't put in value history and don't print
newline
print -- Print value of expression EXP
print-object -- Ask an Objective-C object to print itself
printf -- Printf "printf format string"
ptype -- Print definition of type TYPE
restore -- Restore the contents of FILE to target memory
set -- Evaluate expression EXP and assign result to variable VAR
set variable -- Evaluate expression EXP and assign result to variable
VAR
undisplay -- Cancel some expressions to be displayed when program
stops
whatis -- Print data type of expression EXP
x -- Examine memory: x/FMT ADDRESS

(gdb) run
The program being debugged has been started already.
Start it from the beginning? (y or n) y
Starting program: /home/ables/main2
```

```
Breakpoint 1, palinAux (str=0x80485b8 "cat", start=1, stop=3) at
palbug.c:27
27          if (start >= stop)
(gdb) continue
Continuing.
palindrome ("cat") = 0

Breakpoint 1, palinAux (str=0x80485d5 "noon", start=1, stop=4) at
palbug.c:27
27          if (start >= stop)
(gdb) print str
$1 = 0x80485d5 "noon"
(gdb) print start
$2 = 1
(gdb) print stop
$3 = 4
(gdb) quit
The program is running. Exit anyway? (y or n) y
$ _
```

11.8.8   The Epiphany

If we continue to step through the program while processing the "noon" string, we see we come to line 30 where we return FALSE (i.e., that "noon" is not a palindrome). Here's a good place to look at some variables, because something clearly isn't right.

```
(gdb) step
30              return (FALSE);
(gdb) print str[1]
$1 = 111 'o'
(gdb) print str[2]
$2 = 111 'o'
(gdb) print str[3]
$3 = 110 'n'
(gdb) print str[4]
$4 = 0 '\0'
(gdb) print str[0]
$5 = 110 'n'
(gdb) quit
The program is running. Exit anyway? (y or n) y
$
```

Do you see the problem? When we entered the palinAux () function, the start and stop variables were 1 and 4, respectively, which seemed reasonable since there are four characters in the string "noon". But those values are not correct, they are both 1 greater than they should be. It's a very common error to forget that C array indices begin at zero rather than one. We should be testing locations 0–3 of our string, not 1–4!

The bug is on line 15 in the main program. Rather than starting to index into the string at element one, we should be starting at zero. The last location is not actually the same number as the length of the string, it is should be one less than the length of the string. If we correct line 15 to read:

```
return (palinAux (str, 0, strlen (str) - 1));
```

and recompile the program, it should work:

```
$ make
cc -g -c -o palbug.o palbug.c
gcc main2.o reverse.o palbug.o -o main2
$ ./main2
palindrome ("cat") = 0
palindrome ("noon") = 1                    ...whoo hoo!
$ _
```

11.9 When You're Done: strip

The debugger and profile utilities both require you compile a program using special options, each of which adds code to the executable file. To remove this extra code after you are finished debugging and profiling, use the **strip** utility (Figure 11–17).

Synopsis: **strip** { *fileName* }+

strip removes all of the symbol table, relocation, debugging, and profiling information from the named files.

Figure 11–17   Description of the **strip** command.

Here's an example of how much space you can save:

```
$ ls -lG main2                 ...look at original file.
-rwxr-xr-x   1 ables      16997 Jan  8 22:18 main2*
$ strip main2                  ...strip out spurious information.
$ ls -lG main2                 ...look at stripped version.
-rwxr-xr-x   1 ables       3416 Jan  8 23:17 main2*
$ _
```

CHAPTER REVIEW

Checklist

In this chapter, I described utilities that:

- compile C programs
- manage the compilation of multimodule programs

- maintain archives
- profile a program
- debug a program

Quiz

1. What is the benefit of the **-q** option of **ar**?
2. Can the **make** utility use object modules stored in an archive file?
3. What does the term "reusable function" mean?
4. Why would you profile a program?
5. Which file is larger, a statically linked binary or a dynamically linked binary?
6. How can you trick **make** into rebuilding all modules of your program?
7. Describe briefly what the **strip** utility does.

Exercises

1. Create a shared library with a simple function that returns an integer value. Then write a program to call this function and print its return value. After compiling and running the program, make a change to the library function that will change the return value of the function. Now rebuild the library, and relink your already compiled .o file(s) with it and run the program again. Which return value do you see this time? What happens if you rename the function in the shared library and try to relink your program? [level: *easy*]
2. Compile "reverse.c" and "palindrome.c" and place them into an archive called "string.a". Write a main program in "prompt.c" that prompts the user for a string and then prints 1 if the string is a palindrome, and 0 if it is not. Create a makefile for the program that links "prompt.o" with the reverse () and palindrome () functions stored in "string.a". Use **gdb** to debug your code if any bugs exist. [level: *medium*]

Project

1. Replace the original version of palindrome () stored in "palindrome" with a pointer-based version. [level: *medium*].

12

Systems Programming

Motivation

If you're a C programmer and you wish to take advantage of the Linux multitasking and inter-process communication facilities, it's essential that you have a good knowledge of the Linux system calls.

Prerequisites

In order to understand this chapter, you should have a good working knowledge of C. For the networking section of this chapter, it helps if you have read Chapter 9, "Networking and the Internet."

Objectives

In this chapter, I'll explain and demonstrate the most commonly used Linux system calls, including those that support I/O, process management, and interprocess communication.

Presentation

The information in this section is presented in the form of several sample programs. Most example code is available online; see the Preface for more information.

Utilities

This chapter introduces the following utility:

mkfifo

System calls and library functions

This section contains the following system calls and library functions, listed in alphabetical order:

accept	fchown	ioctl	pipe
alarm	fcntl	kill	read
bind	fork	lchown	readdir
bzero	fstat	link	setegid
chdir	ftruncate	listen	seteuid
chmod	getegid	lseek	setgid
chown	geteuid	lstat	setpgid
close	getgid	memset	setuid
closedir	gethostbyname	mkdir	signal
connect	gethostname	mkfifo	socket
dup	getpgid	mknod	stat
dup2	getpid	nice	sync
execl	getppid	ntohl	truncate
execlp	getuid	ntohs	unlink
execv	htonl	open	wait
execvp	htons	opendir	write
exit	inet_addr	pause	
fchmod	inet_ntoa	perror	

12.1 Introduction

In order to make use of services such as file creation, process duplication, and interprocess communication, application programs must talk to the operating system. They can do this via a collection of routines called *system calls*, which are the programmer's functional interface to the Linux kernel. To the programmer, they're just like library functions (in fact, some are library functions that, in turn, make true system calls) except that they perform a subroutine call directly into the heart of Linux.

The Linux system calls can be loosely grouped into three main categories:

• file management
• process management
• error handling

Interprocess communication (IPC) is in fact a subset of file management, since Linux treats IPC mechanisms as special files. Figure 12–1 illustrates the file management system call hierarchy.

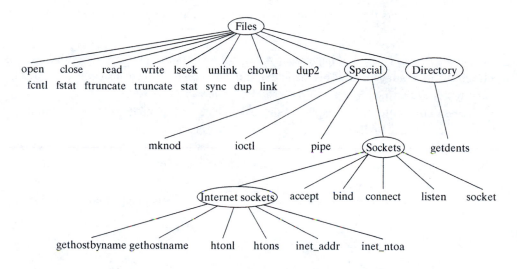

Figure 12-1 File management system call hierarchy.

The process management system call hierarchy includes routines for duplicating, differentiating, and terminating processes (Figure 12-2).

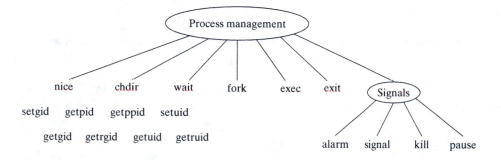

Figure 12-2 Process management system call hierarchy.

The only system call that supports error handling is perror (), which I'll put it in a hierarchy just to be consistent (Figure 12-3).

Figure 12-3 Error handling hierarchy.

This chapter covers the system calls shown in these hierarchy diagrams in the following order:

- **Error handling.** I start the chapter with a description of perror ().
- **Regular file management.** This includes information on how to create, open, close, read, and write regular files. We'll also see a short overview of STREAMS.
- **Process management**. This explains how to duplicate, differentiate, suspend, and terminate processes and briefly discusses multithreaded processes.
- **Signals.** Although the signal facility could come under the heading of either process management or interprocess communication, it's a significant enough topic to warrant a section of its own.
- **Interprocess communications.** This section describes IPC via pipes (both unnamed and named) and sockets.

12.2 Error Handling: perror ()

Most system calls are capable of failing in some way. For example, the open () system call will fail if you try to open a nonexistent file for reading. By convention, all system calls return -1 if an error occurs. However, this doesn't tell you much about *why* the error occurred; the open () system call can fail for one of several different reasons. If you want to deal with system call errors in a systematic way, you must know about two things:

- **errno**, a global variable that holds the numeric code of the last system call error
- perror (), a subroutine that describes system call errors

Every process contains a global variable called **errno**, which is originally set to zero when the process is created. When a system call error occurs, **errno** is set to the numeric code associated with the cause of the error. For example, if you try to open a file that doesn't exist for reading, **errno** is set to 2. These predefined error codes are defined in a C program by including the file "/usr/include/errno.h" (which itself includes other platform-specific files). The names of the error codes are also listed in the **errno** man page. Here's a snippet of the file "/usr/include/asm/errno.h" on my system, where the error constants are defined:

```
#define      EPERM      1   /* Operation not permitted */
#define      ENOENT     2   /* No such file or directory */
#define      ESRCH      3   /* No such process */
#define      EINTR      4   /* Interrupted system call */
#define      EIO        5   /* I/O error */
```

The value of **errno** only has a meaning following an unsuccessful system call which overwrites the current value of **errno**. A successful system call is *not* guaranteed to leave **errno** unmodified (as it is in some versions of UNIX). To access **errno** from your program, include <errno.h>. The perror () subroutine converts the current value of **errno** into a text description (Figure 12–4).

Library Function: void **perror** (char* *str*)

perror () displays the string *str*, followed by a colon, followed by a description of the last system call error. If there is no error to report, it displays the string "Error 0." Actually, perror () isn't a system call—it's a standard C library function.

Figure 12–4 Description of the perror () system call.

Your program should check system calls for a return value of -1 and then deal with the error. One of the first things to do in these situations, especially during debugging, is to call perror () for a description of the error.

In the following example, I forced a couple of system call errors to demonstrate perror (), and then demonstrated that **errno** did not retain the last system call error code after a subsequent successful call was made. Don't worry about how open () works; I'll describe it later in this chapter.

```
$ cat showErrno.c
#include <stdio.h>
#include <fcntl.h>
#include <errno.h>
main ()
{
 int fd;
  /* Open a nonexistent file to cause an error */
 fd = open ("nonexist.txt", O_RDONLY);
 if (fd == -1) /* fd == -1 =, an error occurred */
    {
    printf ("errno = %d\n", errno);
    perror ("main");
    }
 fd = open ("/", O_WRONLY); /* Force a different error */
 if (fd == -1)
    {
    printf ("errno = %d\n", errno);
    perror ("main");
    }
 /* Execute a successful system call */
 fd = open ("nonexist.txt", O_RDONLY | O_CREAT, 0644);
 printf ("errno = %d\n", errno); /* Display after successful call */
 perror ("main");
 errno = 0; /* Manually reset error variable */
 perror ("main");
}
```

Here's the output from the program shown above:

```
$ ./showErrno                  ...run the program.
errno = 2
main: No such file or directory
errno = 21
main: Is a directory
errno = 29         ...even after a successful call
main: Illegal seek
main: Success   ...after we reset manually.
$ _
```

12.3 Regular File Management

My description of file management system calls is split up into subsections:

- A primer that describes the main concepts behind Linux files and file descriptors.
- A description of the basic file management system calls, using a sample program called "reverse" that reverses the lines of a file.
- An explanation of a few advanced system calls, using a sample program called "monitor," which periodically scans directories and displays the names of files within them that have changed since the last scan.
- A description of the remaining file management system calls, using some miscellaneous snippets of source code.

12.3.1   A File Management Primer

The file management system calls allow you to manipulate the full collection of regular, directory, and special files, including:

- disk-based files
- terminals
- printers
- interprocess communication facilities, such as pipes and sockets

In most cases, open () is used to initially access or create a file. If the system call succeeds, it returns a small integer called a *file descriptor* that is used in subsequent I/O operations on that file. If open () fails, it returns -1. Here's a snippet of code that illustrates a typical sequence of events:

```
int fd; /* File descriptor */
...
fd = open (fileName, ...); /* Open file, return file descriptor */
if (fd == -1) {  /* deal with error condition */ }
...
fcntl (fd, ...); /* Set some I/O flags if necessary */
...
read (fd, ...);  /* Read from file */
...
```

```
write (fd, ...); /* Write to file */
...
lseek (fd, ...); /* Seek within file*/
...
close (fd); /* Close the file, freeing file descriptor */
```

When a process no longer needs to access an open file, it should close it using the close () system call. All of a process's open files are automatically closed when the process terminates. Although this means that you may often omit an explicit call to close (), it's better programming practice to explicitly close your files.

File descriptors are numbered sequentially, starting from zero. By convention, the first three file descriptor values have a special meaning (Figure 12–5).

Value	Meaning
0	standard input (stdin)
1	standard output (stdout)
2	standard error (stderr)

Figure 12–5 File descriptor values for standard I/O channels.

For example, the printf () library function always sends its output using file descriptor 1, and scanf () always reads its input using file descriptor 0. When a reference to a file is closed, the file descriptor is freed and may be reassigned by a subsequent open (). Most I/O system calls require a file descriptor as their first argument so that they know which file to operate on.

A single file may be opened several times and thus have several file descriptors associated with it (Figure 12–6).

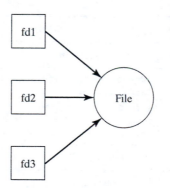

Figure 12–6 Many file descriptors, one file.

Each file descriptor has its own private set of properties that have nothing to do with the file that it is associated with, including:

• A file pointer that records the offset in the file where it is reading/writing. When a file descriptor is created, its file pointer is positioned at offset 0 in the file (the first character) by default. As the process reads and/or writes, the file pointer is updated accordingly. For example, if a process opened a file and then read 10 bytes from the file, the file pointer would end up positioned at offset 10. If the process then wrote 20 bytes, the bytes at offset 10..29 in the file would be overwritten and the file pointer would end up positioned at off-set 30.

• A flag that indicates whether the descriptor should be automatically closed if the process calls exec (). exec () is described in the "Process Management" on page 473.

• A flag that indicates whether all of the output to the file should be appended to the end of the file.

In addition to these values, some other values are meaningful only if the file is a special one such as a pipe or a socket:

• A flag that indicates whether a process should block on input from the file if the file doesn't currently contain any input.

• A number that indicates a process ID or process group that should be sent a SIGIO signal if input becomes available on the file. Signals and process groups are discussed later in this chapter.

The system calls open () and fcntl () allow you to manipulate these flags, and are described later in this section.

12.3.2   First Example: reverse

In this first section, I'll describe the most basic I/O system calls. Figure 12–7 lists them, together with a brief description of their function.

Name	Function
open	Opens/creates a file.
read	Reads bytes from a file into a buffer.
write	Writes bytes from a buffer to a file.
lseek	Moves to a particular offset in a file.
close	Closes a file.
unlink	Removes a file.

Figure 12–7   Linux system calls for basic I/O operations.

To illustrate the use of these system calls, I'll use a small utility program called "reverse.c" (Figure 12–8). As well as being a good vehicle for my presentation, it also doubles as a nice example of how to write a utility.

Utility: **reverse** -c [*fileName*]

reverse reverses the lines of its input and displays them to standard output. If no file name is specified, **reverse** reverses its standard input. When the **-c** option is used, **reverse** also reverses the characters in each line.

Figure 12–8   Description of the **reverse** program.

Here's an example of **reverse** in action:

```
$ gcc reverse.c -o reverse      ...compile the program.
$ cat test                      ...list the test file.
Christmas is coming,
The days that grow shorter,
Remind me of seasons I knew in the past.
$ ./reverse test                ...reverse the file.
Remind me of seasons I knew in the past.
The days that grow shorter,
Christmas is coming,
$ ./reverse -c test             ...reverse the lines too.
.tsap eht ni wenk I snosaes fo em dnimeR
,retrohs worg taht syad ehT
,gnimoc si samtsirhC
$ cat test | ./reverse          ...pipe output to "reverse".
Remind me of seasons I knew in the past.
The days that grow shorter,
Christmas is coming,
$ _
```

12.3.3   How reverse Works

The **reverse** utility works by performing two passes over its input. During the first pass, it notes the starting offset of each line in the file and stores this information in an array. During the second pass, it jumps to the start of each line in reverse order, copying it from the original input file to its standard output.

If no file name is specified on the command line, **reverse** reads from its standard input during the first pass and copies it into a temporary file for the second pass. When the program is finished, the temporary file is removed.

Figure 12–9 gives an overview of the program flow, together with a list of the functions that are associated with each action, and a list of the system calls used by each step.

Step	Action	Functions	System calls
1	Parse command line.	parseCommandLine, processOptions	open
2	If reading from standard input, create temporary file to store input; otherwise open input file for reading.	pass1	open
3	Read from file in chunks, storing the starting offset of each line in an array. If reading from standard input, copy each chunk to the temporary file.	pass1, trackLines	read, write
4	Read the input file again, backward, copying each line to standard output. Reverse the line if the -c option was chosen.	pass2, processLine, reverseLine	lseek
5	Close file, removing it if it was a temporary file.	pass2	close

Figure 12–9   Description of algorithm used in reverse.c.

The next several pages provide a complete listing of "reverse.c," the source code of **reverse**. I suggest that you skim through it and then read the description of the system calls that follow. This code is also available online; see the Preface for more information.

12.3.4   reverse.c: Listing

```
1   #include <fcntl.h>  /* For file mode definitions */
2   #include <stdio.h>
3   #include <stdlib.h>
4
5
6   /* Enumerator */
7   enum { FALSE, TRUE }; /* Standard false and true values */
8   enum { STDIN, STDOUT, STDERR }; /* Standard I/O channel indices */
9
10
11  /* #define Statements */
12  #define BUFFER_SIZE    4096    /* Copy buffer size */
13  #define NAME_SIZE      12
14  #define MAX_LINES      100000 /* Max lines in file */
15
16
17  /* Globals */
18  char *fileName = 0; /* Points to file name */
19  char tmpName [NAME_SIZE];
20  int charOption = FALSE; /* Set to true if -c option is used */
```

```
21  int standardInput = FALSE; /* Set to true if reading stdin */
22  int lineCount = 0; /* Total number of lines in input */
23  int lineStart [MAX_LINES]; /* Store offsets of each line */
24  int fileOffset = 0; /* Current position in input */
25  int fd; /* File descriptor of input */
26
27  /****************************************************************/
28
29  main (argc, argv)
30
31  int argc;
32  char* argv [];
33
34  {
35    parseCommandLine (argc,argv); /* Parse command line */
36    pass1 (); /* Perform first pass through input */
37    pass2 (); /* Perform second pass through input */
38    return (/* EXITSUCCESS */ 0); /* Done */
39  }
40
41  /****************************************************************/
42
43  parseCommandLine (argc, argv)
44
45  int argc;
46  char* argv [];
47
48  /* Parse command-line arguments */
49
50  {
51    int i;
52
53    for (i= 1; i < argc; i++)
54      {
55        if(argv[i][0] == '-')
56          processOptions (argv[i]);
57        else if (fileName == 0)
58          fileName= argv[i];
59        else
60          usageError (); /* An error occurred */
61      }
62
63    standardInput = (fileName == 0);
64  }
65
66  /****************************************************************/
67
68  processOptions (str)
```

```
69
70   char* str;
71
72   /* Parse options */
73
74   {
75     int j;
76
77     for (j= 1; str[j] != 0; j++)
78       {
79         switch(str[j]) /* Switch on command-line flag */
80           {
81             case 'c':
82               charOption = TRUE;
83               break;
84
85             default:
86               usageError ();
87               break;
88           }
89       }
90   }
91
92   /***************************************************************/
93
94   usageError ()
95
96   {
97     fprintf (stderr, "Usage: reverse -c [filename]\n");
98     exit (/* EXITFAILURE */ 1);
99   }
100
101  /***************************************************************/
102
103  pass1 ()
104
105  /* Perform first scan through file */
106
107  {
108    int tmpfd, charsRead, charsWritten;
109    char buffer [BUFFER_SIZE];
110
111    if (standardInput) /* Read from standard input */
112      {
113        fd = STDIN;
114        sprintf (tmpName, ".rev.%d",getpid ()); /* Random name */
115        /* Create temporary file to store copy of input */
116        tmpfd = open (tmpName, O_CREAT | O_RDWR, 0600);
```

```
117          if (tmpfd == -1) fatalError ();
118        }
119     else /* Open named file for reading */
120        {
121          fd = open (fileName, O_RDONLY);
122          if (fd == -1) fatalError ();
123        }
124
125     lineStart[0] = 0; /* Offset of first line */
126
127     while (TRUE) /* Read all input */
128        {
129          /* Fill buffer */
130          charsRead = read (fd, buffer, BUFFER_SIZE);
131          if (charsRead == 0) break; /* EOF */
132          if (charsRead == -1) fatalError (); /* Error */
133          trackLines (buffer, charsRead); /* Process line */
134          /* Copy line to temporary file if reading from stdin */
135          if (standardInput)
136            {
137              charsWritten = write (tmpfd, buffer, charsRead);
138              if(charsWritten != charsRead) fatalError ();
139            }
140        }
141
142     /* Store offset of trailing line, if present */
143     lineStart[lineCount + 1] = fileOffset;
144
145     /* If reading from standard input, prepare fd for pass2 */
146     if (standardInput) fd = tmpfd;
147   }
148
149   /*****************************************************************/
150
151   trackLines (buffer, charsRead)
152
153   char* buffer;
154   int charsRead;
155
156   /* Store offsets of each line start in buffer */
157
158   {
159     int i;
160
161     for (i = 0; i < charsRead; i++)
162        {
163          ++fileOffset; /* Update current file position */
164          if (buffer[i] == '\n') lineStart[++lineCount] = fileOffset;
```

```
165       }
166  }
167
168  /**************************************************************/
169
170  int pass2 ()
171
172  /* Scan input file again, displaying lines in reverse order */
173
174  {
175    int i;
176
177    for (i = lineCount - 1; i >= 0; i--)
178      processLine (i);
179
180    close (fd); /* Close input file */
181    if (standardInput) unlink (tmpName); /* Remove temp file */
182  }
183
184  /**************************************************************/
185
186  processLine (i)
187
188  int i;
189
190  /* Read a line and display it */
191
192  {
193    int charsRead;
194    char buffer [BUFFER_SIZE];
195
196    lseek (fd, lineStart[i], SEEK_SET); /* Find line and read */
197    charsRead = read (fd, buffer, lineStart[i+1] - lineStart[i]);
198    /* Reverse line if -c option was selected */
199    if (charOption) reverseLine (buffer, charsRead);
200    write (1, buffer, charsRead); /* Write it to standard output */
201  }
202
203  /**************************************************************/
204
205  reverseLine (buffer, size)
206
207  char* buffer;
208  int size;
209
210  /* Reverse all the characters in the buffer */
211
212  {
```

```
213    int start = 0, end = size - 1;
214    char tmp;
215
216    if (buffer[end] == '\n') --end; /* Leave trailing newline */
217
218    /* Swap characters in a pairwise fashion */
219    while (start < end)
220       {
221         tmp = buffer[start];
222         buffer[start] = buffer[end];
223         buffer[end] = tmp;
224         ++start; /* Increment start index */
225         --end; /* Decrement end index */
226       }
227  }
228
229  /***************************************************************/
230
231  fatalError ()
232
233  {
234    perror ("reverse: "); /* Describe error */
235    exit (1);
236  }
```

12.3.5   Opening a File: open ()

The **reverse** utility begins by executing parseCommandLine () [43] that sets various flags depending on which options are chosen. If a filename is specified, the variable *fileName* is set to point to the name and *standardInput* is set to FALSE; otherwise, *fileName* is set to a zero-length string and *standardInput* is set to TRUE. Next, pass1 () [103] is executed, which performs one of the following actions:

- If **reverse** is reading from standard input, a temporary file is created. The file is created with read and write permissions for the owner, and no permissions for anyone else (octal mode 600). It is opened in read/write mode, and is used to store a copy of the standard input for use during pass 2. During pass 1, the input is taken from standard input, and so the file descriptor **fd** is set to STDIN, defined to be 0 at the top of the program. Recall that standard input is always file descriptor zero.
- If **reverse** is reading from a named file, the file is opened in read-only mode so that its contents may be read during pass 1 using the file descriptor **fd**.

Each action uses the open () system call; the first action uses it to create a file, and the second action uses it to access an existing file (Figure 12–10).

System Call: int **open** (char* *fileName*, int *mode* [, int *permissions*])

open () allows you to open or create a file for reading and/or writing. *fileName* is an absolute or relative pathname and *mode* is a bitwise or'ing of a read/write flag together with zero or more miscellaneous flags. *permissions* is a number that encodes the value of the file's permission flags, and should only be supplied when a file is being created. It is usually written using the octal encoding scheme described in Chapter 3, "GNU Utilities for Nonprogrammers." The *permissions* value is affected by the process's umask value, described in Chapter 5, "The Linux Shells." The values of the predefined read/write and miscellaneous flags are defined in "/usr/include/fcntl.h". The read/write flags are as follows:

FLAG	MEANING
O_RDONLY	Open for read-only.
O_WRONLY	Open for write-only.
O_RDWR	Open for read and write.

The miscellaneous flags are as follows:

FLAG	MEANING
O_APPEND	Position the file pointer at the end of the file before each write ().
O_CREAT	If the file doesn't exist, create the file, and set the owner ID to the process's effective user ID. The umask value is used when determining the initial permission flag settings.
O_EXCL	If O_CREAT is set and the file exists, then open () fails.
O_NONBLOCK or O_NDELAY	This setting works only for named pipes. If set, an open for read-only will return immediately, regardless of whether the write end is open, and an open for write-only will fail if the read end isn't open. If clear, an open for read-only or write-only will block until the other end is also open.
O_TRUNC	If the file exists, it is truncated to length zero.

open () returns a non-negative file descriptor if successful; otherwise, it returns -1.

Figure 12-10 Description of the open () system call.

12.3.5.1 Creating a File

To create a file, use the O_CREAT flag as part of the mode flags, and supply the initial file permission flag settings as an octal value. For example, lines 114..117 create a temporary file with read and write permission for the owner, and then open it for reading and writing:

```
114    sprintf (tmpName, ".rev.%d", getpid ()); /* Random name */
115    /* Create temporary file to store copy of input */
116    tmpfd = open (tmpName, O_CREAT | O_RDWR, 0600);
117    if (tmpfd == -1) fatalError ();
```

The getpid () function is a system call that returns the process's ID number (PID), which is guaranteed to be unique. This is a handy way to generate unique temporary filenames. For more details on this system call, see the section "Process Management" on page 473. Note that I chose the name of the temporary file to begin with a period, making it a hidden file, so that it doesn't show up in an ls listing.

12.3.5.2 Opening an Existing File

To open an existing file, specify the mode flags only. Lines 121..122 open a named file for read-only:

```
121    fd = open (fileName, O_RDONLY);
122    if (fd == -1) fatalError ();
```

12.3.5.3 Other Open Flags

The other more complicated flag settings for open (), such as O_NONBLOCK, are intended for use with the pipes, sockets, and STREAMS that are described later in this chapter. Right now, the O_CREAT flag is probably the only miscellaneous flag that you'll need.

12.3.6 Reading From a File: read ()

Once **reverse** has initialized the file descriptor **fd** for input, it reads chunks of input and processes them until the end of the file is reached. To read bytes from a file, it uses the read () system call (Figure 12–11).

System Call: ssize_t **read** (int *fd*, void* *buf*, size_t *count*)

[*Note*: This synopsis describes how read () operates when reading a regular file. For information on reading from special files, please refer to later sections of this chapter.]

read () copies *count* bytes from the file referenced by the file descriptor *fd* into the buffer *buf*. The bytes are read from the current file position, which is then updated accordingly.

read () copies as many bytes from the file as it can, up to the number specified by *count*, and returns the number of bytes actually copied. If a read () is attempted after the last byte has already been read, it returns 0, which indicates end-of-file.

If successful, read () returns the number of bytes that it read; otherwise, it returns -1.

Figure 12–11 Description of the read () system call.

The read () system call performs low-level input, and has none of the formatting capabilities of scanf (). The benefit of read () is that it bypasses the additional layer of buffering supplied by the C library functions, and is therefore very fast. Although I could have read one character of input at a time, this would have resulted in a large number of system calls, thus slowing down the execution of my program considerably. Instead, I used read () to read up to BUFFER_SIZE characters at a time. BUFFER_SIZE was chosen to be a multiple of the disk block size, for efficient copying. Lines 130..132 perform the read and test the return result:

```
130     charsRead = read (fd, buffer, BUFFER_SIZE);
131     if (charsRead == 0) break; /* EOF */
132     if (charsRead == -1) fatalError (); /* Error */
```

As each chunk of input is read, it is passed to the trackLines () function. This function scans the input buffer for newlines and stores the offset of the first character in each line in the *lineStart* array. The variable *fileOffset* is used to maintain the current file offset. The contents of *lineStart* are used during the second pass.

12.3.7   Writing to a File: write ()

When **reverse** is reading from standard input, it creates a copy of the input for use during pass two. To do this, it sets the file descriptor **tmpfd** to refer to a temporary file, and then writes each chunk of input to the file during the read loop. To write bytes to a file, it uses the write () system call (Figure 12–12).

System Call: ssize_t **write** (int *fd*, void* *buf*, size_t *count*)

[*Note*: This synopsis describes how write () operates when writing to a regular file. For information on writing to special files, please refer to later sections of this chapter.]

write () copies *count* bytes from a buffer *buf* to the file referenced by the file descriptor *fd*. The bytes are written at the current file position, which is then updated accordingly. If the O_APPEND flag was set for *fd*, the file position is set to the end of the file before each write.

write () copies as many bytes from the buffer as it can, up to the number specified by *count*, and returns the number of bytes actually copied. Your process should always check the return value. If the return value isn't *count*, then the disk probably filled up and no space was left.

If successful, write () returns the number of bytes that were written; otherwise, it returns -1.

Figure 12–12   Description of the write () system call.

The write () system call performs low-level output, and has none of the formatting capabilities of printf (). The benefit of write () is that it bypasses the additional layer of buffering supplied by the C library functions, and is therefore very fast. Lines 134..139 perform the write operation:

```
134     /* Copy line to temporary file if reading standard input */
135     if (standardInput)
136        {
137           charsWritten = write (tmpfd, buffer, charsRead);
```

```
138        if (charsWritten != charsRead) fatalError ();
139     }
```

12.3.8   Moving in a File: lseek ()

Once the first pass has completed, the array *lineStart* contains the offsets of the first character of each line of the input file. During pass two, the lines are read in reverse order and displayed to standard output. In order to read the lines out of sequence, the program makes use of lseek (), which is a system call that allows a descriptor's file pointer to be changed (Figure 12–13).

System Call: off_t **lseek** (int *fd*, off_t *offset*, int *mode*)

lseek () allows you to change a descriptor's current file position. *fd* is the file descriptor, offset is a long integer, and mode describes how *offset* should be interpreted. The three possible values of mode are defined in "/usr/include/stdio.h," and have the following meaning:

VALUE	MEANING
SEEK_SET	*offset* is relative to the start of the file.
SEEK_CUR	*offset* is relative to the current file position.
SEEK_END	*offset* is relative to the end of the file.

lseek () fails if you try to move before the start of the file.
    If successful, lseek () returns the current file position; otherwise, it returns -1.

Figure 12–13   Description of the lseek () system call.

Lines 196..197 seek to the start of a line and then read in all of its characters. Note that the number of characters to read is calculated by subtracting the start offset of the next line from the start offset of the current line.

```
196  lseek (fd, lineStart[i], SEEK_SET); /* Find line and read it */
197  charsRead = read (fd, buffer, lineStart[i+1] - lineStart[i]);
```

If you want to find out your current location without moving, use an offset value of zero relative to the current position:

```
currentOffset = lseek (fd, 0, SEEK_CUR);
```

If you move past the end of the file and then perform a write (), the kernel automatically extends the size of the file and treats the intermediate file area as if it were filled with NULL (ASCII 0) characters. Interestingly enough, it doesn't allocate disk space for the intermediate area, which is confirmed by the following example:

```
$ cat sparse.c                    ...list the test file.
#include <fcntl.h>
#include <stdio.h>
```

```
#include <stdlib.h>
/******************************************************/
main ()
{
 int i, fd;
  /* Create a sparse file */
 fd = open ("sparse.txt", O_CREAT | O_RDWR, 0600);
 write (fd, "sparse", 6);
 lseek (fd, 60006, SEEK_SET);
 write (fd, "file", 4);
 close (fd);
  /* Create a normal file */
 fd = open ("normal.txt", O_CREAT | O_RDWR, 0600);
 write (fd, "normal", 6);
 for (i = 1; i <= 60000; i++)
   write (fd, "/0", 1);
 write (fd, "file", 4);
 close (fd);
}
$ sparse                    ...execute the file.
$ ls -lG *.txt              ...look at the files.
-rw-r--r--   1 ables        60010 Aug 16 15:06 normal.txt
-rw-r--r--   1 ables        60010 Aug 16 15:06 sparse.txt
$ ls -s *.txt                   ...list their block usage.
  64 normal.txt    12 sparse.txt
$ _
```

Files that contain "gaps" like this are termed "sparse" files. For details on how they are actually stored, consult Chapter 13, "Linux Internals."

12.3.9   Closing a File: close ()

When pass two is over, reverse uses the close () system call to free the input file descriptor. Figure 12–14 gives a description of close ().

System Call: int **close** (int *fd*)

close () frees the file descriptor *fd*. If *fd* is the last file descriptor associated with a particular open file, the kernel resources associated with the file are deallocated. When a process terminates, all of its file descriptors are automatically closed, but it's better programming practice to close a file when you're done with it. If you close a file descriptor that's already closed, an error occurs.

   If successful, close () returns zero; otherwise, it returns -1.

Figure 12–14   Description of the close () system call.

Line 180 contains the call to close ():

```
180    close (fd); /* Close input file */
```

When a file is closed, it does not guarantee that the file's buffers are immediately flushed to disk. For more information on file buffering, consult Chapter 13, "Linux Internals."

12.3.10 Deleting a File: unlink ()

If **reverse** reads from standard input, it stores a copy of the input in a temporary file. At the end of pass two, it removes this file using the unlink () system call (Figure 12–15).

System Call: int **unlink** (const char* *fileName*)

unlink () removes the hard link from the name *fileName* to its file. If *fileName* is the last link to the file, the file's resources are deallocated. In this case, if any process's file descriptors are currently associated with the file, the directory entry is removed immediately but the file is only deallocated after all of the file descriptors are closed. This means that an executable file can unlink itself during execution and still continue to completion.

   If successful, unlink () returns zero; otherwise, it returns -1.

Figure 12–15   Description of the unlink () system call.

Line 181 contains the call to unlink ():

```
181    if (standardInput) unlink (tmpName); /* Remove temp file */
```

For more information about hard links, consult Chapter 13, "Linux Internals."

12.3.11 Second Example: monitor

This section provides a description of some more advanced system calls (Figure 12–16).

Name	Function
stat	Obtains status information about a file.
fstat	Works just like stat.
readdir	Obtains directory entries.

Figure 12–16   Advanced Linux I/O system calls.

These calls are demonstrated in the context of a program called "monitor," which allows a user to monitor a series of named files and obtain information whenever any of them are modified. Figure 12–17 describes **monitor**.

Utility: **monitor** [-t *delay*] [-l *count*]{ *fileName* }+

monitor scans all of the specified files every *delay* seconds and displays information about any of the specified files that were modified since the last scan. If *fileName* is a directory, all of the files inside that directory are scanned. File modification is indicated in one of three ways:

LABEL	MEANING
ADDED	Indicates that the file was created since the last scan. Every file in the file list is given this label during the first scan.
CHANGED	Indicates that the file was modified since the last scan.
DELETED	Indicates that the file was deleted since the last scan.

By default, **monitor** will scan forever, although you can specify the total number of scans by using the **-l** option. The default delay time is 10 seconds between scans, although this may be overridden by using the **-t** option.

Figure 12–17   Description of the **monitor** program.

In the following example, I monitored a directory, storing the output of monitor into a temporary file. Notice how the contents of the "monitor.out" file reflected the additions, modifications, and deletions in the monitored directory:

```
% mkdir tmp
% ./monitor tmp >& monitor.out &
[1] 15771
% cat >tmp/a                    ...create a file in ./tmp.
hi there
^D
% cat tmp/a tmp/b               ...and another.
% vim tmp/b                     ...change one.
...
% cat >tmp/file.txt             ...create one more.
more data
^D
% rm tmp/a                      ...then remove them.
% rm tmp/b
% jobs
```

```
[1]   + Running              ./monitor tmp >& monitor.out
% kill %1                      ...kill monitor.
%
[1]      Terminated          ./monitor tmp >& monitor.out
%
% cat monitor.out
ADDED tmp/a size 9bytes, mod. time = Sun Aug 29 17:47:10 2004
ADDED tmp/b size 9 bytes, mod. time = Sun Aug 29 17:47:18 2004
CHANGED tmp/b size 9 bytes, mod. time = Sun Aug 29 17:47:41 2004
ADDED tmp/file.txt size 10 bytes, mod. time = Sun Aug 29 17:47:52 2004
DELETED tmp/a
DELETED tmp/b
% _
```

12.3.12 How monitor Works

The **monitor** utility continually scans the specified files and directories for modifications. It uses the stat () system call to obtain status information about named files, including their type and last modification time, and uses the readdir () system call to scan directories. It maintains a status table called **stats**, which holds the following information about each file that it finds:

- the name of the file
- the status information obtained by the stat ()
- a record of whether the file was present during the present scan and the previous scan

During a scan, **monitor** processes each file as follows:

- If the file isn't currently in the scan table, it's added and the message "ADDED" is displayed.
- If the file is already in the scan table and has been modified since the last scan, the message "CHANGED" is displayed.

At the end of a scan, all entries that were present during the previous scan but not during the current scan are removed from the table and the message "DELETED" is displayed.

Following is a complete listing of "monitor.c", the source code of **monitor**. I suggest that you skim through it and then read the descriptions of the system calls that follow.

12.3.13 Monitor.c: Listing

```
1 #include <stdio.h>           /* For printf, fprintf */
2 #include <string.h>          /* For strcmp */
3 #include <ctype.h>           /* For isdigit */
4 #include <fcntl.h>           /* For O_RDONLY */
5 #include <dirent.h>          /* For readdir */
6 #include <sys/stat.h>        /* For IS macros */
7 #include <sys/types.h>       /* For modet */
8 #include <time.h>            /* For localtime, asctime */
9
```

```
10
11 /* #define Statements */
12 #define MAX_FILES            100
13 #define MAX_FILENAME         50
14 #define NOT_FOUND            -1
15 #define FOREVER              -1
16 #define DEFAULT_DELAY_TIME   10
17 #define DEFAULT_LOOP_COUNT   FOREVER
18
19
20 /* Booleans */
21 enum { FALSE, TRUE };
22
23
24 /* Status structure, one per file. */
25 struct statStruct
26 {
27   char fileName [MAX_FILENAME]; /* File name */
28   int lastCycle, thisCycle; /* To detect changes */
29   struct stat status; /* Information from stat () */
30 };
31
32
33 /* Globals */
34 char* fileNames [MAX_FILES]; /* One per file on command line */
35 int fileCount; /* Count of files on command line */
36 struct statStruct stats [MAX_FILES]; /* One per matching file */
37 int loopCount = DEFAULT_LOOP_COUNT; /* Number of times to loop */
38 int delayTime = DEFAULT_DELAY_TIME; /* Seconds between loops */
39
40 /******************************************************************/
41
42 main (argc, argv)
43
44 int argc;
45 char* argv [];
46
47 {
48   parseCommandLine (argc, argv); /* Parse command line */
49   monitorLoop (); /* Execute main monitor loop */
50   return (/* EXIT_SUCCESS */ 0);
51 }
52
53 /******************************************************************/
54
```

```
55 parseCommandLine (argc, argv)
56
57 int argc;
58 char* argv [];
59
60 /* Parse command-line arguments */
61
62 {
63   int i;
64
65   for (i = 1; ( (i < argc) && (i < MAX_FILES) ); i++)
66     {
67       if (argv[i][0] == '-')
68         processOptions (argv[i]);
69       else
70         fileNames[fileCount++] = argv[i];
71     }
72
73   if (fileCount == 0) usageError ();
74 }
75
76 /*****************************************************************/
77
78 processOptions (str)
79
80 char* str;
81
82 /* Parse options */
83
84 {
85   int j;
86
87   for (j = 1; str[j] != 0; j++)
88     {
89       switch(str[j]) /* Switch on option letter */
90         {
91           case 't':
92             delayTime = getNumber (str, &j);
93             break;
94
95           case 'l':
96             loopCount = getNumber (str, &j);
97             break;
98         }
99     }
```

```
100 }
101
102 /****************************************************************/
103
104 getNumber (str, i)
105
106 char* str;
107 int* i;
108
109 /* Convert a numeric ASCII option to a number */
110
111 {
112     int number = 0;
113     int digits = 0; /* Count the digits in the number */
114
115     while (isdigit (str[(*i) + 1])) /* Convert chars to ints */
116       {
117         number = number * 10 + str[++(*i)] - '0';
118         ++digits;
119       }
120
121     if (digits == 0) usageError (); /* There must be a number */
122     return (number);
123 }
124
125 /****************************************************************/
126
127 usageError ()
128
129 {
130     fprintf (stderr, "Usage: monitor -t<seconds> -l<loops> {filename}+\n");
131     exit (/* EXIT_FAILURE */ 1);
132 }
133
134 /****************************************************************/
135
136 monitorLoop ()
137
138 /* The main monitor loop */
139
140 {
141     do
142       {
143         monitorFiles (); /* Scan all files */
144         fflush (stdout); /* Flush standard output */
```

```
145            fflush (stderr); /* Flush standard error */
146            sleep (delayTime); /* Wait until next loop */
147         }
148     while (loopCount == FOREVER || --loopCount > 0);
149 }
150
151 /*****************************************************************/
152
153 monitorFiles ()
154
155 /* Process all files */
156
157 {
158     int i;
159
160     for (i = 0; i < fileCount; i++)
161       monitorFile (fileNames[i]);
162
163     for (i = 0; i< MAX_FILES; i++) /* Update stat array */
164        {
165          if (stats[i].lastCycle && !stats[i].thisCycle)
166            printf ("DELETED %s\n", stats[i].fileName);
167
168          stats[i].lastCycle = stats[i].thisCycle;
169          stats[i].thisCycle = FALSE;
170        }
171 }
172
173 /*****************************************************************/
174
175 monitorFile (fileName)
176
177 char* fileName;
178
179 /* Process a single file/directory*/
180
181 {
182     struct stat statBuf;
183     mode_t mode;
184     int result;
185
186     result = stat (fileName, &statBuf); /* Obtain file status */
187
188     if (result == -1) /* Status was not available */
```

```
189        {
190          fprintf (stderr, "Cannot stat %s\n", fileName);
191          return;
192        }
193
194     mode = statBuf.st_mode; /* Mode of file */
195
196     if(S_ISDIR (mode)) /* Directory */
197        processDirectory (fileName);
198     else if (S_ISREG (mode) || S_ISCHR (mode) || S_ISBLK (mode))
199        updateStat (fileName, &statBuf); /* Regular file */
200 }
201
202 /****************************************************************/
203
204 processDirectory (dirName)
205
206 char* dirName;
207
208 /* Process all files in the named directory */
209
210 {
211     struct dirent *dirEntry;
212     DIR *dp;
213     char fileName [MAX_FILENAME];
214
215     if ((dp = opendir(dirName)) == NULL ) {
216             fatalError ();
217     }
218
219     dirEntry = readdir(dp);
220
221     while ( dirEntry != NULL ) /* Read all directory entries */
222       {
223         if (strcmp (dirEntry->d_name, ".") != 0&&
224             strcmp (dirEntry->d_name, "..") != 0) /* Skip . and .. */
225           {
226             sprintf (fileName, "%s/%s", dirName, dirEntry->d_name);
227             monitorFile (fileName); /* Call recursively */
228           }
229
230         dirEntry = readdir(dp);
231       }
232
233     closedir(dp);
```

```
234 }
235
236 /****************************************************************/
237
238 updateStat (fileName, statBuf)
239
240 char* fileName;
241 struct stat* statBuf;
242
243 /* Add a status entry if necessary */
244
245 {
246    int entryIndex;
247
248    entryIndex = findEntry (fileName); /* Find existing entry */
249
250    if (entryIndex == NOT_FOUND)
251      entryIndex = addEntry (fileName, statBuf); /* Add new entry */
252    else
253      updateEntry (entryIndex, statBuf); /* Update existing entry */
254
255    if (entryIndex != NOT_FOUND)
256      stats[entryIndex].thisCycle = TRUE; /* Update status array */
257 }
258
259 /****************************************************************/
260
261 findEntry (fileName)
262
263 char* fileName;
264
265 /* Locate the index of a named filein the status array */
266
267 {
268    int i;
269
270    for (i = 0; i < MAX_FILES; i++)
271      if (stats[i].lastCycle &&
272          strcmp (stats[i].fileName, fileName) == 0) return (i);
273
274    return (NOT_FOUND);
275 }
276
277 /****************************************************************/
278
279 addEntry (fileName, statBuf)
```

```
280
281 char* fileName;
282 struct stat* statBuf;
283
284 /* Add a new entry into the status array */
285
286 {
287     int index;
288
289     index = nextFree (); /* Find the next free entry */
290     if (index == NOT_FOUND) return (NOT_FOUND); /* None left */
291     strcpy (stats[index].fileName, fileName); /* Add filename */
292     stats[index].status = *statBuf; /* Add status information */
293     printf ("ADDED "); /* Notify standard output */
294     printEntry (index); /* Display status information */
295     return (index);
296 }
297
298 /***************************************************************/
299
300 nextFree ()
301
302 /* Return the nextfree index in the status array */
303
304 {
305     int i;
306
307     for (i = 0; i < MAX_FILES; i++)
308         if (!stats[i].lastCycle && !stats[i].thisCycle) return (i);
309
310     return (NOT_FOUND);
311 }
312
313 /***************************************************************/
314
315 updateEntry (index, statBuf)
316
317 int index;
318 struct stat* statBuf;
319
320 /*Display information if the file has been modified */
321
322 {
323     if (stats[index].status.st_mtime != statBuf->st_mtime)
324         {
```

```
325            stats[index].status = *statBuf; /* Store stat information */
326            printf ("CHANGED "); /* Notify standard output */
327            printEntry (index);
328        }
329 }
330
331 /*****************************************************************/
332
333 printEntry (index)
334
335 int index;
336
337 /* Display an entry of the status array */
338
339 {
340    printf ("%s ", stats[index].fileName);
341    printStat (&stats[index].status);
342 }
343
344 /*****************************************************************/
345
346 printStat (statBuf)
347
348 struct stat* statBuf;
349
350 /* Display a status buffer */
351
352 {
353    printf ("size %lu bytes, mod. time = %s", statBuf->st_size,
354                asctime (localtime (&statBuf->st_mtime)));
355 }
356
357 /*****************************************************************/
358
359 fatalError ()
360
361 {
362    perror ("monitor: ");
363    exit (/* EXIT_FAILURE */ 1);
364 }
```

12.3.14 Obtaining File Information: stat ()

monitor obtains its file information by calling stat () (Figure 12–18).

System Call: int **stat** (const char* *name*, struct stat* *buf*)

      int **lstat** (const char* *name*, struct stat* *buf*)

      int **fstat** (int *fd*, struct stat* *buf*)

stat () fills the buffer *buf* with information about the file *name*. The **stat** structure is defined in "/usr/include/sys/stat.h". lstat () returns information about a symbolic link itself rather than the file it references. fstat () performs the same function as stat (), except that it takes the file descriptor of the file to be stat'ed as its first parameter. The **stat** structure contains the following members:

NAME	MEANING
st_dev	the device number
st_ino	the inode number
st_mode	the permission flags
st_nlink	the hard link count
st_uid	the user ID
st_gid	the group ID
st_size	the file size
st_atime	the last access time
st_mtime	the last modification time
st_ctime	the last status change time

There are some predefined macros defined in "/usr/include/sys/stat.h" that take **st_mode** as their argument and return true (1) for the following file types:

MACRO	RETURNS TRUE FOR FILE TYPE
S_ISDIR	directory
S_ISCHR	character-oriented special device
S_ISBLK	block-oriented special device
S_ISREG	regular file
S_ISFIFO	pipe

The time fields may be decoded using the standard C library asctime () and localtime () subroutines.

     stat () and fstat () return 0 if successful and -1 otherwise.

Figure 12–18 Description of the stat () system call.

The **monitor** utility invokes stat () from monitorFile () [175] on line 186:

```
186    result = stat (fileName, &statBuf); /* Obtain file status */
```

It examines the mode of the file using the S_ISDIR, S_ISREG, S_ISCHR, and S_ISBLK macros, processing directory files and other files as follows:

- If the file is a directory file, it calls processDirectory () [204], which applies monitorFile () recursively to each of its directory entries.
- If the file is a regular file, character-oriented special file, or block-oriented special file, it calls updateStat () [238], which either adds or updates the file's status entry. If the status changes in any way, updateEntry () [315] is called to display the file's new status. The decoding of the time fields is performed by the localtime () and asctime () routines in printStat () [346].

12.3.15 Reading Directory Information: opendir (), readdir (), and closedir ()

processDirectory () [204] opens a directory file with opendir () and then uses readdir () to obtain every entry in the directory (Figure 12–19).

Library Function: DIR * **opendir** (char * *fileName*)
      struct dirent * **readdir** (DIR **dir*)
      int **closedir** (DIR **dir*)

opendir () opens a directory file for reading and returns a pointer to a stream descriptor which is used as the argument to readdir () and closedir (). readdir () returns a pointer to a **dirent** structure containing information about the next directory entry each time it is called. closedir () is used to close the directory. The **dirent** structure is defined in the system header file "/usr/include/dirent.h"

NAME	MEANING
d_ino	the inode number
d_off	the offset of the next directory entry
d_reclen	the length of the directory entry structure
d_name	the filename

opendir () returns the directory stream pointer when successful, NULL when not successful. readdir () returns 1 when a directory entry has been successfully read, 0 when the last directory entry has already been read, and -1 in the case of an error. closedir () returns 0 on success, -1 on failure.

Figure 12–19 Description of the opendir (), readdir (), and closedir () library functions.

processDirectory () is careful not to trace into the "." and ".." directories. When the directory has been completely searched, it is closed.

12.3.16 Miscellaneous File Management System Calls

There now follows a brief description of the following miscellaneous file management system calls (Figure 12–20).

Name	Function
chown	Changes a file's owner and/or group.
chmod	Changes a file's permission settings.
dup	Duplicates a file descriptor.
dup2	Similar to dup.
fchown	Works just like chown.
fchmod	Works just like chmod.
fcntl	Gives access to miscellaneous file characteristics.
ftruncate	Works just like truncate.
ioctl	Controls a device.
link	Creates a hard link.
mknod	Creates a special file.
sync	Schedules all file buffers to be flushed to disk.
truncate	Truncates a file.

Figure 12–20 Linux file management system calls.

12.3.17 Changing a File's Owner and/or Group: chown ()

chown () changes the owner and/or group of a file (Figure 12–21).

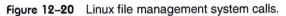

> *System Call*: int **chown** (const char* *fileName*, uid_t *ownerId*, gid_t *groupId*)
>   int **lchown** (const char* *fileName*, uid_t *ownerId*, gid_t *groupId*)
>   int **fchown** (int *fd*, uid_t *ownerId*, gid_t *groupId*)
>
> chown () causes the owner and group IDs of *fileName* to be changed to *ownerId* and *groupId*, respectively. A value of -1 in a particular field means that its associated value should remain unchanged.
>
>   Only a super-user can change the ownership of a file, and a user may change the group only to another group that he/she is a member of. If *fileName* is a symbolic link, the owner and group of the link are changed instead of the file that the link is referencing.
>
>   fchown () is just like chown () except that it takes an open descriptor as an argument instead of a filename.
>
>   lchown () changes the ownership of a symbolic link itself rather than the file the link references.
>
>   They both return -1 if unsuccessful, and 0 otherwise.

Figure 12–21   Description of the chown () system call.

In the following example, I changed the group of the file "test.txt" from "music" to "cs," which has group ID number 62. For more information about group IDs and how to locate them, consult Chapter 14, "System Administration."

```
$ cat mychown.c                  ...list the file.
main ()
{
 int flag;
 flag = chown ("test.txt", -1, 62); /* Leave user ID unchanged */
 if (flag == -1) perror("mychown.c");
}
$ ls -l test.txt                 ...examine file before.
-rw-r--r--  1 glass     music      3 May 25 11:42 test.txt
$ ./mychown                      ...run program.
$ ls -l test.txt                 ...examine file after.
-rw-r--r--  1 glass     cs         3 May 25 11:42 test.txt
$ _
```

12.3.18 Changing a File's Permissions: chmod ()

The system call chmod () changes a file's permission flags (Figure 12–22).

System Call: int **chmod** (const char* *fileName*, int *mode*)
     int **fchmod** (int *fd*, mode_t *mode*);

chmod () changes the mode of *fileName* to *mode*, where *mode* is usually supplied as an octal number as described in Chapter 3, "GNU Utilities for Nonprogrammers." The "set user ID" and "set group ID" flags have the octal values 4000 and 2000, respectively. To change a file's mode, you must either own it or be a super-user.
     fchmod () works just like chmod () except that it takes an open file descriptor as an argument instead of a filename.
     They both return -1 if unsuccessful, and 0 otherwise.

Figure 12-22   Description of the chmod () system call.

In the following example, I changed the permission flags of the file "test.txt" to 600 octal, which corresponds to read and write permission for the owner only:

```
$ cat mychmod.c               ...list the file.
main ()
{
 int flag;
 flag = chmod ("test.txt", 0600); /* Use an octal encoding */
 if (flag == -1) perror ("mychmod.c");
}
$ ls -lG test.txt             ...examine file before.
-rw-r--r--  1 glass           3 May 25 11:42 test.txt
$ ./mychmod                   ...run the program.
$ ls -lG test.txt             ...examine file after.
-rw-------  1 glass           3 May 25 11:42 test.txt
$ _
```

12.3.19 Duplicating a File Descriptor: dup ()
The system call dup () allows you to duplicate file descriptors (Figure 12-23).

System Call: int **dup** (int *oldFd*)
     int **dup2** (int *oldFd*, int *newFd*)

dup () finds the smallest free file descriptor entry and points it to the same file as *oldFd*. dup2 () closes *newFd* if it's currently active and then points it to the same file as *oldFd*. In both cases, the original and copied file descriptors share the same file pointer and access mode.
     They both return the index of the new file descriptor if successful, and -1 otherwise.

Figure 12-23   Description of the dup () system call.

The shells use dup2 () to perform redirection and piping. For examples that show how this is done, see "Process Management" on page 473.

In the following example, I created a file called "test.txt" and wrote to it via four different file descriptors:

- The first file descriptor was the original descriptor.
- The second descriptor was a copy of the first, allocated in slot 4.
- The third descriptor was a copy of the first, allocated in slot 0 that was freed by the close (0) statement (the standard input channel).
- The fourth descriptor was a copy of descriptor 3, copied over the existing descriptor in slot 2 (the standard error channel).

```
$ cat mydup.c                   ...list the file.
#include <stdio.h>
#include <fcntl.h>
main ()
{
 int fd1, fd2, fd3;
  fd1 = open ("test.txt", O_RDWR | O_TRUNC);
 printf ("fd1 = %d\n", fd1);
 write (fd1, "what's", 6);
  fd2 = dup (fd1); /* Make a copy of fd1 */
 printf ("fd2 = %d\n", fd2);
 write (fd2, " up", 3);
  close (0); /* Close standard input */
 fd3 = dup (fd1); /* Make another copy of fd1 */
 printf ("fd3 = %d\n", fd3);
 write (0, " doc", 4);
  dup2 (3, 2); /* Duplicate channel 3 to channel 2 */
 write (2, "?\n", 2);
}
$ ./mydup               ...run the program.
fd1 = 3
fd2 = 4
fd3 = 0
$ cat test.txt          ...list the output file.
what's up doc?
$ _
```

12.3.20 File Descriptor Operations: fcntl ()

The system call fcntl () directly controls the settings of the flags associated with a file descriptor (Figure 12–24).

System Call: int **fcntl** (int *fd*, int *cmd*, int *arg*)

fcntl () performs the operation encoded by *cmd* on the file associated with the file descriptor *fd*. *arg* is an optional argument for *cmd*. Here are the most common values of *cmd*:

VALUE	OPERATION
F_SETFD	Set the close-on-exec flag to the lowest bit of *arg* (0 or 1).
F_GETFD	Return a number whose lowest bit is 1 if the close-on-exec flag is set, and 0 otherwise.
F_GETFL	Return a number corresponding to the current file status flags and access modes.
F_SETFL	Set the current file status flags to *arg*.
F_GETOWN	Return the process ID or process group that is currently set to receive SIGIO/SIGURG signals. If the returned value is positive, it refers to a process ID. If it's negative, its absolute value refers to a process group.
F_SETOWN	Set the process ID or process group that should receive SIGIO/SIGURG signals to *arg*. The encoding scheme is as described for F_GETOWN.

fcntl () returns -1 if unsuccessful.

Figure 12-24   Description of the fcntl () system call.

In the following example, I opened an existing file for writing and overwrote the initial few letters with the phrase "hi there." I then used fcntl () to set the file descriptor's APPEND flag, which instructed it to append all further writes. This caused "guys" to be placed at the end of the file, even though I moved the file position pointer back to the start with lseek ():

```
$ cat myfcntl.c                  ...list the program.
#include <stdio.h>
#include <fcntl.h>
main ()
{
 int fd;
 fd = open ("test.txt", O_WRONLY); /* Open file for writing */
write (fd, "hi there\n", 9);
 lseek (fd, 0, SEEK_SET); /* Seek to beginning of file */
fcntl (fd, F_SETFL, O_WRONLY | O_APPEND); /* Set APPEND flag */
```

```
write (fd, " guys\n", 6);
close (fd);
}
```
```
$ cat test.txt              ...list the original file.
here are the contents of
the original file.
$ ./myfcnt1                 ...run the program.
$ cat test.txt              ...list the new contents.
hi there
the contents of
the original file.
guys                        ...note that "guys" is at the end.
$ _
```

12.3.21 Controlling Devices: ioctl ()

Figure 12–25 describes the ioctl () system call.

System Call: int **ioctl** (int *fd*, int *cmd*, int *arg*)

ioctl () performs the operation encoded by *cmd* on the file associated with the file descriptor *fd*. *arg* is an optional argument for *cmd*. The valid values of *cmd* depend on the device that *fd* refers to, and are typically documented in the manufacturer's operating instructions. I therefore supply no examples for this system call.

    ioctl () returns -1 if unsuccessful.

Figure 12–25   Description of the ioctl () system call.

12.3.22 Creating Hard Links: link ()

The system call link () creates a hard link to an existing file (Figure 12–26).

System Call: int **link** (const char* *oldPath*, const char* *newPath*)

link () creates a new label *newPath* and links it to the same file as the label *oldPath*. The hard link count of the associated file is incremented by one. If *oldPath* and *newPath* reside on different physical devices, a hard link cannot be made and link () fails. For more information about hard links, consult the description of **ln** in Chapter 4, "GNU Utilities for Power Users."

    link () returns -1 if unsuccessful, and 0 otherwise.

Figure 12–26   Description of the link () system call.

In the following example, I created the filename "another.txt" and linked it to the file referenced by the existing name "original.txt". I then demonstrated that both labels were linked to the same file.

```
$ cat mylink.c                     ...list the program.
main ()
{
 link ("original.txt", "another.txt");
}
$ cat original.txt                 ...list original file.
this is a file.
$ ls -lG original.txt another.txt     ...examine files before.
another.txt not found
-rw-r--r--  1 glass             16 May 25 12:18 original.txt
$ ./mylink                         ...run the program.
$ ls -lG original.txt another.txt     ...examine files after.
-rw-r--r--  2 glass             16 May 25 12:18 another.txt
-rw-r--r--  2 glass             16 May 25 12:18 original.txt
$ cat >> another.txt               ...alter "another.txt".
hi
^D
$ ls -lG original.txt another.txt     ...both labels reflect change.
-rw-r--r--  2 glass             20 May 25 12:19 another.txt
-rw-r--r--  2 glass             20 May 25 12:19 original.txt
$ rm original.txt              ...remove original label.
$ ls -lG original.txt another.txt     ...examine labels.
original.txt not found
-rw-r--r--  1 glass             20 May 25 12:19 another.txt
$ cat another.txt         ...list contents via other label.
this is a file.
hi
$ _
```

12.3.23 Creating Special Files: mknod (), mkdir (), and mkfifo ()

The system call mknod () allows you to create a special file, mkdir () allows you to create a directory, and they work as described in Figure 12–27.

System Call: int **mknod** (const char* *fileName*, mode_t *type*, dev_t *device*)

int **mkdir** (const char* *fileName*, mode_t *mode*)

mknod () creates a new regular, directory, or special file called *fileName* whose type can be one of the following:

VALUE	MEANING
S_IFDIR	directory
S_IFCHR	character-oriented special file
S_IFBLK	block-oriented special file
S_IFREG	regular file
S_IFIFO	named pipe

Only a super-user can use mknod () to create directories or special files.

mkdir () creates a directory with permission setting created by a logical AND of *mode* with the process's current umask setting.

It is now typical to use the mkdir () system call to create directories and mkfifo () (see below) to make named pipes rather than mknod ().

Both mknod () and mkdir () return -1 if unsuccessful, and 0 otherwise.

Figure 12–27 Description of the mknod () and mkdir () system calls.

While it is possible to create a named pipe with mknod (), Linux provides the more specialized library function mkfifo () for this purpose (Figure 12–28).

Library Function: int **mkfifo** (const char* *fileName*, mode_t *mode*)

mkfifo () creates a named pipe called *fileName* with permission setting created by a logical AND of *mode* with the process's current umask setting.

Figure 12–28 Description of the mkfifo () library function.

12.3.24 Flushing the File System Buffer: sync ()

The system call sync () flushes the file system buffers (Figure 12–29).

System Call: void **sync** ()

sync () schedules all of the file system buffers to be written to disk. For more information on the buffer system, consult Chapter 13, "Linux Internals." sync () should be performed by any programs that bypass the file system buffers and examine the raw file system.

      sync () always succeeds.

Figure 12–29 Description of the sync () system call.

12.3.25 Truncating a File: truncate ()

The system call truncate () sets the length of a file (Figure 12–30).

System Call: int **truncate** (const char* *fileName*, off_t *length*)
        int **ftruncate** (int *fd*, off_t *length*)

truncate () sets the length of the file *fileName* to be *length* bytes. If the file is longer than *length*, it is truncated. If it is shorter than *length*, it is padded with ASCII nulls.

      ftruncate () works just like truncate () except that it takes an open file descriptor as an argument instead of a filename.

      They both return -1 if unsuccessful, and 0 otherwise.

Figure 12–30 Description of the truncate () system call.

    In the following example, I set the length of two files to 10 bytes; one of the files was originally shorter than that, and the other was longer:

```
$ cat truncate.c               ...list the program.
main ()
{
 truncate ("file1.txt", 10);
 truncate ("file2.txt", 10);
}
$ cat file1.txt                ...list "file1.txt".
short
$ cat file2.txt                ...list "file2.txt".
```

```
long file with lots of letters

$ ls -lG file*.txt               ...examine both files.
-rw-r--r--  1 glass          6 May 25 12:16 file1.txt
-rw-r--r--  1 glass         32 May 25 12:17 file2.txt
$ ./truncate                     ...run the program.
$ ls -lG file*.txt               ...examine both files again.
-rw-r--r--  1 glass         10 May 25 12:16 file1.txt
-rw-r--r--  1 glass         10 May 25 12:17 file2.txt
$ cat file1.txt                  ..."file1.txt" is longer.
short
$ cat file2.txt                  ..."file2.txt" is shorter.
long file $ _
```

12.4 Process Management

A Linux process is a unique instance of a running or runable program. Every process in a Linux system has the following attributes:

- some code (a.k.a. text)
- some data
- a stack
- a unique process ID number (PID)

When Linux is first started, there's only one visible process in the system. This process is called "init," and is PID 1. The only way to create a new process in Linux is to duplicate an existing process, so "init" is the ancestor of all subsequent processes. When a process duplicates, the parent and child processes are virtually identical (except for things like PIDs, PPIDs, and runtimes); the child's code, data, and stack are a copy of the parent's, and they even continue to execute the same code. A child process may, however, replace its code with that of another executable file, thereby differentiating itself from its parent. When a child process terminates, its death is communicated to its parent so that the parent may take some appropriate action.

It's very common for a parent process to suspend until one of its children terminates. For example, when a shell executes a utility in the foreground, it duplicates into two shell processes; the child shell process replaces its code with that of the utility, whereas the parent shell waits for the child process to terminate. When the child terminates, the original parent process awakens and presents the user with the next shell prompt.

Figure 12–31 illustates the way that a shell executes a utility; I've indicated the system calls that are responsible for each phase of the execution.

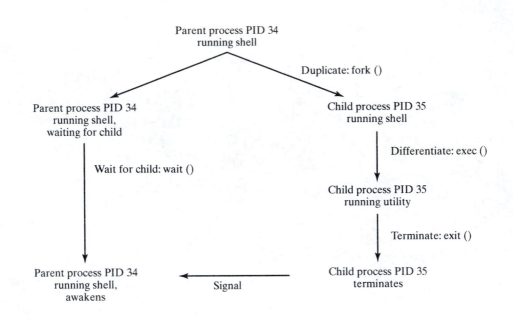

Figure 12-31 How a shell runs a utility.

Let's look at some simple programs that introduce the system calls one by one. The next few subsections describe the system calls listed in Figure 12–32.

Name	Function
fork	Duplicates a process.
getpid	Obtains a process's ID number.
getppid	Obtains a parent process's ID number.
exit	Terminates a process.
wait	Waits for a child process.
exec..	Replaces the code, data, and stack of a process.

Figure 12-32 Linux process-oriented system calls.

12.4.1 Creating a New Process: fork ()
A process may duplicate itself by using fork () (Figure 12–33).

System Call: pid_t **fork** (void)

fork () causes a process to duplicate. The child process is an almost-exact duplicate of the original parent process; it inherits a copy of its parent's code, data, stack, open file descriptors, and signal table. However, the parent and child have different process ID numbers and parent process ID numbers.

   If fork () succeeds, it returns the PID of the child to the parent process, and returns 0 to the child process. If it fails, it returns -1 to the parent process, and no child is created.

Figure 12–33   Description of the fork () system call.

fork () is a strange system call, because one process (the original) calls it, but two processes (the original and its child) return from it. Both processes continue to run the same code concurrently, but they have completely separate stack and data spaces.

   This reminds me of a great sci-fi story I read once, about a man who comes across a fascinating booth at a circus. The vendor at the booth tells the man that the booth is a matter-replicator; anyone who walks through the booth is duplicated. The original person walks out of the booth unharmed, but the duplicate person walks out onto the surface of Mars as a slave of the Martian construction crews. The vendor then tells the man that he'll be given a million dollars if he allows himself to be replicated, and he agrees. He happily walks through the machine, looking forward to collecting the million dollars ... and walks out onto the surface of Mars. Meanwhile, back on Earth, his duplicate is walking off with a stash of cash. The question is this: If you came across the booth, what would you do?

   Linux adds a clone () system call that is, for most uses, the same as fork (). clone () provides for parts of the execution context to be shared (rather than merely copied as with fork ()) between parent and child.

   A process may obtain its own process ID and parent process ID numbers by using the getpid () and getppid () system calls, respectively (Figure 12–34).

System Call: pid_t **getpid** (void)
      pid_t **getppid** (void)

getpid () and getppid () return a process's ID and parent process's ID numbers, respectively. They always succeed. The parent process ID number of PID 1 is 1.

Figure 12–34   Description of the getpid () and getppid () system calls.

To illustrate the operation of fork (), here's a small program that duplicates and then branches based on the return value of fork ():

```
$ cat myfork.c                    ...list the program.
#include <stdio.h>
main ()
{
 int pid;
 printf ("I'm the original process with PID %d and PPID %d.\n",
         getpid (), getppid ());
 pid = fork (); /* Duplicate. Child and parent continue from here */
 if (pid != 0) /* pid is non-zero, so I must be the parent */
   {
     printf ("I'm the parent process with PID %d and PPID %d.\n",
             getpid (), getppid ());
     printf ("My child's PID is %d\n", pid);
   }
 else /* pid is zero, so I must be the child */
   {
     printf ("I'm the child process with PID %d and PPID %d.\n",
             getpid (), getppid ());
   }
 printf ("PID %d terminates.\n", getpid () ); /* Both processes
execute this */
}
$ ./myfork                        ...run the program.
I'm the original process with PID 13292 and PPID 13273.
I'm the parent process with PID 13292 and PPID 13273.
My child's PID is 13293.
I'm the child process with PID 13293 and PPID 13292.
PID 13293 terminates.          ...child terminates.
PID 13292 terminates.          ...parent terminates.
$ _
```

The PPID of the parent refers to the PID of the shell that executed the "myfork" program.

Here is a warning: As you will soon see, it is dangerous for a parent to terminate without waiting for the death of its child. The only reason that the parent doesn't wait for its child in this example is because I haven't yet described the wait () system call!

12.4.2   Orphan Processes

If a parent dies before its child, the child is automatically adopted by the original "init" process, PID 1. To illustrate this, I modified the previous program by inserting a sleep statement into the child's code. This ensured that the parent process terminated before the child.

Here's the program and the resultant output:

```
$ cat orphan.c                    ...list the program.
#include <stdio.h>
```

```
main ()
{
  int pid;
   printf ("I'm the original process with PID %d and PPID %d.\n",
         getpid (), getppid ());
  pid = fork (); /* Duplicate. Child and parent continue from here */
  if (pid != 0) /* Branch based on return value from fork () */
     {
        /* pid is nonzero, so I must be the parent */
        printf ("I'm the parent process with PID %d and PPID %d.\n",
              getpid (), getppid ());
        printf ("My child's PID is %d\n", pid);
     }
  else
     {
        /* pid is zero, so I must be the child */
        sleep (5); /* Make sure that the parent terminates first */
        printf ("I'm the child process with PID %d and PPID %d.\n",
              getpid (), getppid ());
     }
   printf ("PID %d terminates.\n", getpid () ); /* Both processes
execute this */
}
$ ./orphan                    ...run the program.
I'm the original process with PID 13364 and PPID 13346.
I'm the parent process with PID 13364 and PPID 13346.
PID 13364 terminates.
I'm the child process with PID 13365 and PPID 1.    ...orphaned!
PID 13365 terminates.
$ _
```

Figure 12–35 illustrates the orphaning effect:

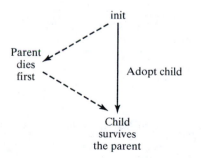

Figure 12–35 Process adoption.

12.4.3   Terminating a Process: exit ()

A process may terminate at any time by executing exit () (Figure 12–36).

System Call: void **exit** (int *status*)

exit () closes all of a process's file descriptors, deallocates its code, data, and stack, and then terminates the process. When a child process terminates, it sends its parent a SIGCHLD signal and waits for its termination code *status* to be accepted. Only the lower eight bits of *status* are used, so values are limited to 0–255. A process that is waiting for its parent to accept its return code is called a *zombie* process. A parent accepts a child's termination code by executing wait (), which is described shortly.

    The kernel ensures that all of a terminating process's children are orphaned and adopted by "init" by setting their PPID to 1. The "init" process always accepts its children's termination codes.

      exit () never returns.

Figure 12–36   Description of the exit () system call.

    The termination code of a child process may be used for a variety of purposes by the parent process. Shells may access the termination code of their last child process via one of their special variables. For example, the C shell stores the termination code of the last command in the variable $status:

```
% cat myexit.c                    ...list the program.
#include <stdio.h>
main ()
{
 printf ("I'm going to exit with return code 42\n");
 exit (42);
}
% ./myexit                        ...run the program.
I'm going to exit with return code 42
% echo $status                    ...display the termination code.
42
% _
```

In all other shells, the return value is returned in the special shell variable $?.

12.4.4   Zombie Processes

A process that terminates cannot leave the system until its parent accepts its return code. If its parent process is already dead, it will already have been adopted by the "init" process, which always accepts its children's return codes. However, if a process's parent is alive but never executes a wait (), the process's return code will never be accepted and the process will remain a zombie. A zombie process doesn't have any code, data, or stack, so it doesn't use up many system resources, but it does continue to inhabit the system's task list. Too many zombie processes can require the system administrator to intervene; see Chapter 14, "System Administration," for more details.

The following program created a zombie process, which was indicated in the output from the **ps** utility. When I killed the parent process, the child was adopted by "init" and allowed to rest in peace.

```
$ cat zombie.c              ...list the program.
#include <stdio.h>
main ()
{
  int pid;
  pid = fork (); /* Duplicate */
  if (pid != 0) /* Branch based on return value from fork () */
    {
      while (1)  /* Never terminate, and never execute a wait () */
        sleep (1000);
    }
  else
    {
      exit (42); /* Exit with a silly number */
    }
}
$ ./zombie &     ...execute the program in the background.
[1] 15896
$ ps                            ...obtain process status.
PID    TTY          TIME CMD
15870 pts2        00:00:00 bash             ...the shell.
15896 pts2        00:00:00 zombie           ...the parent.
15897 pts2        00:00:00 zombie <defunct>   ...the zombie.
15898 pts2        00:00:00 ps
$ kill 15896                    ...kill the parent process.
[1] +   Terminated      ./zombie
$ ps                    ...notice the zombie is gone now.
PID    TTY          TIME CMD
15870 pts2        00:00:00 bash
15901 pts2        00:00:00 ps
$ _
```

12.4.5   Waiting for a Child: wait ()

A parent process may wait for one of its children to terminate and then accept its child's termination code by executing wait () (Figure 12–37).

System Call: pid_t **wait** (int* *status*)

wait () causes a process to suspend until one of its children terminates. A successful call to wait () returns the pid of the child that terminated and places a status code into *status* that is encoded as follows:

If the rightmost byte of status is zero, the leftmost byte contains the low eight bits of the value returned by the child's call to exit () or return ().

If the rightmost byte is nonzero, the rightmost seven bits are equal to the number of the signal that caused the child to terminate, and the remaining bit of the rightmost byte is set to 1 if the child produced a core dump.

If a process executes a wait () and has no children, wait () returns immediately with -1. If a process executes a wait () and one or more of its children are already zombies, wait () returns immediately with the status of one of the zombies.

Figure 12-37 Description of the wait () system call.

In the following example, the child process terminated before the end of the program by executing an exit () with return code 42. Meanwhile, the parent process executed a wait () and suspended until it received its child's termination code. At this point, the parent displayed information about its child's demise and executed the rest of the program:

```
$ cat mywait.c                        ...list the program.
#include <stdio.h>
main ()
{
  int pid, status, childPid;
  printf ("I'm the parent process and my PID is %d\n", getpid ());
  pid = fork (); /* Duplicate */
  if (pid != 0) /* Branch based on return value from fork () */
    {
      printf ("I'm the parent process with PID %d and PPID %d\n",
              getpid (), getppid ());
      childPid = wait (&status); /* Wait for a child to terminate. */
      printf ("A child with PID %d terminated with exit code %d\n",
              childPid, status >> 8);
    }
  else
    {
      printf ("I'm the child process with PID %d and PPID %d\n",
              getpid (), getppid ());
      exit (42); /* Exit with a silly number */
    }
  printf ("PID %d terminates\n", getpid () );
}
```

```
$ ./mywait                                ...run the program.
I'm the parent process and my PID is 13464
I'm the child process with PID 13465 and PPID 13464
I'm the parent process with PID 13464 and PPID 13409
A child with PID 13465 terminated with exit code 42
PID 13465 terminates
$ _
```

12.4.6   Differentiating a Process: exec

A process may replace its current code, data, and stack with those of another executable by using one of the exec family of system calls. When a process executes an exec, its PID and PPID numbers stay the same—only the code that the process is executing changes. The exec family of system calls work as described in Figure 12–38.

Library Function: int **execl** (const char* *path*, const char* *arg0*, const char* *arg1*, ..., const char* *argn*, NULL)

   int **execv** (const char* *path*, const char* *argv[ ]*)

   int **execlp** (const char* *path*, const char* *arg0*, const char* *arg1*,..., const char* *argn*, NULL)

   int **execvp** (const char* *path*, const char* *argv[ ]*)

The exec family of library functions replace the calling process's code, data, and stack from the executable whose pathname is stored in *path*.

   execvl () is identical to execlp (), and execv () is identical to execvp (), except that execl () and execv () require the absolute or relative pathname of the executable file to be supplied, whereas execlp () and execvp () use the $PATH environment variable to find *path*.

   If the executable is not found, the system call returns -1; otherwise, the calling process replaces its code, data, and stack from the executable and starts to execute the new code. A successful call to any of the exec system calls never returns.

   execl () and execlp () invoke the executable with the string arguments pointed to by *arg1..argn*. *arg0* must be the name of the executable file itself, and the list of arguments must be null terminated.

   execv () and execvp () invoke the executable with the string arguments pointed to by *argv[1]..argv[n]*, where *argv[n+1]* is NULL. *argv[0]* must be the name of the executable file itself.

Figure 12–38   Description of the exec family of library functions.

The exec family listed in Figure 12–38 aren't really system calls—they're C library functions that invoke the execve () system call. execve () is hardly ever used directly, as it contains some rarely used options.

In the following example, the program displayed a small message and then replaced its code with that of the "ls" executable. Note that the execl () was successful and therefore never returned:

```
$ cat myexec.c                      ...list the program.
#include <stdio.h>
main ()
{
 printf ("I'm process %d and I'm about to exec an ls -l\n",getpid ());
 execl ("/bin/ls", "ls", "-l", NULL); /* Execute ls */
 printf ("This line should never be executed\n");
}
$ ./myexec                          ...run the program.
I'm process 13623 and I'm about to exec an ls -l
total 125
-rw-r--r--  1 glass     cs      277 Feb 15 00:47 myexec.c
-rwxr-xr-x  1 glass     cs    24576 Feb 15 00:48 myexec
$ _
```

12.4.7 Changing Directories: chdir ()

Every process has a *current working directory* that is used when processing a relative pathname. A child process inherits its current working directory from its parent. For example, when a utility is executed from a shell, its process inherits the shell's current working directory. To change a process' current working directory, use chdir () (Figure 12–39).

System Call: int **chdir** (const char* *pathname*)

chdir () sets a process's current working directory to the directory *pathname*. The process must have execute permission from the directory to succeed.

   chdir () returns 0 if successful; otherwise, it returns -1.

Figure 12–39 Description of the chdir () system call.

In the following example, the process printed its current working directory before and after executing chdir () by executing **pwd** using the system () library function:

```
$ cat mychdir.c            ...list the source code.
#include <stdio.h>
main ()
{
 system ("pwd"); /* Display current working directory */
 chdir ("/"); /* Change working directory to root directory */
 system ("pwd"); /* Display new working directory */
 chdir ("/home/glass"); /* Change again */
 system ("pwd"); /* Display again */
}
```

```
$ ./mychdir                ...execute the program.
/home/glass
/
/home/glass
$ _
```

12.4.8 Changing Priorities: nice ()

Every process has a priority value between -20 and +19 that affects the amount of CPU time that it's allocated. In general, the smaller the priority value, the faster the process will run. Only super-user and kernel processes (described in Chapter 13, "Linux Internals") can have a negative priority value, and login shells start with priority 0.

A child process inherits its priority value from its parent, and may change it by using nice () (Figure 12–40).

Library Function: int **nice** (int *delta*)

nice () adds *delta* to a process's current priority value. Only a super-user may specify a *delta* that leads to a negative priority value. Legal priority values lie between -20 and +19. If a *delta* is specified that takes a priority value beyond a limit, the priority value is truncated to the limit.

If nice () succeeds, it returns the new nice value; otherwise it returns -1. Note that this can cause problems, since a nice value of -1 is legal.

Figure 12–40 Description of the nice () library function.

In the following example, the process executes **ps** commands before and after a couple of nice () calls. Notice that when the process's priority changes, the next invocation of the **ps** command also has the lower priority.

```
$ cat mynice.c              ...list the source code.
#include <stdio.h>
main ()
{
 printf ("original priority\n");
 system ("ps -l"); /* Execute a ps */
 nice (0); /* Add 0 to my priority */
 printf ("running at priority 0\n");
 system ("ps -l"); /* Execute another ps */
 nice (10); /* Add 10 to my priority */
 printf ("running at priority 10\n");
 system ("ps -l"); /* Execute the last ps */
}
$ mynice                    ...execute the program.
original priority
F S   UID   PID  PPID  C PRI  NI ADDR SZ WCHAN   TTY    CMD
0 S   500  1290  1288  0  76   0 -    552 rt_sig pts/4 ksh
```

```
0 S   500  1549  1290  0 76   0 -   583 wait4  pts/4 a.out
0 S   500  1550  1549  0 80   0 -   889 -      pts/4 ps
running at priority 0        ...adding 0 doesn't change it.
F S   UID   PID  PPID  C PRI  NI ADDR SZ WCHAN  TTY   CMD
0 S   500  1290  1288  0 76   0 -   552 rt_sig pts/4 ksh
0 S   500  1549  1290  0 75   0 -   583 wait4  pts/4 a.out
0 S   500  1551  1549  0 78   0 -   638 -      pts/4 ps
running at priority 10       ...adding 10 makes them run slower.
F S   UID   PID  PPID  C PRI  NI ADDR SZ WCHAN  TTY   CMD
0 S   500  1290  1288  0 76   0 -   552 rt_sig pts/4 ksh
0 S   500  1549  1290  0 90  10 -   583 wait4  pts/4 a.out
0 S   500  1552  1549  0 87  10 -   694 -      pts/4 ps
$ _
```

12.4.9   Accessing User and Group IDs

Figure 12–41 lists the system calls that allow you to read a process's real and effective IDs.

System Call: uid_t **getuid** ()

      uid_t **geteuid** ()

      gid_t **getgid** ()

      gid_t **getegid** ()

getuid () and geteuid () return the calling process's real and effective user ID, respectively. getgid () and getegid () return the calling process's real and effective group ID, respectively. The ID numbers correspond to the user and group IDs listed in the "/etc/passwd" and "/etc/group" files.

      These calls always succeed.

Figure 12–41   Description of the getuid (), geteuid (), getgid (), and getegid () system calls.

Figure 12–42 lists the system calls that allow you to set a process's real and effective IDs.

System Call: int **setuid** (uid_t *id*)

      int **seteuid** (uid_t *id*)

      int **setgid** (gid_t *id*)

      int **setegid** (gid_t *id*)

seteuid () and setegid () set the calling process's effective user and group ID, respectively. setuid () and setgid () set the calling process's effective and real user and group ID, respectively, to the specified value.

      These calls succeed only if executed by a super-user, or if *id* is the real or effective user (group) ID of the calling process. They return 0 if successful; otherwise, they return -1.

Figure 12–42   Description of the setuid (), seteuid (), setgid (), and setegid () system calls.

12.4.10 Sample Program: Background Processing

Here's a sample program that makes use of fork () and exec () to execute a program in the background. The original process creates a child to "exec" the specified executable and then terminates. The orphaned child is automatically adopted by "init." Notice how I craftily passed the argument list from main () to execvp () by passing &argv[1] as the second argument to execvp (). Note also that I used execvp () instead of execv () so that the program could use $PATH to find the executable file:

```
$ cat background.c              ...list the program.
#include <stdio.h>
main (argc, argv)
int argc;
char* argv [];
{
  if (fork () == 0) /* Child */
    {
      execvp (argv[1], &argv[1]); /* Execute other program */
      fprintf (stderr, "Could not execute %s\n", argv[1]);
    }
}
$ background sleep 60    ...run the program.
$ ps                    ...confirm that it is in background.
PID    TTY         TIME CMD
10742 pts0    00:00:00 bash
10936 pts0    00:00:01 ksh
15669 pts0    00:00:00 csh
16073 pts0    00:00:00 sleep 60
16074 pts0    00:00:00 ps
$ _
```

12.4.11 Redirection

When a process forks, the child inherits a copy of its parent's file descriptors. When a process execs, all non-close-on-exec file descriptors remain unaffected, including the standard input, output, and error channels. The Linux shells use these two pieces of information to implement redirection. For example, say you type the following command at a terminal:

```
$ ls > ls.out
```

To perform the redirection, the shell performs the following series of actions:

- The parent shell forks and then waits for the child shell to terminate.
- The child shell opens the file "ls.out," creating it or truncating it as necessary.
- The child shell then duplicates the file descriptor of "ls.out" to the standard output file descriptor, number 1, and then closes the original descriptor of "ls.out". All standard output is therefore redirected to "ls.out".

- The child shell then exec's the ls utility. Since the file descriptors are inherited during an exec (), all of the standard output of ls goes to "ls.out".
- When the child shell terminates, the parent resumes. The parent's file descriptors are unaffected by the child's actions, as each process maintains its own private descriptor table.

To redirect the standard error channel in addition to standard output, the shell would simply have to duplicate the "ls.out" descriptor twice; once to descriptor 1 and once to descriptor 2.

Here's a small program that does approximately the same kind of redirection as a Linux shell. When invoked with the name of a file as the first parameter and a command sequence as the remaining parameters, the program "redirect" redirects the standard output of the command to the named file.

```
$ cat redirect.c               ...list the program.
#include <stdio.h>
#include <fcntl.h>
main (argc, argv)
int argc;
char* argv [];
{
 int fd;
 /* Open file for redirection */
 fd = open (argv[1], O_CREAT | O_TRUNC | O_WRONLY, 0600);
 dup2 (fd, 1); /* Duplicate descriptor to standard output */
 close (fd); /* Close original descriptor to save descriptor space */
 execvp (argv[2], &argv[2]); /* Invoke program; will inherit stdout */
 perror ("main"); /* Should never execute */
}
$ redirect ls.out ls -lG       ...redirect "ls -lG" to "ls.out".
$ cat ls.out                   ...list the output file.
total 5
-rw-r-xr-x   1 glass          0 Feb 15 10:35 ls.out
-rw-r-xr-x   1 glass        449 Feb 15 10:35 redirect.c
-rwxr-xr-x   1 glass       3697 Feb 15 10:33 redirect
$ _
```

12.5 Signals

Programs must sometimes deal with unexpected or unpredictable events, such as:

- a floating-point error
- a power failure
- an alarm clock "ring" (discussed soon)
- the death of a child process
- a termination request from a user (i.e., a *Control-C*)
- a suspend request from a user (i.e., a *Control-Z*)

These kind of events are sometimes called *interrupts*, as they must interrupt the regular flow of a program in order to be processed. When Linux recognizes that such an event has occurred, it sends the corresponding process a signal. There is a unique, numbered signal for each possible event. For example, if a process causes a floating point error, the kernel sends the offending process signal number 8 (Figure 12–43).

Figure 12–43 Floating-point error signal.

The kernel isn't the only one that can send a signal; any process can send any other process a signal, as long as it has permission. The rules regarding permissions are discussed shortly.

A programmer may arrange for a particular signal to be ignored or to be processed by a special piece of code called a *signal handler*. In the latter case, the process that receives the signal suspends its current flow of control, executes the signal handler, and then resumes the original flow of control when the signal handler finishes.

By learning about signals, you can "protect" your programs from *Control-C*, arrange for an alarm clock signal to terminate your program if it takes too long to perform a task, and learn how Linux uses signals during everyday operations.

12.5.1 Signal Types

Linux supports two types of signals: standard signals—the traditional UNIX signals—and real-time—or queued—signals. Traditional signals are delivered to a process by setting a bit in a bitmap, one for each signal. Therefore, multiple instances of the same signal cannot be represented, because the bitmap can only be one (signal) or zero (no signal).

POSIX 1003.1b also defines queued signals for real-time processes where successive instances of the same signal are significant and need to be properly delivered. In order to use queued signals, you must use the sigaction () system call, rather than signal (), which is described in the rest of this section.

12.5.2 Defined Signals

Signals are defined in "/usr/include/signal.h" and the other platform-specific header files it includes (the actual signal definitions are in "/usr/include/asm/signal.h" on my system). A programmer may choose that a particular signal triggers a user-supplied signal handler, triggers the default kernel-supplied handler, or is ignored. The default handler usually performs one of the following actions:

- terminates the process and generates a dump of memory in a core file (*core*)
- terminates the process without generating a core image file (*quit*)

• ignores and discards the signal (*ignore*)
• suspends the process (*stop*)
• resumes the process

12.5.3   POSIX Signals

Figure 12–44 is a list of the standard POSIX signals defined in Linux along with their macro definition, numeric value, process's default action, and a brief description.

Macro	#	Default action	Description
SIGHUP	1	quit	Hangup or death of controlling process.
SIGINT	2	quit	Keyboard interrupt.
SIGQUIT	3	core	Quit.
SIGILL	4	core	Illegal instruction.
SIGABRT	6	core	Abort.
SIGFPE	8	core	Arithmetic exception.
SIGKILL	9	quit	Kill (cannot be caught, blocked, or ignored).
SIGUSR1	10	quit	User-defined signal.
SIGSEGV	11	core	Segmentation violation (out of range address).
SIGUSR2	12	quit	User-defined signal.
SIGPIPE	13	quit	Write on a pipe or other socket with no one to read it.
SIGALRM	14	quit	Alarm clock.
SIGTERM	15	quit	Software termination signal (default signal sent by *kill*).
SIGCHLD	17	ignore	Status of child process has changed.
SIGCONT	18	none	Continue if stopped.
SIGSTOP	19	stop	Stop (suspend) the process.
SIGTSTP	20	stop	Stop from the keyboard.
SIGTTIN	21	stop	Background read from tty device.
SIGTTOU	22	stop	Background write to tty device.

Figure 12–44   POSIX signals.

Other signals are supported by Linux. For information on other signals, see the man page for signal in section 7 ("man 7 signal").

12.5.4 Terminal Signals

The easiest way to send a signal to a foreground process is by pressing *Control-C* or *Control-Z* from the keyboard. When the terminal driver (the piece of software that supports the terminal) recognizes a *Control-C*, it sends a SIGINT signal to all of the processes in the current foreground job. Similarly, *Control-Z* causes it to send a SIGTSTP signal to all of the processes in the current foreground job. By default, SIGINT terminates a process and SIGTSTP suspends a process. Later in this section, I'll show you how to perform similar actions from a C program.

12.5.5 Requesting an Alarm Signal: alarm ()

One of the simplest ways to see a signal in action is to arrange for a process to receive an alarm clock signal, SIGALRM, by using alarm (). The default handler for this signal displays the message "Alarm clock" and terminates the process. Figure 12–45 describes how alarm () works.

System Call: unsigned int alarm (unsigned int *count*)

alarm () instructs the kernel to send the SIGALRM signal to the calling process after *count* seconds. If an alarm had already been scheduled, it is overwritten. If *count* is 0, any pending alarm requests are cancelled.

 alarm () returns the number of seconds that remain until the alarm signal is sent.

Figure 12–45 Description of the alarm () system call.

Here's a small program that uses alarm (), together with its output:

```
$ cat alarm.c                    ...list the program.
#include <stdio.h>
main ()
{
 alarm (3); /* Schedule an alarm signal in three seconds */
 printf ("Looping forever...\n");
 while (1);
 printf ("This line should never be executed\n");
}
$ ./alarm                  ...run the program.
Looping forever...
Alarm clock              ...occurs three seconds later.
$ _
```

The next section shows you how you override a default signal handler and make your program respond specially to a particular signal.

12.5.6   Handling Signals: signal ()

The last example program reacted to the alarm signal SIGALRM in the default manner. The signal () system call may be used to override the default action (Figure 12–46).

System Call: void (***signal** (int *sigCode*, void (**func*)(int))) (int)

signal () allows a process to specify the action that it will take when a particular signal is received. The parameter *sigCode* specifies the number of the signal that is to be reprogrammed, and *func* may be one of several values:

- SIG_IGN, which indicates that the specified signal should be ignored and discarded.
- SIG_DFL, which indicates that the kernel's default handler should be used.
- an address of a user-defined function, which indicates that the function should be executed when the specified signal arrives.

   The valid signal numbers are included from "/usr/include/signal.h" (and the other header files that includes, the actual signal definitions are in "/usr/include/asm/signal.h" on my Linux machine). The signals SIGKILL and SIGSTP may not be reprogrammed. A child process inherits the signal settings from its parent during a fork (). When a process performs an exec (), previously ignored signals remain ignored but installed handlers are set back to the default handler.

   With the exception of SIGCHLD, signals are not stacked. This means that if a process is sleeping and three identical signals are sent to it, only one of the signals is actually processed.

   signal () returns the previous *func* value associated with *sigCode* if successful; otherwise it returns -1.

Figure 12–46   Description of the signal () system call.

   I made a couple of changes to the previous program so that it caught and processed the SIGALRM signal efficiently:

- I installed my own signal handler, alarmHandler (), by using signal ().
- I made the while loop less draining on the timesharing system by making use of a system call called pause (). The old version of the while loop had an empty code body which caused it to loop very fast and soak up CPU resources. The new version of the while loop suspends each time through the loop until a signal is received.

Before I show you the updated program, let's look at a description of pause () (Figure 12–47).

System Call: int **pause** (void)

pause () suspends the calling process and returns when the calling process receives a signal. It is most often used to wait efficiently for an alarm signal. pause () doesn't return anything useful.

Figure 12–47   Description of the pause () system call.

Here's the updated version:

```
$ cat handler.c                        ...list the program.
#include <stdio.h>
#include <signal.h>
int alarmFlag = 0; /* Global alarm flag */
void alarmHandler (); /* Forward declaration of alarm handler */
/**************************************************************/
main ()
{
  signal (SIGALRM, alarmHandler); /* Install signal handler */
  alarm (3); /* Schedule an alarm signal in three seconds */
  printf ("Looping...\n");
  while (!alarmFlag) /* Loop until flag set */
    {
       pause (); /* Wait for a signal */
    }
  printf ("Loop ends due to alarm signal\n");
}
/**************************************************************/
void alarmHandler ()
{
  printf ("An alarm clock signal was received\n");
  alarmFlag = 1;
}
$ ./handler                            ...run the program.
Looping...
An alarm clock signal was received  ...occurs three seconds later.
Loop ends due to alarm signal
$ _
```

12.5.7   Protecting Critical Code and Chaining Interrupt Handlers

The same techniques that I just described may be used to protect critical pieces of code against *Control-C* attacks and other such signals. In these cases, it's common to save the previous value of the handler so that it can be restored after the critical code has executed. Here's the source code of a program that protects itself against SIGINT signals:

```
$ cat critical.c                       ...list the program.
#include <stdio.h>
#include <signal.h>
main ()
{
  void (*oldHandler) (); /* To hold old handler value */
   printf ("I can be Control-C'ed\n");
  sleep (3);
  oldHandler = signal (SIGINT, SIG_IGN); /* Ignore Control-C */
  printf ("I'm protected from Control-C now\n");
  sleep (3);
```

```
signal (SIGINT, oldHandler); /* Restore old handler */
printf ("I can be Control-C'ed again\n");
sleep (3);
printf ("Bye!\n");
}
$ ./critical                    ...run the program.
I can be Control-C'ed
^C                              ...Control-C works here.
$ ./critical                    ...run the program again.
I can be Control-C'ed
I'm protected from Control-C now
^C                              ...Control-C is ignored.
I can be Control-C'ed again
Bye!
$ _
```

12.5.8   Sending Signals: kill ()

A process may send a signal to another process by using the kill () system call (Figure 12–48). kill () is a misnomer, since many of the signals that it can send do not terminate a process. It's called kill () for historical reasons; back when UNIX was first designed, the main use of signals was to terminate processes.

System Call: int **kill** (pid_t *pid*, int *sigCode*)

kill () sends the signal with value *sigCode* to the process with PID *pid*. kill () succeeds and the signal is sent as long as at least one of the following conditions is satisfied:

- The sending process and the receiving process have the same owner.
- The sending process is owned by a super-user.

There are a few variations on the way that kill () works:

- If *pid* is 0, the signal is sent to all of the processes in the sender's process group.
- If *pid* is -1 and the sender is owned by a super-user, the signal is sent to all processes, including the sender.
- If *pid* is -1 and the sender is not a super-user, the signal is sent to all of the processes owned by the same owner as the sender, excluding the sending process.
- If the *pid* is negative and not -1, the signal is sent to all of the processes in the process group.

Process groups are discussed later in this chapter. If kill () manages to send at least one signal successfully, it returns 0; otherwise, it returns -1.

Figure 12–48   Description of the kill () system call.

12.5.9   Death of Children

When a parent's child terminates, the child process sends its parent a SIGCHLD signal. A parent process often installs a handler to deal with this signal, which typically executes a wait () to accept the child's termination code and let the child de-zombify.[1]

Alternatively, the parent can choose to ignore SIGCHLD signals, in which case the child de-zombifies automatically. One of the socket programs that follows later in this chapter makes use of this feature.

The next example illustrates a SIGCHLD handler, and allows a user to limit the amount of time that a command takes to execute. The first parameter of "limit" is the maximum number of seconds allowed for execution, and the remaining parameters are the command itself. The program works by performing the following steps:

1. The parent process installs a SIGCHLD handler that is executed when its child process terminates.
2. The parent process forks a child process to execute the command.
3. The parent process sleeps for the specified number of seconds. When it wakes up, it sends its child process a SIGINT signal to kill it.
4. If the child terminates before its parent finishes sleeping, the parent's SIGCHLD handler is executed, causing the parent to terminate immediately.

Here are the source code and sample output from the program:

```
$ cat limit.c                   ...list the program.
#include <stdio.h>
#include <signal.h>
int delay;
void childHandler ();
/***************************************************************/
main (argc, argv)
int argc;
char* argv[];
{
 int pid;
 signal (SIGCHLD, childHandler); /* Install death-of-child handler */
 pid = fork (); /* Duplicate */
 if (pid == 0) /* Child */
   {
     execvp (argv[2], &argv[2]); /* Execute command */
     perror ("limit"); /* Should never execute */
   }
 else /* Parent */
```

---

1.   This means that the child is completely laid to rest and is no longer a zombie.

```
  {
    sscanf (argv[1], "%d", &delay); /* Read delay from command line */
    sleep (delay); /* Sleep for the specified number of seconds */
    printf ("Child %d exceeded limit and is being killed\n", pid);
    kill (pid, SIGINT); /* Kill the child */
  }
}
/*********************************************************************/
void childHandler () /* Executed if the child dies before the parent */
{
 int childPid, childStatus;
 childPid = wait (&childStatus); /* Accept child's termination code */
 printf ("Child %d terminated within %d seconds\n", childPid, delay);
 exit (/* EXITSUCCESS */ 0);
}
$ ./limit 5 ls        ...run the program; command finishes OK.
a.out         alarm        critical      handler        limit
alarm.c       critical.c   handler.c     limit.c
Child 4030 terminated within 5 seconds
$ ./limit 4 sleep 100    ...run it again; command takes too long.
Child 4032 exceeded limit and is being killed
$ _
```

12.5.10 Suspending and Resuming Processes

The SIGSTOP and SIGCONT signals suspend and resume a process, respectively. They are used by the Linux shells to support job control to implement built-in commands like *stop, fg,* and *bg.*

In the following example, the main program created two children that both entered an infinite loop and displayed a message every second. The main program waited for three seconds and then suspended the first child. The second child continued to execute as usual. After another three seconds, the parent restarted the first child, waited a little while longer, and then terminated both children.

```
$ cat pulse.c           ...list the program.
#include <signal.h>
#include <stdio.h>
main ()
{
 int pid1;
 int pid2;
  pid1 = fork ();
 if (pid1 == 0) /* First child */
   {
```

```
        while (1) /* Infinite loop */
          {
            printf ("pid1 is alive\n");
            sleep (1);
          }
      }
  pid2 = fork (); /* Second child */
  if (pid2 == 0)
    {
      while (1) /* Infinite loop */
        {
          printf ("pid2 is alive\n");
          sleep (1);
        }
    }
  sleep (3);
  kill (pid1, SIGSTOP); /* Suspend first child */
  sleep (3);
  kill (pid1, SIGCONT); /* Resume first child */
  sleep (3);
  kill (pid1, SIGINT); /* Kill first child */
  kill (pid2, SIGINT); /* Kill second child */
}
```

```
$ ./pulse               ...run the program.
pid1 is alive           ...both run in first three seconds.
pid2 is alive
pid1 is alive
pid2 is alive
pid1 is alive
pid2 is alive
pid2 is alive                   ...just the second child runs now.
pid2 is alive
pid2 is alive
pid1 is alive                   ...the first child is resumed.
pid2 is alive
pid1 is alive
pid2 is alive
pid1 is alive
pid2 is alive
$ _
```

12.5.11 Process Groups and Control Terminals

When you're in a shell and you execute a program that creates several children, a single *Control-C* from the keyboard will normally terminate the program and its children and then return you to the shell. There are several features that produce this behavior:

- In addition to having a unique process ID number, every process is also a member of a *process group*. Several processes can be members of the same process group. When a process forks, the child inherits its process group from its parent. A process may change its process group to a new value by using setpgid (). When a process execs, its process group remains the same.
- Every process can have an associated *control terminal*. This is typically the terminal where the process was started. When a process forks, the child inherits its control terminal from its parent. When a process execs, its control terminal stays the same.
- Every terminal can be associated with a single *control* process. When a metacharacter such as a *Control-C* is detected, the terminal sends the appropriate signal to all of the processes in the process group of its control process.
- If a process attempts to read from its control terminal and is not a member of the same process group as the terminal's control process, the process is sent a SIGTTIN signal, which normally suspends the process.

Here's how a shell uses these features:

- When an interactive shell begins, it is the control process of a terminal and has that terminal as its control terminal. How this occurs is beyond the scope of this book.
- When a shell executes a foreground process, the child shell places itself in a different process group before exec'ing the command, and takes control of the terminal. Any signals generated from the terminal thus go to the foreground command rather than the original parent shell. When the foreground command terminates, the original parent shell takes back control of the terminal.
- When a shell executes a background process, the child shell places itself in a different process group before exec'ing, but does not take control of the terminal. Any signals generated from the terminal continue to go to the shell. If the background process tries to read from its control terminal, it is suspended by a SIGTTIN signal.

Figure 12–49 illustrates a typical setup. Assume that process 145 and process 230 are the process leaders of background jobs, and that process 171 is the process leader of the foreground job.

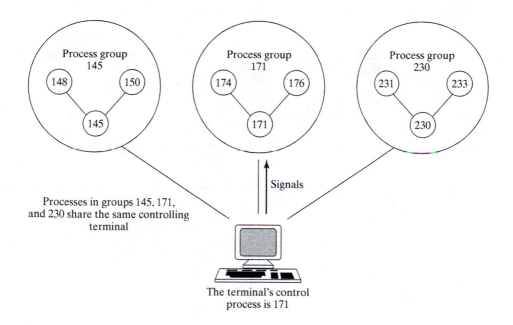

Figure 12-49   Control terminals and process groups.

setpgid () changes a process's group (Figure 12–50).

System Call: pid_t **setpgid** (pid_t *pid*, pid_t *pgrpId*)

setpgid () sets the process group ID of the process with PID *pid* to *pgrpId*. If *pid* is zero, the caller's process group ID is set to *pgrpId*. In order for setpgid () to succeed and set the process group ID, at least one of the following conditions must be met:

• The caller and the specified process must have the same owner.
• The caller must be owned by a super-user.

When a process wants to start its own unique process group, it typically passes its own process ID number as the second parameter to setpgid ().

    If setpgid () fails, it returns -1.

Figure 12-50   Description of the setpgid () system call.

A process may find out its current process group ID by using getpgid () (Figure 12–51).

System Call: pid_t **getpgid** (pid_t *pid*)

getpgid () returns the process group ID of the process with PID pid. If *pid* is zero, the process group ID of the caller is returned.

Figure 12–51   Description of the getpgid () system call.

The following example illustrates the fact that a terminal distributes signals to all of the processes in its control process's process group. Since the child inherited its process group from its parent, both the parent and child caught the SIGINT signal:

```
$ cat pgrp1.c                        ...list program.
#include <signal.h>
#include<stdio.h>
void sigintHandler ();
main ()
{
 signal (SIGINT, sigintHandler); /* Handle Control-C */
 if (fork () == 0)
   printf ("Child PID %d PGRP %d waits\n", getpid (),getpgid (0));
 else
printf ("Parent PID %d PGRP %dwaits\n", getpid (), getpgid (0));
 pause (); /* Wait for asignal */
}
void sigintHandler ()
{
 printf ("Process %d got a SIGINT\n",getpid ());
}
$ ./pgrp1                     ...run the program.
Parent PID 24583 PGRP 24583 waits
Child PID 24584 PGRP 24583 waits
^C                           ...press Control-C.
Process 24584 got a SIGINT
Process 24583 got a SIGINT
$ _
```

If a process places itself into a different process group, it is no longer associated with the terminal's control process, and does not receive signals from the terminal. In the following example, the child process was not affected by a *Control-C*:

```
$ cat pgrp2.c                    ...list the program.
#include <signal.h>
#include <stdio.h>
void sigintHandler ();
main()
{
 int i;
  signal (SIGINT, sigintHandler); /* Install signal handler */
 if (fork () == 0)
   setpgid (0, getpid ()); /* Place child in its own process group */
 printf ("Process PID %d PGRP %d waits\n", getpid (), getpgid (0));
 for (i = 1; i <= 3; i++) /* Loop three times */
   {
     printf ("Process %d is alive\n", getpid ());
     sleep(1);
   }
}
void sigintHandler ()
{
 printf ("Process %d got a SIGINT\n", getpid ());
 exit (1);
}
$ ./pgrp2         ...run the program.
Process PID 24591 PGRP 24591 waits
Process PID 24592 PGRP 24592 waits
^C        ...Control-C
Process 24591 got a SIGINT          ...parent receives signal.
Process 24592 is alive              ...child carries on.
Process 24592 is alive
Process 24592 is alive
$ _
```

If a process attempts to read from its control terminal after it disassociates itself from the terminal's control process, it is sent a SIGTTIN signal, which suspends the receiver by default. In the following example, I trapped SIGTTIN with my own handler to make the effect a little clearer:

```
$ cat pgrp3.c          ...list the program.
#include <signal.h>
#include <stdio.h>
#include <sys/termio.h>
#include <fcntl.h>
void sigttinHandler ();
main ()
{
 int status;
 char str [100];
  if (fork () == 0) /* Child */
    {
      signal (SIGTTIN, sigttinHandler); /* Install handler */
      setpgid (0, getpid ()); /* Place myself in a new process group */
      printf ("Enter a string: ");
      scanf ("%s", str); /* Try to read from control terminal */
      printf ("You entered %s\n", str);
    }
  else /* Parent */
    {
      wait (&status); /* Wait for child to terminate */
    }
}
void sigttinHandler ()
{
 printf ("Attempted inappropriate read from control terminal\n");
 exit (1);
}
$ ./pgrp3          ...run the program.
Enter a string: Attempted inappropriate read from control terminal
$ _
```

12.6 Interprocess Communication

Interprocess communication (IPC) is the generic term describing how two processes may exchange information with each other. In general, the two processes may be running on the same machine or different machines, although some IPC mechanism may only support local usage (e.g., signals and pipes). This communication may be an exchange of data, where two or more processes are cooperatively processing the data or synchronization information to help two independent, but related, processes schedule work so they do not destructively overlap.

12.6.1   Pipes

Pipes are an interprocess communication mechanism allowing two or more processes to send information to each other. They are commonly used from within shells to connect the standard output of one utility to the standard input of another. For example, here's a simple shell command that determines how many users are on the system:

```
$ who | wc -1
```

The **who** utility generates one line of output per user. This output is then "piped" into the wc utility, which, when invoked with the **-1** option, outputs the total number of lines in its input. Thus, the pipelined command craftily calculates the total number of users by counting the number of lines that **who** generates. Figure 12–52 is a diagram of the pipeline.

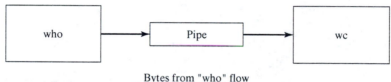

Bytes from "who" flow
through the pipe to "wc"

Figure 12–52   A simple pipe.

It's important to realize that both the writer process and the reader process of a pipeline execute concurrently; a pipe automatically buffers the output of the writer and suspends the writer if the pipe gets too full. Similarly, if a pipe empties, the reader is suspended until some more output becomes available.

Linux provides two types of pipes. The simplest is the *unnamed* pipe, which is what the shell uses to pipe data between processes. A *named* pipe allows two independent processes to find the pipe. In this section, I'll show you how to construct each kind of pipe, starting with unnamed pipes.

12.6.1.1 Unnamed Pipes: pipe ()

An unnamed pipe is a unidirectional communications link that automatically buffers its input and may be created using the pipe () system call. Each end of a pipe has an associated file descriptor. The "write" end of the pipe may be written to using write (), and the "read" end may be read from using read (). When a process has finished with a pipe's file descriptor, it should close it using close (). Figure 12–53 describes how pipe () works.

System Call: int pipe (int *fd* [2])

pipe () creates an unnamed pipe and returns two file descriptors; the descriptor associated with the "read" end of the pipe is stored in *fd*[0], and the descriptor associated with the "write" end of the pipe is stored in *fd*[1].

The following rules apply to processes that read from a pipe:

- If a process reads from a pipe whose write end has been closed, the read () returns a 0, indicating end-of-input.
- If a process reads from an empty pipe whose write end is still open, it sleeps until some input becomes available.
- If a process tries to read more bytes from a pipe than are present, all of the current contents are returned and read () returns the number of bytes actually read.

The following rules apply to processes that write to a pipe:

- If a process writes to a pipe whose read end has been closed, the write fails and the writer is sent a SIGPIPE signal. The default action of this signal is to terminate the writer.
- If a process writes fewer bytes to a pipe than the pipe can hold, the write () is guaranteed to be atomic; that is, the writer process will complete its system call without being preempted by another process. If a process writes more bytes to a pipe than the pipe can hold, no similar guarantees of atomicity apply.

Since access to an unnamed pipe is via the file descriptor mechanism, typically only the process that creates a pipe and its descendants may use the pipe.[a] lseek () has no meaning when applied to a pipe.

If the kernel cannot allocate enough space for a new pipe, pipe () returns -1; otherwise, it returns 0.

a. In advanced situations, it is actually possible to pass file descriptors to unrelated processes via a pipe.

Figure 12-53   Description of the pipe () system call.

If the following code were executed:

```
int fd [2];
pipe (fd);
```

then the data structures shown in Figure 12–54 would be created.

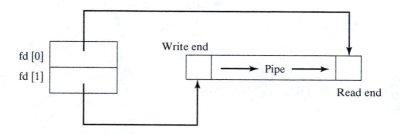

Figure 12–54 An unnamed pipe.

Unnamed pipes are usually used for communication between a parent process and its child, with one process writing and the other process reading. The typical sequence of events is as follows:

1. The parent process creates an unnamed pipe using pipe ().
2. The parent process forks.
3. The writer closes its read end of the pipe, and the designated reader closes its write end of the pipe.
4. The processes communicate by using write () and read () calls.
5. Each process closes its active pipe descriptor when finished with it.

Bidirectional communication is only possible by using two pipes.

Here's a small program that uses a pipe to allow the parent to read a message from its child:

```
$ cat talk.c                      ...list the program.
#include <stdio.h>
#define READ    0       /* The index of the read end of the pipe */
#define WRITE   1       /* The index of the write end of the pipe */
char* phrase = "Stuff this in your pipe and smoke it";
main ()
{
 int fd [2], bytesRead;
 char message [100]; /* Parent process' message buffer */
  pipe (fd); /*Create an unnamed pipe */
 if (fork () == 0) /* Child, writer */
    {
      close(fd[READ]); /* Close unused end */
      write (fd[WRITE],phrase, strlen (phrase) + 1); /* include NULL*/
      close (fd[WRITE]); /* Close used end*/
    }
 else /* Parent, reader*/
    {
      close (fd[WRITE]); /* Close unused end */
```

```
        bytesRead = read (fd[READ], message, 100);
        printf ("Read %d bytes: %s\n", bytesRead, message); /* Send */
        close (fd[READ]); /* Close used end */
     }
}
```
```
$ ./talk                                    ...run the program.
Read 37 bytes: Stuff this in your pipe and smoke it
$ _
```

Notice that the child included the phrase's NULL terminator as part of the message so that the parent could easily display it. When a writer process sends more than one variable-length message into a pipe, it must use a protocol to indicate to the reader an end-of-message. Methods for doing this include:

- sending the length of a message (in bytes) before sending the message itself
- ending a message with a special character such as a newline or a NULL

The Linux shells use unnamed pipes to build pipelines. They use a trick similar to the redirection mechanism described in "Process Management" on page 473 to connect the standard output of one process to the standard input of another. To illustrate this approach, here's the source code of a program that executes two named programs, connecting the standard output of the first to the standard input of the second. It assumes that neither program is invoked with options, and that the names of the programs are listed on the command line.

```
$ cat connect.c                             ...list the program.
#include <stdio.h>
#define READ   0
#define WRITE  1
main (argc, argv)
int argc;
char* argv [];
{
  int fd [2];
    pipe (fd); /* Create an unnamed pipe */
    if (fork () != 0) /* Parent, writer */
      {
        close (fd[READ]); /* Close unused end */
        dup2 (fd[WRITE], 1); /* Duplicate used end to stdout */
        close (fd[WRITE]); /* Close original used end */
        execlp (argv[1], argv[1], NULL); /* Execute writer program */
        perror ("connect");  /* Should never execute */
      }
  else /* Child, reader */
      {
        close (fd[WRITE]); /* Close unused end */
        dup2 (fd[READ], 0); /* Duplicate used end to stdin */
```

```
        close (fd[READ]); /* Close original used end */
        execlp (argv[2], argv[2], NULL); /* Execute reader program */
        perror ("connect"); /* Should never execute */
    }
}
$ who                          ...execute "who" by itself.
glass     pts/1      Feb 15 18:45   (:0.0)
$ ./connect who wc             ...pipe "who" through "wc".
       1       6      42      ...1 line, 6 words, 42 chars.
$ _
```

12.6.1.2 Named Pipes

Named pipes (referred to in Linux as FIFOs, meaning "first in, first out") are less restricted than unnamed pipes, and offer the following advantages:

- They have a name that exists in the file system.
- They may be used by unrelated processes.
- They exist until explicitly deleted.

All of the pipe rules mentioned in the "Unnamed Pipes" section apply to named pipes.

Because named pipes exist as special files in the file system, processes using them to communicate need not have a common ancestry as they do when using unnamed pipes. A named pipe (FIFO) may be created in one of two ways:

- by using the Linux **mkfifo** utility
- by using the mkfifo () system call

Figure 12–55 describes the mkfifo utility.

Utility: **mkfifo** fileName

mkfifo creates a named pipe called *fileName*.

Figure 12–55 Description of the **mkfifo** utility.

UNIX used **mknod** and mknod () to create named pipes, and this still works on Linux, but **mkfifo** and mkfifo () are the preferred methods.

The mode of the named pipe may be set using **chmod**, allowing others to access the pipe that you create. Here's an example of this procedure:

```
$ mkfifo myPipe                    ...create pipe.
$ chmod ug+rw myPipe               ...update permissions.
$ ls -l myPipe                     ...examine attributes.
 prw-rw----   1 glass      cs      0 Feb 27 12:38 myPipe
$ _
```

Note that the type of the named pipe is "p" in the ls listing.

Here's a line of C code that creates a named pipe with read and write permission for the owner and group:

```
mkfifo ("myPipe", 0660);   /* Create a named pipe */
```

Regardless of how you go about creating a named pipe, the end result is the same: a special file is added into the file system. Once a named pipe is opened using open (), write () adds data at the start of the FIFO queue, and read () removes data from the end of the FIFO queue. When a process has finished using a named pipe, it should close it using close (), and when a named pipe is no longer needed, it should be removed from the file system using unlink ().

Like an unnamed pipe, a named pipe is intended for use only as a unidirectional link. Writer processes should open a named pipe for write-only, and reader processes should open for read-only. Although a process could open a named pipe for both reading and writing, this doesn't have much practical application. Before I show you an example program that uses named pipes, here are a couple of special rules concerning their use:

- If a process tries to open a named pipe for read-only and no process currently has it open for writing, the reader will wait until a process opens it for writing, unless O_NONBLOCK or O_NDELAY is set, in which case open () succeeds immediately.
- If a process tries to open a named pipe for write-only and no process currently has it open for reading, the writer will wait until a process opens it for reading, unless O_NONBLOCK or O_NDELAY is set, in which case open () fails immediately.
- Named pipes will not work across a network.

The following example uses two programs, "reader" and "writer", and they work like this:

- A single reader process is executed, which creates a named pipe called "aPipe". It then reads and displays NULL-terminated lines from the pipe until the pipe is closed by all of the writing processes.
- One or more writer processes are executed, each of which opens the named pipe called "aPipe" and sends three messages to it. If the pipe does not exist when a writer tries to open it, the writer retries every second until it succeeds. When all of a writer's messages are sent, the writer closes the pipe and exits.

The following are the source code for each file and some sample output:

```
$ ./reader & ./writer & ./writer &  ...start 1 reader, 2 writers.
[1] 4698              ...reader process.
[2] 4699              ...first writer process.
```

```
[3] 4700                ...second writer process.
Hello from PID 4699
Hello from PID 4700
Hello from PID 4699
Hello from PID 4700
Hello from PID 4699
Hello from PID 4700
[2] -   Done            ./writer    ...first writer exits.
[3] +   Done            ./writer    ...second writer exits.
[1]     Done            ./reader    ...reader exits.
$ _
```

The reader.c program looks like this:

```
#include <stdio.h>
#include <sys/types.h>
#include <fcntl.h>
/**********************************************************************/
main ()
{
 int fd;
 char str[100];
 mkfifo ("aPipe", 0660); /* Create named pipe */
 fd = open ("aPipe", O_RDONLY); /* Open it for reading */
  while (readLine (fd, str)) /* Display received messages */
   printf ("%s\n", str);
   close (fd); /* Close pipe */
}
/**********************************************************************/
readLine (fd, str)
int fd;
char* str;
/* Read a single NULL-terminated line into str from fd */
/* Return 0 when the end-of-input is reached and 1 otherwise */
{
 int n;
  do /* Read characters until NULL or end-of-input */
   {
     n = read (fd, str, 1); /* Read one character */
   }
 while (n > 0 && *str++ != 0);
 return (n > 0); /* Return false if end-of-input */
}
```

The writer.c program looks like this:

```
#include <stdio.h>
#include <fcntl.h>
/*****************************************************************/
main ()
{
 int fd, messageLen, i;
 char message [100];
  /* Prepare message */
 sprintf (message, "Hello from PID %d", getpid ());
 messageLen = strlen (message) + 1;
  do /* Keep trying to open the file until successful */
    {
      fd = open ("aPipe", O_WRONLY); /* Open named pipe for writing */
      if (fd == -1) sleep (1); /* Try again in 1 second */
    }
 while (fd == -1);
  for (i = 1; i <= 3; i++) /* Send three messages */
    {
      write (fd, message, messageLen); /* Write message down pipe */
      sleep (3); /* Pause a while */
    }
   close (fd); /* Close pipe descriptor */
}
```

12.6.2   Sockets

A socket is an interprocess communication mechanism that allows processes to talk to each other even if they're on different machines. It is this cross-network capability that makes them so useful. For example, the **rlogin** utility, which allows a user on one machine to log into a remote host, is implemented using sockets. Other common uses of sockets include:

- printing a file on one machine from another machine
- transferring files from one machine to another machine

Process communication via sockets is based on the client-server model. One process, known as a server process, creates a socket whose name is known by other client processes. These client processes can talk to the server process via a connection to its named socket. To do this, a client process first creates an unnamed socket and then requests that it be connected to the server's named socket. A successful connection returns one file descriptor to the client and one to the server, both of which may be used for reading and writing. Note that, unlike pipes, socket connections are bidirectional. Figure 12–56 illustrates the process.

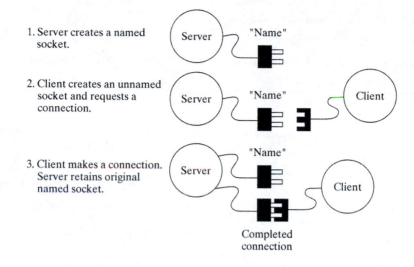

1. Server creates a named socket.

2. Client creates an unnamed socket and requests a connection.

3. Client makes a connection. Server retains original named socket.

Completed connection

figure 12–56 The socket connection.

Once a socket connection is made, it's quite common for the server process to fork a child process to converse with the client, while the original parent process continues to accept other client connections. A typical example of this is a remote print server: the server process accepts a client that wishes to send a file for printing, and then forks a child to perform the file transfer. The parent process meanwhile waits for more client print requests.

In the coming sections, we'll take a look at the following topics:

• the different kinds of sockets
• how a server creates a named socket and waits for connections
• how a client creates an unnamed socket and requests a connection from a server
• how a server and client communicate after a socket connection is made
• how a socket connection is closed.
• how a server can create a child process to converse with the client

12.6.2.1 Socket Types

The various kinds of sockets may be classified according to three attributes:

• the *domain*
• the *type*
• the *protocol*

Domains   The domain of a socket indicates where the server and client sockets may reside; the domains that are currently supported include:

- PF_LOCAL (the clients and server must be in the same machine, also called PF_UNIX)
- PF_INET (the clients and server are on the network)
- PF_INET6 (the clients and server are on an IPv6 network)

Other domains are listed in the socket man page. PF stands for "Protocol Family." This book contains examples of PF_LOCAL and PF_INET sockets.

Types   The type of a socket determines the type of communication that can exist between the client and server; the two main types that are currently supported are:

- SOCK_STREAM: sequenced, reliable, two-way connection based, variable-length streams of bytes
- SOCK_DGRAM: like telegrams; connectionless, unreliable, fixed-length messages

Other types that are either in the planning stages or implemented only in some domains include:

- SOCK_SEQPACKET: sequenced, reliable, two-way connection based, fixed-length packets of bytes
- SOCK_RAW: provides access to internal network protocols and interfaces

This book contains information only on how to use SOCK_STREAM sockets, which are the most common. They are both intuitive and easy to use.

Protocols   The protocol value specifies the low-level means by which the socket type is implemented. System calls that expect a protocol parameter accept 0 as meaning "the correct protocol"; in other words, the protocol value is something that you generally won't have to worry about. Most systems support only protocols other than 0 as an optional extra, so I'll use the default protocol in all the examples.

Writing Socket Programs   Any program that uses sockets must include "/usr/include/sys/types.h" and "/usr/include/sys/socket.h".

To illustrate the way a program that uses sockets is written I'll build my description of the socket-oriented system calls around a small client/server example that uses PF_LOCAL sockets. Once I've done this, I'll show you another example that uses PF_INET sockets. The PF_LOCAL example is comprised of two programs:

- "chef," the server, which creates a named socket called "recipe" and writes the recipe to any clients who request it. The recipe is a collection of variable-length NULL-terminated strings.
- "cook," the client, which connects to the named socket called "recipe" and reads the recipe from the server. It displays the recipe to standard output as it reads it, and then terminates.

The chef server process runs in the background. Any client cook processes that connect to the server cause the server to fork a duplicate server to handle the recipe transfer, allowing the original server to accept other incoming connections. Here's some sample output from the chef/cook example:

```
$ ./chef &            ...run the server in the background.
[1] 5684
$ ./cook              ...run a client--display the recipe.
spam, spam, spam, spam,
spam, and spam.
$ ./cook              ...run another client--display the recipe.
spam, spam, spam, spam,
spam, and spam.
$ kill %1             ...kill the server.
[1]    Terminated           chef
$ _
```

12.6.2.2 Chef/Cook Listings

This section contains the complete listing of the chef and cook programs. I suggest that you quickly skim through the code and then read the sections that follow for details on how they both work. I have purposely left out a great deal of error checking in the interest of space. This code may be downloaded from the Prentice Hall web site, please see the Preface for details.

Here is the code for the "chef.c" server program:

```
1   #include <stdio.h>
2   #include <signal.h>
3   #include <sys/types.h>
4   #include <sys/socket.h>
5   #include <sys/un.h>        /* for sockaddr_un struct */
6
7   #define DEFAULT_PROTOCOL   0
8
9   /****************************************************************/
10
11  main ()
12
13  {
14    int serverFd, clientFd, serverLen, clientLen;
15    struct sockaddr_un serverAddress;/* Server address */
16    struct sockaddr_un clientAddress; /* Client address */
17    struct sockaddr* serverSockAddrPtr; /* Ptr to server address */
18    struct sockaddr* clientSockAddrPtr; /* Ptr to client address */
19
20    /* Ignore death-of-child signals to prevent zombies */
21    signal (SIGCHLD, SIG_IGN);
22
23    serverSockAddrPtr = (struct sockaddr*) &serverAddress;
24    serverLen = sizeof (serverAddress);
```

```
25
26      clientSockAddrPtr = (struct sockaddr*) &clientAddress;
27      clientLen = sizeof (clientAddress);
28
29      /* Create a socket, bidirectional, default protocol */
30      serverFd = socket (PF_LOCAL, SOCK_STREAM, DEFAULT_PROTOCOL);
31      serverAddress.sun_family = PF_LOCAL; /* Set domain type */
32      strcpy (serverAddress.sun_path, "recipe"); /* Set name */
33      unlink ("recipe"); /* Remove file if it already exists */
34      bind (serverFd, serverSockAddrPtr, serverLen); /* Create file */
35      listen (serverFd, 5); /* Maximum pending connection length */
36
37      while (1) /* Loop forever */
38        {
39          /* Accept a client connection */
40          clientFd = accept (serverFd, clientSockAddrPtr, &clientLen);
41
42          if (fork () == 0) /* Create child to send recipe */
43            {
44                writeRecipe (clientFd); /* Send the recipe */
45                close (clientFd); /* Close the socket */
46                exit (/* EXIT_SUCCESS */ 0); /* Terminate */
47            }
48          else
49            close (clientFd); /* Close the client descriptor */
50        }
51    }
52
53    /***************************************************************/
54
55    writeRecipe (fd)
56
57    int fd;
58
59    {
60      static char* line1 = "spam, spam, spam, spam,";
61      static char* line2 = "spam, and spam.";
62      write (fd, line1, strlen (line1) + 1); /* Write first line */
63      write (fd, line2, strlen (line2) + 1); /* Write second line */
64    }
```

Here is the code for the "cook.c" client program:

```
1   #include <stdio.h>
2   #include <signal.h>
3   #include <sys/types.h>
4   #include <sys/socket.h>
5   #include <sys/un.h>                    /* for sockaddr_un struct*/
6
7   #define DEFAULT_PROTOCOL    0
8
9   /*********************************************************************/
10
11  main ()
12
13  {
14    int clientFd, serverLen, result;
15    struct sockaddr_un serverAddress;
16    struct sockaddr* serverSockAddrPtr;
17
18    serverSockAddrPtr = (struct sockaddr*) &serverAddress;
19    serverLen = sizeof (serverAddress);
20
21    /* Create a socket, bidirectional, default protocol */
22    clientFd = socket (PF_LOCAL, SOCK_STREAM, DEFAULT_PROTOCOL);
23    serverAddress.sun_family = PF_LOCAL; /* Server domain */
24    strcpy (serverAddress.sun_path, "recipe"); /* Server name */
25
26    do /* Loop until a connection is made with the server */
27      {
28        result = connect (clientFd, serverSockAddrPtr, serverLen);
29        if (result == -1) sleep (1); /* Wait and then try again */
30      }
31    while (result == -1);
32
33    readRecipe (clientFd); /* Read the recipe */
34    close (clientFd); /* Close the socket */
35    exit (/* EXIT_SUCCESS */ 0); /* Done */
36  }
37
38  /*********************************************************************/
```

```
39
40   readRecipe (fd)
41
42   int fd;
43
44   {
45     char str[200];
46
47     while (readLine (fd, str)) /* Read lines until end-of-input */
48       printf ("%s\n", str); /* Echo line from socket */
49   }
50
51   /***************************************************************/
52
53   readLine (fd, str)
54
55   int fd;
56   char* str;
57
58   /* Read a single NULL-terminated line */
59
60   {
61     int n;
62
63     do /* Read characters until NULL or end-of-input */
64       {
65         n = read (fd,str, 1); /* Read one character */
66       }
67     while (n > 0 && *str++ != 0);
68     return (n > 0); /* Return false if end-of-input */
69   }
```

12.6.2.3 Analyzing the Source Code

Now that you've glanced at the program, it's time to go back and analyze it. We will examine each of the following steps that are performed when our programs are executed:

- create a server socket
- name a server socket
- specify the maximum number of pending connections to a server socket
- accept connections on a server socket
- create a client socket

- connect a client socket to the server socket
- communicate via sockets

12.6.2.4 The Server

A server is the process that is responsible for creating a named socket and accepting connections to it. To accomplish this, it must use the system calls listed in Figure 12–57 in their presented order.

Name	Meaning
socket	Creates an unnamed socket.
bind	Gives the socket a name.
listen	Specifies the maximum number of pending connections.
accept	Accepts a socket connection from a client.

Figure 12–57 System calls used by a typical Linux daemon process.

12.6.2.5 Creating a Socket: socket ()

A process may create a socket by using socket () (Figure 12–58).

System Call: int **socket** (int *domain*, int *type*, int *protocol*)

socket () creates an unnamed socket of the specified domain, type, and protocol. The legal values of these parameters were described earlier in this section.

    If socket () is successful, it returns a file descriptor associated with the newly created socket; otherwise, it returns -1.

Figure 12–58 Description of the socket () system call.

The chef server creates its unnamed socket on line 30:

```
30      serverFd = socket (PF_LOCAL, SOCK_STREAM, DEFAULT_PROTOCOL);
```

12.6.2.6 Naming a Socket: bind ()

Once the server has created an unnamed socket, it must bind it to a name by using bind (), which works as described in Figure 12–59.

System Call: int **bind** (int *fd*, const struct sockaddr* *address*, size_t *addressLen*)

bind () associates the unnamed socket represented by file descriptor *fd* with the socket address stored in *address*. *addressLen* must contain the length of the address structure. The type and value of the incoming address depend on the socket domain.

If the socket is in the PF_LOCAL domain, a pointer to a **sockaddr_un** structure (defined in "/usr/include/sys/un.h") must be cast to a (**sockaddr***) and passed in as *address*. This structure has two fields that should be set as follows:

FIELD	ASSIGN THE VALUE
sun_family	PF_LOCAL
sun_path	the full pathname of the socket (absolute or relative), up to 108 characters long

If the named PF_LOCAL socket already exists, an error occurs, so it's a good idea to unlink () a name before attempting to bind to it.

If the socket is in the PF_INET domain, a pointer to a **sockaddr_in** structure must be cast to a (**sockaddr***) and passed in as *address*. This structure has four fields, which should be set as follows:

FIELD	ASSIGN THE VALUE
sin_family	PF_INET
sin_port	the port number of the Internet socket
sin_addr	a structure of type in_addr that holds the Internet address
sin_zero	leave empty

For more information about Internet ports and addresses, please consult the Internet-specific part of this section.

If bind () succeeds, it returns a 0; otherwise, it returns -1.

Figure 12-59 Description of the bind () system call.

The chef server assigns the **sockaddr_un** fields and performs a bind () on lines 31..34:

```
31    serverAddress.sun_family = PF_LOCAL; /* Set domain type */
32    strcpy (serverAddress.sun_path, "recipe"); /* Set name */
33    unlink ("recipe"); /* Remove file if it already exists */
34    bind (serverFd, serverSockAddrPtr, serverLen); /* Create file */
```

12.6.2.7 Creating a Socket Queue: listen ( )

When a server process is servicing a client connection, it's always possible that another client will also attempt a connection. The listen () system call allows a process to specify the number of pending connections that may be queued (Figure 12–60).

System Call: int **listen** (int *fd*, int *queueLength*)

listen () allows you to specify the maximum number of pending connections on a socket. Right now, the maximum queue length is 5. If a client attempts a connection to a socket whose queue is full, it is denied.

Figure 12–60   Description of the listen () system call

The chef server listens to its named socket on line 35:

```
35      listen (serverFd, 5); /* Maximum pending connection length */
```

12.6.2.8 Accepting a Client: accept ()

Once a socket has been created, named, and its queue size specified, the final step is to accept client connection requests. To do this, the server must use accept () (Figure 12–61).

System Call: int **accept** (int *fd*, struct sockaddr* *address*, int* *addressLen*)

accept () listens to the named server socket referenced by *fd* and waits until a client connection request is received. When this occurs, accept () creates an unnamed socket with the same attributes as the original named server socket, connects it to the client's socket, and returns a new file descriptor that may be used for communication with the client. The original named server socket may be used to accept more connections.

The *address* structure is filled with the address of the client, and is normally only used in conjunction with Internet connections. The *addressLen* field should be initially set to point to an integer containing the size of the structure pointed to by *address*. When a connection is made, the integer that it points to is set to the actual size, in bytes, of the resulting *address*.

If accept () succeeds, it returns a new file descriptor that may be used to talk with the client; otherwise, it returns -1.

Figure 12–61   Description of the accept () system call.

The chef server accepts a connection on line 40:

```
40            clientFd = accept (serverFd, clientSockAddrPtr, &clientLen);
```

12.6.2.9 Serving a Client

When a client connection succeeds, the most common sequence of events is this:

- The server process forks.
- The parent process closes the newly formed client file descriptor and loops back to accept (), ready to service new client connection requests.
- The child process talks to the client using read () and write (). When the conversation is complete, the child process closes the client file descriptor and exits.

The chef server process follows this series of actions on lines 37..50:

```
37    while (1) /* Loop forever */
38      {
39        /* Accept a client connection */
40        clientFd = accept (serverFd, clientSockAddrPtr, &clientLen);
41
42        if (fork () == 0) /* Create child to send recipe */
43          {
44            writeRecipe (clientFd); /* Send the recipe */
45            close (clientFd); /* Close the socket */
46            exit (/*EXIT_SUCCESS */ 0); /* Terminate */
47          }
48        else
49          close (clientFd); /* Close the client descriptor */
50      }
```

Note that the server chose to ignore SIGCHLD signals on line 21 so that its children can die immediately without requiring the parent to accept their return codes. If the server had not done this, it would had to have installed a SIGCHLD handler, which would have been more tedious.

12.6.2.10 The Client

Now that you've seen how a server program is written, let's take a look at the construction of a client program. A client is a process that's responsible for creating an unnamed socket and then attaching it to a named server socket. To accomplish this, it must use the system calls listed in Figure 12–62 in their presented order.

Name	Meaning
socket	Creates an unnamed socket.
connect	Attaches an unnamed client socket to a named server socket.

Figure 12–62   System calls used by a typical Linux client process.

The way that a client uses socket () to create an unnamed socket is the same as the way that the server uses it. The domain, type, and protocol of the client socket must match those of the targeted server socket. The cook client process creates its unnamed socket on line 22:

```
22    clientFd = socket (PF_LOCAL, SOCK_STREAM, DEFAULT_PROTOCOL);
```

12.6.2.11 Making the Connection: connect ()

To connect to a server's socket, a client process must fill a structure with the address of the server's socket and then use connect () (Figure 12–63).

System Call: int **connect** (int *fd*, struct sockaddr* *address*, int *addressLen*)

connect () attempts to connect to a server socket whose address is contained within a structure pointed to by *address*. If successful, fd may be used to communicate with the server's
socket. The type of structure that *address* points to must follow the same rules as those stated
in the description of bind ():

- If the socket is in the PF_LOCAL domain, a pointer to a **sockaddr_un** structure must
  be cast to a (**sockaddr***) and passed in as *address*.
- If the socket is in the PF_INET domain, a pointer to a **sockaddr_in** structure must be
  cast to a (**sockaddr***) and passed in as *address*.

addressLen must be equal to the size of the address structure.

     If the connection is made, connect () returns 0. If the server socket doesn't exist or its
pending queue is currently filled, connect () returns -1.

Figure 12–63   Description of the connect () system call.

     The cook client process calls connect () until a successful connection is made in lines 26..31:

```
26   do /* Loop until a connection is made with the server */
27      {
28         result = connect (clientFd, serverSockAddrPtr, serverLen);
29         if (result == -1) sleep (1); /* Wait and then try again */
30      }
31   while (result == -1);
```

12.6.2.12 Communicating via Sockets

Once the server socket and client socket have connected, their file descriptors may be used by
write () and read (). In the example program, the server uses write () in lines 55..64:

```
55   writeRecipe (fd)
56
57   int fd;
58
59   {
60      static char* line1 = "spam, spam, spam, spam,";
61      static char* line2 = "spam, and spam.";
62      write (fd, line1, strlen (line1) + 1); /* Write first line */
63      write (fd, line2, strlen (line2) + 1); /* Write second line*/
64   }
```

and the client uses read () in lines 53..69:

```
53   readLine (fd, str)
54
```

```
55  int fd;
56  char* str;
57
58  /* Read a single NULL-terminated line */
59
60  {
61    int n;
62
63    do /* Read characters until NULL or end-of-input */
64      {
65        n = read (fd, str, 1); /* Read one character */
66      }
67    while (n > 0 && *str++ != 0);
68    return (n > 0); /* Return false if end-of-input */
69  }
```

The server and client should be careful to close their socket file descriptors when they are no longer needed.

12.6.2.13 Internet Sockets

The PF_LOCAL sockets that you've seen so far are OK for learning about sockets, but they aren't where the action is. Most of the useful stuff involves communicating between machines on the Internet, and so the rest of this chapter is dedicated to PF_INET sockets. If you haven't already read about networking in Chapter 9, "Networking and the Internet," now would be a good time to do so.

An Internet socket is specified by two values: a 32-bit IP (v4) address, which specifies a single unique Internet host, and a 16-bit port number, which specifies a particular port on the host. This means that an Internet client must know not only the IP address of the server, but also the server's port number.

As I mentioned in Chapter 9, "Networking and the Internet," several standard port numbers are reserved for system use. For example, port 13 is always served by a process that echoes the host's time of day to any client that's interested. The first Internet socket example allows you to connect to port 13 of any Internet host in the world and find out the "remote" time of day. It allows three kinds of Internet address:

- If you enter "s", it automatically means the local host.
- If you enter something that starts with a digit, it's assumed to be an A.B.C.D format IP address, and is converted into a 32-bit IP address by software.
- If you enter a string, it's assumed to be a symbolic host name, and is converted into a 32-bit IP address by software.

Here's some sample output from the "Internet time" program. The third address that I entered is the IP address of "ddn.nic.mil," the national Internet database server. Notice the one-hour time difference between my local host's time and the database server host's time.

```
$ ./inettime                         ...run the program.
Host name (q= quit, s = self): s     ...what's my time?
Self host name is csservr2
Internet Address = 129.110.42.1
The time on the target port is 09 FEB 2005 10:02:01 CST
Host name (q = quit, s= self): wotan         ...time on "wotan"?
Internet Address = 129.110.2.1
The time on the target port is 09 FEB 2005 10:03:45 CST
Host name (q = quit, s = self): 192.112.36.5    ...IP address.
The time on the target port is 09 FEB 2005 11:03:17 EST
Host name (q = quit, s = self): q          ...quit program.
$ _
```

Here is a listing of the code for the Internet time program:

```
 1  #include <stdio.h>
 2  #include <signal.h>
 3  #include <ctype.h>
 4  #include <sys/types.h>
 5  #include <sys/socket.h>
 6  #include <netinet/in.h>                    /* For PF_INET sockets */
 7  #include <arpa/inet.h>
 8  #include <netdb.h>
 9
10  #define DAYTIME_PORT           13          /* Standard port # */
11  #define DEFAULT_PROTOCOL        0
12
13  unsigned long promptForINETAddress ();
14  unsigned long nameToAddr ();
15
16  /*****************************************************************/
17
18  main ()
19
20  {
21     int clientFd; /* Client socket file descriptor */
22     int serverLen; /* Length of server address structure */
23     int result; /* From connect () call */
24     struct sockaddr_in serverINETAddress; /* Server address */
25     struct sockaddr* serverSockAddrPtr; /* Pointer to address */
26     unsigned long inetAddress; /* 32-bit IP address */
27
28     /* Set the two server variables */
29     serverSockAddrPtr = (struct sockaddr*) &serverINETAddress;
30     serverLen = sizeof (serverINETAddress); /* Length of address */
31
32     while (1) /* Loop until break */
```

```
33      {
34          inetAddress = promptForINETAddress (); /* Get 32-bit IP */
35          if (inetAddress == 0) break; /* Done */
36          /* Start by zeroing out the entire address structure */
37      memset ((char*)&serverINETAddress,0,sizeof(serverINETAddress));
38          serverINETAddress.sin_family = PF_INET; /* Use Internet */
39          serverINETAddress.sin_addr.s_addr = inetAddress; /* IP */
40          serverINETAddress.sin_port = htons (DAYTIME_PORT);
41          /* Now create the client socket */
42          clientFd = socket (PF_INET, SOCK_STREAM, DEFAULT_PROTOCOL);
43          do /* Loop until a connection is made with the server */
44            {
45              result = connect (clientFd,serverSockAddrPtr,serverLen);
46              if (result == -1) sleep (1); /* Try again in 1 second */
47            }
48          while (result == -1);
49
50          readTime (clientFd); /* Read the time from the server */
51          close (clientFd); /* Close the socket */
52        }
53
54    exit (/* EXIT_SUCCESS */ 0);
55  }
56
57  /*****************************************************************/
58
59  unsigned long promptForINETAddress ()
60
61  {
62    char hostName [100]; /* Name from user: numeric or symbolic */
63    unsigned long inetAddress; /* 32-bit IP format */
64
65    /* Loop until quit or a legal name is entered */
66    /* If quit, return 0 else return host's IP address */
67    do
68      {
69        printf ("Host name (q = quit, s = self): ");
70        scanf ("%s", hostName); /* Get name from keyboard */
71        if (strcmp (hostName, "q") == 0) return (0); /* Quit */
72        inetAddress = nameToAddr (hostName); /* Convert to IP */
73        if (inetAddress == 0) printf ("Host name not found\n");
74      }
75    while (inetAddress == 0);
76    return (inetAddress);
77  }
78  /*****************************************************************/
79
80  unsigned long nameToAddr (name)
```

```
81
82   char* name;
83
84   {
85     char hostName [100];
86     struct hostent* hostStruct;
87     struct in_addr* hostNode;
88
89     /* Convert name into a 32-bit IP address */
90
91     /* If name begins with a digit, assume it's a valid numeric */
92     /* Internet address of the form A.B.C.D and convert directly */
93     if (isdigit (name[0])) return (inet_addr (name));
94
95     if (strcmp (name, "s") == 0) /* Get host name from database */
96       {
97         gethostname (hostName,100);
98         printf ("Self host name is %s\n", hostName);
99       }
100    else /* Assume name is a valid symbolic host name */
101      strcpy (hostName, name);
102
103    /* Now obtain address information from database */
104    hostStruct = gethostbyname (hostName);
105    if (hostStruct == NULL) return (0); /* Not Found */
106    /* Extract the IP Address from the hostent structure */
107    hostNode = (struct in_addr*) hostStruct->h_addr;
108    /* Display a readable version for fun */
109    printf ("Internet Address = %s\n", inet_ntoa (*hostNode));
110    return (hostNode->s_addr); /* Return IP address */
111  }
112
113  /*****************************************************************/
114
115  readTime (fd)
116
117  int fd;
118
119  {
120    char str [200]; /* Line buffer */
121
122    printf ("The time on the target port is ");
123    while (readLine (fd, str)) /* Read lines until end-of-input */
124      printf ("%s\n", str); /* Echo line from server to user */
125  }
126
127  /*****************************************************************/
128
```

```
129   readLine (fd, str)
130
131   int fd;
132   char* str;
133
134   /* Read a single NEWLINE-terminated line */
135
136   {
137     int n;
138
139     do /* Read characters until NULL or end-of-input */
140       {
141         n = read (fd, str, 1); /* Read one character */
142       }
143     while (n > 0 && *str++ != '\n');
144     return (n > 0); /* Return false if end-of-input */
145   }
```

12.6.2.14 Analyzing the Source Code

Now that you've had a brief look through the Internet socket source code, it's time to examine the interesting bits. This program focuses mostly on the client side of an Internet connection, so I'll describe that portion first.

12.6.2.15 Internet Clients

The procedure for creating an Internet client is the same as that of a PF_LOCAL client, except for the initialization of the socket address. I mentioned earlier in this section during the discussion of bind () that an Internet socket address structure is of type **struct sockaddr_in**, and has four fields:

- **sin_family**, the domain of the socket, which should be set to PF_INET
- **sin_port**, the port number, which in this case is 13
- **sin_addr**, the 32-bit IP number of the client/server
- **sin_zero**, which is padding and is not set

When creating the client socket, the only tricky bit is determining the server's 32-bit IP address. promptForINETAddress () [59] gets the host's name from the user and then invokes nameToAddr () [80] to convert it into an IP address. If the user enters a string starting with a digit, inet_addr () is invoked to perform the conversion. Figure 12–64 shows how it works.

Library Function: in_addr_t **inet_addr** (const char* *string*)

inet_addr () returns the 32-bit IP address that corresponds to the A.B.C.D format *string*. The IP address is in network byte order.

Figure 12–64   Description of the inet_addr () library function.

Network byte order is a host-neutral ordering of bytes in the IP address. This is necessary, because the order of multibyte values can differ from machine to machine, which would make IP addresses nonportable.

If the string doesn't start with a digit, the next step is to see if it's "s," which means the local host. The name of the local host is obtained by gethostname () [97], which works as shown in Figure 12–65.

System Call: int **gethostname** (char* *name*, int *nameLen*)

gethostname () sets the character array pointed to by *name* of length *nameLen* to a null-terminated string equal to the local host's name.

Figure 12–65 Description of the gethostname () system call.

Once the symbolic name of the host is determined, the next stage is to look it up in the network host file, "/etc/hosts." This is performed by gethostbyname () [104] (Figure 12–66).

Library Function: struct hostent* **gethostbyname** (const char* *name*)

gethostbyname () searches the "/etc/hosts" file (and/or DNS database if the host is a DNS client) and returns a pointer to a **hostent** structure that describes the file entry associated with the string *name*.

If *name* is not found in the "/etc/hosts" file, NULL is returned.

Figure 12–66 Description of the gethostbyname () library function.

The hostent structure has several fields, but the only one we're interested in is a field of type (**struct in_addr***) called **h_addr**. This field contains the host's associated IP number in a subfield called **s_addr**. Before returning this IP number, the program displays a string description of the IP address by calling inet_ntoa () [109] (Figure 12–67).

Library Function: char* **inet_ntoa** (struct in_addr *address*)

inet_ntoa () takes a structure of type *in_addr* as its argument and returns a pointer to a string that describes the address in the format A.B.C.D.

Figure 12–67 Description of the inet_ntoa () library function.

The final 32-bit address is then returned by line 110. Once the IP address **inetAddress** has been determined, the client's socket address fields are filled by lines 37..40.

```
37  memset ((char*)&serverINETAddress,0,sizeof(serverINETAddress));
38  serverINETAddress.sin_family = PF_INET; /* Use Internet */
39  serverINETAddress.sin_addr.s_addr = inetAddress; /* IP */
40  serverINETAddress.sin_port = htons (DAYTIME_PORT);
```

memset () clears the socket address structure's contents before its fields are assigned (Figure 12–68).

Library Function: void **memset** (void* *buffer*, int *value*, size_t *length*)

memset () fills the array *buffer* of size *length* with the value of *value*.

Figure 12–68 Description of the memset () library function.

memset () is defined by the POSIX standard and was originally part of System V UNIX. If you port or look at BSD UNIX application code, you may also find a similar library function called bzero () (Figure 12–69).

Library Function: void **bzero** (void* *buffer*, size_t *length*)

bzero () fills the array *buffer* of size *length* with zeroes (ASCII NULL).

Figure 12–69 Description of the bzero () library function.

Both functions are supported by Linux, but bzero () is deprecated, thus memset () should be used in new code. memset () is preferable since it can be used to set values other than zero.

Like the IP address, the port number is also converted to a network byte ordering by htons () (Figure 12–70).

Library Function: in_addr_t **htonl** (in_addr_t *hostLong*)
    in_port_t **htons** (in_port_t *hostShort*)
    in_addr_t **ntohl** (in_addr_t *networkLong*)
    in_port_t **ntohs** (in_port_t *networkShort*)

Each of these functions performs a conversion between a host-format number and a network-format number. For example, htonl () returns the network-format equivalent of the host-format unsigned long *hostLong*, and ntohs () returns the host-format equivalent of the network-format unsigned short *networkShort*.

Figure 12–70 Description of the htonl (), htons (), ntohl (), and ntohs () library functions.

The final step is to create the client socket and attempt the connection. The code for this is almost the same as for PF_LOCAL sockets:

```
42      clientFd = socket (PF_INET, SOCK_STREAM, DEFAULT_PROTOCOL);
43      do /* Loop until a connection is made with the server */
44        {
45          result = connect (clientFd,serverSockAddrPtr,serverLen);
46          if (result == -1) sleep (1); /* Try again in 1 second */
47        }
48      while (result == -1);
```

The rest of the program contains nothing new. Now it's time to look at how an Internet server is built.

12.6.2.16 Internet Servers

Constructing an Internet server is actually pretty easy. The **sin_family, sin_port,** and **sin_zero** fields of the socket address structure should be filled in, as they were in the client example. The only difference is that the **s_addr** field should be set to the network byte ordered value of the constant INADDR_ANY, which means "accept any incoming client requests." The following is an example of how to create a server socket address:

```
int serverFd; /* Server socket
struct sockaddr_in serverINETAddress; /* Server Internet address */
struct sockaddr* serverSockAddrPtr; /* Pointer to server address */
struct sockaddr_in clientINETAddress; /* Client Internet address */
struct sockaddr* clientSockAddrPtr; /* Pointer to client address */
int port = 13; /* Set to the port that you wish to serve */
int serverLen; /* Length of address structure */

serverFd = socket (PF_INET, SOCK_STREAM, DEFAULT_PROTOCOL);/* Create */
serverLen = sizeof (serverINETAddress); /* Length of structure */

bzero ((char*) &serverINETAddress, serverLen); /* Clear structure */
serverINETAddress.sin_family = PF_INET; /* Internet domain */
serverINETAddress.sin_addr.s_addr = htonl (INADDR_ANY);/* Accept all */
serverINETAddress.sin_port = htons (port); /* Server port number */
```

When the address is created, the socket is bound to the address, and its queue size is specified in the usual way:

```
serverSockAddrPtr = (struct sockaddr*) &serverINETAddress;
bind (serverFd, serverSockAddrPtr, serverLen);
listen (serverFd, 5);
```

The final step is to accept client connections. When a successful connection is made, the client socket address is filled with the client's IP address and a new file descriptor is returned:

```
clientLen = sizeof (clientINETAddress);
clientSockAddrPtr = (struct sockaddr*) clientINETAddress;
clientFd = accept (serverFd, clientSockAddrPtr, &clientLen);
```

As you can see, an Internet server's code is very similar to that of a PF_LOCAL server.

CHAPTER REVIEW

Checklist

In this chapter, I described:

- all of the common file management system calls
- the system calls for duplicating, terminating, and differentiating processes
- how a parent may wait for its children
- the terms *orphan* and *zombie*
- threaded processes
- how signals may be trapped and ignored
- the way to kill processes
- how processes may be suspended and resumed
- IPC mechanisms: unnamed pipes, named pipes, and sockets
- the client/server paradigm
- local domain and Internet domain sockets

Quiz

1. How can you tell when you've reached the end of a file?
2. What is a file descriptor?
3. What's the quickest way to move to the end of a file?
4. Why is the system call to delete a file called unlink () instead of delete ()?
5. Describe the way that shells implement I/O redirection.
6. What is an orphaned process?
7. Under what circumstances do zombies accumulate?
8. How can a parent find out how its children died?
9. What's the difference between execv () and execvp ()?
10. Why is the name of the system call kill () a misnomer?
11. If a process does not handle a specific signal, what are the default reactions the process may have upon receiving that signal?
12. How can you protect critical code?
13. Must you be the super-user to lower your process's nice value (i.e., to raise the process's priority)?
14. What is the purpose of process groups?

15. What happens when a process attempts to read from its controlling terminal but it is not a member of the same process group as the terminal's control process?
16. What happens when a writer tries to overflow a pipe?
17. How can you create a named pipe?
18. What is meant by "network byte order"?
19. Describe the client/server paradigm.
20. Describe the stages that a client and a server go through to establish a connection.

Exercises

1. Write a program to catch all signals sent to it and print out which signal was sent. Then issue a "kill -9" command to the process. How is SIGKILL different from the other signals? [level: *easy*]

2. Write a program that takes a single integer argument *n* from the command line and creates a binary tree of processes of depth *n*. When the tree is created, each process should display the phrase "I am process x" and then terminate. The nodes of the process tree should be numbered according to a breadth-first traversal. For example, if the user entered this:

```
$ tree 4                    ...build a tree of depth 4.
```

then the process tree would look like this:

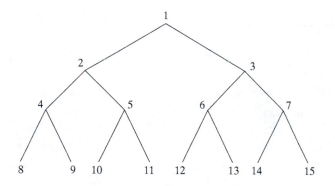

and the output would be:

```
I am process 1
I am process 2
...
I am process 15
```

Make sure that the original parent process does not terminate until all of its children have died. This is so that you can terminate the parent and its children from your terminal with a *Control-C*. [level: *medium*]

3. Write a program that creates a ring of three processes connected by pipes. The first process should prompt the user for a string and then send it to the second process. The second process should reverse the string and send it to the third process. The third process should convert the string to uppercase and send it back to the first process. When the first process gets the processed string, it should display it to the terminal. When this is done, all three processes should terminate. Here's an illustration of the process ring:

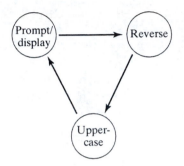

Here's an example of the program in action:

```
$ ring                                  ...run the program.
Please enter a string: ole
Processed string is: ELO
$ _
```

[level: *medium*]

4. Rewrite the "ghoul" exercise of Chapter 6, "The Bourne Again Shell," using the C language. [level: *medium*]

5. Write a program that uses setuid () to access a file that he/she could not normally access. [level: *medium*]

Projects

1. Write a suite of programs that run in parallel and interact to play the "Paper, Scissors, Rock" game. In this game, two players secretly choose either paper, scissors, or rock. They then reveal their choice. A referee decides who wins as follows:

   • Paper beats rock (by covering it).
   • Rock beats scissors (by blunting it).
   • Scissors beats paper (by cutting it).
   • Matching choices draw.

The winning player gets a point. In a draw, no points are awarded. Your program should simulate such a game, allowing the user to choose how many iterations are performed, observe the game, and see the final score. Here's an example of a game:

```
$ ./play 3                          ...play three iterations.
Paper, Scissors, Rock: 3 iterations
Player 1: ready
Player 2: ready
Go Players [1]
 Player 1: Scissors
 Player 2: Rock
Player 2 wins
Go Players [2]
 Player 1: Paper
 Player 2: Rock
Player 1 wins
Go Players [3]
 Player 1: Paper
 Player 2: Paper
Players draw.
Final score:
 Player 1: 1
 Player 2: 1
Players Draw
$ _
```

You should write three programs, which operate as follows:

a. One program is the main program, which fork/execs one referee process and two player processes. It then waits until all three terminate. It should check that the command-line parameter that specifies the number of turns is legal and pass it to the referee process as a parameter to exec ().

b. One program is a referee program, which plays the role of the server. This program should prepare a socket and then listen for both players to send the string "READY", which means that they're ready to make a choice. It should then tell each player to make a choice by sending them both the string "GO". Their responses are then read, and their scores are calculated and updated. This process should be repeated until all of the turns have been taken, at which point the referee should send both players the string "STOP", which causes them to terminate.

c. One program is a player program, which plays the role of the client. This program is executed twice by the main program, and should start by connecting to the referee's socket. It should then send the "READY" message. When it receives the "GO" message back from the referee, it should make a choice and send it as a string to the referee. When it receives the string "STOP", it should kill itself.

These programs will almost certainly share some functions. To do a good job, create a makefile that separately compiles these common functions and links them into the executables that use them. Do not avoid sending strings by encoding them as one-byte numbers—sending strings is part of the exercise. [level: *medium*]

2. Rewrite Exercise 1 using unnamed pipes instead of sockets. Which do you think was easier to write? Which is easier to understand? [level: *medium*]

3. Rewrite Exercise 1 to allow the players to reside on different machines on the network. Each component of the game should be able to start separately. [level: *hard*]

This is an example of how 3 will work.

```
...execute this command on vanguard.
$ ./referee 5000            ...use local port 5000.
...execute this command on csservr2.
$ ./player vanguard.5000    ...player is on a remote port.
...execute this command on wotan.
$ ./player vanguard.5000    ...player is on a remote port.
```

13

Linux Internals

Motivation

The predecessor to Linux, UNIX, was one of the best-designed operating systems of its time. Many of the underlying operating system concepts embedded in UNIX have been adopted by other operating systems, including Windows and Linux. Knowledge of how the system works can aid in designing high-performance Linux applications. For example, knowledge of the internals of the virtual memory system can help you arrange data structures so that the amount of information transferred between main and secondary memory is minimized. In summary, knowledge of Linux internals is useful for two reasons: as a source of reusable information that may help you in designing other similar systems, and to help you design high-performance applications.

Prerequisites

You should already have read Chapter 12, "Systems Programming." It also helps to have a good knowledge of data structures such as pointers and linked lists.

Objectives

In this chapter, I describe the mechanisms that Linux uses to support the file system, processes, memory management, input/output, and interprocess communications. I also explain some of the main kernel data structures and algorithms.

Presentation

The information in this chapter is presented in several sections, each of which describes a portion of the Linux kernel.

13.1 Introduction

The Linux kernel is the core of a Linux system. In order to understand it well, it's necessary to break it down into manageable portions and to tackle each portion in a layered fashion. Here's a description of each section of this chapter:

- *Kernel Basics*, which discusses system calls and interrupts.
- *The File System*, which describes how the directory hierarchy, regular files, peripherals, and multiple file systems are managed.
- *Process Management*, which explains how processes share the CPU.
- *Virtual Memory Management*, which explains how processes access and share memory.
- *Input/Output*, which describes how processes access files.
- *Interprocess Communication* (IPC), which explains the mechanisms that allow processes to communicate with each other, even if they're on different machines.

13.2 Kernel Basics

The Linux kernel is the part of the operating system that contains the code for:

- sharing the CPU and RAM between competing processes
- processing system calls
- transferring data between processes and peripheral devices (including the network), and between processes

The kernel is a program that is loaded from disk into RAM when the computer is first turned on. It always stays in RAM, and runs until the system is turned off (or crashes). Although it's mostly written in C, some parts of the kernel were written in assembly language for efficiency reasons. User programs make use of the kernel via the system call interface.

13.2.1   Kernel Subsystems

The kernel facilities may be divided into several subsystems:

- memory management
- process management
- interprocess communication (IPC)
- input/output
- file management

These subsystems interact in a fairly hierarchical way. Figure 13–1 illustrates the layering.

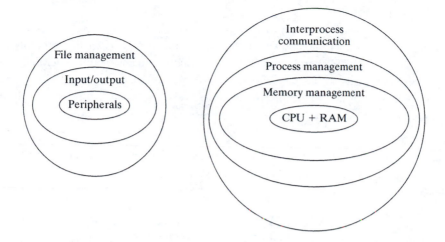

Figure 13–1   Linux kernel subsystems.

13.2.2   Processes and Files

The Linux kernel supports the concepts of processes and files. Processes are the "life forms" that live in the computer and make decisions. Files are containers of information that processes read and write. In addition, processes may talk to each other via several different kinds of interprocess communication mechanisms, including signals, pipes, and sockets. Figure 13–2 is an illustration of what I mean.

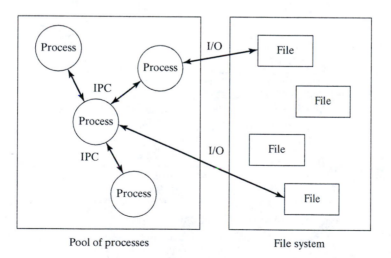

Figure 13–2   Linux supports processes and files.

13.2.3   Talking to the Kernel

Processes access kernel functions via the system call interface, and peripherals (special files) communicate with the kernel via hardware interrupts. Linux also provides the /proc file system (discussed in Chapter 14, "System Administration"), which is an abstraction layer that provides access to "live" kernel data.

Since systems calls and interrupts are obviously very important, I'll begin the discussion of Linux internals with a description of each mechanism.

13.2.4   System Calls

System calls are the programmer's functional interface to the kernel. They are subroutines that reside inside the Linux kernel, and support basic system functions such as the ones listed in Figure 13–3.

Function	System call
open a file	open
close a file	close
perform I/O	read/write
send a signal	kill
create a pipe	pipe
create a socket	socket
duplicate a process	fork/clone
overlay a process	execl/execv
terminate a process	exit

Figure 13–3   Common Linux system calls.

System calls may be loosely grouped into three main categories, as illustrated in Figure 13–4.

13.2.5   User Mode and Kernel Mode

The kernel contains several data structures that are essential to the functioning of the system. Examples include:

- a *task list*, which is a doubly linked list of objects representing each process
- a *file list,* which is a doubly linked list of objects representing each open file

These data structures reside in the kernel's memory space, which is protected from user processes by a memory management system that I'll describe to you later. User processes therefore cannot accidentally corrupt these important kernel data structures. System call routines are

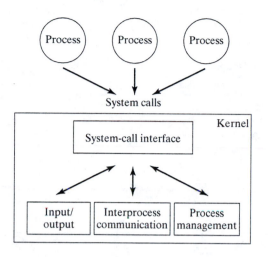

Figure 13–4   Major system call subsystems.

different from regular functions because they *can* directly manipulate kernel data structures, albeit in a carefully controlled manner.

When a user process is running, it operates in a special machine mode called *user mode*. This mode prevents a process from executing certain privileged machine instructions, including those that would allow it to access the kernel data structures. The other machine mode is called *kernel mode*. A kernel-mode process may execute any machine instruction.

The only way for a user process to enter kernel mode is to execute a system call. Every system call is allocated a code number, starting from 1. When a process invokes a system call, the C runtime library version of the system call places the system call parameters and the system call code number into some machine registers, and then executes a *trap* machine instruction. The trap instruction flips the machine into kernel mode and uses the system call code number to find the proper function. The code corresponding to the indexed function executes in kernel mode, modifying kernel data structures as necessary, and then performs a special *return* instruction that flips the machine back into user mode and returns to the user process's code.

Why not just use a client/server model with a kernel server process that services system requests from client user processes? This avoids the need for user processes to directly execute kernel code. The reason is pure and simple—speed. In current architectures, the overhead of swapping between processes is too great to make the client/server approach practical. However, it's interesting to note that some of the modern microkernel systems are taking the latter approach.

From a programmer's standpoint, using a system call is easy; you call the C function with the correct parameters, and the function returns when complete. If an error occurs, the function returns -1 and the global variable **errno** is set to indicate the cause of the error. Figure 13–5 illustrates the flow of control during a system call.

User process

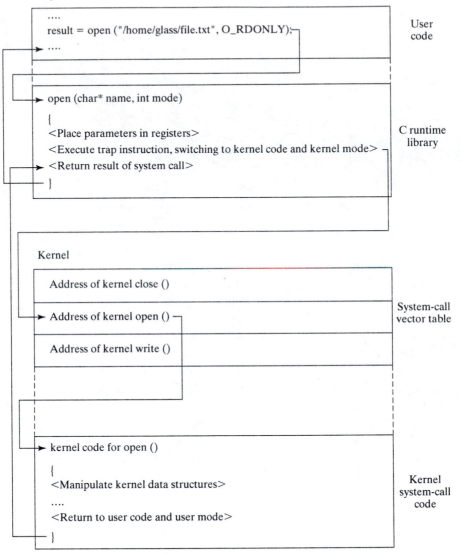

Figure 13–5   User mode and kernel mode.

13.2.6   Synchronous Versus Asynchronous Processing

When a process performs a system call, it cannot usually be preempted. This means that the scheduler will not assign the CPU to another process during the operation of a system call. However, some system calls request I/O operations from a device, which can take a while to complete. To avoid leaving the CPU idle during the wait for I/O completion, the kernel sends the waiting process to sleep and wakes it up again only when a hardware interrupt signaling I/O completion is received. The scheduler does not allocate a sleeping process any CPU time, and so allocates the CPU to other processes while the hardware device is servicing the I/O request.

An interesting consequence of the way that Linux handles read () and write () is that user processes experience synchronous execution of system calls, whereas the kernel experiences asynchronous behavior (Figure 13–6).

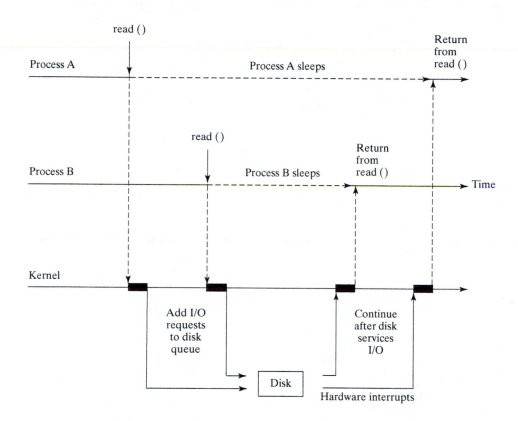

Figure 13–6   Synchronous and asynchronous events

13.2.6.1 Interrupts

Interrupts are the way that hardware devices notify the kernel that they would like some attention. In the same way that processes compete for CPU time, hardware devices compete for interrupt processing. Devices are allocated an interrupt priority based on their relative importance. For example, interrupts from the system clock have a higher priority than those from the keyboard. Figure 13–7 illustrates interrupt processing.

When an interrupt occurs, the current process is suspended and the kernel determines the source of the interrupt. It then examines its interrupt vector table (called irq_action in the kernel), to find the location of the code that processes the interrupt. This "interrupt handler" code is then executed. When the interrupt handler completes, the current process is resumed.

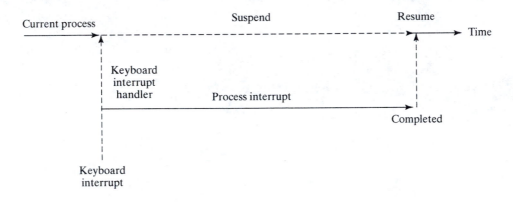

Figure 13–7   Interrupt processing.

13.2.7   Interrupting Interrupts

Interrupt processing may itself be interrupted! If an interrupt of a higher priority than the current interrupt arrives, a similar sequence of events occurs, and the lower-priority interrupt handler is suspended until the higher-priority interrupt completes (Figure 13–8).

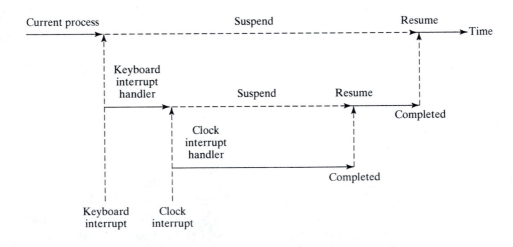

Figure 13–8   Interrupts may be interrupted.

13.3 The File System

Linux uses files for long-term storage and RAM for short-term storage. Programs, data, and text are all stored in files. Files are usually stored on hard disks, but can also be stored on other media such as tape and floppy disks. Linux files are organized by a hierarchy of labels, commonly known as a *directory structure*. The files referenced by these labels may be of three kinds:

- *Regular files*, which contain a sequence of bytes generally corresponding to code or data. They may be referenced via the standard I/O system calls.
- *Directory files*, which are stored on disk in a special format and form the backbone of the file system. They may be referenced only via directory-specific system calls.
- *Special files,* which correspond to peripherals such as printers and disks, and interprocess communication mechanisms such as pipes and sockets. They may be referenced via the standard I/O system calls.

Conceptually, a Linux file is a linear sequence of bytes. The Linux kernel does not support any higher order of file structure, such as records and/or fields, as some older operating systems did. This is evident if you consider the lseek () system call, which allows you to position the file pointer only in terms of a byte offset.

While most of the concepts in this section apply to any file system supported by Linux, we will specifically examine the Native Linux (ext2) file system. But first, let's examine the hardware architecture of the most common file system medium: the disk drive.

13.3.1   Disk Architecture

Figure 13–9 is a diagram of a typical disk architecture.

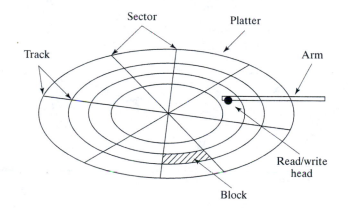

Figure 13–9   Disk architecture.

A disk is split up in two ways: it's sliced like a pizza into areas called *sectors*, and further subdivided into concentric rings called *tracks*. The individual areas bounded by the intersection of sectors and tracks are called *blocks*, and form the basic unit of disk storage. A typical disk block can hold 4K bytes. A single read/write head accesses information as the disk rotates and its surface passes underneath. A special chip called a *disk controller* moves the read/write head in response to instructions from the disk device driver, which is a special piece of software located in the Linux kernel.

There are several variations of this simple disk architecture. Many disk drives actually contain several platters, stacked one upon the other. In these systems, the collection of tracks with the same index number is called a *cylinder*. In most multiplatter systems, the disk arms are connected to each other so that the read/write heads all move synchronously, rather like a comb moving through hair (Figure 13–10). The read/write heads of such disk systems therefore move through cylinders of media.

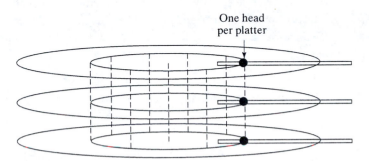

Figure 13–10   A multiplatter architecture.

Notice that the blocks on the outside track are larger than the blocks on the inside track, due to the way that a disk is partitioned. If a disk always rotates at the same speed, the density of data on outer blocks is less than it could be, thus wasting potential storage (Figure 13–11).

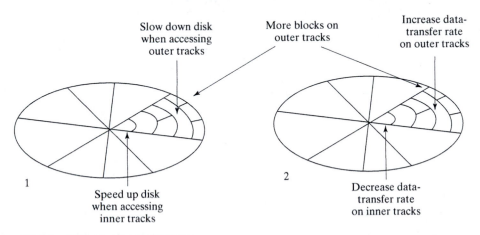

Figure 13–11   Disk storage techniques.

13.3.1.1 Interleaving

When a sequence of contiguously numbered blocks is read, there's a latency delay between each block due to the overhead of the communication between the disk controller and the device driver. Logically contiguous blocks are therefore spaced apart on the surface of the disk so that, by the time the latency delay is over, the head is positioned over the correct area. The spacing between blocks due to this delay effect is called the *interleave factor*. Figure 13–12 illustrates two different interleave factors.

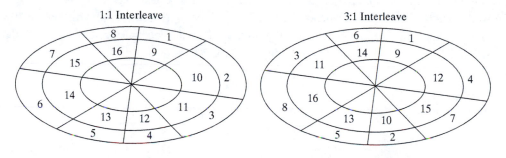

Figure 13–12 Disk interleaving.

13.3.1.2 Block I/O

Input and output to and from the disk is always performed in whole blocks. If you issue a read () system call to read the first byte of data from a file, the device driver issues an I/O request to the disk controller to read the first 4K block into a kernel buffer, and then copies the first byte from the buffer to your process. More information about I/O buffering is presented later in this chapter.

Most disk controllers handle one block I/O request at a time. When a disk controller completes the current block I/O request, it issues a hardware interrupt back to the device driver to signal completion. At this point, the device driver usually makes the next block I/O request. Figure 13–13 illustrates the sequence of events that might occur during a 9K read ().

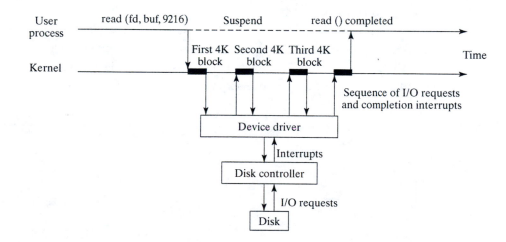

Figure 13–13 Block I/O.

13.3.1.3 Fragmentation

Block size can be specified at 1K, 2K, or 4K, when the file system is created with the **mkfs** utility (if not specified, **mkfs** will pick a size suitable to the size of the file system). Assuming a 4K block size, a single 9K file requires 3 blocks of storage—one to hold the first 4K, one to hold the next 4K, and the last to hold the remaining 1K. As a file is modified, blocks are added to and removed from the file as data is added and deleted. Disk blocks are rarely contiguous on the disk device and, over time, the disk blocks making up the file tend to become scattered all over the disk (Figure 13–14). This situation is called *fragmentation*.

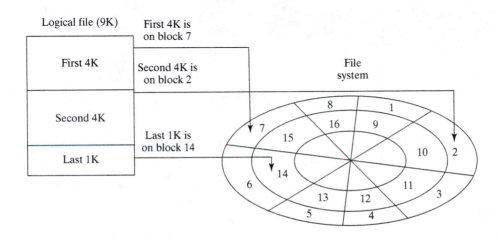

Figure 13–14 A file's blocks are scattered.

13.3.2   Virtual File System

The central connection between the Linux kernel and all file systems is the Virtual File System (VFS) abstraction layer. The Linux kernel knows nothing of the details of any particular file system, it simply talks to the VFS to deal with any file system. Every file system provides a standard interface that hooks into VFS. Figure 13–15 shows the relationship between a process and a file system.

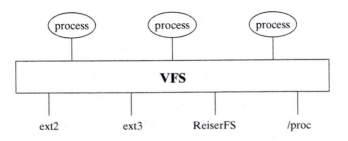

Figure 13–15 The VFS layer between process and file system.

This abstraction not only allows many different types of real file system to be plugged in underneath and run smoothly, it also allows a file system interface to be created for data structures other than file systems. The /proc file system (discussed in Chapter 14, "System Administration") is an example of such a use and is a good example of the power of VFS. A file system interface to kernel data provides an easy-to-navigate interface into a running kernel.

13.3.3 Inodes

Linux uses a structure called an *inode* (**Index Node**) to store information about each file. The inode of a regular or directory file contains pointers to the locations of its disk blocks, and the inode of a special file contains information that allows the peripheral to be identified. Each inode also holds other information about the file.

An inode is a fixed size structure containing pointers to disk blocks and additional indirect pointers (for large files). Every inode in a particular file system is allocated a unique inode number and every file has exactly one inode (Figure 13–16).

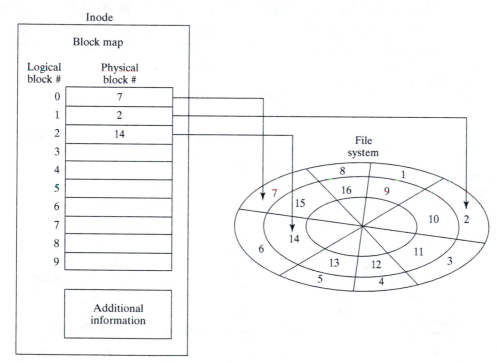

Figure 13–16 Every file has an inode.

Each inode contains information about the file such as:

• the type of the file: regular, directory, block-oriented or character-oriented special, etc.
• file permissions (mode)

- the owner and group ID of the file
- a hard link count (described later in this chapter)
- the last modification and last access times
- if it's a regular or directory file, the location of the blocks
- if it's a special file, the major and minor device numbers (described later in this chapter)
- if it's a symbolic link, the value of the symbolic link (unless it's so long it must be in a data block)

In other words, an inode contains most of the information that you see when you perform an "ls -l," except the filename.

Only the locations of the first 12 blocks of a file are stored directly in the inode. Many Linux files are smaller than 48K in size, so in a 4K-block file system, this is sufficient for many files. An indirect accessing scheme is used for addressing larger files. In this scheme, a disk block is used to hold the locations of other data blocks. This block is called an *indirect block*. Its location is stored in the inode, and it is used to address the next group of blocks in the file. If this is still insufficient to hold references to all the required data blocks for a file, a *double-indirect block* is used. This block points to a group of indirect blocks, which in turn point to data blocks. A Linux inode contains a place to store references to one indirect, one double-indirect, and one triple-indirect block as shown in Figure 13–17.

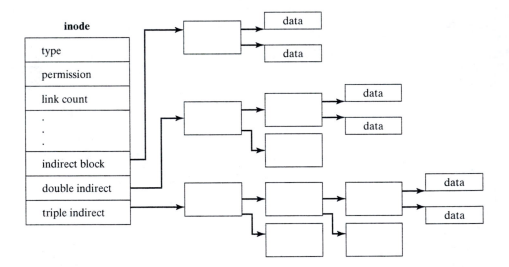

Figure 13–17 A file's blocks are scattered.

Note that, as the file gets larger, the amount of indirection required to access a particular block increases. This overhead is minimized by buffering the contents of the inode and commonly referenced indirect blocks in RAM.

13.3.4 File System Layout

The first logical block of a disk is called the *boot block,* and contains some executable code that is used when Linux is first activated. See Chapter 2, "Installing Your Linux System," and Chapter 14, "System Administration," for more information.

The remainder of the file system is a repeated series of *block groups*, each containing a group of inodes, disk blocks, and some housekeeping information about them.

Each block group contains the following data:

- a copy of the file system's superblock
- group descriptors
- block bitmap
- inode bitmap
- the inode table
- data blocks

Figure 13–18 is a simplified diagram of the layout of the ext2 file system.

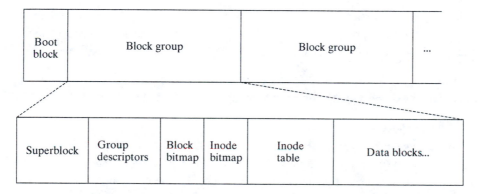

Figure 13–18 Simplified view of the ext2 file system layout.

13.3.4.1 The Superblock

The superblock contains information pertaining to the entire file system, such as:

- a "magic number" denoting type of file system
- number of inodes in the file system
- number of currently free inodes
- number of blocks in the file system
- number of currently free blocks
- the size of a block (in bytes) used by the file system
- number of data blocks per block group
- number of inodes per block group

Without the superblock, the file system could not be used. Therefore, multiple copies of the superblock are maintained throughout the file system area in case of a failure of the primary copy. A copy of the superblock is maintained at the started of each block group.

13.3.4.2 Group Descriptors

The group descriptor is a sort of superblock for the individual block group. As in superblock, a copy of all group descriptors is stored in each block group, so this area contains a copy of all group descriptors in the file system. Information stored here includes:

- pointer to a disk block containing the block allocation bitmap
- pointer to a disk block containing the inode allocation bitmap
- pointer to the beginning of the inode table
- free block count
- free inode count
- used directory count

13.3.4.3 Block and Inode Bitmaps

The block and inode bitmaps are each a string of bits corresponding to each block and inode, respectively, in the block group. If the bit is set to 1, then block or inode is allocated, otherwise it is available. These bitmaps are used during allocation and deallocation of block and inodes.

13.3.4.4 Inode Table

The *inode table* is simply an array of inode structures for each inode defined in the block group.

13.3.5   Bad Blocks

A disk always contains several blocks that, for one reason or another, are not fit for use. Many disk drives map out bad blocks internally, but those that are not can be mapped out by the file system itself. The utilities that create a new file system also create a single "worst nightmare" file composed of all the bad blocks on the disk and record the locations of all these blocks in inode number 1. This prevents the blocks from being allocated to other files. When **fsck** runs to check the file system, bad blocks can be added to this file and thus mapped out of the file system.

13.3.6   Directories

Inode number 2 contains the location of the block(s) containing the root directory of the file system. A directory contains a list of associations between filenames and inode numbers. When a directory is created, it is automatically allocated entries for "..", its parent directory, and ".", itself. Since a <filename, inode number> pair effectively links a name to a file, these associations are termed "hard links." Since filenames are stored in the directory blocks, they are not stored in a file's inode. In fact, it wouldn't make any sense to store the name in the inode, as a file may have more than one name. Because of this observation, it's more accurate to think of the directory hierarchy as being a hierarchy of *file labels*, rather than a hierarchy of *files*. Most file systems allow filenames up to 255 characters in length.

Figure 13–19 is an illustration of the root inode corresponding to a simple root directory. The inode numbers associated with each filename are shown as subscripts.

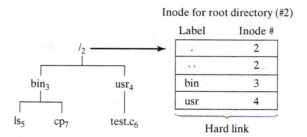

figure 13–19 The root directory is associated with inode two.

13.3.7 Translating Pathnames into Inode Numbers

System calls such as open () must obtain a file's inode from its pathname. They perform the translation as follows:

1. The inode from which to start the pathname search is located. If the pathname is absolute, the search starts from inode #2. If the pathname is relative, the search starts from the inode corresponding to the process's current working directory.
2. The components of the pathname are then processed from left to right. Every component except the last should correspond to either a directory or a symbolic link. Let's call the inode from which the pathname search is started the *current inode*.
3. If the current inode corresponds to a directory, the directory corresponding to the current inode is searched to see if the current pathname component is there. If it's not found, an error occurs—otherwise, the value of the current inode number becomes the inode number associated with the located pathname component.
4. If the current inode corresponds to a symbolic link, the pathname up to and including the current path component is replaced by the contents of the symbolic link, and the pathname is reprocessed.
5. The inode corresponding to the final pathname component is the inode of the file referenced by the entire pathname.

To illustrate this algorithm, I'll list the steps required to translate the pathname "/usr/test.c" into an inode number. Figure 13–20 contains the disk layout that I assume during the translation process. It indicates the translation path using bold lines, and the final destination using a circle.

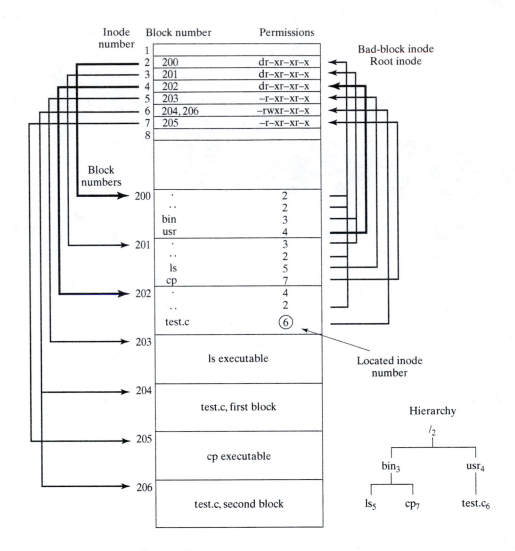

Figure 13–20   A sample directory layout.

Here's the logic that the kernel uses to translate the pathname "/usr/test.c" into an inode number:

1. The pathname is absolute, so the current inode number is 2.
2. The directory corresponding to inode 2 is searched for the pathname component "usr." The matching entry is found, and the current inode number is set to 4.

3. The directory corresponding to inode 4 is searched for the pathname component "test.c". The matching entry is found, and the current inode number is set to 6.

4. "test.c" is the final pathname component, so the algorithm returns the inode number 6.

As you can see, the translation bounces between inodes and directory blocks until the pathname is fully processed.

13.3.8   Mounting File Systems

When Linux is booted, the directory hierarchy corresponds to the file system located on a single disk called the *root device*. Linux allows you to create file systems on other devices and attach them to the original directory hierarchy using a mechanism termed *mounting*. The **mount** utility allows a super-user to splice the root directory of a file system into the existing directory hierarchy. The hierarchy of a large Linux system may be spread across many devices, each containing a subtree of the total hierarchy. For example, the "/usr" subtree is commonly stored on a device other than the root device. Non-root file systems are usually mounted automatically at boot time. See Chapter 14, "System Administration," for more details. For example, assume that a file system is stored on a floppy disk in the "/dev/fd0" device. To attach it to the "/mnt" subdirectory of the main hierarchy, you'd execute the command:

```
$ mount /dev/fd0 /mnt
```

Figure 13–21 illustrates the effect of this command.

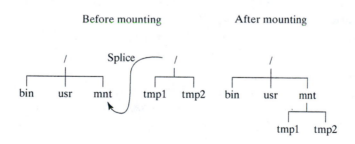

Figure 13–21   Mounting directories.

File systems may be detached from the main hierarchy by using the **umount** utility. The following command would detach the file system stored in "/dev/fd0":

```
$ umount /dev/fd0
```

or

```
$ umount /mnt
```

13.4 Process Management

In this section, I describe the way that the kernel shares the CPU and RAM among competing processes. The area of the kernel that shares the CPU is called the *scheduler*, and the area of the kernel that shares RAM is called the *memory manager*. This section also contains information about process-oriented system calls, including exec (), fork (), and exit ().

13.4.1   Executable Files

When the source code of a program is compiled, it is stored in a special format on disk. The first few bytes of the file are known as the *magic number*, and are used by the kernel to identify the type of the executable file. For example, if the first two bytes of the file are the characters "#!", the kernel knows that the executable file contains shell text, and invokes a shell to execute the text. In addition to recognizing a specific magic number, Linux recognizes the following executable file formats:

- a.out—old-style format for backward compatibility
- ELF—Executable and Linking Format, the typical executable format
- EM86—allows Intel binaries to run on Alpha platforms
- Java—executes Java class files without specifying a Java bytecode interpreter

13.4.2   The First Processes

Linux runs a program by creating a process and then associating it with a named executable file. Surprisingly enough, there's no system call that allows you to say "create a new process to run program X"; instead, you must duplicate an existing process and then associate the newly created child process with the executable file "X."

The first process, sched, has process ID (PID) 0, and is created by Linux during boot time. This process immediately forks (creating PID 1), and that process execs the **init** program. This is known as a "fork and exec."

The purpose of these processes is described later in this chapter. All other processes in the system are descendants of the *init* process. For more information concerning the boot sequence, see Chapter 14, "System Administration."

13.4.3   Kernel Processes and User Processes

Most processes execute in user mode except when they make a system call, at which point they flip temporarily into kernel mode. However, the *sched* daemon (PID 0) executes permanently in kernel mode due to its importance and is called a *kernel process*. In contrast to user processes, kernel process code is linked directly into the kernel and does not reside in a separate executable file. In addition, kernel processes are never preempted.

13.4.4   The Process Hierarchy

When a process duplicates by using fork (), the original process is known as the parent of the new process, or *child process*. The *init* process, PID 1, is the process from which all user processes are descended. Parent and child processes are therefore related in a hierarchy, with the *init* process as the root of the hierarchy. Figure 13–22 illustrates a process hierarchy involving four processes.

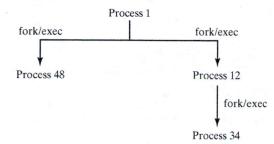

Figure 13–22 Process hierarchy.

13.4.5 Process States

Every process in the system can be in one of six possible states, as follows:

- *Running*, which means that the process is currently using the CPU.
- *Running/runable*, which means that the process is in the run queue and can make use of the CPU as soon as it becomes available.
- *Waiting/sleeping*, which means that the process is waiting for an event to occur and it may be interrupted. For example, if a process executes a read () system call, it sleeps until the I/O request completes.
- *Waiting/uninterruptible*, which means that the process is waiting for a event to occur, but it has disabled signals, so it cannot be interrupted.
- *Suspended/stopped*, which means that the process has been "frozen" by a signal such as SIGSTOP. It will resume only when sent a SIGCONT signal. For example, a *Control-Z* from the keyboard suspends all of the processes in the foreground job.
- *Zombified*, which means that the process has terminated but its parent has not accepted its exit code. A process remains in existence as a zombie process until its parent accepts its return code using the wait () system call.

13.4.6 Process Kernel Data

In addition to the code and data of a running process, every process in the system has some additional associated "housekeeping" information that is maintained by the kernel for process management. This data is stored in the kernel's data region and is accessible only by the kernel; user processes may not access their process's housekeeping data. Data within a process's user area includes:

- a record of how the process should react to each kind of signal
- a record of the process's open file descriptors
- a record of the process's virtual memory pages

Most of this data is maintained in individual structures, which themselves are parts of a doubly linked list that the kernel uses to track all of a type of resource in the system. For example, a single process (or task, as it is called in the Linux kernel code) is represented by a task_struct structure, shown in Figure 13–23.

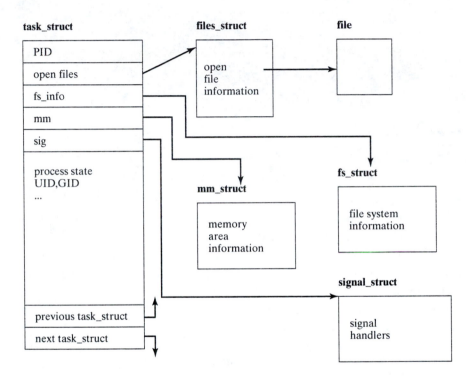

Figure 13–23   A user process's task_struct.

Each process or task has a kernel structure that contains information about all the files the process is currently using, or *open files*, as shown in Figure 13–24.

Whenever the open () system call succeeds and a new file is opened, a new file structure is created, a pointer is added to the files_struct of the process that opened the file, and the file structure is linked into the doubly linked list of open files on the system. Rather than constantly allocating and deallocating these structures in kernel memory, when a file structure is no longer needed, it is added to a free list and reused in the future.

f_op points to a file_operations structure which contains pointers to all I/O operations that are defined for the device driver of the device containing the file. This is used when a user program executes a system call like read (), write (), or lseek ().

files_struct

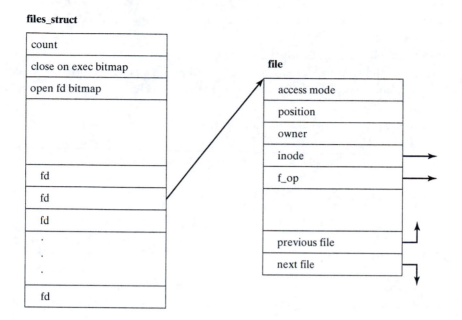

Figure 13–24 Open file information for a task.

13.4.7 The Task List

The kernel keeps track of all processes in the system by virtue of their being linked together into what is called the *task list* (this is analogous to the UNIX process table). The kernel keeps a pointer to the head of the list, the task_struct for the *init* process, and from there it can find all other processes in the system (Figure 13–25).

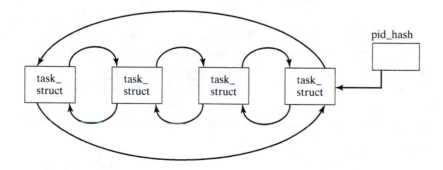

Figure 13–25 The Linux task list.

13.4.8 The Scheduler

The kernel is responsible for sharing CPU time between competing processes. A section of the kernel code called the *scheduler* performs this duty, and maintains a special data structure called a *run queue* that allows it to schedule processes efficiently. The run queue is a linked list of the runable processes that are ready to use the CPU.

Processes are allocated CPU time in a round-robin fashion in proportion to their importance or what the Linux kernel calls "goodness." Scheduling policy differs for traditional processes and real-time processes, which Linux supports. All real-time processes have a higher priority than any regular process.

The scheduler periodically walks the task list looking for processes that are ready to run to add to the run queue. Then it goes through the run queue to see which process should get CPU access next. Some of the factors the scheduler uses to determine goodness are:

- process type (real-time or normal)
- priority (can be affected by the **nice** utility or nice () system call)
- amount of time process has already used (it's "less good" if it's been running)

If the scheduler selects the currently running process, then nothing changes. If it selects a different process, then important information about the running process is saved and the new process is given access to the CPU. This is known as a *context switch*. The old process is put at the end of the run queue (if it is still ready to run) and will get CPU time again after other runable processes have had their turn.

A process can voluntarily give up the CPU in a situation where it will wait for system resources. In this case, it sleeps and the scheduler immediately finds a new process to which to allocate the CPU. An interactive process will tend to have good response time, because while it waits for user action, it uses no CPU time, so its priority increases.

13.5 Virtual Memory Management

The Linux kernel also manages fair access to physical memory on behalf of all user processes. Processes have their own view of system memory that is not exactly reality, so a process is said to use a *virtual memory* space rather than a physical memory space. The beauty of this scheme is that each process sees system memory as an area that can be much larger than the amount of physical memory actually in the system. The addressing always begins at zero (rather than some varying and large number where the process might begin if it were in a physical memory space) and the process has no access to any other process's memory space, so all processes are protected from being overwritten by any other process.

13.5.1 The Page Table

For the sake of convenience, memory is (conceptually) divided into regions called *pages*, analogous to disk blocks. In fact, the size of a memory page is usually the same as the size of a disk block to facilitate moving data back and forth between the two efficiently. For example, memory pages on an Alpha platform are 8K, but 4K on an Intel platform.

The virtual memory manager in the Linux kernel, often with hardware assistance from the Memory Management Unit (MMU) if available, maps the address of a virtual page of memory from the user process's address space to the address of a physical page of memory on the system. This is accomplished through the use of a *page table*, as shown in Figure 13–26.

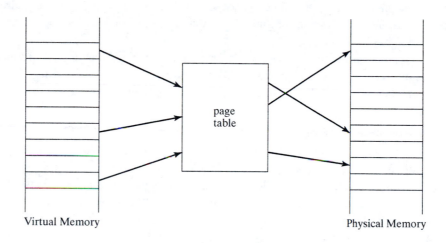

Figure 13–26 The page table maps virtual to physical memory addresses.

This is an oversimplification of a Linux page table. Linux uses a *three-level page table* to map from a virtual to a physical memory address. The first level is a *page directory,* which is a list of pointers to other page directories, which in turn are lists of pointers to page tables. On platforms where the MMU only supports two-level page tables (e.g., Intel platforms), Linux makes the middle directory of length one.

A page-table entry in the memory management system is analogous to an inode in the file system, as each tracks the location of individual storage units. Each page-table entry contains information about an individual page of memory, including:

- valid flag (invalid means page is in swap area)
- physical page address
- access control information (executable or shared data, modified flag, last time used, etc.)

When the proper page-table entry has been identified, the memory page can be accessed and the data transferred to the proper location in memory or read from memory and transferred back to the process. We'll see uses for the other information in the page-table entry a bit later.

13.5.2 Paging

When a process is running, not all of its memory pages need to be resident in physical memory. In fact, since the virtual memory space may be larger than the physical memory space, this might well be impossible. The only pages that must be in physical memory are those the process is actually using. Linux uses a scheme called *demand paging* to bring memory pages into memory as they are needed.

When a running process makes a request of an address in a page of memory that is not currently in physical memory (i.e., its valid bit is not set), it generates a *page fault*. This causes the kernel to bring the required data into memory and update the page tables to reflect where the page is located in physical memory.

If there is no room in physical memory to bring in a new page, then a page currently in physical memory (either a page belonging to this process that it is no longer using or a page belonging to another process) will need to be removed to make room. We'll see the algorithm for this a bit later.

13.5.3   Memory-Mapped Files

Data from files that needs to be loaded into memory (such as executables or shared libraries) is treated a bit differently. Rather than loading it and then treating it as memory space, the data is mapped into memory directly from the file. Such a file is a *memory-mapped file,* since its contents are mapped into the virtual memory space of the process. Whenever a page fault occurs on a page from a memory-mapped file, the page is paged in directly from the disk file. The kernel also maintains a *page cache* so that recently used pages can be obtained again without having to go back to disk.

13.5.4   Swapping

The term *swapping* refers to the opposite of paging in memory—that is, to page it out. The name is somewhat historical and harkens back to a time when you had to swap an entire process with another one in order to run the new one. Some people use the terms "swapping in" and "swapping out," which are essentially the same as "paging in" and "paging out."

If a process needs to bring a new page into physical memory but there is no physical memory left in which to store it, then some existing page of memory must be paged out first. This is accomplished by the swapper, the kernel process *kswapd*, which is started by *init* when the system boots.

The swapper will run anytime real memory falls below a certain threshold (the kernel value free_pages_low) and will try to release memory until the number of free pages is back up to the value of free_pages_high. It looks at each process to see what pages might be swapped out. Some of the criteria the swapper uses to decide to swap out or release a memory page include:

- if the page hasn't been used for some time
- if the page hasn't been modified, especially if is still in the *swap cache*
- if the page is from a memory-mapped file, especially if it is still in the page cache

If the page is still available in a cache, then it could easily be brought back in without having to be read from disk. If it is not easily available, then it must be saved to the *swap area* before it can be released from memory and that space in memory can be used by another process. The swap area is a disk partition created solely for use by the kernel to store copies of memory pages.

If a page is a memory-mapped page from a disk file or data that has not been modified since the last time it was brought in from the swap area, the page does not need to be saved in the swap area and may simply be discarded, since a copy of the page as it currently exists in memory is still available on the disk.

13.5.5   Allocation and Deallocation

Linux maintains a list of free pages of physical memory, so that when a process requests one or more new pages, the request can be quickly fulfilled. When pages are deallocated and added back into the list of free pages, the memory manager attempts to group them into larger contiguous groups whenever possible so that memory does not become badly fragmented. It accomplishes this with the free_area data structure shown in Figure 13–27.

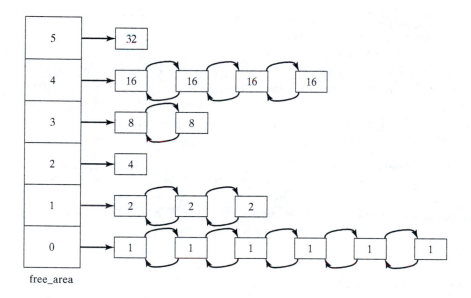

free_area

Figure 13–27   The free_area list of free memory pages.

The free_area is an array of pointers to groups of pages. free_area[0] points to a doubly linked list of single pages that are available. free_area[1] points to a doubly linked list of groups of two pages that are free. Each successive entry points to a doubly linked list of groups of pages whose size increases by powers of two, up to the sixth entry, free_area[5], that points to a doubly linked list of groups of 32 pages.

When a process allocates new memory and requests free pages from the kernel, the kernel looks in the free_area structure to find the largest contiguous group of pages of memory to give the process. If the largest page group is more pages than the process is requesting, the extra pages are removed from the group and put back into the proper list in the free_area, depending on how many pages are involved. If there is no single page group that will satisfy the process, then multiple smaller groups are selected until the process receives what it requested.

When a process releases memory or is swapped out (so that its real memory is returned to the system), its pages are deallocated and returned to the free_area. The memory manager attempts to recombine these pages with adjacent groups of pages of equal size to form a contiguous page group of the next larger size. For example, when returning a single page of memory, it checks to see if the page on either side of the page to be returned is also in the list pointed to by free_area[0]. If one is, its next step is to create a page group with the two pages. Then go through the same process and check to see if the two pages on either side of these two make up a group of pages listed in free_area[1]. If not, then add the group into the list pointed to by free_area[1]. If one of the adjacent two-page groups is also free, combine them into a four-page group and continue. This way, the freed pages are recombined into the largest possible contiguous group of free pages and put in the appropriate list in the free_area array.

13.5.6   Loading an Executable: execl ()/execv ()

When a process performs an execl () or execv (), the kernel creates new page tables for the process. At this point, all of the code and initialized data resides on disk in the executable file, and so the page-table entries are set to contain the locations of the corresponding disk blocks of the memory-mapped file. When the process accesses one of these pages for the first time, its corresponding block is copied from disk into memory, and the page-table entry is updated with the physical memory page number.

13.5.7   Duplicating a Process: fork ()

When a process forks, the child process must be allocated a copy of its parent's memory space. Unfortunately, a process often immediately follows a fork () by an execl (), thereby deallocating its previous memory areas. To avoid any unnecessary and costly copying suggested by these two observations, the kernel puts off copying the entire context of the process until absolutely necessary.

When the fork occurs, the child inherits a page table of its own that points to the same pages of memory, but they are marked read-only (for both processes). If the process later tries to write to an individual memory location, the fact that the page is marked read-only will trigger a page fault. The memory manager will see that the page is valid and only then will it create an entirely new copy of the page for the process trying to write. This is known as *copy-on-write*. In many cases, the child process simply execs a new program, so none of this ever takes place and an unnecessary copy is avoided. If the child process really does continue to run the current program, it does get its very own copy, just not at the moment of the fork.

13.6 Input and Output

In this section, I'll describe the data structures and algorithms that the Linux kernel uses to support I/O-related system calls. Specifically, I'll look at the implementation of these calls in relation to three main types of file:

- *regular* files
- *directory* files
- *special* files (i.e., peripherals, pipes, and sockets)

13.6.1 I/O Objects

I like to think of files as being special kinds of objects that have I/O capabilities. Linux I/O objects may be arranged according to the hierarchy in Figure 13–28.

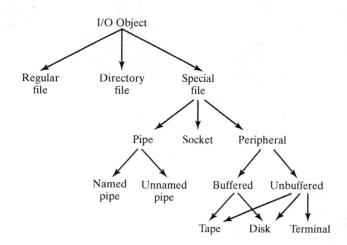

Figure 13–28 The I/O object hierarchy.

13.6.2 I/O System Calls

As I described in Chapter 12, "Systems Programming," the I/O system calls may be applied in a uniform way to all I/O objects. A few exceptions exist; for example, you can't use lseek () on a pipe or a socket. Here's a list of the system calls that are described in this section:

close	mkdir	umount
dup	mount	unlink
ioctl	open	write
link	read	
lseek	sync	

13.6.3 I/O Buffering

The kernel avoids unnecessary device I/O by buffering most I/O in a fixed-size, systemwide data structure call the *buffer cache*. The buffer cache is a collection of buffers that are used for caching file blocks in RAM.

When a process reads from a block for the very first time, the block is copied from the file or device into the buffer cache and then copied from there into the process's data space. Subsequent reads from the same block are serviced directly from RAM. Similarly, if a process writes to a block that isn't in the buffer cache, the block is copied from the file into the cache and then the buffered copy is modified. If the block is already in the cache, the buffered version is modified without any need for physical I/O. Several hash lists based on the block's device and block number are maintained for the buffers in the cache so that the kernel can quickly locate a buffered block.

It's tempting to think that the kernel copies all of a file's modified buffered blocks back to disk when the file is closed, but it may not. It is not necessary to write the buffered blocks back to the device until the buffer needs to be reused for another stream of data. This scheme delays physical I/O until the last possible moment. If another process performs I/O on the same data block, it will receive data from the buffer cache or write its own data into the buffer as long as it is associated with the file or device. When the buffer is disassociated from the file or device, the entire contents of the buffer is written to the device or *flushed*.

Linux includes a kernel daemon called *bdflush*, the buffer-dirty flush daemon, that period-ically flushes "dirty" buffers (buffers that have data that needs to be written to disk).

13.6.3.1 sync ()
sync () causes the kernel to flush all of the buffers to disk.

13.6.4   Regular File I/O
The next few sections describe the implementation of *regular* file I/O, including the implemen-tations of open (), read (), write (), lseek (), close (), dup (), and unlink ().

13.6.4.1 open ()
Let's take a look at what happens when a process opens an existing regular file for read-only access. Later, we'll examine the way the kernel creates a new file. Assume that the process is the first process to open the file since the system was last rebooted, and that it executes the following code:

```
fd = open ("/home/glass/sample.txt", O_RDONLY);
```

The kernel begins by translating the filename into an inode number, using the algorithm described earlier in this chapter. If the inode of the file is not found, an error code is returned. Otherwise, the kernel takes an available *file* structure from the free list to hold information about the file and adds a pointer to it to the process's files_struct structure and links it into the kernel's open file list. Finally, the kernel returns the index of the file descriptor entry as the return value of open ().

If a process opens a nonexistent file and specifies the O_CREAT option, the kernel creates the named file. To do this, it allocates a free inode from the file system's inode list, sets the fields within it to indicate that the file is empty, and then adds a hard link to the appropriate directory file. Recall that a hard link is an entry consisting of a filename and its associated inode number.

Now that you've seen the way the kernel handles an open () system call, I'll describe the read (), write (), lseek (), and close () system calls. For now, assume that the example file is being accessed by just one process.

13.6.4.2 read ()

Let's see what happens when the example process executes the following sequence of read () system calls:

```
read (fd, buf1, 100);    /* read 100 bytes into buffer buf1 */
read (fd, buf2, 200);    /* read 200 bytes into buffer buf2 */
read (fd, buf3, 5000);   /* read 5000 bytes into buffer buf3 */
```

Here's the sequence of events that would occur:

- The data requested by the first read () resides in the first block of the file. The kernel determines that the block is not in the buffer cache, and so copies it from disk into a free buffer. It then copies the first 100 bytes from the buffer into **buf1**. Finally, the file position stored in the file struct is updated to its new value of 100.
- The data requested by the second read () also resides in the first block of the file. The kernel finds that the block is already in the buffer cache, and so copies the next 200 bytes from the buffer into **buf2**. It then updates the file position to 300.
- The data requested by the third read resides partly in the first block of the file and partly in the second block. The kernel transfers the remainder of the first block (3796 bytes) from the buffer cache into **buf3**. It then copies the second block from disk into a free buffer in the cache and copies the remaining data (1204 bytes) from the buffer cache into **buf3**. Finally, it updates the file position to 5300.

Note that a single read may cause more than one block to be copied from disk into the buffer cache. If a process reads from a block that does not have an allocated user block (see Chapter 12, "Systems Programming," for a discussion of sparse files), then read () doesn't buffer anything, but instead treats the block as if it were filled with NULL (ASCII 0) characters.

13.6.4.3 write ()

The example process now executes the following series of write () system calls:

```
write (fd, buf4, 100);    /* write 100 bytes from buffer buf4 */
write (fd, buf5, 4000);   /* write 4000 bytes from buffer buf5 *
```

Recall that the current value of the file position is 5300, which is situated near the start of the file's second block. Recall also that this block is currently buffered, courtesy of the last read (). Here's the sequence of events that would occur:

- The data to be overwritten by the first write () resides entirely in the second block. This block is already in the buffer cache, and so 100 bytes of **buf4** are copied into the appropriate bytes of the buffered second block.
- The data to be overwritten by the second write () resides partly in the second block and partly in the third block. The kernel copies the first 3792 bytes of **buf5** into the remaining

3792 bytes of the buffered second block. Then it copies the third block from the file into a free buffer. Finally, it copies the remaining 208 bytes of **buf5** into the first 208 bytes of the buffered third block.

13.6.4.4 lseek ()

The implementation of lseek () is trivial. The kernel simply changes the value of the descriptor's associated file position, located in the file struct. Note that no physical I/O is necessary. Changing the current location to 3000 is performed by the following code:

```
lseek (fd, 3000, SEEK_SET);
```

13.6.4.5 close ()

When a file descriptor is closed and it's the only one associated with a particular file, the kernel copies the file's inode back to disk and then marks the corresponding file structure as *free*. When a process terminates, the kernel automatically closes all of its open file descriptors.

As I mentioned earlier, the kernel has special mechanisms to support multiple file descriptors associated with the same file. To implement these mechanisms, the kernel keeps a *reference count* field in the structure representing each open file as well as the file's inode structure. When a file is opened for the first time, the reference count is set to one. Subsequent opens by other processes increment the reference count.

Multiple file structures can point to the same inode, in which case the inode's reference count will be greater than one. Multiple fds, either in a process or in multiple processes, can point to the same file structure, in which case its reference count will be greater than one.

The algorithm for close () handles the reference count fields as follows: when a file descriptor is closed, the kernel decrements the reference count field in its associated file struct. If the reference count remains greater than zero, nothing else occurs. If the reference count drops to zero, the file struct is marked as free and the reference count field in the file's inode structure is decremented. If the inode structure's reference count remains greater than zero, nothing else happens. If the inode's reference count drops to zero, the inode is copied back to disk and the inode structure is freed.

13.6.4.6 dup ()

The implementation of dup () is simple; it copies the specified file descriptor into the next free file descriptor array entry and increments the corresponding file structure reference count.

13.6.4.7 unlink ()

unlink () removes a hard link from a directory and decrements its associated inode's hard link count. If the hard link count drops to zero, the file's inode and data blocks are deallocated when the last process using it exits. Notice that this means that a process may unlink a file and continue to access it until the process exits (and all the while it will not be visible in the directory).

13.6.5   Directory File I/O

Directory files are different from regular files in a few ways:

- They may only be created using mknod () or mkdir ().
- They may only be read using readdir ().
- They may only be modified using link ().

This ensures the integrity of the directory hierarchy. Directory files may be opened just like regular files. Let's take a look at the implementation of mkdir () and link ().

13.6.5.1   mkdir ()

mkdir () creates a directory by allocating a new inode on disk, setting its type field accordingly, and adding it via a hard link into the directory hierarchy. A user block is associated with the inode and filled with the default "." and ".." entries. Here's an example of mkdir ():

```
mkdir ("/home/glass/tmpdir", 0666);
```

13.6.5.2   link ()

link () adds a hard link into a directory. Here's an example of link ():

```
link ("/home/glass/file1.c", "/home/glass/file2.c");
```

In this example, the kernel would find the inode number of the source filename "/home/glass/file1.c" and then associate it with the label "file2.c" in the destination directory "/home/glass." It would then increment the inode's hard link count. Only a super-user may link directories, to prevent unwary users from creating circular directory structures.

13.6.6   Mounting File Systems

The kernel maintains a data structure called the *mount table* that allows multiple file systems to be accessed via a single directory hierarchy. The mount () and umount () system calls modify this table, and are executable only by a super-user.

13.6.6.1   mount ()

When a file system is mounted using mount (), an entry is added to the mount table containing the following fields:

- the number of the device that contains the newly mounted file system
- a pointer to the root inode of the newly mounted file system
- a pointer to the inode of the mount point
- a pointer to the mount data structure specific to the newly mounted file system

The directory associated with the *mount point* becomes synonymous with the root node of the newly mounted file system, and its previous contents become inaccessible to processes until the file system is later unmounted. To enable the correct translation of pathnames that cross mount points, the inode of the mount directory is marked as a mount point, and is set to point to the associated mount-table entry. For example, Figure 13–29 shows the effect of the following system call, which mounts the file system contained on the "/dev/da0" device onto the "/mnt" directory:

```
mount ("/dev/da0", "/mnt", 0);
```

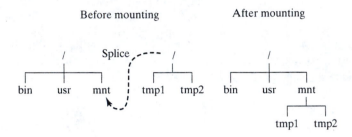

Before mounting   After mounting

Figure 13–29   Mounting a directory.

13.6.7   Translation of Filenames

The name-translation algorithm uses the contents of the mount table when translating pathnames that cross mount points. This can occur when moving up or down the directory hierarchy. For example, consider the following example:

```
$ cd /mnt/tmp1
$ cd ../../bin
```

The first *cd* command crosses from the root device to the "/dev/da0" device, and the second *cd* command crosses back across to the root device. Here's how the algorithm incorporates mounted file systems into the translation process:

- When an inode is encountered during the translation process that is a mount point, a pointer to the root inode of the mounted file system is returned instead. For example, when the "/mnt" portion of the "/mnt/dir1" is translated, a pointer to the root node of the mounted file system is returned. This pointer is used as the starting point for the rest of the pathname translation.
- When a ".." pathname component is encountered, the kernel checks to see whether a mount point is about to be crossed. If the current inode pointer of the translation process points to a root node and ".." also points to a root node, then a crossing point has been reached (Figure 13–30). It replaces the current inode pointer of the translation process with a pointer to the inode of the mount point in the parent file system, which it finds by scanning the mount table for the entry corresponding to the device number of the current inode.

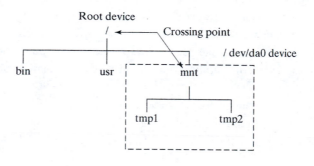

Figure 13–30 Crossing point.

13.6.7.1 umount ()

When unmounting a file system, there are several things that the kernel must do:

- It checks that there are no open files in the file system about to be unmounted. If any open files are found, the system call fails.
- It flushes the superblock and buffered inodes back to the file system.
- It removes the mount-table entry and removes the mount-point mark from the mount-point directory.

13.6.8 Special File I/O

Most special files correspond to peripherals such as printers, terminals, and disk drives, so for the rest of this section I'll use the terms *special file* and *peripheral* synonymously.

Every peripheral in the system has an associated *device driver*, which is a custom-crafted piece of software that contains all of the peripheral-specific code. For example, a tape drive's device driver contains the code for rewinding and retensioning the tape. A single device driver may control all instances of a particular kind of peripheral. In other words, three tape drives of the same type can share a single device driver. The device drivers can be linked into the kernel during configuration of the kernel or can be in loadable kernel modules and loaded only when they need to run.

13.6.8.1 Device Interface

A peripheral's device driver supplies the peripheral's *interface*, which can come in two flavors:

- *block-oriented*, which means that I/O is buffered, and that physical I/O is performed on a block-by-block basis. Disk drives and tape drives have a block-oriented interface.
- *character-oriented*, which means that I/O is unbuffered, and that physical I/O occurs on a character-by-character basis. A character-oriented interface is sometimes known as a *raw* interface. All peripherals usually have a raw interface, including disk drives and tape drives.

A peripheral's device driver sometimes contains both kinds of interfaces. The kind of interface that you choose depends on how you're going to access the device. When performing random access and repeated access to a common set of blocks, it makes good sense to access the peripheral via its block-oriented interface. However, if you're going to access the blocks in a single linear sequence, as you would when making a backup tape, it makes more sense to access the peripheral via its character-oriented interface. This avoids the overhead of the kernel's internal buffering mechanism and sometimes allows the kernel to use the hardware's Direct Memory Access (DMA) capabilities.

It's perfectly possible, although not advisable, to access a single device simultaneously via both interfaces. The trouble with this is that the character-oriented interface bypasses the buffering system, possibly leading to confusing I/O results. Here's an example:

- Process A opens a floppy disk using its block-oriented interface, "/dev/fd0." It then writes 1000 bytes to the disk. This output is stored in the buffer cache, and marked for delayed writing.
- Process B then opens the same floppy disk using its character-oriented interface, "/dev/rfd0." When it reads 1000 bytes from the disk, the data that was written by process A is ignored, since it's still in the buffer cache.

The solution to this problem is easy: Don't open a device via different interfaces simultaneously!

13.6.8.2 Major/Minor Numbers

The *major* and *minor* device numbers are used to locate the device driver associated with a particular device. The major device number specifies which device driver configured into the kernel will be used to access the device. The minor device number specifies which one of the (possibly many) devices will be used. For example, if you have three tape drives on a system, and the device driver for the tape drive corresponds to major number 15, if you use the **ls** command to list the block-oriented tape devices, you might see:

```
brw--w--w-  1      root  15,  0 Feb 13 14:27 /dev/mt0
brw--w--w-  1      root  15,  1 Feb 13 14:29 /dev/mt1
brw--w--w-  1      root  15,  2 Feb 13 14:27 /dev/mt2
```

From this, we see that all three tape drives are accessed by the same device driver (signified by the index of 15), and each minor number uniquely identifies a specific tape drive. The major and minor numbers are used to index into switch tables to locate the appropriate device driver.

13.6.8.3 Device Access

All Linux device drivers provide a set of standard operational functions that perform open, close, read, and write operations on the peripheral device. Pointers to these functions are maintained in the *file* structure of each open file. In this way, when a process requests an operation on a special file, the proper function in the device driver gets called to perform the I/O operation.

lseek (), chmod (), and stat () work the same way for special files as they do for regular files. For block-oriented devices, blocks of data are buffered in the buffer cache.

13.6.8.4 Terminal I/O

Although terminals are a kind of peripheral, terminal device drivers are special even for special files. The main difference between terminal device drivers and other device drivers is that they must support several different kinds of pre- and post-processing on their input and output, respectively. Each variety of processing is called a *line discipline*. A terminal's line discipline can be set using ioctl (). Most terminal drivers support the following three common line disciplines:

- *raw mode*, which performs no special processing at all. Characters entered at the keyboard are made available to the reading process based on the ioctl () parameters. Key sequences such as *Control-C* do not generate any kind of special action, and are passed as regular ASCII characters. For example, *Control-C* would be read as the character with ASCII value 3. Raw mode is used by applications such as editors that prefer to do all of their own character processing.
- *cbreak mode*, which processes only some key sequences specially. For example, flow control via *Control-S* and *Control-Q* remains active. Similarly, *Control-C* generates an interrupt signal for every process in the foreground job. As with raw mode, all other characters are available to the reading process based on the ioctl () parameters.
- *cooked mode* (sometimes known as *canonical mode*), which performs full pre- and post-processing. In this mode, the delete and backspace keys take on their special meanings, together with the less common word-erase and line-erase characters. Input is made available to a reading process only when the *Enter* key is pressed. Similarly, tabs have a special meaning when output, and are expanded by the line discipline to the correct number of spaces. A newline character is expanded into a carriage return/newline pair.

Terminal devices are controlled through the use of the ioctl () system call and *termios*, a group of library functions provided by Linux especially for driving terminal I/O.

13.7 Interprocess Communication

In this section, I describe the data structures and algorithms that the Linux kernel uses to support the basic IPC using signals and more sophisticated forms of IPC using pipes and sockets.

13.7.1 Signals

Signals inform processes of asynchronous events like keyboard input, error conditions, and job control. Linux supports the following types of signals:

- traditional UNIX signals (non-real-time)
- real-time or *queued* signals (mandated by POSIX 1003.1b)

Using queued signals, multiple instances (i.e., duplicates) of the same signal can be delivered to a process, unlike traditional signals where only one of each signal type can be pending at any time (and you can lose subsequent signals if you're still handling a previous one).

The kernel or root can send a signal to any process. Only user processes that have the same UID and GID can signal each other.

The data structures that support signals are stored in the task_struct and signal_struct associated with the process. Every process includes the following data structures associated with signal handling:

- a pointer to the signal_structure which contains an array of pointers to *signal handler* functions (that process each signal)
- a *signal bitmap*, used to specify, one bit per type of signal, that a particular type of signal has arrived for processing
- a *blocked signal bitmap*, used to specify, one bit per type of signal, that a particular type of signal should not be processed yet (except SIGSTOP and SIGKILL)
- a *signal queue* (sigqueue), used to keep track of queued signals
- a *process group ID*, which is used when distributing signals

Note that the signal bitmaps are one machine word in size and therefore dictate how many signals can be processed on a particular machine. Most common 32-bit architectures (e.g., PCs) use 32-bit bitmaps, so 32 signals are supported. On 64-bit architectures, like Itanium and Alpha, as many as 64 signals can be supported.

Blocked signals remain as pending in the signal bitmap until they are unblocked and processed or ignored. A signal handler function pointer that is SIG_DFL (zero) will cause the kernel to perform the default action for that signal (see "man 7 signal"). Set the pointer to SIG_IGN to ignore the particular signal.

13.7.1.1 setpgrp ()
setpgrp () sets the calling process's process group number to its own PID, thereby placing it in its own unique process group. A fork'ed process inherits its parent's process group. setpgrp () works by changing the process group number entry in the task struct. The process group number is used by kill (), as you'll see later.

13.7.1.2 signal ()
signal () sets the way that a process responds to a particular type of signal. There are three options: ignore the signal, perform the default kernel action, or execute a user-installed signal handler. The entries in the signal handler array are set as follows:

- If the signal is to be ignored, the entry is set to 1.
- If the signal is to cause the default action, the entry is set to 0.
- If the signal is to be processed using a user-installed handler, the entry is set to the address of the handler.

When a signal is sent to a process, the kernel sets the appropriate bit in the receiving process's signal bitmap or adds the signal to the process's sigqueue, depending on the type of signal. If the receiving process is sleeping at an interruptible priority, it is awakened so that it may process the signal. The kernel checks a process's signal bitmap for pending signals whenever the process returns from kernel mode to user mode (i.e., when returning from a system call) or when the process returns from a sleep state.

When using non-real-time signals, the pending signal bitmap does not keep a *count* of how many of a particular type of signal are pending. This means that if three SIGINT signals arrive in close succession, it's possible that only one of them will be noticed.

13.7.1.3 Signals After a fork or an exec

A fork'ed process inherits the contents of its parent's signal handler array. When a process execs, the signals that were originally ignored continue to be ignored, and all others are set to their default setting. In other words, all entries equal to 1 are unchanged, and all others are set to 0.

13.7.1.4 Processing a Signal

When the kernel detects that a process has a pending signal, it either ignores it, performs the default action, or invokes a user-installed handler. To invoke the handler, it appends a new stack frame to the process's stack and modifies the process's program counter to make the receiving process act as if it had called the signal handler from its current program location. When the kernel returns the process to user mode, the process executes the handler and then returns from the function back to the previous program location. The "death of a child" signal (SIGCHLD) is processed slightly differently, as you'll see when I describe the wait () system call.

13.7.1.5 exit ()

When a process terminates, it leaves its exit code in a field (exit_code) in its task_struct, and is marked as a zombie process. This exit code is obtainable by the parent process via the wait () system call. The kernel always informs a parent process that one of its children has died by sending it a "death of child" (SIGCHLD) signal.

The reason you can't kill a zombie process by sending it a SIGKILL is that it never again looks at its signal bitmap. A zombie process is merely a task_struct in the task list, but it is no longer a running process, so nothing can check the signal bitmap and process it.

13.7.1.6 wait ()

wait () returns in one of two conditions; either the calling process has no children, in which case it returns an error code, or one of the calling process's children has terminated, in which case it returns the child process's PID and exit code. The way that the kernel processes a wait () system call may be split up into a three-step algorithm:

1. If a process calls wait () and doesn't have any children, wait () returns an error code.
2. If a process calls wait () and one or more of its children are already zombies, the kernel picks a child at random, removes it from the task list, and returns its PID and exit code.
3. If a process calls wait () and none of its children is a zombie, the wait call goes to sleep. It is awakened by the kernel when *any* signals are received, at which point it resumes from step 1.

Although this algorithm would work as it stands, there's one small problem; if a process chose to ignore SIGCHLD signals, all of its children would remain zombies, and this could clog up the task list. To avoid this problem, the kernel treats ignorance of the SIGCHLD signal as a special case. If a SIGCHLD signal is received and the signal is ignored, the kernel immediately removes all the parent's zombie children from the task list and then allows the wait () system call to proceed as normal. When the wait () call resumes, it doesn't find any zombie children, and so it goes back to sleep. Eventually, when the last child's death signal is ignored, the wait () system call returns with an error code to signify that the calling process has no child processes.

13.7.1.7 kill ()

kill () makes use of the real user ID and process group ID fields in the task list. For example, when the following line of code is executed:

```
kill (0, SIGINT);
```

the kernel sets the bit in the signal bitmap corresponding to SIGINT in every process whose process group ID matches that of the calling process. Linux uses this facility to distribute the signals triggered by *Control-C* and *Control-Z* to all of the processes in the control terminal's process group.

13.7.2   Pipes

There are two kinds of pipes in Linux: *unnamed* pipes and *named* pipes (called FIFOs in Linux). Unnamed pipes are created by pipe (), and named pipes are created using mkfifo () or mknod () and with the **mkfifo** utility. Data written to a pipe is stored in the file system. When either kind of pipe is created, the kernel allocates a VFS inode, two open file entries, and two file descriptors. Originally, the inode describes an empty file. If the pipe is named, a hard link is made from the specified directory to the pipe's inode; otherwise, no hard link is created and the pipe remains anonymous.

The kernel maintains the current write position and current read position of each pipe in its inode, rather than in the file list structure. This ensures that each byte in the pipe is read by exactly one process. It also keeps track of the number of processes reading from the pipe and writing to the pipe. As you'll soon see, it needs both of these counts to process a close () properly.

13.7.2.1 Writing to a Pipe

When data is written to a pipe, the kernel allocates disk blocks and increments the current write position as necessary, until the last direct block has been allocated. For reasons of simplicity and efficiency, a pipe is never allocated indirect blocks, thereby limiting the size of a pipe to about 40K, depending on the file system's block size. If a write to a pipe would overflow its storage capacity, the writing process writes as much as it can to the pipe and then sleeps until some of the data is drained by reader processes. If a writer tries to write past the end of the last direct block, the write position "wraps around" to the beginning of the file, starting at offset 0. Thus, the direct blocks are treated like a circular buffer. Although it might seem that using the file system for implementing pipes would be slow, remember that disk blocks are buffered in the buffer cache, and so most pipe I/O is buffered in RAM.

13.7.2.2 Reading from a Pipe

As data is read from a pipe, its current read position is updated accordingly. The kernel ensures that the read position never overtakes the write position. If a process attempts to read from an empty pipe, it is sent to sleep until output becomes available.

13.7.2.3 Closing a Pipe

When a pipe's file descriptor is closed, the kernel does some special processing:

- It updates the count of the pipe's reader and writer processes.
- If the writer count drops to zero and there are processes trying to read from the pipe, they return from read () with an error condition.
- If the reader count drops to zero and there are processes trying to write to the pipe, they are sent a signal.
- If the reader and writer counts drop to zero, all of the pipe's blocks are deallocated and the inode's current write and read positions are reset. If the pipe is unnamed, the inode is also deallocated.

13.7.3   Sockets

We examined sockets from the application point of view in Chapter 12, "Systems Programming," on page 508. Now we want to see how things work in the kernel to support this.

When a socket is created using socket (), the system creates a sock structure that holds all of the information pertaining to the socket, like the socket domain and socket protocol. A VFS inode is created that points to the socket structure and it is associated with an open file in the process's file structure. The associated file descriptor is returned to the calling process.

Then a socket works much like a pipe. Data can be written to the socket and is buffered by the file system until read by the other end of the socket. One difference is the data is encapsulated in a socket buffer (sk_buff) that contains other data needed by the network layers. The file structure contains pointers to socket driver operator functions that are used when performing I/O on the socket.

CHAPTER REVIEW

Checklist

In this chapter, I described:

- the layering of kernel subsystems
- the difference between user mode and kernel mode.
- the implementation of system calls and interrupt handlers
- the physical and logical layout of the file system
- inodes
- the algorithm that the kernel uses for translating pathnames into inode numbers
- the process hierarchy
- process states

- how the scheduler decides to allocate the CPU
- memory management
- the I/O subsystem and buffering
- interprocess communication via pipes and sockets

Quiz

1. Why do system calls make use of kernel mode?
2. Where is the name of a file stored?
3. What information does the superblock contain?
4. How does Linux avoid using bad blocks?
5. Why is inode #2 special?
6. What is the meaning of the term *magic number?*
7. What is the meaning of the term *context switch?*
8. If a signal is sent to a process that is suspended, where is it stored?
9. What does the swapper do?
10. What is the purpose of the *task list?*
11. How does Linux copy a parent's data to its child?
12. What is the meaning of the term "copy-on-write"?
13. What is the purpose of the open *file list?*

Exercises

1. Using **ps**, find the process on the system with the lowest process ID (PID). What is the process and why does it have this PID? [level: *easy*]
2. Delayed writing normally causes a modified buffer to be flushed when its RAM is needed, not when its file is closed. An alternative method is to flush modified buffers when disk traffic is low, thereby making the best use of the idle time. Critique this strategy. [level: *medium*]

Projects

1. Investigate some other operating systems such as Mac OS X and Windows XP. How do they compare to Linux? [level: *medium*]
2. If you know object-oriented techniques, design a basic object-oriented kernel where system services are provided by a collection of system objects. How does the design of your kernel differ from the Linux kernel? [level: *hard*]

14

System Administration

Motivation

Several administrative duties must be performed on a Linux system to keep it running smoothly. Without them, files may be irrecoverably lost, utilities may become out of date, and the system may run slower than its potential speed. Many Linux installations are large enough that they warrant a full-time system administrator. Smaller Linux installations, such as your home system, do not. Regardless of whether you're destined to perform administrative duties, this chapter contains valuable information on how to oversee a Linux installation.

Prerequisites

In order to understand this chapter, you should have read Chapter 1, "What Is Linux?," and Chapter 3, "GNU Utilities for Nonprogrammers." It also helps if you've read Chapter 5, "The Linux Shells," and Chapter 9, "Networking and the Internet."

Objectives

In this chapter, I describe the main tasks that a system administrator must perform in order to keep a Linux system running smoothly.

Presentation

The information presented in this section is in the form of several small, self-contained subsections.

Utilities

This chapter mentions the following utilities, listed in alphabetical order:

df	mknod	sysctl
du	rpm	useradd
fsck	shutdown	userdel
ifconfig	su	
mkfs	sudo	

14.1 Introduction

A system administrator must regularly perform a variety of tasks to keep a Linux system running properly. These tasks involve starting and stopping the system, maintaining user accounts, monitoring system resources, installing new hardware and software, managing the network, and maintaining security.

Almost all of these tasks require the administrator to be in super-user mode, as they access and modify privileged information. If you don't have access to the super-user password, you'll just have to use your imagination. Even in this case, however, being aware of these functions increases your overall understanding of how Linux works. Many of these programs are installed in the /sbin directory, which is not typically included in a user's path, so you may have to explicitly type "/sbin/command" or add /sbin to your path in order to run the utilities.

To cover each of these topics in depth would require an entire book, so this chapter simply presents an overview of system administration. For more detailed information on managing Linux systems, I can highly recommend [Nemeth, 2002].

14.2 Becoming the Super-User

The *super-user* is a special user ID (0) that has permission to do practically anything on a Linux system. Because of this, you can see how important it is for not "just anyone" to have this access, especially anyone with any malicious intentions. Most administration tasks require that you have super-user powers, and there are three common ways to get them:

• Login as "root," the username of the super-user.
• Use the **su** utility, described in Chapter 4, "GNU Utilities for Power Users," to create a child shell owned by "root."
• Use the **sudo** utility to run a single command as the super-user.

Although the first method is very direct, there are some dangers associated with it. If you log in as "root," every single command that you execute will have super-user privileges—even the ones with errors in them. Imagine typing "rm -r * .bak" instead of "rm -r *.bak" while in the "/" directory! Because of this, I strongly recommend that you avoid this method. Most distributions of Linux will actually ask you if you mean to login as "root" or put up a warning (like a red background) if you attempt to do so.

14.2.1   Using su

A major advantage of using the **su** command (described in Chapter 4, "GNU Utilities for Power Users" on page 147) is that it logs who uses it and when. In an environment with more than one system administrator, it is sometimes hard to make sure the super-user password is given only to those who really need it. Having a log to examine helps you see who is using root privileges.

14.2.2   Using sudo

An alternative method of becoming the super-user available in most Linux systems is the **sudo** command, which works like this:

Utility: **sudo** [-u *username*] *commandLine*

sudo causes the command *commandLine* to be run as the user *username* (if specified) or by root if no **-u** argument and username are specified. The user who executed the **sudo** command is logged along with the time and command executed.

   sudo allows a user to execute commands as another user only if the user is listed in the /etc/sudoers file. The first time you run **sudo**, you must authenticate yourself to gain access by providing your own password (not the root password or that of the specified username). After that, a configurable timeout clock starts (5 minutes by default), in which time another command can be run with **sudo** without your having to provide your password again.

   Attempts to use **sudo** by a user not listed in /etc/sudoers are reported to the system administrator.

Figure 14–1   Description of **sudo** command.

The advantages of **sudo** over **su** are many. **sudo** simplifies the process of becoming the super-user when you need to and so encourages you not to be super-user when you don't need it. It also provides more configurable access to root privileges. Those needing super-user access do not need to know the root password and, if necessary, can take away someone's super-user rights without having to change the root password.

   The only real disadvantage is that now your system can be compromised not only by someone obtaining the root password but also by someone obtaining the password of *any* of the users listed in the /etc/sudoers file. So if you choose to use **sudo**, you must be sure those who will be listed protect their own passwords as judiciously as they would the root password.

14.3 Starting Linux

Like most computer systems, when you apply power to a Linux system, it *boots*. Booting is the process of "bootstrapping" a small program, then another, until the main operating system is loaded and running. If your system has installed a Linux boot loader (LILO or GRUB) into the Master Boot Record (MBR), this program will load Linux and boot it into multi-user mode. For information on boot loaders, see Chapter 2, "Installing Your Linux System."

When you start a Linux system, the following sequence of events occurs:

1. The hardware performs diagnostic self-tests.
2. The Linux kernel is loaded from the /boot directory on the root device.
3. The kernel starts running and initializes itself.
4. The kernel starts **init**, the first user-mode process.

14.3.1   The Linux Kernel

The Linux kernel is the core program that runs a Linux system. The kernel is simply a file in the /boot directory on the root drive (maybe in the root file system, or /boot is sometimes in its own partition; see Chapter 2, "Installing Your Linux System," for more information).

The kernel itself is named vmlinuz-*version*. The version number is generally in the form:

```
major.minor.build
```

Some distributions add their own version information after that. This is not the version of the Linux distribution (which is unique to each vendor) but the version of the Linux kernel included with that distribution. This version is assigned by Linus and the others who produce the kernel itself.

14.3.2   Run Levels

Once booted, a Linux system can run in several different ways. Linux adopts the UNIX System V concept of *run levels*. Run levels define the desired state of the system. Linux allows 10 run levels (0–9), although not all of them are used. Each run level can have its own specific boot scripts and can be configured to suit your local needs. For example, you might configure run level 4 to be everything your system normally runs in operational mode except your company's production database application. This would allow you to do database maintenance on the database while allowing the rest of the system to be used normally.

Run levels are defined in "/etc/inittab." The commonly predefined run levels are:

- 0—halt
- 1—single-user (i.e., maintenance)
- 2—multi-user without networking
- 3—server (full multi-user)
- 5—workstation (full multi-user, graphical login)
- 6—reboot

Depending on your Linux distribution, other run levels could have other meanings.

14.3.3   init

The first user-mode process started after the kernel is **init**, the parent of all other processes. **init**'s job is to start other programs required on a running system.

init controls the run levels and the specific scripts associated with each run level. These scripts, usually referred to as *boot scripts*, check system integrity and start required services as appropriate for each run level.

init can be run by the super-user and provided a new run level for the system. **init** will then run the appropriate scripts to take the system to its new run level, including run level zero, which halts the system.

14.3.4   Boot Scripts

When **init** is started at boot or run by the super-user, its job is to take the system to a new run level. The normal default when the system boots is run level 5.

The scripts run by **init** are in the directory "/etc/rc.d" and are organized by run level. The regular files in /etc/rc.d are boot scripts run once at boot time. Names vary between different Linux distributions, but are usually one or more of:

- rc.sysinit
- rc.boot
- rc.modules
- rc.local (for local additions, runs after all other boot scripts)

Scripts specific to run levels (and symbolic links to scripts when shared by multiple run levels) are stored in subdirectories in /etc/rc.d, named with the number of the run level as rcN.d. In other words, all scripts specific to run level 6 can be found in the "/etc/rc.d/rc6.d" directory. In that directory, you will find scripts whose names begin with either "S" or "K." The "S" scripts are startup scripts, the "K" scripts are kill scripts, which are run when shutting the system down to kill the programs that were started by the "S" scripts.

The scripts for various run levels start (or stop) the appropriate services for each run level. For example, run level 3 startup scripts check the file system consistency using **fsck** (described later in this chapter) and mount file systems.

14.4 Stopping Linux

No computer can be turned off the way you turn off other electrical appliances. A Linux computer has running processes and open files, and a sudden loss of power can cause problems in the file system or even hardware failures. You should always gracefully shut down a Linux system.

The traditional way to stop a Linux system is to change the run level to 0 (halt). To reboot, change the run level to 6. This can be done on a Linux system with the **init** and/or **telinit** commands.

However, a more graceful method to stop a Linux system is to use the **shutdown** utility (Figure 14–2). **shutdown** can be used to either halt Linux, place it into single-user mode (run level 1), or place it into multi-user mode. It allows the shutdown or reboot to be scheduled at some point in the future and it emits warning messages prior to the shutdown so that users may log out before the system changes state.

Utility: **shutdown** -hkr *time* [*message*]

shutdown shuts down the system in a graceful way. The shutdown time must be specified in one of three ways:

- *now*: the system is shut down immediately.
- *+minutes*: the system is shut down in the specified number of minutes.
- *hours:minutes*: the system is shut down at the specified time (24-hour format).

The specified warning message (or a default one if none is specified) is displayed periodically as the time of shutdown approaches. Logins are disabled five minutes prior to shutdown.

If neither **-h** nor **-k** is specified, **shutdown** brings the system down to single-user mode by signaling **init** to change to run level 1. Using the **-h** option causes **shutdown** to change the run level to 0 (halt). The **-r** option causes **shutdown** to change the run level to 6 (reboot). The **-k** option is funny; it causes **shutdown** to behave as if were going to shut down the system, but when the shutdown time arrives, it does nothing. The "k" stands for "just kidding"!

Figure 14–2   Description of the **shutdown** command.

14.5 Maintaining the File System

Several regular activities are required to assure the proper functioning of the file systems on your system. In addition to this, there may be instances where you need to add new file systems to the system.

14.5.1   File System Integrity

When the system first boots, all run level's boot scripts run a utility called **fsck** to check the integrity of the file system (Figure 14–3).

> *Utility*: **fsck** -p [*fileSystem*]*
>
> **fsck** (file system check) scans the specified file systems and checks them for consistency. The kind of consistency errors that can exist include:
>
> - A block is marked as free in the bitmap but is also referenced from an inode.
> - A block is marked as used in the bitmap but is never referenced from an inode.
> - More than one inode refers to the same block.
> - An invalid block number.
> - An inode's link count is incorrect.
> - A used inode is not referenced from any directory.
>
> If the **-p** option is used, **fsck** automatically corrects any errors that it finds. Without the **-p** option, it prompts the user for confirmation of any corrections that it suggests. If **fsck** finds a block that is used but is not associated with a named file, it connects it to a file whose name is equal to the block's inode number in the "/lost+found" directory.
>
> If no file systems are specified, **fsck** checks the standard file systems listed in "/etc/fstab."
>
> Linux has specialized **fsck** programs for different types of file systems. For example, when checking an ext2 or ext3 file system, **fsck** act as a front-end to **e2fsck**, which is the program that actually checks the file system.
>
> For information about inodes, see Chapter 13, "Linux Internals."

Figure 14–3   Description of the **fsck** command.

Fortunately, **fsck** is very good at correcting errors. This means that you'll probably never have the joy of patching disk errors by hand as was done in "the good old days."

14.5.2   Disk Space

As I just mentioned, disk errors are uncommon and are generally corrected automatically. Disk usage problems, on the other hand, are very common. Many users treat the file system as if it were infinitely large, and create huge numbers of files without much thought. When I taught UNIX at UT Dallas, the disks would invariably fill up on the last day of the semester, just as everyone was trying to complete his project. Students would try to save their work from **vi**, and **vi** would respond with a "disk full" message. When they quit from **vi**, they would find that their file had been deleted.

To avoid running out of disk space, it's wise to run a shell script from **cron** that periodically runs the **df** utility to check the available disk space (Figure 14–4).

> *Utility*: **df** [*fileSystem*]*
>
> **df** (disk free) displays a table of used and available disk space on the specified mounted file systems. If no file system is specified, all mounted file systems are described.

Figure 14–4   Description of the **df** command.

The exact format varies a bit between Linux distributions, partly because of the way file systems are mounted and named. Here's an example of **df** in action from Mandrake Linux:

```
$ df                     ...list information about all file systems.
Filesystem              Size  Used Avail Use% Mounted on
 /dev/ide/host0/bus0/target0/lun0/part7
                        2.4G  1.5G  795M  66% /
 /dev/ide/host0/bus0/target0/lun0/part5
                        198M  7.6M  180M   5% /boot
 /dev/ide/host0/bus0/target0/lun0/part1
                         16G  2.7G   14G  17% /mnt/windows
$ _
```

Here's output from **df** on a SuSE Linux system:

```
$ df
Filesystem           1K-blocks      Used Available Use% Mounted on
/dev/hda6             3635216    1759508   1691044 51% /
tmpfs                   95744         16     95728  1% /dev/shm
$ _
```

You can find out how much disk space is left on the device where your home directory resides just as easily:

```
$ df .
Filesystem           1K-blocks      Used Available Use% Mounted on
/dev/hda6             3635216    1759508   1691044 51% /
$ _
```

If **df** reports that a disk is greater than 95% full, your script could detect this and send you some e-mail. Even better, your script could then run the **du** utility to determine which users are using the most disk space, and then automatically send them mail suggesting that they remove some files (Figure 14–5).

Utility: **du** [-h] [-s] [*fileName*]*

du displays the number of kilobytes that are allocated to each of the specified filenames. If a filename refers to a directory, its files are recursively described. When the **-h** option is used, the numeric values are changed to more human-readable values (i.e., 63844 blocks is displayed as 63M). When used with the **-s** option, **du** displays only the grand total (summary) for each file or directory. If no filenames are specified, the current directory is scanned.

Figure 14–5 Description of the **du** command.

In the following example, I used **du** to find out how many kilobytes my current directory and all its files were using up. I then obtained a file-by-file breakdown of the disk usage:

```
$ du -s -h          ...obtain grand total of current directory.
9M    .
$ du .                   ...obtain file-by-file listing.
91    ./proj/fall.89
158   ./proj/summer.89/proj4
159   ./proj/summer.89
181   ./proj/spring.90/proj2
21    ./proj/spring.90/proj1
204   ./proj/spring.90
455   ./proj
...                      ...other files were listed here.
38    ./sys5
859   ./sys6
9291  .
$ _
```

14.5.3   Creating New File Systems

If you add a new disk drive to your system, you must do a few things before your system can use it as part of the file system:

1. Partition and format the drive if necessary (as discussed in Chapter 2, "Installing Your Linux System").
2. Create a file system on the medium.
3. Mount the disk into the file system hierarchy.

Create a file system on the medium using **mkfs** (Figure 14–6).

Utility: **mkfs** -t *type specialFile* [*sectorCount*]

mkfs creates a new file system on the specified special file. A new file system consists of a superblock, an inode list, a root directory, and a "lost+found" directory. The file system is built to be *sectorCount* sectors in size. Only a super-user can use this command.

As with **fsck**, **mkfs** is really a front-end to a specific file system creator for each specific file system supported (e.g., **mke2fs**), determined by the file system type specified by *type*.

Figure 14–6   Description of the **mkfs** command.

Once the file system is created, it may be connected to the root file system by using the **mount** utility described on page 157 in Chapter 4, "GNU Utilities for Power Users."

14.5.4 Backing up File Systems

Making a backup copy of file system information is the most important and most frequently overlooked task a system administrator should perform. It's frustrating to spend time at it, since you believe you'll never need the backup. But just like buying insurance on your car, you should do it, because if you ever do need it, not having it will be a big problem. The procedure and utilities for backing up the file system are described in Chapter 4, "GNU Utilities for Power Users."

Some distributions install **dump** and **restore** (they may be called **e2fsdump** and **e2fsrestore**), which are backup and restore utilities based on the Berkeley **dump** and **restore** utilities. **dump** (or **e2fsdump**) will work only on an ext2 or ext3 file system, as it is specific to those file systems, so these utilities are not generally useful if you might ever use other types of file systems.

14.6 Maintaining User Accounts

One of a system administrator's most common tasks is to add a new user to the system. To do this, you must:

- Add a new entry to the password file (and shadow password file if in use).
- Add a new entry to the group file.
- Create a home directory for the user.
- Provide the user with some appropriate startup files.

Most distributions of Linux provide the **useradd** command to take care of the details, so you don't have to do this manually. Others provide a GUI-based method in addition to **useradd** or in its place. To run **useradd**, you must be the super-user.

Utility: **useradd** [-d *directory*] [-s *shell*] *userName*

useradd creates a new user on the system called *userName*. When **-d** is specified, make the new user's home *directory*. If **-s** is specified, make the new user's login *shell*. The next available UID is assigned to the new user.

Figure 14–7   The **useradd** command.

To delete a user, use the **userdel** command:

Utility: **userdel** [-r] *userName*

userdel removes a user account from the system. If **-r** is specified, the user's home directory is removed as well.

Figure 14–8   The **userdel** command.

You should always remove old accounts from a system. An unused but active account represents a security risk.

14.6.1   The Password File

Every user of the system has an entry in the password file (usually "/etc/passwd") in the following format:

```
username:password:userId:groupId:personal:homedir:startup
```

where each field has the meaning given in Figure 14–9.

Field	Meaning
username	The user's login name.
password	The encrypted version of the user's password or "x" if a shadow password file is in use.
userId	The unique integer allocated to the user.
groupId	The integer corresponding to the user's group.
personal	The description of the user that is displayed by the **finger** utility.
homedir	The home directory of the user.
startup	The program that is run for the user at login.

Figure 14–9   Fields in the Linux password file.

Since the password field is an encrypted value, putting any single character in that field is equivalent to disallowing logins on that account. Since there is no string you could type which would encrypt into the text "*" (for example), nothing that could be typed will match when encrypted and compared against such a password field. Here's a snippet from a real-life password file:

```
$ head -5 /etc/passwd          ...look at first five lines.
root:x:0:0:root:/root:/bin/bash
bin:x:1:1:bin:/bin:/sbin/nologin
daemon:x:2:2:daemon:/sbin:/sbin/nologin
adm:x:3:4:adm:/var/adm:/sbin/nologin
lp:x:4:7:lp:/var/spool/lpd:/sbin/nologin
$ _
```

I used **grep** to find my own entry:

```
$ grep ables /etc/passwd              ...find my line.
ables:x:500:500:King Ables:/home/ables:/bin/bash
$ _
```

The "x" in the password field indicates that a *shadow password file* ("/etc/shadow") is in use. A shadow password file is an extra security mechanism to prevent regular users from reading even the encrypted strings in the standard password file. While difficult, it is possible to crack a given encrypted password by repetitively encrypting random (or systematic) strings until a match is found. A shadow password file eliminates this option for a would-be intruder by storing the encrypted password in a separate file that is inaccessible to regular users.

14.6.2   The Group File

To add a new user, you must decide which group the user will belong to and then search the group file to find the associated group ID. As an example, I'll show you how to add a new user called "simon" into the "cs4395" group.

Every group in the system has an entry in the group file ("/etc/group") in the following format:

```
groupname:groupPassword:groupId:users
```

where each field is defined as in Figure 14–10.

Field	Meaning
groupname	The name of the group.
groupPassword	The encrypted password for the group.
groupId	The unique integer corresponding to the group.
users	A list of the users in the group, separated by commas.

Figure 14–10   Fields in the Linux group file.

Here's a snippet from a real-life "/etc/group" file:

```
$ head -5 /etc/group        ...look at start of group file.
cs4395:*:91:glass
cs5381:*:92:glass
wheel:*:0:posey,aicklen,shrid,dth,moore,lippke,rsd,garner
daemon:*:1:daemon
sys:*:3:
$ _
```

As you can see, the "cs4395" group has an associated group ID number of 91. To add Simon as a new user, I allocated him the unique user ID number 10, a group ID of 91, and left his password field empty. Here's what his entry looked like:

```
simon::101:91:Simon Pritchard:/home/simon:/bin/ksh
```

Once the entry was added to the password file, I added Simon onto the end of the "cs4395" list in the "/etc/group" file.

14.7 Installing New Software

Installing new software or updates to existing software is an important task of a system administrator. Most Linux distributions use the Red Hat Package Manager (RPM) to install new software packages. Even those that don't (e.g., Debian, Slackware) provide their own tools that can read RPM-format package files. Linux software is almost always distributed as an RPM package file. Software can also be packaged using **tar** or **cpio**.

Often, new software for your Linux system will be available in an RPM file. Install an RPM package with the **rpm** utility:

Utility: **rpm** -aiqU *packageName*

rpm installs or updates an RPM package in the file *packageName* depending on whether **-i** or **-U** is specified. If the **-q** option is specified, the system is queried to see if *packageName* is currently installed. If **-q** is used with **-a**, all packages installed on the system are listed.

Figure 14–11   The **rpm** utility

RPM packages maintain dependency information, so when you attempt to install a package, if it depends on other packages that have not been installed, the installation fails and tells you what dependency is not met.

If you install your Linux system and later want to install a package that you did not install, it is fairly simple to go back to the CDs and find the proper package and install it and anything it depends on. RPM package files are usually named in the form *packagename-version*.rpm.

14.8 Peripheral Devices

Let's assume that you've just bought a new device and you wish to connect it to your system. For the system to be able to "talk to" a new device the hardware must be connected and the software must be installed or activated. If the device is already recognized by Linux (as is most common PC hardware), this may be simple. Some devices require that new drivers be loaded into the kernel and the kernel rebuilt, others may use dynamically loadable device drivers where the driver will be loaded into the kernel when the device is accessed. The basic steps of device installation are as follows:

1. Install the device driver if it isn't currently in the kernel and loadable device drivers are not used.
2. Determine the device's major and minor numbers.
3. Use **mknod** to associate a filename in "/dev" with the new device.

Once the device driver is installed and the major and minor numbers are known, you must use **mknod** to create the special file (Figure 14–12).

Utility: **mknod** *fileName* [c] [b] *majorNumber minorNumber*
     mknod *fileName* p

mknod creates the special file *fileName* in the file system. The first form of **mknod** allows a super-user to create either a character-oriented or block-oriented special file with the specified major and minor numbers. The major number identifies the class of the device, and the minor number identifies the instance of the device. The second form of **mknod** creates a named pipe, and may be used by anyone (or the **mkfifo** command may also be used).

Figure 14–12   Description of the **mknod** command.

In the following example, I installed the thirteenth instance of a terminal whose major number was 1:

```
$ mknod /dev/tty12 c 1 12  ...note the 13th instance is index 12.
$ _
```

The "c" indicated that the terminal was a character-oriented device. In the next example, I installed the first instance of a disk drive whose major number was 2:

```
$ mknod /dev/dk1 b 2 0      ...note the 1st instance is index 0.
$ _
```

The "b" indicated that the terminal was a block-oriented device.

Major and minor numbers are the fourth and fifth fields, respectively, in an "ls -lG" listing. In the following example, I obtained a long listing of the "/dev" directory:

```
$ ls -lG /dev      ...get a long listing of the device directory.
crw--w--w-  1     root  1,  0 Feb 13 14:21 /dev/tty0
crw--w--w-  1     root  1,  1 Feb 13 14:27 /dev/tty1
brw--w--w-  1     root  2,  0 Feb 13 14:29 /dev/dk0
crw--w--w-  1     root  3,  0 Feb 13 14:27 /dev/rmt0
...
$ _
```

14.9 The Network Interface

An important aspect of system administration is getting a Linux machine connected to the local network so that other machines and all users can communicate with it. Some of the basic concepts and tools used to do this were discussed in Chapter 9, "Networking and the Internet." Networking is a huge subject, and this will only be an overview. For a detailed view, I strongly recommend [Nemeth, 2002].

Unless you are using wireless networking, some kind of network cable will have to be connected to your Linux computer in order for it to talk to the network. Your machine will have to have an IP address and hostname assigned to it, and the rest of the network will need to be made aware of this name and address (by updating the local host table or DNS database).

The **ifconfig** command is used to configure the network interface. The typical way to activate a network interface is:

```
$ ifconfig eth0 194.27.1.14 up
```

This causes the interface called "eth0" to be assigned the IP address 194.27.1.14 and configured to be up. Other IP attributes can also be configured with **ifconfig**. While you can issue this command by hand at a terminal, it is usually found in boot scripts that initialize all network interfaces. When you add a network interface, you'll have to add the appropriate configuration command to the appropriate boot file.

For your Linux machine to communicate with any other computer that is not directly connected to the same network cable (segment), routing information on your machine will need to be specified. The **route** command is used to specify routers that provide a path to other networks. Generally, you only have to make sure a "default" route is established. A packet will be sent to this router when the destination is not on the local network. The packet is sent to the default router with the assumption that upstream routers will know how to get to the destination.

14.10 Automating Tasks

There are several system tasks that are fairly simple but tedious to perform. For example:

- checking disk space usage
- performing incremental backups
- cleaning up temporary directories (/tmp) and old "core" files

One of the powers of Linux is its capacity to run simple shell scripts or C programs you've written to automate tasks that you currently perform by hand. I recommend that you automate as many of these chores as you can. Tasks that must be executed on a periodic basis can be scheduled by the **cron** utility. The **cron** utility allows you to schedule a program to run anywhere from once every minute to once every year. This is accomplished by using the **crontab** command (discussed on page 135 of Chapter 4, "GNU Utilities for Power Users"). Any messages generated by the program are sent via e-mail to the user who registered the program to be run.

For example, a simple script to see if any of your file systems are at 90% capacity or greater might be:

```
#!/bin/sh
#
df | egrep "9[0-9]%|100%"
```

If this script is registered by "root" with **cron** to be run every hour, nothing (visible) happens until a file system reaches 90% capacity or greater. The script is run every hour but no output is generated. When a file system reaches 90%, the search pattern specified to the **egrep** command will be satisfied by the line in the **df** output corresponding to the offending file system, so the script will generate a line of output. This line will be e-mailed to "root," so within one hour of the file system's hitting 90%, you'll know about it.

You can write all kinds of simple shell scripts to monitor nearly anything about your system and only send e-mail when some threshold is reached that triggers concern.

14.11 Tunable Kernel Parameters

The Linux kernel has many constant values that may be examined to find out how things are working or modified in order to improve the performance of the system. Altering kernel parameters to improve performance is referred to as system *tuning*. In addition to modifying kernel source code or header files, recompiling the kernel, and rebooting the system (as was required in "the old days"), Linux provides two more manageable methods of examining and modifying kernel parameters.

14.11.1 The /proc File System

The /proc file system is not really a file system at all, but an abstraction of kernel data with an interface that resembles a file system. By registering itself with the Linux virtual file system (VFS), the /proc file system looks just like a normal part of the Linux file system. Most "files" in the /proc file system are read-only, but the super-user can modify some of them.

Each process has its own directory in the /proc file system, named with its process ID (PID). That pseudodirectory contains other files that provide access to information about the running process.

Other named directories contain files whose contents are computed from live kernel data when the file is opened. For example, to find information about the CPU on the system, you can look at the file /proc/cpuinfo.

Most of the interesting kernel-related data is found in /proc/sys. For example, to find and change the maximum number of open files allowed on the system, I might do this:

```
# cat /proc/sys/fs/file-max
18999
# echo 25000 >/proc/sys/fs/file-max
# cat /proc/sys/fs/file-max
25000
# _
```

Note that when you modify a kernel parameter this way, it is modified only in the live running kernel. When the system reboots, it will return to its default value. To make a modification permanent, you must add the command to a boot script so it is executed every time the system is booted.

14.11.2 The sysctl Utility

As convenient it is to modify kernel parameters through the /proc file system, it lacks a bit as a user interface. So Linux also provides the BSD 4.4-inspired **sysctl** utility as a command-line interface to data in /proc/sys.

Utility: **sysctl** -aw { *parameter=value* }
      sysctl -p *file*

The **sysctl** utility provides a convenient command-line interface to the kernel parameters available in /proc/sys. When the **-a** option is used, **sysctl** prints all the kernel parameter names and their values. When the **-w** option is used, subsequent *parameter=value* specifications are used to modify the parameter in the running kernel (when run as root). When the **-p** option is used, *parameter=value* specifications are read from the named file. By default, this file is "/etc/sysctl.conf" and can be used to reset kernel parameters at boot time.

Figure 14-13 The **sysctl** utility.

The **sysctl** command equivalent to the modification I made manually in the previous section would be:

```
# sysctl -w fs.file-max=25000
fs.file-max = 25000
# _
```

The same restriction applies: unless this change is made at boot time (e.g., added to /etc/sysctl.conf), the kernel will revert to its previous setting after a reboot.

14.12 Security Issues

Security is another topic to which one might devote an entire book. As you are no doubt aware, Linux systems are not 100% secure. No computer connected to any network can be. With the explosion of Internet connectivity, the problems have grown as well.

UNIX was not originally designed with security in mind. The original UNIX environments were places where everyone trusted each other and there was no need. Linux improves on many of these problems, but it is still far from bulletproof.

While there are many aspects to Linux security, the ones with which every user has experience are passwords and file permissions. These mechanisms are tough for a regular user to break but not so hard for experienced hackers. The best that a system administrator can do is to read about as many of the known security loopholes as possible and adopt strategies to stop them. To give you an idea of what you're up against, here are a couple of common password-nabbing techniques:

- If you have a regular account and desire a super-user account, you begin by obtaining a copy of the one-way encryption algorithm that is used by the Linux **passwd** utility. You also buy an electronic dictionary. Next, you copy the "/etc/passwd" file to your home PC and compare the encrypted versions of every word in the dictionary against the encrypted root password. If one of the dictionary entries matches, you've cracked the password! Other common passwords to test for include names of friends, pets, places, anything that is a known favorite of the person whose account you're trying to crack. This brute-force technique is very powerful, and may be defended against by asking everyone to pick non-English, nonobvious, nontrivial passwords.

• A scheming user can use the command-superseding technique described on page 203 to trick a super-user into executing the wrong version of **su**. To use this Trojan horse technique, set $PATH so that the shell looks in your own "bin" directory before the standard "bin" directories. Next, write a shell script called **su** that pretends to offer a super-user login, but really stores the super-user password in a safe place, displays "wrong password", and then erases itself. When this script is prepared, call a super-user and tell him/her that there's a nasty problem with your terminal that requires super-user powers to fix. When the administrator types **su** to enter super-user mode, *your* **su** script executes instead of the standard **su** utility, and the super-user password is captured. The super-user sees the "wrong password" message and tries **su** again. This time, it succeeds, as your Trojan horse script has already erased itself. The super-user password is now yours! The way to defeat this technique is never to execute commands using a relative pathname when you're at an unfamiliar terminal. In other words, execute "/bin/su" instead of just "su".

The best ways to improve your knowledge of cunning schemes are to network with other system administrators and to read specialized system administration and security books such as [Nemeth, 2002] and [Toxen, 2003].

CHAPTER REVIEW

Checklist
In this chapter, I described:

- how to obtain super-user powers
- how to start and stop Linux
- the difference between single- and multi-user modes
- some useful disk-utilization utilities
- installing software
- how to create a new file system
- how to add and delete user accounts
- an overview of how a device is installed
- configuring a network interface
- tunable kernel parameters
- some common security problems

Quiz

1. Why should you shut down a Linux system instead of simply turning it off?
2. Why do most versions of Linux now use a "shadow" password file in addition to the normal /etc/passwd file?
3. Why is it better to use **su** to become the super-user than to simply log in as "root"?
4. How can you put Linux into single-user mode?
5. Which files must be modified when you add a new user?
6. What does the **ifconfig** command do?
7. Describe the "Trojan horse" technique for capturing a super-user password.

Exercises

1. Try using **cpio** and **tar** to transfer some files to and from whatever removable media are available on your system (or to a file in /tmp if no removable media are available). Which of these utilities do you prefer? Why? [level: *easy*]
2. Use **du** to examine your disk usage. Write a script that prints out the full pathnames of your files that are over a specified size. [level: *medium*]
3. Fill in the functionality of the skeleton script you wrote in Exercise 1 of Chapter 7, "The Korn Shell," so that it will perform the system administration tasks in your menu-driven interface. Useful tasks to automate include:

   • automatic deletion of core files
   • automatic warnings to users that use a lot of CPU time or disk space
   • automatic archiving

   [level: *medium*]

Project

1. Find an optional package (in RPM format) on your Linux distribution CD or on the Internet and install it on your system. [level: *easy*]
2. Explore the /proc file system and find out the kind of data a normal user can access. Why is it useful to be able to read this data? [level: *medium*]

Appendix

A

A.1 Regular Expressions

Regular expressions are character sequences that describe a family of matching strings. They are accepted as arguments to many GNU utilities, such as **grep, egrep, gawk, sed,** and **vim**. Note that the filename substitution wildcards used by the shells are *not* examples of regular expressions, as they use different matching rules.

Regular expressions are formed out of a sequence of normal character and special characters. Figure A–1 is a list of special characters, sometimes called *metacharacters*, together with their meaning.

Metacharacter	Meaning
.	Matches any single character.
[ ]	Matches any of the single characters enclosed in brackets. A hyphen may be used to represent a range of characters. If the first character after the [is a ^, then any character *not* enclosed in brackets is matched. The *, ^, $, and \ metacharacters lose their normal special meaning when used inside brackets.
*	May follow any character, and denotes zero or more occurrences of the character that precedes it.
^	Matches the beginning of a line only.
$	Matches the end of a line only.
\	The meaning of any metacharacter may be inhibited by preceding it with a \.

Figure A–1 Regular expression metacharacters.

A regular expression matches the longest pattern that it can. For example, when the pattern "y.*ba" is searched for in the string "yabadabadoo", the match occurs against the substring "yabad-aba" and not "yaba". The next page contains some examples of regular expressions in action.

To illustrate the use of these metacharacters, here is a piece of text followed by the lines of text that would match various regular expressions. The portion of each line that satisfies the regular expression is italicized.

A.1.1   Text

```
Well you know it's your bedtime,
So turn off the light,
Say all your prayers and then,
Oh you sleepy young heads dream of wonderful things,
Beautiful mermaids will swim through the sea,
And you will be swimming there too.
```

A.1.2   Patterns

Figure A–2 lists lines that match regular expression patterns.

Pattern	Lines that match
the	So turn off *the* light, Say all your prayers and *then*, Beautiful mermaids will swim through *the* sea, And you will be swimming *the*re too.
.nd	Say all your prayers *and* then, Oh you sleepy young heads dream of w*ond*erful things, *And* you will be swimming there too.
^.nd	*And* you will be swimming there too.
sw.*ng	And you will be *swimming* there too.
[A-D]	*B*eautiful mermaids will swim through the sea, *A*nd you will be swimming there too.
\.	And you will be swimming there too. *(the "." matches)*
a.	S*ay* all your prayers and then, Oh you sleepy young he*ad*s dream of wonderful things, Be*au*tiful mermaids will swim through the sea,
a.$	Beautiful mermaids will swim through the se*a*,
[a-m]nd	Say all your prayers *and* then,
[^a-m]nd	Oh you sleepy young heads dream of w*ond*erful things, *And* you will be swimming there too.

Figure A–2   Lines matching regular expression patterns.

A.2 Extended Regular Expressions

Some utilities such as **egrep** support an extended set of metacharacters, which are described in Figure A–3.

Metacharacter	Meaning
+	Matches one or more occurrences of the single preceding character.
?	Matches zero or one occurrence of the single preceding character.
| (pipe symbol)	If you place a pipe symbol between two regular expressions, a string that matches either expression will be accepted. In other words, a | acts like an "or" operator.
()	If you place a regular expression in parentheses, you may use the *, +, or ? metacharacters to operate on the entire expression, rather than just a single character.

Figure A–3 Extended regular expression metacharacters.

Figure A–4 lists some examples of full regular expressions, using the example file from Section A.1.1.

Pattern	Lines that match
s.*w	Oh you *sleepy young heads dream of w*onderful things, Beautiful mermaid*s will sw*im through the sea, And you will be *sw*imming there too.
s.+w	Oh you *sleepy young heads dream of w*onderful things, Beautiful mermaid*s will sw*im through the sea,
off|will	So turn *off* the light, Beautiful mermaids *will* swim through the sea, And you *will* be swimming there too.
im*ing	And you will be sw*imming* there too.
im?ing	\<no matches\>

Figure A–4 Lines matching extended regular expression patterns.

A.3 Modified Backus-Naur Notation

The syntax of the GNU utilities and Linux system calls in this book are presented in a modified version of a language known as Backus-Naur Form, or BNF for short. In a BNF description, the sequences in Figure A–5 have a special meaning.

The last sequence is the Linux/GNU-oriented modification, which allows me to avoid placing large numbers of brackets around command-line options. To indicate a [, {, |, or - without its special meaning, I precede it with a \ character.

Sequence	Meaning
[strings]	Strings may appear zero or one time.
{ strings }*	Strings may appear zero or more times.
{ strings }+	Strings may appear one or more times.
string1|string2	string1 or string2 may appear.
-optionlist	Zero or more options may follow a dash.

Figure A–5   BNF notations used in this book.

Some variations of commands depend on which option you choose. I indicate this by supplying a separate syntax description for each variation. For example, take a look at the syntax description of the **at** utility (Figure A–6).

Utility: **at** -csm *time* [*date* [, *year*]][+*increment*][*script*]
  at -r { *jobId*}+
  at -l { *jobId*}*

Figure A–6   Example description of the **at** command

The first version of the **at** utility is selected by any combination of the command-line options **-c, -s,** and **-m.** These must then be followed by a time and an optional date specifier. The optional date specifier may be followed by an optional year specifier. Additionally, an increment may be specified and/or a script name.

The second version of **at** is selected by a **-r** option, and may be followed by one or more job ID numbers.

The third version of **at** is selected by the **-l** option, and may be followed by zero or more job ID numbers.

A.4   Utilities and Shell Built-In Commands

Here is an alphabetized list of references to each Linux utility or shell built-in where it is described in this book.

Name	Synopsis	Described on page
alias	display or define command aliases	217, 255, 308
ar	archive files	408
at	run commands at a future time	130
bg	run or resume a process in the background	274
builtin	run the specified built-in shell command even if a function of the same name is defined	234
cancel	cancel a print job	64
case	test a set of expressions	226
cat	display or concatenate the contents of a file	54
cd	change your current working directory to a new directory	59, 238, 284
chdir	change current working directory	329
chgrp	change a file's group	73
chmod	change a file's mode (protection specification)	74
chown	change a file's owner	76
chsh	change login shell	169
clear	clear the screen	45
cmp	compare files	116
cp	copy a file	61
cpio	archive files	122
crontab	add or remove commands for scheduled execution via cron	128
date	print the date and time	44
declare	define a variable or variable array	209
df	display a table of free disk space	581
diff	display differences between files	117
dirs	list the contents of the directory stack	239, 330

Name	Synopsis	Described on page
du	display disk usage information	582
dump	dump the contents of a file system to backup media	127
echo	print text	171
egrep	similar to **grep**	109
emacs	screen editor	93
env	display environment variables or designate a shell variable as an environment variable and assign a value	212, 252
eval	execute output of a command as a shell command itself	197
exec	replace the current process with a new program	198
exit	terminate the shell process	196
export	display environment variables or designate a shell variable as an environment variable	212, 251
fc	edit and re-execute commands in the Korn shell	260
fg	run or resume a process in the foreground	275
fgrep	similar to **grep**	109
file	display type of a file	70
find	find files	119
finger	display information about users on the system	346
for	process a loop	229
foreach	process in a loop	315
fsck	check the file system for consistency problems	581
ftp	transfer files to another system via the File Transfer Protocol	352
function	define function	232, 269
gawk	sophisticated text processor	132
gcc	compile a C program	402
gdb	debug a program	420

Name	Synopsis	Described on page
glob	print variables after they've been processed by the shell's metacharacter mechanisms	329
goto	transfer control to a specified location in a script	315
gprof	profile an executable program	418
grep	filter lines of text based on patterns	109
groups	list groups of which user is a member	73
gunzip	GNU utility to restore a compressed file to its original contents	141
gzip	GNU utility to compress the contents of a file	141
head	display the beginning of a file	57
history	display shell command history	218, 311
host	find IP address or hostname via DNS	365
hostname	display or set the hostname of the system	346
if	test a set of expressions	228, 316
ifconfig	configure a network interface	589
jobs	display a list of running jobs belonging to the current shell	240, 273
kill	send a signal to a process	192, 242, 275
let	perform integer arithmetic	265
ln	create links to files	137
local	define a shell variable to be inaccessible outside the current function	234
logout	terminate a login shell	328
lp	print a file	64
lpq	display status of printer queue	66
lpr	queue print a file	65
lprm	remove a queued print job	66
lpstat	get printer status	64

Name	Synopsis	Described on page
ls	list directory contents	55
mail	send and receive electronic mail messages	99
make	tool to build applications based on dependencies of modified files	412
man	display manual pages	45
mesg	allow or disallow write access to your tty device by other users	347
mkdir	create a new directory	58
mkfifo	create a named pipe	505
mkfs	create a file system	583
mknod	create a device node	588
more	display a file one page at a time	57
mount	mount a file system	150
mv	move or rename a file	58
newgrp	change a user's group membership	77
nice	change a process' priority	327
nohup	make a process immune to a SIGHUP (hangup signal)	191, 327
notify	inform about changes in job's state	328
od	octal dump	148
onintr	process an interrupt	317
passwd	change your password	49
perl	flexible scripting language	152
popd	pop a directory from the directory stack	239, 330
print	print text to the terminal or an output stream	287
ps	display process status	189
pushd	push a directory onto the directory stack	239, 330
pwd	print the current working directory	52

Name	Synopsis	Described on page
rcp	copy files to a remote host	351
read	read one line from standard input	211, 288
readonly	designate a shell variable unchangeable	213, 252
rehash	rebuild the shell's hash table	331
repeat	repeat a command multiple times	318
restore	restore files backed up with the dump utility	127
return	return from a function	233, 270
rlogin	login to a remote system	355
rm	remove a file	63
rmdir	remove a directory	62
rpm	install a Linux package	587
rsh	execute a shell command on a remote system	356
scp	securely copy files to a remote host	351
sed	stream editor	142
select	create menu selection	236, 267
set	display or set shell options	220, 285, 298
setenv	define an environment variable	302
sftp	securely transfer files to another system via the File Transfer Protocol	352
shift	shift the shell's positional parameters	198
shutdown	shut down the system	580
sleep	cause a process to be idle	189
slogin	securely log in to a remote system	355
sort	sort lines in a file	113
source	execute shell commands from a file in the current shell	236, 329

Name	Synopsis	Described on page
ssh	securely execute a shell command on a remote system	356
stop	stop a process	326
strip	remove debugging and profiling information from binary to make it smaller	429
stty	display and modify terminal settings	81
su	become a new user	140
suspend	suspend a process	327
switch	branch based on expression	318
tail	display the end of a file	57
talk	carry on a real-time conversation with another user via the screen	349
tar	archive files	124
tee	write text to standard output as well as to a file	177
telnet	connect to another system to login	357
time	display time used by a program	151
touch	update modification time of files	416
tr	translate characters	146
trap	catch signals	231, 289
tset	determine and/or set terminal type	78
tty	display device name of terminal	151
typeset	format shell variables	281
ul	change underlining so it displays properly	147
umask	display or set the shell's umask value	200
umount	unmount a file system	150
unalias	remove a defined command alias	217, 256, 309
unhash	disable the shell's hashing capability	331

Name	Synopsis	Described on page
uniq	eliminate redundant text	112
unset	deallocate a variable	211
until	process in a loop	230
useradd	add a user to the system	584
userdel	delete a user from the system	584
users	display users on the system	344
vim	screen editor	82
w	display information about local users on the system	345
wait	wait for a child process to terminate	193
wall	write to all users	350
wc	count words in a file	67
while	process in a loop	230, 320
who	display users on the system	345
whoami	display user information	139
write	write a message to another user's screen	348
xclock	clock tool for the X Window System	390
xhost	defines access to the local X server by users of other systems	379
xrdb	query and modify the X server's resource database	396
xterm	terminal window client for the X Window System	391
zcat	GNU utility to produce the original contents of a compressed file	141

A.5 System Calls and Library Functions

Here is an alphabetized list of pages on which each system call or library function is described in Chapter 12, "Systems Programming."

Name	Synopsis	Described on page
accept	accepts a connection request from a client socket	517
alarm	sets a process "alarm clock"	489
bind	binds a socket to a name	516
bzero	fills an array with values of zero	526
chdir	changes a process's current working directory	482
chmod	changes a file's permission settings	466
chown	changes a file's owner and/or group	465
close	closes a file	450
closedir	close a directory stream	463
connect	connects to a named server socket	519
dup	duplicates a file descriptor	466
dup2	similar to *dup* ()	466
execl	replaces the calling process with an executable file	481
execlp	similar to *execl* ()	481
execv	similar to *execl* ()	481
execvp	similar to *execl* ()	481
exit	terminates a process	478
fchmod	similar to *chmod* ()	466
fchown	similar to *chown* ()	465
fcntl	gives access to miscellaneous file characteristics	468
fork	duplicates a process	475
fstat	similar to *stat* ()	462
ftruncate	similar to *truncate* ()	472
getegid	returns a process's effective group ID	484
geteuid	returns a process's effective user ID	484
getgid	returns a process's real group ID	484
gethostbyname	returns a structure describing an Internet host	525

Name	Synopsis	Described on page
gethostname	returns the name of the host	525
getpgid	returns a process's process group ID	498
getpid	returns a process's ID number	475
getppid	returns a parent process's ID number	475
getuid	returns a process's real user ID	484
htonl	converts a host-format number to a network-format number	526
htons	similar to *htonl* ()	526
inet_addr	returns a 32-bit value IP address	524
inet_ntoa	returns a string-format IP address	525
ioctl	controls a device	469
kill	sends a signal to a specified process or group of processes	492
lchown	similar to *chown* ()	465
link	creates a hard link	469
listen	sets the maximum number of pending socket connections	517
lseek	moves to a particular offset in a file	449
lstat	similar to *stat* ()	462
memset	fills an array with a specific value	526
mkdir	create a directory	471
mkfifo	create a named pipe	505
mknod	creates a special file	471
nice	changes a process's priority	483
ntohl	converts a network-format number to a host-format number	526
ntohs	similar to *ntohl* ()	526
open	opens or creates a file	446
opendir	open a directory stream for reading with *readdir* ()	463

Name	Synopsis	Described on page
pause	suspends the calling process and returns when a signal is received	490
perror	displays message text from most recent system call error	435
pipe	creates an unnamed pipe	502
read	reads bytes from a file into a buffer	447
readdir	read a directory entry from an open stream	463
setegid	sets a process's effective group ID	484
seteuid	sets a process's effective user ID	484
setgid	sets a process's real and effective group ID	484
setpgid	sets a process's real and effective group ID	497
setuid	sets a process's real and effective user ID	484
signal	specifies the action that will be taken when a particular signal arrives	490
socket	creates an unnamed socket	515
stat	returns status information about a file	462
sync	schedules all file buffers to be flushed to disk	472
sysctl	examine or modify kernel parameters	591
truncate	truncates a file	472
unlink	removes a file	451
wait	waits for a child process	480
write	writes bytes from a buffer to a file	448

Bibliography

1. [Anderson, 1986] Anderson, Gail and Paul Anderson. *The UNIX C Shell Field Guide*. Prentice Hall, 1986.
2. [Anderson, 1995] Anderson, Bart (Editor), Bryan Costales, and Harry Henderson. *The Waite Group's UNIX Communications and the Internet*. Sams, 1995.
3. [Bar, 2000] Bar, Moshe. *Linux Internals*. McGraw-Hill, 2000.
4. [Bar, 2001] Bar, Moshe. *Linux File Systems*. Osborne/McGraw-Hill, 2001.
5. [Bolsky, 1995] Bolsky, Morris I. and David G. Korn. *The New Korn Shell Command and Programming Language*, Second Edition. Prentice Hall PTR, 1995.
6. [Bovet, 2002] Bovet, Daniel P. and Marco Cesati. *Understanding the Linux Kernel*, Second Edition. O'Reilly & Associates, 2002.
7. [Cheswick, 1994] Cheswick, William R. and Steven M. Bellovin. *Firewalls and Internet Security*. Addison-Wesley, 1994.
8. [Curry, 1992] Curry, David A. *UNIX System Security: A Guide for Users and System Administrators*. Addison-Wesley, 1992.
9. [Fink, 2003] Fink, Martin. *The Business and Economics of Linux and Open Source*. Prentice Hall, 2003.
10. [Garfinkel, 1996] Garfinkel, Simson and Gene Spafford. *Practical UNIX and Internet Security*, Second Edition. O'Reilly & Associates, 1996.
11. [Horspool, 1992] Horspool, R. Nigel. *The Berkeley UNIX Environment*, Second Edition. Prentice Hall, 1992.
12. [Kernighan , 1992] Kernighan, Brian and Rob Pike. *The UNIX Programming Environment*. Prentice Hall, 1992.
13. [Maxwell, 2001] Maxwell, Scott. *Linux Core Kernel Commentary*, Second Edition. The Coriolis Group, 2001.
14. [Medinets, 1996] Medinets, David. *Perl 5 by Example*. Que, 1996.
15. [Nemeth, 2002] Nemeth, Evi, Garth Snyder, and Trent R. Hein, with Adam Boggs, Matt Crosby, and Ned McClain. *Linux Administration Handbook*. Prentice Hall PTR, 2002.
16. [Oram, 1991] Oram, Andrew and Steve Talbott. *Managing Projects With make*, Second Edition. O'Reilly & Associates, 1991.
17. [Quercia, 1993] Quercia, Valerie and Tim O'Reilly. *X Window System User's Guide—OSF/Motif Edition*, Second Edition. O'Reilly & Associates, 1993.

18.   [Roberts, 1991] Roberts, Ralph, Mark Boyd, Stephen G. Kochan, and Patrick H. Wood. *UNIX Desktop Guide to EMACS*. Sams, 1991.

19.   [Rochkind, 1986] Rochkind, Marc J. *Advanced UNIX Programming*. Prentice Hall PTR, 1986.

20.   [Sage, 1986] Sage, Russell G. *Tricks of the UNIX Masters*. Sams, 1986.

21.   [Salus, 1994] Salus, Peter H. *A Quarter Century of UNIX*. Addison-Wesley, 1994.

22.   [Sarwar, 2003] Sarwar, Syed Mansoor, and Khaled Al-Saqabi. *Linux and UNIX Programming Tools: A Primer for Software Developers*. Addison-Wesley, 2003.

23.   [Stevens, 1992] Stevens, W. Richard. *Advanced Programming in the UNIX Environment*. Addison-Wesley, 1992.

24.   [Stevens, 1998] Stevens, W. Richard. *UNIX Network Programming*, Second Edition. Prentice Hall PTR, 1998.

25.   [Toxen, 2003] Toxen, Bob. *Real World Linux Security*, Second Edition. Prentice Hall PTR, 2003.

26.   [Waite, 1987] Waite Group and Michael Waite (Editor). *UNIX Papers*. Sams, 1987.

27.   [Wall, 1996] Wall, Larry, Tom Christiansen, Randal L. Schwartz, and Stephen Potter. *Programming Perl*, Second Edition. O'Reilly & Associates, 1996.

28.   [Welsh, 2002] Welsh, Matt, Lar Kaufman, Matthias Kalle Dalheimer, and Terry Dawson. *Running Linux*, Fourth Edition. O'Reilly & Associates, 2002.

29.   [Williams, 2002] Williams, Sam. *Free As In Freedom: Richard Stallman's Crusade For Free Software*. O'Reilly & Associates, 2002.

Index